The Reign Of Henry The Eighth
Vol. 1

by

James Anthony Froude

The Reign Of Henry The Eighth
Vol. 1
by James Anthony Froude

ISBN: 978-93-59393-00-1

Published by

DOUBLE 9 BOOKS

2/13-B, Ansari Road
Daryaganj, New Delhi – 110002
info@double9books.com
www.double9books.com
Tel. 011-40042856

ABOUT THE AUTHOR

James Anthony Froude was a prominent English historian, biographer, and essayist, born on April 23, 1818, in Dartington, Devon, England. He is best known for his works on the history of England and his biographies of significant figures from the Tudor period. Froude was educated at Westminster School and Oriel College, Oxford. He developed a keen interest in history and literature, particularly in the period of the English Reformation. His writings often reflect his controversial views on religious and political matters, which garnered both acclaim and criticism. One of Froude's most notable works is "The History of England from the Fall of Wolsey to the Defeat of the Spanish Armada," a monumental historical series spanning six volumes. In this series, Froude provides a vivid and dramatic account of the tumultuous events during the reigns of the Tudor monarchs, including Henry VIII and Elizabeth I. Aside from his historical writings, Froude also penned biographies of notable figures such as Thomas Carlyle. His works often tackled complex themes and explored the intersection of politics, religion, and society. James Anthony Froude's writings continue to be studied and debated by scholars, making him a significant figure in the field of historical literature.

CONTENTS

INTRODUCTION

James Anthony Froude was born at Dartington Rectory, the youngest son of the Archdeacon of Totnes, on April 23, 1818. His father was a clergyman of the old school, as much squire as parson. In the concluding chapter to his *History of England*, Froude wrote that "for a hundred and forty years after the Revolution of 1688, the Church of England was able to fulfil with moderate success the wholesome functions of a religious establishment. Theological doctrinalism passed out of fashion; and the clergy, merged as they were in the body of the nation, and no longer endeavouring to elevate themselves into a separate order, were occupied healthily in impressing on their congregations the meaning of duty and moral responsibility to God." Of this sane and orthodox, but not over-spiritual, clergy, Archdeacon Froude was an excellent and altogether wholesome type. He was a stiff Tory; his hatred of Dissent was so uncompromising that he would not have a copy of the *Pilgrim's Progress* in the rectory. A stern, self-contained, reticent man, he never, in word of deed, confessed his affection for his youngest son. He was a good horseman, and was passionately fond of open-air exercises and especially of hunting. His one accomplishment was drawing, and his sketches in after years earned the praise of Ruskin.

Cast in the same mould, but fashioned by different circumstances, the archdeacon's eldest son, Richard Hurrell Froude, was a man of greater intellectual brilliance and even more masterful character. He was one of the pioneers of the Oxford Movement, and it was only his early death that deposed him from his place of equality with Newman and Keble and Pusey. Anthony was a sickly child, and from his earliest years lacked the loving care of a mother. He was brought up with Spartan severity by his father and his aunt. The most venial self-indulgence was regarded as criminal. From the age of three he was inured to hardship by being ducked every morning in a trough of ice-cold water. Hurrell Froude felt no tenderness for the ailing lad. Once, in order to rouse a manly spirit in his little brother, he took him by the heels, plunged him like another Achilles into a stream, and stirred with his head the mud at the bottom. Froude has been accused, and not without justice, of not feeling a proper aversion to acts of cruelty. The horrible Boiling Act of Henry VIII. excites neither disgust nor hatred in him; and he makes smooth excuses for the illegal tortures of the rack and the screw which were inflicted on prisoners by Elizabeth and her ministers. He had himself been reared in a hardy school; he had been trained to be indifferent to pain. It may well be that his callousness in speaking of Tudor cruelties is to be traced to the influences that surrounded his loveless childhood and youth.

Hurrell Froude was the idol of his younger brothers. He was a man of brilliant parts, and a born leader of men. His hatred of Radicals and Dissenters transcended even his father's dislike of them. His conception of the Church differed widely from that in which the archdeacon had been reared. To him a clergyman was a priest who belonged to a sacerdotal caste, and who ought not "to merge himself in the body of the nation." To him the Reformation was an infamous crime, and Henry VIII. was worse than the Bluebeard of the nursery. His hero was Thomas à Becket. He wrote a sketch of his life and career, which he did not live to finish. His friends ill-advisedly published it after his death. His ideal ecclesiastical statesman of modern times was Archbishop Laud. Charles I. was a martyr, and the Revolution of 1688 an inglorious blunder. To the day of his death—in spite of the harsh discipline which he received at his hands in boyhood, in spite of wide divergence of opinion in later years in all matters secular and religious—Froude never ceased to worship at his brother's shrine. Out of regard for his memory, more than from any passionate personal conviction, he associated himself while at Oxford with the Anglican movement. His affectionate admiration for Newman, neither time nor change served to impair. If Carlyle was his prophet in later years, his influence happily did not affect his style. That was based on the chaste model of Newman. He owed his early friendship with Newman to that great man's association with Hurrell Froude. Many years after, when Freeman had venomously accused him of "dealing stabs in the dark at a brother's almost forgotten fame"—poor Froude's offence was that he dared to write an essay on Thomas à Becket—he defended himself with rare emotion against the charge. "I look back upon my brother," he said, "as on the whole the most remarkable man I have ever met in my life. I have never seen any person—not one—in whom, as I now think him, the excellences of intellect and character were combined in fuller measure."

As Froude's powers developed and matured, and as his experience of the world broadened, he cast away his brother's yoke, and reverted more to his father's school of thought. As his father was to him the ideal clergyman of the Church of England, so the Church before 1828 remained to him the model of what an established religion should be. He was a thorough Erastian, who believed in the subordination of the Church to the state. He detested theological doctrinalism of all kinds; he revolted against the idea that the clergy should form a separate order. The pretensions of Whitgift and Laud, the High Anglican school of Keble and Pusey, the whole conception of the Church and the priesthood which underlay the Oxford Movement, were things obnoxious to him. In a characteristic passage in the chapter on the Massacre of St. Bartholomew he reveals his hatred and distrust of dogmatism. "Whenever the doctrinal aspect of Christianity has been prominent above the practical," he wrote, "whenever the first duty of the believer has been held to consist in holding particular opinions on the functions and nature of his Master, and only the second in obeying his Master's commands, then always, with a uniformity more remarkable than is obtained in any other historical phenomena, there have followed dissension, animosity, and in later ages bloodshed. Christianity, as a principle of life, has been the most powerful check upon the passions of mankind. Christianity as a speculative system of opinion has converted them into monsters of cruelty."

Holding such decided views on doctrinalism, it might have been thought that Froude would have visited all the warring sects of the sixteenth century with equal judgment. No Church was more doctrinal than that of Geneva; no Calvinist ever was more dogmatic than John Knox. But the men who fought the battle of the Reformation in England and Scotland were, in the main, the Calvinists; and to Froude the Reformation was the beginning of a new and better era, when the yoke of the priest had been finally cast away. "Calvinism," he said in one of his addresses at St. Andrews, "was the spirit which rises in revolt against untruth." John Knox was too heroic a figure not to rouse the artistic sense in Froude. "There lies one," said the Regent Morton over his coffin, "who never feared the face of mortal man." Froude has made this epitaph the text of the noblest eulogy ever delivered on Knox. "No grander figure can be found, in the entire history of the Reformation in this island, than that of Knox." He surpassed Cromwell and Burghley in integrity of purpose and in purity of methods. He towered above the Regent Murray in intellect, and he worked on a larger scale than Latimer. "His was the voice that taught the peasant of the Lothians that he was a free man, the equal in the sight of God with the proudest peer or prelate that had trampled on his forefathers. He was the one antagonist whom Mary Stuart could not soften nor Maitland deceive. He it was who had raised the poor commons of his country into a stern and rugged people, who might be hard, narrow, superstitious, and fanatical, but who nevertheless were men whom neither king, noble, nor priest could force again to submit to tyranny." Yet even here, Froude could not refrain from quoting the sardonic comment of the English ambassador at Edinburgh: Knox behaved, said Randolph, "as though he were of God's privy council."

It is certain, at least, that other reformers, who were not greatly inferior to Knox in capacity, and not at all in piety and honesty, have not met the same generous treatment at his hands. He sneers at Hooper because he had scruples about wearing episcopal robes at his consecration as Bishop of Worcester, though he himself in a famous passage asserts the anomalous position of bishops in the Church of England. Hooper, as a Calvinist, was in the right in objecting, and though the point upon which he took his stand was nominally one of form, there lay behind it a protest against the Anglican conception of a bishop. He speaks slightingly of Ridley and Ferrars, though he makes ample amends to them and to Hooper, when he comes to describe the manner of their death. To the reformers who fled from the Marian persecution, including men like Jewel and Grindal, he refers with scornful contempt, though he has no word of criticism to apply to Knox for retiring to England and to the continent when the flame of persecution was certainly not more fierce. Latimer is one of his favourites,—a plain, practical man, not given to abstract speculation or theological subtleties, but one who was content to do his duty day by day without the fear of man before his eyes. Latimer, though he was looked upon as a Protestant in the earliest years of the English Reformation, believed in the Real Presence up to a short time before his death. But of all English ecclesiastics Thomas Cranmer was perhaps most to Froude's liking. Cranmer was, like Froude himself, an artist in words. The English liturgy owes its charm and beauty to his sense of style, his grace of expression, and his cultured piety. That he was a great man few will be found in these days to maintain; fewer still will believe that he deserved the scathing invective of Macaulay. But no one can read the account given by Froude of his last years without feeling that the first Protestant Archbishop of Canterbury was neither saint nor martyr. If ever there was one, he was a timeserver. He pronounced the divorce of Catherine of Arragon, though he had sworn fealty to the Pope. He never raised a protest against any of the political murders of Henry VIII.—with the notable exception of his courageous attempt to save his friend, Thomas Cromwell. Even in that case, however, he lies under the suspicion of having interfered through fear that his own fate was involved in that of the *malleus monachorum*. In the days of Edward VI. he aimed at the liberty, if not at the life, of Bonner and Gardiner, without semblance of legal right: He recanted in the reign of Mary when he thought he could purchase his miserable life. It was only when all hope of pardon was past that he re-affirmed his belief in the reformed faith. Indeed, he waited until the day of his execution before withdrawing his recantation, and confounded his enemies on the way to the stake. To a master of dramatic narrative the last scene of Cranmer's life came as a relief and an inspiration. "So perished Cranmer," wrote Froude, in a memorable passage: "he was brought out, with the eyes of his soul blinded, to make sport for his enemies, and in his death he brought upon them a wider destruction than he had effected by his teaching while alive. Pole was appointed the next day to the See of Canterbury; but in other respects the court had over-reached themselves by their cruelty. Had they been contented to accept the recantation, they would have left the archbishop to die broken-hearted, pointed at by the finger of pitying scorn; and the Reformation would have been disgraced in its champion. They were tempted, by an evil spirit of revenge, into an act unsanctioned even by their own bloody laws; and they gave him an opportunity of writing his name in the roll of martyrs. The worth of a man must be measured by his life, not by his failure under a single and peculiar peril. The Apostle, though forewarned, denied his Master on the first alarm of danger; yet that Master, who knew his nature in its strength and its infirmity, chose him for the rock on which he would build his Church."

With this conscious and avowed bias in favour of undogmatic Christianity, Froude came to write the story of the transition of England from a Catholic to a Protestant country. He was not without sympathy with the old order of things. We cannot but feel a thrill as we read his incomparable description of the change which was effected in men's thoughts and ideas by the translation of the mediæval into the modern world? "For, indeed, a change was coming upon the world, the meaning and direction of which even still is hidden from us, a change from era to era. The paths trodden by the footsteps of ages were broken up; old things were passing away, and the faith and the life of ten centuries were dissolving like a dream. Chivalry was dying; the abbey and the castle were soon together to crumble into ruins; and all the forms, desires, beliefs, convictions, of the old world were passing away, never to return. A new continent had risen up beyond the western sea. The floor of heaven, inlaid with stars, had sunk back into an infinite abyss of immeasurable space; and the firm earth itself, unfixed from its foundations, was seen to be but a small atom in the awful vastness of the universe. In the fabric of habit which they had so laboriously built for themselves, mankind were to remain no longer. And now it is all gone—like an unsubstantial pageant faded; and between us and the old English there lies a gulf of mystery which the prose of the historian will never adequately bridge. They cannot come to us, and our imagination can but feebly penetrate to them. Only among the aisles of the cathedral, only as we gaze upon their silent figures sleeping on their tombs, some faint conceptions float before us of what these men were when they were alive; and perhaps in the sound of church bells, that peculiar creation of mediæval age, which falls upon the ear like the echo of a vanished world." Froude was once asked what was the greatest and most essential quality of an historian. He replied that it was imagination. It was a true and a just saying, and Froude himself possessed the faculty in abundance.

It was not only with the old order that Froude showed his sympathy. He is seldom ungenerous in his references to individual Catholics, however mistaken in his sight their opinions may have been. With Wolsey and Warham, Fisher and More, even with Gardiner and Bonner he deals fairly and with some amount of real sympathy. The heroic death of Campian moves him to pity just as much as the death of Latimer; the strenuous labours of Father Parsons to overthrow Elizabeth and Protestantism failed to remove him beyond the pale of Froude's charitable judgment. One English Catholic alone was reserved for the historian's harsh and sometimes petulant criticism. For Cardinal Pole Froude felt the angriest contempt. He was descended from the blood royal, both of England and of Wales. On his father's side he was descended in direct line from the ancient princes of Powis; on his mother's from the Plantagenets and the Nevilles. He was the most learned and illustrious Englishman of his age. He had stood high in King Henry's favour; he was destined for the greatest offices in the state. He was not without natural ambition. Yet he forfeited all that he had—the favour of his prince, the society of his mother whom he loved, and the kindred who were proud of him, the hope of promotion and of power, his friends, his home, and his country, for conscience' sake. He remained true to the ancient faith in which he was reared. With unerring instinct he foresaw that, once England was severed from the Papacy, it would be impossible for king or parliament to stem the flood of the Reformation. For twenty years he remained an exile on the continent. He returned an old and broken man, to witness the overthrow of his cherished plans. He was repudiated by the Pope whose authority he had sacrificed everything to maintain, and in his old age he suffered the humiliation of being accused of heresy in the court of Rome. He died the same day as Mary died, with the knowledge that all his life's labours and sacrifices were come to naught, and that the dominion of the Roman Church in England was gone for ever. Froude saw none of the pathos or tragedy of Pole's life. To him the cardinal was a renegade, a traitor to his country, a mercenary of the Pope, a foreign potentate, a "hysterical dreamer," who vainly imagined that he was "the champion of heaven, and the destroyer of heresy."

Froude was, above all, an Englishman. His strongest sympathies went out to the "God's Englishmen" of Elizabeth's reign, who broke the power of Rome and Spain, and who made England supreme in Europe. In his first chapter he describes the qualities of Englishmen with a zest and gusto that drew the comment from Carlyle that "this seems to me exaggerated: what we call John Bullish." He described them as "a sturdy, high-hearted race, sound in body and fierce in spirit which, under the stimulus of those great shins of beef, their common diet, were the wonder of the age." Carlyle's advice when he read this passage in proof was characteristic:—"Modify a little: Frederick the Great was brought up on beer-sops; Robert Burns on oatmeal porridge; and Mahomet and the Caliphs conquered the world on barley meal." But the passage stood unmodified, in spite of Froude's regard for his master.

How this fierce and turbulent people fought their way to world-wide empire was a problem which Froude thought he was able to solve. It was, in the main, because they broke down the power of the priests, and insisted on the supremacy of state over Church. Therefore all his filial affection, his patriotism, and his ecclesiastical prejudices were arrayed on the same side. If history be an exact science, then Froude can lay no claim to the title of historian. He was a brilliant advocate, a man of letters endowed with a matchless style, writing of matters which interested him deeply, and in the investigation of which he spent twenty years of his life. Froude himself would have been the first to repudiate the idea that history is philosophy teaching by examples, or that an historian has necessarily a greater insight into the problems of the present than any other observant student of affairs. "Gibbon," he once wrote, "believed that the era of conquerors was at an end. Had he lived out the full life of man, he would have seen Europe at the feet of Napoleon. But a few years ago we believed the world had grown too civilised for war, and the Crystal Palace in Hyde Park was to be the inauguration of a new era. Battles, bloody as Napoleon's, are now the familiar tale of every day; and the arts which have made the greatest progress are the arts of destruction."

It is absurd to attack Froude on the ground that he was biassed. No man has ever yet written a living history without being biassed. Thucydides detested the radicalism of Cleon as heartily as Gibbon hated the Christianity of Rome. It was once the fashion of the Oxford school to decry Froude as being unworthy of the name of historian. Stubbs, indeed, did pay public tribute to Froude's "great work," but he stood almost alone of his school. Freeman for many years pursued and persecuted Froude with a persistent malevolence which happily has no parallel in the story of English scholarship. It is not necessary in this place to do more than refer to that unpleasant episode. Since the publication of the brilliant vindication of Froude in Mr. Herbert Paul's *Life*, it would be superfluous to go into the details of that unhappy controversy. The only difference between Froude and other historians is that Froude's partisanship is always obvious. He was not more favourable to Henry VIII. than Stubbs was to Thomas à Becket. But Froude openly avowed his preferences and his dislikes. Catholicism was to him "a dying superstition," Protestantism "a living truth." Freeman went further, and charged Froude with having written a history which was not "*un livre de bonne joy.*" It is only necessary to recall the circumstances under which the *History* was written to dispose of that odious charge. In order to obtain material for his *History*, Froude spent years of his life in the little Spanish village of Simancas. "I have worked in all," he said in his Apologia, "through nine hundred volumes of letters, notes, and other papers, private and official, in five languages and in different handwritings. I am not rash enough to say that I have never misread a word, or overlooked a passage of importance. I profess only to have dealt with my materials honestly to the best of my ability." Few, indeed, have had to encounter such difficulties as met Froude in his exploration of the archives at Simancas. "Often at the end of a page," he wrote many years after, "I have felt as after descending a precipice, and have wondered how I got down. I had to cut my way through a jungle, for no one had opened the road for me. I have been turned into rooms piled to the window-sill with bundles of dust-coloured despatches, and told to make the best of it. Often have I found the sand glistening on the ink where it had been sprinkled when a page was turned. There the letter had lain, never looked at again since it was read and put away." Of these difficulties not a trace is discoverable in Froude's easy and effortless narrative. When he was approaching the completion of his *History*, he vowed that his account of the Armada should be as interesting as a novel. He succeeded not only with that portion of his task, but with all the stirring story that he set out to narrate. But the ease of his style only concealed the real pains which he had taken. Of Freeman's charge Froude has long been honourably acquitted. The Simancas MSS. have since been published in the Rolls Series, and Mr. Martin Hume, in his Introduction, has paid his tribute to the care, accuracy, and good faith of their first transcriber. Long before this testimony could be given, Scottish historians who disagreed with Froude's conclusions on many points,—men such as Skelton and Burton— had been profoundly impressed with the care, skill, and conscientiousness with which Froude handled the mass of tangled materials relating to the history of Scotland.

This does not mean that Froude is free from minor inaccuracies, or that he is innocent of graver faults which flowed from his abundant quality of imagination. He constantly quotes a sentence inaccurately in his text, while it is accurately transcribed in a footnote. He is careless in matters which are important to students of Debrett, as for instance, he indiscriminately describes Lord Howard as Lord William Howard and Lord Howard. But Froude was sometimes guilty of something worse than these trivial "howlers." Lecky exposed, with calm ruthlessness, some of Froude's exaggerations—to call them by no worse name—in his *Story of the English in Ireland*. When his *Erasmus* was translated into Dutch, the countrymen of Erasmus accused him of constant, if not deliberate, inaccuracy. Lord Carnarvon once sent Froude to South Africa as an informal special commissioner. When he returned to this country he wrote an article on the South African problem in the *Quarterly Review*. Sir Bartle Frere, who knew South Africa as few men did, said of it that it was an "essay in which for whole pages a truth expressed in brilliant epigrams alternates with mistakes or misstatements which would scarcely be pardoned in a special war correspondent hurriedly writing against time." So dangerous is the quality of imagination in a writer!

Truth to tell, Froude was a literary man with a fondness for historical investigation, and an artist's passion for the dramatic in life and story. He wrote with a purpose—that purpose being to defend the English Reformation against the attacks of the neo-Catholic-Anglicans, under whose influence he had himself been for a time in his youth. To him, therefore, Henry VIII. was "the majestic lord who broke the bonds of Rome." This is not the occasion, nor is the present writer the man, to analyse that complex and masterful personality. Froude started to defend the English Reformation against the vile charge that it was the outcome of kingly lust. That charge he has finally dispelled. Henry VIII. was not the monster that Lingard painted. He beheaded two queens, but few will be found to assert to-day that either Anne Boleyn or Catherine Howard were innocent martyrs. People must agree to differ to the crack of doom as to the justice of Catherine's divorce. It is one of those questions which different men will continue to answer in different ways. But one thing is abundantly clear. If Henry was actuated merely by passion for Anne Boleyn, he would scarcely have waited for years before putting Queen Catherine away. Henry divorced Anne of Cleves, but Anne, who survived the dissolution of her marriage and remained in England for twenty years, made no complaint of her treatment, and she has had no champions either among Catholic or Protestant writers. Her divorce is only remembered as the occasion of the downfall of the greatest statesman of his age, Thomas Cromwell, Earl of Essex. But in his eagerness to proclaim the truth, Froude went on to defend a paradox. Once free from the charge of lust,—and compared with Francis of France or Charles V., Henry was a continent man—Henry became to Froude the ideal monarch.

Some one has said that Henry VIII. was the greatest king that ever lived, because he always got his own way. If that be the test, then Henry was indeed "every inch a king." He broke with Rome; he deposed the Pope from his supremacy over England; he dissolved the monasteries; he sent the noblest and wisest in England to the scaffold; he reduced Wales to law and order and gave her a constitution; he married and unmarried as he liked; he disposed of the succession to the throne of England by his will; and his people never murmured. Only once, when the Pilgrimage of Grace broke out, was his throne in any danger, and that insurrection he easily suppressed. He made war with France; he invaded Scotland more than once, and every time with striking success. He played his vigorous part in European politics, and at his death he left his realm inviolate. It is an amazing record, which might well dazzle a writer of Froude's temperament and training. But there are dark shades in the picture, which Froude was content to make little of, if not to ignore. He is fond of contrasting Henry's way with conspirators with that of his daughter Elizabeth. He sneers at her "tenderness" towards high-born traitors, and never ceases to reproach her with her one act of repression after the Yorkshire rising. But he had not a word to say against the tyrannical murders of Henry VIII. Elizabeth truly boasted that she never punished opinion: Henry sent to the scaffold better men than himself for holding academical opinions contrary to his own. Cardinal Fisher may have been— after the publication of Chappuys's letters it is not possible to deny that he was—technically guilty of treason. But he was a saint and an old man past eighty, and "the earth on the edge of the grave was already crumbling under his feet." The king spared neither age nor worth nor innocence. He had been the familiar friend of More; he had walked through his gardens at Chelsea leaning on his arm; More had been his chancellor; he was still the greatest of his subjects; while frankly admitting that he differed in opinion from the king on the question of the royal supremacy, he promised that he would not try to influence others. Henry was inexorable. He not only condemned him to die a traitor's death,—he added a callous message, which still rouses the indignation of every generous soul, that he should "not use many words on the scaffold." Thomas Cromwell had served him as few ministers have served a king; to him was due—or, at least, he was the capable instrument of—the policy which has given distinction to Henry's reign; but he was delivered over to his enemies when the king's caprice had shifted to another quarter. Even Froude finds it difficult to excuse the execution of More and Cromwell. But, having once made up his mind to make a hero of Henry, he goes on with it bravely to the end. He hides nothing, he excuses nothing, he extenuates nothing. Neither the death of the aged Countess of Salisbury or of the gallant Earl of Surrey, nor the illegal imprisonment of the aged Norfolk, the hero of Flodden, shakes his faith in his hero-king. He even relates, with minute detail, how a few days before the king's death, four poor persons, one of whom was a tailor, were burnt at the stake for denying the Real Presence. But his final comment on it all was: "His personal faults were great, and he shared, besides them, in the errors of his age; but far deeper blemishes would be but scars upon the features of a sovereign who in trying times sustained nobly the honour of the English name, and carried the commonwealth securely through the hardest crisis in its history."

When a young man Froude had been elected Fellow of Exeter College, Oxford. This entailed his taking holy orders, though he does not seem to have regularly performed the duties of a clergyman. In 1849 he published his first book, *The Nemesis of Faith*, now happily forgotten. It raised an immediate commotion. It was denounced as heretical, and the senior tutor of Exeter burnt it during a lecture in the College Hall. Froude resigned his Fellowship, and his connection with the university was severed for thirty-three years. He was one of the first to take advantage of the alteration of the law which enabled a clergyman to resign his orders. In 1892 he went back to Oxford as Regius Professor of Modern History. "The temptation of going back to Oxford in a respectable way," he said, "was too much for me." He died on October 20, 1894, and on his tombstone he is simply described, by his own wish, as Professor of Modern History in the University of Oxford.

The writer is indebted for information with regard to Froude's life to Mr. Pollard's article in the *Dictionary of National Biography*, and to Mr. Herbert Paul's admirable *Life of Froude* (Pitman).

W. LLEWELYN WILLIAMS.

November 16, 1908.

The following is a list of the published works of J.A. Froude:

Life of St. Neot (Lives of the English Saints, edited by J.H. Newman), 1844; Shadows of the Clouds (Tales), by Zeta (*pseud.*), 1847; A Sermon (on 2 Cor. vii. 10) preached at St. Mary's Church on the Death of the Rev. George May Coleridge, 1847; Article on Spinoza (*Oxford and Cambridge Review*), 1847; The Nemesis of Faith (Tale), 1849; England's Forgotten Worthies (*Westminster Review*), 1852; Book of Job (*Westminster Review*), 1853; Poems of Matthew Arnold (*Westminster Review*), 1854; Suggestions on the Best Means of Teaching English History (Oxford Essays, etc.), 1855; History of England, 12 vols., 1856-70; The Influence of the Reformation on the Scottish Character, 1865; Inaugural Address delivered to the University of St. Andrews, March 19, 1869, 1869; Short Studies on Great Subjects, 1867, 2 vols., series 2-4, 1871-83 (articles from *Fraser's Magazine, Westminster Review*, etc.); The Cat's Pilgrimage, 1870;

Calvinism: Address at St. Andrews, 1871; The English in Ireland, 3 vols., 1872-74; Bunyan (English Men of Letters), 1878; Cæsar: a Sketch, 1879; Two Lectures on South Africa, 1880; Thomas Carlyle (a history of the first forty years of his life, etc.), 2 vols., 1882; Luther: a Short Biography, 1883; Thomas Carlyle (a history of his life in London, 1834-81), 2 vols., 1884; Oceana, 1886; The English in the West Indies, 1888; Liberty and Property: an Address [1888]; The Two Chiefs of Dunboy, 1889; Lord Beaconsfield (a Biography), 1890; The Divorce of Catherine of Aragon, 1891; The Spanish Story of the Armada, 1892; Life and Letters of Erasmus, 1894; English Seamen in the Sixteenth Century, 1895; Lectures on the Council of Trent, 1896; My Relations with Carlyle, 1903.

CHAPTER I.
SOCIAL CONDITION OF ENGLAND IN THE SIXTEENTH CENTURY

In periods like the present, when knowledge is every day extending, and the habits and thoughts of mankind are perpetually changing under the influence of new discoveries, it is no easy matter to throw ourselves back into a time in which for centuries the European world grew upon a single type, in which the forms of the father's thoughts were the forms of the son's, and the late descendant was occupied in treading into paths the footprints of his distant ancestors. So absolutely has change become the law of our present condition, that it is identified with energy and moral health; to cease to change is to lose place in the great race; and to pass away from off the earth with the same convictions which we found when we entered it, is to have missed the best object for which we now seem to exist.

It has been, however, with the race of men as it has been with the planet which they inhabit. As we look back over history, we see times of change and progress alternating with other times when life and thought have settled into permanent forms; when mankind, as if by common consent, have ceased to seek for increase of knowledge, and, contented with what they possess, have endeavoured to make use of it for purposes of moral cultivation. Such was the condition of the Greeks through many ages before the Persian war; such was that of the Romans till the world revenged itself upon its conquerors by the introduction among them of the habits of the conquered; and such again became the condition of Europe when the Northern nations grafted the religion and the laws of the Western empire on their own hardy natures, and shaped out that wonderful spiritual and political organisation which remained unshaken for a thousand years.

The aspirant after sanctity in the fifteenth century of the Christian era found a model which he could imitate in detail in the saint of the fifth. The gentleman at the court of Edward IV. or Charles of Burgundy could imagine no nobler type of heroism than he found in the stories of King Arthur's knights. The forms of life had become more elaborate—the surface of it more polished—but the life itself remained essentially the same; it was the development of the same conception of human excellence; just as the last orders of Gothic architecture were the development of the first, from which the idea had worked its way till the force of it was exhausted.

A condition of things differing alike both outwardly and inwardly from that into which a happier fortune has introduced ourselves, is necessarily obscure to us. In the alteration of our own character, we have lost the key which would interpret the characters of our fathers, and the great men even of our own English history before the Reformation seem to us almost like the fossil skeletons of another order of beings. Some broad conclusions as to what they were are at least possible to us, however; and we are able to determine, with tolerable certainty, the social condition of the people of this country, such as it was before the movements of the sixteenth century, and during the process of those movements.

The extent of the population can only be rudely conjectured. A rough census was taken at the time of the Armada, when it was found to be something under five millions; but anterior to this I can find no authority on which I can rely with any sort of confidence. It is my impression, however, from a number of reasons—each in itself insignificant, but which taken together leave little doubt upon my mind—that it had attained that number by a growth so slow as to be scarcely perceptible, and had nearly approached to it many generations before. Simon Fish, in *The Supplication of Beggars*, 1 says that the number of households in England in 1531 was 520,000. His calculation is of the most random kind; for he rates the number of parishes at 52,000, with ten households on an average in each parish. A mistake so preposterous respecting the number of parishes shows the great ignorance of educated men upon the subject. The ten households in each parish may, probably (in some parts of the country), have been a correct computation; but this tells us little with respect to the aggregate numbers, for the households were very large—the farmers, and the gentlemen also, usually having all the persons whom they employed residing under their own roof. Neither from this, therefore, nor from any other positive statement which I have seen, can I gather any conclusion that may be depended upon. But when we remember the exceeding slowness with which the population multiplied in a time in which we can accurately measure it—that is to say, from 1588 to the opening of the last century—under circumstances in every way more favourable to an increase, I think we may assume that the increase was not so great between 1500 and 1588, and that, previous to 1500, it did not more than keep pace with the waste from civil and foreign war. The causes, indeed, were wholly wanting which lead to a rapid growth of numbers. Numbers now increase with the increase of employment and with the facilities which are provided by the modern system of labour for the establishment of independent households. At present, any able-bodied unskilled labourer earns, as soon as he has arrived at man's estate, as large an amount of wages as he will earn at any subsequent time; and having no connection with his employer beyond the receiving the due amount of weekly money from him, and thinking himself as well able to marry as he is likely to be, he takes a wife, and is usually the father of a family before he is thirty. Before the Reformation, not only were early marriages determinately discouraged, but the opportunity for them did not exist. A labourer living in a cottage by himself was a rare exception to the rule; and the work of the field was performed generally, as it now is in the large farms in America and Australia, by servants who lived in the families of the squire or the farmer, and who, while in that position, commonly remained single, and married only when by prudence they had saved a sufficient sum to enable them to enter some other position.

Checked by circumstances of this kind, population would necessarily remain almost stationary, and a tendency to an increase was not of itself regarded by the statesmen of the day as any matter for congratulation or as any evidence of national prosperity. Not an increase of population, which would facilitate production and beat down wages by competition, but the increase of the commonwealth, the sound and healthy maintenance of the population already existing, were the chief objects which the government proposed to itself; and although Henry VIII. carefully nursed his manufactures, there is sufficient proof in the grounds alleged for the measures to which he resorted, that there was little redundancy of occupation.

In a statute, for instance, for the encouragement of the linen manufactures, it is said 2 that—"The King's Highness, calling to his most blessed remembrance the great number of idle people daily increasing throughout this his Realm, supposeth that one great cause thereof is by the continued bringing into the same the great number of wares and merchandise made, and brought out and from, the parts beyond the sea into this his Realm, ready wrought by manual occupation; amongst the which wares one kind of merchandise in great quantity, which is linen cloth of divers sorts made in divers countries beyond the sea, is daily conveyed into this Realm; which great quantity of linen cloth so brought is consumed and spent within the same; by reason whereof not only the said strange countries where the said linen cloth is made, by the policy and industry of making and vending the same are greatly enriched; and a marvellous great number of their people, men, women, and children, are set on work and occupation, and kept from idleness, to the great furtherance and advancement of their commonwealth; but also contrariwise the inhabitants and subjects of this Realm, for lack of like policy and industry, are compelled to buy all or most part of the linen cloth consumed in the same, amounting to inestimable sums of money. And also the people of this Realm, as well men as women, which should and might be set on work, by exercise of like policy and craft of spinning, weaving, and making of cloth, lies now in idleness and otiosity, to the high displeasure of Almighty God, great diminution of the King's people, and extreme ruin, decay, and impoverishment of this Realm. Therefore, for reformation of these things, the King's most Royal Majesty intending, like a most virtuous Prince, to provide remedy in the premises; nothing so much coveting as the increase of the Commonwealth of this his Realm, with also the virtuous exercise of his most loving subjects and people, and to avoid that most abominable sin of idleness out of the Realm, hath, by the advice and consent of his Lords and Commons in Parliament assembled, ordained and enacted that every person occupying land for tillage, shall for every sixty acres which he hath under the plough, sow one quarter of an acre in flax or hemp."

This Act was designed immediately to keep the wives and children of the poor in work in their own houses; 3 but it leaves no doubt that manufactures in England had not of themselves that tendency to self-development which would encourage an enlarging population. The woollen manufactures similarly appear, from the many statutes upon them, to have been vigorous at a fixed level, but to have shown no tendency to rise beyond that level. With a fixed market and a fixed demand, production continued uniform.

A few years subsequent, indeed, to the passing of the Act which I have quoted, a very curious complaint is entered in the statute book, from the surface of which we should gather, that so far from increasing, manufactures had alarmingly declined. The fact mentioned may bear another meaning, and a meaning far more favourable to the state of the country; although, if such a phenomenon were to occur at the present time, it could admit of but one interpretation. In the 18th and 19th of the 32nd of Henry VIII., all the important towns in England, from the Tweed to the Land's End, are stated, one by one, to have fallen into serious decay. Usually when we meet with language of this kind, we suppose it to mean nothing more than an awakening to the consciousness of evils which had long existed, and which had escaped notice only because no one was alive to them. In the present instance, however, the language was too strong and too detailed to allow of this explanation; and the great body of the English towns undoubtedly were declining in wealth and in the number of their inhabitants. "Divers and many beautiful houses of habitation," these statutes say, "built in tyme past within their walls and liberties, now are fallen down and decayed, and at this day remain unre-edified, and do lie as desolate and vacant grounds, many of them nigh adjoining to the High-streets, replenished with much uncleanness and filth, with pits, sellers, and vaults lying open and uncovered, to the great perill and danger of the inhabitants and other the King's subjects passing by the same; and some houses be very weak and feeble, ready to fall down, and therefore dangerous to pass by, to the great decay and hinderance of the said boroughs and towns." 4

At present, the decay of a town implies the decay of the trade of the town; and the decay of all towns simultaneously would imply a general collapse of the trade of the whole country. Walled towns, however, before the Reformation, existed for other purposes than as the centre points of industry: they existed for the protection of property and life: and although it is not unlikely that the agitation of the Reformation itself did to some degree interrupt the occupation of the people, yet I believe that the true account of the phenomenon which then so much disturbed the parliament, is, that one of their purposes was no longer required; the towns flagged for a time because the country had become secure. The woollen manufacture in Worcestershire was spreading into the open country, 5 and, doubtless, in other counties as well; and the "beautiful houses" which had fallen into decay, were those which, in the old times of insecurity, had been occupied by wealthy merchants and tradesmen, who were now enabled, by a strong and settled government, to dispense with the shelter of locked gates and fortified walls, and remove their residences to more convenient situations. It was, in fact, the first symptom of the impending social revolution. Two years before the passing of this Act, the magnificent Hengrave Hall, in Suffolk, had been completed by Sir Thomas Kitson, "mercer of London," 6 and Sir Thomas Kitson was but one of many of the rising merchants who were now able to root themselves on the land by the side of the Norman nobility, first to rival, and then slowly to displace them.

This mighty change, however, was long in silent progress before it began to tell on the institutions of the country. When city burghers bought estates, the law insisted jealously on their accepting with them all the feudal obligations. Attempts to use the land as "a commodity" were, as we shall presently see, angrily repressed; while, again, in the majority of instances, such persons endeavoured, as they do at present, to cover the recent origin of their families by adopting the manners of the nobles, instead of transferring the habits of the towns to the parks and chases of the English counties. The old English organisation maintained its full activity; and the duties of property continued to be for another century more considered than its rights.

Turning, then, to the tenure of land—for if we would understand the condition of the people, it is to this point that our first attention must be directed—we find that through the many complicated varieties of it there was one broad principle which bore equally upon every class, that the land of England must provide for the defence of England. The feudal system, though practically modified, was still the organising principle of the nation, and the owner of land was bound to military service for his country whenever occasion required. Further, the land was to be so administered, that the accustomed number of families supported by it should not be diminished, and that the State should suffer no injury from the carelessness or selfishness of the owners. 7 Land never was private property in that personal sense of property in which we speak of a thing as our own, with which we may do as we please; and in the administration of estates, as indeed in the administration of all property whatsoever, duty to the State was at all times supposed to override private interest or inclination. Even tradesmen, who took advantage of the fluctuations of the market, were rebuked by parliament for "their greedy and covetous minds," "as more regarding their own singular lucre and profit than the commonweal of the Realm;" 8 and although in an altered world, neither industry nor enterprise will thrive except under the stimulus of self-interest, we may admire the confidence which in another age expected every man to prefer the advantage of the community to his own. All land was held upon a strictly military principle. It was the representative of authority, and the holder or the owner took rank in the army of the State according to the nature of his connection with it. It was first broadly divided among the great nobility holding immediately under the crown, who, above and beyond the ownership of their private estates, were the Lords of the Fee throughout their presidency, and possessed in right of it the services of knights and gentlemen who held their manors under them, and who followed their standard in war. Under the lords of manors, again, small freeholds and copyholds were held of various extent, often forty shilling and twenty shilling value, tenanted by peasant occupiers, who thus, on their own land, lived as free Englishmen, maintaining by their own free labour themselves and their families. There was thus a descending scale of owners, each of whom possessed his separate right, which the law guarded and none might violate; yet no one of whom, again, was independent of an authority higher than himself; and the entire body of the English free possessors of the soil was interpenetrated by a coherent organisation which converted them into a perpetually subsisting army of soldiers. The extent of land which was held by the petty freeholders was very large, and the possession of it was jealously treasured; the private estates of the nobles and gentlemen were either cultivated by their own servants, or let out, as at present, to free tenants; or (in earlier times) were occupied by villains, a class who, without being bondmen, were expected to furnish further services than those of the field, services which were limited by the law, and recognised by an outward ceremony, a solemn oath and promise from the villain to his lord. Villanage, in the reign of Henry VIII., had practically ceased. The name of it last appears upon the statute book in the early years of the reign of Richard II., when the disputes between villains and their liege lords on their relative rights had furnished matter for cumbrous lawsuits, and by general consent the relation had merged of itself into a more liberal form. Thus serfdom had merged or was rapidly merging into free servitude; but it did not so merge that labouring men, if they pleased, were allowed to live in idleness. Every man was regimented somewhere; and although the peasantry, when at full age, were allowed, under restrictions, their own choice of masters, yet the restrictions both on masters and servants were so severe as to prevent either from taking advantage of the necessities of the other, or from terminating through caprice or levity, or for any insufficient reason, a connection presumed to be permanent. 9

Through all these arrangements a single aim is visible, that every man in England should have his definite place and definite duty assigned to him, and that no human being should be at liberty to lead at his own pleasure an unaccountable existence. The discipline of an army was transferred to the details of social life, and it issued in a chivalrous perception of the meaning of the word duty, and in the old characteristic spirit of English loyalty.

From the regulations with respect to land, a coarser advantage was also derived, of a kind which at the present time will be effectively appreciated. It is a common matter of dispute whether landed estates should be large or small; whether it is better that the land should be divided among small proprietors, cultivating their own ground, or that it should follow its present tendency, and be shared by a limited and constantly diminishing number of wealthy landlords. The advocates for a peasant proprietary tell us truly, that a landed monopoly is dangerous; that the possession of a spot of ground, though it be but a few acres, is the best security for loyalty, giving the state a pledge for its owner, and creating in the body of the nation a free, vigorous, and manly spirit. The advocates for the large estates tell us, that the masses are too ill-educated to be trusted with independence; that without authority over them, these small proprietors become wasteful, careless, improvident; that the free spirit becomes a democratic and dangerous spirit; and finally, that the resources of the land cannot properly be brought out by men without capital to cultivate it. Either theory is plausible. The advocates of both can support their arguments with an appeal to experience; and the verdict of fact has not as yet been pronounced emphatically.

The problem will be resolved in the future history of this country. It was also nobly and skilfully resolved in the past. The knights and nobles retained the authority and power which was attached to the lordships of the fees. They retained extensive estates in their own hands or in the occupation of their immediate tenants; but the large proportion of the lands was granted out by them to smaller owners, and the expenditure of their own incomes in the wages and maintenance of their vast retinues left but a small margin for indulgence in luxuries. The necessities of their position obliged them to regard their property rather as a revenue to be administered in trust, than as "a fortune" to be expended in indulgence. Before the Reformation, while the differences of social degree were enormous, the differences in habits of life were comparatively slight, and the practice of men in these things was curiously the reverse of our own. Dress, which now scarcely suffices to distinguish the master from his servant, was then the symbol of rank, prescribed by statute to the various orders of society as strictly as the regimental uniform to officers and privates; diet also was prescribed, and with equal strictness; but the diet of the nobleman was ordered down to a level which was then within the reach of the poorest labourer. In 1336, the following law was enacted by the Parliament of Edward III.: 10 "Whereas, heretofore through the excessive and over-many sorts of costly meats which the people of this Realm have used more than elsewhere, many mischiefs have happened to the people of this Realm—for the great men by these excesses have been sore grieved; and the lesser people, who only endeavour to imitate the great ones in such sort of meats, are much impoverished, whereby they are not able to aid themselves, nor their liege lord, in time of need, as they ought; and many other evils have happened, as well to their souls as their bodies—our Lord the King, desiring the common profit as well of the great men as the common people of his Realm, and considering the evils, grievances, and mischiefs aforesaid, by the common assent of the prelates, earls, barons, and other nobles of his said Realm, and of the commons of the same Realm, hath ordained and established that no man, of what estate or condition soever he be, shall cause himself to be served, in his house or elsewhere, at dinner, meal, or supper, or at any other time, with more than two courses, and each mess of two sorts of victuals at the utmost, be it of flesh or fish, with the common sorts of pottage, without sauce or any other sorts of victuals. And if any man choose to have sauce for his mess, he may, provided it be not made at great cost; and if fish or flesh be to be mixed therein, it shall be of two sorts only at the utmost, either fish or flesh, and shall stand instead of a mess, except only on the principal feasts of the year, on which days every man may be served with three courses at the utmost, after the manner aforesaid."

Sumptuary laws are among the exploded fallacies which we have outgrown, and we smile at the unwisdom which could expect to regulate private habits and manners by statute. Yet some statutes may be of moral authority when they cannot be actually enforced, and may have been regarded, even at the time at which they were issued, rather as an authoritative declaration of what wise and good men considered to be right, than as laws to which obedience could be compelled. This act, at any rate, witnesses to what was then thought to be right by "the great persons" of the English realm; and when great persons will submit themselves of their free will to regulations which restrict their private indulgence, they are in little danger of disloyalty from those whom fortune has placed below them.

Such is one aspect of these old arrangements; it is unnecessary to say that with these, as with all other institutions created and worked by human beings, the picture admits of being reversed. When by the accident of birth men are placed in a position of authority, no care in their training will prevent it from falling often to singularly unfit persons. The command of a permanent military force was a temptation to ambition, to avarice, or hatred, to the indulgence of private piques and jealousies, to political discontent on private and personal grounds. A combination of three or four of the leading nobles was sufficient, when an incapable prince sate on the throne, to effect a revolution; and the rival claims of the houses of York and Lancaster to the crown, took the form of a war unequalled in history for its fierce and determined malignancy, the whole nation tearing itself in pieces in a quarrel in which no principle was at stake, and no national object was to be gained. A more terrible misfortune never befel either this or any other country, and it was made possible only in virtue of that loyalty with which the people followed the standard, through good and evil, of their feudal superiors. It is still a question, however, whether the good or the evil of the system predominated; and the answer to such question is the more difficult because we have no criterion by which, in these matters, degrees of good and evil admit of being measured. Arising out of the character of the nation, it reflected this character in all its peculiarities; and there is something truly noble in the coherence of society upon principles of fidelity. Fidelity of man to man is among the rarest excellences of humanity, and we can tolerate large evils which arise out of such a cause. Under the feudal system men were held together by oaths, free acknowledgments, and reciprocal obligations, entered into by all ranks, high and low, binding servants to their masters, as well as nobles to their kings; and in the frequent forms of the language in which the oaths were sworn we cannot choose but see that we have lost something in exchanging these ties for the harsher connecting links of mutual self-interest.

"When a freeman shall do fealty to his lord," the statute says, "he shall hold his right hand upon the book, and shall say thus:—Hear you, my lord, that I shall be to you both faithful and true, and shall owe my faith to you for the land that I hold, and lawfully shall do such customs and services as my duty is to you, at the times assigned, so help me God and all his saints."

"The villain," also, "when he shall do fealty to his lord, shall hold his right hand over the book, and shall say:—Hear you, my lord, that I from this day forth unto you shall be true and faithful, and shall owe you fealty for the land which I hold of you in villanage; and that no evil or damage will I see concerning you, but I will defend and warn you to my power. So help me God and all his saints." 11

Again, in the distribution of the produce of land, men dealt fairly and justly with each other; and in the material condition of the bulk of the people there is a fair evidence that the system worked efficiently and well. It worked well for the support of a sturdy high-hearted race, sound in body and fierce in spirit, and furnished with thews and sinews which, under the stimulus of those "great shins of beef," 12 their common diet, were the wonder of the age. "What comyn folke in all this world," says a state paper in 1515 13 "may compare with the comyns of England in riches, freedom, liberty, welfare, and all prosperity? What comyn folke is so mighty, so strong in the felde, as the comyns of England?" The relative numbers of the French and English armies which fought at Cressy and Agincourt may have been exaggerated, but no allowance for exaggeration will effect the greatness of those exploits; and in stories of authentic actions under Henry VIII., where the accuracy of the account is undeniable, no disparity of force made Englishmen shrink from enemies wherever they could meet them. Again and again a few thousands of them carried dismay into the heart of France. Four hundred adventurers, vagabond apprentices, from London, 14 who formed a volunteer corps in the Calais garrison, were for years the terror of Normandy. In the very frolic of conscious power they fought and plundered, without pay, without reward, except what they could win for themselves; and when they fell at last they fell only when surrounded by six times their number, and were cut to pieces in careless desperation. Invariably, by friend and enemy alike, the English are described as the fiercest people in all Europe (the English wild beasts, Benvenuto Cellini calls them); and this great physical power they owed to the profuse abundance in which they lived, and to the soldier's training in which every man of them was bred from childhood. The state of the working classes can, however, be more certainly determined by a comparison of their wages with the prices of food. Both were regulated, so far as regulation was possible, by act of parliament, and we have therefore data of the clearest kind by which to judge. The majority of agricultural labourers lived, as I have said, in the houses of their employers; this, however, was not the case with all, and if we can satisfy ourselves as to the rate at which those among the poor were able to live who had cottages of their own, we may be assured that the rest did not live worse at their masters' tables.

Wheat, the price of which necessarily varied, averaged in the middle of the fourteenth century tenpence the bushel; 15 barley averaging at the same time three shillings the quarter. With wheat the fluctuation was excessive; a table of its possible variations describes it as ranging from eighteenpence the quarter to twenty shillings; the average, however, being six and eightpence. 16 When the price was above this sum, the merchants might import to bring it down; 17 when it was below this price the farmers were allowed to export to the foreign markets. 18 The same scale, with a scarcely appreciable tendency to rise, continued to hold until the disturbance in the value of the currency. In the twelve years from 1551 to 1562, although once before harvest wheat rose to the extraordinary price of forty-five shillings a quarter, it fell immediately after to five shillings and four. 19 Six and eightpence continued to be considered in parliament as the average; 20 and on the whole it seems to have been maintained for that time with little variation. 21

Beef and pork were a halfpenny a pound—mutton was three farthings. They were fixed at these prices by the 3rd of the 24th of Hen. VIII. But the act was unpopular both with buyers and with sellers. The old practice had been to sell in the gross, and under that arrangement the rates had been generally lower. Stow says, 22 "It was this year enacted that butchers should sell their beef and mutton by weight—beef for a halfpenny the pound, and mutton for three farthings; which being devised for the great commodity of the realm (as it was thought), hath proved far otherwise: for at that time fat oxen were sold for six and twenty shillings and eightpence the piece; fat wethers for three shillings and fourpence the piece; fat calves at a like price; and fat lambs for twelvepence. The butchers of London sold penny pieces of beef for the relief of the poor—every piece two pound and a half, sometimes three pound for a penny; and thirteen and sometimes fourteen of these pieces for twelvepence; mutton eightpence the quarter, and an hundred weight of beef for four shillings and eightpence." The act was repealed in consequence of the complaints against it, 23 but the prices never fell again to what they had been, although beef sold in the gross could still be had for a halfpenny a pound in 1570. 24 Other articles of food were in the same proportion. The best pig or goose in a country market could be bought for fourpence; a good capon for threepence or fourpence; a chicken for a penny; a hen for twopence. 25

Strong beer, such as we now buy for eighteenpence a gallon, was then a penny a gallon; 26 and table-beer less than a halfpenny. French and German wines were eightpence the gallon. Spanish and Portuguese wines a shilling. This was the highest price at which the best wines might be sold; and if there was any fault in quality or quantity, the dealers forfeited four times the amount. 27 Rent, another important consideration, cannot be fixed so accurately, for parliament did not interfere with it. Here, however, we are not without very tolerable information. "My father," says Latimer, 28 "was a yeoman, and had no lands of his own; only he had a *farm of three or four pounds by the year* at the uttermost, and hereupon he tilled so much as kept half-a-dozen men. He had walk for a hundred sheep, and my mother milked thirty kine. He was able, and did find the king a harness with himself and his horse. I remember that I buckled on his harness when he went to Blackheath field. He kept me to school, or else I had not been able to have preached before the King's Majesty now. He married my sisters with five pounds, or twenty nobles, each, having brought them up in godliness and fear of God. He kept hospitality for his poor neighbours, and some alms he gave to the poor; and all this he did of the said farm." If "three or four pounds at the uttermost" was the rent of a farm yielding such results, the rent of labourers' cottages is not likely to have been considerable. 29

Some uncertainty is unavoidable in all calculations of the present nature; yet, after making the utmost allowances for errors, we may conclude from such a table of prices that a penny, in terms of the labourer's necessities, must have been nearly equal in the reign of Henry VIII. to the present shilling. For a penny, at the time of which I write, the labourer could buy as much bread, beef, beer, and wine—he could do as much towards finding lodging for himself and his family—as the labourer of the nineteenth century can for a shilling. I do not see that this admits of question. Turning, then, to the table of wages, it will be easy to ascertain his position. By the 3rd of the 6th of Henry VIII. it was enacted that master carpenters, masons, bricklayers, tylers, plumbers, glaziers, joiners, and other employers of such skilled workmen, should give to each of their journeymen, if no meat or drink was allowed, sixpence a day for the half year, fivepence a day for the other half; or fivepence-halfpenny for the yearly average. The common labourers were to receive fourpence a day for half the year, for the remaining half, threepence. 30 In the harvest months they were allowed to work by the piece, and might earn considerably more; 31 so that, in fact (and this was the rate at which their wages were usually estimated), the day labourer, if in full employment, received on an average fourpence a day for the whole year. Allowing a deduction of one day in a fortnight for a saint's day or a holiday, he received, therefore, steadily and regularly, if well conducted, an equivalent of something near to twenty shillings a week, the wages at present paid in English colonies: and this is far from being a full account of his advantages. Except in rare instances, the agricultural labourer held land in connection with his house, while in most parishes, if not in all, there were large ranges of common and unenclosed forest land, which furnished his fuel to him gratis, where pigs might range, and ducks and geese; where, if he could afford a cow, he was in no danger of being unable to feed it; and so important was this privilege considered, that when the commons began to be largely enclosed, parliament insisted that the working man should not be without some piece of ground on which he could employ his own and his family's industry. 32 By the 7th of the 31st of Elizabeth, it was ordered that no cottage should be built for residence without four acres of land at lowest being attached to it for the sole use of the occupants of such cottage.

It will, perhaps, be supposed that such comparative prosperity of labour was the result of the condition of the market in which it was sold, that the demand for labour was large and the supply limited, and that the state of England in the sixteenth century was analogous to that of Australia or Canada at the present time. And so long as we confine our view to the question of wages alone, it is undoubted that legislation was in favour of the employer. The Wages Act of Henry VIII. was unpopular with the labourers, and was held to deprive them of an opportunity of making better terms for themselves. 33 But we shall fall into extreme error if we translate into the language of modern political economy the social features of a state of things which in no way correspond to our own. There was this essential difference, that labour was not looked upon as a market commodity; the government (whether wisely or not, I do not presume to determine) attempting to portion out the rights of the various classes of society by the rule, not of economy, but of equity. Statesmen did not care for the accumulation of capital; they desired to see the physical well-being of all classes of the commonwealth maintained at the highest degree which the producing power of the country admitted; and population and production remaining stationary, they were able to do it. This was their object, and they were supported in it by a powerful and efficient majority of the nation. On the one side parliament interfered to protect employers against their labourers; but it was equally determined that employers should not be allowed to abuse their opportunities; and this directly appears from the 4th of the 5th of Elizabeth, by which, on the most trifling appearance of a depreciation in the currency, it was declared that the labouring man could no longer live on the wages assigned to him by the act of Henry; and a sliding scale was instituted by which, for the future, wages should be adjusted to the price of food. 34

The same conclusion may be gathered also, indirectly, from other acts, interfering imperiously with the rights of property where a disposition showed itself to exercise them selfishly. The city merchants, as I have said, were becoming landowners; and some of them attempted to apply the rules of trade to the management of landed estates. While wages were ruled so high, it answered better as a speculation to convert arable land into pasture; but the law immediately stepped in to prevent a proceeding which it regarded as petty treason to the commonwealth. Self-protection is the first law of life; and the country relying for its defence on an able-bodied population, evenly distributed, ready at any moment to be called into action, either against foreign invasion or civil disturbance, it could not permit the owners of land to pursue for their own benefit a course of action which threatened to weaken its garrisons. It is not often that we are able to test the wisdom of legislation by specific results so clearly as in the present instance. The first attempts of the kind which I have described were made in the Isle of Wight, early in the reign of Henry VII. Lying so directly exposed to attacks from France, the Isle of Wight was a place which it was peculiarly important to keep in a state of defence, and the following act was therefore the consequence:—

"Forasmuch as it is to the surety of the Realm of England that the Isle of Wight, in the county of Southampton, be well inhabited with English people, for the defence as well of our antient enemies of the Realm of France as of other parties; the which Isle is late decayed of people by reason that many towns and villages have been let down, and the fields dyked and made pasture for beasts and cattle, and also many dwelling-places, farms, and farmholds have of late time been used to be taken into one man's hold and hands, that of old time were wont to be in many several persons' holds and hands, and many several households kept in them; and thereby much people multiplied, and the same Isle thereby well inhabited, which now, by the occasion aforesaid, is desolate and not inhabited, but occupied with beasts and cattle, so that if hasty remedy be not provided, that Isle cannot long be kept and defended, but open and ready to the hands of the king's enemies, which God forbid. For remedy hereof, it is ordained and enacted that no manner of person, of what estate, degree, or condition soever, shall take any several farms more than one, whereof the yearly value shall not exceed the sum of ten marks; and if any several leases afore this time have been made to any person or persons of divers and sundry farmholds, whereof the yearly value shall exceed that sum, then the said person or persons shall choose one farmhold at his pleasure, and the remnant of his leases shall be utterly void." 35

An act, tyrannical in form, was singularly justified by its consequences. The farms were rebuilt, the lands reploughed, the island repeopled; and in 1546, when a French army of sixty thousand men attempted to effect a landing at St. Helen's, they were defeated and driven off by the militia of the island and a few levies transported from Hampshire and the adjoining counties. 36 The money-making spirit, however, lay too deep to be checked so readily. The trading classes were growing rich under the strong rule of the Tudors. Increasing numbers of them were buying or renting land; and the symptoms complained of broke out in the following reign in many parts of England. They could not choose but break out indeed; for they were the outward marks of a vital change, which was undermining the feudal constitution, and would by and bye revolutionise and destroy it. Such symptoms it was impossible to extinguish; but the government wrestled long and powerfully to hold down the new spirit; and they fought against it successfully, till the old order of things had finished its work, and the time was come for it to depart. By the 1st of the 7th of Henry VIII., the laws of feudal tenure were put in force against the landed traders. Wherever lands were converted from tillage to pasture, the lords of the fee had authority to seize half of all profits until the farm-buildings were reconstructed. If the immediate lord did not do his duty, the lord next above him was to do it; and the evil still increasing, the act, twenty years later, was extended further, and the king had power to seize. 37 Nor was this all. Sheep-farming had become an integral branch of business; and falling into the hands of men who understood each other, it had been made a monopoly, affecting seriously the prices of wool and mutton. 38 Stronger measures were therefore now taken, and the class to which the offenders belonged was especially pointed out by parliament.

"Whereas," says the 13th of the 25th of Henry VIII., "divers and sundry persons of the king's subjects of this Realm, to whom God of his goodness hath disposed great plenty and abundance of moveable substance, now of late, within few years, have daily studied, practised, and invented ways and means how they might accumulate and gather together into few hands, as well great multitude of farms as great plenty of cattle, and in especial, sheep, putting such lands as they can get to pasture and not to tillage; whereby they have not only pulled down churches and towns and enhanced the old rates of the rents of the possessions of this Realm, or else brought it to such excessive fines that no poor man is able to meddle with it, but also have raised and enhanced the prices of all manner of corn, cattle, wool, pigs, geese, hens, chickens, eggs, and such other commodities, almost double above the prices which hath been accustomed, by reason whereof a marvellous multitude of the poor people of this realm be not able to provide meat, drink, and clothes necessary for themselves, their wives, and children, but be so discouraged with misery and poverty, that they fall daily to theft, robbery, and other inconveniences, or pitifully die for hunger and cold; and it is thought by the king's humble and loving subjects, that one of the greatest occasions that moveth those greedy and covetous people so to accumulate and keep in their hands such great portions and parts of the lands of this Realm from the occupying of the poor husbandmen, and so to use it in pasture and not in tillage, is the great profit that cometh of sheep which be now come into a few persons' hands, in respect of the whole number of the king's subjects; it is hereby enacted, that no person shall have or keep on lands not their own inheritance more than 2000 sheep; that no person shall occupy more than two farms; and that the 19th of the 4th of Henry VII., and those other acts obliging the lords of the fees to do their duty, shall be re-enacted and enforced." 39

By these measures the money-making spirit was for a time driven back, and the country resumed its natural course. I am not concerned to defend the economic wisdom of such proceedings; but they prove, I think, conclusively, that the labouring classes owed their advantages not to the condition of the labour market, but to the care of the state; and that when the state relaxed its supervision, or failed to enforce its regulations, the labourers being left to the market chances, sank instantly in the unequal struggle with capital.

The government, however, remained strong enough to hold its ground (except during the discreditable interlude of the reign of Edward VI.) for the first three quarters of the century; and until that time the working classes of this country remained in a condition more than prosperous. They enjoyed an abundance far beyond what in general falls to the lot of that order in long-settled countries; incomparably beyond what the same class were enjoying at that very time in Germany or France. The laws secured them; and that the laws were put in force we have the direct evidence of successive acts of the legislature justifying the general policy by its success: and we have also the indirect evidence of the contented loyalty of the great body of the people at a time when, if they had been discontented, they held in their own hands the means of asserting what the law acknowledged to be their right. The government had no power to compel submission to injustice, as was proved by the fate of an attempt to levy a "benevolence" by force, in 1525. The people resisted with a determination against which the crown commissioners were unable to contend, and the scheme ended with an acknowledgment of fault by Henry, who retired with a good grace from an impossible position. If the peasantry had been suffering under any real grievances we should not have failed to have heard of them when the religious rebellions furnished so fair an opportunity to press those grievances forward. Complaint was loud enough when complaint was just, under the Somerset protectorate. 40

The incomes of the great nobles cannot be determined, for they varied probably as much as they vary now. Under Henry IV. the average income of an earl was estimated at £2000 a year. 41 Under Henry VIII. the great Duke of Buckingham, the wealthiest English peer, had £6000. 42 And the income of the Archbishop of Canterbury was rated at the same amount. 43 But the establishments of such men were enormous; their ordinary retinues in time of peace consisting of many hundred persons; and in war, when the duties of a nobleman called him to the field, although in theory his followers were paid by the crown, yet the grants of parliament were on so small a scale that the theory was seldom converted into fact, and a large share of the expenses was paid often out of private purses. The Duke of Norfolk, in the Scotch war of 1523, declared (not complaining of it, but merely as a reason why he should receive support) that he had spent all his private means upon the army; and in the sequel of this history we shall find repeated instances of knights and gentlemen voluntarily ruining themselves in the service of their country. The people, not universally, but generally, were animated by a true spirit of sacrifice; by a true conviction that they were bound to think first of England, and only next of themselves; and unless we can bring ourselves to understand this, we shall never understand what England was under the reigns of the Plantagenets and Tudors. The expenses of the court under Henry VII. were a little over £14,000 a year, out of which were defrayed the whole cost of the king's establishment, the expenses of entertaining foreign ambassadors, the wages and maintenance of the yeomen of the guard, the retinues of servants, and all necessary outlay not incurred for public business. Under Henry VIII., of whose extravagance we have heard so much, and whose court was the most magnificent in the world, these expenses were £19,894 16s. 8d., 44 a small sum when compared with the present cost of the royal establishment, even if we adopt the relative estimate of twelve to one, and suppose it equal to £240,000 a year of our money. But indeed it was not equal to £240,000; for, although the proportion held in articles of common consumption, articles of luxury were very dear indeed. 45

Passing down from the king and his nobles, to the body of the people, we find that the income qualifying a country gentleman to be justice of the peace was £20 a year, 46 and if he did his duty, his office was no sinecure. We remember Justice Shallow and his clerk Davy, with his novel theory of magisterial law; and Shallow's broad features have so English a cast about them, that we may believe there were many such, and that the duty was not always very excellently done. But the Justice Shallows were not allowed to repose upon their dignity. The justice of the peace was required not only to take cognisance of open offences, but to keep surveillance over all persons within his district, and over himself in his own turn there was a surveillance no less sharp, and penalties for neglect prompt and peremptory. 47 Four times a year he was to make proclamation of his duty, and exhort all persons to complain against him who had occasion.

Twenty pounds a year, and heavy duties to do for it, represented the condition of the squire of the parish. 48 By the 2nd of the 2nd of Henry V., "the wages" of a parish priest were limited to £5 6s. 8d., except in cases where there was special licence from the bishop, when they might be raised as high as £6. Priests were probably something better off under Henry VIII., but the statute remained in force, and marks an approach at least to their ordinary salary. 49 The priest had enough, being unmarried, to supply him in comfort with the necessaries of life. The squire had enough to provide moderate abundance for himself and his family. Neither priest nor squire was able to establish any steep difference in outward advantages between himself and the commons among whom he lived.

The habits of all classes were open, free, and liberal. There are two expressions corresponding one to the other, which we frequently meet with in old writings, and which are used as a kind of index, marking whether the condition of things was or was not what it ought to be. We read of "merry England;"—when England was not merry, things were not going well with it. We hear of "the glory of hospitality," England's pre-eminent boast,-by the rules of which all tables, from the table of the twenty-shilling freeholder to the table in the baron's hall and abbey refectory, were open at the dinner hour to all comers, without stint or reserve, or question asked: 50 to every man, according to his degree, who chose to ask for it there was free fee and free lodging; bread, beef, and beer for his dinner; for his lodging, perhaps, only a mat of rushes in a spare corner of the hall, with a billet of wood for a pillow, 51 but freely offered and freely taken, the guest probably faring much as his host fared, neither worse nor better. There was little fear of an abuse of such licence, for suspicious characters had no leave to wander at pleasure; and for any man found at large and unable to give a sufficient account of himself, there were the ever-ready parish stocks or town gaol. The "glory of hospitality" lasted far down into Elizabeth's time; and then, as Camden says, "came in great bravery of building, to the marvellous beautifying of the realm, but to the decay" of what he valued more.

In such frank style the people lived, hating three things with all their hearts: idleness, want, and cowardice; and for the rest carrying their hearts high, and having their hands full. The 52 hour of rising, winter and summer, was four o'clock, with breakfast at five, after which the labourers went to work and the gentlemen to business, of which they had no little. In the country every unknown face was challenged and examined—if the account given was insufficient, he was brought before the justice; if the village shopkeeper sold bad wares, if the village cobbler made "unhonest" shoes, if servants and masters quarrelled, all was to be looked to by the justice; there was no fear lest time should hang heavy with him. At twelve he dined; after dinner he went hunting, or to his farm or to what he pleased. 53 It was a life unrefined, perhaps, but coloured with a broad, rosy, English health.

Of the education of noblemen and gentlemen we have contradictory accounts, as might be expected. The universities were well filled, by the sons of yeomen chiefly. The cost of supporting them at the colleges was little, and wealthy men took a pride in helping forward any boys of promise. 54 It seems clear also, as the Reformation drew nearer, while the clergy were sinking lower and lower, a marked change for the better became perceptible in a portion at least of the laity. The more old-fashioned of the higher ranks were slow in moving; for as late as the reign of Edward VI. 55 there were peers of parliament unable to read; but on the whole, the invention of printing, and the general ferment which was commencing all over the world, had produced marked effects in all classes. Henry VIII. himself spoke four languages, and was well read in theology and history; and the high accomplishments of More and Sir T. Elliott, of Wyatt and Cromwell, were but the extreme expression of a temper which was rapidly spreading, and which gave occasion, among other things to the following reflection in Erasmus. "Oh, strange vicissitudes of human things," exclaims he. "Heretofore the heart of learning was among such as professed religion. Now, while they for the most part give themselves up, *ventri luxui pecuniæque*, the love of learning is gone from them to secular princes, the court and the nobility. May we not justly be ashamed of ourselves? The feasts of priests and divines are drowned in wine, are filled with scurrilous jests, sound with intemperate noise and tumult, flow with spiteful slanders and defamation of others; while at princes' tables modest disputations are held concerning things which make for learning and piety."

A letter to Thomas Cromwell from his son's tutor will not be without interest on this subject; Cromwell was likely to have been unusually careful in his children's training, and we need not suppose that all boys were brought up as prudently. Sir Peter Carew, for instance, being a boy at about the same time, and giving trouble at the High School at Exeter, was led home to his father's house at Ottery, coupled between two foxhounds. 56 Yet the education of Gregory Cromwell is probably not far above what many young men of the middle and higher ranks were beginning to receive. Henry Dowes was the tutor's name, beyond which fact I know nothing of him. His letter is as follows:—

"After that it pleased your mastership to give me in charge, not only to give diligent attendance upon Master Gregory, but also to instruct him with good letters, honest manners, pastyme of instruments, and such other qualities as should be for him meet and convenient, pleaseth it you to understand that for the accomplishment thereof I have endeavoured myself by all ways possible to excogitate how I might most profit him. In which behalf, through his diligence, the success is such as I trust shall be to your good contentation and pleasure, and to his no small profit. But for cause the summer was spent in the service of the wild gods, [and] it is so much to be regarded after what fashion youth is brought up, in which time that that is learned for the most part will not be wholly forgotten in the older years, I think it my duty to acertain your mastership how he spendeth his time. And first after he hath heard mass he taketh a lecture of a dialogue of Erasmus' *Colloquies*, called *Pietas Puerilis*, wherein is described a very picture of one that should be virtuously brought up; and for cause it is so necessary for him, I do not only cause him to read it over, but also to practise the precepts of the same. After this he exerciseth his hand in writing one or two hours, and readeth upon Fabyan's *Chronicle* as long. The residue of the day he doth spend upon the lute and virginals. When he rideth, as he doth very oft, I tell him by the way some history of the Romans or the Greeks, which I cause him to rehearse again in a tale. For his recreation he useth to hawk and hunt and shoot in his long bow, which frameth and succeedeth so well with him that he seemeth to be thereunto given by nature." 57

I have spoken of the organisation of the country population, I have now to speak of that of the towns, of the trading classes and manufacturing classes, the regulations respecting which are no less remarkable and no less illustrative of the national character. If the tendency of trade to assume at last a form of mere self-interest be irresistible, if political economy represent the laws to which in the end it is forced to submit itself, the nation spared no efforts, either of art or policy, to defer to the last moment the unwelcome conclusion.

The names and shadows linger about London of certain ancient societies, the members of which may still occasionally be seen in quaint gilt barges pursuing their own difficult way among the swarming steamers; when on certain days, the traditions concerning which are fast dying out of memory, the Fishmongers' Company, the Goldsmiths' Company, the Mercers' Company, make procession down the river for civic feastings at Greenwich or Blackwall. The stately tokens of ancient honour still belong to them, and the remnants of ancient wealth and patronage and power. Their charters may be read by curious antiquaries, and the bills of fare of their ancient entertainments. But for what purpose they were called into being, what there was in these associations of common trades to surround with gilded insignia, and how they came to be possessed of broad lands and church preferments, few people now care to think or to inquire. Trade and traders have no dignity any more in the eyes of any one, except what money lends to them; and these outward symbols scarcely rouse even a passing feeling of curiosity. And yet these companies were once something more than names. They are all which now remain of a vast organisation which once penetrated the entire trading life of England—an organisation set on foot to realise that most necessary, if most difficult, condition of commercial excellence under which man should deal faithfully with his brother, and all wares offered for sale, of whatever kind, should honestly be what they pretend to be. 58 I spoke of the military principle which directed the distribution and the arrangements of land. The analogy will best explain a state of things in which every occupation was treated as the division of an army; regiments being quartered in every town, each with its own self-elected officers, whose duty was to exercise authority over all persons professing the business to which they belonged; who were to see that no person undertook to supply articles which he had not been educated to manufacture; who were to determine the prices at which such articles ought justly to be sold; above all, who were to take care that the common people really bought at shops and stalls what they supposed themselves to be buying; that cloth put up for sale was true cloth, of true texture and full weight: that leather was sound and well tanned; wine pure, measures honest; flour unmixed with devil's dust;—who were generally to look to it that in all contracts between man and man for the supply of man's necessities, what we call honesty of dealing should be truly and faithfully observed. 59 An organisation for this purpose did once really exist in England, 60 really trying to do the work which it was intended to do, as half the pages of our early statutes witness. In London, as the metropolis, a central council sate for every branch of trade, and this council was in communication with the Chancellor and the Crown. It was composed of the highest and most respectable members of the profession, and its office was to determine prices, fix wages, arrange the rules of apprenticeship, and discuss all details connected with the business on which legislation might be required. Further, this council received the reports of the searchers—high officers taken from their own body, whose business was to inspect, in company with the lord mayor or some other city dignitary, the shops of the respective traders; to receive complaints, and to examine into them. In each provincial town local councils sate in connection with the municipal authorities, who fulfilled in these places the same duties; and their reports being forwarded to the central body, and considered by them, representations on all necessary matters were then made to the privy council; and by the privy council, if requisite, were submitted to parliament. If these representations were judged to require legislative interference, the statutes which were passed in consequence were returned through the Chancellor to the mayors of the various towns and cities, by whom they were proclaimed as law. No person was allowed to open a trade or to commence a manufacture, either in London or the provinces, unless he had first served his apprenticeship; unless he could prove to the satisfaction of the authorities that he was competent in his craft; and unless he submitted as a matter of course to their supervision. The legislature had undertaken not to let that indispensable task go wholly unattempted, of distributing the various functions of society by the rule of capacity; of compelling every man to do his duty in an honest following of his proper calling, securing to him that he in his turn should not be injured by his neighbour's misdoings.

The state further promising for itself that all able-bodied men should be found in work, 61 and not allowing any man to work at a business for which he was unfit, insisted as its natural right that children should not be allowed to grow up in idleness, to be returned at mature age upon its hands. Every child, so far as possible, was to be trained up in some business or calling, 62 idleness "being the mother of all sin," and the essential duty of every man being to provide honestly for himself and his family. The educative theory, for such it was, was simple but effective: it was based on the single principle that, next to the knowledge of a man's duty to God, and as a means towards doing that duty, the first condition of a worthy life was the ability to maintain it in independence. Varieties of inapplicable knowledge might be good, but they were not essential; such knowledge might be left to the leisure of after years, or it might be dispensed with without vital injury. Ability to labour could not be dispensed with, and this, therefore, the state felt it to be its own duty to see provided; so reaching, I cannot but think, the heart of the whole matter. The children of those who could afford the small entrance fees were apprenticed to trades, the rest were apprenticed to agriculture; and if children were found growing up idle, and their fathers or their friends failed to prove that they were able to secure them an ultimate maintenance, the mayors in towns and the magistrates in the country had authority to take possession of such children, and apprentice them as they saw fit, that when they grew up "they might not be driven" by want or incapacity "to dishonest courses." 63

Such is an outline of the organisation of English society under the Plantagenets and Tudors. A detail of the working of the trade laws would be beyond my present purpose. It is obvious that such laws could be enforced only under circumstances when production and population remained (as I said before) nearly stationary; and it would be madness to attempt to apply them to the changed condition of the present. It would be well if some competent person would make these laws the subject of a special treatise. I will run the risk, however, of wearying the reader with two or three illustrative statutes, which I have chosen, not as being more significant than many others, but as specimens merely of the discipline under which, for centuries, the trade and manufactures of England contrived to move;

showing on one side the good which the system effected, on the other the inevitable evils under which it finally sank.

The first which I shall quote concerns simply the sale of specific goods and the means by which tradesmen were prevented from enhancing prices. The Act is the 6th of the 24th of Henry VIII., and concerns the sale of wines, the statute prices of which I have already mentioned.

"Because," says this Act, "that divers merchants inhabiting within the city of London have of late not only presumed to bargain and sell in gross to divers of the king's subjects great quantities of wines of Gascony, Guienne, and French wines, some for five pounds per tonne, some for more and some for less, and so after the rate of excessive prices contrary to the effect of a good and laudable statute lately made in this present parliament; that is to say, contrary to and above the prices thereof set by the Right Honourable Lord Chancellor, Lord Treasurer, Lord President of the King's most honourable Council, Lord Privy Seal, and the two Chief Justices of either bench, whereby they be fallen into the penalties limited by the said statute; as by due proof made by examination taken is well known—but also having in their hands great abundance of wine, by them acquired and bought to be sold, obstinately and maliciously, since their said attemptate and defaults proved, have refused to bargain and sell to many of the king's subjects any of their said wines remaining and being in their hands; purposing and intending thereby their own singular and unreasonable lucres and profits, to have larger and higher prices of their said wines, to be set according to their insatiable appetites and minds; it is therefore ordained and enacted, by authority of this present parliament, that every merchant now having, or which shall hereafter have, wines to be sold, and refusing to sell or deliver, or not selling and delivering any of the said wines for ready money therefore to be paid, according to the price or prices thereof being set, shall forfeit and lose the value of the wine so required to be bought.... For due execution of which provision, and for the relief of the king's subjects, it shall be lawful to all and singular justices of the peace, mayors, bailiffs, and other head officers in shires, cities, boroughs, towns, etc., at the request of any person to whom the said merchant or merchants have refused to sell, to enter into the cellars and other places where such wines shall lie or be, and to sell and deliver the same wine or wines desired to be bought to the person or persons requiring to buy the same; taking of the buyer of the wine so sold to the use and satisfaction of the proprietor aforesaid, according to the prices determined by the law."

The next which I select is the eleventh of the second and third of Philip and Mary; and falling in the midst of the smoke of the Smithfield fires, and the cruelties of that melancholy time, it shines like a fair gleam of humanity, which will not lose anything of its lustre because the evils against which it contends have in our times, also, furnished matter for sorrow and calamity—calamity which we unhappily have been unable even to attempt to remedy. It is termed "An Act touching Weavers," and runs:

"Forasmuch as the weavers of this realm have, as well at this present parliament as at divers other times, complained that the rich and wealthy clothiers do in many ways oppress them—some by setting up and keeping in their houses divers looms, and keeping and maintaining them by journeymen and persons unskilful, to the decay of a great number of artificers which were brought up in the said science of weaving, with their families and their households—some by engrossing of looms into their hands and possession, and letting them out at such unreasonable rents, as the poor artificers are not able to maintain themselves, much less maintain their wives, families, and children—some also by giving much less wages and hire for weaving and workmanship than in times past they did, whereby they are enforced utterly to forsake their art and occupation wherein they have been brought up; It is, therefore, for remedy of the premises, and for the avoiding of a great number of inconveniences which may grow if in time it be not foreseen, ordained and enacted by authority of this present parliament, that no person using the feat or mystery of cloth-making, and dwelling out of a city, borough, market-town, or corporate town, shall keep, or retain, or have in his or their houses or possession, any more than one woollen loom at a time; nor shall by any means, directly or indirectly, receive or take any manner of profit, gain, or commodity, by letting or setting any loom, or any house wherein any loom is or shall be used or occupied, which shall be together by him set or let, upon pain of forfeiture for every week that any person shall do the contrary to the tenor and true meaning hereof, twenty shillings."

A provision then follows, limiting weavers living in towns to two looms—the plain intention being to prevent the cloth manufacture from falling into the power of large capitalists employing "hands;" and to enable as many persons as possible to earn all in their own homes their own separate independent living. I suppose that the parliament was aware that by pursuing this policy the cost of production was something increased; that cloth was thus made dearer than it would have been if trade had been left to follow its own course. It considered, however, that the loss was compensated to the nation by retaining its people in the condition not of "hands," but of men; by rendering them independent of masters, who only sought to make their own advantage at the expense of labour; and enabling them to continue to maintain themselves in manly freedom. The weak point of all such provisions did not lie, I think, in the economic aspect of them, but in a far deeper difficulty. The details of trade legislation, it is obvious, could only be determined by persons professionally conversant with those details; and the indispensable condition of success with such legislation is, that it be conducted under the highest sense of the obligations of honesty. No laws are of any service which are above the working level of public morality; and the deeper they are carried down into life, the larger become the opportunities of evasion. That the system succeeded for centuries is evident from the organisation of the companies remaining so long in its vitality; but the efficiency of this organisation for the maintenance of fair dealing could exist only so long as the companies themselves—their wardens and their other officials, who alone, *quisque in suâ arte*, were competent to judge what was right and what was wrong—could be trusted, at the same time being interested parties, to give a disinterested judgment. The largeness of the power inevitably committed to the councils was at once a temptation and an opportunity to abuse those powers; and slowly through the statute book we find the traces of the poison as it crept in and in. Already in the 24th of Henry VIII., we meet with complaints in the leather trade of the fraudulent conduct of the searchers, whose duty was to affix their seal upon leather ascertained to be sound, before it was exposed for sale, "which mark or print, for corruption and lucre, is commonly set and put by such as take upon them the search and sealing, as well upon leather insufficiently tanned, as upon leather well tanned, to the great deceit of the buyers thereof." About the same time, the "craft wardens" of the various fellowships, "out of sinister mind and purpose," were levying excessive fees on the admission of apprentices; and when parliament interfered to bring them to order, they "compassed and practised by cautill and subtle means to delude the good and wholesome statutes passed for remedy." 64 The old proverb, *Quis custodiat custodes*, had begun to verify itself, and the symptom was a fatal one. These evils, for the first half of the century, remained within compass; but as we pass on we find them increasing steadily. In the 7th and the 8th of Elizabeth, there are indications of the truck system; and towards her later years, the multiplying statutes and growing complaints and difficulties show plainly that the companies had lost their healthy vitality, and, with other relics of feudalism, were fast taking themselves away. There were no longer tradesmen to be found in sufficient numbers who were possessed of the necessary probity; and it is impossible not to connect such a phenomenon with the deep melancholy which in those years settled down on Elizabeth herself.

For, indeed, a change was coming upon the world, the meaning and direction of which even still is hidden from us, a change from era to era. The paths trodden by the footsteps of ages were broken up; old things were passing away, and the faith and the life of ten centuries were dissolving like a dream. Chivalry was dying; the abbey and the castle were soon together to crumble into ruins; and all the forms, desires, beliefs, convictions of the old world were passing away, never to return. A new continent had risen up beyond the western sea. The floor of heaven, inlaid with stars, had sunk back into an infinite abyss of immeasurable space; and the firm earth itself, unfixed from its foundations, was seen to be but a small atom in the awful vastness of the universe. In the fabric of habit in which they had so laboriously built for themselves, mankind were to remain no longer.

And now it is all gone—like an unsubstantial pageant faded; and between us and the old English there lies a gulf of mystery which the prose of the historian will never adequately bridge. They cannot come to us, and our imagination can but feebly penetrate to them. Only among the aisles of the cathedral, only as we gaze upon their silent figures sleeping on their tombs, some faint conceptions float before us of what these men were when they were alive; and perhaps in the sound of church bells, that peculiar creation of mediæval age, which falls upon the ear like the echo of a vanished world.

The transition out of this old state is what in this book I have undertaken to relate. As yet there were uneasy workings below the surface; but the crust was unbroken, and the nation remained outwardly unchanged as it had been for centuries. I have still some few features to add to my description.

Nothing, I think, proves more surely the mutual confidence which held together the government and the people, than the fact that all classes were armed. Every man, as I have already said, was a soldier; and every man was ready equipped at all times with the arms which corresponded to his rank. By the great statute of Winchester, 65 which was repeated and expanded on many occasions in the after reigns, it was enacted, "That every man have harness in his house to keep the peace after the antient assise—that is to say, every man between fifteen years of age and sixty years shall be assessed and sworn to armour according to the quantity of his lands and goods—that is, to wit, for fifteen pounds lands and forty marks goods, a hauberke, a helmet of iron, a sword, a dagger, and a horse. For ten pounds of lands and twenty marks goods, a hauberke, a helmet, a sword, and a dagger. For five pounds lands, a doublet, a helmet of iron, a sword, and a dagger. For forty shillings lands, a sword, a bow and arrows, and a dagger. And all others that may shall have bows and arrows. Review of armour shall be made every year two times, by two constables for every hundred and franchise thereunto appointed; and the constables shall present, to justices assigned for that purpose, such defaults as they do find."

As the archery was more developed, and the bow became the peculiar weapon of the English, regular practice was ordered, and shooting became at once the drill and the amusement of the people. Every hamlet had its pair of butts; and on Sundays and holidays 66 all able-bodied men were required to appear in the field, to employ their leisure hours "as valyant Englishmen ought to do," "utterly leaving the play at the bowls, quoits, dice, kails, and other unthrifty games;" magistrates, mayors, and bailiffs being responsible for their obedience, under penalty, if these officers neglected their duty, of a fine of twenty shillings for each offence. On the same days, the tilt-yard at the Hall or Castle was thrown open, and the young men of rank amused themselves with similar exercises. Fighting, or mock fighting—and the imitation was not unlike the reality—was at once the highest enjoyment and the noblest accomplishment of all ranks in the state; and over that most terrible of human occupations they had flung the enchanted halo of chivalry, decorating it with all the fairest graces, and consecrating it with the most heroic aspirations.

The chivalry, with much else, was often perhaps something ideal. In the wars of the Roses it had turned into mere savage ferocity; and in forty years of carnage the fighting propensities had glutted themselves. A reaction followed, and in the early years of Henry VIII. the statutes were growing obsolete, and the "unlawful games" rising again into favour. The younger nobles, or some among them, were shrinking from the tilt-yard, and were backward on occasions even when required for war. Lord Surrey, when waiting on the Border, expecting the Duke of Albany to invade the northern counties, in 1523, complained of the growing "slowness" of the young lords "to be at such journeys," 67 and of their "inclination to dancing, carding, and dicing." The people had followed the example, and were falling out of archery practice, exchanging it for similar amusements. Henry VIII., in his earlier days an Englishman after the old type, set himself resolutely to oppose these downward tendencies, and to brace again the slackened sinews of the nation. In his own person he was the best rider, the best lance, and the best archer in England; and while a boy he was dreaming of fresh Agincourts, and even of fresh crusades. In 1511, when he had been king only three years, parliament re-enacted the Winchester statute, with new and remarkable provisions; and twice subsequently in the course of his reign he returned back upon the subject, insisting upon it with increasing stringency. The language of the Act of 1511 is not a little striking. "The King's Highness," so the words run, "calling to his gracious remembrance that by the feats and exercise of the subjects of his realm in shooting in long bows, there had continually grown and been within the same great numbers and multitudes of good archers, which hath not only defended the realm and the subjects thereof against the cruel malice and dangers of their enemies in times heretofore past, but also, with little numbers and puissance in regard of their opposites, have done many notable acts and discomfitures of war against the infidels and others; and furthermore reduced divers regions and countries to their due obeysance, to the great honour, fame, and surety of this realm and subjects, and to the terrible dread and fear of all strange nations, anything to attempt or do to the hurt or damage of them: Yet nevertheless that archery and shooting in long bows is but little used, but daily does minish and decay, and abate more and more; for that much part of the commonalty and poor people of this realm, whereby of old time the great number and substance of archers had grown and multiplied, be not of power nor ability to buy them long bows of yew to exercise shooting in the same, and to sustain the continual charge thereof; and also because, by means and occasions of customable usage of tennis play, bowles, claish and other unlawful games, prohibited by many good and beneficent statutes, much impoverishment hath ensued: Wherefore, the King's Highness, of his great wisdom and providence, and also for zeal to the public weal, surety, and defence of this his realm, and the antient fame in this behalf to be revived, by the assent of his Lords Spiritual and Temporal, and his Commons in this present parliament assembled, hath enacted and established that the statute of Winchester for archers be put in due execution; and over that, that every man being the king's subject, not lame, decrepit, or maimed, being within the age of sixty years, except spiritual men, justices of the one bench and of the other, justices of the assize, and barons of the exchequer, do use and exercise shooting in long bows, and also do have a bow and arrows ready continually in his house, to use himself in shooting. And that every man having a man child or men children in his house, shall provide for all such, being of the age of seven years and above, and till they shall come to the age of seventeen years, a bow and two shafts, to learn them and bring them up in shooting; and after such young men shall come to the age of seventeen years, every of them shall provide and have a bow and four arrows continually for himself, at his proper costs and charges, or else of the gift and provision of his friends, and shall use the same as afore is rehearsed." Other provisions are added, designed to suppress the games complained of, and to place the bows more within the reach of the poor, by cheapening the prices of them.

The same statute 68 (and if this be a proof that it had imperfectly succeeded, it is a proof also of Henry's confidence in the general attachment of his subjects) was re-enacted thirty years later, at the crisis of the Reformation, when the northern counties were fermenting in a half-suppressed rebellion, and the catholics at home and abroad were intriguing to bring about a revolution. In this subsequent edition of it 69 some particulars are added which demand notice. In the directions to the villages for the maintaining each "a pair of buttes," it is ordered that no person above the age of twenty-four shall shoot with the light flight arrow at a distance under two hundred and twenty yards. Up to two hundred and twenty yards, therefore, the heavy war arrow was used, and this is to be taken as the effective range for fighting purposes of the old archery. 70 No measures could have been invented more effective than this vigorous arming to repress the self-seeking tendencies in the mercantile classes which I have mentioned as beginning to show themselves. Capital supported by force may make its own terms with labour; but capital lying between a king on one side resolved to prevent oppression, and a people on the other side in full condition to resist, felt even prudence dictate moderation, and reserved itself for a more convenient season.

Looking, therefore, at the state of England as a whole, I cannot doubt that under Henry the body of the people were prosperous, well-fed, loyal, and contented. In all points of material comfort they were as well off as they had ever been before; better off than they have ever been in later times.

Their amusements, as prescribed by statute, consisted in training themselves as soldiers. In the prohibitions of the statutes we see also what their amusements were inclined to be. But besides "the bowles and the claish," field sports, fishing, shooting, hunting, were the delight of every one, and although the forest laws were terrible, they served only to enhance the excitement by danger. Then, as now, no English peasant could be convinced that there was any moral crime in appropriating the wild game. It was an offence against statute law, but no offence against natural law; and it was rather a trial of skill between the noble who sought to monopolise a right which seemed to be common to all, and those who would succeed, if they could, in securing their own share of it. The Robin Hood ballads reflect the popular feeling and breathe the warm genial spirit of the old greenwood adventurers. If deer-stealing was a sin, it was more than compensated by the risk of the penalty to which those who failed submitted, when no other choice was left. They did not always submit, as the old northern poem shows of *Adam Bell, Clym of the Clough, and William of Cloudislee*, with its most immoral moral; yet I suppose there was never pedant who could resist the spell of those ringing lines, or refuse with all his heart to wish the rogues success, and confusion to the honest men.

But the English peasantry had pleasures of less ambiguous propriety, and less likely to mislead our sympathies. The chroniclers have given us many accounts of the masques and plays which were acted in the court, or in the castles of the noblemen. Such pageants were but the most splendid expression of a taste which was national and universal. As in ancient Greece, generations before the rise of the great dramas of Athens, itinerant companies wandered from village to village, carrying their stage furniture in their little carts, and acted in their booths and tents the grand stories of the mythology; so in England the mystery players haunted the wakes and fairs, and in barns or taverns, taprooms, or in the farmhouse kitchen, played at saints and angels, and transacted on their petty stage the drama of the Christian faith. To us, who can measure the effect of such scenes only by the impression which they would now produce upon ourselves, these exhibitions can seem but unspeakably profane; they were not profane when tendered in simplicity, and received as they were given. They were no more profane than those quaint monastic illuminations which formed the germ of Italian art; and as out of the illuminations arose those paintings which remain unapproached and unapproachable in their excellence, so out of the mystery plays arose the English drama, represented in its final completeness by the creations of a poet who, it now begins to be supposed, stands alone among mankind. We allow ourselves to think of Shakspeare or of Raphael or of Phidias, as having accomplished their work by the power of their own individual genius; but greatness like theirs is never more than the highest degree of an excellence which prevails widely round it, and forms the environment in which it grows. No single mind in single contact with the facts of nature could have created out of itself a Pallas, a Madonna, or a Lear; such vast conceptions are the growth of ages, the creations of a nation's spirit; and artist and poet, filled full with the power of that spirit, have but given them form, and nothing more than form. Nor would the form itself have been attainable by any isolated talent. No genius can dispense with experience; the aberrations of power, unguided or ill-guided, are ever in proportion to its intensity, and life is not long enough to recover from inevitable mistakes. Noble conceptions already existing, and a noble school of execution which will launch mind and hand at once upon their true courses, are indispensable to transcendent excellence; and Shakspeare's plays were as much the offspring of the long generations who had pioneered his road for him, as the discoveries of Newton were the offspring of those of Copernicus.

No great general ever arose out of a nation of cowards; no great statesman or philosopher out of a nation of fools; no great artist out of a nation of materialists; no great dramatist except when the drama was the passion of the people. Acting was the especial amusement of the English, from the palace to the village green. It was the result and expression of their power over themselves, and power over circumstances. They were troubled with no subjective speculations; no social problems vexed them with which they were unable to deal; and in the exuberance of vigour and spirits they were able, in the strict and literal sense of the word, to play with the materials of life. The mystery plays came first; next the popular legends; and then the great figures of English history came out upon the stage, or stories from Greek and Roman writers; or sometimes it was an extemporised allegory. Shakspeare himself has left us many pictures of the village drama. Doubtless he had seen many a Bottom in the old Warwickshire hamlets; many a Sir Nathaniel playing "Alissander," and finding himself "a little o'erparted." He had been with Snug the joiner, Quince the carpenter, and Flute the bellows-mender, when a boy we will not question, and acted with them, and written their parts for them; had gone up with them in the winter's evenings to the Lucy's Hall before the sad trouble with the deer-stealing; and afterwards, when he came to London and found his way into great society, he had not failed to see Polonius burlesquing Cæsar on the stage, as in his proper person Polonius burlesqued Sir William Cecil. The strolling players in *Hamlet* might be met at every country wake or festival; it was the direction in which the especial genius of the people delighted to revel. As I desire in this chapter not only to relate what were the habits of the people, but to illustrate them also, within such compass as I can allow myself, I shall transcribe out of Hall 71 a description of a play which was acted by the boys of St. Paul's School, in 1527, at Greenwich, adding some particulars, not mentioned by Hall, from another source. 72 It is a good instance of the fantastic splendour with which exhibitions of this kind were got up, and it possesses also a melancholy interest of another kind, as showing how little the wisest among us can foresee our own actions, or assure ourselves that the convictions of to-day will alike be the convictions of to-morrow. The occasion was the despatch of a French embassy to England, when Europe was outraged by the Duke of Bourbon's capture of Rome, when the children of Francis I. were prisoners in Spain, and Henry, with the full energy of his fiery nature, was flinging himself into a quarrel with Charles V. as the champion of the Holy See.

At the conclusion of a magnificent supper "the king led the ambassadors into the great chamber of disguisings; and in the end of the same chamber was a fountain, and on one side was a hawthorne tree, all of silk, with white flowers, and on the other side was a mulberry tree full of fair berries, all of silk. On the top of the hawthorne were the arms of England, compassed with the collar of the order 73 of St. Michael, and in the top of the mulberry tree stood the arms of France within a garter. The fountain was all of white marble, graven and chased; the bases of the same were balls of gold, supported by ramping beasts wound in leaves of gold. In the first work were gargoylles of gold, fiercely faced with spouts running. The second receit of this fountain was environed with winged serpents, all of gold, which griped it; and on the summit of the same was a fair lady, out of whose breasts ran abundantly water of marvellous delicious savour. About this fountain were benches of rosemary, fretted in braydes laid on gold, all the sides set with roses, on branches as they were growing about this fountain. On the benches sate eight fair ladies in strange attire, and so richly apparelled in cloth of gold, embroidered and cut over silver, that I cannot express the cunning workmanship thereof. Then when the king and queen were set, there was played before them, by children, in the Latin tongue, a manner of tragedy, the effect whereof was that the pope was in captivity and the church brought under foot. Whereupon St. Peter appeared and put the cardinal (Wolsey) in authority to bring the pope to his liberty, and to set up the church again. And so the cardinal made intercession with the kings of England and France that they took part together, and by their means the pope was delivered. Then in came the French king's children, and complained to the cardinal how the emperour kept them as hostages, and would not come to reasonable point with their father, whereupon they desired the cardinal to help for their deliverance; which wrought so with the king his master and the French king that he brought the emperour to a peace, and caused the two young princes to be delivered." So far Hall relates the scene, but there was more in the play than he remembered or cared to notice, and I am able to complete this curious picture of a pageant once really and truly a living spectacle in the old palace at Greenwich, by an inventory of the dresses worn by the boys and a list of the *dramatis personæ*.

The school-boys of St. Paul's were taken down the river with the master in six boats, at the cost of a shilling a boat—the cost of the dresses and the other expenses amounting in all to sixty-one shillings.

The characters were—

An orator in apparel of cloth of gold.

Religio, Ecclesia, Veritas, like three widows, in garments of silk, and suits of lawn and Cyprus.

Heresy and False Interpretation, like sisters of Bohemia, apparelled in silk of divers colours.

The heretic Luther, like a party friar, in russet damask and black taffety.

Luther's wife, like a frow of Spiers in Almayn, in red silk.

Peter, Paul, and James, in habits of white sarsnet, and three red mantles, and lace of silver and damask, and pelisses of scarlet.

A Cardinal in his apparel.

Two Sergeants in rich apparel.

The Dolphin and his brother in coats of velvet embroidered with gold, and capes of satin bound with velvet.

A Messenger in tinsel satin.

Six men in gowns of grey sarsnet.

Six women in gowns of crimson velvet.

War, in rich cloth of gold and feathers, armed.

Three Almeyns, in apparel all cut and holed in silk.

Lady Peace in lady's apparel white and rich.

Lady Quietness and Dame Tranquillity richly beseen in lady's apparel.

It is a strange world. This was in November, 1527. In November, 1530, but three brief years after, Wolsey lay dying in misery, a disgraced man, at Leicester Abbey; "the Pope's Holiness" was fast becoming in English eyes plain Bishop of Rome, held guilty towards this realm of unnumbered enormities, and all England was sweeping with immeasurable velocity towards the heretic Luther. So history repeats the lesson to us, not to boast ourselves of the morrow, for we know not what a day may bring forth.

Before I conclude this survey, it remains for me to say something of the position of the poor, and of the measures which were taken for the solution of that most difficult of all problems, the distinguishing the truly deserving from the worthless and the vagabond. The subject is one to which in the progress of this work I shall have more than one occasion to return; but inasmuch as a sentimental opinion prevails that an increase of poverty and the consequent enactment of poor-laws was the result of the suppression of the religious houses, and that adequate relief had been previously furnished by these establishments, it is necessary to say a few words for the removal of an impression which is as near as possible the reverse of the truth. I do not doubt that for many centuries these houses fulfilled honestly the intentions with which they were established; but as early as the reign of Richard II. it was found necessary to provide some other means for the support of the aged and impotent; the monasteries not only having then begun to neglect their duty; but by the appropriation of benefices having actually deprived the parishes of their local and independent means of charity. 74 Licences to beg were at that time granted to deserving persons; and it is noticeable that this measure was in a few years followed by the petition to Henry IV. for the secularisation of ecclesiastical property. 75 Thus early in our history had the regular clergy forgotten the nature of their mission, and the object for which the administration of the nation's charities had been committed to them. Thus early, while their houses were the nurseries of dishonest mendicancy, 76 they had surrendered to lay compassion, those who ought to have been their especial care. I shall unhappily have occasion hereafter to illustrate these matters in detail. I mention them in this place only in order to dissipate at once a foolish dream. At the opening of the sixteenth century, before the suppression of the monasteries had suggested itself in a practical form, pauperism was a state question of great difficulty, and as such I have at present to consider it.

For the able-bodied vagrant, it is well known that the old English laws had no mercy. When wages are low, and population has outgrown the work which can be provided for it, idleness may be involuntary and innocent; at a time when all industrious men could maintain themselves in comfort and prosperity, "when a fair day's wages for a fair day's work" was really and truly the law of the land, it was presumed that if strong capable men preferred to wander about the country, and live upon the labour of others, mendicancy was not the only crime of which they were likely to be guilty; while idleness itself was justly looked upon as a high offence, and misdemeanour. The penalty of God's laws against idleness, as expressed in the system of nature, was starvation; and it was held intolerable that any man should be allowed to escape a divine judgment by begging under false pretences, and robbing others of their honest earnings.

In a country also the boast of which was its open-handed hospitality, it was necessary to take care that hospitality was not brought to discredit by abuse; and when every door was freely opened to a request for a meal or a night's lodging, there was an imperative duty to keep a strict eye on whatever persons were on the move. We shall therefore be prepared to find "sturdy and valiant beggars" treated with summary justice as criminals of a high order; the right of a government so to treat them being proportioned to the facilities with which the honestly disposed can maintain themselves.

It might have been expected, on the other hand, that when wages were so high, and work so constant, labourers would have been left to themselves to make provision against sickness and old age. To modern ways of thinking on these subjects, there would have seemed no hardship in so leaving them; and their sufferings, if they had suffered, would have appeared but as a deserved retribution. This, however, was not the temper of earlier times. Charity has ever been the especial virtue of Catholic States, and the aged and the impotent were always held to be the legitimate objects of it. Men who had worked hard while they were able to work were treated like decayed soldiers, as the discharged pensionaries of society; they were held entitled to wear out their age (under restrictions) at the expense of others; and so readily did society acquiesce in this aspect of its obligations, that on the failure of the monasteries to do their duty, it was still sufficient to leave such persons to voluntary liberality, and legislation had to interfere only to direct such liberality into its legitimate channels. In the 23rd of Edw. III. cap. 7, a prohibition was issued against giving alms to "valiant beggars," and this proving inadequate, and charity being still given indiscriminately, in the twelfth year of Richard II. the system of licences was introduced, and a pair of stocks was erected by order in every town or village, to "justify" persons begging unpermitted. The monasteries growing more and more careless, the number of paupers continued to multiply, and this method received successive expansions, till at length, when the Reformation was concluded, it terminated, after many changes of form, in the famous Act of Elizabeth. We can thus trace our poor law in the whole course of its growth, and into two stages through which it passed I must enter with some minuteness. The 12th of the 22nd of Henry VIII., and the 25th of the 27th, are so remarkable in their tone, and so rich in their detail, as to furnish a complete exposition of English thought at that time upon the subject; while the second of these two acts, and probably the first also, has a further interest for us, as being the composition of Henry himself, and the most finished which he has left to us. 77

"Whereas," says the former of these two Acts, "in all places throughout this realm of England, vagabonds and beggars have of long time increased, and daily do increase in great and excessive numbers, by the occasion of idleness, mother and root of all vices; whereby hath insurged and sprung, and daily insurgeth and springeth, continual thefts, murders, and other heinous offences and great enormities, to the high displeasure of God, the inquietation and damage of the king's people, and to the marvellous disturbance of the common weal of this realm; and whereas, strait statutes and ordinances have been before this time devised and made, as well by the king our sovereign lord, as also by divers his most noble progenitors, kings of England, for the most necessary and due reformation of the premises; yet that notwithstanding, the said number of vagabonds and beggars be not seen in any part to be diminished, but rather daily augmented and increased into great routs or companies, as evidently and manifestly it doth and may appear: Be it therefore enacted by the king our sovereign lord, and by the Lords Spiritual and Temporal, and the Commons, in this present parliament assembled, that the justices of the peace of all and singular the shires of England within the limits of their commission, and all other justices of the peace, mayors, sheriffs, bailiffs, and other officers of every city, borough, or franchise, shall from time to time, as often as need shall require, make diligent search and inquiry of all aged, poor, and impotent persons, which live, or of necessity be compelled to live by alms of the charity of the people;

and such search made, the said officers, every of them within the limits of their authorities, shall have power, at their discretions, to enable to beg within such limits as they shall appoint, such of the said impotent persons as they shall think convenient; and to give in commandment to every such impotent beggar (by them enabled) that none of them shall beg without the limits so appointed to them. And further, they shall deliver to every such person so enabled a letter containing the name of that person, witnessing that he is authorised to beg, and the limits within which he is appointed to beg, the same letter to be sealed with the seal of the hundred, rape, wapentake, city, or borough, and subscribed with the name of one of the said justices or officers aforesaid. And if any such impotent person do beg in any other place than within such limits, then the justices of the peace, and all other the king's officers and ministers, shall by their discretions punish all such persons by imprisonment in the stocks, by the space of two days and two nights, giving them only bread and water."

Further, "If any such impotent person be found begging without a licence, at the discretion of the justices of the peace, he shall be stripped naked from the middle upwards, and whipped within the town in which he be found, or within some other town, as it shall seem good. Or if it be not convenient so to punish him, he shall be set in the stocks by the space of three days and three nights."

Such were the restrictions under which impotency was allowed support. Though not in itself treated as an offence, and though its right to maintenance by society was not denied, it was not indulged, as we may see, with unnecessary encouragement. The Act then proceeds to deal with the genuine vagrant.

"And be it further enacted, that if any person or persons, being whole and mighty in body and able to labour, be taken in begging in any part of this realm; and if any man or woman, being whole and mighty in body, having no land, nor master, nor using any lawful merchandry, craft, or mystery whereby he might get his living, be vagrant, and can give none account how he doth lawfully get his living, then it shall, be lawful to the constables and all other king's officers, ministers, and subjects of every town, parish, and hamlet, to arrest the said vagabonds and idle persons, and bring them to any justice of the peace of the same shire or liberty, or else to the high constable of the hundred; and the justice of the peace, high constable, or other officer, shall cause such idle person so to him brought, to be had to the next market town or other place, and there to be tied to the end of a cart, naked, and be beaten with whips throughout the same town till his body be bloody by reason of such whipping; and after such punishment of whipping had, the person so punished shall be enjoined upon his oath to return forthwith without delay, in the next and straight way, to the place where he was born, or where he last dwelled before the same punishment, by the space of three years; and then put himself to labour like a true man ought to do; and after that done, every such person so punished and ordered shall have a letter, sealed with the seal of the hundred, rape, or wapentake, witnessing that he hath been punished according to this estatute, and containing the day and place of his punishment, and the place where unto he is limited to go, and by what time he is limited to come thither: for that within that time, showing the said letter, he may lawfully beg by the way, and otherwise not; and if he do not accomplish the order to him appointed by the said letter, then to be eftsoons taken and whipped; and so often as there be fault found in him, to be whipped till he has his body put to labour for his living, or otherwise truly get his living, so long as he is able to do so."

Then follow the penalties against the justices of the peace, constables, and all officers who neglect to arrest such persons; and a singularly curious catalogue is added of certain forms of "sturdy mendicancy," which, if unspecified, might have been passed over as exempt, but to which Henry had no intention of conceding further licence. It seems as if, in framing the Act, he had Simon Fish's petition before him, and was commencing at last the rough remedy of the cart's-tail, which Fish had dared to recommend for a very obdurate evil. 78 The friars of the mendicant orders were tolerated for a few years longer; but many other spiritual persons may have suffered seriously under the provisions of the present statute.

"Be it further enacted," the Act continues, "that scholars of the Universities of Oxford and Cambridge, that go about begging, not being authorised under the seal of the said universities, by the commissary, chancellor, or vice-chancellor of the same; and that all and singular shipmen pretending losses of their ships and goods, going about the country begging without sufficient authority, shall be punished and ordered in manner and form as is above rehearsed of strong beggars; and that all proctors and pardoners, and all other idle persons going about in counties or abiding in any town, city, or borough, some of them using divers subtle, crafty, and unlawful games and plays, and some of them feigning themselves to have knowledge in physick, physnamye, and palmistry, or other crafty science, whereby they bear the people in hand that they can tell their destinies, dreams, and fortunes, and such other like fantastical imaginations, to the great deceit of the king's subjects, shall, upon examination had before two justices of the peace, if by provable witness they be found guilty of such deceits, be punished by whipping at two days together, after the manner before rehearsed. And if they eftsoons offend in the same or any like offence, to be scourged two days, and the third day to be put upon the pillory, from nine o'clock till eleven the forenoon of the same day, and to have the right ear cut off; and if they offend the third time, to have like punishment with whipping and the pillory, and to have the other ear cut off."

It would scarcely have been expected that this Act would have failed for want of severity in its penalties; yet five years later, for this and for some other reasons, it was thought desirable to expand the provisions of it, enhancing the penalties at the same time to a degree which has given a bloody name in the history of English law to the statutes of Henry VIII. Of this expanded statute 79 we have positive evidence, as I said, that Henry was himself the author. The merit of it, or the guilt of it—if guilt there be—originated with him alone. The early clauses contain practical amendments of an undoubtedly salutary kind. The Act of 1531 had been defective in that no specified means had been assigned for finding vagrants in labour, which, with men of broken character, was not immediately easy. The smaller monasteries having been suppressed in the interval, and sufficient funds being thus placed at the disposal of the government, public works 80 were set on foot throughout the kingdom, and this difficulty was obviated.

Another important alteration was a restriction upon private charity. Private persons were forbidden, under heavy penalties, to give money to beggars, whether deserving or undeserving. The poor of each parish might call at houses within the boundaries for broken meats; but this was the limit of personal almsgiving; and the money which men might be disposed to offer was to be collected by the churchwardens on Sundays and holidays in the churches. The parish priest was to keep an account of receipts and of expenditure, and relief was administered with some approach to modern formalities. A further excellent but severe enactment empowered the parish officers to take up all idle children above the age of five years, "and appoint them to masters of husbandry or other craft or labour to be taught;" and if any child should refuse the service to which he was appointed, or run away "without cause reasonable being shown for it," he might be publicly whipped with rods, at the discretion of the justice of the peace before whom he was brought.

So far, no complaint can be urged against these provisions: they display only that severe but true humanity, which, in offering fair and liberal maintenance for all who will consent to be honest, insists, not unjustly, that its offer shall be accepted, and that the resources of charity shall not be trifled away. On the clause, however, which gave to the Act its especial and distinguishing character, there will be large difference of opinion. "The sturdy vagabond," who by the earlier statute was condemned on his second offence to lose the whole or a part of his right ear, was condemned by the amended Act, if found a third time offending, with the mark upon him of his mutilation, "to suffer pains and execution of death, as a felon and as an enemy of the commonwealth." So the letter stands. For an able-bodied man to be caught a third time begging was held a crime deserving death, and the sentence was intended, on fit occasions, to be executed. The poor man's advantages, which I have estimated at so high a rate, were not purchased without drawbacks. He might not change his master at his will, or wander from place to place. He might not keep his children at his home unless he could answer for their time. If out of employment, preferring to be idle, he might be demanded for work by any master of the "craft" to which he belonged, and compelled to work whether he would or no. If caught begging once, being neither aged nor infirm, he was whipped at the cart's tail. If caught a second time, his ear was slit, or bored through with a hot iron. If caught a third time, being thereby proved to be of no use upon this earth, but to live upon it only to his own hurt and to that of others, he suffered death as a felon. So the law of England remained for sixty years. First drawn by Henry, it continued unrepealed through the reigns of Edward and of Mary, subsisting, therefore, with the deliberate approval of both the great parties between whom the country was divided. Reconsidered under Elizabeth, the same law was again formally passed; and it was, therefore, the expressed conviction of the English nation, that it was better for a man not to live at all than to live a profitless and worthless life. The vagabond was a sore spot upon the commonwealth, to be healed by wholesome discipline if the gangrene was not incurable; to be cut away with the knife if the milder treatment of the cart-whip failed to be of profit. 81

A measure so extreme in its severity was partly dictated by policy. The state of the country was critical; and the danger from questionable persons traversing it unexamined and uncontrolled was greater than at ordinary times. But in point of justice, as well as of prudence, it harmonised with the iron temper of the age, and it answered well for the government of a fierce and powerful people, in whose hearts lay an intense hatred of rascality, and among whom no one need have lapsed into evil courses except by deliberate preference for them. The moral substance of the English must have been strong indeed when it admitted of such hardy treatment; but on the whole, the people were ruled as they preferred to be ruled; and if wisdom may be tested by success, the manner in which they passed the great crisis of the Reformation is the best justification of their princes.

The era was great throughout Europe. The Italians of the age of Michael Angelo; the Spaniards who were the contemporaries of Cortez; the Germans who shook off the pope at the call of Luther; and the splendid chivalry of Francis I. of France, were no common men. But they were all brought face to face with the same trials, and none met them as the English met them. The

English alone never lost their self-possession; and if they owed something to fortune in their escape from anarchy, they owed more to the strong hand and steady purpose of their rulers.

To conclude this chapter then.

In the brief review of the system under which England was governed, we have seen a state of things in which the principles of political economy were, consciously or unconsciously, contradicted; where an attempt, more or less successful, was made to bring the production and distribution of wealth under the moral rule of right and wrong; and where those laws of supply and demand, which we are now taught to regard as immutable ordinances of nature, were absorbed or superseded by a higher code. It is necessary for me to repeat that I am not holding up the sixteenth century as a model which the nineteenth might safely follow. The population has become too large, employment has become too complicated and fluctuating, to admit of external control; while, in default of control, the relapse upon self-interest as the one motive principle is certain to ensue, and when it ensues is absolute in its operations. But as, even with us, these so-called ordinances of nature in time of war consent to be suspended, and duty to his country becomes with every good citizen a higher motive of action than the advantages which he may gain in an enemy's market; so it is not uncheering to look back upon a time when the nation was in a normal condition of militancy against social injustice; when the government was enabled by happy circumstances to pursue into detail a single and serious aim at the well-being—well-being in its widest sense—of all members of the commonwealth. The world, indeed, was not made particularly pleasant. Of liberty, in the modern sense of the word, of the supposed right of every man "to do what he will with his own" or with himself, there was no idea. To the question, if ever it was asked, May I not do what I will with my own? there was the brief answer, No man may do what is wrong, either with that which is his own or with that which is another's. Workmen were not allowed to take advantage of the scantiness of the labour market to exact extravagant wages. Capitalists were not allowed to drive the labourers from their holdings, and destroy their healthy independence. The antagonism of interests was absorbed into a relation of which equity was something more than the theoretic principle, and employers and employed were alike amenable to a law which both were compelled to obey. The working man of modern times has bought the extension of his liberty at the price of his material comfort. The higher classes have gained in luxury what they have lost in power. It is not for the historian to balance advantages. His duty is with the facts.

CHAPTER II.
THE LAST YEARS OF THE
ADMINISTRATION OF WOLSEY

Times were changed in England since the second Henry walked barefoot through the streets of Canterbury, and knelt while the monks flogged him on the pavement in the Chapter-house, doing penance for Becket's murder. The clergy had won the battle in the twelfth century because they deserved to win it. They were not free from fault and weakness, but they felt the meaning of their profession. Their hearts were in their vows, their authority was exercised more justly, more nobly, than the authority of the crown; and therefore, with inevitable justice, the crown was compelled to stoop before them. The victory was great; but, like many victories, it was fatal to the conquerors. It filled them full with the vanity of power; they forgot their duties in their privileges; and when, a century later, the conflict recommenced, the altering issue proved the altering nature of the conditions under which it was fought. The laity were sustained in vigour by the practical obligations of life; the clergy sunk under the influence of a waning religion, the administration of the forms of which had become their sole occupation; and as character forsook them, the Mortmain Act, 82 the Acts of Premunire, and the repeatedly recurring Statutes of Provisors mark the successive defeats that drove them back from the high post of command which character alone had earned for them. If the Black Prince had lived, or if Richard II. had inherited the temper of the Plantagenets, the ecclesiastical system would have been spared the misfortune of a longer reprieve. Its worst abuses would have then terminated, and the reformation of *doctrine* in the sixteenth century would have been left to fight its independent way unsupported by the moral corruption of the church from which it received its most powerful impetus. The nation was ready for sweeping remedies. The people felt little loyalty to the pope, as the language of the Statutes of Provisors 83 conclusively proves, and they were prepared to risk the sacrilege of confiscating the estates of the religious houses—a complete measure of secularisation being then, as I have already said, 84 the expressed desire of the House of Commons. 85 With an Edward III. on the throne such a measure would very likely have been executed, and the course of English history would have been changed. It was ordered otherwise, and doubtless wisely. The church was allowed a hundred and fifty more years to fill full the measure of her offences, that she might fall only when time had laid bare the root of her degeneracy, and that faith and manners might be changed together.

The history of the time is too imperfect to justify a positive conclusion. It is possible, however, that the success of the revolution effected by Henry IV. was due in part to a reaction in the church's favour; and it is certain that this prince, if he did not owe his crown to the support of the church, determined to conciliate it. He confirmed the Statutes of Provisors, 86 but he allowed them to sink into disuse. He forbade the further mooting of the confiscation project; and to him is due the first permission of the bishops to send heretics to the stake. 87 If English tradition is to be trusted, the clergy still felt insecure; and the French wars of Henry V. are said to have been undertaken, as we all know from Shakspeare, at the persuasion of Archbishop Chichele, who desired to distract his attention from reverting to dangerous subjects. Whether this be true or not, no prince of the house of Lancaster betrayed a wish to renew the quarrel with the church. The battle of Agincourt, the conquest and re-conquest of France, called off the attention of the people; while the rise of the Lollards, and the intrusion of speculative questions, the agitation of which has ever been the chief aversion of English statesmen, contributed to change the current; and the reforming spirit must have lulled before the outbreak of the wars of the Roses, or one of the two parties in so desperate a struggle would have scarcely failed to have availed themselves of it. Edward IV. is said to have been lenient towards heresy; but his toleration, if it was more than imaginary, was tacit only; he never ventured to avow it. It is more likely that in the inveterate frenzy of those years men had no leisure to remember that heresy existed.

The clergy were thus left undisturbed to go their own course to its natural end. The storm had passed over them without breaking; and they did not dream that it would again gather. The immunity which they enjoyed from the general sufferings of the civil war contributed to deceive them; and without anxiety for the consequences, and forgetting the significant warning which they had received, they sank steadily into that condition which is inevitable from the constitution of human nature, among men without faith, wealthy, powerful, and luxuriously fed, yet condemned to celibacy, and cut off from the common duties and common pleasures of ordinary life. On the return of a settled government, they were startled for a moment in their security; the conduct of some among them had become so unbearable, that even Henry VII., who inherited the Lancastrian sympathies, was compelled to notice it; and the following brief act was passed by his first parliament, proving by the very terms in which it is couched the existing nature of church discipline. "For the more sure and likely reformation," it runs, "of priests, clerks, and religious men, culpable, or by their demerits openly noised of incontinent living in their bodies, contrary to their order, be it enacted, ordained, and established, that it be lawful to all archbishops and bishops, and other ordinaries having episcopal jurisdiction, to punish and chastise such religious men, being within the bounds of their jurisdiction, as shall be convict before them, by lawful proof, of adultery, fornication, incest, or other fleshly incontinency, by committing them to ward and prison, there to remain for such time as shall be thought convenient for the quality of their trespasses." 88

Previous to the passing of this act, therefore, the bishops, who had power to arrest laymen on suspicion of heresy, and detain them in prison untried, 89 had no power to imprison priests, even though convicted of adultery or incest. The legislature were supported by the Archbishop of Canterbury. Cardinal Morton procured authority from the pope to visit the religious houses, the abominations of which had become notorious; 90 and in a provincial synod held on the 24th of February, 1486, he laid the condition of the secular clergy before the assembled prelates. Many priests, it was stated, spent their time in hawking or hunting, in lounging at taverns, in the dissolute enjoyment of the world. They wore their hair long like laymen; they were to be seen lounging in the streets with cloak and doublet, sword and dagger. By the scandal of their lives they imperilled the stability of their order. 91 A number of the worst offenders, in London especially, were summoned before the synod and admonished; 92 certain of the more zealous among the learned (*complures docti*) who had preached against clerical abuses were advised to be more cautious, for the avoiding of scandal; 93 but the archbishop, taking the duty upon himself, sent round a circular among the clergy of his province, exhorting them to general amendment. 94

Yet this little cloud again disappeared. Henry VII. sat too insecurely on his throne to venture on a resolute reform, even if his feelings had inclined him towards it, which they did not. Morton durst not resolutely grapple with the evil. He rebuked and remonstrated; but punishment would have caused a public scandal. He would not invite the inspection of the laity into a disease which, without their assistance, he had not the strength to encounter; and his incipient reformation died away ineffectually in words. The church, to outward appearance, stood more securely than ever. The obnoxious statutes of the Plantagenets were in abeyance, their very existence, as it seemed, was forgotten; and Thomas à Becket never desired more absolute independence for the ecclesiastical order than Archbishop

Warham found established when he succeeded to the primacy. He, too, ventured to repeat the experiment of his predecessor. In 1511 he attempted a second visitation of the monasteries, and again exhorted a reform; but his efforts were even slighter than Morton's, and in their results equally without fruit. The maintenance of his order in its political supremacy was of greater moment to him than its moral purity: a decent veil was cast over the clerical infirmities, and their vices were forgotten as soon as they ceased to be proclaimed. 95 Henry VIII., a mere boy on his accession, was borne away with the prevailing stream; and trained from his childhood by theologians, he entered upon his reign saturated with theological prepossessions. The intensity of his nature recognising no half measures, he was prepared to make them the law of his life; and so zealous was he, that it seemed as if the church had found in him a new Alfred or a Charlemagne. Unfortunately for the church, institutions may be restored in theory; but theory, be it never so perfect, will not give them back their life; and Henry discovered, at length, that the church of the sixteenth century as little resembled the church of the eleventh, as Leo X. resembled Hildebrand, or Warham resembled St. Anselm.

If, however, there were no longer saints among the clergy, there could still arise among them a remarkable man; and in Cardinal Wolsey the king found an adviser who was able to retain him longer than would otherwise have been possible in the course which he had entered upon; who, holding a middle place between an English statesman and a catholic of the old order, was essentially a transition minister; and who was qualified, above all men then living, by a combination of talent, honesty, and arrogance, to open questions which could not again be closed when they had escaped the grasp of their originator. Under Wolsey's influence Henry made war with Louis of France, In the pope's quarrel, entered the polemic lists with Luther, and persecuted the English protestants. But Wolsey could not blind himself to the true condition of the church. He was too wise to be deceived with outward prosperity; he knew well that there lay before it, in Europe and at home, the alternative of ruin or amendment; and therefore he familiarised Henry with the sense that a reformation was inevitable, and dreaming that it could be effected from within, by the church itself inspired with a wiser spirit, he himself fell first victim of a convulsion which he had assisted to create, and which he attempted too late to stay.

His intended measures were approaching maturity, when all Europe was startled by the news that Rome had been stormed by the Imperial army, that the pope was imprisoned, the churches pillaged, the cardinals insulted, and all holiest things polluted and profaned. A spectator, judging only by outward symptoms, would have seen at that strange crisis in Charles V.

the worst patron of heresy, and the most dangerous enemy of the Holy See; while the indignation with which the news of these outrages was received at the English court, would have taught him to look on Henry as the one sovereign in Europe on whom that See might calculate most surely for support in its hour of danger. If he could have pierced below the surface, he would have found that the pope's best friend was the prince who held him prisoner; that Henry was but doubtfully acquiescing in the policy of an unpopular minister; and that the English nation would have looked on with stoical resignation if pope and papacy had been wrecked together. They were not inclined to heresy; but the ecclesiastical system was not the catholic faith; and this system, ruined by prosperity, was fast pressing its excesses to the extreme limit, beyond which it could not be endured. Wolsey talked of reformation, but delayed its coming; and in the mean time, the persons to be reformed showed no fear that it would come at all. The monasteries grew worse and worse. The people were taught only what they could teach themselves. The consistory courts became more oppressive. Pluralities multiplied, and non-residence and profligacy. Favoured parish clergy held as many as eight benefices. 96 Bishops accumulated sees, and, unable to attend to all, attended to none. Wolsey himself, the church reformer (so little did he really know what a reformation meant), was at once Archbishop of York, Bishop of Winchester, of Bath, and of Durham, and Abbot of St. Alban's. In Latimer's opinion, even twenty years later, and after no little reform in such matters, there was but one bishop in all England who was ever at his work and ever in his diocese. "I would ask a strange question," he said, in an audacious sermon at Paul's Cross, "Who is the most diligent bishop and prelate in all England, that passeth all the rest in doing of his office? 97 I can tell, for I know him who it is; I know him well. But now I think I see you listening and hearkening that I should name him. There is one that passeth all the others, and is the most diligent prelate and preacher in all England. And will ye know who it is? I will tell you. It is the devil. Among all the pack of them that have cure, the devil shall go for my money, for he applieth his business. Therefore, ye unpreaching prelates, learn of the devil to be diligent in your office. If ye will not learn of God, for shame learn of the devil." 98

Under such circumstances, we need not be surprised to find the clergy sunk low in the respect of the English people. Sternly intolerant of each other's faults, the laity were not likely to be indulgent to the vices of men who ought to have set an example of purity; and from time to time, during the first quarter of the century, there were explosions of temper which might have served as a warning if any sense or judgment had been left to profit by it.

In 1514 a London merchant was committed to the Lollards' Tower for refusing to submit to an unjust exaction of mortuary; 99 and a few days after was found dead in his cell. An inquest was held upon the body, when a verdict of wilful murder was returned against the chancellor of the Bishop of London; and so intense was the feeling of the city, that the bishop applied to Wolsey for a special jury to be chosen on the trial. "For assured I am," he said, "that if my chancellor be tried by any twelve men in London, they be so maliciously set *in favorem hæreticæ pravitatis*, that they will cast and condemn any clerk, though he were as innocent as Abel." 100 Fish's famous pamphlet also shows the spirit which was seething; and though we may make some allowance for angry rhetoric, his words have the clear ring of honesty in them; and he spoke of what he had seen and knew. The monks, he tells the king, "be they that have made a hundred thousand idle dissolute women in your realm, who would have gotten their living honestly in the sweat of their faces had not their superfluous riches allured them to lust and idleness. These be they that when they have drawn men's wives to such incontinency, spend away their husbands' goods, make the women to run away from their husbands, bringing both man, wife, and children to idleness, theft, and beggary. Yea, who is able to number the great broad bottomless ocean sea full of evils that this mischievous generation may bring upon us if unpunished?" 101

Copies of this book were strewed about the London streets; Wolsey issued a prohibition against it, with the effect which such prohibitions usually have. Means were found to bring it under the eyes of Henry himself; and the manner in which it was received by him is full of significance, and betrays that the facts of the age were already telling on his understanding. He was always easy of access and easy of manner; and the story, although it rests on Foxe's authority, has internal marks of authenticity.

"One Master Edmund Moddis, being with the king in talk of religion, and of the new books that were come from beyond the seas, said that if it might please his Highness to pardon him, and such as he would bring to his Grace, he should see such a book as it was a marvel to hear of. The king demanded who they were? He said 'Two of your merchants—George Elliot and George Robinson.' The king appointed a time to speak with them. When they came before his presence in a privy closet, he demanded what they had to say or to shew him. One of them said that there was a book come to their hands which they had there to shew his Grace. When he saw it he demanded if any of them could read it. 'Yea,' said George Elliot, 'if it please your Grace to hear it.' 'I thought so,' said the king; 'if need were, thou couldst say it without book.'

"The whole book being read out, the king made a long pause, and then said, 'If a man should pull down an old stone wall, and should begin at the lower part, the upper part thereof might chance to fall upon his head.' Then he took the book, and put it in his desk, and commanded them, on their allegiance, that they should not tell any man that he had seen it." 102

Symptoms such as these boded ill for a self-reform of the church, and it was further imperilled by the difficulty which it is not easy to believe that Wolsey had forgotten. No measures would be of efficacy which spared the religious houses, and they would be equally useless unless the bishops, as well as the inferior clergy, were comprehended in the scheme of amendment. But neither with monks nor bishops could Wolsey interfere except by a commission from the pope, and the laws were unrepealed which forbade English subjects, under the severest penalties, to accept or exercise within the realm an authority which they had received from the Holy See. Morton had gone beyond the limits of the statute of provisors in receiving powers from Pope Innocent to visit the monasteries. But Morton had stopped short with inquiry and admonition. Wolsey, who was in earnest with the work, had desired and obtained a full commission as legate, but he could only make use of it at his peril. The statute slumbered, but it still existed. 103 He was exposing not himself only, but all persons, lay and clerical, who might recognise his legacy to a Premunire; and he knew well that Henry's connivance, or even expressed permission, could not avail him if his conduct was challenged. He could not venture to appeal to parliament. Parliament was the last authority whose jurisdiction a churchman would acknowledge in the concerns of the clergy; and his project must sooner or later have sunk, like those of his two predecessors, under its own internal difficulties, even if the accident had not arisen which brought the dispute to a special issue in its most vital point, and which, fostered by Wolsey for his own purposes, precipitated his ruin.

It is never more difficult to judge equitably the actions of public men than when private as well as general motives have been allowed to influence them, or when their actions may admit of being represented as resulting from personal inclination, as well as from national policy. In life, as we actually experience it, motives slide one into the other, and the most careful analysis will fail adequately to sift them. In history, from the effort to make our conceptions distinct, we pronounce upon these intricate matters with unhesitating certainty, and we lose sight of truth in the desire to make it truer than itself. The difficulty is further complicated by the different points of view which are chosen by contemporaries and by posterity. Where motives are mixed, men all naturally dwell most on those which approach nearest to themselves: contemporaries whose interests are at stake overlook what is personal in consideration of what is to them of broader moment; posterity, unable to realise political embarrassments which have ceased to concern them, concentrate their attention on such features of the story as touch their own sympathies, and attend exclusively to the private and personal passions of the men and women whose character they are considering.

These natural, and to some extent inevitable tendencies, explain the difference with which the divorce between Henry VIII. and Catherine of Arragon has been regarded by the English nation in the sixteenth and in the nineteenth centuries. In the former, not only did the parliament profess to desire it, urge it, and further it, but we are told by a contemporary 104 that "all indifferent and discreet persons" judged that it was right and necessary. In the latter, perhaps, there is not one of ourselves who has not been taught to look upon it as an act of enormous wickedness. In the sixteenth century, Queen Catherine was an obstacle to the establishment of the kingdom, an incentive to treasonable hopes. In the nineteenth, she is an outraged and injured wife, the victim of a false husband's fickle appetite. The story is a long and painful one, and on its personal side need not concern us here further than as it illustrates the private character of Henry. Into the public bearing of it I must enter at some length, in order to explain the interest with which the nation threw itself into the question, and to remove the scandal with which, had nothing been at stake beyond the inclinations of a profligate monarch, weary of his queen, the complaisance on such a subject of the lords and commons of England would have coloured the entire complexion of the Reformation.

The succession to the throne, although determined in theory by the ordinary law of primogeniture, was nevertheless, subject to repeated arbitrary changes. The uncertainty of the rule was acknowledged and deplored by the parliament, 105 and there was no order of which the nation, with any unity of sentiment, compelled the observance. An opinion prevailed—not, I believe, traceable to statute, but admitted by custom, and having the force of statute in the prejudices of the nation—that no stranger born out of the realm could inherit. 106 Although the descent in the female line was not formally denied, no female sovereign had ever, in fact, sat upon the throne. 107 Even Henry VII. refused to strengthen his title by advancing the claims of his wife: and the uncertainty of the laws of marriage, and the innumerable refinements of the Romish canon law, which affected the legitimacy of children, 108 furnished, in connection with the further ambiguities of clerical dispensations, perpetual pretexts, whenever pretexts were needed, for a breach of allegiance. So long, indeed, as the character of the nation remained essentially military, it could as little tolerate an incapable king as an army in a dangerous campaign can bear with an inefficient commander; and whatever might be the theory of the title, when the sceptre was held by the infirm hand of an Edward II., a Richard II., or a Henry VI., the difficulty resolved itself by force, and it was wrenched by a stronger arm from a grasp too feeble to retain it. The consent of the nation was avowed, even in the authoritative language of a statute, 109 as essential to the legitimacy of a sovereign's title; and Sir Thomas More, on examination by the Solicitor-General, declared as his opinion that parliament had power to depose kings if it so pleased. 110 So many uncertainties on a point so vital had occasioned fearful episodes in English history; the most fearful of them, which had traced its character in blood in the private records of every English family, having been the long struggle of the preceding century, from which the nation was still suffering, and had but recovered sufficiently to be conscious of what it had endured. It had decimated itself for a question which involved no principle and led to no result, and perhaps the history of the world may be searched in vain for any parallel to a quarrel at once so desperate and so unmeaning.

This very unmeaning character of the dispute increased the difficulty of ending it. In wars of conquest or of principle, when something definite is at stake, the victory is either won, or it is lost; the conduct of individual men, at all events, is overruled by considerations external to themselves which admit of being weighed and calculated. In a war of succession, where the great families were divided in their allegiance, and supported the rival claimants in evenly balanced numbers, the inveteracy of the conflict increased with its duration, and propagated itself from generation to generation. Every family was in blood feud with its neighbour; and children, as they grew to manhood, inherited the duty of revenging their fathers' deaths.

No effort of imagination can reproduce to us the state of this country in the fatal years which intervened between the first rising of the Duke of York and the battle of Bosworth; and experience too truly convinced Henry VII. that the war had ceased only from general exhaustion, and not because there was no will to continue it. The first Tudor breathed an atmosphere of suspended insurrection, and only when we remember the probable effect upon his mind of the constant dread of an explosion, can we excuse or understand, in a prince not generally cruel, the execution of the Earl of Warwick. The danger of a bloody revolution may present an act of arbitrary or cowardly tyranny in the light of a public duty.

Fifty years of settled government, however, had not been without their effects. The country had collected itself; the feuds of the families had been chastened, if they had not been subdued; while the increase of wealth and material prosperity had brought out into obvious prominence those advantages of peace which a hot-spirited people, antecedent to experience, had not anticipated, and had not been able to appreciate. They were better fed, better cared for, more justly governed than they had ever been before; and though abundance of unruly tempers remained, yet the wiser portion of the nation, looking back from their new vantage-ground, were able to recognise the past in its true hatefulness. Thenceforward a war of succession was the predominating terror with English statesmen, and the safe establishment of the reigning family bore a degree of importance which it is possible that their fears exaggerated, yet which in fact was the determining principle of their action.

It was therefore with no little anxiety that the council of Henry VIII. perceived his male children, on whom their hopes were centred, either born dead, or dying one after another within a few days of their birth, as if his family were under a blight. When the queen had advanced to an age which precluded hope of further offspring, and the heir presumptive was an infirm girl, the unpromising prospect became yet more alarming. The life of the Princess Mary was precarious, for her health was weak from her childhood. If she lived, her accession would be a temptation to insurrection; if she did not live, and the king had no other children, a civil war was inevitable. At present such a difficulty would be disposed of by an immediate and simple reference to the collateral branches of the royal family; the crown would descend with even more facility than the property of an intestate to the next of kin. At that time, if the rule had been recognised, it would only have increased the difficulty, for the next heir in blood was James of Scotland; and, gravely as statesmen desired the union of the two countries, in the existing mood of the people, the very stones in London streets, it was said, 111 would rise up against a king of Scotland who claimed to enter England as sovereign. Even the parliament itself declared in formal language that they would resist any attempt on the part of the Scottish king "to the uttermost of their power." 112

As little, however, as the English would have admitted James's claims, would James himself have acknowledged their right to reject them. He would have pleaded the sacred right of inheritance, refusing utterly the imaginary law which disentitled him: he would have pressed his title with all Scotland to back him, and probably with the open support of France. Centuries of humiliation remained unrevenged, which both France and Scotland had endured at English hands. It was not likely that they would waste an opportunity thrust upon them by Providence. The country might, it is true, have encountered this danger, serious as it would have been, if there had been hope that it would itself have agreed to any other choice. England had many times fought successfully against the same odds, and would have cared little for a renewal of the struggle, if united in itself: but the prospect on this side, also, was fatally discouraging. The elements of the old factions were dormant, but still smouldering. Throughout Henry's reign a White Rose agitation had been secretly fermenting; without open success, and without chance of success so long as Henry lived, but formidable in a high degree if opportunity to strike should offer itself. Richard de la Pole, the representative of this party, had been killed at Pavia, but his loss had rather strengthened their cause than weakened it, for by his long exile he was unknown in England; his personal character was without energy; while he made place for the leadership of a far more powerful spirit in the sister of the murdered Earl of Warwick, the Countess of Salisbury, mother of Reginald Pole. This lady had inherited, in no common degree, the fierce nature of the Plantagenets; born to command, she had rallied round her the Courtenays, the Nevilles, and all the powerful kindred of Richard the King Maker, her grandfather. Her Plantagenet descent was purer than the king's; and if Mary died and Henry left no other issue, half England was likely to declare either for one of her sons, or for the Marquis of Exeter, the grandson of Edward IV.

In 1515, when Giustiniani, 113 the Venetian ambassador, was at the court, the Dukes of Buckingham, of Suffolk, and of Norfolk, were also mentioned to him as having each of them hopes of the crown. Buckingham, meddling prematurely in the dangerous game, had lost his life for it; but in his death he had strengthened the chance of Norfolk, who had married his daughter. Suffolk was Henry's brother-in-law; 114 chivalrous, popular, and the ablest soldier of his day; and Lady Margaret Lennox, also, daughter of the Queen of Scotland by her second marriage, would not have wanted supporters, and early became an object of intrigue. Indeed, as she had been born in England, it was held in parliament that she stood next in order to the Princess Mary. 115

Many of these claims were likely to be advanced if Henry died leaving a daughter to succeed him. They would all inevitably be advanced if he died childless; and no great political sagacity was required to foresee the probable fate of the country if such a moment was chosen for a French and Scottish invasion. The very worst disasters might be too surely looked for, and the hope of escape, precarious at the best, hung upon the frail thread of a single life. We may therefore imagine the dismay with which the nation saw this last hope failing them—and failing them even in a manner more dangerous than if it had failed by death; for it did but add another doubt, when already there were too many. In order to detach France from Scotland, and secure, if possible, its support for the claims of the princess, it had been proposed to marry the Princess Mary to a son of the French king. The negotiations were conducted through the Bishop of Tarbês, 116 and at the first conference the Bishop raised a question in the name of his government, on the validity of the papal dispensation granted by Julius the Second, to legalise the marriage from which she was sprung. The abortive marriage Scheme perished in its birth, but the doubt which had been raised could not perish with it. Doubt on such a subject once mooted might not be left unresolved, even if the raising it thus publicly had not itself destroyed the frail chance of an undisputed succession. If the relations of Henry with Queen Catherine had been of a cordial kind, it is possible that he would have been contented with resentment; that he would have refused to reconsider a question which touched his honour and his conscience; and, united with parliament, would have endeavoured to bear down all difficulties with a high hand. This at least he might have himself attempted. Whether the parliament, with so precarious a future before them, would have consented, is less easy to say. Fortunately or unfortunately, the interests of the nation pointed out another road, which Henry had no unwillingness to enter.

On the death of Prince Arthur, five months after his marriage, Henry VII. and the father of the Princess alike desired that the bond between their families thus broken should be re-united; and, as soon as it became clear that Catherine had not been left pregnant (a point which, tacitly at least, she allowed to be considered uncertain at the time of her husband's decease), it was proposed that she should be transferred, with the inheritance of the crown, to the new heir. A dispensation was reluctantly granted by the pope, 117 and reluctantly accepted by the English ministry. The Prince of Wales, who was no more than twelve years old at the time, was under the age at which he could legally sue for such an object; and a portion of the English council, the Archbishop of Canterbury among them, were unsatisfied, 118 both with the marriage itself, and with the adequacy of the forms observed in a matter of so dubious an import. The betrothal took place at the urgency of Ferdinand. In the year following Henry VII. became suddenly ill; Queen Elizabeth died; and superstition working on the previous hesitation, misfortune was construed into an indication of the displeasure of Heaven. The intention was renounced, and the prince, as soon as he had completed his fourteenth year, was invited and required to disown, by a formal act, the obligations contracted in his name. 119 Again there was a change. The king lived on, the alarm yielded to the temptations of covetousness. Had he restored Catherine to her father he must have restored with her the portion of her dowry which had been already received; he must have relinquished the prospect of the moiety which had yet to be received. The negotiation was renewed. Henry VII. lived to sign the receipts for the first instalment of the second payment; 120 and on his death, notwithstanding much general murmuring, 121 the young Henry, then a boy of eighteen, proceeded to carry out his father's ultimate intentions. The princess-dowager, notwithstanding what had passed, was still on her side willing;—and the difference of age (she was six years older than Henry) seeming of little moment when both were comparatively young, they were married. For many years all went well; opposition was silenced by the success which seemed to have followed, and the original scruples were forgotten. Though the marriage was dictated by political convenience, Henry was faithful, with but one exception, to his wife's bed—no slight honour to him, if he is measured by the average royal standard in such matters; and, if his sons had lived to grow up around his throne, there is no reason to believe that the peace of his married life would have been interrupted, or that, whatever might have been his private feelings, he would have appeared in the world's eye other than acquiescent in his condition.

But his sons had not lived; years passed on, bringing with them premature births, children born dead, or dying after a few days or hours, 122 and the disappointment was intense in proportion to the interests which were at issue. The especial penalty denounced against the marriage with a brother's wife 123 had been all but literally enforced; and the king found himself growing to middle life and his queen passing beyond it with his prayers unheard, and no hope any longer that they might be heard. The disparity of age also was more perceptible as time went by, while Catherine's constitution was affected by her misfortunes, and differences arose on which there is no occasion to dwell in these pages—differences which in themselves reflected no discredit either on the husband or the wife, but which were sufficient to extinguish between two infirm human beings an affection that had rested only upon mutual esteem, but had not assumed the character of love.

The circumstances in which Catherine was placed were of a kind which no sensitive woman could have endured without impatience and mortification; but her conduct, however natural, only widened the breach which personal repugnance and radical opposition of character had already made too wide. So far Henry and she were alike that both had imperious tempers, and both were indomitably obstinate; but Henry was hot and impetuous, Catherine was cold and self-contained—Henry saw his duty through his wishes; Catherine, in her strong Castilian austerity, measured her steps by the letter of the law; the more her husband withdrew from her, the more she insisted upon her relation to him as his wife; and continued with fixed purpose and immovable countenance 124 to share his table and his bed long after she was aware of his dislike for her.

If the validity of so unfortunate a connection had never been questioned, or if no national interests had been dependent on the continuance or the abolition of it, these discomforts were not too great to have been endured in silence. They were not originally occasioned by any latent inclination on the part of the king for another woman. They had arisen to their worst dimensions before he had ever seen Anne Boleyn, and were produced by causes of a wholly independent kind; and even if it had not been so, when we remember the tenor of his early life we need not think that he would have been unequal to the restraint which ordinary persons in similar circumstances are able to impose on their caprices. The legates spoke no more than the truth when they wrote to the pope, saying that "it was mere madness to suppose that the king would act as he was doing merely out of dislike of the queen, or out of inclination, for another person; he was not a man whom harsh manners and an unpleasant disposition (*duri mores et injucunda consuetudo*) could so far provoke; nor could any sane man believe him to be so infirm of character that sensual allurements would have led him to dissolve a connexion in which he had passed the flower of youth without stain or blemish, and in which he had borne himself in his trial so reverently and honourably." 125 I consider this entirely true in a sense which no great knowledge of human nature is required to understand. The king's personal dissatisfaction was great: if this had been all, however, it would have been extinguished or endured; but the interests of the nation, imperilled as they were by the maintenance of the marriage, entitled him to regard his position under another aspect. Even if the marriage in itself had never been questioned, he might justly have desired the dissolution of it; and when he recalled the circumstances under which it was contracted, the hesitation of the council, the reluctance of the pope, the alarms and vacillation of his father, we may readily perceive how scruples of conscience must have arisen in a soil well prepared to receive them—how the loss of his children must have appeared as a judicial sentence on a violation of the Divine law. The divorce presented itself to him as a moral obligation, when national advantage combined with superstition to encourage what he secretly desired; and if he persuaded himself that those public reasons, without which, in truth and fact, he would not have stirred, were those that alone were influencing him, the self-deceit was of a kind with which the experience of most men will probably have made them too familiar. In those rare cases where inclination coincides with right, we cannot be surprised if mankind should mislead themselves with the belief that the disinterested motives weigh more with them than the personal.

A remarkable and very candid account of Henry's feelings is furnished by himself in one of the many papers of instructions 126 which he forwarded to his secretary at Rome. Hypocrisy was not among his faults, and in detailing the arguments which were to be laid before the pope he has exhibited a more complete revelation of what was passing in himself—and indirectly of his own nature in its strength and weakness—than he perhaps imagined while he wrote. The despatch is long and perplexed; the style that of a man who saw his end clearly, and was vexed with the intricate and dishonest trifling with which his way was impeded, and which nevertheless he was struggling to tolerate. The secretary was to say, "that the King's Highness having above all other things his intent and mind ever founded upon such respect unto Almighty God as to a Christian and catholic prince doth appertain, knowing the fragility and uncertainty of all earthly things, and how displeasant unto God, how much dangerous to the soul, how dishonourable and damageable to the world it were to prefer vain and transitory things unto those that be perfect and certain, hath in this cause, doubt, and matter of matrimony, whereupon depend so high and manifold consequences of greatest importance, always cast from his conceit the darkness and blundering confusion of falsity, and specially hath had and put before his eyes the light and shining brightness of truth; upon which foundation as a most sure base for perpetual tranquillity of his conscience his Highness hath expressly resolved and determined with himself to build and establish all his acts, deeds, and cogitations touching this matter; without God did build the house, in vain they laboured that went about to build it; and all actions grounded upon that immovable fundament of truth, must needs therein be firm, sound, whole, perfect, and worthy of a Christian man; which if truth were put apart, they could not for the same reason be but evil, vain, slipper, uncertain, and in nowise permanent or endurable." He then laboured to urge on the pope the duty of straightforward dealing; and dwelt in words which have a sad interest for us (when we consider the manner in which the subject of them has been dealt with) on the judgment bar, not of God only, but of human posterity, at which his conduct would be ultimately tried.

"The causes of private persons dark and doubtful be sometimes," the king said, "pretermitted and passed over as things more meet at some seasons to be dissimuled than by continual strife and plea to nourish controversies. Yet since all people have their eyes conject upon princes, whose acts and doings not only be observed in the mouths of them that now do live, but also remain in such perpetual memory to our posterity [so that] the evil, if any there be, cannot but appear and come to light, there is no reason for toleration, no place for dissimulation; but [there is reason] more deeply, highly, and profoundly to penetrate and search for the truth, so that the same may vanquish and overcome, and all guilt, craft, and falsehood clearly be extirpate and reject."

I am anticipating the progress of the story in making these quotations; for the main burden of the despatch concerns a forged document which had been introduced by the Roman lawyers to embarrass the process, and of which I shall by-and-bye have to speak directly; but I have desired to illustrate the spirit in which Henry entered upon the general question— assuredly a more calm and rational one than historians have usually represented it to be. In dealing with the obstacle which had been raised, he displayed a most efficient mastery over himself, although he did not conclude without touching the pith of the matter with telling clearness. The secretary was to take some opportunity of speaking to the pope privately; and of warning him, "as of himself," that there was no hope that the king would give way: he was to "say plainly to his Holiness that the king's desire and intent *convolare ad secundas nuptias non patitur negativum*; and whatsoever should be found of bull, brief, or otherwise, his Highness found his conscience so inquieted, his succession in such danger, and his most royal person in such perplexity for things unknown and not to be spoken, that other remedy there was not but his Grace to come by one way or other, and specially at his hands, if it might be, to the desired end; and that all concertation to the contrary should be vain and frustrate."

So peremptory a conviction and so determined a purpose were of no sudden growth, and had been probably maturing in his mind for years, when the gangrene was torn open by the Bishop of Tarbês, and accident precipitated his resolution. The momentous consequences involved, and the reluctance to encounter a probable quarrel with the emperor, might have long kept him silent, except for some extraneous casualty; but the tree being thus rudely shaken, the ripe fruit fell. The capture of Rome occurring almost at the same moment, Wolsey caught the opportunity to break the Spanish alliance; and the prospect of a divorce was grasped at by him as a lever by which to throw the weight of English power and influence into the papal scale, to commit Henry definitely to the catholic cause. Like his acceptance of legatine authority, the expedient was a desperate one, and if it failed it was ruinous. The nation at that time was sincerely attached to Spain. The alliance with the house of Burgundy was of old date; the commercial intercourse with Flanders was enormous, Flanders, in fact, absorbing all the English exports; and as many as 15,000 Flemings were settled in London. Charles himself was personally popular; he had been the ally of England in the late French war; and when in his supposed character of leader of the anti-papal party in Europe he allowed a Lutheran army to desecrate Rome, he had won the sympathy of all the latent discontent which was fermenting in the population. France, on the other hand, was as cordially hated as Spain was beloved. A state of war with France was the normal condition of England; and the reconquest of it the universal dream from the cottage to the castle. Henry himself, early in his reign, had shared in this delusive ambition; and but three years before the sack of Rome, when the Duke of Suffolk led an army into Normandy, Wolsey's purposed tardiness in sending reinforcements had alone saved Paris. 127

There could be no doubt, therefore, that a breach with the emperor would in a high degree be unwelcome to the country. The king, and probably such members of the council as were aware of his feelings, shrank from offering an open affront to the Spanish people., and anxious as they were for a settlement of the succession, perhaps trusted that advantage might be taken of some political contingency for a private arrangement; that Catherine might be induced by Charles himself to retire privately, and sacrifice herself, of her free will, to the interests of the two countries. This, however, is no more than conjecture; I think it probable, because so many English statesmen were in favour at once of the divorce and of the Spanish alliance—two objects which, only on some such hypothesis, were compatible. The fact cannot be ascertained, however, because the divorce itself was not discussed at the council table until Wolsey had induced the king to change his policy by the hope of immediate relief.

Wolsey has revealed to us fully his own objects in a letter to Sir Gregory Cassalis, his agent at Rome. He shared with half Europe in an impression that the emperor's Italian campaigns were designed to further the Reformation; and of this central delusion he formed the keystone of his conduct. "First condoling with his Holiness," he wrote, "on the unhappy position in which, with the college of the most reverend cardinals, he is placed, 128 you shall tell him how, day and night, I am revolving by what means or contrivance I may bring comfort to the church of Christ, and raise the fallen state of our most Holy Lord. I care not whit it may cost me, whether of expense or trouble; nay, though I have to shed my blood, or give my life for it, assuredly so long as life remains to me for this I will labour. And how let me mention the great and marvellous effects which have been wrought by my instrumentality on the mind of my most excellent master the king, whom I have persuaded to unite himself with his Holiness in heart and soul. I urged innumerable reasons to induce him to part him from the emperor, to whom he clung with much tenacity. The most effective of them all was the constancy with which I assured him of the good-will and affection which were felt for him by his Holiness, and the certainty that his Holiness would furnish proof of his friendship in conceding his said Majesty's requests, in such form as the church's treasure and the authority of the Vicar of Christ shall permit, or so far as that authority extends or may extend. I have undertaken, moreover, for all these things in their utmost latitude, pledging my salvation, my faith, my honour and soul upon them. I have said that his demands shall be granted amply and fully, without scruple, without room or occasion being left for after-retractation; and the King's Majesty, in consequence, believing on these my solemn asseverations that the Pope's Holiness is really and indeed well inclined towards him, accepting what is spoken by me as spoken by the legate of the Apostolic See, and therefore, as in the name of his Holiness, has determined to run the risk which I have pressed upon him; he will spare no labour or expense, he will disregard the wishes of his subjects, and the private interest of his Realm, to attach himself cordially and constantly to the Holy See." 129

These were the words of a man who loved England well, but who loved Rome better; and Wolsey has received but scanty justice from catholic writers, since he sacrificed himself for the catholic cause. His scheme was bold and well laid, being weak only in that it was confessedly in contradiction to the instincts and genius of the nation, by which, and by which alone, in the long run, either this or any other country has been successfully governed. And yet he might well be forgiven if he ventured on an unpopular course in the belief that the event would justify him; and that, in uniting with France to support the pope, he was not only consulting the true interest of England, but was doing what England actually desired, although blindly aiming at her object by other means. The French wars, however traditionally popular, were fertile only in glory. The rivalry of the two countries was a splendid folly, wasting the best blood of both countries for an impracticable chimera; and though there was impatience of ecclesiastical misrule, though there was jealousy of foreign interference, and general irritation with the state of the church, yet the mass of the people hated protestantism even worse than they hated the pope, the clergy, and the consistory courts. They believed — and Wolsey was, perhaps, the only leading member of the privy council, except Archbishop Warham, who was not under the same delusion — that it was possible for a national church to separate itself from the unity of Christendom, and at the same time to crush or prevent innovation of doctrine; that faith in the sacramental system could still be maintained, though the priesthood by whom those mysteries were dispensed should minister in gilded chains. This was the English historical theory handed down from William Rufus, the second Henry, and the Edwards; yet it was and is a mere phantasm, a thing of words and paper fictions, as Wolsey saw it to be. Wolsey knew well that an ecclesiastical revolt implied, as a certainty, innovation of doctrine; that plain men could not and would not continue to reverence the office of the priesthood, when the priests were treated as the paid officials of an earthly authority higher than their own. He was not to be blamed if he took the people at their word; if he believed that, in their doctrinal conservatism, they knew and meant what they were saying: and the reaction which took place under Queen Mary, when the Anglican system had been tried and failed, and the alternative was seen to be absolute between a union with Rome or a forfeiture of catholic orthodoxy, prove after all that he was wiser than in the immediate event he seemed to be; that if his policy had succeeded, and if, strengthened by success, he had introduced into the church those reforms which he had promised and desired, 130 he would have satisfied the substantial wishes of the majority of the nation.

Like other men of genius, Wolsey also combined practical sagacity with an unmeasured power of hoping. As difficulties gathered round him, he encountered them with the increasing magnificence of his schemes; and after thirty years' experience of public life, he was as sanguine as a boy. Armed with this little lever of the divorce, he saw himself, in imagination, the rebuilder of the catholic faith and the deliverer of Europe. The king being remarried, and the succession settled, he would purge the Church of England, and convert the monasteries into intellectual garrisons of pious and learned men, occupying the land from end to end. The feuds with France should cease for ever, and, united in a holy cause, the two countries should restore the papacy, put down the German heresies, depose the emperor, and establish in his place some faithful servant of the church. Then Europe once more at peace, the hordes of the Crescent, which were threatening to settle the quarrels of Christians in the West as they had settled them in the East—by the extinction of Christianity itself,—were to be hurled back into their proper barbarism. 131 These magnificent visions fell from him in conversations with the Bishop of Bayonne, and may be gathered from hints and fragments of his correspondence. Extravagant as they seem, the prospect of realising them was, humanly speaking, neither chimerical nor even improbable. He had but made the common mistake of men of the world who are the representatives of an old order of things at the time when that order is doomed and dying. He could not read the signs of the times; and confounded the barrenness of death with the barrenness of a winter which might be followed by a new spring and summer; he believed that the old life-tree of Catholicism, which in fact was but cumbering the ground, might bloom again in its old beauty. The thing which he called heresy was the fire of Almighty God, which no politic congregation of princes, no state machinery, though it were never so active, could trample out; and as in the early years of Christianity the meanest slave who was thrown to the wild beasts for his presence at the forbidden mysteries of the gospel, saw deeper, in the divine power of his faith, into the future even of this earthly world than the sagest of his imperial persecutors, so a truer political prophet than Wolsey would have been found in the most ignorant of those poor men, for whom his myrmidons were searching in the purlieus of London, who were risking death and torture in disseminating the pernicious volumes of the English Testament.

If we look at the matter, however, from a more earthly point of view, the causes which immediately defeated Wolsey's policy were not such as human foresight could have anticipated. We ourselves, surveying the various parties in Europe with the light of our knowledge of the actual sequel, are perhaps able to understand their real relations; but if in 1527 a political astrologer had foretold that within two years of that time the pope and the emperor who had imprisoned him would be cordial allies, that the positions of England and Spain toward the papacy would be diametrically reversed, and that the two countries were on the point of taking their posts, which they would ever afterwards maintain, as the champions respectively of the opposite principles to those which at that time they seemed to represent, the prophecy would have been held scarcely less insane than a prophecy six or even three years before the event, that in the year 1854 England would be united with an Emperor Napoleon for the preservation of European order.

Henry, then, in the spring of the year 1527, definitively breaking the Spanish alliance, formed a league with Francis I., the avowed object of which was the expulsion of the Imperialists from Italy; with a further intention—if it could be carried into effect—of avenging the outrage offered to Europe in the pope's imprisonment, by declaring vacant the imperial throne. Simultaneously with the congress at Amiens where the terms of the alliance were arranged, confidential persons were despatched into Italy to obtain an interview—if possible—with the pope, and formally laying before him the circumstances of the king's position, to request him to make use of his powers to provide a remedy. It is noticeable that at the outset of the negotiation the king did not fully trust Wolsey. The latter had suggested, as the simplest method of proceeding, that the pope should extend his authority as legate, granting him plenary power to act as English vicegerent so long as Rome was occupied by the Emperor's troops. Henry, not wholly satisfied that he was acquainted with his minister's full intentions in desiring so large a capacity, sent his own secretary, unknown to Wolsey, with his own private propositions—requesting simply a dispensation to take a second wife, his former marriage being allowed to stand with no definite sentence passed upon it; or, if that were impossible, leaving the pope to choose his own method, and settle the question in the manner least difficult and least offensive. 132

Wolsey, however, soon satisfied the king that he had no sinister intentions. By the middle of the winter we find the private messenger associated openly with Sir Gregory Cassalis, the agent of the minister's communications; 133 and a series of formal demands were presented jointly by these two persons in the names of Henry and the legate; which, though taking many forms, resolved themselves substantially into one. The pope was required to make use of his dispensing power to enable the King of England to marry a wife who could bear him children, and thus provide some better security than already existed for the succession to the throne. This demand could not be considered as in itself unreasonable; and if personal feeling was combined with other motives to induce Henry to press it, personal feeling did not affect the general bearing of the question. The king's desire was publicly urged on public grounds, and thus, and thus only, the pope was at liberty to consider it. The marriages of princes have ever been affected by other considerations than those which influence such relations between private persons. Princes may not, as "unvalued persons" may, "carve for themselves;" they pay the penalty of their high place, in submitting their affections to the welfare of the state; and the same causes which regulate the formation of these ties must be allowed to influence the continuance of them. The case which was submitted to the pope was one of those for which his very power of dispensing had been vested in him; and being, as he called himself, the Father of Christendom, the nation thought themselves entitled to call upon him to make use of that power. A resource of the kind must exist somewhere—the relation between princes and subjects indispensably requiring it. It had been vested in the Bishop of Rome, because it had been presumed that the sanctity of his office would secure an impartial exercise of his authority. And unless he could have shown (which he never attempted to show) that the circumstances of the succession were not so precarious as to call for his interference, it would seem that the express contingency had arisen which was contemplated in the constitution of the canon law; 134 and that where a provision had been made by the church of which he was the earthly head, for difficulties of this precise description, the pope was under an obligation either to make the required concessions in virtue of his faculty, or, if he found himself unable to make those concessions, to offer some distinct explanation of his refusal. I speak of the question as nakedly political. I am not considering the private injuries of which Catherine had so deep a right to complain, nor the complications subsequently raised on the original validity of the first marriage. A political difficulty, on which alone he was bound to give sentence, was laid before the pope in his judicial capacity, in the name of the nation; and the painful features which the process afterwards assumed are due wholly to his original weakness and vacillation.

Deeply, however, as we must all deplore the scandal and suffering which were occasioned by the dispute, it was in a high degree fortunate, that at the crisis of public dissatisfaction in England with the condition of the church, especially in the conduct of its courts of justice, a cause should have arisen which tested the whole question of church authority in its highest form; where the dispute between the laity and the ecclesiastics was represented in a process in which the pope sat as judge; in which the king was the appellant, and the most vital interests of the nation were at stake upon the issue. It was no accident which connected a suit for divorce with the reformation of religion. The ecclesiastical jurisdiction was upon its trial, and the future relations of church and state depended upon the pope's conduct in a matter which no technical skill was required to decide, but only the moral virtues of probity and courage. The time had been when the clergy feared only to be unjust, and when the functions of judges might safely be entrusted to them. The small iniquities of the consistory courts had shaken the popular faith in the continued operation of such a fear; and the experience of an Alexander VI., a Julius II., and a Leo X. had induced a suspicion that even in the highest quarters justice had ceased to be much considered. It remained for Clement VII. to disabuse men of their alarms, or by confirming them to forfeit for ever the supremacy of his order in England. Nor can it be said for him that the case was one in which it was unusually difficult to be virtuous. Justice, wounded dignity, and the interests of the See pointed alike to the same course. Queen Catherine's relationship to the emperor could not have recommended her to the tenderness of the pope, and the policy of assenting to an act which would infallibly alienate Henry from Charles, and therefore attach him to the Roman interests, did not require the eloquence of Wolsey to make it intelligible. If, because he was in the emperor's power, he therefore feared the personal consequences to himself, his cowardice of itself disqualified him to sit as a judge.

It does not fall within my present purpose to detail the first stages of the proceedings which followed. In substance they are well known to all readers of English history, and may be understood without difficulty as soon as we possess the clue to the conduct of Wolsey. I shall, however, in a few pages briefly epitomise what passed.

At the outset of the negotiation, the pope, although he would take no positive steps, was all, in words, which he was expected to be. Neither he nor the cardinals refused to acknowledge the dangers which threatened the country. He discussed freely the position of the different parties, the probabilities of a disputed succession, and the various claimants who would present themselves, if the king died without an heir of undisputed legitimacy. 135 Gardiner writes to Wolsey, 136 "We did even more inculcate what speed and celerity the thing required, and what danger it was to the realm to have this matter hang in suspense. His Holiness confessed the same, and thereupon began to reckon what divers titles might be pretended by the King of Scots and others, and granted that, without an heir male, with provision to be made by consent of the state for his succession, and unless that what shall be done herein be established in such fashion as nothing may hereafter be objected thereto, the realm was like to come to dissolution."

In stronger language the Cardinal-Governor of Bologna declared that "he knew the gyze of England as well as few men did, and if the king should die without heirs male, he was sure it would cost two hundred thousand men's lives. Wherefore he thought, supposing his Grace should have no more children by the queen, and that by taking of another wife he might have heirs male, the bringing to pass that matter, and by that to avoid the mischiefs afore written, he thought would deserve Heaven." 137 Whatever doubt their might be, therefore, whether the original marriage with Catherine was legal, it was universally admitted that there was none about the national desirableness of the dissolution of it; and if the pope had been free to judge only by the merits of the case, it is impossible to doubt that he would have cut the knot, either by granting a dispensation to Henry to marry a second wife—his first being formally, though not judicially, separated from him—or in some other way. 138 But the emperor was "a lion in his path;" the question of strength between the French and the Spaniards remained undecided, and Clement would come to no decision until he was assured of the power of the allies to protect him from the consequences. Accordingly he said and unsaid, sighed, sobbed, beat his breast, shuffled, implored, threatened; 139 in all ways he endeavoured to escape from his dilemma, to say yes and to say no, to do nothing, to offend no one, and above all to gain time, with the weak man's hope that "something might happen" to extricate him. Embassy followed embassy from England, each using language more threatening than its predecessor. The thing, it was said, must be done, and should be done. If it was not done by the pope it would be done at home in some other way, and the pope must take the consequences. 140 Wolsey warned him passionately of the rising storm, 141 a storm which would be so terrible when it burst "that it would be better to die than to live." The pope was strangely unable to believe that the danger could be real, being misled perhaps by other information from the friends of Queen Catherine, and by an over-confidence in the attachment of the people to the emperor. He acted throughout in a manner natural to a timid amiable man, who found himself in circumstances to which he was unequal; and as long as we look at him merely as a man we can pity his embarrassment. He forgot, however, that only because he was supposed to be more than a man had kings and emperors consented to plead at his judgment seat—a fact of which Stephen Gardiner, then Wolsey's secretary, thought it well to remind him in the following striking language:—

"Unless," said the future Bishop of Winchester in the council, at the close of a weary day of unprofitable debating, "unless some other resolution be taken than I perceive you intend to make, hereupon shall be gathered a marvellous opinion of your Holiness, of the college of cardinals, and of the authority of this See. The King's Highness, and the nobles of the realm who shall be made privy to this, shall needs think that your Holiness and these most reverend and learned councillors either will not answer in this cause, or cannot answer. If you will not, if you do not choose to point out the way to an erring man, the care of whom is by God committed to you, they will say, 'Oh race of men most ungrateful, and of your proper office most oblivious! You who should be simple as doves are full of all deceit, and craft, and dissembling. If the king's cause be good, we require that you pronounce it good. If it be bad, why will you not say that it is bad, so to hinder a prince to whom you are so much bounden from longer continuing with it? We ask nothing of you but justice, which the king so loves and values, that whatever sinister things others may say or think of him, he will follow that with all his heart; that, and nothing else, whether it be for the marriage or against the marriage.'

"But if the King's Majesty," continued Gardiner, hitting the very point of the difficulty, "if the King's Majesty and the nobility of England, being persuaded of your good will to answer if you can do so, shall be brought to doubt of your ability, they will be forced to a harder conclusion respecting this See—namely, that God has taken from it the key of knowledge; and they will begin give better ear to that opinion of some persons to which they have as yet refused to listen, that those papal laws which neither the pope himself nor his council can interpret, deserve only to be committed to the flames." "I desired his Holiness," he adds, "to ponder well this matter." 142

Clement was no hero, but in his worst embarrassments his wit never failed him. He answered that he was not learned, and "to speak truth, albeit there was a saying in the canon law, that *Pontifex habet omnia jura in scrinio pectoris* (the pope has all laws locked within his breast), yet God had never given him the key to open that lock." He was but "seeking pretexts" for delay, as Gardiner saw, till the issue of the Italian campaign of the French in the summer of 1528 was decided. He had been liberated, or had been allowed to escape from Rome, in the fear that if detained longer he might nominate a vicegerent; and was residing at an old ruined castle at Orvieto, waiting upon events, leaving the Holy City still occupied by the Prince of Orange. In the preceding autumn, immediately after the congress at Amiens, M. de Lautrec, accompanied by several English noblemen, had led an army across the Alps. He had defeated the Imperialists in the north of Italy in several minor engagements; and in January his success appeared so probable, that the pope took better heart, and told Sir Gregory Cassalis, that if the French would only approach near enough to enable him to plead compulsion, he would grant a commission to Wolsey, with plenary power to conclude the cause. 143 De Lautrec, however, foiled in his desire to bring the Imperialists to a decisive engagement, wasted his time and strength in ineffectual petty sieges; and finally, in the summer, on the unhealthy plains of Naples, a disaster more fatal in its consequences than the battle of Pavia, closed the prospects of the French to the south of the Alps; and with them all Wolsey's hopes of realising his dream. Struck down, not by a visible enemy, but by the silent hand of fever, the French general himself, his English friends, and all his army melted away from off the earth. The pope had been wise in time. He had committed himself in words and intentions; but he had done nothing which he could not recall. He obtained his pardon from the emperor by promising to offend no more; and from that moment never again entertained any real thought of concession. Acting under explicit directions, he made it his object thenceforward to delay and to procrastinate. Charles had no desire to press matters to extremities. War had not yet been declared 144 against him by Henry; nor was he anxious himself to precipitate a quarrel from which, if possible, he would gladly escape. He had a powerful party in England, which it was unwise to alienate by hasty, injudicious measures; and he could gain all which he himself desired by a simple policy of obstruction. His object was merely to protract the negotiation and prevent a decision, in the hope either that Henry would be wearied into acquiescence, or that Catherine herself would retire of her own accord, or, finally, that some happy accident might occur to terminate the difficulty. It is, indeed, much to the honour of Charles V. that he resolved to support the queen. She had thrown herself on his protection; but princes in such matters consider prudence more than feeling, and he could gain nothing by defending her: while, both for himself and for the church he risked the loss of much. He over-rated the strength of his English connection, and mistook the English character; but he was not blind to the hazard which he was incurring, and would have welcomed an escape from the dilemma perhaps as warmly as Henry would have welcomed it himself. The pope, who well knew his feelings, told Gardiner, "It would be for the wealth of Christendom if the queen were in her grave; and he thought the emperor would be thereof most glad of all;" saying, also, "that he thought like as the emperor had destroyed the temporalities of the church, so should she be the destruction of the spiritualities." 145

In the summer of 1528, before the disaster at Naples, Cardinal Campeggio had left Rome on his way to England, where he was to hear the cause in conjunction with Wolsey. An initial measure of this obvious kind it had been impossible to refuse; and the pretexts under which it was for many months delayed, were exhausted before the pope's ultimate course had been made clear to him. But Campeggio was instructed to protract his journey to its utmost length, giving time for the campaign to decide itself. He loitered into the autumn, under the excuse of gout and other convenient accidents, until the news reached him of De Lautrec's death, which took place on the 21st of August; and then at length proceeding, he betrayed to Francis I., on passing through Paris, that he had no intention of allowing judgment to be passed upon the cause. 146 Even Wolsey was beginning to tremble at what he had attempted, and was doubtful of success. 147 The seeming relief came in time, for Henry's patience was fast running out. He had been over-persuaded into a course which he had never cordially approved. The majority of the council, especially the Duke of Norfolk and the Duke of Suffolk, were traditionally imperial, and he himself might well doubt whether he might not have found a nearer road out of his difficulties by adhering to Charles. Charles, after all, was not ruining the papacy, and had no intention of ruining it; and his lightest word weighed more at the court of Rome than the dubious threats and prayers of France. The Bishop of Bayonne, resident French ambassador in London, whose remarkable letters transport us back into the very midst of that unquiet and stormy scene, tells us plainly that the French alliance was hated by the country, that the nobility were all for the emperor, and that among the commons the loudest discontent was openly expressed against Wolsey from the danger of the interruption of the trade with Flanders. Flemish ships had been detained in London, and English ships in retaliation had been arrested in the Zealand ports; corn was unusually dear, and the expected supplies from Spain and Germany were cut off; 148 while the derangement of the woollen trade, from the reluctance of the merchants to venture purchases, was causing distress all over the country, and Wolsey had been driven to the most arbitrary measures to prevent open disturbance. 149 He had set his hopes upon the chance of a single cast which he would not believe could fail him, but on each fresh delay he was compelled to feel his declining credit, and the Bishop of Bayonne wrote, on the 20th of August, 1528, that the cardinal was in bad spirits, and had told him in confidence, that "if he could only see the divorce arranged, the king remarried, the succession settled, and the laws and the manners and customs of the country reformed, he would retire from the world and would serve God the remainder of his days." 150 To these few trifles he would be contented to confine himself — only to these; he was past sixty, he was weary of the world, and his health was breaking, and he would limit his hopes to the execution of a work for which centuries imperfectly sufficed. It seemed as if he measured his stature by the lengthening shadow, as his sun made haste to its setting. Symptoms of misgiving may be observed in the many anxious letters which he wrote while Campeggio was so long upon his road; and the Bishop of Bayonne, whose less interested eyes could see more deeply into the game, warned him throughout that the pope was playing him false. 151 Only in a revulsion from violent despondency could such a man as Wolsey have allowed himself, on the mere arrival of the legate, and after a few soft words from him, to write in the following strain to Sir Gregory Cassalis:—

"You cannot believe the exultation with which at length I find myself successful in the object for which these many years, with all my industry, I have laboured. At length I have found means to bind my most excellent sovereign and this glorious realm to the holy Roman see in faith and obedience for ever. Henceforth will this people become the most sure pillar of support to bear up the sacred fabric of the church. Henceforth, in recompense for that enduring felicity which he has secured to it, our most Holy Lord has all England at his devotion. In brief time will this noble land make its grateful acknowledgments to his clemency at once for the preservation of the most just, most wise, most excellent of princes, and for the secure establishment of the realm and the protection of the royal succession." 152

This letter was dated on the fourth of October, and was written in the hope that the pope had collected his courage, and that the legate had brought powers to proceed to judgment. In a few days the prospect was again clouded, and Wolsey was once more in despair. 153 Campeggio had brought with him instructions if possible to arrange a compromise,—if a compromise was impossible, to make the best use of his ingenuity, and do nothing and allow nothing to be done. In one of two ways, however, it was hoped that he might effect a peaceful solution. He urged the king to give way and to proceed no further; and this failing, as he was prepared to find, he urged the same thing upon the queen. 154 He invited Catherine, or he was directed to invite her, in the pope's name, 155 for the sake of the general interests of Christendom, to take the vows and enter what was called *religio laxa*, a state in which she might live unincumbered by obligations except the easy one of chastity, and free from all other restrictions either of habit, diet, or order. The proposal was Wolsey's, and was formed when he found the limited nature of Campeggio's instructions; 156 but it was adopted by the latter; and I cannot but think (though I have no proof of it) that it was not adopted without the knowledge of the emperor. Whatever were his own interests, Charles V. gave Catherine his unwavering support: he made it his duty to maintain her in the ignominious position in which she was placed, and submitted his own conduct to be guided by her wishes. It cannot be doubted, however, from the pope's words, and also from the circumstances of the case, that if she could have prevailed upon herself to yield, it would have relieved him from a painful embarrassment. As a prince, he must have felt the substantial justice of Henry's demand, and in refusing to allow the pope to pass a judicial sentence of divorce, he could not but have known that he was compromising the position of the Holy See: while Catherine herself, on the other hand, if she had yielded, would have retired without a stain; no opinion would have been pronounced upon her marriage; the legitimacy of the Princess Mary would have been left without impeachment; and her right to the succession, in the event of no male heir following from any new connection which the king might form, would have been readily secured to her by act of parliament. It may be asked why she did not yield, and it is difficult to answer the question. She was not a person who would have been disturbed by the loss of a few court vanities. Her situation as Henry's wife could not have had many charms for her, nor can it be thought that she retained a personal affection for him. If she had loved him, she would have suffered too deeply in the struggle to have continued to resist, and the cloister would have seemed a paradise. Or if the cloister had appeared too sad a shelter for her, she might have gone back to the gardens of the Alhambra, where she had played as a child, carrying with her the affectionate remembrance of every English heart, and welcomed by her own people as an injured saint. Nor again can we suppose that the possible injury of her daughter's prospects from the birth of a prince by another marriage could have seemed of so vast moment to her. Those prospects were already more than endangered, and would have been rather improved than brought into further peril.

It is not for us to dictate the conduct which a woman smarting under injuries so cruel ought to have pursued. She had a right to choose the course which seemed the best to herself, and England especially could not claim of a stranger that readiness to sacrifice herself which it might have demanded and exacted of one of its own children. We may regret, however, what we are unable to censure; and the most refined ingenuity could scarcely have invented a more unfortunate answer than that which the Queen returned to the legate's request. She seems to have said that she was ready to take vows of chastity if the king would do the same. It does not appear whether the request was *formally* made, or whether it was merely suggested to her in private conversation. That she told the legates, however, what her answer would be, appears certain from the following passage, sadly indicating the "devices of policy" to which in this unhappy business honourable men allowed themselves to be driven:—

"Forasmuch as it is like that the queen shall make marvellous difficulty, and in nowise be conformable to enter religion 157 or take vows of chastity, but that to induce her thereunto, there must be ways and means of high policy used, and all things possible devised to encourage her to the same; wherein percase she shall resolve that she in no wise will condescend so to do, unless that the King's Highness also do the semblable for his part; the king's said orators shall therefore in like wise ripe and instruct themselves by their secret learned council in the court of Rome, if, for so great a benefit to ensue unto the king's succession, realm, and subjects, with the quiet of his conscience, his Grace should promise so to enter religion on vows of chastity for his part, only thereby to conduce the queen thereunto, whether in that case the Pope's Holiness may dispense with the King's Highness for the same promise, oath, or vow, discharging his Grace clearly of the same." 158

The explanation of the queen's conduct lies probably in regions into which it is neither easy nor well to penetrate; in regions of outraged delicacy and wounded pride, in a vast drama of passion which had been enacted behind the scenes. From the significant hints which are let fall of the original cause of the estrangement, it was of a kind more difficult to endure than the ordinary trial of married women, the transfer of a husband's affection to some fairer face; and a wife whom so painful a misfortune had failed to crush would be likely to have been moved by it to a deeper and more bitter indignation even, because while she could not blame herself, she knew not whom she might rightly allow herself to blame. And if this were so, the king is not likely to have allayed the storm when at length, putting faith in Wolsey's promises, he allowed himself openly to regard another person as his future wife, establishing her in the palace at Greenwich under the same roof with the queen, with reception rooms, and royal state, and a position openly acknowledged, 159 the gay court and courtiers forsaking the gloomy dignity of the actual wife for the gaudy splendour of her brilliant rival. Tamer blood than that which flowed in the veins of a princess of Castile would have boiled under these indignities; and we have little reason to be surprised if policy and prudence were alike forgotten by Catherine in the bitterness of the draught which was forced upon her, and if her own personal wrongs outweighed the interests of the world. Henry had proceeded to the last unjustifiable extremity as soon as the character of Campeggio's mission had been made clear to him, as if to demonstrate to all the world that he was determined to persevere at all costs and hazards. 160 Taking the management of the negotiation into his own keeping, he sent Sir Francis Bryan, the cousin of Anne Boleyn, to the pope, to announce that what he required must be done, and to declare peremptorily, no more with covert hints, but with open menace, that in default of help from Rome, he would lay the matter before parliament, to be settled at home by the laws of his own country.

Meanwhile, the emperor, who had hitherto conducted himself with the greatest address, had fallen into his first error. He had retreated skilfully out of the embarrassment in which the pope's imprisonment involved him, and mingling authority and dictation with kindness and deference, he had won over the Holy See to his devotion, and neutralised the danger to which the alliance of France and England threatened to expose him. His correspondence with the latter country assured him of the unpopularity of the course which had been pursued by the cardinal; he was aware of the obstruction of trade which it had caused, and of the general displeasure felt by the people at the breach of an old friendship; while the league with France in behalf of the Roman church had been barren of results, and was made ridiculous by the obvious preference of the pope for the enemy from whom it was formed to deliver him. If Charles had understood the English temper, therefore, and had known how to avail himself of the opportunity, events might have run in a very different channel. But he was not aware of the earnestness with which the people were bent upon securing the succession, nor of their loyal attachment to Henry. He supposed that disapproval of the course followed by Wolsey to obtain the divorce implied an aversion to it altogether; and trusting to his interest in the privy council, and to his commercial connection with the city, he had attempted to meet menace with menace; he had replied to the language addressed by Henry to the pope with an attempt to feel the pulse of English disaffection, and he opened a correspondence with the Earl of Desmond for an Irish revolt. 161

The opportunity for a movement of this kind had not yet arrived. There was, in England at least, as yet no wide disaffection; but there was a chance of serious outbreaks; and Henry instantly threw himself upon the nation. He summoned the peers by circular to London, and calling a general meeting, composed of the nobility, the privy council, the lord mayor, and the great merchants of the city, he laid before them a specific detail of his objects in desiring the divorce; 162 and informed them of the nature of the measures which had been taken. 163 This, the French ambassador informs us, gave wide satisfaction and served much to allay the disquiet; but so great was the indignation against Wolsey, that disturbances in London were every day anticipated; and at one time the danger appeared so threatening, that an order of council was issued, commanding all strangers to leave the city, and a general search was instituted for arms. 164 The strangers aimed at were the Flemings, whose numbers made them formidable, and who were, perhaps, supposed to be ready to act under instruction from abroad.

The cloud, however, cleared away; the order was not enforced; and the propitious moment for treason had not yet arrived. The emperor had felt so confident that, in the autumn of 1528, he had boasted that, "before the winter was over, he would fling Henry from his throne by the hands of his own Subjects." The words had been repeated to Wolsey, who mentioned them openly at his table before more than a hundred gentlemen. A person present exclaimed, "That speech has lost the emperor more than a hundred thousand hearts among us;" 165 an expression which reveals at once the strength and the weakness of the imperial party. England might have its own opinions of the policy of the government, but it was in no humour to tolerate treason, and the first hint of revolt was followed by an instant recoil. The discovery of more successful intrigues in Scotland and Ireland completed the destruction of Charles's influence; 166 and the result of these ill-judged and premature efforts was merely to unite the nation in their determination to prosecute the divorce.

Thus were the various parties in the vast struggle which was about to commence gravitating into their places; and mistake combined with policy to place them in their true positions. Wolsey, in submitting "the king's matter" to the pope, had brought to issue the question whether the papal authority should be any longer recognised in England; and he had secured the ruin of that authority by the steps through which he hoped to establish it; while Charles, by his unwise endeavours to foment a rebellion, severed with his own hand the links of a friendship which would have been seriously embarrassing if it had continued. By him, also, was dealt the concluding stroke in this first act of the drama; and though we may grant him credit for the ingenuity of his contrivance, he can claim it only at the expense of his probity. The pope, when the commission was appointed for the trial of the cause in England, had given a promise in writing that the commission should not be revoked. It seemed, therefore, that the legates would be compelled, in spite of themselves, to pronounce sentence; and that the settlement of the question, in one form or other, could not long be delayed. At the pressure of the crisis in the winter of 1528-9, a document was produced alleged to have been found in Spain, which furnished a pretext for a recall of the engagement, and opening now questions, indefinite and inexhaustible, rendered the passing of a sentence in England impossible. Unhappily, the weight of the king's claim (however it had been rested on its true merits in conversation and in letters) had, by the perverse ingenuity of the lawyers, been laid on certain informalities and defects in the original bull of dispensation, which had been granted by Julius II. for the marriage of Henry and Catherine. At the moment when the legates' court was about to be opened, a copy of a brief was brought forward, bearing the same date as the bull, exactly meeting the objection. The authenticity of this brief was open, on its own merits, to grave doubt; and suspicion becomes certainty when we find it was dropped out of the controversy so soon as the immediate object was gained for which it was produced. But the legates' hands were instantly tied by it. The "previous question" of authenticity had necessarily to be tried before they could take another step; and the "original" of the brief being in the hands of the emperor, who refused to send it into England, but offered to send it to Rome, the cause was virtually transferred to Rome, where Henry, as he knew, was unlikely to consent to plead, or where he could himself rule the decision. He had made a stroke of political finesse, which answered not only the purpose that he immediately intended, but answered, also, the purpose that he did not intend—of dealing the hardest blow which it had yet received to the supremacy of the Holy See.

The spring of 1529 was wasted in fruitless efforts to obtain the brief. At length, in May, the proceedings were commenced; but they were commenced only in form, and were never more than an illusion. Catherine had been instructed in the course which she was to pursue. She appealed from the judgment of the legates to that of the pope; and the pope, with the plea of the new feature which had arisen in the case, declared that he could not refuse to revoke his promise. Having consented to the production of the brief, he had in fact no alternative; nor does it appear what he could have urged in excuse of himself. He may have suspected the forgery; nay, it is certain that in England he was believed to be privy to it; but he could not ignore an important feature of necessary evidence, especially when pressed upon him by the emperor; and it was in fact no more than an absurdity to admit the authority of a papal commission, and to refuse to permit an appeal from it to the pope in person. We may thank Clement for dispelling a chimera by a simple act of consistency. The power of the See of Rome in England was a constitutional fiction, acknowledged only on condition that it would consent to be inert. So long as a legate's court sat in London, men were able to conceal from themselves the fact of a foreign jurisdiction, and to feel that, substantially, their national independence was respected; when the fiction aspired to become a reality, but one consequence was possible. If Henry himself would have stooped to plead at a foreign tribunal, the spirit of the nation would not have permitted him to inflict so great a dishonour on the free majesty of England.

So fell Wolsey's great scheme, and with it fell the last real chance of maintaining the pope's authority in England under any form. The people were smarting under the long humiliation of the delay, and ill-endured to see the interests of England submitted, as they virtually were, to the arbitration of a foreign prince. The emperor, not the pope, was the true judge who sat to decide the quarrel; and their angry jealousy refused to tolerate longer a national dishonour.

"The great men of the realm," wrote the legates, "are storming in bitter wrath at our procrastination. Lords and commons alike complain that they are made to expect at the hands of strangers things of vital moment to themselves and their fortunes. And many persons here who would desire to see the pope's authority in this country diminished or annulled, are speaking in language which we cannot repeat without horror." 167

And when, being in such a mood, they were mocked, after two weary years of negotiation, by the opening of a fresh vista of difficulties, when they were informed that the further hearing of the cause was transferred to Italy, even Wolsey, with certain ruin before him, rose in protest before such a dream of shame. He was no more the Roman legate, but the English minister.

"If the advocation be passed," he wrote to Cassalis, 168 "or shall now at any time hereafter pass, with citation of the king in person, or by proctor, to the court of Rome, or with any clause of interdiction or excommunication, *vel cum invocatione brachii sæcularis*, whereby the king should be precluded from taking his advantage otherwise, the dignity and prerogative royal of the king's crown, whereunto all the nobles and subjects of this realm will adhere and stick unto the death, may not tolerate nor suffer that the same be obeyed. And to say the truth, in so doing the pope should not only show himself the king's enemy, but also as much as in him is, provoke all other princes and people to be the semblable. Nor shall it ever be seen that the king's cause shall be ventilated or decided in any place out of his own realm; *but that if his Grace should come at any time to the Court of Rome, he would do the same with such a main and army royal as should be formidable to the pope and all Italy.*" 169

Wolsey, however, failed in his protest; the advocation was passed, Campeggio left England, and he was lost. A crisis had arrived, and a revolution of policy was inevitable. From the accession of Henry VII., the country had been governed by a succession of ecclesiastical ministers, who being priests as well as statesmen, were essentially conservative; and whose efforts in a position of constantly increasing difficulty had been directed towards resisting the changing tendencies of the age, and either evading a reformation of the church while they admitted its necessity, or retaining the conduct of it in their own hands, while they were giving evidence of their inability to accomplish the work. It was now over; the ablest representative of this party, in a last desperate effort to retain power, had decisively failed. Writs were issued for a parliament when the legate's departure was determined, and the consequences were inevitable. Wolsey had known too well the unpopularity of his foreign policy, to venture on calling a parliament himself. He relied on success as an ultimate justification; and inasmuch as success had not followed, he was obliged to bear the necessary fate of a minister who, in a free country, had thwarted the popular will and whom fortune deserted in the struggle. The barriers which his single hand had upheld suddenly gave way, the torrent had free course, and he himself was the first to be swept away. In modern language, we should describe what took place as a change of ministry, the government being transferred to an opposition, who had been irritated by long depression under the hands of men whom they despised, and who were borne into power by an irresistible force in a moment of excitement and danger. The king, who had been persuaded against his better judgment to accept Wolsey's schemes, admitted the rising spirit without reluctance, contented to moderate its action, but no longer obstructing or permitting it to be obstructed. Like all great English statesmen, he was constitutionally conservative, but he had the tact to perceive the conditions under which, in critical times, conservatism is possible; and although he continued to endure for himself the trifling of the papacy, he would not, for the sake of the pope's interest, delay further the investigation of the complaints of the people against the church; while in the future prosecution of his own cause, he resolved to take no steps except with the consent of the legislature, and in a question of national moment, to consult only the nation's wishes.

The new ministry held a middle place between the moving party in the commons and the expelled ecclesiastics, the principal members of it being the chief representatives of the old aristocracy, who had been Wolsey's fiercest opponents, but who were disinclined by constitution and sympathy from sweeping measures. An attempt was made, indeed, to conciliate the more old-fashioned of the churchmen, by an offer of the seals to Warham, Archbishop of Canterbury, probably because he originally opposed the marriage between the king and his sister-in-law, and because it was hoped that his objections remained unaltered. Warham, however, as we shall see, had changed his mind: he declined, on the plea of age, and the office of chancellor was given to Sir Thomas More, perhaps the person least disaffected to the clergy who could have been found among the leading laymen. The substance of power was vested in the Dukes of Norfolk and Suffolk, the great soldier-nobles of the age, and Sir William Fitz-William, lord admiral; to all of whom the ecclesiastical domination had been most intolerable, while they had each of them brilliantly distinguished themselves in the wars with France and Scotland. According to the French ambassador, we must add one more minister, supreme, if we may trust him, above them all. "The Duke of Norfolk," he writes, "is made president of the council, the Duke of Suffolk vice-president, and above them both is Mistress Anne;" 170 this last addition to the council being one which boded little good to the interests of the See that had so long detained her in expectation. So confident were the destructive party of the temper of the approaching parliament, and of the irresistible pressure of the times, that the general burden of conversation of the dinner-tables in the great houses in London was an exulting expectation of a dissolution of the church establishment, and a confiscation of ecclesiastical property; the king himself being the only obstacle which was feared by them. "These noble lords imagine," continues the same writer, "that the cardinal once dead of ruined, they will incontinently plunder the church, and strip it of all its wealth," adding that there was no occasion for him to write this in cipher, for it was everywhere openly spoken of. 171

Movements, nevertheless, which are pregnant with vital change, are slow in assuming their essential direction, even after the stir has commenced. Circumstances do not immediately open themselves; the point of vision alters gradually; and fragments of old opinions, and prepossessions, and prejudices remain interfused with the new, even in the clearest minds, and cannot at a moment be shaken off. Only the unwise change suddenly; and we can never too often remind ourselves, when we see men stepping forward with uncertainty and hesitation over a road, where to us, we know the actual future, all seems so plain, that the road looked different to the actors themselves, who were beset with imaginations of the past, and to whom the gloom of the future appeared thronged with phantoms of possible contingencies. The hasty expectations of the noble lords were checked by Henry's prudence; and though parties were rapidly arranging themselves, there was still confusion. The city, though disinclined to the pope and the church, continued to retain an inclination for the emperor; and the pope had friends among Wolsey's enemies, who, by his overthrow, were pressed forward into prominence, and divided the victory with the reformers. The presence of Sir Thomas More in the council was a guarantee that no exaggerated measures against the church would be permitted so long as he held the seals; and Henry, perhaps, was anxious to leave room for conciliation, which he hoped that the pope would desire as much as himself, so soon as the meeting of parliament had convinced him that the mutinous disposition of the nation had not been overstated by his own and Wolsey's letters.

The impression conceived two years before of the hostile relations between the pope and Charles had not yet been wholly effaced; and even as late as September, 1529, after the closing of the legates' court, in the very heat of the public irritation, there were persons who believed that when Clement met his imperial captor face to face, and the interview had taken place which had been arranged for the ensuing January, his eyes would be opened, and that he would fall back upon England. 172 At the same time, the incongruities in the constitution of the council became so early apparent, that their agreement was thought impossible, and Wolsey's return to power was discussed openly as a probability 173—a result which Anne Boleyn, who, better than any other person, knew the king's feelings, never ceased to fear, till, a year after his disgrace, the welcome news were brought to her that he had sunk into his long rest, where the sick load of office and of obloquy would gall his back no more.

There was a third party in the country, unconsidered as yet, who had a part to play in the historical drama: a party which, indeed, if any one had known it, was the most important of all; the only one which, in a true, high sense, was of importance at all; and for the sake of which, little as it then appeared to be so, the whole work was to be done—composed at that time merely of poor men, poor cobblers, weavers, carpenters, trade apprentices, and humble artisans, men of low birth and low estate, who might be seen at night stealing along the lanes and alleys of London, carrying with them some precious load of books which it was death to possess; and giving their lives gladly, if it must be so, for the brief tenure of so dear a treasure. These men, for the present, were likely to fare ill from the new ministry. They were the disturbers of order, the anarchists, the men disfigured *pravitate hereticâ*, by monstrous doctrines, and consequently by monstrous lives—who railed at authorities, and dared to read New Testaments with their own eyes—who, consequently, by their excesses and extravagances, brought discredit upon liberal opinions, and whom moderate liberals (as they always have done, and always will do while human nature remains itself) held it necessary for their credit's sake to persecute, that a censorious world might learn to make no confusion between true wisdom and the folly which seemed to resemble it. The Protestants had not loved Wolsey, and they had no reason to love him; but it was better to bear a fagot of dry sticks in a procession when the punishment was symbolic, than, lashed fast to a stake in Smithfield, amidst piles of the same fagots kindled into actual flames, to sink into a heap of blackened dust and ashes; and before a year had passed, they would gladly have accepted again the hated cardinal, to escape from the philosophic mercies of Sir Thomas More. The number of English Protestants at this time it is difficult to conjecture. The importance of such men is not to be measured by counting heads. In 1526, they were organised into a society, calling themselves "the Christian brotherhood," 174 with a central committee sitting in London; with subscribed funds, regularly audited, for the purchase of Testaments and tracts; and with paid agents, who travelled up and down the country to distribute them. Some of the poorer clergy belonged to the society; 175 and among the city merchants there were many well inclined to it, and who, perhaps, attended its meetings "by night, secretly, for fear of the Jews." But, as a rule, "property and influence" continued to hold aloof in the usual haughty style, and the pioneers of the new opinions had yet to win their way along a scorched and blackened path of suffering, before the State would consent to acknowledge them. We think bitterly of these things, and yet we are but quarrelling with what is inevitable from the constitution of the world. New doctrines ever gain readiest hearing among the common people; not only because the interests of the higher classes are usually in some degree connected with the maintenance of existing institutions; but because ignorance is itself a protection against the many considerations which embarrass the judgment of the educated. The value of a doctrine cannot be determined on its own apparent merits by men whose habits of mind are settled in other forms; while men of experience know well that out of the thousands of theories which rise in the fertile soil below them, it is but one here and one there which grows to maturity; and the precarious chances of possible vitality, where the opposite probabilities are so enormous, oblige them to discourage and repress opinions which threaten to disturb established order, or which, by the rules of existing beliefs, imperil the souls of those who entertain them. Persecution has ceased among ourselves, because we do not any more believe that want of theoretic orthodoxy in matters of faith is necessarily fraught with the tremendous consequences which once were supposed to be attached to it. If, however, a school of Thugs were to rise among us, making murder a religious service; if they gained proselytes, and the proselytes put their teaching in execution, we should speedily begin again to persecute opinion. What teachers of Thuggism would appear to ourselves, the teachers of heresy actually appeared to Sir Thomas More, only being as much more hateful as the eternal death of the soul is more terrible than the single and momentary separation of it from the body. There is, I think, no just ground on which to condemn conscientious Catholics on the score of persecution, except only this: that as we are now convinced of the injustice of the persecuting laws, so among those who believed them to be just, there were some who were led by an instinctive protest of human feeling to be lenient in the execution of those laws; while others of harder nature and more narrow sympathies enforced them without reluctance, and even with exultation. The heart, when it is rightly constituted, corrects the folly of the head; and wise good men, even though they entertain no conscious misgiving as to the soundness of their theories, may be delivered from the worst consequences of those theories, by trusting their more genial instincts. And thus, and thus only, are we justified in censuring those whose names figure largely in the persecuting lists. Their defence is impregnable to logic. We blame them for the absence of that humanity which is deeper than logic, and which should have taught them to refuse the conclusions of their speculative creed.

Such, then, was the state of parties in the autumn of 1529. The old conservatives, the political ecclesiastics, had ceased to exist, and the clergy as a body were paralysed by corruption. There remained—

The English party who had succeeded to power, and who were bent upon a secular revolt.

The papal party, composed of theoretic theologians, like Fisher, Bishop of Rochester, and represented on the council by Sir Thomas More.

And both of these were united in their aversion to the third party, that of the doctrinal Protestants, who were still called heretics.

These three substantially divided what was sound in England; the first composed of the mass of the people, representing the principles of prudence, justice, good sense, and the working faculties of social life: the two last sharing between them the higher qualities of nobleness, enthusiasm, self-devotion; but in their faith being without discretion, and in their piety without understanding. The problem of the Reformation was to reunite virtues which could be separated only to their mutual confusion; and to work out among them such inadequate reconciliation as the wilfulness of human nature would allow.

Before I close this chapter, which is intended as a general introduction, I have to say something of two prominent persons whose character antecedent to the actions in which we are to find them engaged it is desirable that we should understand; I mean Henry VIII. himself, and the lady whom he had selected to fill the place from which Catherine of Arragon was to be deposed.

If Henry VIII. had died previous to the first agitation of the divorce, his loss would have been deplored as one of the heaviest misfortunes which had ever befallen the country; and he would have left a name which would have taken its place in history by the side of that of the Black Prince or of the conqueror of Agincourt. Left at the most trying age, with his character unformed, with the means at his disposal of gratifying every inclination, and married by his ministers when a boy to an unattractive woman far his senior, he had lived for thirty-six years almost without blame, and bore through England the reputation of an upright and virtuous king. Nature had been prodigal to him of her rarest gifts. In person he is said to have resembled his grandfather, Edward IV., who was the handsomest man in Europe. His form and bearing were princely; and amidst the easy freedom of his address, his manner remained majestic. No knight in England could match him in the tournament except the Duke of Suffolk: he drew with ease as strong a bow as was borne by any yeoman of his guard; and these powers were sustained in unfailing vigour by a temperate habit and by constant exercise. Of his intellectual ability we are not left to judge from the suspicious panegyrics of his contemporaries. His state papers and letters may be placed by the side of those of Wolsey or of Cromwell, and they lose nothing in the comparison. Though they are broadly different, the perception is equally clear, the expression equally powerful, and they breathe throughout an irresistible vigour of purpose. In addition to this he had a fine musical taste, carefully cultivated; he spoke and wrote in four languages; and his knowledge of a multitude of other subjects, with which his versatile ability made him conversant, would have formed the reputation of any ordinary man. He was among the best physicians of his age; he was his own engineer, inventing improvements in artillery, and new constructions in ship-building; and this not with the condescending incapacity of a royal amateur, but with thorough workmanlike understanding. His reading was vast, especially in theology, which has been ridiculously ascribed by Lord Herbert to his father's intention of educating him for the Archbishopric of Canterbury; as if the scientific mastery of such a subject could have been acquired by a boy of twelve years of age, for he was no more when he became Prince of Wales. He must have studied theology with the full maturity of his intellect; and he had a fixed and perhaps unfortunate interest in the subject itself. 176

In all directions of human activity Henry displayed natural powers of the highest order, at the highest stretch of industrious culture. He was "attentive," as it is called, "to his religious duties," being present at the services in chapel two or three times a day with unfailing regularity, and showing to outward appearance a real sense of religious obligation in the energy and purity of his life. In private he was good-humoured and good-natured. His letters to his secretaries, though never undignified, are simple, easy, and unrestrained; and the letters written by them to him are similarly plain and businesslike, as if the writers knew that the person whom they were addressing disliked compliments, and chose to be treated as a man. Again, from their correspondence with one another, when they describe interviews with him, we gather the same pleasant impression. He seems to have been always kind, always considerate; inquiring into their private concerns with genuine interest, and winning, as a consequence, their warm and unaffected attachment.

As a ruler he had been eminently popular. All his wars had been successful. He had the splendid tastes in which the English people most delighted, and he had substantially acted out his own theory of his duty which was expressed in the following words:—

"Scripture taketh princes to be, as it were, fathers and nurses to their subjects, and by Scripture it appeareth that it appertaineth unto the office of princes to see that right religion and true doctrine be maintained and taught, and that their subjects may be well ruled and governed by good and just laws; and to provide and care for them that all things necessary for them may be plenteous; and that the people and commonweal may increase; and to defend them from oppression and invasion, as well within the realm as without; and to see that justice be administered unto them indifferently; and to hear benignly all their complaints; and to show towards them, although they offend, fatherly pity. And, finally, so to correct them that be evil, that they had yet rather save them than lose them if it were not for respect of justice, and maintenance of peace and good order in the commonweal." 177

These principles do really appear to have determined Henry's conduct in his earlier years. His social administration we have partially seen in the previous chapter. He had more than once been tried with insurrection, which he had soothed down without bloodshed, and extinguished in forgiveness; and London long recollected the great scene which followed "evil Mayday," 1517, when the apprentices were brought down to Westminster Hall to receive their pardons. There had been a dangerous riot in the streets, which might have provoked a mild government to severity; but the king contented himself with punishing the five ringleaders, and four hundred other prisoners, after being paraded down the streets in white shirts with halters round their necks, were dismissed with an admonition, Wolsey weeping as he pronounced it. 178

It is certain that if, as I said, he had died before the divorce was mooted, Henry VIII., like that Roman Emperor said by Tacitus to have been *consensu omnium dignus imperii nisi imperasset*, would have been considered by posterity as formed by Providence for the conduct of the Reformation, and his loss would have been deplored as a perpetual calamity. We must allow him, therefore, the benefit of his past career, and be careful to remember it, when interpreting his later actions. Not many men would have borne themselves through the same trials with the same integrity; but the circumstances of those trials had not tested the true defects in his moral constitution. Like all princes of the Plantagenet blood, he was a person of a most intense and imperious will. His impulses, in general nobly directed, had never known contradiction; and late in life, when his character was formed, he was forced into collision with difficulties with which the experience of discipline had not fitted him to contend. Education had done much for him, but his nature required more correction than his position had permitted, whilst unbroken prosperity and early independence of control had been his most serious misfortune. He had capacity, if his training had been equal to it, to be one of the greatest of men. With all his faults about him, he was still perhaps the greatest of his contemporaries; and the man best able of all living Englishmen to govern England, had been set to do it by the conditions of his birth.

The other person whose previous history we have to ascertain is one, the tragedy of whose fate has blotted the remembrance of her sins—if her sins were, indeed, and in reality, more than imaginary. Forgetting all else in shame and sorrow, posterity has made piteous reparation for her death in the tenderness with which it has touched her reputation; and with the general instincts of justice, we have refused to qualify our indignation at the wrong which she experienced, by admitting either stain or shadow on her fame. It has been with Anne Boleyn as it has been with Catherine of Arragon—both are regarded as the victims of a tyranny which catholics and protestants unite to remember with horror; and each has taken the place of a martyred saint in the hagiology of the respective creeds. Catholic writers have, indeed, ill repaid, in their treatment of Anne, the admiration with which the mother of Queen Mary has been remembered in the Church of England; but the invectives which they have heaped upon her have defeated their object by their extravagance. It has been believed that matter failed them to sustain a just accusation, when they condescended to outrageous slander. Inasmuch, however, as some natural explanation can usually be given of the actions of human beings in this world without supposing them to have been possessed by extraordinary wickedness, and if we are to hold Anne Boleyn entirely free from fault, we place not the king only, but the privy council, the judges, the Lords and Commons, and the two Houses of Convocation, in a position fatal to their honour and degrading to ordinary humanity; we cannot without inquiry acquiesce in so painful a conclusion. The English nation also, as well as she, deserves justice at our hands; and it must not be thought uncharitable if we look with some scrutiny at the career of a person who, except for the catastrophe with which it was closed, would not so readily have obtained forgiveness for having admitted the addresses of the king, or for having received the homage of the court as its future sovereign, while the king's wife, her mistress, as yet resided under the same roof, with the title and the position of queen, and while the question was still undecided, of the validity of the first marriage. If in that alone she was to blame, her fault was, indeed, revenged a thousandfold,—and yet no lady of true delicacy would have accepted such a position; and feeling for Queen Catherine should have restrained her, if she was careless of respect for herself. It must, therefore, be permitted me, out of such few hints and scattered notices as remain, to collect such information as may be trusted respecting her early life before her appearance upon the great stage. These hints are but slight, since I shall not even mention the scandals of Sanders, any more than I shall mention the panegyrics of Foxe; stories which, as far as I can learn, have no support in evidence, and rest on no stronger foundation than the credulity of passion.

Anne Boleyn was the second daughter of Sir Thomas Boleyn, a gentleman of noble family, though moderate fortune; 179 who, by a marriage with the daughter of the Duke of Norfolk, was brought into connection with the highest blood in the realm. The year of her birth has not been certainly ascertained, but she is supposed to have been seven years old 180 in 1514, when she accompanied the Princess Mary into France, on the marriage of that lady with Louis XII. Louis dying a few months subsequently, the princess married Sir Charles Brandon, afterwards created Duke of Suffolk, and returned to England. Anne Boleyn did not return with her; she remained in Paris to become accomplished with the graces and elegancies, if she was not contaminated by the vices, of that court, which, even in those days of loyal licentiousness, enjoyed an undesirable pre-eminence in profligacy. In the French capital she could not have failed to see, to hear, and to become familiar with occurrences with which no young girl can be brought in contact with impunity, and this poisonous atmosphere she continued to breathe for nine years. She came back to England in 1525, to be maid of honour to Queen Catherine, and to be distinguished at the court, by general consent, for her talents, her accomplishments, and her beauty. Her portraits, though all professedly by Holbein, or copied from pictures by him, are singularly unlike each other. The profile in the picture which is best known is pretty, innocent, and piquant, though rather insignificant: there are other pictures, however, in which we see a face more powerful, though less prepossessing. In these the features are full and languid. The eyes are large; but the expression, though remarkable, is not pleasing, and indicates cunning more than thought, passion more than feeling; while the heavy lips and massive chin wear a look of sensuality which is not to be mistaken. Possibly all are like the original, but represented her under different circumstances, or at different periods of her life. Previous to her engagement with the king, she was the object of fleeting attentions from the young noblemen about the court. Lord Percy, eldest son of Lord Northumberland, as we all know, was said to have been engaged to her. He was in the household of Cardinal Wolsey; and Cavendish, who was with him there, tells a long romantic story of the affair, which, if his account be true, was ultimately interrupted by Lord Northumberland himself. The story is not without its difficulties, since Lord Percy had been contracted, several years previously, to a daughter of the Earl of Shrewsbury, 181 whom he afterwards married, and by the law he could not have formed a second engagement so long as the first was undissolved. And again, he himself, when subsequently examined before the privy council, denied solemnly on his oath that any contract of the kind had existed. 182 At the same time, we cannot suppose Cavendish to have invented so circumstantial a narrative, and Percy would not have been examined if there had been no reason for suspicion. Something, therefore, probably had passed between him and the young maid of honour, though we cannot now conjecture of what nature; and we can infer only that it was not openly to her discredit, or she would not have obtained the position which cost her so dear. She herself confessed subsequently, before Archbishop Cranmer, to a connection of some kind into which she had entered before her acquaintance with Henry. No evidence survives which will explain to what she referred, for the act of parliament which mentions the fact furnishes no details. 183 But it was of a kind which made her marriage with the king illegal, and illegitimatised the offspring of it; and it has been supposed, therefore, that, in spite of Lord Percy's denial, he had really engaged himself to her, and was afraid to acknowledge it. 184 This supposition, however, is not easy to reconcile with the language of the act, which speaks of the circumstance, whatever it was, as only "recently known;" nor could a contract with Percy have invalidated her marriage with the king, when Percy having been pre-contracted to another person, it would have been itself invalid. A light is thrown upon the subject by a letter found among Cromwell's papers, addressed by some unknown person to a Mr. Melton, also unknown, but written obviously when "Mistress Anne" was a young lady about the court, and before she had been the object of any open attention from Henry.

"MR. MELTON.—This shall be to advertise you that Mistress Anne is changed from that she was at when we three were last together. Wherefore I pray you that ye be no devil's sakke, but according to the truth ever justify, as ye shall make answer before God; and do not suffer her in my absence to be married to any other man. I must go to my master, wheresoever he be, for the Lord Privy Seal desireth much to speak with me, whom if I should speak with in my master's absence, it would cause me to lose my head; and yet I know myself as true a man to my prince as liveth, whom (as my friend informeth me) I have offended grievously in my words. No more to you, but to have me commended unto Mistress Anne, and bid her remember her promise, which none can loose, but God only, to whom I shall daily during my life commend her." 185

The letter must furnish its own interpretation; for it receives little from any other quarter. Being in the possession of Cromwell, however, it had perhaps been forwarded to him at the time of Queen Anne's trial, and may have thus occasioned the investigation which led to the annulling of her marriage.

From the account which was written of her by the grandson of Sir Thomas Wyatt the poet, we still gather the impression (in spite of the admiring sympathy with which Wyatt writes) of a person with whom young men took liberties, 186 however she might seem to forbid them. In her diet she was an epicure, fond of dainty and delicate eating, and not always contented if she did not obtain what she desired. When the king's attentions towards her became first marked, Thomas Heneage, afterwards lord chamberlain, wrote to Wolsey, that he had one night been "commanded down with a dish for Mistress Anne for supper"; adding that she caused him "to sup with her, and she wished she had some of Wolsey's good meat, as carps, shrimps, and others." 187 And this was not said in jest, since Heneage related it as a hint to Wolsey, that he might know what to do, if he wished to please her. In the same letter he suggested to the cardinal that she was a little displeased at not having received a token or present from him; she was afraid she was forgotten, he said, and "the lady, her mother, desired him to send unto his Grace, and desire his Grace to bestow a morsel of tunny upon her." Wolsey made her presents also at times of a more valuable character, as we find her acknowledging in language of exaggerated gratitude; 188 and, perhaps the most painful feature in all her earlier history lies in the contrast between the servility with which she addressed the cardinal so long as he was in power, and the bitterness with which the Bishop of Bayonne (and, in fact, all contemporary witnesses) tells us, that she pressed upon his decline. Wolsey himself spoke of her under the title of "the night-crow," 189 as the person to whom he owed all which was most cruel in his treatment; as "the enemy that never slept, but studied and continually imagined, both sleeping and waking, his utter destruction." 190

Taking these things together, and there is nothing to be placed beside them of a definitely pleasing kind, except beauty and accomplishments, we form, with the assistance of her pictures, a tolerable conception of this lady; a conception of her as a woman not indeed questionable, but as one whose antecedents might lead consistently to a future either of evil or of good; and whose character removes the surprise which we might be inclined to feel at the position with respect to Queen Catherine in which she consented to be placed. A harsh critic would describe her, on this evidence, as a self-indulgent coquette, indifferent to the obligations of gratitude, and something careless of the truth. From the letter referring to her, preserved by Cromwell, it appears that she had broken a definite promise at a time when such promises were legally binding, and that she had really done so was confirmed by her subsequent confession. The breach of such promises by a woman who could not be expected to understand the grounds on which the law held them to be sacred, implies no more than levity, and levity of this kind has been found compatible with many high qualities. Levity, however, it does undoubtedly imply, and the symptom, if a light one, must be allowed the weight which is due to it.

It is a miserable duty to be compelled to search for these indications of human infirmities; above all when they are the infirmities of a lady whose faults, let them have been what they would, were so fearfully and terribly expiated; and, if there were nothing else at issue but poor questions of petty scandal, it were better far that they perished in forgetfulness, and passed away out of mind and memory for ever. The fortunes of Anne Boleyn were unhappily linked with those of men to whom the greatest work ever yet accomplished in this country was committed; and the characters of a king of England, and of the three estates of the realm, are compromised in the treatment which she received from them.

CHAPTER III.
THE PARLIAMENT OF 1529

No Englishman can look back uninterested on the meeting of the parliament of 1529. The era at which it assembled is the most memorable in the history of this country, and the work which it accomplished before its dissolution was of larger moment politically and spiritually than the achievements of the Long Parliament itself. For nearly seven years it continued surrounded by intrigue, confusion, and at length conspiracy, presiding over a people from whom the forms and habits by which they had moved for centuries were falling like the shell of a chrysalis. While beset with enemies within the realm and without, it effected a revolution which severed England from the papacy, yet it preserved peace unbroken and prevented anarchy from breaking bounds; and although its hands are not pure from spot, and red stains rest on them which posterity have bitterly and long remembered; yet if we consider the changes which it carried through, and if we think of the price which was paid by other nations for victory in the same struggle, we shall acknowledge that the records of the world contain no instance of such a triumph, bought at a cost so slight and tarnished by blemishes so trifling.

The letters of the French Ambassador 191 describe to us the gathering of the members into London, and the hum of expectation sounding louder and louder as the day of the opening approached. In order that we may see distinctly what London felt on this occasion, that we may understand in detail the nature of those questions with which parliament was immediately to deal, we will glance at some of the proceedings which had taken place in the Bishops' Consistory Courts during the few preceding years. The duties of the officials of these courts resembled in theory the duties of the censors under the Roman Republic. In the middle ages, a lofty effort had been made to overpass the common limitations of government, to introduce punishment for sins as well as crimes, and to visit with temporal penalties the breach of the moral law. The punishment best adapted for such offences was some outward expression of the disapproval with which good men regard acts of sin; some open disgrace; some spiritual censure; some suspension of communion with the church, accompanied by other consequences practically inconvenient, to be continued until the offender had made reparation, or had openly repented, or had given confirmed proof of amendment. The administration of such a discipline fell, as a matter of course, to the clergy. The clergy were the guardians of morality; their characters were a claim to confidence, their duties gave them opportunities of observation which no other men could possess; while their priestly office gave solemn weight to their sentences. Thus arose throughout Europe a system of spiritual surveillance over the habits and conduct of every man, extending from the cottage to the castle, taking note of all wrong dealing, of all oppression of man by man, of all licentiousness and profligacy, and representing upon earth, in the principles by which it was guided, the laws of the great tribunal of Almighty God.

Such was the origin of the church courts, perhaps the greatest institutions ever yet devised by man. But to aim at these high ideals is as perilous as it is noble; and weapons which may be safely trusted in the hands of saints become fatal implements of mischief when saints have ceased to wield them. For a time, we need not doubt, the practice corresponded to the intention. Had it not been so, the conception would have taken no root, and would have been extinguished at its birth. But a system which has once established itself in the respect of mankind will be tolerated long after it has forfeited its claim to endurance, as the name of a great man remains honoured though borne by worthless descendants; and the Consistory courts had continued into the sixteenth century with unrestricted jurisdiction, although they had been for generations merely perennially flowing fountains, feeding the ecclesiastical exchequer. The moral conduct of every English man and woman remained subject to them. Each private person was liable to be called in question for every action of his life; and an elaborate network of canon law perpetually growing, enveloped the whole surface of society. But between the original design and the degenerate counterfeit there was this vital difference,—that the censures were no longer spiritual. They were commuted in various gradations for pecuniary fines, and each offence against morality was rated at its specific money value in the episcopal tables. Suspension and excommunication remained as ultimate penalties; but they were resorted to only to compel unwilling culprits to accept the alternative.

The misdemeanours of which the courts took cognisance 192 were "offences against chastity," "heresy," or "matter sounding thereunto," "witchcraft," "drunkenness," "scandal," "defamation," "impatient words," "broken promises," "untruth," "absence from church," "speaking evil of saints," "non-payment of offerings," and other delinquencies incapable of legal definition; matters, all of them, on which it was well, if possible, to keep men from going wrong; but offering wide opportunities for injustice;

while all charges, whether well founded or ill, met with ready acceptance in courts where innocence and guilt alike contributed to the revenue. 193 "Mortuary claims" were another fertile matter for prosecution; and probate duties and legacy duties; and a further lucrative occupation was the punishment of persons who complained against the constitutions of the courts themselves; to complain against the justice of the courts being to complain against the church, and to complain against the church being heresy. To answer accusations on such subjects as these, men were liable to be summoned, at the will of the officials, to the metropolitan courts of the archbishops, hundreds of miles from their homes. 194 No expenses were allowed; and if the charges were without foundation, it was rare that costs could be recovered. Innocent or guilty, the accused parties were equally bound to appear. 195 If they failed, they were suspended for contempt. If after receiving notice of their suspension, they did not appear, they were excommunicated; and no proof of the groundlessness of the original charge availed to relieve them from their sentence, till they had paid for their deliverance.

Well did the church lawyers understand how to make their work productive. Excommunication seems but a light thing when there are many communions. It was no light thing when it was equivalent to outlawry; when the person excommunicated might be seized and imprisoned at the will of the ordinary; when he was cut off from all holy offices; when no one might speak to him, trade with him, or show him the most trivial courtesy; and when his friends, if they dared to assist him, were subject to the same penalties. In the *Register* of the Bishop of London 196 there is more than one instance to be found of suspension and excommunication for the simple crime of offering shelter to an excommunicated neighbour; and thus offence begot offence, guilt spread like a contagion through the influence of natural humanity, and a single refusal of obedience to a frivolous citation might involve entire families in misery and ruin.

The people might have endured better to submit to so enormous a tyranny, if the conduct of the clergy themselves had given them a title to respect, or if equal justice had been distributed to lay and spiritual offenders. "Benefit of clergy," unhappily, as at this time interpreted, was little else than a privilege to commit sins with impunity. The grossest moral profligacy in a priest was passed over with indifference; and so far from exacting obedience in her ministers to a higher standard than she required of ordinary persons, the church extended her limits under fictitious pretexts as a sanctuary for lettered villany. Every person who could read was claimed by prescriptive usage as a clerk, and shielded under her protecting mantle; nor was any clerk amenable for the worst crimes to the secular jurisdiction, until he had been first tried and degraded by the ecclesiastical judges. So far was this preposterous exemption carried, that previous to the passing of the first of the 23rd of Henry the Eighth, 197 those who were within the degrees might commit murder with impunity, the forms which it was necessary to observe in degrading a priest or deacon being so complicated as to amount to absolute protection. 198

Among the clergy, properly so called, however, the prevailing offence was not crime, but licentiousness. A doubt has recently crept in among our historians as to the credibility of the extreme language in which the contemporary writers spoke upon this painful topic. It will scarcely be supposed that the picture has been overdrawn in the act books of the Consistory courts; and as we see it there it is almost too deplorable for belief, as well in its own intrinsic hideousness as in the unconscious connivance of the authorities. Brothels were kept in London for the especial use of priests; 199 the "confessional" was abused in the most open and abominable manner. 200 Cases occurred of the same frightful profanity in the service of the mass, which at Rome startled Luther into Protestantism; 201 and acts of incest between nuns and monks were too frequently exposed to allow us to regard the detected instances as exceptions. 202 It may be said that the proceedings upon these charges prove at least that efforts were made to repress them. The bishops must have the benefit of the plea, and the two following instances will show how far it will avail their cause. In the Records of the London Court I find a certain Thomas Wyseman, priest, summoned for fornication and incontinency. He was enjoined for penance, that on the succeeding Sunday, while high mass was singing, he should offer at each of the altars in the Church of St. Bartholomew a candle of wax, value one penny, saying therewith five *Paternosters*, five *Ave Marys*, and five *Credos*. On the following Friday he was to offer a candle of the same price before the crucifix, standing barefooted, and one before the image of cur Lady of Grace. This penance accomplished he appeared again at the court and compounded for absolution, paying six shillings and eightpence. 203

An exposure too common to attract notice, and a fine of six and eightpence was held sufficient penalty for a mortal sin.

Even this, however, was a severe sentence compared with the sentence passed upon another priest who confessed to incest with the prioress of Kilbourn. The offender was condemned to bear a cross in a procession in his parish church, and was excused his remaining guilt for three shillings and fourpence. 204

I might multiply such instances indefinitely; but there is no occasion for me to stain my pages with them. 205

An inactive imagination may readily picture to itself the indignation likely to have been felt by a high-minded people, when they were forced to submit their lives, their habits, their most intimate conversations and opinions to a censorship conducted by clergy of such a character; when the offences of these clergy themselves were passed over with such indifferent carelessness. Men began to ask themselves who and what these persons were who retained the privileges of saints, 206 and were incapable of the most ordinary duties; and for many years before the burst of the Reformation the coming storm was gathering. Priests were hooted, or "knocked down into the kennel," 207 as they walked along the streets—women refused to receive the holy bread from hands which they thought polluted, 208 and the appearance of an apparitor of the courts to serve a process or a citation in a private house was a signal for instant explosion. Violent words were the least which these officials had to fear, and they were fortunate if they escaped so lightly. A stranger had died in a house in St. Dunstan's belonging to a certain John Fleming, and an apparitor had been sent "to seal his chamber and his goods" that the church might not lose her dues. John Fleming drove him out, saying loudly unto him, "Thou shalt seale no door here; go thy way, thou stynkyng knave, ye are but knaves and brybours everych one of you." 209 Thomas Banister, of St. Mary Wolechurch, when a process was served upon him, "did threaten to slay the apparitor." "Thou horson knave," he said to him, "without thou tell me who set thee awork to summon me to the court, by Goddis woundes, and by this gold, I shall brake thy head." 210 A "waiter, at the sign of the Cock," fell in trouble for saying that "the sight of a priest did make him sick," also, "that he would go sixty miles to indict a priest," saying also in the presence of many—"horsyn priests, they shall be indicted as many as come to my handling." 211 Often the officers found threats convert themselves into acts. The apparitor of the Bishop of London went with a citation into the shop of a mercer of St. Bride's, Henry Clitheroe by name. "Who does cite me?" asked the mercer. "Marry, that do I," answered the apparitor, "if thou wilt anything with it;" whereupon, as the apparitor deposeth, the said Henry Clitheroe did hurl at him from off his finger that instrument of his art called the "thymmelle," and he, the apparitor, drawing his sword, "the said Henry did snatch up his virga, Anglice, his yard, and did pursue the apparitor into the public streets, and after multiplying of many blows did break the head of the said apparitor." 212 These are light matters, but they were straws upon the stream; and such a scene as this which follows reveals the principles on which the courts awarded their judgment. One Richard Hunt was summoned for certain articles implying contempt, and for vilipending his lordship's jurisdiction. Being examined, he confessed to the words following: "That all false matters were bolstered and clokyd in this court of Paul's Cheyne; moreover he called the apparitor, William Middleton, false knave in the full court, and his father's dettes, said he, by means of his mother-in-law and master commissary, were not payd; and this he would abide by, that he had now in this place said no more but truth." Being called on to answer further, he said he would not, and his lordship did therefore excommunicate him. 213 From so brief an entry we cannot tell on which side the justice lay; but at least we can measure the equity of a tribunal which punished complaints against itself with excommunication, and dismissed the confessed incest of a priest with a fine of a few shillings.

Such then were the English consistory courts. I have selected but a few instances from the proceedings of a single one of them. If we are to understand the weight with which the system pressed upon the people, we must multiply the proceedings at St. Paul's by the number of the English dioceses; the number of dioceses by the number of archdeaconries; we must remember that in proportion to the distance from London the abuse must have increased indefinitely from the absence of even partial surveillance; we must remember that appeals were permitted only from one ecclesiastical court to another; from the archdeacon's court to that of the bishop of the diocese, from that of the bishop to the Court of Arches; that any language of impatience or resistance furnished suspicion of heresy, and that the only security therefore was submission. We can then imagine what England must have been with an archdeacon's commissary sitting constantly in every town; exercising an undefined jurisdiction over general morality; and every court swarming with petty lawyers who lived upon the fees which they could extract. Such a system for the administration of justice was perhaps never tolerated before in any country.

But the time of reckoning at length was arrived; slowly the hand had crawled along the dial plate; slowly as if the event would never come: and wrong was heaped on wrong; and oppression cried, and it seemed as if no ear had heard its voice; till the measure of the circle was at length fulfilled, the finger touched the hour, and as the strokes of the great hammer rang out above the nation, in an instant the mighty fabric of iniquity was shivered into ruins. Wolsey had dreamed that it might still stand, self-reformed as he hoped to see it; but in his dread lest any hands but those of friends should touch the work, he had "prolonged its sickly days," waiting for the convenient season which was not to be; he had put off the meeting of parliament, knowing that if parliament were once assembled, he would be unable to resist the pressure which would be brought to bear upon him; and in the impatient minds of the people he had identified himself with the evils which he alone for the few last years had hindered from falling. At length he had fallen himself, and his disgrace was celebrated in London with enthusiastic rejoicing as the inauguration of the new era. On the eighteenth of October, 1529, Wolsey delivered up the seals. He was ordered to retire to Esher; and, "at the taking of his barge," Cavendish saw no less than a thousand boats full of men and women of the city of London, "waffeting up and down in Thames," to see him sent, as they expected, to the Tower. 214 A fortnight later the same crowd was perhaps again assembled on a wiser occasion, and with truer reason for exultation, to see the king coming up in his barge from Greenwich to open parliament.

"According to the summons," says Hall, "the King of England began his high court of parliament the third day of November, on which day he came by water to his palace of Bridewell, and there he and his nobles put on their robes of Parliament, and so came to the Black Friars Church, where a mass of the Holy Ghost was solemnly sung by the king's chaplain; and after the mass, the king, with all his Lords and Commons which were summoned to appear on that day, came into the Parliament. The king sate on his throne or seat royal, and Sir Thomas More, his chancellor, standing on the right hand of the king, made an eloquent oration, setting forth the causes why at that time the king so had summoned them." 215

"Like as a good shepherd," More said, "which not only keepeth and attendeth well his sheep, but also foreseeth and provideth for all things which either may be hurtful or noysome to his flock; so the king, which is the shepherd, ruler, and governor of his realm, vigilantly foreseeing things to come, considers how that divers laws, before this time made, are now, by long continuance of time and mutation of things, become very insufficient and imperfect; and also, by the frail condition of man, divers new enormities are sprung amongst the people, for the which no law is yet made to reform the same. For this cause the king at this time has summoned his high court of parliament; and I liken the king to a shepherd or herdsman, because if a prince be compared to his riches, he is but a rich man; if a prince be compared to his honour, he is but an honourable man; but compare him to the multitude of his people, and the number of his flock, then he is a ruler, a governor of might and puissance; so that his people maketh him a prince, as of the multitude of sheep cometh the name of a shepherd.

"And as you see that amongst a great flock of sheep some be rotten and faulty, which the good shepherd sendeth from the good sheep; so the great wether which is of late fallen, as you all know, so craftily, so scabedly, yea, so untruly juggled with the king, that all men must needs guess that he thought in himself, either the king had no wit to perceive his crafty doings, or else that he would not see nor know them.

"But he was deceived, for his Grace's sight was so quick and penetrable that he saw him; yea, and saw through him, both within and without; and according to his desert he hath had a gentle correction, which small punishment the king will not to be an example to other offenders; but clearly declareth that whosoever hereafter shall make like attempt, or shall commit like offence, shall not escape with like punishment.

"And because you of the Commons House be a gross multitude, and cannot all speak at one time, the king's pleasure is, that you resort to the Nether House, and then amongst yourselves, according to the old and antient custom, choose an able person to be your common mouth and speaker." 216

The invective against "the great wether" was not perhaps the portion of the speech to which the audience listened with least interest. In the minds of contemporaries, principles are identified with persons, who form, as it were, the focus on which the passions concentrate. At present we may consent to forget Wolsey, and fix our attention on the more permanently essential matter—the reform of the laws. The world was changing; how swiftly, how completely, no living person knew;—but a confusion no longer tolerable was a patent fact to all men; and with a wise instinct it was resolved that the grievances of the nation, which had accumulated through centuries, should be submitted to a complete ventilation, without reserve, check, or secrecy.

For this purpose it was essential that the Houses should not be interfered with, that they should be allowed full liberty to express their wishes and to act upon them. Accordingly, the practice then usual with ministers, of undertaking the direction of the proceedings, was clearly on this occasion foregone. In the House of Commons then, as much as now, there was in theory unrestricted liberty of discussion, and free right for any member to originate whatever motion he pleased. "The discussions in the English Parliament," wrote Henry himself to the pope, "are free and unrestricted; the crown has no power to limit their debates or to controul the votes of the members. They determine everything for themselves, as the interests of the commonwealth require." 217 But so long as confidence existed between the crown and the people, these rights were in great measure surrendered. The ministers prepared the business which was to be transacted; and the temper of the Houses was usually so well understood, that, except when there was a demand for money, it was rare that a measure was proposed the acceptance of which was doubtful, or the nature of which would provoke debate. So little jealousy, indeed, was in quiet times entertained of the power of the crown, and so little was a residence in London to the taste of the burgesses and the country gentlemen, that not only were their expenses defrayed by a considerable salary, but it was found necessary to forbid them absenting themselves from their duties by a positive enactment. 218

In the composition of the House of Commons, however, which had now assembled, no symptoms appeared of such indifference. The election had taken place in the midst of great and general excitement; and the members chosen, if we may judge from their acts and their petitions, were men of that broad resolved temper, who only in times of popular effervescence are called forward into prominence. It would have probably been unsafe for the crown to attempt dictation or repression at such a time, if it had desired to do so. Under the actual circumstances, its interest was to encourage the fullest expression of public feeling.

The proceedings were commenced with a formal "act of accusation" against the clergy, which was submitted to the king in the name of the Commons of England, and contained a summary of the wrongs of which the people complained. This remarkable document must have been drawn up before the opening of parliament, and must have been presented in the first week of the session,—probably on the first day on which the House met to transact business. 219 There is appearance of haste in the composition, little order being observed in the catalogue of grievances; but inasmuch as it contains the germ of all the acts which were framed in the following years for the reform of the church, and is in fact the most complete exhibition which we possess of the working of the church system at the time when it ceased to be any more tolerable, I have thought it well to insert it uncurtailed. Although the fact of the presentation of this petition has been well known, it has not been accurately described by any of our historians, none of them appearing to have seen more than incorrect and imperfect epitomes of it. 220

"TO THE KING OUR SOVEREIGN LORD

"In most humble wise show unto your Highness and your most prudent wisdom your faithful, loving, and most obedient servants the Commons in this your present parliament assembled; that of late, as well through new fantastical and erroneous opinions grown by occasion of frantic seditious books compiled, imprinted, published, and made in the English tongue, contrary and against the very true Catholic and Christian faith; as also by the extreme and uncharitable behaviour and dealing of divers ordinaries, their commissaries and sumners, which have heretofore had, and yet have the examination in and upon the said errours and heretical opinions; much discord, variance, and debate hath risen, and more and more daily is like to increase and ensue amongst the universal sort of your said subjects, as well spiritual as temporal, each against the other—in most uncharitable manner, to the great inquietation, vexation, and breach of your peace within this your most Catholic Realm:

"The special particular griefs whereof, which most principally concern your Commons and lay subjects, and which are, as they undoubtedly suppose, the very chief fountains, occasions, and causes that daily breedeth and nourisheth the said seditious factions, deadly hatred, and most uncharitable part taking, of either part of said subjects spiritual and temporal against the other, followingly do ensue.—

"I. First the prelates and spiritual ordinaries of this your most excellent Realm of England, and the clergy of the same, have in their convocations heretofore made or caused to be made, and also daily do make many and divers fashions of laws, constitutions, and ordinances; without your knowledge or most Royal assent, and without the assent and consent of any of your lay subjects; unto the which laws your said lay subjects have not only heretofore been and daily be constrained to obey, in their bodies, goods, and possessions; but have also been compelled to incur daily into the censures of the same, and been continually put to importable charges and expenses, against all equity, right, and good conscience. And yet your said humble subjects ne their predecessors could ever be privy to the said laws; ne any of the said laws have been declared unto them in the English tongue, or otherwise published, by knowledge whereof they might have eschewed the penalties, dangers, or censures of the same; which laws so made your said most humble and obedient servants, under the supportation of your Majesty, suppose to be not only to the diminution and derogation of your imperial jurisdiction and prerogative royal, but also to the great prejudice, inquietation, and damage of your said subjects.

"II. Also now of late there hath been devised by the Most Reverend Father in God, William, Archbishop of Canterbury, that in the courts which he calleth his Courts of the Arches and Audience, shall only be ten proctors at his deputation, which be sworn to preserve and promote the only jurisdiction of his said courts; by reason whereof, if any of your lay subjects should have any lawful cause against the judges of the said courts, or any doctors or proctors of the same, or any of their friends and adherents, they can ne may in nowise have indifferent counsel: and also all the causes depending in any of the said courts may by the confederacy of the said few proctors be in such wise tracted and delayed, as your subjects suing in the same shall be put to importable charges, costs, and expense. And further, in case that any matter there being preferred should touch your crown, your regal jurisdiction, and prerogative Royal, yet the same shall not be disclosed by any of the said proctors for fear of the loss of their offices. Your most obedient subjects do therefore, under protection of your Majesty, suppose that your Highness should have the nomination of some convenient number of proctors to be always attendant upon the said Courts of Arches and Audience, there to be sworn to the preferment of your jurisdiction and prerogative, and to the expedition of the causes of your lay subjects repairing and suing to the same.

"III. And also many of your said most humble and obedient subjects, and *specially those that be of the poorest sort*, within this your Realm, be daily convented and called before the said spiritual ordinaries, their commissaries and substitutes, *ex officio*; sometimes, at the pleasure of the said ordinaries, for malice without any cause; and sometimes at the only promotion and accusement of their summoners and apparitors, being light and undiscreet persons; without any lawful cause of accusation, or credible fame proved against them, and without any presentment in the visitation: and your said poor subjects be thus inquieted, disturbed, vexed, troubled, and put to excessive and importable charges for them to bear—and many times be suspended and excommunicate for small and light causes upon the only certificate of the proctors of the adversaries, made under a feigned seal which every proctor hath in his keeping; whereas the party suspended or excommunicate many times never had any warning; and yet when he shall be absolved, if it be out of court, he shall be compelled to pay to his own proctor twenty 221 *pence*; to the proctor which is against him other twenty pence, and twenty pence to the scribe, besides a privy reward that the judge shall have, to the great impoverishing of your said poor lay subjects.

"IV. Also your said most humble and obedient servants find themselves grieved with the great and excessive fees taken in the said spiritual courts, and especially in the said Courts of the Arches and Audience; where they take for every citation two shillings and sixpence; for every inhibition six shillings and eightpence; for every proxy sixteen pence; for every certificate sixteen pence; for every libel three shillings and fourpence; for every answer for every libel three shillings and fourpence; for every act, if it be but two words according to the register, fourpence; for every personal citation or decree three shillings and fourpence; for every sentence or judgment, to the judge twenty-six shillings and eightpence; for every testament upon such sentence or judgment twenty-six shillings and eightpence; for every significavit twelve shillings; for every commission to examine witnesses twelve shillings, which charges be thought importable to be borne by your said subjects, and very necessary to be reformed.

"V. And also the said prelates and ordinaries daily do permit and suffer the parsons, vicars, curates, parish priests, and other spiritual persons having cure of souls within this your Realm, to exact and take of your humble servants divers sums of money for the sacraments and sacramentals of Holy Church, sometimes denying the same without they be first paid 222 the said sums of money, which sacraments and sacramentals your said most humble and obedient subjects, under protection of your Highness, do suppose and think ought to be in most reverend, charitable, and godly wise freely ministered unto them at all times requisite, without denial, or exaction of any manner sums of money to be demanded or asked for the same.

"VI. And also in the spiritual courts of the said prelates and ordinaries there be limited and appointed so many judges, scribes, apparitors, summoners, appraysers, and other ministers for the approbation of Testaments, which covet so much their own private lucres, and the satisfaction and appetites of the said prelates and ordinaries, that when any of your said loving subjects do repair to any of the said courts for the probate of any Testaments, they do in such wise make so long delays, or excessively do take of them so large fees and rewards for the same as is importable for them to bear, directly against all justice, law, equity, and good conscience. Therefore your most humble and obedient subjects do, under your gracious correction and supportation, suppose it were very necessary that the said ordinaries in their deputation of judges should be bound to appoint and assign such discreet, gracious, and honest persons, having sufficient learning, wit, discretion, and understanding; and also being endowed with such spiritual promotion, stipend, and salary; as they being judges in their said courts might and may minister to every person repairing to the same, justice—without taking any manner of fee or reward for any manner of sentence or judgment to be given before them.

"VII. And also divers spiritual persons being presented as well by your Highness as others within this your Realm to divers benefices or other spiritual promotions, the said ordinaries and their ministers do not only take of them for their letters of institution and induction many large sums of money and rewards; but also do pact and covenant with the same, taking sure bonds for their indemnity to answer to the said ordinaries for the firstfruits of their said benefices after their institution—so as they, being once presented or promoted, as aforesaid, are by the said ordinaries very uncharitably handled, to their no little hindrance and impoverishment; which your said subjects suppose not only to be against all laws, right, and good conscience, but also to be simony, and contrary to the laws of God.

"VIII. And also *the said spiritual ordinaries do daily confer and give sundry benefices unto certain young folks, calling them their nephews or kinsfolk*, being in their minority and within age, not apt ne able to serve the cure of any such benefice: whereby the said ordinaries do keep and detain the fruits and profits of the same benefices in their own hands, and thereby accumulate to themselves right great and large sums of money and yearly profits, to the most pernicious example of your said lay subjects—and so the cures and promotions given unto such infants be only employed to the enriching of the said ordinaries; and the poor silly souls of your people, which should be taught in the parishes given as aforesaid, for lack of good curates [be left] to perish without doctrine or any good teaching.

"IX. Also, a great number of holydays now at this present time, with very small devotion, be solemnised and kept throughout this your Realm, upon the which many great, abominable, and execrable vices, idle and wanton sports, be used and exercised, which holydays, if it may stand with your Grace's pleasure, and specially such as fall in the harvest, might, by your Majesty, with the advice of your most honourable council, prelates, and ordinaries, be made fewer in number; and those that shall be hereafter ordained to stand and continue, might and may be the more devoutly, religiously, and reverendly observed, to the laud of Almighty God, and to the increase of your high honour and favour.

"X. And furthermore the said spiritual ordinaries, their commissaries and substitutes, sometimes for their own pleasure, sometimes by the sinister procurement of other spiritual persons, use to make out process against divers of your said subjects, and thereby compel them to appear before themselves, to answer at a certain day and place to such articles as by them shall be, *ex officio*, then proposed; and that secretly and not in open places; 223 and forthwith upon their appearance, without any declaration made or showed, commit and send them to ward, sometimes for [half] a year, sometimes for a whole year or more, before they may in anywise know either the cause of their imprisonment or the name of their accuser; 224 and finally after their great costs and charges therein, when all is examined and nothing can be proved against them, but they clearly innocent for any fault or crime that can be laid unto them, they be again set at large without any recompence or amends in that behalf to be towards them adjudged.

"XI. And also if percase upon the said process and appearance any party be upon the said matter, cause, or examination, brought forth and named, either as party or witness, and then upon the proof and trial thereof be not able to prove and verify the said accusation and testimony against the party accused, then the person so accused is for the more part without any remedy for his charges and wrongful vexation to be towards him adjudged and recovered.

"XII. Also upon the examination of the said accusation, if heresy be ordinarily laid unto the charge of the parties so accused, then the said ordinaries or their ministers use to put to them such subtle interrogatories concerning the high mysteries of our faith, as are able quickly to trap a simple unlearned, or yet a well-witted layman without learning, and bring them by such sinister introductions soon to their own confusion. And further, if there chance any heresy to be by such subtle policy, by any person confessed in words, and yet never committed neither in thought nor deed, then put they, without further favour, the said person either to make his purgation, and so thereby to lose his honesty and credence for ever; or else as some simple silly soul [may do], the said person may stand precisely to the testimony of his own well-known conscience, rather than confess his innocent truth in that behalf [to be other than he knows it to be], and so be utterly destroyed. And if it fortune the said party so accused to deny the said accusation, and to put his adversaries to prove the same as being untrue, forged and imagined against him, then for the most part such witnesses as are brought forth for the same, be they but two in number, never so sore diffamed, of little truth or credence, they shall be allowed and enabled, only by discretion of the said ordinaries, their commissaries or substitutes; and thereupon sufficient cause be found to proceed to judgment, to deliver the party so accused either to secular hands, after abjuration, 225 without remedy; or afore if he submit himself, as best happeneth, he shall have to make his purgation and bear a faggot, to his extreme shame and undoing.

"In consideration of all these things, most gracious Sovereign Lord, and forasmuch as there is at this present time, and by a few years past hath been outrageous violence on the one part and much default and lack of patient sufferance, charity, and good will on the other part; and consequently a marvellous disorder [hath ensued] of the godly quiet, peace, and tranquillity in which this your Realm heretofore, ever hitherto, has been through your politic wisdom, most honourable fame, and catholic faith inviolably preserved; it may therefore, most benign Sovereign Lord, like your excellent goodness for the tender and universally indifferent zeal, benign love and favour which your Highness beareth towards both the said parties, that the said articles (if they shall be by your most clear and perfect judgment, thought any instrument of the said disorders and factions), being deeply and weightily, after your accustomed ways and manner, searched and considered; graciously to provide (all violence on both sides utterly and clearly set apart) some such necessary and behoveful remedies as may effectually reconcile and bring in perpetual unity, your said subjects, spiritual and temporal; and for the establishment thereof, to make and ordain on both sides such strait laws against transgressors and offenders as shall be too heavy, dangerous, and weighty for them, or any of them, to bear, suffer, and sustain.

"Whereunto your said Commons most humbly and entirely beseech your Grace, as the only Head, Sovereign Lord and Protector of both the said parties, in whom and by whom the only and sole redress, reformation, and remedy herein absolutely resteth [of your goodness to consent]. By occasion whereof all your Commons in their conscience surely account that, beside the marvellous fervent love that your Highness shall thereby engender in their hearts towards your Grace, ye shall do the most princely feat, and show the most honourable and charitable precedent and mirrour that ever did sovereign lord upon his subjects; and therewithal merit and deserve of our merciful God eternal bliss—whose goodness grant your Grace in goodly, princely, and honourable estate long to reign, prosper, and continue as the Sovereign Lord over all your said most humble and obedient servants." 226

But little comment need be added in explanation of this petition, which, though drawn with evident haste, is no less remarkable for temper and good feeling, than for the masterly clearness with which the evils complained of are laid bare. Historians will be careful for the future how they swell the charges against Wolsey with quoting the lamentations of Archbishop Warham, when his Court of Arches was for a while superseded by the Legate's Court, and causes lingering before his commissaries were summarily dispatched at a higher tribunal. 227 The archbishop professed, indeed, that he derived no personal advantage from his courts, 228 and as we have only the popular impression to the contrary to set against his word, we must believe him; yet it was of small moment to the laity who were pillaged, whether the spoils taken from them filled the coffers of the master, or those of his followers and friends.

When we consider, also, the significant allusion 229 to the young folks whom the bishops called their nephews, we cease to wonder at their lenient dealing with the poor priests who had sunk under the temptations of frail humanity; and still less can we wonder at the rough handling which was soon found necessary to bring back these high dignitaries to a better mind.

The House of Commons, in casting their grievances into the form of a petition, showed that they had no desire to thrust forward of themselves violent measures of reform; they sought rather to explain firmly and decisively what the country required. The king, selecting out of the many points noticed those which seemed most immediately pressing, referred them back to the parliament, with a direction to draw up such enactments as in their own judgment would furnish effective relief. In the meantime he submitted the petition itself to the consideration of the bishops, requiring their immediate answer to the charges against them, and accompanied this request with a further important requisition. The legislative authority of convocation lay at the root of the evils which were most complained of. The bishops and clergy held themselves independent of either crown or parliament, passing canons by their own irresponsible and unchecked will, irrespective of the laws of the land, and sometimes in direct violation of them; and to these canons the laity were amenable without being made acquainted with their provisions, learning them only in the infliction of penalties for their unintended breach. The king required that thenceforward the convocation should consent to place itself in the position of parliament, and that his own consent should be required and received before any law passed by convocation should have the force of statute. 230

Little notion, indeed, could the bishops have possessed of the position in which they were standing. It seemed as if they literally believed that the promise of perpetuity which Christ had made to his church was a charm which would hold them free in the quiet course of their injustice; or else, under the blinding influence of custom, they did not really know that any injustice adhered to them. They could see in themselves only the ideal virtues of their saintly office, and not the vices of their fragile humanity; they believed that they were still holy, still spotless, still immaculate, and therefore that no danger might come near them. It cannot have been but that, before the minds of such men as Warham and Fisher, some visions of a future must at times have floated, which hung so plainly before the eyes of Wolsey and of Sir Thomas More. 231 They could not have been wholly deaf to the storm in Germany; and they must have heard something of the growls of smothered anger which for years had been audible at home, to all who had ears to hear. 232 Yet if any such thoughts at times did cross their imagination, they were thrust aside as an uneasy dream, to be shaken off like a nightmare, or with the coward's consolation, "It will last my time." If the bishops ever felt an uneasy moment, there is no trace of uneasiness in the answer which they sent in to the king, and which now, when we read it with the light which is thrown back out of the succeeding years, seems like the composition of mere lunacy. Perhaps they had confidence in the support of Henry. In their courts they were in the habit of identifying an attack upon themselves with an attack upon the doctrines of the Church; and reading the king's feelings in their own, they may have considered themselves safe under the protection of a sovereign who had broken a lance with Luther, and had called himself the Pope's champion. Perhaps they thought that they had bound him to themselves by a declaration which they had all signed in the preceding summer in favour of the divorce. 233 Perhaps they were but steeped in the dulness of official lethargy. The defence is long, wearying the patience to read it; wearying the imagination to invent excuses for the falsehoods which it contains. Yet it is well to see all men in the light in which they see themselves; and justice requires that we allow the bishops the benefit of their own reply. It was couched in the following words:— 234

"After our most humble wise, with our most bounden duty of honour and reverence to your excellent Majesty, endued from God with incomparable wisdom and goodness. Please it the same to understand that we, your orators and daily bounden bedemen, have read and perused a certain supplication which the Commons of your Grace's honourable parliament now assembled have offered unto your Highness, and by your Grace's commandment delivered unto us, that we should make answer thereunto. We have, as the time hath served, made this answer following, beseeching your Grace's indifferent benignity graciously to hear the same.

"And first for that discord, variance, and debate which, in the preface of the said supplication they do allege to have risen among your Grace's subjects, spiritual and temporal, occasioned, as they say, by the uncharitable behaviour and demeanour of divers ordinaries: to this we, the ordinaries, answer, assuring your Majesty that in our hearts there is no such discord or variance ort our part against our brethren in God and ghostly children your subjects, as is induced in this preface; but our daily prayer is and shall be that all peace and concord may increase among your Grace's true subjects our said children, whom God be our witness we love, have loved, and shall love ever with hearty affection; never intending any hurt ne harm towards any of them in soul or body; ne have we ever enterprised anything against them of trouble, vexation, or displeasure; but only have, with all charity, exercised the spiritual jurisdiction of the Church, as we are bound of duty, upon certain evil-disposed persons infected with the pestilent poison of heresy. And to have peace with such had been against the Gospel of our Saviour Christ, wherein he saith, *Non veni mittere pacem sed gladium*. Wherefore, forasmuch as we know well that there be as well disposed and well-conscienced men of your Grace's Commons in no small number assembled, as ever we knew at any time in parliament; and with that consider how on our part there is given no such occasion why the whole number of the spirituality and clergy should be thus noted unto your Highness; we humbling our hearts to God and remitting the judgment of this our inquietation to Him, and trusting, as his Scripture teacheth, that if we love him above all, *omnia cooperabuntur in bonum*, shall endeavour to declare to your Highness the innocency of us, your poor orators.

"And where, after the general preface of the same supplication, your Grace's Commons descend to special particular griefs, and first to those divers fashions of laws concerning temporal things, whereon, as they say, the clergy in their convocation have made and daily do make divers laws, to their great trouble and inquietation, which said laws be sometimes repugnant to the statutes of your Realm, with many other complaints thereupon: 235 To this we say, that forasmuch as we repute and take our authority of making of laws to be grounded upon the Scriptures of God and the determination of Holy Church, which must be the rule and square to try the justice and righteousness of all laws, as well spiritual as temporal, we verily trust that in such laws as have been made by us, or by our predecessors, the same being sincerely interpreted, and after the meaning of the makers, there shall be found nothing contained in them but such as may be well justified by the said rule and square. And if it shall otherwise appear, as it is our duty whereunto we shall always most diligently apply ourselves to reform our ordinances to God's commission, and to conform our statutes to the determination of Scripture and Holy Church; *so we hope in God, and shall daily pray for the same, that your Highness will, if there appear cause why, with the assent of your people, temper your Grace's laws accordingly; whereby shall ensue a most sure and hearty conjunction and agreement; God being lapis angularis.*

"And as concerning the requiring of your Highness's royal assent to the authorising of such laws as have been made by our predecessors, or shall be made by us, in such points and articles, as we have authority to rule and order; we knowing your Highness's wisdom, virtue, and learning, nothing doubt but that the same perceiveth how the granting thereunto dependeth not upon our will and liberty, *and that we may not submit the execution of our charges and duty certainly prescribed to us by God to your Highness's assent;* although, indeed, the same is most worthy for your most princely and excellent virtues, not only to give your royal assent, but also to devise and command what we should for good order or manners by statutes and laws provide in the church. Nevertheless, we considering we may not so nor in such sort restrain the doing of our office in the feeding and ruling of Christ's people, we most humbly desire your Grace (as the same hath done heretofore) to show your Grace's mind and opinion unto us, which we shall most gladly hear and follow if it shall please God to inspire us so to do; and with all humility we therefore beseech your Grace, following the steps of your most noble progenitors, to maintain and defend such laws and ordinances as we, according to our calling and by the authority of God, shall for his honour make to the edification of virtue and the maintaining of Christ's faith, whereof your Highness is defender in name, and hath been hitherto indeed a special protector.

"Furthermore, where there be found in the said supplication, with mention of your Grace's person, other griefs that some of the said laws extend to the goods and possessions of your said lay subjects, declaring the transgressors not only to fall under the terrible censure of excommunication, but also under the detestable crime of heresy:

"To this we answer that we remember no such, and yet if there be any such, it is but according to the common law of the Church, and also to your Grace's law, which determine and decree that every person spiritual or temporal condemned of heresy shall forfeit his moveables or immoveables to your Highness, or to the lord spiritual or temporal that by law hath right to them. 236 Other statutes we remember none that toucheth lands or goods. If there be, it were good that they were brought forth to be weighed and pondered accordingly.

"Item as touching the second principal article of the said supplication, where they say that divers and many of your Grace's obedient subjects, and especially they that be of the poorest sort, be daily called before us or before our substitutes ex officio; sometimes at the pleasure of us, the ordinaries, without any probable cause, and sometimes at the only promotion of our summoner, without any credible fame first proved against them, and without presentment in the visitation or lawful accusation:

"On this we desire your high wisdom and learning to consider that albeit in the ordering of Christ's people, your Grace's subjects, God of His spiritual goodness assisteth his church, and inspireth by the Holy Ghost as we verily trust such rules and laws as tend to the wealth of his elect folk; yet upon considerations to man unknown, his infinite wisdom leaveth or permitteth men to walk in their infirmity and frailty; so that we cannot ne will arrogantly presume of ourselves, as though being in name spiritual men, we were also in all our acts and doings clean and void from all temporal affections and carnality of this world, or that the laws of the church made for spiritual and ghostly purpose be not sometime applied to worldly intent. This we ought and do lament, as becometh us, very sure. Nevertheless, as the evil deeds of men be the mere defaults of those particular men, and not of the whole order of the clergy, nor of the law wholesomely by them made; our request and petition shall be with all humility and reverence; that laws well made be not therefore called evil because by all men and at all times they be not well executed; and that in such defaults as shall appear such distribution may be used *ut unusquisque onus suum portet*, and remedy be found to reform the offenders; unto the which your Highness shall perceive as great towardness in your said orators as can be required upon declaration of particulars. And other answer than this cannot be made in the name of your whole clergy, for though *in multis offendimus omnes*, as St. James saith, yet not 'in omnibus offendimus omnes;' and the whole number can neither justify ne condemn particular acts to them unknown but thus. He that calleth a man ex officio for correction of sin, doeth well. He that calleth men for pleasure or vexation, doeth evil. Summoners should be honest men. If they offend in their office, they should be punished. To prove first [their faults] before men be called, is not necessary. He that is called according to the laws ex officio or otherwise, cannot complain. He that is otherwise ordered should have by reason convenient recompence and so forth; that is well to be allowed, and misdemeanour when it appeareth to be reproved.

"Item where they say in the same article that upon their appearance ex officio at the only pleasure of the ordinaries, they be committed to prison without bail or mainprize; and there they lie some half a year or more before they come to their deliverance; to this we answer,—

"That we use no prison before conviction but for sure custody, and only of such as be suspected of heresy, in which crime, thanked be God, there hath fallen no such notable person in our time, or of such qualities as hath given occasion of any sinister suspicion to be conceived of malice or hatred to his person other than the heinousness of their crime deserveth. *Truth it is that certain apostates, friars, monks, lewd priests, bankrupt merchants, vagabonds, and lewd idle fellows of corrupt intent, have embraced the abominable and erroneous opinions lately sprung in Germany;* and by them some have been seduced in simplicity and ignorance. Against these, if judgment has been exercised according to the laws of the church, and conformably to the laws of this realm, we be without blame. If we have been too remiss and slack, we shall gladly do our duty from henceforth. If any man hath been, under pretence of this [crime], particularly offended, it were pity to suffer any man to be wronged; and thus it ought to be, and otherwise we cannot answer, no man's special case being declared in the said petition.

"Item where they say further that they so appearing ex officio, be condemned to answer to many subtle questions by the which a simple, unlearned, or else a well-witted layman without learning sometimes is, and commonly may be trapped and induced into peril of open penance to their shame, or else [forced] to redeem their penance for money, as is commonly used; to this we answer that we should not use subtlety, for we should do all things plainly and openly; and if we do otherwise, we do amiss. We ought not to ask questions, but after the capacities of the man. Christ hath defended his true doctrine and faith in his Catholic church from all subtlety, and so preserved good men in the same, as they have not (blessed be God) been vexed, inquieted, or troubled in Christ's church. Thereupon evil men fall in danger by their own subtlety; we protest afore God we have neither known, read, nor heard of any one man damaged or prejudiced by spiritual jurisdiction in this behalf, neither in this realm nor any other, but only by his own deserts. Such is the goodness of God in maintaining the cause of his Catholic faith.

"Item where they say they be compelled to do open penance, or else redeem the same for money; as for penance, we answer it consisteth in the arbitre of a judge who ought to enjoin such penance as might profit for correction of the fault. Whereupon we disallow that judge's doing who taketh money for penance for lucre or advantage, not regarding the reformation of sin as he ought to do. But when open penance may sometimes work in certain persons more hurt than good, it is commendable and allowable in that case to punish by the purse, and preserve the fame of the party; foreseeing always the money be converted *in usus pios et eleemosynam*, and thus we think of the thing, and that the offenders should be punished.

"Item where they complain that two witnesses be admitted, be they never so defamed, of little truth or credence, adversaries or enemies to the parties; yet in many cases they be allowed by the discretion of the ordinaries to put the party defamed, ex officio, to open penance, and then to redemption for money; so that every of your subjects, upon the only will of the ordinaries or their substitutes, without any accuser, proved fame, or presentment, is or may be infamed, vexed, and troubled, to the peril of their lives, their shames, costs, and expenses:

"To this we reply, *the Gospel of Christ teacheth us to believe two witnesses; and as the cause is, so the judge must esteem the quality of the witness; and in heresy no exception is necessary to be considered if their tale be likely; which hath been highly provided lest heretics without jeopardy might else plant their heresies in lewd and light persons, and taking exception to the witnesses, take boldness to continue their folly. This is the universal law of Christendom, and hath universally done good. Of any injury done to any man thereby we know not.*

"Item where they say it is not intended by them to take away from us our authority to correct and punish sins, and especially the detestable crime of heresy:

"To this we answer, in the prosecuting heretics we regard our duty and office whereunto we be called, and if God will discharge us thereof, or cease that plague universal, as, by directing the hearts of princes, and specially the heart of your Highness (laud and thanks be unto Him), His goodness doth commence and begin to do, we should and shall have great cause to rejoice; as being our authority therein costly, dangerous, full of trouble and business, without any fruit, pleasure, or commodity worldly, but a continued conflict and vexation with pertinacity, wilfulness, folly, and ignorance, whereupon followeth their bodily and ghostly destruction, to our great sorrow.

"Item where they desire that by assent of your Highness (if the laws heretofore made be not sufficient for the repression of heresy) more dreadful and terrible laws may be made; this We think is undoubtedly a more charitable request than as we trust necessary, considering that by the aid of your Highness, and the pains of your Grace's statutes freely executed, your realm may be in short time clean purged from the few small dregs that do remain, if any do remain.

"Item where they desire some reasonable declaration may be made to your people, how they may, if they will, avoid the peril of heresy. No better declaration, we say, can be made than is already by our Saviour Christ, the Apostles, and the determination of the church, which if they keep, they shall not fail to eschew heresy.

"Item where they desire that some charitable fashion may be devised by your wisdom for the calling of any of your subjects before us, that it shall not stand in the only will and pleasure of the ordinaries at their own imagination, without lawful accusation by honest witness, according to your law; to this we say that a better provision cannot be devised than is already devised by the clergy in our opinion; and if any default appear in the execution, it shall be amended on declaration of the particulars, and the same proved.

"Item where they say that your subjects be cited out of the diocese which they dwell in, and many times be suspended and excommunicate for light causes upon the only certificate devised by the proctors, and that all your subjects find themselves grieved with the excessive fees taken in the spiritual courts:

"To this article, for because it concerneth specially the spiritual courts of me the Archbishop of Canterbury, please it your Grace to understand that about twelve months past I reformed certain things objected here; and now within these ten weeks I reformed many other things in my said courts, as I suppose is not unknown unto your Grace's Commons; and some of the fees of the officers of my courts I have brought down to halves, some to the third part, and some wholly taken away and extincted; and yet it is objected to me as though I had taken no manner of reformation therein. Nevertheless I shall not cease yet; but in such things as I shall see your Commons most offended I will set redress accordingly, so as, I trust, they will be contented in that behalf. And I, the said archbishop, beseech your Grace to consider what service the doctors in civil law, which have had their practice in my courts, have done your Grace concerning treaties, truces, confederations, and leagues devised and concluded with outward princes; and that without such learned men in civil law your Grace could not have been so conveniently served as at all times you have been, which thing, perhaps, when such learned men shall fail, will appear more evident than it doth now. The decay whereof grieveth me to foresee, not so greatly for any cause concerning the pleasure or profit of myself, being a man spent, and at the point to depart this world, and having no penny of any advantage by my said courts, but principally for the good love which I bear to the honour of your Grace and of your realm. And albeit there is, by the assent of the Lords Temporal and the Commons of your Parliament, an act passed thereupon already, the matter depending before your Majesty by way of supplication offered to your Highness by your said Commons; 237 yet, forasmuch as we your Grace's humble chaplains, the Archbishops of Canterbury and York, be bounden by oath to be intercessors for the rights of our churches; and forasmuch as the spiritual prelates of the clergy, being of your Grace's parliament, consented to the said act for divers great causes moving their conscience, we your Grace's said chaplains show unto your Highness that it hath appertained to the Archbishops of Canterbury and York for the space of four hundred years or thereabouts to have spiritual jurisdiction over all your Grace's subjects dwelling within the provinces; and to have authority to call before them, not only in spiritual causes devolved to them by way of appeal, but also by way of querimony and complaint; which right and privilege pertaineth not only to the persons of the said archbishops, but also to the pre-eminences of their churches. Insomuch that when the archbishop of either of the sees dieth, the said privileges do not only remain to his successor (by which he is named Legatus natus), but also in the meantime of vacation the same privilege resteth in the churches of Canterbury and York; and is executed by the prior, dean and chapter of the said churches, and so the said act is directly against the liberty and privileges of the churches of Canterbury and York; and what dangers be to them which study and labour to take away the liberties and privileges of the church, whoso will read the general councils of Christendom and the canons of the fathers of the Catholic church ordained in that behalf, shall soon perceive. And further, we think verily that our churches, to which the said privileges were granted, can give no cause why the pope himself (whose predecessors granted that privilege) or any other (the honour of your Grace ever except) may justly take away the same privileges so lawfully prescribed from our churches, though we [ourselves] had greatly offended, abusing the said privileges. But when in our persons we trust we have given no cause why to lose that privilege, we beseech your Grace of your goodness and absolute power to set such orders in this behalf as we may enjoy our privileges lawfully admitted so long.

"Item where they complain that there is exacted and demanded in divers parishes of this your realm, other manner of tythes than hath been accustomed to be paid this hundred years past; and in some parts of this your realm there is exacted double tythes, that is to say, threepence, or twopence-halfpenny, for one acre, over and beside the tythe for the increase of cattle that pastureth the same:

"To this we say, that tythes being due by God's law, be so duly paid (thanked be God), by all good men, as there needeth not exaction in the most parts of this your Grace's realm. As for double tythes, they cannot be maintained due for one increase; whether in any place they be unduly exacted in fact we know not. This we know in learning, that neither a hundred years, nor seven hundred of non-payment, may debar the right of God's law. The manner of payment, and person unto whom to pay, may be in time altered, but the duty cannot by any means be taken away.

"Item where they say that when a mortuary is due, curates sometimes, before they will demand it, will bring citation for it; and then will not receive the mortuaries till they may have such costs as they say they have laid out for the suit of the same; when, indeed, if they would first have charitably demanded it, they needed not to have sued for the same, for it should have been paid with good will:

"We answer that curates thus offending, if they were known, ought to be punished, but who thus doeth we know not.

"Item where they say that divers spiritual persons being presented to benefices within this your realm, we and our ministers do take of them great sums of money and reward; we reply that this is a particular abuse, and he that taketh reward doeth not well; and if any penny be exacted above the accustomed rate and after convenient proportion, it is not well done. But in taking the usual fee for the sealing, writing, and registering the letters, which is very moderate, we cannot think it to be reputed as any offence; neither have we heard any priests in our days complain of any excess therein.

"And where they say in the same article that such as be presented be delayed without reasonable cause, to the intent that we the ordinaries may have the profit of the benefice during the vacation, unless they will pact and convent with us by temporal bonds, whereof some bonds contain that we should have part of the profit of the said benefice, which your said subjects suppose to be not only against right and conscience, but also seemeth to be simony, and contrary to the laws of God:

"To this we do say that a delay without reasonable cause, and for a lucrative intent, is detestable in spiritual men, and the doers cannot eschew punishment: but otherwise a delay is sometimes expedient to examine the clerk, and sometimes necessary when the title is in variance. All other bargains and covenants being contrary to the law ought to be punished, as the quality is of the offence more or less, as simony or inordinate covetousness.

"Item where they say that we give benefices to our nephews and kinsfolk, being in young age or infants, whereby the cure is not substantially looked into, nor the parishioners taught as they should be; we reply to this that the thing which is not lawful in others is in spiritual men more detestable. Benefices should be disposed of not *secundum carnem et sanguinem, sed secundum merita*. And when there is a default it is not authorised by the clergy as good, but reproved; whereupon in this the clergy is not to be blamed, but the default as it may appear must be laid to particular men.

"And where they say that we take the profit of such benefices for the time of the minority of our said kinsfolk, if it be done to our own use and profit it is not well; *if it be bestowed to the bringing up and use of the same parties*, or applied to the maintenance of the church and God's service, or distributed among the poor, we do not see but that it may be allowed.

"Item where they say that divers and many spiritual persons, not contented with the convenient livings and promotions of the church, daily intromit and exercise themselves in secular offices and rooms, as stewards, receivers, auditors, bailiffs, and other temporal occupations, withdrawing themselves from the good contemplative lives that they have professed, not only to the damage but also to the perilous example of your loving and obedient subjects; to this we your bedesmen answer that beneficed men may lawfully be stewards and receivers to their own bishops, as it evidently appeareth in the laws of the church; and we by the same laws ought to have no other And as for priests to be auditors and bailiffs, we know none such.

"And where, finally, they, in the conclusion of their supplication, do repeat and say that forasmuch as there is at this present time, and by a few years past hath been much misdemeanour and violence upon the one part, and much default and lack of patience, charity, and good will on the other part; and marvellous discord in consequence of the quiet, peace, and tranquillity in which this your realm hath been ever hitherto preserved through your politic wisdom:

"To the first part as touching such discord as is reported, and also the misdemeanour which is imputed to us and our doings, we trust we have sufficiently answered the same, humbly beseeching your Grace so to esteem and weigh such answer with their supplication as shall be thought good and expedient by your high wisdom. Furthermore we ascertain your Grace as touching the violence which they seem to lay to our charge, albeit divers of the clergy of this your realm have sundry times been *rigorously handled, and with much violence entreated by certain ill-disposed and seditious persons of the lay fee, have been injured in their bodies, thrown down in the kennel in the open streets at mid-day,* even here within your city and elsewhere, to the great rebuke and disquietness of the clergy of your realm, the great danger of the souls of the said misdoers, and perilous example of your subjects. Yet we think verily, and do affirm the same, that no violence hath been so used on our behalf towards your said lay subjects in any case; unless they esteem this to be violence that we do use as well for the health of their souls as for the discharge of our duties in taking, examining, and punishing heretics according to the law: wherein we doubt not but that your Grace, and divers of your Grace's subjects, do understand well what charitable entreaty we have used with such as have been before us for the same cause of heresy; and what means we have devised and studied for safeguard specially of their souls; and that charitably, as God be our judge, and without violence as [far as] we could possibly devise. In execution thereof, and also of the laws of the church for repression of sin, and also for reformation of mislivers, it hath been to our great comfort that your Grace hath herein of your goodness, assisted and aided us in this behalf for the zeal and love which your Grace beareth to God's church and to His ministers; especially in defence of His faith whereof your Grace only and most worthily amongst all Christian princes beareth the title and name. And for that marvellous discord and grudge among your subjects as is reported in the supplication of your Commons, we beseech your Majesty, all the premises considered, to repress those that be misdoers; protesting in our behalf that we ourselves have no grudge nor displeasure towards your lay subjects our ghostly children. We intreat your Grace of your accustomed goodness to us your bedemen to continue our chief protector, defender, and aider in and for the execution of our office and duty; specially touching repression of heresy, reformation of sin, and due behaviour and order of all your Grace's subjects, spiritual and temporal; which (no doubt thereof) shall be much to the pleasure of God, great comfort to men's souls, quietness and unity of all your realm; and, as we think, most principally to the great comfort of your Grace's Majesty. Which we beseech lowly upon our knees, so entirely as we can, to be the author of unity, charity, and concord as above, for whose preservation we do and shall continually pray to Almighty God long to reign and prosper in most honourable estate to his pleasure."

This was the bishops' defence; the best which, under the circumstances, they considered themselves capable of making. The House of Commons had stated their complaints in the form of special notorious facts; the bishops replied with urging the theory of their position, and supposed that they could relieve the ecclesiastical system from the faults of its ministers, by laying the sole blame on the unworthiness of individual persons. The degenerate representatives of a once noble institution could not perhaps be expected to admit their degeneracy, and confess themselves, as they really were, collectively incompetent; yet the defence which they brought forward would have been valid only so long as the blemishes were the rare exceptions in the working of an institution which was still generally beneficent. It was no defence at all when the faults had become the rule, and when there was no security in the system itself for the selection of worth and capacity to exercise its functions. The clergy, as I have already said, claimed the privileges of saints, while their conduct fell below the standard of that of ordinary men; and the position taken in this answer was tenable only on the hypothesis which it, in fact, deliberately asserted, that the judicial authority of the church had been committed to it by God Himself; and that no misconduct of its ministers in detail could forfeit their claims or justify resistance to them.

There is something touching in the bishops' evidently sincere unconsciousness that there could be real room for blame. Warham, who had been Archbishop of Canterbury thirty years, took credit to himself for the reforms which, under the pressure of public opinion, he had introduced, in the last few weeks or months; and did not know that in doing so he had passed sentence on a life of neglect. In the opinion of the entire bench no infamy, however notorious, could shake the testimony of a witness in a case of heresy; no cruelty was unjust when there was suspicion of so horrible a crime; while the appointment of minors to church benefices (not to press more closely the edge of the accusation) they admitted while they affected to deny it; since they were not ashamed to defend the appropriation of the proceeds of benefices occupied by such persons, if laid out on the education and maintenance of the minors themselves.

Yet these things were as nothing in comparison with the powers claimed for convocation; and the prelates of the later years of Henry's reign must have looked back with strange sensations at the language which their predecessors had so simply addressed to him. If the canons which convocation might think good to enact were not consistent with the laws of the Realm, "His Majesty" was desired to produce the wished-for uniformity by altering the laws of the Realm; and although the bishops might not submit their laws to His Majesty's approval, they would be happy, they told him, to consider such suggestions as he might think proper to make. The spirit of the Plantagenets must have slumbered long before such words as these could have been addressed to an English sovereign, and little did the bishops dream that these light words were the spell which would burst the charm, and bid that spirit wake again in all its power and terror.

The House of Commons in the mean time had not been idle. To them the questions at issue were unincumbered with theoretic difficulties. Enormous abuses had been long ripe for dissolution, and there was no occasion to waste time in unnecessary debates. At such a time, with a House practically unanimous, business could be rapidly transacted, the more rapidly indeed in proportion to its importance. In six weeks, for so long only the session lasted, the astonished church authorities saw bill after bill hurried up before the Lords, by which successively the pleasant fountains of their incomes would be dried up to flow no longer; or would flow only in shallow rivulets along the beds of the once abundant torrents, The jurisdiction of the spiritual courts was not immediately curtailed, and the authority which was in future to be permitted to convocation lay over for further consideration, to be dealt with in another manner. But probate duties and legacy duties, hitherto assessed at discretion, were dwarfed into fixed proportions, 238 not to touch the poorer laity any more, and bearing even upon wealth with a reserved and gentle hand. Mortuaries were shorn of their luxuriance; when effects were small, no mortuary should be required; when large, the clergy should content themselves with a modest share. No velvet cloaks should be stripped any more from strangers' bodies to save them from a rector's grasp; 239 no shameful battles with apparitors should disturb any more the recent rest of the dead. 240 Such sums as the law would permit should be paid thenceforward in the form of decent funeral fees for householders dying in their own parishes, and there the exactions should terminate. 241

The carelessness of the bishops in the discharge of their most immediate duties obliged the legislature to trespass also in the provinces purely spiritual, and undertake the discipline of the clergy. The Commons had complained in their petition that the clergy, instead of attending to their duties, were acting as auditors, bailiffs, stewards, or in other capacities, as laymen; they were engaged in trade also, in farming, in tanning, in brewing, in doing anything but the duties which they were paid for doing; while they purchased dispensations for non-residence on their benefices; and of these benefices, in favoured cases, single priests held as many as eight or nine. It was thought unnecessary to wait for the bishops' pleasure to apply a remedy here. If the clergy were unjustly accused of these offences, a law of general prohibition would not touch them. If the belief of the House of Commons was well founded, there was no occasion for longer delay. It was therefore enacted 242—"for the more quiet and virtuous increase and maintenance of divine service, the preaching and teaching the Word of God with godly and good example, for the better discharge of cures, the maintenance of hospitality, the relief of poor people, the increase of devotion and good opinion of the lay fee towards spiritual persons"—that no such persons thenceforward should take any land to farm beyond what was necessary, *bonâ fide,* for the support of their own households; that they should not buy merchandise to sell again; that they should keep no tanneries or brewhouses, or otherwise directly or indirectly trade for gain. Pluralities were not to be permitted with benefices above the yearly value of eight pounds, and residence was made obligatory under penalty in cases of absence without special reason, of ten pounds for each month of such absence. The law against pluralities was limited as against existing holders, each of whom, for their natural lives, might continue to hold as many as four benefices. But dispensations, either for non-residence or for the violation of any other provision of the act, were made penal in a high degree, whether obtained from the bishops or from the court of Rome.

These bills struck hard and struck home. Yet even persons who most disapprove of the Reformation will not at the present time either wonder at their enactment or complain of their severity. They will be desirous rather to disentangle their doctrine from suspicious connection, and will not be anxious to compromise their theology by the defence of unworthy professors of it.

The bishops, however, could ill tolerate an interference with the privileges of the ecclesiastical order. The Commons, it was exclaimed, were heretics and schismatics; 243 the cry was heard everywhere, of Lack of faith, Lack of faith; and the lay peers being constitutionally conservative, and perhaps instinctively apprehensive of the infectious tendencies of innovation, it seemed likely for a time that an effective opposition might be raised in the Upper House. The clergy commanded an actual majority in that House from their own body, which they might employ if they dared; and although they were not likely to venture alone on so bold a measure, yet a partial support from the other members was a sufficient encouragement. The aged Bishop of Rochester was made the spokesman of the ecclesiastics on this occasion. "My Lords," he said, "you see daily what bills come hither from the Commons House, and all is to the destruction of the church. For God's sake see what a realm the kingdom of Bohemia was; and when the church went down, then fell the glory of that kingdom. Now with the Commons is nothing but Down with the church, and all this meseemeth is for lack of faith only." 244 "In result," says Hall, "the acts were sore debated; the Lords Spiritual would in no wise consent, and committees of the two Houses sate continually for discussion." The spiritualty defended themselves by prescription and usage, to which a Gray's Inn lawyer something insolently answered, on one occasion, "the usage hath ever been of thieves to rob on Shooter's Hill, *ergo*, it is lawful." "With this answer," continues Hall, "the spiritual men were sore offended because their doings were called robberies, but the temporal men stood by their sayings, insomuch that the said gentlemen declared to the Archbishop of Canterbury, that both the exaction of probates of testaments and the taking of mortuaries were open robbery and thefts."

At length, people out of doors growing impatient, and dangerous symptoms threatening to show themselves, the king summoned a meeting in the Star-chamber between eight members of both Houses. The lay peers, after some discussion, conclusively gave way; and the bishops, left without support, were obliged to yield. They signified their unwilling consent, and the bills, "somewhat qualified," were the next day agreed to—"to the great rejoicing of the lay people, and the great displeasure of the spiritual persons." 245

Nor were the House of Commons contented with the substance of victory. The reply to their petition had perhaps by that time been made known to them, and at any rate they had been accused of sympathy with heresy, and they would not submit to the hateful charge without exacting revenge. The more clamorous of the clergy out of doors were punished probably by the stocks; from among their opponents in the Upper House, Fisher was selected for special and signal humiliation. The words of which he had made use were truer than the Commons knew; perhaps the latent truth of them was the secret cause of the pain which they inflicted; but the special anxiety of the English reformers was to disconnect themselves, with marked emphasis, from the movement in Germany, and they determined to compel the offending bishop to withdraw his words.

They sent the speaker, Sir Thomas Audeley, to the king, who "very eloquently declared what dishonour it was to his Majesty and the realm, that they which were elected for the wisest men in the shires, cities, and boroughs within the realm of England, should be declared in so noble a presence to lack faith." It was equivalent to saying "that they were infidels, and no Christians—as ill as Turks and Saracens." Wherefore he "most humbly besought the King's Highness to call the said bishop before him, and to cause him to speak more discreetly of such a number as was in the Commons House." 246 Henry consented to their request, it is likely with no great difficulty, and availed himself of the opportunity to read a lesson much needed to the remainder of the bench. He sent for Fisher, and with him for the Archbishop of Canterbury, and for six other bishops. The speaker's message was laid before them, and they were asked what they had to say. It would have been well for the weak trembling old men if they could have repeated what they believed and had maintained their right to believe it. Bold conduct is ever the most safe; it is fatal only when there is courage but for the first step, and fails when a second is required to support it. But they were forsaken in their hour of calamity, not by courage only, but by prudence, by judgment, by conscience itself. The Bishop of Rochester stooped to an equivocation too transparent to deceive any one; he said that "he meant only the doings of the Bohemians were for lack of faith, and not the doings of the Commons House"—"which saying was confirmed by the bishops present." The king allowed the excuse, and the bishops were dismissed; but they were dismissed into ignominy, and thenceforward, in all Henry's dealings with them, they were treated with contemptuous disrespect. For Fisher himself we must feel only sorrow. After seventy-six years of a useful and honourable life, which he might have hoped to close in a quiet haven, he was launched suddenly upon stormy waters, to which he was too brave to yield, which he was too timid to contend against; and the frail vessel drifting where the waves drove it, was soon piteously to perish.

Thus triumphant on every side, the parliament, in the middle of December, closed its session, and lay England celebrated its exploits as a national victory. "The king removed to Greenwich, and there kept his Christmas with the queen with great triumph, with great plenty of viands, and disguisings, and interludes, to the great rejoicing of his people;" 247 the members of the House of Commons, we may well believe, following the royal example in town and country, and being the little heroes of the day. Only the bishops carried home sad hearts within them, to mourn over the perils of the church and the impending end of all things; Fisher, unhappily for himself, to listen to the wailings of the Nun of Kent, and to totter slowly into treason.

Here, for the present leaving the clergy to meditate on their future, and reconsider the wisdom of their answer to the king respecting the ecclesiastical jurisdiction (a point on which they were not the less certain to be pressed, because the process upon it was temporarily suspended), we must turn to the more painful matter which, for a time longer, ran parallel with the domestic reformation, and as yet was unable to unite with it. After the departure of Campeggio, the further hearing of the divorce cause had been advoked to Rome, where it was impossible for Henry to consent to plead; while the appearance of the supposed brief had opened avenues of new difficulty which left no hope of a decision within the limits of an ordinary lifetime. Henry was still, however, extremely reluctant 248 to proceed to extremities, and appeal to the parliament. He had threatened that he would tolerate no delay, and Wolsey had evidently expected that he would not. Queen Catherine's alarm had gone so far, that in the autumn she had procured an injunction from the pope, which had been posted in the churches of Flanders, menacing the king with spiritual censures if he took any further steps. 249 Even this she feared that he would disregard, and in March, 1529-30, a second inhibition was issued at her request, couched in still stronger language. 250 But these measures were needless, or at least premature. Henry expected that the display of temper in the country in the late session would produce an effect both on the pope and on the emperor; and proposing to send an embassy to remonstrate jointly with them on the occasion of the emperor's coronation, which was to take place in the spring at Bologna, he had recourse in the mean time to an expedient which, though blemished in the execution, was itself reasonable and prudent.

Among the many *technical* questions which had been raised upon the divorce, the most serious was on the validity of the original dispensation; a question not only on the sufficiency of the form the defects of which the brief had been invented to remedy; but on the more comprehensive uncertainty whether Pope Julius had not exceeded his powers altogether in granting a dispensation where there was so close affinity. No one supposed that the pope could permit a brother to marry a sister; a dispensation granted in such a case would be *ipso facto* void.—Was not the dispensation similarly void which permitted the marriage of a brother's widow? The advantage which Henry expected from raising this difficulty was the transfer of judgment from the partial tribunal of Clement to a broader court. The pope could not, of course, adjudicate on the extent of his own powers; especially as he always declared himself to be ignorant of the law; and the decision of so general a question rested either with a general council, or must be determined by the consent of Christendom, obtained in some other manner. If such general consent declared against the pope, the cause was virtually terminated. If there was some approach to a consent against him, or even if there was general uncertainty, Henry had a legal pretext for declining his jurisdiction, and appealing to a council.

Thomas Cranmer, then a doctor of divinity at Cambridge, 251 is said to have been the person who suggested this ingenious expedient, and to have advised the king, as the simplest means of carrying it out, to consult in detail the universities and learned men throughout Europe. His notorious activity in collecting the opinions may have easily connected him with the origination of the plan, which probably occurred to many other persons as well as to him; but whoever was the first adviser, it was immediately acted upon, and English agents were despatched into Germany, Italy, and France, carrying with them all means of persuasion, intellectual, moral, and material, which promised to be of most cogent potency with lawyers' convictions.

This matter was in full activity when the Earl of Wiltshire, Anne Boleyn's father, with Cranmer, the Bishop of London, and Edward Lee, afterwards Archbishop of York, was despatched to Bologna to lay Henry's remonstrances before the emperor, who was come at last in person to enjoy his miserable triumph, and receive from the pope the imperial crown. Sir Nicholas Carew, who had been sent forward a few weeks previously, described in piteous language the state to which Italy had been reduced by him. Passing through Pavia, the English emissary saw the children crying about the streets for bread, and dying of hunger; the grapes in midwinter rotting on the vines, because there was no one to gather them; and for fifty miles scarcely a single creature, man or woman, in the fields. "They say," added Carew, "and the pope also showed us the same, that the whole people of that country, with divers other places in Italia, with war, famine, and pestilence, are utterly dead and gone." 252 Such had been the combined work of the vanity of Francis and the cold selfishness of Charles; and now the latter had arrived amidst the ruins which he had made, to receive his crown from the hands of a pope who was true to Italy, if false to all the world besides, and whom, but two years before, he had imprisoned and disgraced. We think of Clement as the creature of the emperor, and such substantially he allowed himself to be; but his obedience was the obedience of fear to a master whom he hated, and the bishop of Tarbès, who was present at the coronation, and stood at his side through the ceremony, saw him trembling under his robes with emotion, and heard him sigh bitterly. 253 Very unwillingly, we may be assured, he was compelled to act his vacillating part to England, and England, at this distance of time, may forgive him for faults to which she owes her freedom, and need not refuse him some tribute of sympathy in his sorrows.

Fallen on evil times, which greater wisdom and greater courage than had for many a century been found in the successors of St. Peter would have failed to encounter successfully, Clement VII. remained, with all his cowardice, a true Italian; his errors were the errors of his age and nation, and were softened by the presence, in more than usual measure, of Italian genius and grace. Benvenuto Cellini, who describes his character with much minuteness, has left us a picture of a hot-tempered, but genuine and kind-hearted man, whose taste was elegant, and whose wit, from the playful spirit with which it was pervaded, and from a certain tendency to innocent levity, approached to humour. He was liable to violent bursts of feeling; and his inability to control himself, his gesticulations, his exclamations, and his tears, all represent to us a person who was an indifferent master of the tricks of dissimulation to which he was reduced, and whose weakness entitles him to pity, if not to respect. The papacy had fallen to him at the crisis of its deepest degradation. It existed as a politically organised institution, which it was convenient to maintain, but from which the private hearts of all men had fallen away; and it depended for its very life upon the support which the courts of Europe would condescend to extend to it. Among these governments, therefore, distracted as they were by mutual hostility, the pope was compelled to make his choice; and the fatality of his position condemned him to quarrel with the only prince on whom, at the outset of these complications, he had a right to depend.

In 1512, France had been on the point of declaring her religious independence; and as late as 1525, Francis entertained thoughts of offering the patriarchate to Wolsey. 254 Charles V., postponing his religious devotion for the leisure of old age, had reserved the choice of his party, to watch events and to wait upon opportunity; while, from his singular position, he wielded in one hand the power of Catholic Spain, in the other that of Protestant Germany, ready to strike with either, as occasion or necessity recommended. If his Spaniards had annexed the New World to the papacy, his German lanzknechts had stormed the Holy City, murdered cardinals, and outraged the pope's person: while both Charles and Francis, alike caring exclusively for their private interests, had allowed the Turks to overrun Hungary, to conquer Rhodes, and to collect an armament at Constantinople so formidable as to threaten Italy itself, and the very Christian faith. Henry alone had shown hitherto a true feeling for religion; Henry had made war with Louis XII. solely in the pope's quarrel; Henry had broken an old alliance with the emperor to revenge the capture of Rome, and had won Francis back to his allegiance. To Henry, if to any one, the Roman bishop had a right to look with confidence. But the power of England was far off, and could not reach to Rome. Francis had been baffled and defeated, his armies destroyed, his political influence in the Peninsula annihilated. The practical choice which remained to Clement lay only, as it seemed, between the emperor and martyrdom; and having, perhaps, a desire for the nobler alternative, yet being without the power to choose it, his wishes and his conduct, his words to private persons and his open actions before the world, were in perpetual contradiction. He submitted while his heart revolted; and while at Charles's dictation he was threatening Henry with excommunication if he proceeded further with his divorce, he was able at that very time to say, in confidence, to the Bishop of Tarbès, that he would be well contented if the King of England would marry on his own responsibility, availing himself of any means which he might possess among his own people, so only that he himself was not committed to a consent or the privileges of the papacy were not trenched upon. 255

Two years later, when the course which the pope would really pursue under such circumstances was of smaller importance, Henry gave him an opportunity of proving the sincerity of this language; and the result was such as he expected it to be. As yet, however, he had not relinquished the hope of succeeding by a more open course.

In March, 1529-30, the English ambassadors appeared at Bologna. Their instructions were honest, manly, and straightforward. They were directed to explain, *ab initio*, the grounds of the king's proceedings, and to appeal to the emperor's understanding of the obligations of princes. Full restitution was to be offered of Catherine's dowry, and the Earl of Wiltshire was provided with letters of credit adequate to the amount. 256 If these proposals were not accepted, they were to assume a more peremptory tone, and threaten the alienation of England; and if menaces were equally ineffectual, they were to declare that Henry, having done all which lay within his power to effect his purpose with the goodwill of his friends, since he could not do as he would, must now do as he could, and discharge his conscience. If the emperor should pretend that he would "abide the law, and would defer to the pope," they were to say, "that the sacking of Rome by the Spaniards and Germans had so discouraged the pope and cardinals, that they feared for body and goods," and had ceased to be free agents; and concluding finally that the king would fear God rather than man, and would rely on comfort from the Saviour against those who abused their authority, they were then to withdraw. 257 The tone of the directions was not sanguine, and the political complications of Europe, on which the emperor's reply must more or less have depended, were too involved to allow us to trace the influences which were likely to have weighed with him. There seems no primâ facie reason, however, why the attempt might not have been successful. The revolutionary intrigues in England had decisively failed, and the natural sympathy of princes, and a desire to detach Henry from Francis, must have combined to recommend a return of the old cordiality which had so long existed between the sovereigns of England and Flanders. But whatever was the cause, the opening interview assured the Earl of Wiltshire that he had nothing to look for. He was received with distant courtesy; but Charles at once objected even to hearing his instructions, as an interested party. 258 The earl replied that he stood there, not as the father of the queen's rival, but as the representative of his sovereign; but the objection declared the attitude which Charles was resolved to maintain, and which, in fact, he maintained throughout. "The emperor," wrote Lord Wiltshire to Henry, "is stiffly bent against your Grace's matter, and is most earnest in it; while the pope is led by the emperor, and neither will nor dare displease him." 259 From that quarter, so long as parties remained in their existing attitude, there was no hope. It seems to have been hinted, indeed, that if war broke out again between Charles and Francis, something might be done as the price of Henry's surrendering the French alliance; 260 but the suggestion, if it was made, was probably ironical; and as Charles was unquestionably acting against his interest in rejecting the English overtures, it is fair to give him credit for having acted on this one occasion of his life, upon generous motives. A respectful compliment was paid to his conduct by Henry himself in the reproaches which he addressed to the pope. 261

So terminated the first and the last overture on this subject which Henry attempted with Charles V. The ambassadors remained but a few days at Bologna, and then discharged their commission and returned. The pope, however, had played his part with remarkable skill, and by finessing dexterously behind the scenes, had contrived to prevent the precipitation of a rupture with himself. His simple and single wish was to gain time, trusting to accident or Providence to deliver him from his dilemma. On the one hand, he yielded to the emperor in refusing to consent to Henry's demand; on the other, he availed himself of all the intricacies to parry Catherine's demand for a judgment in her favour. He even seemed to part with the emperor on doubtful terms. "The latter," said the Bishop of Tarbès, 262 "before leaving Bologna, desired his Holiness to place two cardinals' hats at his disposal, to enable him to reward certain services." His Holiness ventured to refuse. During his imprisonment, he said he had been compelled to nominate several persons for that office whose conduct had been a disgrace to their rank; and when the emperor denied his orders, the pope declared that he had seen them. The cardinals' hats, therefore, should be granted only when they were deserved, "when the Lutherans in Germany had been reduced to obedience, and Hungary had been recovered from the Turks." If this was acting, it was skilfully managed, and it deceived the eyes of the French ambassador.

Still further to gratify Henry, the pope made a public declaration with respect to the dispute which had arisen on the extent of his authority, desiring, or professing to desire, that all persons whatever throughout Italy should be free to express their opinions without fear of incurring his displeasure. This declaration, had it been honestly meant, would have been creditable to Clement's courage: unfortunately for his reputation, his outward and his secret actions seldom corresponded, and the emperor's agents were observed to use very dissimilar language in his name. The double policy, nevertheless, was still followed to secure delay. Delay was his sole aim,— either that Catherine's death, or his own, or Henry's, or some relenting in one or other of the two princes who held their minatory arms extended over him, might spare himself and the church the calamity of a decision. For to the church any decision was fatal. If he declared for Charles, England would fall from it; if for Henry, Germany and Flanders were lost irrecoverably, and Spain itself might follow. His one hope was to procrastinate; and in this policy of hesitation for two more years he succeeded, till at length the patience of Henry and of England was worn out, and all was ended. When the emperor required sentence to be passed, he pretended to be about to yield; and at the last moment, some technical difficulty ever interfered to make a decision impossible. When Henry was cited to appear at Rome, a point of law was raised upon the privilege of kings, threatening to open into other points of law, and so to multiply to infinity. The pope, indeed, finding his own ends so well answered by evasion, imagined that it would answer equally those of the English nation, and he declared to Henry's secretary that "if the King of England would send a mandate ad totam causam, then if his Highness would, there might be given so many delays by reason of matters which his Highness might lay in, and the remissorials that his Grace might ask, ad partes, that peradventure in ten years or longer a sentence should not be given." 263 In point of worldly prudence, his conduct was unexceptionably wise; but something beyond worldly prudence was demanded of a tribunal which claimed to be inspired by the Holy Ghost.

The dreary details of the negotiations I have no intention of pursuing. They are of no interest to any one,—a miserable tissue of insincerity on one side, and hesitating uncertainty on the other. There is no occasion for us to weary ourselves with the ineffectual efforts to postpone an issue which was sooner or later inevitable.

I may not pass over in similar silence another unpleasant episode in this business,—the execution of Cranmer's project for collecting the sentiments of Europe on the pope's dispensing power. The details of this transaction are not wearying only, but scandalous; and while the substantial justice of Henry's cause is a reason for deploring the means to which he allowed himself to be driven in pursuing it, we may not permit ourselves either to palliate those means or to conceal them. The project seemed a simple one, and likely to be effective and useful. Unhappily, the appeal was still to ecclesiastics, to a body of men who were characterised throughout Europe by a universal absence of integrity, who were incapable of pronouncing an honest judgment, and who courted intimidation and bribery by the readiness with which they submitted to be influenced by them. Corruption was resorted to on all sides with the most lavish unscrupulousness, and the result arrived at was general discredit to all parties, and a conclusion which added but one more circle to the labyrinth of perplexities. Croke, 264 a Doctors' Commons lawyer, who was employed in Italy, described the state of feeling in the peninsula as generally in Henry's favour; and he said that he could have secured an all but universal consent, except for the secret intrigues of the Spanish agents, and their open direct menaces, when intrigue was insufficient. He complained bitterly of the treachery of the Italians who were in the English pay; the two Cassalis, Pallavicino, and Ghinucci, the Bishop of Worcester. These men, he said, were betraying Henry when they were pretending to serve him, and were playing secretly into the hands of the emperor. 265 His private despatches were intercepted, or the contents of them by some means were discovered; for the persons whom he named as inclining against the papal claims, became marked at once for persecution. One of them, a Carmelite friar, was summoned before the Cardinal Governor of Bologna, and threatened with death; 266 and a certain Father Omnibow, a Venetian who had been in active co-operation with Dr. Croke, wrote himself to Henry, informing him in a very graphic manner of the treatment to which, by some treachery, he had been exposed. Croke and Omnibow were sitting one morning in the latter's cell, "when there entered upon them the emperor's great ambassador, accompanied with many gentlemen of Spain, and demanded of the Father how he durst be so bold to take upon him to intermeddle in so great and weighty a matter, the which did not only lessen and enervate the pope's authority, but was noyful and odious to all Realms Christened." 267 Omnibow being a man of some influence in Venice, the ambassador warned him on peril of his life to deal no further with such things: there was not the slightest chance that the King of England could obtain a decision in his favour, because the question had been placed in the hands of six cardinals who were all devoted to the emperor: the pope, it was sternly added, had been made aware of his conduct, and was exceedingly displeased, and the general 268 of his order had at the same time issued an injunction, warning all members to desist at their peril from intercourse with the English agents. The Spanish party held themselves justified in resorting to intimidation to defend themselves against English money; the English may have excused their use of money as a defence against Spanish intimidation; and each probably had recourse to their several methods prior to experience of the proceedings of their adversaries, from a certain expectation of what those proceedings would be. Substantially, the opposite manœuvres neutralised each other, and in Catholic countries, opinions on the real point at issue seem to have been equally balanced. The Lutheran divines, from their old suspicion of Henry, were more decided in their opposition to him. "The Italian Protestants," wrote Croke to the king, "be utterly against your Highness in this cause, and have letted as much as with their power and malice they could or might." 269 In Germany Dr. Bames and Cranmer found the same experience. Luther himself had not forgotten his early passage at arms with the English Defender of the Faith, and was coldly hostile; the German theologians, although they expressed themselves with reserve and caution, saw no reason to court the anger of Charles by meddling in a quarrel in which they had no interest; they revenged the studied slight which had been passed by Henry on themselves, with a pardonable indifference to the English ecclesiastical revolt.

If, however, in Germany and Italy the balance of unjust interference lay on the imperial side, it was more than adequately compensated by the answering pressure which was brought to bear in England and in France on the opposite side. Under the allied sovereigns, the royal authority was openly exercised to compel such expressions of sentiment as the courts of London and Paris desired; and the measures which were taken oblige us more than ever to regret the inventive efforts of Cranmer's genius. For, in fact, these manœuvres, even if honestly executed, were all unrealities. The question at issue was one of domestic English politics, and the metamorphosis of it into a question of ecclesiastical law was a mere delusion. The discussion was transferred to a false ground, and however the king may have chosen to deceive himself, was not being tried upon its real merits. A complicated difficulty vitally affecting the interests of a great nation, was laid for solution before a body of persons incompetent to understand or decide it, and the laity, with the alternative before them of civil war, and the returning miseries of the preceding century, could brook no judgment which did not answer to their wishes.

The French king, contemptuously indifferent to justice, submitted to be guided by his interest; feeling it necessary for his safety to fan the quarrel between Henry and the emperor, he resolved to encourage whatever measures would make the breach between them irreparable. The reconciliation of Herod and Pontius Pilate 270 was the subject of his worst alarm; and a slight exercise of ecclesiastical tyranny was but a moderate price by which to ensure himself against so dangerous a possibility.

Accordingly, at the beginning of June, the University of Paris was instructed by royal letters to pronounce an opinion on the extent to which the pope might grant dispensations for marriage within the forbidden degrees. The letters were presented by the grand master, and the latter in his address to the faculty, maintained at the outset an appearance of impartiality. The doctors were required to decide according to their conscience, having the fear of God before their eyes; and no open effort was ventured to dictate the judgment which was to be delivered.

The majority of the doctors understood their duty and their position, and a speedy resolution was anticipated, when a certain Dr. Beda, an energetic Ultramontane, commenced an opposition. He said that, on a question which touched the power of the pope, they were not at liberty to pronounce an opinion without the permission of his Holiness himself; and that the deliberation ought not to go forward till they had applied for that permission and had received it. This view was supported by the Spanish and Italian party in the university. The debate grew warm, and at length the meeting broke up in confusion without coming to a resolution. Beda, when remonstrated with on the course which he was pursuing, did not hesitate to say that he had the secret approbation of his prince; that, however Francis might disguise from the world his real opinions, in his heart he only desired to see the pope victorious. An assertion so confident was readily believed, nor is it likely that Beda ventured to make it without some foundation. But being spoken of openly it became a matter of general conversation, and reaching the ears of the English ambassador, it was met with instant and angry remonstrance. "The ambassador," wrote the grand master to Francis, "has been to me in great displeasure, and has told me roundly that his master is trifled with by us. We give him words in plenty to keep his beak in the water; but it is very plain that we are playing false, and that no honesty is intended. Nor are his words altogether without reason; for many persons declare openly that nothing will be done. If the alliance of England, therefore, appear of importance to your Highness, it would be well for you to write to the Dean of the Faculty, directing him to close an impertinent discussion, and require an answer to the question asked as quickly as possible." 271 The tone of this letter proves, with sufficient clearness, the true feelings of the French government; but at the moment the alternative suggested by the grand master might not be ventured. Francis could not afford to quarrel with England, or to be on less than cordial terms with it, and for a time at least his brother sovereigns must continue to be at enmity. The negotiations for the recovery of the French princes out of their Spanish prison, were on the point of conclusion; and, as Francis was insolvent, Henry had consented to become security for the money demanded for their deliverance. Beda had, moreover, injured his cause by attacking the Gallican liberties; and as this was a point on which the government was naturally sensitive, some tolerable excuse was furnished for the lesson which it was thought proper to adminster to the offending doctor.

On the seventeenth of June, 1530, therefore, Francis wrote as follows to the President of the Parliament of Paris:—

"We have learnt, to our great displeasure, that one Beda, an imperialist, has dared to raise an agitation among the theologians, dissuading them from giving their voices on the cause of the King of England.—On receipt of this letter, therefore, you shall cause the said Beda to appear before you, and you shall show him the grievous anger which he has given us cause to entertain towards him. And further you shall declare to him, laying these our present writings before his eyes that he may not doubt the truth of what you say, that if he does not instantly repair the fault which he has committed, he shall be punished in such sort as that he shall remember henceforth what it is for a person of his quality to meddle in the affairs of princes. If he venture to remonstrate; if he allege that it is matter of conscience, and that before proceeding to pronounce an opinion it is necessary to communicate with the pope; in our name you shall forbid him to hold any such communication: and he and all who abet him, and all persons whatsoever, not only who shall themselves dare to consult the pope on this matter, but who shall so much as entertain the proposal of consulting him, shall be dealt with in such a manner as shall be an example to all the world. The liberties of the Gallican Church are touched, and the independence of our theological council, and there is no privilege belonging to this realm on which we are more peremptorily determined to insist." 272

The haughty missive, a copy of which was sent to England, 273 produced the desired effect. The doctors became obedient and convinced, and the required declaration of opinion in Henry's favour, was drawn up in the most ample manner. They made a last desperate effort to escape from the position in which they were placed when the seal of the university was to be affixed to the decision; but the resistance was hopeless, the authorities were inexorable, and they submitted. It is not a little singular that the English political agent employed on this occasion, and to whose lot it fell to communicate the result to the king, was Reginald Pole. He it was, who behind the scenes, and assisting to work the machinery of the intrigue, first there, perhaps, contracted his disgust with the cause on which he was embarked. There learning to hate the ill with which he was forced immediately into contact, he lost sight of the greater ill to which it was opposed; and in the recoil commenced the first steps of a career, which brought his mother to the scaffold, which overspread all England with an atmosphere of treason and suspicion, and which terminated at last after years of exile, rebellion, and falsehood, in a brief victory of blood and shame. So ever does wrong action beget its own retribution, punishing itself by itself, and wrecking the instruments by which it works. The letter which Pole wrote from Paris to Henry will not be uninteresting. It revealed his distaste for his occupation, though prudence held him silent as to his deeper feelings.

"Please it your Highness to be advertised, that the determination and conclusion of the divines in this university was achieved and finished according to your desired purpose, upon Saturday last past. The sealing of the same has been put off unto this day, nor never could be obtained before for any soliciting on our parts which were your agents here, which never ceased to labour, all that lay in us, for the expedition of it, both with the privy president and with all such as we thought might in any part aid us therein. But what difficulties and stops hath been, to let the obtaining of the seal of the university, notwithstanding the conclusion passed and agreed unto by the more part of the faculty, by reason of such oppositions as the adversary part hath made to embezzle the determination that it should not take effect nor go forth in that same form as it was concluded, it may please your Grace, to be advertised by this bearer, Master Fox; who, with his prudence, diligence, and great exercise in the cause, hath most holp to resist all these crafts, and to bring the matter to that point as your most desired purpose hath been to have it. He hath indeed acted according to that hope which I had of him at the beginning and first breaking of the matter amongst the faculty here, when I, somewhat fearing and foreseeing such contentions, altercations, and empeschements as by most likelihood might ensue, did give your Grace advertisement, how necessary I thought it was to have Master Fox's presence. And whereas I was informed by Master Fox how it standeth with your Grace's pleasure, considering my fervent desire thereon, that, your motion once achieved and brought to a final conclusion in this university, I should repair to your presence, your Grace could not grant me at this time a petition more comfortable unto me. And so, making what convenient speed I may, my trust is shortly to wait upon your Highness. Thus Jesu preserve your most noble Grace to his pleasure, and your most comfort and honour. Written at Paris, the seventh day of July, by your Grace's most humble and faithful servant, REGINALD POLE." 274

We must speak of this transaction as it deserves, and call it wholly bad, unjust, and inexcusable. Yet we need not deceive ourselves into supposing that the opposition which was crushed so roughly was based on any principal of real honesty. In Italy, intrigue was used against intimidation. In France intimidation was used against intrigue; and the absence of rectitude in the parties whom it was necessary to influence, provoked and justified the contempt with which they were treated.

The conduct of the English universities on the same occasion was precisely what their later characters would have led us respectively to expect from them. At Oxford the heads of houses and the senior doctors and masters submitted their consciences to state dictation, without opposition, and, as it seemed, without reluctance. Henry was wholly satisfied that the right was on his own side; he was so convinced of it, that an opposition to his wishes among his own subjects, he could attribute only to disloyalty or to some other unworthy feeling; and therefore, while he directed the convocation, "giving no credence to sinister persuasions, to show and declare their just and true learning in his cause," he was able to dwell upon the answer which he expected from them, as a plain matter of duty; and obviously as not admitting of any uncertainty whatever.

"We will and command you," he said, "that ye, not leaning to wilful and sinister opinions of your own several minds, considering that we be your sovereign liege lord [and] totally giving your time, mind, and affections to the true overtures of divine learning in this behalf, do show and declare your true and just learning in the said cause, like as ye will abide by: wherein ye shall not only please Almighty God, but also us your liege lord. And we, for your so doing, shall be to you and to our university there so good and gracious a lord for the same, as ye shall perceive it well done in your well fortune to come. And in case you do not uprightly, according to divine learning, handle yourselves herein, ye may be assured that we, not without great cause, shall so quickly and sharply look to your unnatural misdemeanour herein, that it shall not be to your quietness and ease hereafter." 275 The admonitory clauses were sufficiently clear; they were scarcely needed, however, by the older members of the university. An enlarged experience of the world which years, at Oxford as well as elsewhere, had not failed to bring with them, a just apprehension of the condition of the kingdom, and a sense of the obligations of subjects in times of political difficulty, sufficed to reconcile the heads of the colleges to obedience; and threats were not required where it is unlikely that a thought of hesitation was entertained. But there was a class of residents which appears to be perennial in that university, composed out of the younger masters; a class of men who, defective alike in age, in wisdom, or in knowledge, were distinguished by a species of theoretic High Church fanaticism; who, until they received their natural correction from advancing years, required from time to time to be protected against their own extravagance by some form of external pressure. These were the persons whom the king was addressing in his more severe language, and it was not without reason that he had recourse to it.

In order to avoid difficulty, and to secure a swift and convenient resolution, it was proposed that both at Oxford and Cambridge the universities should be represented by a committee composed of the heads of houses, the proctors, and the graduates in divinity and law: that this committee should agree upon a form of a reply; and that the university seal should then be affixed without further discussion. This proposition was plausible as well as prudent, for it might be supposed reasonably that young half-educated students were incapable of forming a judgment on an intricate point of law; and to admit their votes was equivalent to allowing judgment to be given by party feeling. The masters who were to be thus excluded refused however to entertain this view of their incapacity. The question whether the committee should be appointed was referred to convocation, where, having the advantage of numbers, they coerced the entire proceedings; and some of them "expressing themselves in a very forward manner" to the royal commissioners, 276 and the heads of houses being embarrassed, and not well knowing what to do, the king found it necessary again to interpose. He was unwilling, as he said, to violate the constitution of the university by open interference, "considering it to exist under grant and charter from the crown as a body politic, in the ruling whereof in things to be done in the name of the whole, the number of private suffrages doth prevail." "He was loth, too," he added, "to show his displeasure, whereof he had so great cause ministered unto him, unto the whole in general, whereas the fault perchance consisted and remained in light and wilful heads," and he trusted that it might suffice if the masters of the colleges used their private influence and authority 277 in overcoming the opposition. For the effecting of this purpose, however, and in order to lend weight to their persuasion, he assisted the convocation towards a conclusion with the following characteristic missive:—

"To our trusty and well-beloved the heads of houses, doctors, and proctors of our University of Oxford:

"Trusty and well-beloved, we greet you well; and of late being informed, to our no little marvel and discontentation, that a great part of the youth of that our university, with contentious and factious manner daily combining together, neither regarding their duty to us their sovereign lord, nor yet conforming themselves to the opinions and orders of the virtuous, wise, sage, and profound learned men of that university, wilfully do stick upon the opinion to have a great number of regents and non-regents to be associate unto the doctors, proctors, and bachelors of divinity for the determination of our question; which we believe hath not been often seen, that such a number of right small learning in regard to the other should be joined with so famous a sort, or in a manner stay their seniors in so weighty a cause. And forasmuch as this, we think, should be no small dishonour to our university there, but most especially to you the seniors and rulers of the same; and as also, we assure you, this their unnatural and unkind demeanour is not only right much to our displeasure, but much to be marvelled of, upon what ground and occasion, they being our mere subjects, should show themselves more unkind and wilful in this matter than all other universities, both in this and all other regions do: we, trusting in the dexterity and wisdom of you and other the said discreet and substantial learned men of that university, be in perfect hope that ye will conduce and frame the said young persons unto order and conformity as it becometh you to do. Whereof we be desirous to hear with incontinent diligence; and doubt you not we shall regard the demeanour of every one of the university according to their merits and deserts. And if the youth of the university will play masteries as they begin to do, we doubt not but they shall well perceive that non est bonum irritare crabrones. 278

"Given under our hand and seal, at our Castle of Windsor,

"HENRY R." 279

It is scarcely necessary to say, that, armed with this letter, the heads of houses subdued the recalcitrance of the overhasty "youth;" and Oxford duly answered as she was required to answer.

The proceedings at Cambridge were not very dissimilar; but Cambridge being distinguished by greater openness and largeness of mind on this as on the other momentous subjects of the day than the sister university, was able to preserve a more manly bearing, and escape direct humiliation. Cranmer had written a book upon the divorce in the preceding year, which, as coming from a well-known Cambridge man, had occasioned a careful ventilation of the question there; the resident masters had been divided by it into factions nearly equal in number, though unharmoniously composed. The heads of houses, as at Oxford, were inclined to the king, but they were embarrassed and divided by the presence on the same side of the suspected liberals, the party of Shaxton, Latimer, and Cranmer himself. The agitation of many months had rendered all members of the university, young and old, so well acquainted (as they supposed) with the bearings of the difficulty, that they naturally resisted, as at the other university, the demand that their power should be delegated to a committee; and the Cambridge convocation, as well as that of Oxford, threw out this resolution when it was first proposed to them. A king's letter having made them more amenable, a list of the intended committee was drawn out, which, containing Latimer's name, occasioned a fresh storm. But the number in the senate house being nearly divided, "the labour of certain friends" turned the scale; the vote passed, and the committee was allowed, on condition that the question should be argued publicly in the presence of the whole university. Finally, judgment was obtained on the king's side, though in a less absolute form than he had required, and the commissioners did not think it prudent to press for a more extreme conclusion. They had been desired to pronounce that the pope had no power to permit a man to marry his brother's widow. They consented only to say that a marriage within those degrees was contrary to the divine law; but the question of the pope's power was left unapproached. 280

It will not be uninteresting to follow this judgment a further step, to the delivery of it into the hands of the king, where it will introduce us to a Sunday at Windsor Castle three centuries ago. We shall find present there, as a significant symptom of the time, Hugh Latimer, appointed freshly select preacher in the royal chapel, but already obnoxious to English orthodoxy, on account of his Cambridge sermons. These sermons, it had been said, contained many things good and profitable, "on sin, and godliness, and virtue," but much also which was disrespectful to established beliefs, the preacher being clearly opposed to "candles and pilgrimages," and "calling men unto the works that God commanded in his Holy Scripture, all dreams and unprofitable glosses set aside and utterly despised." The preacher had, therefore, been cited before consistory courts and interdicted by bishops, "swarms of friars and doctors flocking against Master Latimer on every side." 281 This also was to be noted about him, that he was one of the most fearless men who ever lived. Like John Knox, whom he much resembled, in whatever presence he might be, whether of poor or rich, of laymen or priests, of bishops or kings, he ever spoke out boldly from his pulpit what he thought, directly if necessary to particular persons whom he saw before him respecting their own actions. Even Henry himself he did not spare where he saw occasion for blame; and Henry, of whom it was said that he never was mistaken in a *man*—loving a *man* 282 where he could find him with all his heart—had, notwithstanding, chosen this Latimer as one of his own chaplains.

The unwilling bearer of the Cambridge judgment was Dr. Buckmaster, the vice-chancellor, who, in a letter to a friend, describes his reception at the royal castle.

"To the right worshipful Dr. Edmonds, vicar of Alborne, in Wiltshire, my duty remembered,—

"I heartily commend me unto you, and I let you understand that yesterday week, being Sunday at afternoon, I came to Windsor, and also to part of Mr. Latimer's sermon; and after the end of the same I spake with Mr. Secretary [Cromwell], and also with Mr. Provost; and so after evensong I delivered our letters in the Chamber of Presence, all the court beholding. The king, with Mr. Secretary, did there read them; and did then give me thanks and talked with me a good while. He much lauded our wisdom and good conveyance in the matter, with the great quietness in the same. He showed me also what he had in his hands for our university, according to that which Mr. Secretary did express unto us, and so he departed from me. But by and bye he greatly praised Mr. Latimer's sermon; and in so praising said on this wise: 'This displeaseth greatly Mr. Vice-Chancellor yonder; yon same,' said he to the Duke of Norfolk, 'is Mr. Vice-Chancellor of Cambridge,' and so pointed unto me. Then he spake secretly unto the said duke, which, after the king's departure, came unto me and welcomed me, saying, among other things, the king would speak with me on the next day. And here is the first act. On the next day I waited until it was dinner time; and so at the last Dr. Butts, [king's physician,] came unto me, and brought a reward, twenty nobles for me, and five marks for the junior proctor which was with me, saying that I should take that for a resolute answer, and that I might depart from the court when I would. Then came Mr. Provost, and when I had shewed him of the answer, he said I should speak with the king after dinner for all that, and so he brought me into a privy place where after dinner he would have me wait. I came thither and he both; and by one of the clock the king entered in. It was in a gallery. There were Mr. Secretary, Mr. Provost, Mr. Latimer, Mr. Proctor, and I, and no more. The king then talked with us until six of the clock. I assure you he was scarce contented with Mr. Secretary and Mr. Provost, that this was not also determined, *an Papa possit dispensare*. I made the best, and confirmed the same that they had shewed his Grace before; and how it would never have been so obtained. He opened his mind, saying he would have it determined after Easter, and of the same was counselled awhile.

"Much other communication we had, which were too long here to recite. Then his Highness departed, casting a little holy water of the court; and I shortly after took my leave of Mr. Secretary and Mr. Provost, with whom I did not drink, nor yet was bidden, and on the morrow departed from thence, thinking more than I did say, and being glad that I was out of the court, where many men, as I did both hear and perceive, did wonder at me. And here shall be an end for this time of this fable.

"All the world almost crieth out of Cambridge for this act, and specially on me; but I must bear it as well as I may. I have lost a benefice by it, which I should have had within these ten days; for there hath one fallen in Mr. Throgmorton's 283 gift which he hath faithfully promised unto me many a time, but now his mind is turned and alienate from me. If ye go to court after Easter I pray you have me in remembrance. Mr. Latimer preacheth still,—quod æmuli ejus graviter ferunt.

"Thus fare you well. Your own to his power,
WILLIAM BUCKMASTER. 284
Cambridge, Monday after Easter, 1530."

It does not appear that Cambridge was pressed further, and we may, therefore, allow it to have acquitted itself creditably, If we sum up the results of Cranmer's measure as a whole, it may be said that opinions had been given by about half Europe directly or indirectly unfavourable to the papal claims; and that, therefore, the king had furnished himself with a legal pretext for declining the jurisdiction of the court of Rome, and appealing to a general council. Objections to the manner in which the opinions had been gained could be answered by recriminations equally just; and in the technical aspect of the question a step had certainly been gained. It will be thought, nevertheless, on wider grounds, that the measure was a mistake; that it would have been far better if the legal labyrinth had never been entered, and if the divorce had been claimed only upon those considerations of policy for which it had been first demanded, and which formed the true justification of it. Not only might a shameful chapter of scandal have been spared out of the world's history, but the point on which the battle was being fought lay beside the real issue. Europe was shaken with intrigue, hundreds of books were written, and tens of thousands of tongues were busy for twelve months weaving logical subtleties, and all for nothing. The truth was left unspoken because it was not convenient to speak it, and all parties agreed to persuade themselves and accept one another's persuasions, that they meant something which they did not mean. Beyond doubt the theological difficulty really affected the king. We cannot read his own book 285 upon it without a conviction that his arguments were honestly urged, that his misgivings were real, and that he meant every word which he said. Yet it is clear at the same time that these misgivings would not have been satisfied, if all the wisdom of the world—pope, cardinals, councils, and all the learned faculties together—had declared against him, the true secret of the matter lying deeper, understood and appreciated by all the chief parties concerned, and by the English laity, whose interests were at stake; but in all these barren disputings ignored as if it had no existence.

It was perhaps less easy than it seems to have followed the main road. The bye ways often promise best at first entrance into them, and Henry's peculiar temper never allowed him to believe beforehand that a track which he had chosen could lead to any conclusion except that to which he had arranged that it should lead. With an intellect endlessly fertile in finding reasons to justify what he desired, he could see no justice on any side but his own, or understand that it was possible to disagree with him except from folly of ill-feeling. Starting always with a foregone conclusion, he arrived of course where he wished to arrive. His "Glasse of Truth" is a very picture of his mind. "If the marshall of the host bids us do anything," he said, "shall we do it if it be against the great captain? Again, if the great captain bid us do anything, and the king or the emperor commandeth us to do another, dost thou doubt that we must obey the commandment of the king or emperor, and contemn the commandment of the great captain? Therefore if the king or the emperor bid one thing, and God another, we must obey God, and contemn and not regard neither king nor emperor." And, therefore, he argued, "we are not to obey the pope, when the pope commands what is unlawful." 286 These were but many words to prove what the pope would not have questioned; and either they concluded nothing or the conclusion was assumed.

We cannot but think that among the many misfortunes of Henry's life his theological training was the greatest; and that directly or indirectly it was the parent of all the rest. If in this unhappy business he had trusted only to his instincts as an English statesman; if he had been contented himself with the truth, and had pressed no arguments except those which in the secrets of his heart had weight with him, he would have spared his own memory a mountain of undeserved reproach, and have spared historians their weary labour through these barren deserts of unreality.

CHAPTER IV.
CHURCH AND STATE

The authorities of the church, after the lesson which they had received from the parliament in its first session, were now allowed a respite of two years, during which they might reconsider the complaints of the people, and consult among themselves upon the conduct which they would pursue with respect to those complaints. They availed themselves of their interval of repose in a manner little calculated to recover the esteem which they had forfeited, or to induce the legislature further to stay their hand. Instead of reforming their own faults, they spent the time in making use of their yet uncurtailed powers of persecution; and they wreaked the bitterness of their resentment upon the unfortunate heretics, who paid with their blood at the stake for the diminished revenues and blighted dignities of their spiritual lords and superiors. During the later years of Wolsey's administration, the Protestants, though threatened and imprisoned, had escaped the most cruel consequences of their faith. Wolsey had been a warm-hearted and genuine man, and although he had believed as earnestly as his brother bishops, that Protestantism was a pernicious thing, destructive alike to the institutions of the country and to the souls of mankind, his memory can be reproached with nothing worse than assiduous but humane efforts for the repression of it. In the three years which followed his dismissal, a far more bloody page was written in the history of the reformers; and under the combined auspices of Sir Thomas More's fanaticism, and the spleen of the angry clergy, the stake re-commenced its hateful activity. This portion of my subject requires a full and detailed treatment; I reserve the account of it, therefore, for a separate chapter, and proceed for the present with the progress of the secular changes.

Although, as I said, no further legislative measures were immediately contemplated against the clergy, yet they were not permitted to forget the alteration in their position which had followed upon Wolsey's fall; and as they had shown in the unfortunate document which they had submitted to the king, so great a difficulty in comprehending the nature of that alteration, it was necessary clearly and distinctly to enforce it upon them. Until that moment they had virtually held the supreme power in the state.

The nobility, crippled by the wars of the Roses, had sunk into the second place; the Commons were disorganised, or incapable of a definite policy; and the chief offices of the government had fallen as a matter of course to the only persons who for the moment were competent to hold them. The jealousy of ecclesiastical encroachments, which had shown itself so bitterly under the Plantagenets, had been superseded from the accession of Henry VII. by a policy of studied conciliation, and the position of Wolsey had but symbolised the position of his order. But Wolsey was now gone, and the ecclesiastics who had shared his greatness while they envied it, were compelled to participate also in his change of fortune.

This great minister, after the failure of a discreditable effort to fasten upon him a charge of high treason,—a charge which, vindictively pressed through the House of Lords, was wisely rejected by the Commons,—had been prosecuted with greater justice for a breach of the law, in having exercised the authority of papal legate within the realm of England. His policy had broken down: he had united against him in a common exasperation all orders in the state, secular and spiritual; and the possible consequences of his adventurous transgression had fallen upon him. The parliaments of Edward I., Edward III., Richard II., and Henry IV. had by a series of statutes pronounced illegal all presentations by the pope to any office or dignity in the Anglican church, under penalty of a premunire; the provisions of these acts extending not only to the persons themselves who accepted office under such conditions, but comprehending equally whoever acknowledged their authority, "their executors, procurators, fautors, maintainers, and receivers." 287 The importance attached to these laws was to be seen readily in the frequent re-enactment of them, with language of increasing vehemence; and although the primary object was to neutralise the supposed right of the pope to present to English benefices, and although the office of papal legate is not especially named in any one of the prohibitory clauses, yet so acute a canonist as Wolsey could not have been ignorant that it was comprehended under the general denunciation. The 5th of the 16th of Richard II. was in fact explicitly universal in its language, and dwelt especially on the importance of prohibiting the exercise of any species of jurisdiction which could encroach on the royal authority. He had therefore consciously violated a law on his own responsibility, which he knew to exist, but which he perhaps trusted had fallen into desuetude, and would not again be revived. It cannot be denied that in doing so, being at the time the highest law officer of the crown, he had committed a grave offence, and was justly liable to the full penalties of the broken statute. He had received the royal permission, but it was a plea which could not have availed him, and he did not attempt to urge it. 288 The contingency of a possible violation of the law by the king himself had been expressly foreseen and provided against in the act under which he was prosecuted, 289 and being himself the king's legal adviser, it was his duty to have kept his sovereign 290 informed of the true nature of the statute. He had neglected this, his immediate obligation, in pursuit of the interests of the church, and when Henry's eyes were opened, he did not consider himself called upon to interfere to shield his minister from the penalties which he had incurred, nor is it likely that in the face of the irritation of the country he could have done so if he had desired. It was felt, indeed, that the long services of Wolsey, and his generally admirable administration, might fairly save him (especially under the circumstances of the case) from extremity of punishment; and if he had been allowed to remain unmolested in the affluent retirement which was at first conceded to him, his treatment would not have caused the stain which we have now to lament on the conduct of the administration which succeeded his fall. He indeed himself believed that the final attack upon him was due to no influence of rival statesmen, but to the hatred of Anne Boleyn; and perhaps he was not mistaken. This, however, is a matter which does not concern us here, and I need not pursue it. It is enough that he had violated the law of England, openly and knowingly, and on the revival of the national policy by which that law had been enacted, he reaped the consequences in his own person.

It will be a question whether we can equally approve of the enlarged application of the statute which immediately followed. The guilt of Wolsey did not rest with himself; it extended to all who had recognised him in his capacity of legate; to the archbishops and bishops, to the two Houses of Convocation, to the Privy Council, to the Lords and Commons, and indirectly to the nation itself. It was obvious that such a state of things was not contemplated by the act under which he was tried, and where in point of law all persons were equally guilty, in equity they were equally innocent; the circumstances of the case, therefore, rendered necessary a general pardon, which was immediately drawn out. The government, however, while granting absolution to the nation, determined to make some exceptions in their lenity; and harsh as their resolution appeared, it is not difficult to conjecture the reasons which induced them to form it. The higher clergy had been encouraged by Wolsey's position to commit those excessive acts of despotism which had created so deep animosity among the people. The overthrow of the last ecclesiastical minister was an opportunity to teach them that the privileges which they had abused were at an end; and as the lesson was so difficult for them to learn, the letter of the law which they had broken was put in force to quicken their perceptions. They were to be punished indirectly for their other evil doings, and forced to surrender some portion of the unnumbered exactions which they had extorted from the helplessness of their flocks.

In pursuance of this resolution, therefore, official notice was issued in December, 1530, that the clergy lay all under a premunire, and that the crown intended to prosecute. Convocation was to meet in the middle of January, and this comforting fact was communicated to the bishops in order to divert their attention to subjects which might profitably occupy their deliberations. The church legislature had sate in the preceding years contemporaneously with the sitting of parliament, at the time when their privileges were being discussed, and when their conduct had been so angrily challenged: but these matters had not disturbed their placid equanimity: and while the bishops were composing their answer to the House of Commons, Convocation had been engaged in debating the most promising means of persecuting heretics and preventing the circulation of the Bible. 291 The session had continued into the spring of 1529-30, when the king had been prevailed upon to grant an order in council prohibiting Tyndale's Testament, in the preface of which the clergy were spoken of disrespectfully. 292 His consent had been obtained with great difficulty, on the representation of the bishops that the translation was faulty, and on their undertaking themselves to supply the place of it with a corrected version. But in obtaining the order, they supposed themselves to have gained a victory; and their triumph was celebrated in St. Paul's churchyard with an auto da fé, over which the Bishop of London consented to preside; when such New Testaments as the diligence of the apparitors could discover, were solemnly burned.

From occupation such as this a not unwholesome distraction was furnished by the intimation of the premunire; and that it might produce its due effect, it was accompanied with the further information that the clergy of the province of Canterbury would receive their pardon only upon payment of a hundred thousand pounds—a very considerable fine, amounting to more than a million of our money. Eighteen thousand pounds was required simultaneously from the province of York; and the whole sum was to be paid in instalments spread over a period of five years. 293 The demand was serious, but the clergy had no alternative but to submit or to risk the chances of the law; and feeling that, with the people so unfavourably disposed towards them, they had no chance of a more equitable construction of their position, they consented with a tolerable grace, the Upper House of Convocation first, the Lower following. Their debates upon the subject have not been preserved. It was probably difficult to persuade them that they were treated with anything but the most exquisite injustice; since Wolsey's legatine faculties had been the object of their general dread; and if he had remained in power, the religious orders would have been exposed to a searching visitation in virtue of these faculties, from which they could have promised themselves but little advantage. But their punishment, if tyrannical in form, was equitable in substance, and we can reconcile ourselves without difficulty to an act of judicial confiscation.

The money, however, was not the only concession which the threat of the premunire gave opportunity to extort; and it is creditable to the clergy that the demand which they showed most desire to resist was not that which most touched their personal interests. In the preamble of the subsidy bill, under which they were to levy their ransom, they were required by the council to designate the king by the famous title which gave occasion for such momentous consequences, of "Protector and only Supreme Head of the Church and Clergy of England." 294 It is not very easy to see what Henry proposed to himself by requiring this designation, at so early a stage in the movement. The breach with the pope was still distant, and he was prepared to make many sacrifices before he would even seriously contemplate a step which he so little desired. It may have been designed as a reply to the papal censures: it may have been to give effect to his own menaces, which Clement to the last believed to be no more than words; 295 or perhaps (and this is the most likely) he desired by some emphatic act, to make his clergy understand the relation in which thenceforward they were to be placed towards the temporal authority. It is certain only that this title was not intended to imply what it implied when, four years later, it was conferred by act Of parliament, and when virtually England was severed by it from the Roman communion.

But whatever may have been the king's motive, he was serious in requiring that the title should be granted to him. Only by acknowledging Henry as Head of the Church should the clergy receive their pardon, and the longer they hesitated, the more peremptorily he insisted on their obedience. The clergy had defied the lion, and the lion held them in his grasp; and they could but struggle helplessly, supplicate and submit. Archbishop Warham, just drawing his life to a close, presided for the last time in the miserable scene, imagining that the clouds were gathering for the storms of the latter day, and that Antichrist was coming in his power.

There had been a debate of three days, whether they should or should not consent, when, on the 9th of February, a deputation of the judges appeared in Convocation, to ask whether the Houses were agreed, and to inform them finally that the king had determined to allow no qualifications. The clergy begged for one more day, and the following morning the bishops held a private meeting among themselves, to discuss some plan to turn aside the blow. They desired to see Cromwell, to learn, perhaps, if there was a chance of melting the hard heart of Henry; and after an interview with the minister which could not have been encouraging, they sent two of their number, the Bishops of Exeter and Lincoln, to attempt the unpromising task. It was in vain; the miserable old men were obliged to return with the answer that the king would not see them—they had seen only the judges, who had assured them, in simple language, that the pardon was not to be settled until the supremacy was admitted. The answer was communicated to the House, and again "debated." Submission was against the consciences of the unhappy clergy; to obey their consciences involved forfeiture of property; and naturally in such a dilemma they found resolution difficult. They attempted another appeal, suggesting that eight of their number should hold a conference with the privy council, and "discover, if they might, some possible expedient." But Henry replied, as before, that he would have a clear answer, "*yes*, or *no*." They might say "yes," and their pardon was ready. They might say "no"—and accept the premunire and its penalties. And now, what should the clergy have done? No very great courage was required to answer, "This thing is wrong; it is against God's will, and therefore it must not be, whether premunire come or do not come." They might have said it, and if they could have dared this little act of courage, victory was in their hands. With the cause against them so doubtful, their very attitude would have commanded back the sympathies of half the nation, and the king's threats would have exploded as an empty sound. But Henry knew the persons with whom he had to deal—forlorn shadows, decked in the trappings of dignity—who only by some such rough method could be brought to a knowledge of themselves. "Shrink to the clergy"—I find in a state paper of the time—"Shrink to the clergy, and they be lions; lay their faults roundly and charitably to them, and they be as sheep, and will lightly be reformed, for their consciences will not suffer them to resist." 296

They hesitated for another night. The day following, the archbishop submitted the clause containing the title to the Upper House, with a saving paragraph, which, as Burnet sententiously observes, the nature of things did require to be supposed. 297 "Ecclesiæ et cleri Anglicani," so it ran, "singularem protectorem, et unicum et supremum Dominum, et quantum per legem Christi licet, etiam supremum caput ipsius Majestatem agnoscimus—We recognise the King's Majesty to be our only sovereign lord, the singular protector of the church and clergy of England, and as far as is allowed by the law of Christ, also as our Supreme Head." The words were read aloud by the archbishop, and were received in silence. "Do you assent?" he asked. The House remained speechless. "Whoever is silent seems to consent," the archbishop said. A voice answered out of the crowd, "Then are we all silent." They separated for a few hours to collect themselves. In the afternoon sitting they discussed the sufficiency of the subterfuge; and at length agreeing that it saved their consciences, the clause was finally passed, the Bishop of Rochester, among the rest, giving his unwilling acquiescence.

So for the present terminated this grave matter. The pardon was immediately submitted to parliament, where it was embodied in a statute; 298 and this act of dubious justice accomplished, the Convocation was allowed to return to its usual occupations, and continue the prosecutions of the heretics.

The House of Commons, during their second session, had confined themselves meanwhile to secular business. They had been concerned chiefly with regulations affecting trade and labour; and the proceedings on the premunire being thought for the time to press sufficiently on the clergy, they deferred the further prosecution of their own complaints till the following year. Two measures, however, highly characteristic of the age, must not be passed over, one of which concerned a matter that must have added heavily to the troubles of the Bishop of Rochester at a time when he was in no need of any addition to his burdens.

Fisher was the only one among the prelates for whom it is possible to feel respect. He was weak, superstitious, pedantical; towards the Protestants he was even cruel; but he was a singlehearted man, who lived in honest fear of evil, so far as he understood what evil was; and he alone could rise above the menaces of worldly suffering, under which his brethren on the bench sank so rapidly into meekness and submission. We can therefore afford to compassionate him in the unexpected calamity by which he was overtaken, and which must have tried his failing spirit in no common manner.

He lived, while his duties required his presence in London, at a house in Lambeth, and being a hospitable person, he opened his doors at the dinner hour for the poor of the neighbourhood. Shortly after the matter which I have just related, many of these people who were dependent on his bounty were reported to have become alarmingly ill, and several gentlemen of the household sickened also in the same sudden and startling manner. One of these gentlemen died, and a poor woman also died; and it was discovered on inquiry that the yeast which had been used in various dishes had been poisoned. The guilty person was the cook, a certain Richard Rouse; and inasmuch as all crimes might be presumed to have had motives, and the motive in the present instance was undiscoverable, it was conjectured by Queen Catherine's friends that he had been bribed by Anne Boleyn, or by some one of her party, to remove out of the way the most influential of the English opponents of the divorce. 299 The story was possibly without foundation, although it is not unlikely that Fisher himself believed it.

The shock of such an occurrence may well have unsettled his powers of reasoning, and at all times he was a person whose better judgment was easily harassed into incapacity. The origin of the crime, however, is of less importance than the effect of the discovery upon the nation, in whom horror of the action itself absorbed every other feeling. Murder of this kind was new in England. Ready as the people ever were with sword or lance—incurably given as they were to fighting in the best ordered times—an Englishman was accustomed to face his enemy, man to man, in the open day; and the Italian crime (as it was called) of poisoning had not till recent years been heard of. 300 Even revenge and passion recognised their own laws of honour and fair play; and the cowardly ferocity which would work its vengeance in the dark, and practise destruction by wholesale to implicate one hated person in the catastrophe, was a new feature of criminality. Occurring in a time so excited, when all minds were on the stretch, and imaginations were feverish with fancies, it appeared like a frightful portent, some prodigy of nature, or enormous new birth of wickedness, not to be received or passed by as a common incident, and not to be dealt with by the process of ordinary law. Parliament undertook the investigation, making it the occasion, when the evidence was completed, of a special statute, so remarkable that I quote it in its detail and wording. The English were a stern people—a people knowing little of compassion where no lawful ground existed for it; but they were possessed of an awful and solemn horror of evil things,—a feeling which, in proportion as it exists, inevitably and necessarily issues in tempers of iron. The stern man is ever the most tender when good remains amidst evil, and is still contending with it; but we purchase compassion for utter wickedness only by doubting in our hearts whether wickedness is more than misfortune.

"The King's royal Majesty," says the 9th of the 22nd of Henry VIII., "calling to his most blessed remembrance that the making of good and wholesome laws, and due execution of the same against the offenders thereof, is the only cause that good obedience and order hath been preserved in this realm; and his Highness having most tender zeal for the same, considering that man's life above all things is chiefly to be favoured, and voluntary murders most highly to be detested and abhorred; and specially all kinds of murders by poisoning, which in this realm hitherto, our Lord be thanked, hath been most rare and seldom committed or practised: and now, in the time of this present parliament, that is to say, on the eighteenth day of February, in the twenty-second year of his most victorious reign, one Richard Rouse, late of Rochester, in the county of Kent, cook, otherwise called Richard Cook, of his most wicked and damnable disposition, did cast a certain venom or poison into a vessel replenished with yeast or barm, standing in the kitchen of the reverend father in God, John Bishop of Rochester, at his place in Lambeth

Marsh; with which yeast or barm, and other things convenient, porridge or gruel was forthwith made for his family there being; whereby not only the number of seventeen persons of his said family, which did eat of that porridge, were mortally infected or poisoned, and one of them, that is to say, Bennet Curwan, gentleman, is thereof deceased; but also certain poor people which resorted to the said bishop's place, and were there charitably fed with the remains of the said porridge and other victuals; were in like wise infected; and one poor woman of them, that is to say, Alice Tryppitt, widow, is also thereof now deceased: Our said sovereign lord the king, of his blessed disposition inwardly abhorring all such abominable offences, because that in manner no person can live in surety out of danger of death by that means, if practices thereof should not be eschewed, hath ordained and enacted by authority of this present parliament, that the said poisoning be adjudged and deemed as high treason; and that the said Richard, for the said murder and poisoning of the said two persons, shall stand and be attainted of high treason.

"And because that detestable offence, now newly practised and committed, requireth condign punishment for the same, it is ordained and enacted by authority of this present parliament that the said Richard Rouse shall be therefore boiled to death, without having any advantage of his clergy; and that from henceforth every wilful murder of any person or persons hereafter to be committed or done by means or way of poisoning, shall be reputed, deemed, and judged in the law to be high treason; and that all and every person or persons which shall hereafter be indicted and condemned by order of the law of such treason, shall not be admitted to the benefit of his or their clergy, but shall be immediately after such attainder or condemnation, committed to execution of death by boiling for the same."

The sentence was carried into effect 301 in Smithfield, "on the tenebra Wednesday following, to the terrible example of all others." The spectacle of a living human being boiled to death, was really witnessed three hundred years ago by the London citizens, within the walls of that old cattle-market; an example terrible indeed, the significance of which is not easily to be exhausted. For the poisoners of the soul there was the stake, 302 for the poisoners of the body, the boiling cauldron,—the two most fearful punishments for the most fearful of crimes. The stake at which the heretic suffered was an inherited institution descending through the usage of centuries; the poisoner's cauldron was the fresh expression of the judgment of the English nation on a novel enormity; and I have called attention to it because the temper which this act exhibits is the key to all which has seemed most dark and cruel in the rough years which followed; a temper which would keep no terms with evil, or with anything which, rightly or wrongly, was believed to be evil, but dreadfully and inexorably hurried out the penalties of it.

Following the statute against poisoning, there stands "an act for the banishment out of the country of divers outlandish and vagabond people called Egyptians;" 303 and attached to it another of analogous import, "for the repression of beggars and vagabonds," the number of whom, it was alleged, was increasing greatly throughout the country, and much crime and other inconveniences were said to have been occasioned by them. We may regard these two measures, if we please, as a result of the energetic and reforming spirit in the parliament, which was dragging into prominence all forms of existing disorders, and devising remedies for those disorders. But they indicate something more than this: they point to the growth of a disturbed and restless disposition, the interruption of industry, and other symptoms of approaching social confusion; and at the same time they show us the government conscious of the momentous nature of the struggle into which it was launched; and with timely energy bracing up the sinews of the nation for its approaching trial. The act against the gipsies especially, illustrates one of the most remarkable features of the times. The air was impregnated with superstition; in a half consciousness of the impending changes, all men were listening with wide ears to rumours and prophecies and fantastic fore-shadowings of the future; and fanaticism, half deceiving and half itself deceived, was grasping the lever of the popular excitement to work out its own ends. 304 The power which had ruled the hearts of mankind for ten centuries was shaking suddenly to its foundation. The Infallible guidance of the Church was failing; its light gone out, or pronounced to be but a mere deceitful ignis fatuus; and men found themselves wandering in darkness, unknowing where to turn or what to think or believe. It was easy to clamour against the spiritual courts. From men smarting under the barefaced oppression of that iniquitous jurisdiction, the immediate outcry rose without ulterior thought; but unexpectedly the frail edifice of the church itself threatened under the attack to crumble into ruins; and many gentle hearts began to tremble and recoil when they saw what was likely to follow on their light beginnings. It was true that the measures as yet taken by the parliament and the crown professed to be directed, not to the overthrow of the church, but to the re-establishment of its strength. But the exulting triumph of the Protestants, the promotion of Latimer to a royal chaplaincy, the quarrel with the papacy, and a dim but sure perception of the direction in which the stream was flowing, foretold to earnest Catholics a widely different issue; and the simplest of them knew better than the court knew, that they were drifting from the sure moorings of the faith into the broad ocean of uncertainty. There seems, indeed, to be in religious men, whatever be their creed, and however limited their intellectual power, a prophetic faculty of insight into the true bearings of outward things,—an insight which puts to shame the sagacity of statesmen, and claims for the sons of God, and only for them, the wisdom even of the world. Those only read the world's future truly who have faith in principle, as opposed to faith in human dexterity; who feel that in human things there lies really and truly a spiritual nature, a spiritual connection, a spiritual tendency, which the wisdom of the serpent cannot alter, and scarcely can affect.

Excitement, nevertheless, is no guarantee for the understanding; and these instincts, powerful as they are, may be found often in minds wild and chaotic, which, although they vaguely foresee the future, yet have no power of sound judgment, and know not what they foresee, or how wisely to estimate it. Their wisdom, if we may so use the word, combines crudely with any form of superstition or fanaticism. Thus in England, at the time of which we are speaking, Catholics and Protestants had alike their horoscope of the impending changes, each nearer to the truth than the methodical calculations of the statesmen; yet their foresight did not affect their convictions, or alter the temper of their hearts. They foresaw the same catastrophe, yet their faith still coloured the character of it. To the one it was the advent of Antichrist, to the other the inauguration of the millennium. The truest hearted men on all sides were deserted by their understandings at the moment when their understandings were the most deeply needed: and they saw the realities which were round them transfigured into phantoms through the mists of their hopes and fears. The present was significant only as it seemed in labour with some gigantic issue, and the events of the outer world flew from lip to lip, taking as they passed every shape most wild and fantastical. Until "the king's matter" was decided, there was no censorship upon speech, and all tongues ran freely on the great subjects of the day. Every parish pulpit rang with the divorce, or with the perils of the Catholic faith; at every village ale-house, the talk was of St. Peter's keys, the sacrament, or of the pope's supremacy, or of the points in which a priest differed from a layman. Ostlers quarrelled over such questions as they groomed their masters' horses; old women mourned across the village shopboards of the evil days which were come or coming; while every kind of strangest superstition, fairy stories and witch stories, stories of saints and stories of devils, were woven in and out and to and fro, like quaint, bewildering arabesques, in the tissue of the general imagination. 305

These were the forces which were working on the surface of the English mind; while underneath, availing themselves skilfully of the excitement, the agents of the disaffected among the clergy, or the friars mendicant, who to a man were devoted to the pope and to Queen Catherine, passed up and down the country, denouncing the divorce, foretelling ruin, disaster, and the wrath of God; and mingling with their prophecies more than dubious language on the near destruction or deposition of a prince who was opposing God and Heaven. The soil was manured by treason, and the sowers made haste to use their opportunity. Thus especially was there danger in those wandering encampments of "outlandish people," whose habits rendered them the ready-made missionaries of sedition; whose swarthy features might hide a Spanish heart, and who in telling fortunes might readily dictate policy. 306 Under the disguise of gipsies, the emissaries of the emperor or the pope might pass unsuspected from the Land's End to Berwick-upon-Tweed, penetrating the secrets of families, tying the links of the Catholic organisation: and in the later years of the struggle, as the intrigues became more determined and a closer connection was established between the Continental powers and the disaffected English, it became necessary to increase the penalty against these irregular wanderers from banishment to death. As yet, however, the milder punishment was held sufficient, and even this was imperfectly enforced. 307 The tendencies to treason were still incipient—they were tendencies only, which had as yet shown themselves in no decisive acts; the future was uncertain, the action of the government doubtful. The aim was rather to calm down the excitement of the people, and to extinguish with as little violence as possible the means by which it was fed.

Ominous symptoms of eccentric agitation, however, began to take shape in the confusion, A preacher, calling himself the favourite of the Virgin Mary, had started up at Edinburgh, professing miraculous powers of abstinence from food. This man was sent by James V. to Rome, where, after having been examined by Clement, and having sufficiently proved his mission, he was furnished with a priest's habit and a certificate under leaden seal. 308 Thus equipped, he went a pilgrimage to Jerusalem, and loaded himself with palm-leaves and with stones from the pillar at which Christ was scourged; and from thence making his way to England, he appeared at Paul's Cross an evident saint and apostle, cursing the king and his divorce, denouncing his apostacy, and threatening the anger of Heaven. He was arrested and thrown into prison, where he remained, as it was believed, fifty days without food, or fed in secret by the Virgin, At the close of the time the government thought it prudent to send him back to Scotland, without further punishment. 309

Another more famous prophetess was then in the zenith of her reputation—the celebrated Nun of Kent—whose cell at Canterbury, for some three years, was the Delphic shrine of the Catholic oracle, from which the orders of Heaven were communicated even to the pope himself. This singular woman seems for a time to have held in her hand the balance of the fortunes of England. By the papal party she was universally believed to be inspired. Wolsey believed it, Warham believed it, the bishops believed it, Queen Catherine believed it, Sir Thomas More's philosophy was no protection to him against the same delusion; and finally, she herself believed the world, when she found the world believed in her. Her story is a psychological curiosity; and, interwoven as it was with the underplots of the time, we cannot observe it too accurately.

In the year 1525, there lived in the parish of Aldington, in Kent, a certain Thomas Cobb, bailiff or steward to the Archbishop of Canterbury, who possessed an estate there. Among the servants of this Thomas Cobb was a country girl called Elizabeth Barton—a decent person, so far as we can learn, but of mere ordinary character, and until that year having shown nothing unusual in her temperament. She was then attacked, however, by some internal disease; and after many months of suffering, she was reduced into that abnormal and singular condition, in which she exhibited the phenomena known to modern wonder-seekers as those of somnambulism or clairvoyance. The scientific value of such phenomena is still undetermined, but that they are not purely imaginary is generally agreed. In the histories of all countries and of all times, we are familiar with accounts of young women of bad health and irritable nerves, who have exhibited at recurring periods certain unusual powers; and these exhibitions have had especial attraction for superstitious persons, whether they have believed in God, or in the devil, or in neither. A further feature also uniform in such cases, has been that a small element of truth may furnish a substructure for a considerable edifice of falsehood; human credulity being always an insatiable faculty, and its powers being unlimited when once the path of ordinary experience has been transcended. We have seen in our own time to what excesses occurrences of this kind may tempt the belief, even when defended with the armour of science. In the sixteenth century, when demoniacal possession was the explanation usually received even of ordinary insanity, we can well believe that the temptation must have been great to recognise supernatural agency in a manifestation far more uncommon; and that the difficulty of retaining the judgment in a position of equipoise must have been very great not only to the spectators but still more to the subject of the phenomenon herself. To sustain ourselves continuously under the influence of reason, even when our faculties are preserved in their natural balance, is a task too hard for most of us. We cannot easily make too great allowance for the moral derangement likely to follow, when a weak girl suddenly found herself possessed of powers which she was unable to understand. Bearing this in mind, for it is only just that we should do so, we continue the story.

This Elizabeth Barton, then, "in the trances, of which she had divers and many, 310 consequent upon her illness, told wondrously things done and said in other places whereat she was neither herself present, nor yet had heard no report thereof." To simple-minded people who believed in Romanism and the legends of the saints, the natural explanation of such a marvel was, that she must be possessed either by the Holy Ghost or by the devil. The archbishop's bailiff, not feeling himself able to decide in a case of so much gravity, called in the advice of the parish priest, one Richard Masters; and together they observed carefully all that fell from her. The girl had been well disposed, as the priest probably knew. She had been brought up religiously; and her mind running upon what was most familiar to it, "she spake words of marvellous holiness in rebuke of sin and vice;" 311 or, as another account says, "she spake very godly certain things concerning the seven deadly sins and the Ten Commandments." 312 This seemed satisfactory as to the source of the inspiration. It was clearly not a devil that spoke words against sin, and therefore, as there was no other alternative, it was plain that God had visited her. Her powers were assuredly from heaven; and it was plain, also, by a natural sequence of reasoning, that she held some divine commission, of which her clairvoyance was the miracle in attestation.

An occurrence of such moment was not to be kept concealed in the parish of Aldington. The priest mounted his horse, and rode to Lambeth with the news to the Archbishop of Canterbury; and the story having lost nothing of its marvel by the way, 313 the archbishop, who was fast sinking into dotage, instead of ordering a careful inquiry, and appointing some competent person to conduct it, listened with greedy interest; he assured Father Richard that "the speeches which she had spoken came of God; and bidding him keep him diligent account of all her utterances, directed him to inform her in his name that she was not to refuse or hide the goodness and works of God." Cobb, the bailiff, being encouraged by such high authority, would not keep any longer in his kitchen a prophetess with the archbishop's imprimatur upon her; and as soon as the girl was sufficiently recovered from her illness to leave her bed, he caused her to sit at his own mess with his mistress and the parson. 314 The story spread rapidly through the country; inquisitive foolish people came about her to try her skill with questions; and her illness, as she subsequently confessed, having then left her, and as only her reputation was remaining, she bethought herself whether it might not be possible to preserve it a little longer. "Perceiving herself to be much made of, to be magnified and much set by, by reason of trifling words spoken unadvisedly by idleness of her brain, she conceived in her mind that having so good success, and furthermore from so small an occasion and nothing to be esteemed, she might adventure further to enterprise and essay what she could do, being in good advisement and remembrance." 315 Her fits no longer recurred naturally, but she was able to reproduce either the reality or the appearance of them; and she continued to improvise her oracles with such ability as she could command, and with tolerable success.

In this undertaking she was speedily provided with an efficient coadjutor. The Catholic church had for some time been unproductive of miracles, and as heresy was raising its head and attracting converts, so opportune an occurrence was not to be allowed to sleep. The archbishop sent his comptroller to the Prior of Christ Church at Canterbury, with directions that two monks whom he especially named, Doctor Bocking, the cellarer, and Dan William Hadley, should go to Aldington to observe. 316 At first, not knowing what was before them, both prior and monks were unwilling to meddle with the matter. 317 They submitted, however, "from the obedience which they owed unto their lord;" and they had soon reason to approve the correctness of the archbishop's judgment. Bocking, selected no doubt from previous knowledge of his qualities, was a man devoted to his order, and not over-scrupulous as to the means by which he furthered the interests of it. With instinctive perception he discovered material in Elizabeth Barton too rich to be allowed to waste itself in a country village. Perhaps he partially himself believed in her, but he was more anxious to ensure the belief of others, and he therefore set himself to assist her inspiration towards more effective utterance. Conversing with her in her intervals of quiet, he discovered that she was wholly ignorant, and unprovided with any stock of mental or imaginative furniture; and that consequently her prophecies were without body, and too indefinite to be theologically available. This defect he remedied by instructing her in the Catholic legends, and by acquainting her with the revelations of St. Brigitt and St. Catherine of Sienna. 318 In these women she found an enlarged reflection of herself; the details of their visions enriched her imagery; and being provided with these fair examples, she was able to shape herself into fuller resemblance with the traditionary model of the saints.

As she became more proficient, Father Bocking extended his lessons to the Protestant controversy, initiating his pupil into the mysteries of justification, sacramental grace, and the power of the keys. The ready damsel redelivered his instructions to the world in her moments of possession; and the world discovered a fresh miracle in the inspired wisdom of the untaught peasant. Lists of these pregnant sayings were forwarded 319 regularly to the archbishop, which still possibly lie mouldering in the Lambeth library, to be discovered by curious antiquaries. It is idle to inquire how far she was yet conscious of her falsehood. Conscious wilful deception lies far down the road in a course of this kind; and supported by the assurance of an archbishop, she was in all likelihood deep in lying before she actually knew it. Fanaticism and deceit are strangely near relations to each other, and the deceiver is often the person first deceived, and the last who is aware of the imposture.

The instructions of the Father had made her acquainted with many stories of miraculous cures. The Catholic saints followed the type of the apostles, and to heal diseases by supernatural means was a more orthodox form of credential than clairvoyance or second sight. Being now cured of her real disorder, yet able to counterfeit the appearance of it, she could find no difficulty in arranging in her own case a miracle of the established kind, and so striking an incident would answer a further end. In the parish was a chapel of the Virgin, which was a place of pilgrimage; the pilgrims added something to the income of the priest; and if, by a fresh demonstration of the Virgin's presence at the favoured spot, the number of these pilgrims could be increased, they would add more. For both reasons, therefore, the miracle was desired; and the priest and the monk were agreed that any means were justifiable which would encourage the devotion of the people. 320 Accordingly, the girl announced, in one of her trances, that "she would never take health of her body till such time as she had visited the image of our Lady" in that chapel. The Virgin had herself appeared to her, she said, and had fixed a day for her appearance there, and had promised that on her obedience she would present herself in person and take away her disorder. 321 The day came; and as (under the circumstances) there was no danger of failure, the holy fathers had collected a vast concourse of people to witness the marvel. The girl was conducted to the chapel by a procession of more than two thousand persons, headed by the monk, the clergyman, and many other religious persons, the whole multitude "singing the Litany and saying divers psalms and orations by the way."

"And when she was brought thither 322 and laid before the image of our Lady, her face was wonderfully disfigured, her tongue hanging out, and her eyes being in a manner plucked out and laid upon her cheeks, and so greatly deformed. There was then heard a voice speaking within her belly, as it had been in a tonne, her lips not greatly moving: she all that while continuing by the space of three hours or more in a trance. The which voice, when it told of anything of the joys of heaven, spake so sweetly and so heavenly, that every man was ravished with the hearing thereof; and contrarywise, when it told anything of hell, it spake so horribly and terribly, that it put the hearers in a great fear. It spake also many things for the confirmation of pilgrimages and trentals, hearing of masses and confession, and many other such things. And after she had lyen there a long time, she came to herself again, and was perfectly whole. So this miracle was finished and solemnly sung; and a book was written of all the whole story thereof, and put into print; which ever since that time was commonly sold, and went abroad among the people."

The miracle successfully accomplished, the residence at Aldington was no longer adapted for an acknowledged and favoured saint. The Virgin informed her that she was to leave the bailiff and devote herself to her exclusive service. She was to be Sister Elizabeth, and her especial favourite; and Father Bocking was to be her spiritual father. The priory of St. Sepulchre's, Canterbury, was chosen for the place of her profession; and as soon as she was established in her cell, she became a recognised priestess or prophetess, alternately communicating revelations, or indulging the curiosity of foolish persons, and for both services consenting to be paid. The church had by this time spread her reputation through England. The book of her oracles, which extended soon to a considerable volume, was shown by Archbishop Warham to the king, who sent it to Sir Thomas More, desiring him to look at it. More's good sense had not yet forsaken him; he pronounced it "a right poor production, such as any simple woman might speak of her own wit;" 323 and Henry himself "esteemed the matter as light as it afterwards proved lewd." But the world were less critical censors: the saintly halo was round her head, and her most trivial words caught the reflection of the glory, and seemed divine. "Divers and many, as well great men of the realm as mean men, and many learned men, but specially many religious men, had great confidence in her, and often resorted to her." 324 They "consulted her much as to the will of God touching the heresies and schisms in the realm;" and when the dispute arose between the bishops and the House of Commons, they asked her what judgment there was in heaven "on the taking away the liberties of the church;" to which questions her answers, being dictated by her confessor, were all which the most eager churchman could desire. Her position becoming more and more determined, the eccentric periods of her earlier visions subsided into regularity. Once a fortnight she was taken up into heaven into the presence of God and the saints, with heavenly lights, heavenly voices, heavenly melodies and joys. The place of ascent was usually the priory chapel, to which it was essential, therefore, that she should have continual access: and she was allowed, in consequence, to pass the dormitory door when she pleased—a privilege of which the Statute uncharitably hints that she availed herself for a less respectable purpose. But whatever was her secret conduct, her outward behaviour was in full keeping with her language and profession. She related many startling stories, not always of the most decent kind, of the attempts which the devil made to lead her astray. The devil and the angels were in fact alternate visitors to her cell, and the former, on one occasion, burnt a mark upon her hand, which she exhibited publicly, and to which the monks were in the habit of appealing, when there were any signs of scepticism in the visitors to the priory. On the occasion of these infernal visits, "great stinking smokes" were seen to issue from her chamber, "savouring grievously through all the dorture;" with which, however, it was suspected subsequently that a paper of brimstone and assafœtida, found among her property after her arrest, had been in some way connected. We smile at these stories, looking back at them with eyes enlightened by scientific scepticism; but they furnished matter for something else than smiles when the accounts of them could be exhibited by the clergy as a living proof of the credibility of the Aurea Legenda, — when the subject of them could be held up as a witness, accredited by miracles, to the truth of the old faith, a living evidence to shame the incredulity of the Protestant sectaries. She became a figure of great and singular significance; a "wise woman," to whom persons of the highest rank were not ashamed to have recourse to inquire of her the will of God, and to ask the benefit of her intercessory prayers, for which also they did not fail to pay at a rate commensurate with their credulity. 325

This position the Nun of Kent, as she was now called, had achieved for herself, when the divorce question was first agitated. The monks at the Canterbury priory, of course, eagerly espoused the side of the queen, and the Nun's services were at once in active requisition. Absurd as the stories of her revelations may seem to us, she had already given evidence that she was no vulgar impostor, and in the dangerous career on which she now entered, she conducted herself with the utmost skill and audacity. Far from imitating the hesitation of the pope and the bishops, she issued boldly, "in the name and by the authority of God," a solemn prohibition against the king; threatening that, if he divorced his wife, he should not "reign a month, but should die a villain's death." 326 Burdened with this message, she forced herself into the presence of Henry himself; 327 and when she failed to produce an effect upon Henry's obdurate scepticism, she turned to the hesitating ecclesiastics, and roused their flagging spirits. The archbishop bent under her denunciations, and at her earnest request introduced her to Wolsey, then tottering on the edge of ruin. 328 He, too, in his confusion and perplexity, was frightened, and doubted. She made herself known to the papal ambassadors, and through them she took upon herself to threaten Clement, 329 assuming, in virtue of her divine commission, an authority above all principalities and powers. If it were likely that she could have heard the story of the Maid of Orleans, it might be supposed that her imagination tempted her to play again a similar career on an English stage, and that she fancied herself the destined saviour of the Church of Christ, as the Maid had been the saviour of France.

It would indeed be a libel on the fair fame of Joan of Arc, if she were to be compared to a confessed impostor; but Joan of Arc might have been the reality which the Nun attempted to counterfeit; and the history of the true heroine might have suggested easily to the imitator the outline of her part. A revolution had been effected in Europe by a somnambulist peasant girl; another peasant girl, a somnambulist also, might have seen in the achievement which had been already accomplished, an earnest of what might be done by herself. While we call the Nun, too, an impostor, we are bound to believe that she first imposed upon herself, and that her wildest adventures into falsehood were compatible with a belief that she was really and truly inspired. Nothing short of such a conviction would have enabled her to play a part among kings and queens, and so many of the ablest statesmen of that most able age. Nothing else could have tempted her, on the failure of her prophecies, into the desperate career of treason into which we are soon to see her launched.

Her proceedings were known partially, but partially only, to the king; and the king seems to have been the only person whose understanding was proof against her influence. To him she appeared nothing worse than an excited fanatic, and he allowed her to go her own way, as the best escapement of a frenzy. Until parliament had declared it illegal to discuss the marriage question further, he interfered with no one, and therefore not with her. If her own word was to be taken, he even showed her much personal kindness, having offered to make her an abbess, which is difficult to believe, especially as she said that she had refused his offer. She stated also that at the time of Lord Wiltshire's mission to the emperor, the Countess of Wiltshire endeavoured to persuade her to accept a place at the court, as a companion to Anne; which again is unsupported by other evidence, and sounds improbable. 330 But it is plain, that until she was found to be meditating treason, she experienced no treatment from the government of which she had cause to complain; and thus for the present we may leave her pursuing her machinations with the Canterbury friars, and return to the parliament.

The second session had been longer than the first; it had commenced on the 16th of January, and continued for ten weeks. On the 30th of March, which was to be its last day, Sir Thomas More came down to the House of Commons, and there read aloud to the members the decision of the various universities on the papal power, and the judgment of European learning on the general question of the king's divorce. The country, he said, was much disturbed, and the king desired them each to report what they had heard in their several counties and towns, "in order that all men might perceive that he had not attempted this matter of his own will or pleasure, as some strangers reported, but only for the discharge of his conscience and surety of the succession of his realm." 331 This appears to have been the first time that the subject was mentioned before parliament, and the occasion was reasonably and sensibly chosen. The clergy having possession of the pulpits, had used their opportunity to spread a false impression where the ignorance of the people would allow them to venture the experiment; the king having resolved to fall back upon the support of his subjects, naturally desired the assistance of the country gentlemen and the nobles to counteract the efforts of disaffection, and provided them with accurate information in the simplest manner which he could have chosen.

But the desire expressed by Henry was no more than an unnecessary form, for as a body, the educated laity were as earnestly bent upon the divorce as the king himself could be, and might have been trusted to use all means by which to further it. The parliament was prorogued, but the Lords, shortly after the separation, united with such of the Commons as remained in London, to give a proof of their feeling by a voluntary address to the pope. The meaning of this movement was not to be mistaken. On one side, the Nun of Kent was threatening Clement, speaking, perhaps, the feelings of the clergy and of all the women in England; on the other side, the parliament thought well to threaten him, speaking for the great body of English *men*, for all persons of substance and property, who desired above all things peace and order and a secured succession.

The language of this remarkable document 332 was as follows:—

"To the Most Holy Lord our Lord and Father in Christ, Clement, by Divine Providence the seventh of that name, we desire perpetual happiness in our Lord Jesus Christ.

"Most blessed Father, albeit the cause concerning the marriage of the most invincible prince, our sovereign lord, the King of England and of France, Defender of the Faith, and Lord of Ireland, does for sundry great and weighty reasons require and demand the aid of your Holiness, that it may be brought to that brief end and determination which we with so great and earnest desire have expected, and which we have been contented hitherto to expect, though so far vainly, at your Holiness's hands; we have been unable, nevertheless, to keep longer silence herein, seeing that this kingdom and the affairs of it are brought into so high peril through the unseasonable delay of sentence. His Majesty, who is our head, and by consequence the life of us all, and we through him as subject members by a just union annexed to the head, have with great earnestness entreated your Holiness for judgment; we have however entreated in vain: we are by the greatness of our grief therefore forced separately and distinctly by these our letters most humbly to demand a speedy determination. There ought, indeed, to have been no need of this request on our part. The justice of the cause itself, approved to be just by the sentence of so many learned men, by the suffrage of the most famous universities in England, France, and Italy, should have sufficed alone to have induced your Holiness to confirm the sentence given by others; especially when the interests of a king and kingdom are at stake, which in so many ways have deserved well of the apostolic see. This we say ought to have been motive sufficient with you, without need of petition on our part; and if we had added our entreaties, it should have been but as men yielding to a causeless anxiety, and wasting words for which there was no occasion. Since, however, neither the merit of the cause nor the recollection of the benefits which you have received, nor the assiduous and diligent supplications of our prince have availed anything with your Holiness; since we cannot obtain from you what it is your duty as a father to grant; the load of our grief, increased as it is beyond measure by the remembrance of the past miseries and calamities which have befallen this nation, makes vocal every member of our commonwealth, and compels us by word and letter to utter our complaints.

"For what a misfortune is this,—that a sentence which our own two universities, which the University of Paris, and many other universities in France, which men of the highest learning and probity everywhere, at home and abroad, are ready to defend with word and pen, that such sentence, we say, cannot be obtained from the apostolic see by a prince to whom that see owes its present existence. Amidst the attacks of so many and so powerful enemies, the King of England ever has stood by that see with sword and pen, with voice and with authority. Yet he alone is to reap no benefit from his labours. He has saved the papacy from ruin, that others might enjoy the fruits of the life which he has preserved for it. We see not what answer can be made to this; and meanwhile we perceive a flood of miseries impending over the commonwealth, threatening to bring back upon us the ancient controversy on the succession, which had been extinguished only with so much blood and slaughter. We have now a king most eminent for his virtues, and reigning by unchallenged title, who will secure assured tranquillity to the realm if he leave a son born of his body to succeed him. The sole hope that such a son may be born to him lies in the being found for him some lawful marriage into which he may enter; and to such marriage the only obstacle lies with your Holiness. It cannot be until you shall confirm the sentence of so many learned men on the character of his former connection. This if you will not do, if you who ought to be our father have determined to leave us as orphans, and to treat us as castaways, we shall interpret such conduct to mean only that we are left to care for ourselves, and to seek our remedy elsewhere. We do not desire to be driven to this extremity, and therefore we beseech your Holiness without further delay to assist his Majesty's just and reasonable desires. We entreat you to confirm the judgment of these learned men; and for the sake of that love and fatherly affection which your office requires you to show towards us, not to close your bowels of compassion against us, your most dutiful, most loving, most obedient children. The cause of his Majesty is the cause of each of ourselves; the head cannot suffer, but the members must bear a part. We have all our common share in the pain and in the injury; and as the remedy is wholly in the power of your Holiness, so does the duty of your fatherly office require you to administer it. If, however, your Holiness will not do this, or if you choose longer to delay to do it, our condition hitherto will have been so much the more wretched, that we have so long laboured fruitlessly and in vain. But it will not be wholly irremediable; extreme remedies are ever harsh of application; but he that is sick will by any means be rid of his distemper; and there is hope in the exchange of miseries, when, if we cannot obtain what is good, we may obtain a lesser evil, and trust that time may enable us to endure it.

"These things we beseech your Holiness, in the name of our Lord Jesus Christ, to consider with yourself. You profess that on earth you are His vicar. Endeavour, then, to show yourself so to be, by pronouncing your sentence to the glory and praise of God, and giving your sanction to that truth which has been examined, approved, and after much deliberation confirmed by the most learned men of all nations. We meanwhile will pray the all-good God, whom we know by most sure testimony to be truth itself, that He will deign so to inform and direct the counsels of your Holiness, that we obtaining by your authority what is holy, just, and true, may be spared from seeking it by other more painful methods."

Thus was the great crisis steadily maturing itself, and the cause by this petition was made to rest upon its proper merits. The justification of the demand for the divorce was the danger of civil war; and into civil war the nation had no intention of permitting themselves to be drifted by papal imbecility. Whatever was the origin of Henry's resolution, it was acted out with calmness, and justified by sober reason; and backed by the good sense of his lay subjects, he proceeded bravely, in spite of excommunication, interdict, and the Nun of Kent, towards the object which his country's interests, as well as his own, required.

It would have been well if his private behaviour as a man had been as unobjectionable as his conduct as a sovereign. Hitherto he had remained under the same roof with Queen Catherine, but with that indelicacy which was the singular blemish on his character, he had maintained her rival in the same household with the state of a princess, 333 and needlessly wounded feelings which he was bound to have spared to the utmost which his duty permitted. The circumstances of the case, if they were known to us, though they could never excuse such a proceeding, might perhaps partially palliate it. Catherine was harsh and offensive, and it was by her own determination, and not by Henry's desire, that she was unprovided with an establishment elsewhere. There lay, moreover, as I have said, behind the scenes a whole drama of contention and bitterness, which now is happily concealed from us; but which being concealed, leaves us without the clue to these painful doings. Indelicate, however, the position given to Anne Boleyn could not but be; and, if it was indelicate in Henry to grant such a position, what shall we say of the lady who consented, in the presence of her sovereign and mistress, to wear such ignominious splendour?

But in these most offensive relations there was henceforth to be a change. In June, 1531, two months after the prorogation of parliament, a deputation of the privy council went to the apartments of Catherine at Greenwich, and laying before her the papers which had been read by Sir Thomas More to the two Houses, demanded formally, whether, for the sake of the country, and for the quiet of the king's conscience, she would withdraw her appeal to Rome, and submit to an arbitration in the kingdom. It was, probably, but an official request, proposed without expectation that she would yield. After rejecting a similar entreaty from the pope himself, she was not likely, inflexible as she had ever been, to yield when the pope had admitted her appeal, and the emperor, victorious through Europe, had promised her support. She refused, of course, like herself, proudly, resolutely, gallantly, and not without the scorn which she was entitled to feel. The nation had no claims upon her, and "for the king's conscience," she answered, "I pray God send his Grace good quiet therein, and tell him I say I am his lawful wife, and to him lawfully married; and in that point I will abide till the court of Rome, which was privy to the beginning, hath made thereof a determination and a final ending." 334 The learned councillors retired with their answer. A more passive resistance would have been more dignified; but Catherine was a queen, and a queen she chose to be; and in defence of her own high honour, and of her daughter's, by no act of hers would she abate one tittle of her dignity, or cease to assert her claim to it. Her reply, however, appears to have been anticipated, and the request was only preparatory to ulterior measures. For the sake of public decency, and certainly in no unkind spirit towards herself, a retirement from the court was now to be forced upon her. At Midsummer she accompanied the king to Windsor; in the middle of July he left her there, and never saw her again. She was removed to the More, a house in Hertfordshire, which had been originally built by George Neville, Archbishop of York, and had belonged to Wolsey, who had maintained it with his usual splendour. 335 Once more an attempt was made to persuade her to submit; but with no better result, and a formal establishment was then provided for her at Ampthill, a large place belonging to Henry not far from Dunstable. There at least she was her own mistress, surrounded by her own friends, who were true to her as queen, and she attracted to her side from all parts of England those whom sympathy or policy attached to her cause. The court, though keeping a partial surveillance over her, did not dare to restrict her liberty; and as the measures against the church became more stringent, and a separation from the papacy more nearly imminent, she became the nucleus of a powerful political party. Her injuries had deprived the king and the nation of a right to complain of her conduct. She owed nothing to England. Her allegiance, politically, was to Spain; spiritually she was the subject of the pope; and this dubious position gave her an advantage which she was not slow to perceive. Rapidly every one rallied to her who adhered to the old faith, and to whom the measures of the government appeared a sacrilege. Through herself, or through her secretaries and confessors, a correspondence was conducted which brought the courts of the continent into connection with the various disaffected parties in England, with the Nun of Kent and her friars, with the Poles, the Nevilles, the Courtenays, and all the remaining faction of the White Rose. And so first the great party of sedition began to shape itself, which for sixty years, except in the shortlived interlude of its triumph under Catherine's daughter, held the nation on the edge of civil war. We shall see this faction slowly and steadily organising itself, starting from scattered and small beginnings, till at length it overspread all England and Ireland and Scotland, exploding from time to time in abortive insurrections, yet ever held in check by the tact and firmness of the government, and by the inherent loyalty of the English to the land of their birth. There was a proverb then current that "the treasons of England should never cease." 336 It was perhaps fortunate that the papal cause was the cause of a foreign power, and could only be defended by a betrayal of the independence of the country. In Scotland and Ireland the insurrectionists were more successful, being supported in either instance by the national feeling. But the strength of Scotland had been broken at Flodden; and Ireland, though hating "the Saxons" with her whole heart, was far off and divided. The true danger was at home; and when the extent and nature of it is fairly known and weighed, we shall understand better what is called the "tyranny" of Henry VIII. and of Elizabeth; and rather admire the judgment than condemn the resolution which steered the country safe among those dangerous shoals. Elizabeth's position is more familiar to us, and is more reasonably appreciated because the danger was more palpable. Henry has been hardly judged because he trampled down the smouldering fire, and never allowed it to assume the form which would have justified him with the foolish and the unthinking. Once and once only the flame blazed out; but it was checked on the instant, and therefore it has been slighted and forgotten. But with despatches before his eyes, in which Charles V. was offering James of Scotland the hand of the Princess Mary, with the title for himself of Prince of England and Duke of York 337—with Ireland, as we shall speedily see it, in flame from end to end, and Dublin castle the one spot left within the island on which the banner of St. George still floated—with a corps of friars in hair shirts and chains, who are also soon to be introduced to us, and an inspired prophetess at their head preaching rebellion in the name of God—with his daughter, and his daughter's mother in league against him, some forty thousand clergy to be coerced into honest dealing, and the succession to the crown floating in uncertainty—finally, with excommunication hanging over himself, and at length falling, and his deposition pronounced, Henry, we may be sure, had no easy time of it, and no common work to accomplish; and all these things ought to be present before our minds, as they were present before his mind, if we would see him as he was, and judge him as we would be judged ourselves.

Leaving disaffection to mature itself, we return to the struggle between the House of Commons and the bishops, which recommenced in the following winter; first pausing to notice a clerical interlude of some illustrative importance which took place in the close of the summer. The clergy, as we saw, were relieved of their premunire on engaging to pay 118,000 pounds within five years. They were punished for their general offences; the formal offence for which they were condemned being one which could not fairly be considered an offence at all. When they came to discuss therefore the manner in which the money was to be levied, they naturally quarrelled among themselves as to where the burden of the fine should fairly rest, and a little scene has been preserved to us by Hall, through which, with momentary distinctness, we can look in upon those poor men in their perplexity. The bishops had settled among themselves that each diocese should make its own arrangements; and some of these great persons intended to spare their own shoulders to the utmost decent extremity. With this object, Stokesley, Bishop of London, who was just then very busy burning heretics, and therefore in bad odour with the people, resolved to call a meeting of five or six of his clergy, on whom he could depend; and passing quietly with their assistance such resolutions as seemed convenient, to avoid in this way the more doubtful expedient of a large assembly.

The necessary intimations were given, and the meeting was to be held on the 1st of September, in the Chapter-house of St. Paul's. The bishop arrived at the time appointed, but unhappily for his hopes, not only the chosen six, but with them six hundred of the clergy of Middlesex, accompanied by a mob of the London citizens, all gathered in a crowd at the Chapter-house door, and clamouring to be admitted.

The bishop, trusting in the strength of the chains and bolts, and still hoping to manage the affair officially, sent out a list of persons who might be allowed to take part in the proceedings, and these with difficulty made their way to the entrance. A rush was made by the others as they were going in, and there was a scuffle, which ended for the moment in the victory of the officials: but the triumph was of brief duration; the excluded clergy were now encouraged by the people; they returned vigorously to the attack, broke down the doors, "struck the bishop's officers over the face," and the whole crowd, priests and laity, rushed together, storming and shouting, into the Chapter-house. The scene may be easily imagined; dust flying, gowns torn, heads broken, well-fed faces in the hot September weather steaming with anger and exertion, and every voice in loudest outcry. At length the clamour was partially subdued, and the bishop, beautifully equal to the emergency, arose bland and persuasive.

"My brethren," he said, "I marvel not a little why ye be so heady. Ye know not what shall be said to you, therefore I pray you keep silence, and hear me patiently. My friends, ye all know that we be men, frail of condition and no angels; and by frailty and lack of wisdom we have misdemeaned ourselves towards the king our sovereign lord and his laws; so that all we of the clergy were in premunire, by reason whereof all our promotions, lands, goods, and chattels were to him forfeit, and our bodies ready to be imprisoned. Yet his Grace, moved with pity and compassion, demanded of us what we could say why he should not extend his laws upon us.

"Then the fathers of the clergy humbly besought his Grace for mercy, to whom he answered he was ever inclined to mercy. Then for all our great offences we had but little penance; for when he might, by the rigour of his laws, have taken all our livelihoods, he was contented with one hundred thousand pounds, to be paid in five years. And though this sum may be more than we may easily bear, yet, by the rigour of his law, we should have borne the whole burden; whereupon, my brethren, I charitably exhort you to bear your parts of your livelihood and salary towards payment of this sum granted." 338

The ingenuity of this address deserved all praise; but the beauty of the form was insufficient to disguise the inconclusiveness of the reasoning. It confessed an offence which the hearers knew to be none; the true provocation which had led to the penalty—the unjust extortion of the high church officials—was ignored. The crowd laughed and hooted. The clergy fiercely tightened their purse-strings, and the bishop was heard out with hardly restrained indignation. "My lord," it was shortly answered by one of them, "twenty nobles a year is but a bare living for a priest. Victual and all else is now so dear that poverty enforceth us to say nay. Besides that, my lord, we never meddled with the cardinal's faculties. Let the bishops and abbots which have offended pay." Loud clamour followed and shouts of applause. The bishop's officers gave the priests high words. The priests threw back the taunts as they came; and the London citizens, delighting in the scandalous quarrel, hounded on the opposition. From words they passed to blows; the bedell and vergers tried to keep order, but "were buffeted and stricken," 339 and the meeting broke up in wild uproar and confusion. For this matter five of the lay crowd and fifteen London curates were sent to the Tower by Sir Thomas More; but the undignified manœuvre had failed, and the fruit of it was but fresh disgrace. United, the clergy might have defied the king and the parliament; but in the race of selfishness the bishops and high dignitaries had cared only for their own advantage. They had left the poorer members of their order with no interest in common with that of their superiors, beyond the shield which the courts consented to extend over moral delinquency; and in the hour of danger they found themselves left naked and alone to bear the storm as they were able.

This incident, and it was perhaps but one of many, is not likely to have softened the disposition of the Commons, or induced them to entertain more respectfully the bishops' own estimate of their privileges. The convocation and the parliament met simultaneously, on the 15th of January, and the conflict, which had been for two years in abeyance, recommenced. The initial measure was taken by convocation, and this body showed a spirit still unsubdued, and a resolution to fight in their own feebly tyrannical manner to the last. A gentleman in Gloucestershire had lately died, by name Tracy. In his last testament he had bequeathed his soul to God through the mercies of Christ, declining the mediatorial offices of the saints; and leaving no money to be expended in masses. 340 Such notorious heresy could not be passed over with impunity, and the first step of the assembled clergy 341 was to issue a commission to raise the body and burn it. Their audacity displayed at once the power which they possessed, and the temper in which they were disposed to use it. The Archbishop of Canterbury seems to have been responsible for this monstrous order, which unfortunately was carried into execution before Henry had time to interfere. 342 It was the last act of the kind, however, in which he was permitted to indulge, and the legislature made haste to take away such authority from hands so incompetent to use it. From their debates upon burning the dead Tracy, convocation were proceeding to discuss the possibility of burning the living Latimer, 343 when they were recalled to their senses by a summons to prepare some more reasonable answer than that which the bishops had made for them on their privilege of making laws. Twenty more years of work were to be lived by Latimer before they were to burn him, and their own delinquencies were for the present of a more pressing nature. The House of Commons at the same time proceeded to frame necessary bills on the other points of their complaint.

The first act upon the roll recalls the Constitutions of Clarendon and the famous quarrel between Becket and the Crown. When Catholicism was a living belief, when ordained priests were held really and truly to possess those awful powers which the mystery of transubstantiation assigns to them, they were acknowledged by common consent to be an order apart from the rest of mankind, and being spiritual men, to be amenable only to spiritual jurisdiction. It was not intended that, if they committed crimes, they should escape the retributive consequences of those crimes: offenders against the law might (originally at least) be degraded, if the bishops thought good, and stripped of their commission be delivered thus to the secular arm. But the more appropriate punishment for such persons was of a more awful kind, proportioned to the magnitude of the fault; and was conveyed or held to be conveyed in the infliction of the spiritual death of excommunication. Excommunication was, in real earnest, the death of the soul, at a time when communion with the church was the only means by which the soul could be made partaker of the divine life; and it was a noble thing to believe that there was something worse for a man than legal penalties on his person or on his mortal body; it was beautiful to recognise in an active living form, that the heaviest ill which could befall a man was to be cut off from God. But it is only for periods that humanity can endure the atmosphere of these high altitudes of morality. The early Christians attempted a community of goods, but they were unequal to it for more than a generation. The discipline of Catholicism was assisted by superstition,—it remained vigorous for many hundreds of years, but it languished at last; and although there was so great virtue in a living idea, that its forms preserved the reverence of mankind unabated, even when in their effect and working they had become as evil as they once were noble; yet reverence and endurance were at length exhausted, and these forms were to submit to alteration in conformity with the altered nature of the persons whom they affected.

I have already alluded to the abuse of "benefit of clergy;" 344 we have arrived at the first of those many steps by which at length it was finally put away,—a step which did not, however, as yet approach the heart of the evil, but touched only its extreme outworks. The clergy had monopolised the learning of the middle ages, and few persons external to their body being able to read or write, their privileges became co-extensive, as I above stated, with these acquirements. The exemption from secular jurisdiction, which they obtained in virtue of their sacred character, had been used as a protection in villainy for every scoundrel who could write his name. Under this plea, felons of the worst kind might claim, till this time, to be taken out of the hands of the law judges, and to be tried at the bishops' tribunals; and at these tribunals, such a monstrous solecism had Catholicism become, the payment of money was ever welcomed as the ready expiation of crime. To prevent the escape of the Bishop of Rochester's cook, who was a "clerk," parliament had specially interfered, and sentenced him without trial, by attainder. They now passed a general act, remarkable alike in what it provided as in what, for the present, it omitted to provide. 345 The preamble related the nature of the evil which was to be remedied, and the historical position of it. It dwelt upon the assurances which had been given again and again by the ordinaries that their privileges should not be abused; but these promises had been broken as often as they had been made; so that "continually manifest thieves and murderers, indicted and found guilty of their misdeeds by good and substantial inquests, and afterwards, by the usages of the common lawes of the land, delivered to the ordinaries as clerks convict, were speedily and hastily delivered and set at large by the ministers of the said ordinaries for corruption and lucre; or else because the ordinaries enclaiming such offenders by the liberties of the church would in no wise take the charges in safe keeping of them, but did suffer them to make their purgation by such as nothing knew of their misdeeds, and by such fraud did annull and make void the good and provable trial which was used against such offenders by the king's law; to the pernicious example, increase, and courage of such offenders, if the King's Highness by his authority royal put not speedy remedy thereto."

To provide such necessary remedy, it was enacted that thenceforward no person under the degree of subdeacon, if guilty of felony, should be allowed to plead "his clergy" any more, but should be proceeded against by the ordinary law. So far it was possible to go—an enormous step if we think of what the evil had been; and in such matters to make a beginning was the true difficulty—it was the logical premise from which the conclusion could not choose but follow. Yet such was the mystical sacredness which clung about the ordained clergy, that their patent profligacy had not yet destroyed it—a priest might still commit a murder, and the profane hand of the law might not reach to him.

The measure, however, if imperfect, was excellent in its degree; and when this had been accomplished, the House proceeded next to deal with the Arches Court—the one enormous grievance of the time. The petition of the Commons has already exhibited the condition of this institution; but the act by which the power of it was limited added more than one particular to what had been previously stated, and the first twenty lines of the statute which was now passed 346 may be recommended to the consideration of the modern censors of the Reformation. The framer of the resolution was no bad friend to the bishops, if they had possessed the faculty of knowing who their true friends were, for the statement of complaint was limited, mild, and moderate. Again, as with the "benefit of clergy," the real ground for surprise is that any fraction of a system so indefensible should have been permitted to continue. The courts were nothing else but the vicious sources of unjust revenue; and with the opportunity so fairly offered, it is strange indeed that they were not swept utterly away. But sweeping measures have never found favour in England. There has ever been in English legislation, even when most reforming, that temperate spirit of equity which has refused to visit the sins of centuries upon a single generation. The statute limited its accusations to the points which it was designed to correct, and touched these with a hand firmly gentle.

"Whereas great numbers of the king's subjects," says the preamble, "as well men, wives, servants, or others dwelling in divers dioceses of the realm of England and Wales, heretofore have been at many times called by citations and other processes compulsory to appear in the Arches, Audience, and other high Courts of the archbishops of this realm, far from and out of the dioceses where such persons are inhabitant and dwelling; and many times to answer to surmised and feigned causes and matters, which have been sued more for vexation and malice than from any just cause of suit; and when certificate hath been made by the sumners, apparitors, or any such light litterate persons, that the party against whom such citations have been awarded hath been cited or summoned; and thereupon the same party so certified to be cited or summoned hath not appeared according to the certificate, the same party therefore hath been excommunicated, or, at the least, suspended from all divine service; and thereupon, before that he or she could be absolved, hath been compelled, not only to pay the fees of the court whereunto he or she was so called, amounting to the sum of two shillings, or twenty pence at the least; but also to pay to the sumner, for every mile distant from the place where he or she then dwelled unto the same court whereunto he or she was summoned to appear, twopence; to the great charge and impoverishment of the king's subjects, and to the great occasion of misbehaviour of wives, women, and servants, and to the great impairment and diminution of their good names and honesties—be it enacted——" We ask what?—looking with impatience for some large measure to follow these solemn accusations; and we find parliament contenting itself with forbidding the bishops, under heavy penalties, to cite any man out of his own diocese, except for specified causes (heresy being one of them), and with limiting the fees which were to be taken by the officers of the courts. 347 It could hardly be said that in this parliament there was any bitter spirit against the church. This act showed only mild forbearance and complacent endurance of all tolerable evil.

Another serious matter was dealt with in the same moderate temper. The Mortmain Act had prohibited the church corporations from further absorbing the lands; but the Mortmain Act was evaded in detail, the clergy using their influence to induce persons on their deathbeds to leave estates to provide a priest for ever "to sing for their souls." The arrangement was convenient possibly for both parties, or if not for both, certainly for one; but to tie up lands for ever for a special service was not to the advantage of the country; and it was held unjust to allow a man a perpetual power over the disposition of property to atone for the iniquities of his life. But the privilege was not abolished altogether; it was submitted only to reasonable limitation. Men might still burden their lands to find a priest for twenty years. After twenty years the lands were to relapse for the service of the living, and sinners were expected in equity to bear the consequence in their own persons of such offences as remained after that time unexpiated. 348

Thus, in two sessions, the most flagrant of the abuses first complained of were in a fair way of being remedied. The exorbitant charges for mortuaries, probate duties, legacy duties, the illegal exactions for the sacraments, the worst injustices of the ecclesiastical courts, the non-residence, pluralities, neglect of cures, the secular occupations and extravagant privileges of the clergy, were either terminated or brought within bounds. There remained yet to be disposed of the legislative power of the convocation and the tyrannical prosecutions for heresy. The last of these was not yet ripe for settlement; the former was under reconsideration by the convocation itself, which at length was arriving at a truer conception of its position; and this question was not therefore to be dealt with by the legislature.

One more important measure, however, was passed by parliament before it separated, and it is noticeable as the first step which was taken in the momentous direction of a breach with the See of Rome. A practice had existed for some hundreds of years in all the churches of Europe, that bishops and archbishops, on presentation to their sees, should transmit to the pope, on receiving their bulls of investment, one year's income from their new preferments. It was called the payment of annates, or firstfruits, and had originated in the time of the crusades, as a means of providing a fund for the holy wars. Once established, it had settled into custom, 349 and was one of the chief resources of the papal revenue. From England alone, as much as 160,000 pounds had been paid out of the country in fifty years; 350 and the impost was alike oppressive to individuals and injurious to the state. Men were appointed to bishopricks frequently at an advanced age, and dying, as they often did, within two or three years of their nomination, their elevation had sometimes involved their families and friends in debt and embarrassment; 351 while the annual export of so much bullion was a serious evil at a time when the precious metals formed the only currency, and were so difficult to obtain. Before a quarrel with the court of Rome had been thought of as a possible contingency, the king had laboured with the pope to terminate the system by some equitable composition; and subsequently cessation of payment had been mentioned more than once in cornection with the threats of a separation. The pope had made light of these threats, believing them to be no more than words; there was an opportunity, therefore, of proving that the English government was really in earnest, in a manner which would touch him in a point where he was naturally sensitive, and would show him at the same time that he could not wholly count on the attachment even of the clergy themselves. For, in fact, the church itself was fast disintegrating, and the allegiance even of the bishops and the secular clergy to Rome had begun to waver: they had a stronger faith in their own privileges than in the union of Christendom; and if they could purchase the continuance of the former at the price of a quarrel with the pope, some among them were not disinclined to venture the alternative. The Bishop of Rochester held aloof from such tendencies, and Warham, though he signed the address of the House of Lords to the pope, regretted the weakness to which he had yielded: but in the other prelates there was little seriousness of conviction; and the constitution of the bench had been affected also hy the preferment of Gardinei and Edward Lee to two of the sees made vacant by the death of Wolsey. Both these men had been active agents in the prosecution of the divorce; and Gardiner, followed at a distance by the other, had shaped out, as the pope grew more intractable, the famous notion that the English church could and should subsist as a separate communion, independent of foreign control, self governed, self organised, and at the same time adhering without variation to Catholic doctrine. This principle (if we may so abuse the word) shot rapidly into popularity: a party formed about it strong in parliament, strong in convocation, strong out of doors among the country gentlemen and the higher clergy—a respectable, wealthy, powerful body, trading upon a solecism, but not the less, therefore, devoted to its maintenance, and in their artificial horror of being identified with heresy, the most relentless persecutors of the Protestants. This party, unreal as they were, and influential perhaps in virtue of their unreality, became for the moment the arbiters of the Church of England; and the bishops belonging to it, and each rising ecclesiastic who hoped to be a bishop, welcomed the resistance of the annates as an opportunity for a demonstration of their strength. On this question, with a fair show of justice, they could at once relieve themselves of a burden which pressed upon their purses, and as they supposed, gratify the king. The conservatives were still numerically the strongest, and for a time remained in their allegiance to the Papacy, 352 but their convictions were too feeble to resist the influence brought to bear upon them, and when Parliament re-assembled after the Easter recess, the two Houses of Convocation presented an address to the crown for the abolition of the impost, and with it of all other exactions, direct and indirect,—the indulgences, dispensations, delegacies, and the thousand similar forms and processes by which the privileges of the Church of England were abridged for the benefit of the Church of Rome, and weighty injury of purse inflicted both on the clergy and the laity. 353

That they contemplated a conclusive revolt from Rome as a consequence of the refusal to pay annates, appears positively in the close of their address: "May it please your Grace," they concluded, after detailing their occasions for complaint,—"may it please your Grace to cause the said unjust exactions to cease, and to be foredone for ever by act of your high Court of Parliament; and in case the pope will make process against this realm for the attaining those annates, or else will retain bishops' bulls till the annates be paid; forasmuch as the exaction of the said annates is against the law of God and the pope's own laws, forbidding the buying or selling of spiritual gifts or promotions; and forasmuch as all good Christian men be more bound to obey God than any man; and forasmuch as St. Paul willeth us to withdraw from all such as walk inordinately; may it please your Highness to ordain in this present parliament that the obedience of your Highness and of the people be withdrawn from the See of Rome." 354

It was perhaps cruel to compel the clergy to be the first to mention separation—or the language may have been furnished by the Erastian party in the Church, who hoped to gratify the King by it, and save the annates for themselves; but there was no intention, if the battle was really to be fought, of decorating the clergy with the spoils. The bill was passed, but passed conditionally, leaving power to the Crown if the pope would consent to a compromise of settling the question by a composition. There was a Papal party in the House of Commons whose opposition had perhaps to be considered, 355 and the annates were left suspended before Clement at once as a menace and a bribe.

"Forasmuch," concluded the statute, "as the King's Highness and this his high Court of Parliament neither have nor do intend in this or any other like cause any manner of extremity or violence, before gentle courtesy and friendly ways and means be first approved and attempted, and without a very great urgent cause and occasion given to the contrary; but principally coveting to disburden this Realm of the said great exactions and intolerable charges of annates and firstfruits: [the said Court of Parliament] have therefore thought convenient to commit the final order and determination of the premises unto the King's Highness, so that if it may seem to his high wisdom and most prudent discretion meet to move the Pope's Holiness and the Court of Rome, amicably, charitably, and reasonably, to compound either to extinct the said annates, or by some friendly, loving, and tolerable composition to moderate the same in such way as may be by this his Realm easily borne and sustained, then those ways of composition once taken shall stand in the strength, force, and effect of a law." 356

The business of the session was closing. It remained to receive the reply of convocation on the limitation of its powers. The convocation, presuming, perhaps, upon its concessions on the annates question, and untamed by the premunire, had framed their answer in the same spirit which had been previously exhibited by the bishops. They had re-asserted their claims as resting on divine authority, and had declined to acknowledge the right of any secular power to restrain or meddle with them. 357 The second answer, as may be supposed, fared no better than the first. It was returned with a peremptory demand for submission; and taught by experience the uselessness of further opposition, the clergy with a bad grace complied. The form was again drawn by the bishops, and it is amusing to trace the workings of their humbled spirit in their reluctant descent from their high estate. They still laboured to protect their dignity in the terms of their concession:—

"As concerning such constitutions and ordinances provincial," they wrote, "as shall be made hereafter by your most humble subjects, we having our special trust and confidence in your most excellent wisdom, your princely goodness, and fervent zeal for the promotion of God's honour and Christian religion, and specially in your incomparable learning far exceeding in our judgment the learning of all other kings and princes that we have read of; and not doubting but that the same should still continue and daily increase in your Majesty; do offer and promise here unto the same, that from henceforth we shall forbear to enact, promulge, or put in execution any such constitutions and ordinances so by us to be made in time coming, unless your Highness by your Royal assent shall license us to make, promulge, and execute such constitutions, and the same so made be approved by your Highness's authority.

"And whereas your Highness's most honourable Commons do pretend that divers of the constitutions provincial, which have been heretofore enacted, be not only much prejudicial to your Highness's prerogative royal, but be also overmuch onerous to your said Commons, we, your most humble servants for the consideration before said, be contented to refer all the said constitutions to the judgment of your Grace only. And whatsoever of the same shall finally be found prejudicial and overmuch onerous as is pretended, we offer and promise your Highness to moderate or utterly to abrogate and annul the same, according to the judgment of your Grace. Saving to us always such liberties and immunities of this Church of England as hath been granted unto the same by the goodness and benignity of your Highness and of others your most noble progenitors; with such constitutions provincial as do stand with the laws of Almighty God and of your Realm heretofore made, which we most humbly beseech your Grace to ratify and approve by your most Royal assent for the better execution of the same in times to come." 358

The acknowledgment appeared to be complete, and might perhaps have been accepted without minute examination, except for the imprudent acuteness of the Lower House of Convocation. As it passed through their hands, they discovered—what had no doubt been intended as a loophole for future evasion—that the grounds which were alleged to excuse the submission were the virtues of the reigning king: and therefore, as they sagaciously argued, the submission must only remain in force for his life. They introduced a limitation to that effect. Some further paltry dabbling was also attempted with the phraseology: and at length, impatient with such dishonest trifling, and weary of a discussion in which they had resolved to allow but one conclusion, the king and the legislature thought it well to interfere with a high hand, and cut short such unprofitable folly. The language of the bishops was converted into an act of parliament; a mixed commission was appointed to revise the canon law, and the clergy with a few brief strokes were reduced for ever into their fit position of subjects. 359 Thus with a moderate hand this great revolution was effected, and, to outward appearance, with offence to none except the sufferers, whose misuse of power when they possessed it deprived them of all sympathy in their fall.

But no change of so vast a kind can be other than a stone of stumbling to those many persons for whom the beaten ways of life alone are tolerable, and who, when these ways are broken, are bewildered and lost. Religion, when men are under its influence at all, so absorbs their senses, and so pervades all their associations, that no faults in the ministers of it can divest their persons of reverence; and just and necessary as all these alterations were, many a pious and noble heart was wounded, many a man was asking himself in his perplexity where things would end, and still more sadly, where, if these quarrels deepened, would lie his own duty. Now the Nun of Kent grew louder in her Cassandra wailings. Now the mendicant friars mounted the pulpits exclaiming sacrilege; bold men, who feared nothing that men could do to them, and who dared in the king's own presence, and in his own chapel, to denounce him by name. 360 The sacred associations of twelve centuries were tumbling into ruin; and hot and angry as men had been before the work began, the hearts of numbers sank in them when they "saw what was done;" and they fell away slowly to doubt, disaffection, distrust, and at last treason.

The first outward symptom of importance pointing in this direction, was the resignation of the seals by Sir Thomas More. 361 More had not been an illiberal man; when he wrote the *Utopia*, he seemed even to be in advance of his time. None could see the rogue's face under the cowl clearer than he, or the proud bad heart under the scarlet hat; and few men had ventured to speak their thoughts more boldly. But there was in More a want of confidence in human nature, a scorn of the follies of his fellow creatures which, as he became more earnestly religious, narrowed and hardened his convictions, and transformed the genial philosopher into the merciless bigot. "Heresy" was naturally hateful to him; his mind was too clear and genuine to allow him to deceive himself with the delusions of Anglicanism; and as he saw the inevitable tendency of the Reformation to lead ultimately to a change of doctrine, he attached himself with increasing determination to the cause of the pope and of the old faith. As if with an instinctive prescience of what would follow from it, he had from the first been opposed to the divorce; and he had not concealed his feeling from the king at the time when the latter had pressed the seals on his unwilling acceptance. In consenting to become chancellor, he had yielded only to Henry's entreaties; he had held his office for two years and a half—and it would have been well for his memory if he had been constant in his refusal—for in his ineffectual struggles against the stream, he had attempted to counterpoise the attack upon the church by destroying the unhappy Protestants. At the close of the session, however, the acts of which we have just described, he felt that he must no longer countenance, by remaining in an office so near to the crown, measures which he so intensely disapproved and deplored; it was time for him to retire from a world not moving to his mind; and in the fair tranquillity of his family prepare himself for the evil days which he foresaw. In May, 1532, he petitioned for permission to resign, resting his request unobtrusively on failing health; and Henry sadly consented to lose his services.

Parallel to More's retirement, and though less important, yet still noticeable, is a proceeding of old Archbishop Warham under the same trying circumstances. In the days of his prosperity, Warham had never reached to greatness as a man. He had been a great ecclesiastic, successful, dignified, important, but without those highest qualities which command respect or interest. The iniquities of Warham's spiritual courts were greater than those of any other in England. He had not made them what they were. They grew by their own proper corruption; and he was no more responsible for them than every man is responsible for the continuance of an evil by which he profits, and which he has power to remedy. We must look upon him as the leader of the bishops in their opposition to the reform; and he was the probable author of the famous answer to the Commons' petition, which led to such momentous consequences. 362 These consequences he had lived partially to see. Powerless to struggle against the stream, he had seen swept away one by one those gigantic privileges to which he had asserted for his order a claim divinely sanctioned; and he withdrew himself heartbroken, into his palace at Lambeth, and there entered his solemn protest against all which had been done. Too ill to write, and trembling on the edge of the grave, he dictated to his notaries from his bed these not unaffecting words:—

"In the name of God, Amen. We, William, by Divine Providence Archbishop of Canterbury, Primate of all England, Legate of the Apostolic See, hereby publicly and expressly do protest for ourselves and for our Holy Metropolitan Church of Canterbury, that to any statute passed or hereafter to be passed in this present Parliament, began the third of November, 1529, and continued until this present time; in so far as such statute or statutes be in derogation of the Pope of Rome or the Apostolic See, or be to the hurt, prejudice, or limitation of the powers of the Church, or shall tend to the subverting, enervating, derogating from, or diminishing the laws, customs, privileges, prerogatives, pre-eminence of liberties of our Metropolitan Church of Canterbury; we neither will, nor intend, nor with clear conscience are able to consent to the same, but by these writings we do dissent from, refuse, and contradict them." 363

Thus formally having delivered his soul, he laid himself down and died.

CHAPTER V.
MARRIAGE OF HENRY AND ANNE BOLEYN

Although in the question of the divorce the king had interfered despotically to control the judgment of the universities, he had made no attempt, as we have seen, to check the tongues of the clergy. Nor if he had desired to check them, is it likely that at the present stage of proceedings he could have succeeded. No law had as yet been passed which made a crime of a difference of opinion on the pope's dispensing powers; and so long as no definitive sentence had been pronounced, every one had free liberty to think and speak as he pleased. So great, indeed, was the anxiety to disprove Catherine's assertion that England was a *locus suspectus*, and therefore that the cause could not be equitably tried there, that even in the distribution of patronage there was an ostentatious display of impartiality. Not only had Sir Thomas More been made chancellor, although emphatically on Catherine's side; but Cuthbert Tunstal, who had been her counsel, was promoted to the see of Durham. The Nun of Kent, if her word was to be believed, had been offered an abbey, 364 and that Henry permitted language to pass unnoticed of the most uncontrolled violence, appears from a multitude of informations which were forwarded to the government from all parts of the country. But while imposing no restraint on the expression of opinion, the council were careful to keep themselves well informed of the opinions which were expressed, and an instrument was ready made to their hands, which placed them in easy possession of what they desired. Among the many abominable practices which had been introduced by the ecclesiastical courts, not the least hateful was the system of espionage with which they had saturated English society; encouraging servants to be spies on their masters, children on their parents, neighbours on their neighbours, inviting every one who heard language spoken anywhere of doubtful allegiance to the church, to report the words to the nearest official, as an occasion of instant process. It is not without a feeling of satisfaction, that we find this detestable invention recoiling upon the heads of its authors. Those who had so long suffered under it, found an opportunity in the turning tide, of revenging themselves on their oppressors; and the country was covered with a ready-made army of spies, who, with ears ever open, were on the watch for impatient or disaffected language in their clerical superiors, and furnished steady reports of such language to Cromwell. 365

Specimens of these informations will throw curious light on the feelings of a portion at least of the people. The English licence of speech, if not recognised to the same extent as it is at present, was certainly as fully practised. On the return of the Abbot of Whitby from the convocation at York in the summer of 1532, when the premunire money was voted, the following conversation was reported as having been overheard in the abbey.

The prior of the convent asked the abbot what the news were. "What news," said the abbot, "evil news. The king is ruled by a common — — Anne Boleyn, who has made all the spiritualty to be beggared, and the temporalty also. Further he told the prior of a sermon that he had heard in York, in which it was said, when a great wind rose in the west we should hear news. And he asked what that was; and he said a great man told him at York, and if he knew as much as three in England he would tell what the news were. And he said who were they? and he said the Duke of Norfolk, the Earl of Wiltshire, and the common — — Anne Boleyn." 366

The dates of these papers cannot always be determined; this which follows, probably, is something later, but it shows the general temper in which the clergy were disposed to meet the measures of the government.

"Robert Legate, friar of Furness, deposeth that the monks had a prophecy among them, that 'in England shall be slain the decorate rose in his mother's belly,' and this they interpret of his Majesty, saying that his Majesty shall die by the hands of priests; for the church is the mother, and the church shall slay his Grace. The said Robert maintaineth that he hath heard the monks often say this. Also, it is said among them that the King's Grace was not the right heir to the crown; for that his Grace's father came in by no line, but by the sword. Also, that no secular knave should be head of the church; also that the abbot did know of these treasons, and had made no report thereof." 367

Nor was it only in the remote abbeys of the North that such dangerous language was ventured. The pulpit of St. Paul's rang Sunday after Sunday with the polemics of the divorce; and if "the holy water of the court" made the higher clergy cringing and cowardly, the rank and file, even in London itself, showed a bold English front, and spoke out their thoughts with entire recklessness. Among the preachers on Catherine's side, Father Forest, famous afterward in Catholic martyrologies, began to distinguish himself. Forest was warden of a convent of Observants at Greenwich attached to the royal chapel, and having been Catherine's confessor, remained, with the majority of the friars, faithful to her interests, and fearless in the assertion of them. From their connection with the palace, the intercourse of these monks with the royal household was considerable; their position gave them influence, and Anne Boleyn tried the power of her charms, if possible, to gain them over. She had succeeded with a few of the weaker brothers, but she was unable (and her inability speaks remarkably for Henry's endurance of opposition through the early stages of the controversy) to protect those whose services she had won from the anger of their superiors. One monk in whom she was interested the warden imprisoned, 368 another there was an effort to expel, 369 because he was ready to preach on her side; and Forest himself preached a violent sermon at Paul's Cross, attacking Cromwell and indirectly the king. 370 He was sent for to the court, and the persecuted brothers expected their triumph; but he returned, as one of them wrote bitterly to Cromwell, having been received with respect and favour, as if, after all, the enmity of a brave man found more honour at the court than the complacency of cowardice. Father Forest, says this letter, has been with the king. "He says he spake with the king for half an hour and more, and was well retained by his Grace; and the King's Grace did send him a great piece of beef from his own table; and also he met with my Lord of Norfolk, and he says he took him in his arms and bade him welcome." 371

Forest, unfortunately for himself, misconstrued forbearance into fear, and went his way at last, through treason and perjury, to the stake. In the meantime the Observants were left in possession of the royal chapel, the weak brother died in prison, and the king, when at Greenwich, continued to attend service, submitting to listen, as long as submission was possible, to the admonitions which the friars used the opportunity to deliver to him.

In these more courteous days we can form little conception of the licence which preachers in the sixteenth century allowed themselves, or the language which persons in high authority were often obliged to bear. Latimer spoke as freely to Henry VIII. of neglected duties, as to the peasants in his Wiltshire parish. St. Ambrose did not rebuke the Emperor Theodosius more haughtily than John Knox lectured Queen Mary and her ministers on the vanities of Holyrood; and Catholic priests, it seems, were not afraid to display even louder disrespect.

On Sunday, the first of May, 1532, the pulpit at Greenwich was occupied by Father Peto, afterwards Cardinal Peto, famous through Europe as a Catholic incendiary; but at this time an undistinguished brother of the Observants convent. His sermon had been upon the story of Ahab and Naboth, and his text had been, "Where the dogs licked the blood of Naboth, even there shall they lick thy blood, O king." Henry, the court, and most likely Anne Boleyn herself, were present; the first of May being the great holy-day of the English year, and always observed at Greenwich with peculiar splendour. The preacher had dilated at length upon the crimes and the fall of Ahab, and had drawn the portrait in all its magnificent wickedness. He had described the scene in the court of heaven, and spoken of the lying prophets who had mocked the monarch's hopes before the fatal battle. At the end, he turned directly to Henry, and assuming to himself the mission of Micaiah, he closed his address in the following audacious words:—"And now, O king," he said, "hear what I say to thee. I am that Micaiah whom thou wilt hate, because I must tell thee truly that this marriage is unlawful, and I know that I shall eat the bread of affliction and drink the waters of sorrow, yet because the Lord hath put it in my mouth I must speak it. There are other preachers, yea too many, which preach and persuade thee otherwise, feeding they folly and frail affections upon hopes of their own worldly promotion; and by that means they betray thy soul, thy honour, and thy posterity; to obtain fat benefices, to become rich abbots and bishops, and I know not what. These I say are the four hundred prophets who, in the spirit of lying, seek to deceive thee. Take heed lest thou, being seduced, find Ahab's punishment, who had his blood licked up by the dogs."

Henry must have been compelled to listen to many such invectives. He left the chapel without noticing what had passed; and in the course of the week Peto went down from Greenwich to attend a provincial council at Canterbury, and perhaps to communicate with the Nun of Kent. Meantime a certain Dr. Kirwan was commissioned to preach on the other side of the question the following Sunday.

Kirwan was one of those men of whom the preacher spoke prophetically, since by the present and similar services he made his way to the archbishopric of Dublin and the bishopric of Oxford, and accepting the Erastian theory of a Christian's duty, followed Edward VI. into heresy, and Mary into popery and persecution. He regarded himself as an official of the state religion; and his highest conception of evil in a Christian was disobedience to the reigning authority. We may therefore conceive easily the burden of his sermon in the royal chapel. "He most sharply reprehended Peto," calling him foul names, "dog, slanderer, base beggarly friar, rebel, and traitor," saying "that no subject should speak so audaciously to his prince:" he "commended" Henry's intended marriage, "thereby to establish his seed in his seat for ever;" and having won, as he supposed, his facile victory, he proceeded with his peroration, addressing his absent antagonist. "I speak to thee, Peto," he exclaimed, "to thee, Peto, which makest thyself Micaiah, that thou mayest speak evil of kings; but now art not to be found, being fled for fear and shame, as unable to answer my argument." In the royal chapel at Greenwich there was more reality than decorum. A voice out of the rood-loft cut short the eloquent declamation. "Good sir," it said, "you know Father Peto is gone to Canterbury to a provincial council, and not fled for fear of you; for to-morrow he will return again. In the meantime I am here as another Micaiah, and will lay down my life to prove those things true which he hath taught. And to this combat I challenge thee; thee Kirwan, I say, who art one of the four hundred into whom the spirit of lying is entered, and thou seekest by adultery to establish the succession, betraying thy king for thy own vain glory into endless perdition."

A scene of confusion followed, which was allayed at last by the king himself, who rose from his seat and commanded silence. It was thought that the limit of permissible licence had been transcended, and the following day Peto and Elstowe, the other speaker, were summoned before the council to receive a reprimand. Lord Essex told them they deserved to be sewn into a sack and thrown into the Thames. "Threaten such things to rich and dainty folk, which have their hope in this world," answered Elstowe, gallantly, "we fear them not; with thanks to God we know the way to heaven to be as ready by water as by land." 372 Men of such metal might be broken, but they could not be bent. The two offenders were hopelessly unrepentant and impracticable, and it was found necessary to banish them. They retired to Antwerp, where we find them the following year busy procuring copies of the Bishop of Rochester's book against the king, which was broadly disseminated on the continent, and secretly transmitting them into England; in close correspondence also with Fisher himself, with Sir Thomas More, and for the ill fortune of their friends, with the court at Brussels, between which and the English Catholics the intercourse was dangerously growing. 373

The Greenwich friars, with their warden, went also a bad way. The death of the persecuted brother was attended with circumstances in a high degree suspicious. 374 Henry ordered an enquiry, which did not terminate in any actual exposure; but a cloud hung over the convent, which refused to be dispelled; the warden was deposed, and soon after it was found necessary to dissolve the order.

If the English monks had shared as a body the character of the Greenwich Observants, of the Carthusians of London and Richmond, and of some other establishments, — which may easily be numbered, — the resistance which they might have offered to the government, with the sympathy which it would have commanded, would have formed an obstacle to the Reformation that no power could have overcome. It was time, however, for the dissolution of the monasteries, when the few among them, which on other grounds might have claimed a right to survive, were driven by their very virtues into treason. The majority perished of their proper worthlessness; the few remaining contrived to make their existence incompatible with the safety of the state.

Leaving for the present these disorders to mature themselves, I must now return to the weary chapter of European diplomacy, to trace the tortuous course of popes and princes, duping one another with false hopes; saying what they did not mean, and meaning what they did not say. It is a very Slough of Despond, through which we must plunge desperately as we may; and we can cheer ourselves in this dismal region only by the knowledge that, although we are now approaching the spot where the mire is deepest, the hard ground is immediately beyond.

We shall, perhaps, be able most readily to comprehend the position of the various parties in Europe, by placing them before us as they stood severally in the summer of 1532, and defining briefly the object which each was pursuing.

Henry only, among the great powers, laid his conduct open to the world, declaring truly what he desired, and seeking it by open means. He was determined to proceed with the divorce, and he was determined also to continue the Reformation of the English Church. If consistently with these two objects he could avoid a rupture with the pope, he was sincerely anxious to avoid it. He was ready to make great efforts, to risk great sacrifices, to do anything short of surrendering what he considered of vital moment, to remain upon good terms with the See of Rome. If his efforts failed, and a quarrel was inevitable, he desired to secure himself by a close maintenance of the French alliance; and having induced Francis to urge compliance upon the pope by a threat of separation if he refused, to prevail on him, in the event of the pope's continued obstinacy, to put his threat in execution, and unite with England in a common schism. All this is plain and straightforward—Henry concealed nothing, and, in fact, had nothing to conceal. In his threats, his promises, and his entreaties, we feel entire certainty that he was speaking his real thoughts.

The emperor's position, also, though not equally simple, is intelligible, and commands our respect. Although if he had consented to sacrifice his aunt, he might have spared himself serious embarrassment; although both by the pope and by the consistory such a resolution would probably have been welcomed with passionate thankfulness; yet at all hazards Charles was determined to make her his first object, even with the risk of convulsing Europe. At the same time his position was encumbered with difficulty. The Turks were pressing upon him in Hungary and in the Mediterranean; his relations with Francis—fortunately for the prospects of the Reformation— were those of inveterate hostility; while in Germany he had been driven to make terms with the Protestant princes; he had offended the pope by promising them a general council, in which the Lutheran divines should be represented; and the pope, taught by recent experience, was made to fear that these symptoms of favour towards heresy, might convert themselves into open support.

With Francis the prevailing feeling was rivalry with the emperor, combined with an eager desire to recover his influence in Italy, and to restore France to the position in Europe which had been lost by the defeat of Pavia, and the failure of Lautrec at Naples. This was his first object, to which every other was subsidiary. He was disinclined to a rupture with the pope; but the possibility of such a rupture had been long contemplated by French statesmen. It was a contingency which the pope feared:—which the hopes of Henry pictured as more likely than it was—and Francis, like his rivals in the European system, held the menace of it extended over the chair of St. Peter, to coerce its unhappy occupant into compliance with his wishes. With respect to Henry's divorce, his conduct to the University of Paris, and his assurances repeated voluntarily on many occasions, show that he was sincerely desirous to forward it. He did not care for Henry, or for England, or for the cause itself; he desired only to make the breach between Henry and Charles irreparable; to make it impossible for ever that "his two great rivals" should become friends together; and by inducing the pope to consent to the English demand, to detach the court of Rome conclusively from the imperial interests.

The two princes who disputed the supremacy of Europe, were intriguing one against the other, each desiring to constitute himself the champion of the church; and to compel the church to accept his services, by the threat of passing over to her enemies. By a dexterous use of the cards which were in his hands, the King of France proposed to secure one of two alternatives. Either he would form a league between himself, Henry, and the pope, against the emperor, of which the divorce, and the consent to it, which he would extort from Clement, should be the cement; or, if this failed him, he would avail himself of the vantage ground which was given to him by the English alliance to obtain such concessions for himself at the emperor's expense as the pope could be induced to make, and the emperor to tolerate.

Such, in so far as I can unravel the web of the diplomatic correspondence, appear to have been the open positions and the secret purposes of the great European powers.

There remains the fourth figure upon the board, the pope himself, labouring with such means as were at his disposal to watch over the interests of the church, and to neutralise the destructive ambition of the princes, by playing upon their respective selfishnesses. On the central question, that of the divorce, his position was briefly this. Both the emperor and Henry pressed for a decision. If he decided for Henry, he lost Germany; if he decided for Catherine, while Henry was supported by Francis, France and England threatened both to fall from him. It was therefore necessary for him to induce the emperor to consent to delay, while he worked upon the King of France; and, if France and England could once be separated, he trusted that Henry would yield in despair. This most subtle and difficult policy reveals itself in the transactions open and secret of the ensuing years. It was followed with a dexterity as extraordinary as its unscrupulousness, and with all but perfect success. That it failed at all, in the ordinary sense of failure, was due to the accidental delay of a courier; and Clement, while he succeeded in preserving the allegiance of France to the Roman see, succeeded also—and this is no small thing to have accomplished—in weaving the most curious tissue of falsehood which will be met with even in the fertile pages of Italian subtlety.

With this general understanding of the relation between the great parties in the drama, let us look to their exact position in the summer of 1532.

Charles was engaged in repelling an invasion of the Turks, with an anarchical Germany in his rear, seething with fanatical anabaptists, and clamouring for a general council.

Henry and Francis had been called upon to furnish a contingent against Solyman, and had declined to act with the emperor. They had undertaken to concert their own measures between themselves, if it proved necessary for them to move; and in the meantime Cardinal Grammont and Cardinal Tournon were sent by Francis to Rome, to inform Clement that unless he gave a verdict in Henry's favour, the Kings of France and England, being *une mesme chose*, would pursue some policy with respect to him, 375 to which he would regret that he had compelled them to have recourse. So far their instructions were avowed and open. A private message revealed the secret means by which the pope might escape from his dilemma; the cardinals were to negotiate a marriage between the Duke of Orleans and the pope's niece (afterwards so infamously famous), Catherine de Medicis. The marriage, as Francis represented it to Henry, was beneath the dignity of a prince of France, he had consented to it, as he professed, only for Henry's sake; 376 but the pope had made it palatable by a secret article in the engagement, for the grant of the duchy of Milan as the lady's dowry.

Henry, threatened as we have seen with domestic disturbance, and with further danger on the side of Scotland, which Charles had succeeded in agitating, concluded, on the 23rd of June, a league, offensive and defensive, with Francis, the latter engaging to send a fleet into the Channel, and to land 15,000 troops in England if the emperor should attempt an invasion from the sea. 378 For the better consolidation of this league, and to consult upon the measures which they would pursue on the great questions at issue in Christendom, and lastly to come to a final understanding on the divorce, it was agreed further that in the autumn the two kings should meet at Calais. The conditions of the interview were still unarranged on the 22nd of July, when the Bishop of Paris, who remained ambassador at the English court, wrote to Montmorency to suggest that Anne Boleyn should be invited to accompany the King of England on this occasion, and that she should be received in state. The letter was dated from Ampthill, to which Henry had escaped for a while from his Greenwich friars and other troubles, and where the king was staying a few weeks before the house was given up to Queen Catherine. Anne Boleyn was with him; she now, as a matter of course, attended him everywhere. Intending her, as he did, to be the mother of the future heir to his crown, he preserved what is technically called her honour unimpeached and unimpaired. In all other respects she occupied the position and received the homage due to the actual wife of the English sovereign; and in this capacity it was the desire of Henry that she should be acknowledged by a foreign prince.

The bishop's letter on this occasion is singularly interesting and descriptive. The court were out hunting, he said, every day; and while the king was pursuing the heat of the chase, he and Mademoiselle Anne were posted together, each with a crossbow, at the point to which the deer was to be driven. The young lady, in order that the appearance of her reverend cavalier might correspond with his occupation, had made him a present of a hunting cap and frock, a horn and a greyhound. Her invitation to Calais he pressed with great earnestness, and suggested that Marguerite de Valois, the Queen of Navarre, should be brought down to entertain her. The Queen of France being a Spaniard, would not, he thought, be welcome: "the sight of a Spanish dress being as hateful in the King of England's eyes as the devil himself." In other respects the reception should be as magnificent as possible, "and I beseech you," he concluded, "keep out of the court, *deux sortes de gens*, the imperialists, and the wits and mockers; the English can endure neither of them." 379

Through the tone of this language the contempt is easily visible with which the affair was regarded in the French court. But for Francis to receive in public the rival of Queen Catherine, to admit her into his family, and to bring his sister from Paris to entertain her, was to declare in the face of Europe, in a manner which would leave no doubt of his sincerity, that he intended to countenance Henry. With this view only was the reception of Anne desired by the King of England; with this view it was recommended by the bishop, and assented to by the French court. Nor was this the only proof which Francis was prepared to give, that he was in earnest. He had promised to distribute forty thousand crowns at Rome, in bribing cardinals to give their voices for Henry in the consistory, with other possible benefactions. 380

He had further volunteered his good offices with the court of Scotland, where matters were growing serious, and where his influence could be used to great advantage. The ability of James the Fifth to injure Henry happily fell short of his inclination, but encouraged by secret promises from Clement and from the emperor, he was waiting his opportunity to cross the Border with an army; and in the meantime he was feeding with efficient support a rebellion in Ireland. Of what was occurring at this time in that perennially miserable country I shall speak in a separate chapter. It is here sufficient to mention, that on the 23rd of August, Henry received information that McConnell of the Isles, after receiving knighthood from James, had been despatched into Ulster with four thousand men, 381 and was followed by Mackane with seven thousand more on the 3rd of September. 382 Peace with England nominally continued; but the Kers, the Humes, the Scotts of Buccleugh, the advanced guard of the Marches, were nightly making forays across the Border, and open hostilities appeared to be on the point of explosion. 383 If war was to follow, Henry was prepared for it. He had a powerful force at Berwick, and in Scotland itself a large party were secretly attached to the English interests. The clan of Douglas, with their adherents, were even prepared for open revolt, and open transfer of allegiance. 384 But, although Scottish nobles might be gained over, and Scottish armies might be defeated in the field, Scotland itself, as the experience of centuries had proved, could never be conquered. The policy of the Tudors had been to abstain from aggression, till time should have soothed down the inherited animosity between the two countries; and Henry was unwilling to be forced into extremities which might revive the bitter memories of Flodden. The Northern counties also, in spite of their Border prejudices, were the stronghold of the papal party, and it was doubtful how far their allegiance could be counted upon in the event of an invasion sanctioned by the pope. The hands of the English government were already full without superadded embarrassment, and the offered mediation of Francis was gratefully welcomed.

These were the circumstances under which the second great interview was to take place between Francis the First and Henry of England. 385 Twelve years had passed since their last meeting, and the experience which those years had brought to both of them, had probably subdued their inclination for splendid pageantry. Nevertheless, in honour of the occasion, some faint revival was attempted of the magnificence of the Field of the Cloth of Gold. Anne Boleyn was invited duly; and the Queen of Navarre, as the Bishop of Paris recommended, came down to Boulogne to receive her. The French princes came also to thank Henry in person for their deliverance out of their Spanish prison; and he too, on his side, brought with him his young Marcellus, the Duke of Richmond, his only son—illegitimate unfortunately—but whose beauty and noble promise were at once his father's misery and pride; giving point to his bitterness at the loss of his sons by Catherine; quickening his hopes of what might be, and deepening his discontent with that which was. If this boy had lived, he would have been named to follow Edward the Sixth in the succession, and would have been King of England; 386 but he too passed away in the flower of his loveliness, one more evidence of the blight which rested upon the stem of the Tudors.

The English court was entertained by Francis at Boulogne. The French court was received in return at Calais by the English. The outward description of the scene, the magnificent train of the princes, the tournaments, the feasts, the dances, will be found minutely given in the pages of Hall, and need not be repeated here. To Hall indeed, the outward life of men, their exploits in war, and their pageantries in peace, alone had meaning or interest; and the backstairs secrets of Vatican diplomacy, the questionings of opinion, and all the brood of mental sicknesses then beginning to distract the world, were but impertinent interferences with the true business of existence. But the healthy objectiveness of an old English chronicler is no longer possible for us; we may envy where we cannot imitate; and our business is with such features of the story as are of moment to ourselves

The political questions which were to be debated at the conference, were three; the Turkish Invasion, the General Council, and King Henry's divorce.

On the first, it was decided that there was no immediate occasion for France and England to move. Solyman's retreat from Vienna had relieved Europe from present peril; and the enormous losses which he had suffered, might prevent him from repeating the experiment. If the danger became again imminent, however, the two kings agreed to take the field in person the following year at the head of eighty thousand men.

On the second point they came to no conclusion, but resolved only to act in common.

On the third and most important, they parted with a belief that they understood each other; but their memories, or the memory of one of them, proved subsequently treacherous; and we can only extract what passed between them out of their mutual recriminations.

It was determined certainly that at the earliest convenient moment, a meeting should take place between the pope and Francis; and that at this meeting Francis should urge in person concession to Henry's demands. If the pope professed himself unable to risk the displeasure of the emperor, it should be suggested that he might return to Avignon, where he would be secure under the protection of France and England. If he was still reluctant, and persisted in asserting his right to compel Henry to plead before him at Rome, or if he followed up his citations by inhibitions, suspensions, excommunications, or other form of censure, Francis declared that he would support Henry to the last, whether against the pope himself or against any prince or potentate who might attempt to enforce the sentence. On this point the promises of the King of France were most profuse and decided; and although it was not expressly stated in words, Henry seems to have persuaded himself that, if the pope pressed matters to extremities, Francis had engaged further that the two countries should pursue a common course, and unite in a common schism. The two princes did in fact agree, that if the general council which they desired was refused, they would summon provincial councils on their own authority. Each of them perhaps interpreted their engagements by their own wishes or interests. 387

We may further believe, since it was affirmed by Henry, and not denied by Francis, that the latter advised Henry to bring the dispute to a close, by a measure from which he could not recede; that he recommended him to act on the general opinion of Europe that his marriage with Queen Catherine was null, and at once upon his return to England to make Anne Boleyn his wife. 388

So far the account is clear. This advice was certainly given, and as certainly Francis undertook to support Henry through all the consequences in which the marriage might involve him. But a league for mutual defence fell short of what Henry desired, and fell short also of what Francis, by the warmth of his manner, had induced Henry for the moment to believe that he meant. It is probable that the latter pressed upon him engagements which he avoided by taking refuge in general professions; and no sooner had Henry returned to England, than either misgivings occurred to him as to the substantial results of the interview, or he was anxious to make the French king commit himself more definitely. He sent to him to beg that he would either write out, or dictate and sign, the expressions which he had used; professing to wish it only for the comfort which he would derive from the continual presence of such refreshing words—but surely for some deeper reason. 389

Francis had perhaps said more than he meant; Henry supposed him to have meant more than he said. Yet some promise was made, which was not afterwards observed; and Francis acknowledged some engagement in an apology which he offered for the breach of it. He asserted, in defence of himself, that he had added a stipulation which Henry passed over in silence,—that no steps should be taken towards annulling the marriage with Catherine in the English law courts until the effect had been seen of his interview with the pope, provided the pope on his side remained similarly inactive. 390 Whatever it was which he had bound himself to do, this condition, if made at all, could be reconciled only with his advice that Henry should marry Anne Boleyn without further delay, on the supposition that the interview in question was to take place immediately; for the natural consequences of the second marriage would involve, as a matter of course, some speedy legal declaration with respect to the first. And when on various pretexts the pope postponed the meeting, and on the other part of his suggestion Henry had acted within a few months of his return from Calais, it became impossible that such a condition could be observed. It availed for a formal excuse; but Francis vainly endeavoured to disguise his own infirmity of purpose behind the language of a negotiation which conveyed, when it was used, a meaning widely different.

The conference was concluded on the 1st of November, but the court was detained at Calais for a further fortnight by violent gales in the Channel. In the excited state of public feeling, events in themselves ordinary assumed a preternatural significance. The friends of Queen Catherine, to whom the meeting between the kings was of so disastrous augury, and the nation generally, which an accident to Henry at such a time would have plunged into a chaos of confusion, alike watched the storm with anxious agitation; on the king's return to London, Te Deums were offered in the churches, as if for his deliverance from some extreme and imminent peril. The Nun of Kent on this great occasion was admitted to conferences with angels. She denounced the meeting, under celestial instruction, as a conspiracy against Heaven. The king, she said, but for her interposition, would have proceeded, while at Calais, to his impious marriage; 391 and God was so angry with him, that he was not permitted to profane with his unholy eyes the blessed Sacrament. "It was written in her revelations," says the statute of her attainder, "that when the King's Grace was at Calais, and his Majesty and the French king were hearing mass in the Church of Our Lady, that God was so displeased with the King's Highness, that his Grace saw not at that time the blessed sacrament in the form of bread, for it was taken away from the priest, being at mass, by an angel, and was ministered to the said

Elizabeth, there being present and invisible, and suddenly conveyed and rapt thence again into the nunnery where she was professed." 392

She had an interview with Henry on his return through Canterbury, to try the effect of her Cassandra presence on his fears; 393 but if he still delayed his marriage, it was probably neither because he was frightened by her denunciations, nor from alarm at the usual occurrence of an equinoctial storm. Many motives combined to dissuade him from further hesitation. Six years of trifling must have convinced him that by decisive action alone he could force the pope to a conclusion. He was growing old, and the exigencies of the succession, rendered doubly pressing by the long agitation, required immediate resolution. He was himself satisfied that he was at liberty to marry whom he pleased and when he pleased, his relationship to Catherine, according to his recent convictions, being such as had rendered his connection with her from the beginning invalid and void. His own inclinations and the interests of the nation pointed to the same course. The King of France had advised it. Even the pope himself, at the outset of the discussion, had advised it also. "Marry freely," the pope had said; "fear nothing, and all shall be arranged as you desire." He had forborne to take the pope at his word; he had hoped that the justice of his demands might open a less violent way to him; and he had shrunk from a step which might throw even a causeless shadow over the legitimacy of the offspring for which he longed. The case was now changed; no other alternative seemed to be open to his choice, and it was necessary to bring the matter to a close once and for all.

But Henry, as he said himself, was past the age when passion or appetite would be likely to move him, and having waited so many years, he could afford to wait a little longer, till the effects of the Calais conferences upon the pope should have had time to show themselves. In December, Clement was to meet the emperor at Bologna. In the month following, it might be hoped that he would meet Francis at Marseilles or Avignon, and from their interview would be seen conclusively the future attitude of the papal and imperial courts. Experience of the past forbade anything like sanguine expectation; yet it was not impossible that the pope might be compelled at last to yield the required concessions. The terms of Henry's understanding with Francis were not perhaps made public, but he was allowed to dictate the language which the French cardinals were to make use of in the consistory; 394 and the reception of Anne Boleyn by the French king was equivalent to the most emphatic declaration that if the censures of the church were attempted in defence of Catherine, the enforcement of them would be resisted by the combined arms of France and England.

And the pope did in fact feel himself in a dilemma from which all his address was required to extricate him. He had no support from his conscience, for he knew that he was acting unjustly in refusing the divorce; while to risk the emperor's anger, which was the only honest course before him, was perhaps for that very reason impossible. He fell back upon his Italian cunning, and it did not fail him in his need. But his conduct, though creditable to his ingenuity, reflects less pleasantly on his character; and when it is traced through all its windings, few reasonable persons will think that they have need to blush at the causes which led to the last breach between England and the papacy.

From the time of Catherine's appeal and the retirement of Campeggio, Clement, with rare exceptions, had maintained an attitude of impassive reserve. He had allowed judgment to be delayed on various pretexts, because until that time delay had answered his purposes sufficiently. But to the English agents he had been studiously cold, not condescending even to hold out hopes to them that concession might be possible. Some little time before the meeting at Calais, however, a change was observed in the language both of the pope himself and of the consistory. The cardinals were visibly afraid of the position which had been taken by the French king; questions supposed to be closed were once more admitted to debate in a manner which seemed to show that their resolution was wavering; and one day, at the close of a long argument, the following curious conversation took place between some person (Sir Gregory Cassalis, apparently), who reported it to Henry, and Clement himself. "I had desired a private interview with his Holiness," says the writer, "intending to use all my endeavours to persuade him to satisfy your Majesty. But although I did my best, I could obtain nothing from him; he had an answer for everything which I advanced, and it was in vain that I laboured to remove his difficulties. At length, however, in reply to something which I had proposed, he said shortly,—Multo minus scandalosum fuisset dispensare cum majestate vestrâ super duabus uxoribus, quam ea cedere quæ ego petebam, *it would have created less scandal to have granted your Majesty a dispensation to have two wives than to concede what I was then demanding.* As I did not know how far this alternative would be pleasing to your Majesty, I endeavoured to divert him from it, and to lead him back to what I had been previously saying. He was silent for a while, and then, paying no regard to my interruption, he continued to speak of the 'two wives,' admitting however that there were difficulties in the way of such an arrangement, principally it seemed because the emperor would refuse his consent from the possible injury which it might create to his cousin's prospects of the succession. I replied, that as to the succession, I could not see what right the emperor had to a voice upon the matter. If some lawful means could be discovered by which your Majesty could furnish yourself with male offspring, the emperor could no more justly complain than if the queen were to die and the prospects of the princess were interfered with by a second marriage of an ordinary kind. To this the pope made no answer. I cannot tell what your Majesty will think, nor how far this suggestion of the pope would be pleasing to your Majesty. Nor indeed can I feel sure, in consequence of what he said about the emperor, that he actually would grant the dispensation of which he spoke. I have thought it right, however, to inform you of what passed." 395

This letter is undated, but it was written, as appears from internal evidence, some time in the year 1532. 396

The pope's language was ambiguous, and the writer did not allow himself to derive from it any favourable augury; but the tone in which the suggestions had been made was by many degrees more favourable than had been heard for a very long time in the quarter from which they came, and the symptoms which it promised of a change of feeling were more than confirmed in the following winter.

Charles was to be at Bologna in the middle of December, where he was to discuss with Clement the situation of Europe, and in particular of Germany, with the desirableness of fulfilling the engagements into which he had entered for a general council.

This was the avowed object of the meeting. But, however important the question of holding a council was becoming, it was not immediately pressing; and we cannot doubt that the disquiet occasioned by the alliance of England and France was the cause that the conference was held at so inconvenient a season. The pope left Rome on the 18th of November, having in his train a person who afterwards earned for himself a dark name in English history, Dr. Bonner, then a famous canon lawyer attached to the embassy. The journey in the wild weather was extremely miserable; and Bonner, whose style was as graphic as it was coarse, sent home a humorous account of it to Cromwell. 397 Three wretched weeks the party were upon the road, plunging through mire and water. They reached Bologna on the 8th of December, where, four days after them, arrived Charles V. It is important, as we shall presently see, to observe the dates of these movements. I shall have to compare with them the successive issues of several curious documents. On the 12th of December the pope and the emperor met at Bologna; on the 24th Dr. Bennet, Henry's able secretary, who had been despatched from England to be present at the conference, wrote to report the result of his observations. He had been admitted to repeated interviews with the pope, as well before as after the emperor's arrival; and the language which the former made use of could only be understood, and was of course intended to be understood, as expressing the attitude in which he was placing himself towards the imperial faction. Bennet's letter was as follows:—

"I have been sundry and many times with the pope, as well afore the coming of the emperour as sythen, yet I have not at any time found his Holiness more tractable or propense to show gratuity unto your Highness than now of late,—insomuch that he hath more freely opened his mind than he was accustomed, and said also that he would speak with me frankly without any observance or respect at all. At which time, I greatly lamented (your Highness's cause being so just) no means could be found and taken to satisfy your Highness therein; and I said also that I doubted not but that (if his Holiness would) ways might be found by his wisdom, now at the emperour's being with him, to satisfy your Highness; and that done, his Holiness should not only have your Highness in as much or more friendship than he hath had heretofore, but also procure thereby that thing which his Holiness hath chiefly desired, which is, as he hath said, a universal concord among the princes of Christendom. His Holiness answered, that he would it had cost him a joint of his hand that such a way might be excogitate; and he said also, that the best thing which he could see to be done therein at this present, for a preparation to that purpose, was the thing which is contained in the first part of the cipher. 398 Speaking of the justness of your cause, he called to his remembrance the thing which he told me two years past; which was, that the opinion of the lawyers was more certain, favourable, and helping to your cause than the opinion of the divines; for he said that as far as he could perceive, the lawyers, though they held quod Papa possit dispensare in this case, yet they commonly do agree quod hoc fieri debeat ex maximâ causâ, adhibitâ causæ cognitione, which in this case doth not appear; and he said, that to come to the truth herein he had used all diligence possible, and enquired the opinion of learned men, being of fame and indifferency both in the court here and in other places. And his Holiness promised me that he would herein use all good policy and dexterity to imprint the same in the emperour's head; which done, he reckoneth many things to be invented that may be pleasant and profitable to your Highness; adding yet that this is not to be done with a fury, but with leisure and as occasion shall serve, lest if he should otherwise do, he should let and hinder that good effect which peradventure might ensue thereby." 399

This letter has all the character of truth about it. The secretary had no interest in deceiving Henry, and it is quite certain that, whether honestly or not, the pope had led him to believe that his sympathies were again on the English side, and that he was using his best endeavours to subdue the emperor's opposition.

On the 26th of December, two days later, Sir Gregory Cassalis, who had also followed the papal court to Bologna, wrote to the same effect. He, too, had been with the pope, who had been very open and confidential with him. The emperor, the pope said, had complained of the delay in the process, but he had assured him that it was impossible for the consistory to do more than it had done. The opinion of the theologians was on the whole against the papal power of dispensation in cases of so close relationship; of the canon lawyers part agreed with the theologians, and those who differed from them were satisfied that such a power might not be exercised unless there were most urgent cause, unless, that is, the safety of a kingdom were dependent upon it. Such occasion he had declared that he could not find to have existed for the dispensation granted by his predecessor. The emperor had replied that there had been such occasion: the dispensation had been granted to prevent war between Spain and England; and that otherwise great calamities would have befallen both countries. But this was manifestly untrue; and his Holiness said that he had answered, It was a pity, then, that these causes had not been submitted at the time, as the reason for the demand, which it was clear that they had not been: as the case stood, it was impossible for him to proceed further. Upon which he added, "Se vidisse Cæsarem obstupefactum." "I write the words," continued Sir Gregory, "exactly as the pope related them to me. Whether he really spoke in this way, I cannot tell; of this, however, I am sure, that on the day of our conversation he had taken the blessed sacrament. He assured me further, that he had laboured to induce the emperor to permit him to satisfy your Majesty. I recommended him that when next the emperor spoke with him upon the subject, he should enter at greater length on the question of *justice*, and that some other person should be present at the conference, that there might be no room left for suspicion." 400

The manner of Clement was so unlike what Cassalis had been in the habit of witnessing in him, that he was unable, as we see, wholly to persuade himself that the change was sincere: the letter, however, was despatched to England, and was followed in a few days by Bonner, who brought with him the result of the pope's good will in the form of definite propositions — instructions of similar purport having been forwarded at the same time to the papal nuncio in England. The pope, so Henry was informed, was now really well disposed to do what was required; he had urged upon the emperor the necessity of concessions, and the cause might be settled in one of two ways, to either of which he was himself ready to consent. Catherine had appealed against judgment being passed in England, as a place which was not indifferent. Henry had refused to allow his cause to be heard anywhere but in his own realm; pleading first his privilege as a sovereign prince; and secondly, his exemption as an Englishman. 401 The pope, with appearance of openness, now suggested that Henry should either "send a mandate requiring the remission of his cause to an indifferent place, in which case he would himself surrender his claim to have it tried in the courts at Rome, and would appoint a legate and two auditors to hear the trial elsewhere;" or else, a truce of three or four years being concluded between England, France, and Spain, the pope would "with all celerity indict a general council, to which he would absolutely and wholly remit the consideration of the question." 402

Both proposals carried on their front a show of fair dealing, and if honestly proffered, were an evidence that something more might at length be hoped than words. But the true obstacle to a settlement lay, as had been long evident, rather in the want of an honest will, than in legal difficulties or uncertainty as to the justice of the cause; and while neither of the alternatives as they stood were admissible or immediately desirable, there were many other roads, if the point of honesty were once made good, which would lead more readily to the desired end. Once for all Henry could not consent to plead out of England; while an appeal to a council would occupy more time than the condition of the country could conveniently allow. But the offer had been courteously made; it had been accompanied with language which might be sincere; and the king replied with grace, and almost with cordiality; not wholly giving Clement his confidence, but expressing a hope that he might soon be no longer justified in withholding it. He was unable, he said, to accept the first condition, because it was contrary to his coronation oath; "it so highly touched the prerogative royal of the realm, that though he were minded to do it, yet must he abstain without the assent of the court of parliament, which he thought verily would never condescend to it." 403 The other suggestion he did not absolutely reject, but the gathering of a council was too serious a matter to be precipitated, and the situation of Christendom presented many obstacles to a measure which would be useless unless it were carried through by all the great powers in a spirit of cordial unanimity. He trusted therefore that if the pope's intentions were really such as he pretended to entertain, he would find some method more convenient of proving his sincerity.

It was happy for Henry that experience had taught him to be distrustful. Events proved too clearly that Clement's assumed alteration of tone was no more than a manœuvre designed to entice him to withdraw from the position in which he had entrenched himself, and to induce him to acknowledge that he was amenable to an earthly authority exterior to his own realm. 404

In his offer to refer the cause to a general council, he proved that he was insincere, when in the following year he refused to allow a council to be a valid tribunal for the trial of it. The course which he would have followed if the second alternative had been accepted, may be conjectured from the measures which, as I shall presently show, he was at this very moment secretly pursuing. Henry, however, had happily resolved that he would be trifled with no further; he felt instinctively that only action would cut the net in which he was entangled; and he would not hesitate any longer to take a step which, in one way or another, must bring the weary question to a close. If the pope meant well, he would welcome a resolution which made further procrastination impossible; if he did not mean well, he could not be permitted to dally further with the interests of the English nation. Within a few days, therefore, of Bonner's return from Bologna, he took the final step from which there was no retreat, and "somewhere about St. Paul's day," 405 Anne Boleyn received the prize for which she had thirsted seven long years, in the hand of the King of England. The ceremony was private. No authentic details are known either of the scene of it or the circumstances under which it took place; but it is said to have been performed by the able Rowland Lee, Bishop of Lichfield, summoned up for the purpose from the Welsh Marches, of which he was warden. It was done, however—in one way or other finally done—the cast was thrown, and a match was laid to the train which now at length could explode the spell of intrigue, and set Henry and England free.

We have arrived at a point from which the issue of the labyrinth is clearly visible. The course of it has been very dreary; and brought in contact as we have been with so much which is painful, so much which is discreditable to all parties concerned, we may perhaps have lost our sense of the broad bearings of the question in indiscriminate disgust. It will be well, therefore, to pause for a moment to recapitulate those features of the story which are the main indications of its character, and may serve to guide our judgment in the censure which we shall pass.

It may be admitted, or it ought to be admitted, that if Henry VIII. had been contented to rest his demand for a divorce merely on the interests of the kingdom, if he had forborne, while his request was pending, to affront the princess who had for many years been his companion and his queen; if he had shown her that respect which her high character gave her a right to demand, and which her situation as a stranger ought to have made it impossible to him to refuse; his conduct would have been liable to no imputation, and our sympathies would without reserve have been on his side. He could not have been expected to love a person to whom he had been married as a boy for political convenience, merely because she was his wife; especially when she was many years his senior in age, disagreeable in her person, and by the consciousness of it embittered in her temper. His kingdom demanded the security of a stable succession; his conscience, it may not be doubted, was seriously agitated by the loss of his children; and looking upon it as the sentence of Heaven upon a connection, the legality of which had from the first been violently disputed, he believed that he had been living in incest, and that his misfortunes were the consequence of it. Under these circumstances he had a full right to apply for a divorce. 406

The causa urgentissima of the canon law for which, by the pope's own showing, the dispensing powers had been granted to him, had arisen in an extreme form; and when the vital interests of England were sacrificed to the will of a foreign prince, sufficient reason had arisen for the nation to decline submission to so emphatic injustice, and to seek within itself its own remedies for its own necessities. These considerations must be allowed all their weight; and except for them, it is not to be supposed that Henry would have permitted private distaste or inclination to induce him to create a scandal in Europe. In his conduct, however, as in that of most men, good was chequered with evil, and sincerity with self-deception. Personal feeling can be traced from the first, holding a subsidiary, indeed, but still an influential place, among his motives; and exactly so far as he was influenced by it, his course was wrong, as the consequence miserably proved. The position which, in his wife's presence, he assigned to another woman, however he may have persuaded himself that Catherine had no claim to be considered his wife, admits neither of excuse nor of palliation; and he ought never to have shared his throne with a person who consented to occupy that position. He was blind to the coarseness of Anne Boleyn, because, in spite of his chivalry, his genius, his accomplishments, in his relations with women he was without delicacy himself. He directed, or attempted to direct, his conduct by the broad rules of what he thought to be just; and in the wide margin of uncertain ground where rules of action cannot be prescribed, and where men must guide themselves by consideration for the feelings of others, he—so far as women were concerned—was altogether or almost a stranger. Such consideration is a virtue which can be learned only in the society of equals, where necessity obliges men to practise it. Henry had been a king from his boyhood; he had been surrounded by courtiers who had anticipated all his desires; and exposed as he was to an ordeal from which no human being could have escaped uninjured, we have more cause, after all, to admire him for those excellences which he conquered for himself, than to blame the defects which he retained.

But if in his private relations the king was hasty and careless, towards the pope to whom we must now return, he exhausted all resources of forbearance: and although, when separation from Rome was at length forced upon him, he then permitted no half measures, and swept into his new career with the strength of irresistible will, it was not till he had shown resolution no less great in the endurance of indignity; and of the three great powers in Europe, the prince who was compelled to break the unity of the Catholic church, was evidently the only one who was capable of real sacrifices to preserve it unbroken. Clement comprehended his reluctance, but presumed too far upon it; and if there was sin in the "great schism" of the Reformation, the guilt must rest where it is due. We have now to show the reverse side of the transactions at Bologna, and explain what a person wearing the title of his Holiness, in virtue of his supposed sanctity, had been secretly doing.

In January, 1532, some little time before his conversation with Sir Gregory Cassalis on the subject of the two wives, the pope had composed a pastoral letter to Henry, which had never been issued. From its contents it would seem to have been written on the receipt of an indignant remonstrance of Queen Catherine, in which she had complained of her desertion by her husband, and of the public position which had been given to her rival. She had supposed (and it was the natural mistake of an embittered and injured woman) that Anne Boleyn had been placed in possession of the rights of an actual, and not only of an intended wife; and the pope, accepting her account of the situation, had written to implore the king to abstain, so long as the cause remained undetermined, from creating so great a scandal in Christendom, and to restore his late queen to her place at his side. This letter, as it was originally written, was one of Clement's happiest compositions. 407 He abstained in it from using any expression which could be construed into a threat: he appealed to Henry's honourable character, which no blot had hitherto stained; and dwelling upon the general confusion of the Christian world, he urged with temperate earnestness the ill effects which would be produced by so open a defiance of the injunctions of the Holy See in a person of so high a position. So far all was well. Henry had deserved that such a letter should be written to him; and the pope was more than justified in writing it. The letter, however, if it was sent, produced no effect, and on the 15th of November, three days before Clement's departure to Bologna, where he pretended (we must not forget) that he considered Henry substantially right; he added a postscript, in a tone not contrasting only with his words to the ambassadors, but with the language of the brief itself.

Again urging Henry's delinquencies, his separation from his wife, and the scandal of his connection with another person, he commanded him, under penalty of excommunication, within one month of the receipt of those injunctions, to restore the queen to her place, and to abstain thenceforward from all intercourse with Anne Boleyn pending the issue of the trial. "Otherwise," the pope continued, "when the said term shall have elapsed, we pronounce thee, Henry King of England, and the said Anne, to be *ipso facto* excommunicate, and command all men to shun and avoid your presence; and although our mind shrinks from allowing such a thought of your Serenity, although by ourselves and by our auditory of the Rota an inhibition has been already issued against you; although the act of which you are suspected be in itself forbidden by all laws human and divine, yet the reports which are brought to us do so move us, that once more we do inhibit you from dissolving your marriage with the aforesaid Catherine, or from continuing process, in your own courts, of divorce from her. And we do also hereby warn you, that you presume not to contract any new marriage with the said or with any other woman; we declare such marriage, if you still attempt it, to be vain and of none effect, and so to be regarded by all persons in obedience to the Apostolic see." 408

An inhibitory mandate, was a natural consequence of the conference of Calais, provided that the pope intended to proceed openly and uprightly; and if it had been sent upon the spot, Henry could have complained of nothing worse than of an honourable opposition to his wishes. But the mystery was not yet exhausted. The postscript was not issued, it was not spoken of; it was carried secretly to Bologna, and it bears at its foot a further date of the 23rd of December, the very time, that is to say, at which the pope was representing himself to Bennet as occupied only in devising the best means of satisfying Henry, and to Sir Gregory Cassalis, as so convinced of the justice of the English demands, that he had ventured in defence of them to the edge of rupture with the emperor.

It might be urged that he was sincere both in his brief and in his conversation; that he believed that a verdict ought to be given, and would at last be given, against the original marriage, and that therefore he was the more anxious to prevent unnecessary scandal. Yet a menace of excommunication couched in so haughty a tone, could have been honestly reconciled with his other conduct, only by his following a course with respect to it which he did not follow—by informing the ambassadors openly of what he had done, and transmitting his letter through their hands to Henry himself. This he might have done; and though the issue of such a document at such a time would have been open to question, it might nevertheless have been defended. His Holiness, however, did nothing of the kind. No hint was let fall of the existence of any minatory brief; he sustained his pretence of good will, till there was no longer any occasion for him to counterfeit; and two months later it suddenly appeared on the doors of the churches in Flanders.

Henry at first believed it to be forgery, One forged brief had already been produced by the imperialists in the course of their transactions, and he imagined that this was another; even his past experience of Clement had not prepared him for this last venture of effrontery; he wrote to Bennet, enclosing a copy, and requiring him to ascertain if it were really genuine. 409

The pope could not deny his hand, though the exposure, and the strange irregular character of the brief itself troubled him, and Bonner, who was again at the papal court, said that "he was in manner ashamed, and in great perplexity what he might do therein." 410

His conduct will be variously interpreted, and to attempt to analyse the motives of a double-minded man is always a hazardous experiment; but a comparison of date, the character of Clement himself, the circumstances in which he was placed, and the retrospective evidence from after events, points almost necessarily to but one interpretation. It is scarcely disputable that, frightened at the reception of Anne Boleyn in France, the pope found it necessary to pretend for a time an altered disposition towards Henry; and that the emperor, unable to feel wholly confident that a person who was false to others was true to himself, had exacted the brief from him as a guarantee for his good faith; Charles, on his side, reserving the publication until Francis had been gained over, and until Clement was screened against the danger which he so justly feared, from the consequences of the interview at Calais.

There was duplicity of a kind; this cannot be denied; and if not designed to effect this object, this object in fact it answered. While Clement was talking smoothly to Bennet and Cassalis, secret overtures were advanced at Paris for a meeting at Nice between the pope, the emperor, and the King of France, from which Henry was to be excluded. 411 The emperor made haste with concessions to Francis, which but a few months before would have seemed impossible. He withdrew his army out of Lombardy, and left Italy free; he consented to the marriage which he had so earnestly opposed between Catherine de Medici and the Duke of Orleans, agreeing also, it is probable, to the contingency of the Duchy of Milan becoming ultimately her dowry. And Francis having coquetted with the proposal for the Nice meeting, 412 not indeed accepting, but not absolutely rejecting it, Charles consented also to waive his objections to the interview between Francis and the pope, on which he had looked hitherto with so much suspicion; provided that the pope would bear in mind some mysterious and unknown communication which had passed at Bologna. 413

Thus was Francis won. He cared only, as the pope had seen, for his own interests; and from this time he drew away, by imperceptible degrees, from his engagements to England. He did not stoop to dishonour or treacherous betrayal of confidence, for with all his faults he was, in the technical acceptation of that misused term, a gentleman. He declined only to maintain the attitude which, if he had continued in it, would have compelled the pope to yield; and although he continued honestly to urge him to make concessions, he no longer affected to make them the price of preserving France in allegiance to the Holy See. Nor need we regret that Francis shrank from a resolution which Henry had no right to require of him. To have united with France in a common schism at the crisis of the Reformation would have only embarrassed the free motions of England; and two nations whose interests and whose tendencies were essentially opposite, might not submit to be linked together by the artificial interests of their princes. The populace of England were unconsciously on the rapid road to Protestantism. The populace of France were fanatically Catholic. England was to go her way through a golden era of Elizabeth to Cromwell, the Puritans, and a Protestant republic; a republic to be perpetuated, if not in England herself, yet among her great children beyond the sea. France was to go her way through Bartholomew massacres and the dragonnades to a polished Louis the Magnificent, and thence to the bloody Medea's cauldron of Revolution, out of which she was to rise as now we know her. No common road could have been found for such destinies as these; and the French prince followed the direction of his wiser instincts when he preferred a quiet arrangement with the pope, in virtue of which his church should be secured by treaty the liberties which she desired, to a doubtful struggle for a freedom which his people neither wished nor approved. The interests of the nation were in fact his own. He could ill afford to forsake a religion which allowed him so pleasantly to compound for his amatory indulgences by the estrapade 414 and a zeal for orthodoxy.

It became evident to Henry early in the spring that he was left substantially alone. His marriage had been kept secret with the intention that it should be divulged by the King of France to the pope when he met him at Marseilles; and as the pope had pretended an anxiety that either the King of England should be present in person at that interview, or should be represented by an ambassador of adequate rank, a train had been equipped for the occasion, the most magnificent which England could furnish. Time, meanwhile, passed on; the meeting, which was to have taken place first in January, and then in April, was delayed till October, and in the interval the papal brief had appeared in Flanders; the queen's pregnancy could not admit of concealment; and the evident proof which appeared that France was no longer to be depended upon, convinced the English government that they had nothing to hope for from abroad, and that Henry's best resources were to be found, where in fact they had always been, in the strength and affection of his own people.

From this choking atmosphere, therefore, we now turn back to England and the English parliament; and the change is from darkness to light, from death to life. Here was no wavering, no uncertainty, no smiling faces with false hearts behind them; but the steady purpose of resolute men, who slowly, and with ever opening vision, bore the nation forward to the fair future which was already dawning.

Parliament met at the beginning of February, a few days after the king's marriage, which, however, still remained a secret. It is, I think, no slight evidence of the calmness with which the statesmen of the day proceeded with their work, that in a session so momentous, in a session in which the decisive blow was to be struck of the most serious revolution through which the country as yet had passed, they should have first settled themselves calmly down to transact what was then the ordinary business of legislation, the struggle with the vital evils of society. The first nine statutes which were passed in this session were economic acts to protect the public against the frauds of money-making tradesmen; to provide that shoes and boots should be made of honest leather; that food should be sold at fair prices, that merchants should part with their goods at fair profits; to compel, or as far as the legislature was able to do it, to compel all classes of persons to be true men; to deal honestly with each other, in that high Quixotic sense of honesty which requires good subjects at all times and under all circumstances to consider the interests of the commonwealth as more important than their own. I have already spoken of this economic legislation, and I need not dwell now upon details of it; although under some aspects it may be thought that more which is truly valuable in English history lies in these unobtrusive statutes than in all our noisy wars, reformations, and revolutions. The history of this as of all other nations (or so much of it as there is occasion for any of us to know), is the history of the battles which it has fought and won with evil; not with political evil merely, or spiritual evil; but with all manifestations whatsoever of the devil's power. And to have beaten back, or even to have struggled against and stemmed in ever so small a degree those besetting basenesses of human nature, now held so invincible that the influences of them are assumed as the fundamental axioms of economic science; this appears to me a greater victory than Agincourt, a grander triumph of wisdom and faith and courage than even the English constitution or the English liturgy. Such a history, however, lies beside the purpose which I may here permit myself; and the two acts with which the session closed, alone in this place require our attention.

The first of these is one of the many "Acts of Apparel," which are to be found in the early volumes of the statute book. The meaning of these laws becomes intelligible when we reflect upon the condition of the people.

The English were an organised nation of soldiers; they formed an army perpetually ready for the field, where the degrees were determined by social position; and the dresses prescribed to the various orders of society were the graduated uniforms which indicated the rank of the wearers. When every man was a soldier, and every gentleman was an officer, the same causes existed for marking, by costume, the distinctions of authority, which lead to the answering differences in the modern regiments.

The changing conditions of the country at the time of the Reformation, the growth of a middle class, with no landed possessions, yet made wealthy by trade or other industry, had tended necessarily to introduce confusion; and the policy of this reign, which was never more markedly operative than during the most critical periods of it, was to reinvigorate the discipline of the feudal system; and pending the growth of what might better suit the age, pending the great struggle in which the nation was engaged, to hold every man at his post. The statute specifies its object, and the motives with which it was passed.

"Whereas," says the preamble, "divers laws, ordinances, and statutes have been with great deliberation and advice provided and established for the necessary repressing and avoiding the inordinate excess daily more and more used in the sumptuous and costly array and apparel accustomably worn in this realm, whereof hath ensued, and daily do chance such sundry high and notable inconveniences as be to the great and notorious detriment of the commonweal, the subversion of politic order in knowledge and distinction of people according to their preeminence and degrees, to the utter impoverishment and undoing of many light and inexpert persons inclined to pride, the mother of all vices: Be it enacted," 415—but I need not enter into the particulars of the uniforms worn by the nobles and gentlemen of the court of Henry VIII.; the temper, not the detail, is of importance; and of the wisdom or unwisdom of such enactments, we who live in a changed age should be cautious of forming a hasty opinion. The ends which the old legislation proposed to itself, have in latter ages been resigned as impracticable. We are therefore no longer adequate judges how far those ends may in other times have been attainable, and we can still less judge of the means through which the attainment of them was sought.

The second act of which I have to speak is open to no such ambiguity; it remains among the few which are and will be of perpetual moment in our national history. The conduct of the pope had forced upon the parliament the reconsideration of the character of his supremacy; and when the question had once been asked, in the existing state of feeling but one answer to it was possible.

The authority of the church over the state, the supreme kingship of Christ, and consequently of him who was held to be Christ's vicar, above all worldly sovereignties, was an established reality of mediæval Europe. The princes had with difficulty preserved their jurisdiction in matters purely secular; while in matters spiritual, and in that vast section of human affairs in which the spiritual and the secular glide one into the other, they had been compelled—all such of them as lay within the pale of the Latin communion—to acknowledge a power superior to their own. To the popes was the ultimate appeal in all causes of which the spiritual courts had cognisance. Their jurisdiction had been extended by an unwavering pursuit of a single policy, and their constancy in the twelfth century was rewarded by absolute victory. In England, however, the field was no sooner won than it was again disputed, and the civil government gave way at last only when the danger seemed to have ceased. So long as the papacy was feared, so long as the successors of St. Peter held a sword which could inflict sensible wounds, and enforce obedience by penalties, the English kings had resisted both the theory and the application. While the pope was dangerous he was dreaded and opposed. When age had withered his arm, and the feeble lightnings flickered in harmless insignificance, they consented to withdraw their watchfulness, and his supremacy was silently allowed as an innocent superstition. It existed as some other institutions exist at the present day, with a merely nominal authority; with a tacit understanding, that the power which it was permitted to retain should be exerted only in conformity with the national will.

Under these conditions the Tudor princes became loyal subjects to the Holy See, and so they would have willingly remained, had not Clement, in an evil hour for himself, forgotten the terms of the compact. He laid upon a legal fiction a strain which his predecessors, in their palmiest days, would have feared to attempt; and the nation, after grave remonstrance, which was only received with insults, exorcised the chimæra with a few resolute words for ever. The parliament, in asserting the freedom of England, carefully chose their language. They did not pass a new law, but they passed an act declaratory merely of the law which already existed, and which they were vindicating against illegal encroachment. "Whereas," says the Statute of Appeals, "by divers sundry old authentic histories and chronicles, it is manifestly declared and expressed that this realm of England is an empire, and so hath been accepted in the world; governed by one supreme head and king, having the dignity and royal estate of the imperial crown of the same; unto whom a body politic compact of all sorts and degrees of people, divided in terms by names of spiritualty and temporalty, be bound and ought to bear, next to God, a natural and humble obedience: he being also institute and furnished by the goodness and sufferance of Almighty God with plenary, whole, and entire power, pre-eminence and authority, prerogative and jurisdiction, to render and yield justice and final determination to all manner of folk resident or subject within this his realm, without restraint or provocation to any foreign prince or potentate of the world: the body spiritual whereof having power when any cause of the law divine happened to come in question, or of spiritual learning, [such cause being] declared, interpret, and shewed by that part of the body politic called the spiritualty, now usually called the English church; (which also hath been reported and also found of that sort, that both for knowledge, integrity, and sufficiency of numbers, it hath been always thought to be, and is also at this hour sufficient and meet of itself, without the interfering of any exterior person or persons, to declare and determine all such doubts, and to administer all such offices and duties as to the administration of their rooms spiritual doth appertain): and the laws temporal, for trial of property of lands and goods, and for the conservation of the people of this realm in unity and peace, having been and yet being administered, adjudged, and executed by sundry judges and administers of the said body politic called the temporalty: and seeing that both these authorities and jurisdictions do conjoin together for the due administration of justice, the one to help the other: and whereas the king's most noble progenitors, and the nobility and commons of this said realm at divers and sundry parliaments, as well in the time of King Edward I., Edward III., Richard II., Henry IV., and other noble kings of this realm, made sundry ordinances, laws, and provisions for the conservation of the prerogatives, liberties, and pre-eminences of the imperial crown of this realm, and of the jurisdiction spiritual and temporal of the same, to keep it from the annoyance as well of the see of Rome as from the authority of other foreign potentates attempting the diminution or violation thereof, as often as from time to time any such annoyance or attempt might be known or espied: and notwithstanding the said good statutes and ordinances, and since the making thereof, divers inconveniences and dangers not provided for plainly by the said statutes, have risen and sprung by reason of appeals sued out of this realm to the see of Rome, in causes testamentary, causes of matrimony and divorce, right of tithes, oblations, and obventions, not only to the great inquietation, vexation, trouble, costs, and charges of the King's Highness, and many of his subjects and residents in this his realm; but also to the delay and let of the speedy determination of the said causes, for so much as parties appealing to the said court of Rome most commonly do the same for the delay of justice; and forasmuch as the great distance of way is so far out of this realm, so that the necessary proofs, nor the true knowledge of the causes, can neither there be so well known, nor the witnesses so well examined there as within this realm, so that the parties grieved by means of the said appeals be most times without remedy; in consideration hereof, all testamentary and matrimonial causes, and all suits for tithes, oblations, and obventions shall henceforth be adjudged in the spiritual and temporal courts within the realm, without regard to any process of foreign jurisdiction, or any inhibition, excommunication, or interdict. Persons procuring processes, inhibitions, appeals, or citations from the court of Rome, as well as their fautors, comforters, counsellors, aiders and abettors, all and every of them shall incur the penalties of premunire; and in all such cases as have hitherto admitted of appeal to Rome, the appeals shall be from the Archdeacon's court to the Bishop's court, from the Bishop's court to that of the Archbishop, and no further." 416

The act was carried through Parliament in February, but again, as with the Annates Bill, the king delayed his sanction till the post could reach and return from the Vatican. The Bishop of Bayonne wrote that there was hope that Clement might yet give way, and entreated that the king would send an "excusator," a person formally empowered to protest for him that he could not by the laws of England plead at a foreign tribunal; and that with this imperfect recognition of his authority the pope would be satisfied.

Chastillon, the French ambassador, had an interview with the king, to communicate the bishop's message.

"The morning after," Chastillon wrote, "his Majesty sent for me and desired me to repeat my words before the council. I obeyed; but the majority declared, that there was nothing in them to act upon, and that the king must not put himself in subjection. His Majesty himself, too, I found less warm than in his preceding conversation. I begged the council to be patient. I said everything that I could think of likely to weigh with the king, I promised him a sentence from our Holy Father declaring his first marriage null, his present marriage good. I urged him on all grounds, public and private, to avoid a rupture with the Holy See. Such a sentence, I said, would be the best security for the queen, and the safest guarantee for the unopposed succession of her offspring. If the marriage was confirmed by the Holy Father's authority, the queen's enemies would lose the only ground where they could make a stand. The peace of the realm was now menaced. The emperor talked loudly and made large preparations. Let the king be allied with France, and through France with the Holy See, and the emperor could do him no harm. Thus I said my proposals were for the benefit of the realm of his Majesty, and of the children who might be born to him. The king would act more prudently both for his own interest, and for the interest of his children, in securing himself, than in running a risk of creating universal confusion; and, besides, he owed something to the king his brother, who had worked so long and so hard for him.

"After some further conversation, his Majesty took me aside into a garden, where he told me that for himself he agreed in what I had said; but he begged me to keep his confidence secret. He fears, I think, to appear to condescend too easily.

"He will not, however, publish the acts of parliament till he sees what is done at Rome. The vast sums of money which used to be sent out of the country will go no longer; but in other respects he will be glad to return to good terms. He will send the excusator when he hears again from M. de Paris; and for myself, I think, that although the whole country is in a blaze against the pope, yet with the good will and assistance of the king, the Holy Father will be reinstated in the greater part of his prerogatives."

But the hope that the pope would yield proved again delusive. Henry wrote to him himself in the spirit of his conversation with Chastillon. His letter was presented by Cardinal Tournon, and Clement said all that could be said in acknowledgment without making the one vital concession. But whenever it was put before him that the cause must be heard and decided in England and in no other place, he talked in the old language of uncertainty and impossibilities; 417 and Henry learning at the same time that a correspondence was going forward between Clement and Francis, with the secrets of which he was not made acquainted, went forward upon his own way. April brought with it the certainty that the expected concessions were delusive. Anne Boleyn's pregnancy made further delay impossible. D'Inteville, who had succeeded Chastillon as French ambassador, once more attempted to interfere, but in vain. Henry told him he could not help himself, the pope forced him to the course which he was pursuing, by the answer which he had been pleased to issue; and he could only encounter enmity with its own weapons. "The archbishop," d'Inteville wrote to Francis, "will try the question, and will give judgment. I entreated the king to wait till the conference at Nice, but he would not consent. I prayed him to keep the sentence secret till the pope had seen your Majesty; he replied it was impossible." 418

Thus the statute became law which transferred to the English courts of law the power so long claimed and exercised by the Roman see. There are two aspects under which it may be regarded, as there were two objects for which it was passed. Considered as a national act, few persons will now deny that it was as just in itself as it was politically desirable. If the pope had no jurisdiction over English subjects, it was well that he should be known to have none; if he had, it was equally well that such jurisdiction should cease. The question was not of communion between the English and Roman churches, which might or might not continue, but which this act would not affect. The pope might still retain his rights of episcopal precedency, whatever those might be, with all the privileges attached to it. The parliament merely declared that he possessed no right of interference in domestic disputes affecting persons and property.

But the act had a special as well as a national bearing, and here it is less easy to arrive at a just conclusion. It destroyed the validity of Queen Catherine's appeal; it placed a legal power in the hands of the English judges to proceed to pass sentence upon the divorce; and it is open to the censure which we ever feel entitled to pass upon a measure enacted to meet the particular position of a particular person. When embarrassments have arisen from unforeseen causes, we have a right to legislate to prevent a repetition of those embarrassments. Our instincts tell us that no legislation should be retrospective, and should affect only positions which have been entered into with a full knowledge at the time of the condition of the laws.

The statute endeavours to avoid the difficulty by its declaratory form; but again this is unsatisfactory; for that the pope possessed some authority was substantially acknowledged in every application which was made to him; and when Catherine had married under a papal dispensation, it was a strange thing to turn upon her, and to say, not only that the dispensation in the particular instance had been unlawfully granted, but that the pope had no jurisdiction in the matter by the laws of the land which she had entered.

On the other hand, throughout the entire negotiations King Henry and his ministers had insisted jealously on the English privileges. They had declared from the first that they might, if they so pleased, fall back upon their own laws. In desiring that the cause might be heard by a papal legate in England, they had represented themselves rather as condescending to a form than acknowledging a right; and they had, in fact, in allowing the opening of Campeggio's court, fallen, all of them, even Henry himself, under the penalties of the statutes of provisors. The validity of Catherine's appeal they had always consistently denied. If the papal jurisdiction was to be admitted at all, it could only be through a minister sitting as judge within the realm of England; and the maxim, "Ne Angli extra Angliam litigare cogantur," was insisted upon as the absolute privilege of every English subject.

Yet, if we allow full weight to these considerations, a feeling of painful uncertainty continues to cling to us; and in ordinary cases to be uncertain on such a point is to be in reality certain. The state of the law could not have been clear, or the statute of appeals would not have been required; and explain it as we may, it was in fact passed for a special cause against a special person; and that person a woman.

How far the parliament was justified by the extremity of the case is a further question, which it is equally difficult to answer. The alternative, as I have repeatedly said, was an all but inevitable civil war, on the death of the king; and practically, when statesmen are entrusted with the fortunes of an empire, the responsibility is too heavy to allow them to consider other interests. Salus populi suprema lex, ever has been and ever will be the substantial canon of policy with public men, and morality is bound to hesitate before it censures them. There are some acts of injustice which no national interest can excuse, however great in itself that interest may be, or however certain to be attained by the means proposed. Yet government, in its easiest tax, trenches to a certain extent on natural right and natural freedom; and trenches further and further in proportion to the emergency with which it has to deal. How far it may go in this direction, or whether Henry VIII. and his parliament went too far, is a difficult problem; their best justification is an exceptive clause introduced into the act, which was intended obviously to give Queen Catherine the utmost advantage which was consistent with the liberties of the realm. "In case," says the concluding paragraph, "of any cause, or matter, or contention now depending for the causes before rehearsed, or that hereafter shall come into contention for any of the same causes in any of the foresaid courts, which hath, doth, shall, or may touch the king, his heirs or successors, kings of this realm; in all or every such case or cases the party grieved as aforesaid shall or may appeal from any of the said courts of this realm, to the spiritual prelates and other abbots and priors of the Upper House, assembled and convocate by the king's writ in convocation." 419 If Catherine's cause was as just as Catholics and English high churchmen are agreed to consider it, the English church might have saved her. If Catherine herself had thought first or chiefly of justice, she would not perhaps have accepted the arbitration of the English convocation; but long years before she would have been in a cloister.

Thus it is that while we regret, we are unable to blame; and we cannot wish undone an act, to have shrunk from which might have spared a single heart, but *might* have wrecked the English nation. We increase our pity for Catherine because she was a princess. We measure the magnitude of the evils which human beings endure by their position in the scale of society; and misfortunes which private persons would be expected to bear without excessive complaining, furnish matter for the lamentation of ages when they touch the sacred head which has been circled with a diadem. Let it be so. Let us compensate the queen's sorrows with unstinted sympathy; but let us not trifle with history, by confusing a political necessity with a moral crime.

The English parliament, then, had taken up the gauntlet which the pope had flung to it with trembling fingers: and there remained nothing but for the Archbishop of Canterbury to make use of the power of which by law he was now possessed. And the time was pressing, for the new queen was enciente, and further concealment was not to be thought of. The delay of the interview between the pope and Francis, and the change in the demeanour of the latter, which had become palpably evident, discharged Henry of all promises by which he might have bound himself; and to hesitate before the menaces of the pope's brief would have been fatal.

The act of appeals being passed, convocation was the authority to which the power of determining unsettled points of spiritual law seemed to have lapsed. In the month of April, therefore, Cranmer, now Archbishop of Canterbury, 420 submitted to it the two questions, on the resolution of which the sentence which he was to pass was dependent.

The first had been already answered separately by the bench of bishops and by the universities, and had been agitated from end to end of Europe—was it lawful to marry the widow of a brother dying without issue, but having consummated his marriage; and was the Levitical prohibition of such a marriage grounded on a divine law, with which the pope could not dispense, or on a canon law of which a dispensation was permissible? 421

The pope had declared himself unable to answer; but he had allowed that the general opinion was against the power of dispensing, 422 and there could be little doubt, therefore, of the reply of the English convocation, or at least of the upper house. Fisher attempted an opposition; but wholly without effect. The, question was one in which the interests of the higher clergy were not concerned, and they were therefore left to the dominion of their ordinary understandings. Out of two hundred and sixty-three votes, nineteen only were in the pope's favour. 423

The lower house was less unanimous, as might have been expected, and as had been experienced before; the opposition spirit of the English clergy being usually then, as much as now, in the ratio of their poverty. But there too the nature of the case compelled an overwhelming majority. 424 It was decided by both houses that Pope Julius, in granting a licence for the marriage of Henry and Catherine, had exceeded his authority, and that this marriage was therefore, *ab initio*, void.

The other question to be decided was one of fact; whether the marriage of Catherine with Prince Arthur had or had not been consummated, a matter which the Catholic divines conceived to be of paramount importance, but which to few persons at the present day will seem of any importance whosoever. We cannot even read the evidence which was produced without a sensation of disgust, although in those broader and less conscious ages the indelicacy was less obviously perceptible. And we may console ourselves with the hope that the discussion was not so wounding as might have been expected to the feelings of Queen Catherine, since at all official interviews, with all classes of persons, at all times and in all places, she appeared herself to court the subject. 425 There is no occasion in this place to follow her example. It is enough that Ferdinand, at the time of her first marriage, satisfied himself, after curious inquiry, that he might hope for a grandchild; and that the fact of the consummation was asserted in the treaty between England and Spain, which preceded the marriage with Henry, and in this supposed brief of Pope Julius which permitted it. 426 We cannot in consequence be surprised that the convocation accepted the conclusion which was sanctioned by so high authority, and we rather wonder at the persistency of Catherine's denials. With respect to this vote, therefore, we need notice nothing except that Dr. Clerk, Bishop of Bath and Wells 427 was one of an exceedingly small minority, who were inclined to believe that the denial might be true, and this bishop was one of the four who were associated with Cranmer when he sate at Dunstable for the trial of the cause.

The ground being thus opened, and all preparations being completed, the archbishop composed a formal letter to the king, in which he dwelt upon the uncertain prospects of the succession, and the danger of leaving a question which closely affected it so long unsettled. He expatiated at length on the general anxiety which was felt throughout the realm, and requested permission to employ the powers attached to his office to bring it to some conclusion. The recent alterations had rendered the archbishop something doubtful of the nature of his position; he was diffident and unwilling to offend; and not clearly knowing in the exercise of the new authority which had been granted to him, whether the extension of his power was accompanied with a parallel extension of liberty in making use of it, he wrote two copies of this letter, with slight alterations of language, that the king might select between them the one which he would officially recognise. Both these copies are extant; both were written the same day from the same place; both were folded, sealed, and sent. It seems, therefore, that neither was Cranmer furnished beforehand with a draught of what he was to write; nor was his first letter sent back to him corrected. He must have acted by his own judgment; and a comparison of the two letters is singular and instructive. In the first he spoke of his office and duty in language, chastened indeed and modest, but still language of independence; and while he declared his unwillingness to "enterprise any part of that office" without his Grace's favour obtained, and pleasure therein first known, he implied nevertheless that his request was rather of courtesy than of obligation, and had arisen rather from a sense of moral propriety than because he might not legally enter on the exercise of his duty without the permission of the crown. 428

The moderate gleam of freedom vanishes in the other copy under a few pithy changes, as if Cranmer instinctively felt the revolution which had taken place in the relations of church and state. Where in the first letter he asked for his Grace's favour, in the second he asked for his Grace's favour *and licence*—where in the first he requested to know his Grace's pleasure as to his proceeding, in the second he desired his Most Excellent Majesty to *license* him to proceed. The burden of both letters was the same, but the introduction of the little word license changed all. It implied a hesitating belief that the spiritual judges might perhaps thenceforward be on a footing with the temporal judges and the magistrates; that under the new constitution they were to understand that they held their offices not directly under God as they had hitherto pretended, but under God through the crown.

The answer of Henry indicated that he had perceived the archbishop's uncertainty; and that he was desirous by the emphatic distinctness of his own language to spare him a future recurrence of it. He accepted the deferential version of the petition; but even Cranmer's anticipation of what might be required of him had not reached the reality. In running through the preamble, the king flung into the tone of it a character of still deeper humility; 429 and he conceded the desired licence in the following imperial style. "In consideration of these things,"—*i.e.* of the grounds urged by the archbishop for the petition—"albeit we being your King and Sovereign, do recognise no superior on earth but only God, and not being subject to the laws of any earthly creature; yet because ye be under us, by God's calling and ours, the most principal minister of our spiritual jurisdiction within this our Realm, who we think assuredly is so in the fear of God, and love towards the observance of his laws, to the which laws, we as a Christian king have always heretofore, and shall ever most obediently submit ourself, we will not therefore refuse (our pre-eminence, power, and authority to us and to our successors in this behalf nevertheless saved) your humble request, offer, and towardness—that is, to mean to make an end according to the will and pleasure of Almighty God in our said great cause of matrimony, which hath so long depended undetermined, to our great and grievous unquietness and burden of our conscience. Wherefore we, inclining to your humble petition, by these our letters sealed with our seal, and signed with our sign manual, do license you to proceed in the said cause, and the examination and final determination of the same; not doubting but that ye will have God and the justice of the said cause only before your eyes, and not to regard any earthly or worldly affection therein; for assuredly the thing which we most covet in the world, is so to proceed in all our acts and doings as may be the most acceptable to the pleasure of Almighty God our Creator, to the wealth and honour of us, our successors and posterity, and the surety of our Realm, and subjects within the same." 430

The vision of ecclesiastical independence, if Cranmer had indulged in it, must have faded utterly before his eyes on receiving this letter. As clergy who committed felony were no longer exempted from the penalties of their crimes; so henceforward the courts of the clergy were to fell into conformity with the secular tribunals. The temporal prerogatives of ecclesiastics as a body whose authority over the laity was countervailed with no reciprocal obligation, existed no longer. This is what the language of the king implied. The difficulty which the persons whom he was addressing experienced in realising the change in their position, obliged him to be somewhat emphatic in his assertion of it; and it might be imagined at first sight, that in insisting on his superiority to the officers of the spiritual courts, he claimed a right to dictate their sentences. But to venture such a supposition would be to mistake the nature of English sovereignty and the spirit of the change. The supreme authority in England was the law; and the king no more possessed, or claimed a power of controlling the judgment of the bishops or their ministers, than he could interfere with the jurisdiction of the judges of the bench. All persons in authority, whether in church or state, held their offices thenceforth by similar tenure; but the rule of the proceedings in each remained alike the law of the land, which Henry had no more thought of superseding by his own will than the most constitutional of modern princes.

The closing sentences of his reply to Cranmer are striking, and it is difficult to believe that he did not mean what he was saying. From the first step in the process to the last, he maintained consistently that his only object was to do what was right. He was thoroughly persuaded that the course which he was pursuing was sanctioned by justice—and persons who are satisfied that he was entitled to feel such persuasion, need not refuse him the merit of sincerity, because (to use the language which Cromwell used at the fatal crisis of his life 431) "It may be well that they who medelle in many matters are not able to answer for them all."

Cranmer, then, being fortified with this permission, and taking with him the Bishops of London, Winchester, Lincoln, and Bath and Wells (the latter perhaps having been chosen in consequence of his late conduct in the convocation, to give show of fairness to the proceeding), went down to Dunstable and opened his court there. The queen was at Ampthill, six miles distant, having entered on her sad tenancy, it would seem, as soon as the place had been evacuated by the gaudy hunting party of the preceding summer. The cause being undecided, and her title being therefore uncertain, she was called by the safe name of "the Lady Catherine," and under this designation she was served with a citation from the archbishop to appear before him on Saturday, the 10th of May. The bearers of the summons were Sir Francis Bryan (an unfortunate choice, for he was cousin of the new queen, and insolent in his manner and bearing), Sir Thomas Gage, and Lord Vaux. She received them like herself with imperial sorrow. They delivered their message; she announced that she refused utterly to acknowledge the competency of the tribunal before which she was called; the court was a mockery; the archbishop was a shadow. 432 She would neither appear before him in person, nor commission any one to appear on her behalf.

The court had but one course before it—she was pronounced contumacious, and the trial went forward. None of her household were tempted even by curiosity to be present. "There came not so much as a servant of hers to Dunstable, save such as were brought in as witnesses;" some of them having been required to give evidence in the re-examination which was thought necessary, as to the nature of the relation of their mistress with her first boy husband. As soon as this disgusting question had been sufficiently investigated, nothing remained but to pronounce judgment. The marriage with the king was declared to have been null and void from the beginning, and on the 23rd of May, the archbishop sent to London the welcome news that the long matter was at an end. 433

It was over;—over at last; yet so over, that the conclusion could but appear to the losing party a fresh injustice. To those who were concerned in bringing it to pass, to the king himself, to the nation, to Europe, to every one who heard of it at the time, it must have appeared, as it appears now to us who read the story of it, if a necessity, yet a most unwelcome and unsatisfying one. That the king remained uneasy is evident from the efforts which he continued to make, or which he allowed to be made, notwithstanding the brief of the 23rd of December, to gain the sanction of the pope. That the nation was uneasy, we should not require the evidence of history to tell us. "There was much murmuring in England," says Hall, "and it was thought by the unwise that the Bishop of Rome would curse all Englishmen; that the emperor and he would destroy all the people." And those who had no such fears, and whose judgment in the main approved of what had been done, were scandalised at the presentation to them at the instant of the publication of the divorce, of a new queen, four months advanced in pregnancy. This also was a misfortune which had arisen out of the chain of duplicities, a fresh accident swelling a complication which was already sufficiently entangled. It had been occasioned by steps which at the moment at which they were ventured, prudence seemed to justify; but we the more regret it, because, in comparison with the interests which were at issue, the few months of additional delay were infinitely unimportant.

Nevertheless, we have reason to be thankful that the thing, well or ill, was over; seven years of endurance were enough for the English nation, and may be supposed to have gained even for Henry a character for patience. In some way, too, it is needless to say, the thing must have ended. The life of none of us is long enough to allow us to squander so large a section of it struggling in the meshes of a law-suit; and although there may be a difference of opinion on the wisdom of having first entered upon ground of such a kind, few thinking persons can suggest any other method in which either the nation or the king could have extricated themselves. Meanwhile, it was resolved that such spots and blemishes as hung about the transaction should be forgotten in the splendour of the coronation. If there was scandal in the condition of the queen, yet under another aspect that condition was matter of congratulation to a people so eager for an heir; and Henry may have thought that the sight for the first time in public of so beautiful a creature, surrounded by the most magnificent pageant which London had witnessed since the unknown day on which the first stone of it was laid, and bearing in her bosom the long-hoped-for inheritor of the English crown, might induce a chivalrous nation to forget what it was the interest of no loyal subject to remember longer, and to offer her an English welcome to the throne.

In anticipation of the timely close of the proceedings at Dunstable, notice had been given in the city early in May, that preparations should be made for the coronation on the first of the following month. Queen Anne was at Greenwich, but, according to custom, the few preceding days were to be spent at the Tower; and on the 19th of May, she was conducted thither in state by the lord mayor and the city companies, with one of those splendid exhibitions upon the water which in the days when the silver Thames deserved its name, and the sun could shine down upon it out of the blue summer sky, were spectacles scarcely rivalled in gorgeousness by the world-famous wedding of the Adriatic. The river was crowded with boats, the banks and the ships in the pool swarmed with people; and fifty great barges formed the procession, all blazing with gold and banners. The queen herself was in her own barge, close to that of the lord mayor; and in keeping with the fantastic genius of the time, she was preceded up the water by "a foyst or wafter full or ordnance, in which was a great dragon continually moving and casting wildfire, and round about the foyst stood terrible monsters and wild men, casting fire and making hideous noise." 434 So, with trumpets blowing, cannon pealing, the Tower guns answering the guns of the ships, in a blaze of fireworks and splendour, Anne Boleyn was borne along to the great archway of the Tower, where the king was waiting on the stairs to receive her.

And now let us suppose eleven days to have elapsed, the welcome news to have arrived at length from Dunstable, and the fair summer morning of life dawning in treacherous beauty after the long night of expectation. No bridal ceremonial had been possible; the marriage had been huddled over like a stolen love-match, and the marriage feast had been eaten in vexation and disappointment. These past mortifications were to be atoned for by a coronation pageant which the art and the wealth of the richest city in Europe should be poured out in the most lavish profusion to adorn.

On the morning of the 31st of May, the families of the London citizens were stirring early in all houses. From Temple Bar to the Tower, the streets were fresh strewed with gravel, the footpaths were railed off along the whole distance, and occupied on one side by the guilds, their workmen, and apprentices, on the other by the city constables and officials in their gaudy uniforms, "with their staves in hand for to cause the people to keep good room and order." 435 Cornhill and Gracechurch Street had dressed their fronts in scarlet and crimson, in arras and tapestry, and the rich carpet-work from Persia and the East. Cheapside, to outshine her rivals, was draped even more splendidly in cloth of gold, and tissue, and velvet. The sheriffs were pacing up and down on their great Flemish horses, hung with liveries, and all the windows were thronged with ladies crowding to see the procession pass. At length the Tower guns opened, the grim gates rolled back, and under the archway in the bright May sunshine, the long column began slowly to defile. Two states only permitted their representatives to grace the scene with their presence—Venice and France. It was, perhaps, to make the most of this isolated countenance, that the French ambassador's train formed the van of the cavalcade. Twelve French knights came riding foremost in surcoats of blue velvet with sleeves of yellow silk, their horses trapped in blue, with white crosses powdered on their hangings. After them followed a troop of English gentlemen, two and two, and then the Knights of the Bath, "in gowns of violet, with hoods purfled with miniver like doctors." Next, perhaps at a little interval, the abbots passed on, mitred in their robes; the barons followed in crimson velvet, the bishops then, and then the earls and marquises, the dresses of each order increasing in elaborate gorgeousness. All these rode on in pairs. Then came alone Audeley, lord-chancellor, and behind him the Venetian ambassador and the Archbishop of York; the Archbishop of Canterbury, and Du Bellay, Bishop of Bayonne and of Paris, not now with bugle and hunting-frock, but solemn with stole and crozier. Next, the lord mayor, with the city mace in hand, the Garter in his coat of arms; and then Lord William Howard—Belted Will Howard, of the

Scottish Border, Marshal of England. The officers of the queen's household succeeded the marshal in scarlet and gold, and the van of the procession was closed by the Duke of Suffolk, as high constable, with his silver wand. It is no easy matter to picture to ourselves the blazing trail of splendour which in such a pageant must have drawn along the London streets,—those streets which now we know so black and smoke-grimed, themselves then radiant with masses of colour, gold, and crimson, and violet. Yet there it was, and there the sun could shine upon it, and tens of thousands of eyes were gazing on the scene out of the crowded lattices.

Glorious as the spectacle was, perhaps however, it passed unheeded. Those eyes were watching all for another object, which now drew near. In an open space behind the constable there was seen approaching "a white chariot," drawn by two palfreys in white damask which swept the ground, a golden canopy borne above it making music with silver bells: and in the chariot sat the observed of all observers, the beautiful occasion of all this glittering homage; fortune's plaything of the hour, the Queen of England— queen at last—borne along upon the waves of this sea of glory, breathing the perfumed incense of greatness which she had risked her fair name, her delicacy, her honour, her self-respect, to win; and she had won it.

There she sate, dressed in white tissue robes, her fair hair flowing loose over her shoulders, and her temples circled with a light coronet of gold and diamonds—most beautiful—loveliest—most favoured perhaps, as she seemed at that hour, of all England's daughters. Alas! "within the hollow round" of that coronet—

> Kept death his court, and there the antick sate,
> Scoffing her state and grinning at her pomp.
> Allowing her a little breath, a little scene
> To monarchise, be feared, and kill with looks,
> Infusing her with self and vain conceit,
> As if the flesh which walled about her life
> Were brass impregnable; and humoured thus,
> Bored through her castle walls; and farewell, Queen.

Fatal gift of greatness! so dangerous ever! so more than dangerous in those tremendous times when the fountains are broken loose of the great deeps of thought; and nations are in the throes of revolution;—when ancient order and law and tradition are splitting in the social earthquake; and as the opposing forces wrestle to and fro, those unhappy ones who stand out above the crowd become the symbols of the struggle, and fall the victims of its alternating fortunes. And what if into an unsteady heart and brain, intoxicated with splendour, the outward chaos should find its way, converting the poor silly soul into an image of the same confusion,—if conscience should be deposed from her high place, and the Pandora box be broken loose of passions and sensualities and follies; and at length there be nothing left of all which man or woman ought to value, save hope of God's forgiveness.

Three short years have yet to pass, and again, on a summer morning, Queen Anne Boleyn will leave the Tower of London—not radiant then with beauty on a gay errand of coronation, but a poor wandering ghost, on a sad tragic errand, from which she will never more return, passing away out of an earth where she may stay no longer, into a presence where, nevertheless, we know that all is well—for all of us—and therefore for her.

But let us not cloud her shortlived sunshine with the shadow of the future. She went on in her loveliness, the peeresses following in their carriages, with the royal guard in their rear. In Fenchurch Street she was met by the children of the city schools; and at the corner of Gracechurch Street a masterpiece had been prepared of the pseudo-classic art, then so fashionable, by the merchants of the Styll Yard. A Mount Parnassus had been constructed, and a Helicon fountain upon it playing into a basin with four jets of Rhenish wine. On the top of the mountain sat Apollo with Calliope at his feet, and on either side the remaining Muses, holding lutes or harps, and singing each of them some "posy" or epigram in praise of the queen, which was presented, after it had been sung, written in letters of gold.

From Gracechurch Street, the procession passed to Leadenhall, where there was a spectacle in better taste, of the old English Catholic kind, quaint perhaps and forced, but truly and even beautifully emblematic. There was again a "little mountain," which was hung with red and white roses; a gold ring was placed on the summit, on which, as the queen appeared, a white falcon was made to "descend as out of the sky"—"and then incontinent came down an angel with great melody, and set a close crown of gold upon the falcon's head; and in the same pageant sat Saint Anne with all her issue beneath her; and Mary Cleophas with her four children, of the which children one made a goodly oration to the queen, of the fruitfulness of St. Anne, trusting that like fruit should come of her." 436

With such "pretty conceits," at that time the honest tokens of an English welcome, the new queen was received by the citizens of London. These scenes must be multiplied by the number of the streets, where some fresh fancy met her at every turn. To preserve the festivities from flagging, every fountain and conduit within the walls ran all day with wine; the bells of every steeple were ringing; children lay in wait with song, and ladies with posies, in which all the resources of fantastic extravagance were exhausted; and thus in an unbroken triumph—and to outward appearance received with the warmest affection—she passed under Temple Bar, down the Strand by Charing Cross to Westminster Hall. The king was not with her throughout the day; nor did he intend to be with her in any part of the ceremony. She was to reign without a rival, the undisputed sovereign of the hour.

Saturday being passed in showing herself to the people, she retired for the night to "the king's manour house at Westminster," where she slept. On the following morning, between eight and nine o'clock, she returned to the hall, where the lord mayor, the city council, and the peers were again assembled, and took her place on the high dais at the top of the stairs under the cloth of state; while the bishops, the abbots, and the monks of the abbey formed in the area. A railed way had been laid with carpets across Palace Yard and the Sanctuary to the abbey gates, and when all was ready, preceded by the peers in their robes of parliament, the Knights of the Garter in the dress of the order, she swept out under her canopy, the bishops and the monks "solemnly singing." The train was borne by the old Duchess of Norfolk her aunt, the Bishops of London and Winchester on either side "bearing up the lappets of her robe." The Earl of Oxford carried the crown on its cushion immediately before her. She was dressed in purple velvet furred with ermine, her hair escaping loose, as she usually wore it, under a wreath of diamonds.

On entering the abbey, she was led to the coronation chair Where she sat while the train fell into their places, and the preliminaries, of the ceremonial were despatched. Then she was conducted up to the high altar, and anointed Queen of England, and she received from the hands of Cranmer, fresh come in haste from Dunstable, with the last words of his sentence upon Catherine scarcely silent upon his lips, the golden sceptre, and St. Edward's crown

Did any twinge of remorse, any pang of painful recollection, pierce at that moment the incense of glory which she was inhaling? Did any vision flit across her of a sad mourning figure which once had stood where she was standing, now desolate, neglected, sinking into the darkening twilight of a life cut short by sorrow? Who can tell? At such a time, that figure would have weighed heavily upon a noble mind, and a wise mind would have been taught by the thought of it, that although life be fleeting as a dream, it is long enough to experience strange vicissitudes of fortune. But Anne Boleyn was not noble and was not wise,—too probably she felt nothing but the delicious, all-absorbing, all-intoxicating present, and if that plain, suffering face presented itself to her memory at all, we may fear that it was rather as a foil to her own surpassing loveliness. Two years later, she was able to exult over Catherine's death; she is not likely to have thought of her with gentler feelings in the first glow and flush of triumph.

We may now leave these scenes. They concluded in the usual English style, with a banquet in the great hall, and with all outward signs of enjoyment and pleasure. There must have been but few persons present however who did not feel that the sunshine of such a day might not last for ever, and that over so dubious a marriage no Englishman could exult with more than half a heart. It is foolish to blame lightly actions which arise in the midst of circumstances which are and can be but imperfectly known; and there may have been political reasons which made so much pomp desirable. Anne Boleyn had been the subject of public conversation for seven years, and Henry, no doubt, desired to present his jewel to them in the rarest and choicest setting. Yet to our eyes, seeing, perhaps, by the light of what followed, a more modest introduction would have appeared more suited to the doubtful nature of her position.

At any rate we escape from this scene of splendour very gladly as from something unseasonable. It would have been well for Henry VIII. if he had lived in a world in which women could have been dispensed with; so ill, in all his relations with them, he succeeded. With men he could speak the right word, he could do the right thing; with women he seemed to be under a fatal necessity of mistake.

It was now necessary, however, after this public step, to communicate in form to the emperor the divorce and the new marriage. The king was assured of the rectitude of the motives on which he had himself acted, and he knew at the same time that he had challenged the hostility of the papal world. Yet he did not desire a quarrel if there were means of avoiding it; and more than once he had shown respect for the opposition which he had met with from Charles, as dictated by honourable care for the interests of his kinswoman. He therefore, in the truest language which will be met with in the whole long series of the correspondence, composed a despatch for his ambassador at Brussels, and expressed himself in a tone of honest sorrow for the injury which he had been compelled to commit. Neither the coercion which the emperor had exerted over the pope, nor his intrigues with his subjects in Ireland and England, could deprive the nephew of Catherine of his right to a courteous explanation; and Henry directed Doctor Nicholas Hawkins in making his communication "to use only gentle words;" to express a hope that Charles would not think only of his own honour, but would remember public justice; and that a friendship of long standing, which the interests of the subjects of both countries were concerned so strongly in maintaining, might not be broken. The instructions are too interesting to pass over with a general description. After stating the grounds on which Henry had proceeded, and which Charles thoroughly understood, Hawkins was directed to continue thus:—

"The King of England is not ignorant what respect is due unto the world. How much he hath laboured and travailed therein he hath sufficiently declared and showed in his acts and proceedings. If he had contemned the order and process of the world, or the friendship and amity of your Majesty, he needed not to have sent so often to the pope and to you both, nor continued and spent his time in delays. He might have done what he has done now, had it so liked him, with as little difficulty as now, if without such respect he would have followed his pleasure."

The minister was then to touch the pope's behaviour and Henry's forbearance, and after that to say:—

"Going forward in that way his Highness saw that he could come to no conclusion; and he was therefore compelled to step right forth out of the maze, and so to quiet himself at last. And is it not time to have an end in seven years? It is not to be asked nor questioned whether the matter hath been determined after the common fashion, but whether it hath in it common justice, truth, and equity. For observation of the common order, his Grace hath done what lay in him. Enforced by necessity he hath found the true order which he hath in substance followed with effect, and hath done as becometh him. He doubteth not but your Majesty, remembering his cause from the beginning hitherto, will of yourself consider and think, that among mortal men nothing should be immortal; and suits must once have an end, si possis recte, si non quocunque modo. If his Highness cannot as he would, then must he do as he may; and he that hath a journey to be perfected must, if he cannot go one way, essay another. For his matter with the pope, he shall deal with him apart. Your Majesty he taketh for his friend, and as to a friend he openeth these matters to you, trusting to find your Majesty no less friendly than he hath done heretofore." 437

If courtesy obliged Henry to express a confidence in the stability of the relations between himself and Charles, which it was impossible that he could have felt, yet in other respects this letter has the most pleasant merit of honesty. Hawkins was so much overcome by "the sweetness of it," that "he nothing doubted if that the emperor read the same, by God's grace he should be utterly persuaded;" and although in this expectation he was a little over sanguine, as in calmer moments he would have acknowledged, yet plain speech is never without its value; and Charles himself after he had tried other expedients, and they had not succeeded with him, found it more prudent to acquiesce in what could no longer be altered, and to return to cordiality.

For the present he remained under the impression that by the great body of the English the divorce was looked upon with coldness and even with displeasure, that the king was supported only by the complacency of a few courtiers, and that the nation were prepared to compel him to undo the wrong which had been inflicted upon Catherine and the princess. So he was assured by the Spanish party in England; so all the disaffected assured him, who were perhaps themselves deceived. He had secured Ireland, and Scotland also in so far as James's promises could secure it; 438 and he was not disposed to surrender for the present so promising a game till he had tried his strength and proved his weakness. He replied coldly to Hawkins, "That for the King of England's amity he would be glad thereof, so the said king would do works according. The matter was none of his; but the lady, whose rights had been violated, was his aunt and an orphan, and that he must see for her, and for her daughter his cousin." 439

The scarcely ambiguous answer was something softened the following day; perhaps only, however, because it was too plain a betrayal of his intentions. He communicated at once with Catherine, and Henry speedily learnt the nature of the advice which he had given to her. After the coronation had passed off so splendidly, when no disturbance had risen, no voice had been raised for her or for her daughter, the poor queen's spirit for the moment had sunk; she had thought of leaving the country, and flying with the Princess Mary to Spain. The emperor sent to urge her to remain a little longer, guaranteeing her, if she could command her patience, an ample reparation for her injuries. Whatever might appear upon the surface, the new queen, he was assured, was little loved by the people, and "they were ready to join with any prince who would espouse her quarrel." 440 All classes, he said, were agreed in one common feeling of displeasure. They were afraid of a change of religion; they were afraid of the wreck of their commerce; and the whole country was fast ripening towards insurrection. The points on which he relied as the occasion of the disaffection betrayed the sources of his information. He was in correspondence with the regular clergy through Peto at Antwerp, and through his Flemish subjects with merchants of London. Among both these classes, as well as among the White Rose nobles, he had powerful adherents; and it could not have been forgotten in the courts, either of London or Brussels, that within the memory of living men, a small band of exiles, equipped by a Duke of Burgundy, had landed at a Yorkshire village, and in a month had revolutionised the kingdom.

In the eyes of Charles there was no reason why an attempt which had succeeded once might not succeed again under circumstances seemingly of far fairer promise. The strength of a party of insurrection is a power which official statesmen never justly comprehend. It depends upon moral influences, which they are professionally incapable of appreciating. They are able complacently to ignore the existence of substantial disaffection though all society may be undermined; they can build their hopes, When it suits their convenience, on the idle trifling of superficial discontent. In the present instance there was some excuse for the mistake. That in England there really existed an active and organised opposition, prepared, when opportunity offered, to try the chances of rebellion, was no delusion of persons who measured facts by their desires; it was an ascertained peril of serious magnitude, which might be seriously calculated upon; and if the experiment was tried, reasonable men might fairly be divided in opinion on the result to be expected.

In the meantime the government had been obliged to follow up the coronation of the new queen by an act which the situation of the kingdom explained and excused; but which, if Catherine had been no more than a private person, would have been wanton cruelty. Among the people she still bore her royal title; but the name of queen, so long as she was permitted to retain it, was an allowed witness against the legality of the sentence at Dunstable. There could not be "two queens" in England, 441 and one or other must retire from the designation. A proclamation was therefore issued by the council, declaring, that in consequence of the final proofs that the Lady Catherine had never been lawfully married to the king, she was to bear thenceforward the title which she had received after the death of her first husband, and be called the Princess Dowager.

Harsh as this measure was, she had left no alternative to the government by which to escape the enforcement of it, by her refusal to consent to any form of compromise. If she was queen, Anne Boleyn was not queen. If she was queen, the Princess Mary remained the heir to the crown, and the expected offspring of Anne would be illegitimate. If the question had been merely of names, to have moved it would have been unworthy and wicked; but where respect for private feeling was incompatible with the steps which a nation felt necessary in order to secure itself against civil convulsions, private feeling was compelled not unjustly to submit to injury. Mary, though still a girl, had inherited both her father's will and her mother's obstinacy. She was in correspondence, as we have seen, with the Nun of Kent, and aware at least, if she was not further implicated in it, of a conspiracy to place her on the throne. Charles was engaged in the same designs; and it will not be pretended that Catherine was left without information of what was going forward, or that her own conduct was uninfluenced by policy. These intrigues it was positively necessary to stifle, and it was impossible to leave a pretext of which so powerful a use might be made in the hands of a party whose object was not only to secure to the princess her right to succeed her father, but to compel him by arms either to acknowledge it, or submit to be deposed. 442

Our sympathies are naturally on the side of the weak and the unsuccessful. State considerations lose their force after the lapse of centuries, when no interests of our own are any longer in jeopardy; and we feel for the great sufferers of history only in their individual capacity, without recalling or caring for the political exigencies to which they were sacrificed. It is an error of disguised selfishness, the counterpart of the carelessness with which in our own age, when we are ourselves constituents of an interested public, we ignore what it is inconvenient to remember.

Thus, therefore, on one hot Midsummer Sunday in this year 1533, the people gathering to church in every parish through the English counties, read, nailed upon the doors, a paper signed Henry R., setting forth that the Lady Catherine of Spain, heretofore called Queen of England, was not to be called by that title any more, but was to be called Princess Dowager, and so to be held and esteemed. The proclamation, we may suppose, was read with varying comments; of the reception of it in the northern counties, the following information was forwarded to the crown. The Earl of Derby, lord-lieutenant of Yorkshire, wrote to inform the council that he had arrested a certain "lewd and naughty priest," James Harrison by name, on the charge of having spoken unfitting and slanderous words of his Highness and the Queen's Grace. He had taken the examinations of several witnesses, which he had sent with his letter, and which were to the following effect:—

Richard Clark deposeth that the said James Harrison reading the proclamation, said that Queen Catherine was queen, Nan Bullen should not be queen, nor the king should be no king but on his bearing.

William Dalton deposeth, that in his hearing the above-named James said, I will take none for queen but Queen Catherine—who the devil made Nan Bullen, that hoore, queen? I will never take her for queen—and he the said William answered, "Hold thy peace, thou wot'st not what thou sayest—but that thou art a priest I should punish thee, that others should take example."

Richard Sumner and John Clayton depose, that they came in company with the said James from Perbalt to Eccleston, when the said James did say, "This is a marvellous world—the king will put down the order of priests and destroy the Sacrament, but he cannot reign long, for York will be in London hastily." 443

Here was the later growth of the spirit which we saw a few months previously in the monks of Furness. The mutterings of discontent had developed into plain open treason, confident of success, and scarcely caring to conceal itself—and Yorkshire was preparing for rebellion and "the Pilgrimage of Grace."

There is another quarter also into which we must follow the proclamation, and watch the effect of the royal order in a scene where it is well that we should for a few moments rest. Catherine was still at Ampthill, surrounded by her own attendants, who formed an inner circle, shielding her retirement against impertinent curiosity. She rarely or never allowed herself to be seen; Lord Mountjoy, with an official retinue, was in attendance in the house; but the occupation was not a pleasant one, and he was as willing to respect the queen's seclusion as she to remain secluded. Injunctions arrived however from the court at the end of June, which compelled him to request an interview; a deputation of the privy council had come down to inform the ex-queen of the orders of the government, and to desire that they might be put in force in her own family. Aware probably of the nature of the communication which was to be made to her, she refused repeatedly to admit them to her presence. At length, however, she nerved herself for the effort, and on the 3rd of July Mountjoy and the state commissioners were informed that she was ready to receive them.

As they entered her room she was lying on a sofa. She had a bad cough, and she had hurt her foot with a pin, and was unable to stand or walk. Her attendants were all present by her own desire; she was glad to see around her some sympathising human faces, to enable her to endure the cold hard eyes of the officials of the council.

She inquired whether the message was to be delivered in writing or by word of mouth.

They replied that they had brought with them instructions which they were to read, and that they were further charged with a message which was to be delivered verbally. She desired that they would read their written despatch. It was addressed to the Princess Dowager, and she at once excepted to the name. She was not Princess Dowager, she said, but queen, and the king's true wife. She came to the king a clear maid for any bodily knowledge of Prince Arthur; she had borne him lawful issue and no bastard, and therefore queen she was, and queen she would be while she lived.

The commissioners were prepared for the objection, and continued, without replying, to read. The paper contained a statement of worn-out unrealities; the old story of the judgment of the universities and the learned men, the sentence of convocation, and of the houses of parliament; and, finally, the fact of substantial importance, that the king, acting as he believed according to the laws of God, had married the Lady Anne Boleyn, who was now his lawful wife, and anointed Queen of England.

Oh yes, she answered when they had done, we know that, and "we know the authority by which it has been done — more by power than justice." The king's learned men were learned heretics; the honest learning was for her. As for the seals of the universities there were strange stories about the way in which they had been obtained. The universities and the parliament had done what the king bade them; and they had gone against their consciences in doing it; but it was of no importance to her—she was in the hands of the pope, who was God's vicar, and she acknowledged no other judge.

The commissioners informed her of the decision of the council that she was no longer to bear the title of queen. It stood, they said, neither with the laws of God nor man, nor with the king's honour, to have two queens named within the realm; and in fact, there was but one queen, the king's lawful wife, to whom he was now married.

She replied shortly that she was the king's lawful queen, and none other.

There was little hope in her manner that anything which could be said would move her; but her visitors were ordered to try her to the uttermost.

The king, they continued, was surprised that she could be so disobedient; and not only that she was disobedient herself, but that she allowed and encouraged her servants in the same conduct.

She was ready to obey the king; she answered, when she could do so without disobeying God; but she could not damn her soul even for him. Her servants, she said, must do the best they could; they were standing round her as she was speaking; and she turned to them with an apology, and a hope that they would pardon her. She would hinder her cause, she said; and put her soul in danger, if on their account she were to relinquish her name, and she could not do it.

The deputation next attempted her on her worldly side. If she would obey, they informed her that she would be allowed not only her jointure as Princess Dowager and her own private fortune, but all the settlements which had been made upon her on her marriage with the king.

She "passed not upon possessions, in regard of this matter," she replied. It touched her conscience, and no worldly considerations were of the slightest moment.

In disobeying the king, they said; seeing that she was none other than his subject, she might give cause for dissension and disturbance; and she might lose the favour of the people.

She "trusted not," she replied—she "never minded it, nor would she"—she "desired only to save her right; and if she should lose the favour of the people in defending that right, yet she trusted to go to heaven cum famâ et infamiâ."

Promises and persuasions being unavailing, they tried threats. She was told that if she persisted in so obstinate a course, the king would be obliged to make known to the world the offers which he had made to her, and the ill reception which they had met with—and then he would perhaps withdraw those offers, and conceive some evil opinions of high displeasure towards her.

She answered that there was no manner of offers neither of lands nor goods that she had respect unto in comparison of her cause—and as to the loss of the king's affection, she trusted to God, to whom she would daily pray for him.

The learned council might as well have reasoned with the winds; or threatened the waves of the sea. But they were not yet weary, and their next effort was as foolish as it was ungenerous. They suggested, "that if she did reserve the name of queen, it was thought that she would do it of a vain desire and appetite of glory; and further, she might be an occasion that the king would withdraw his love from her most dear daughter the Lady Princess, which should chiefly move her, if none other cause did."

They must have known little of Catherine, if they thought she could be influenced by childish vanity. It was for no vain glory that she cared, she answered proudly; she was the king's true wife, and her conscience forbade her to call herself otherwise; the princess was his true begotten child; and as God hath given her to them, so for her part she would render her again; neither for daughter, family, nor possessions, would she yield in her cause; and she made a solemn protestation, calling on every one present to bear witness to what she said, that the king's wife she was, and such she would take herself to be, and that she would never surrender the name of queen till the pope had decided that she must bear it no longer.

So ended the first interview. Catherine, before the commissioners left her, desired to have a copy of the proposals which they had brought, that she might translate and send them to Rome. They returned with them the next day, when she requested to see the report which they intended to send to the council of the preceding conversation. It was placed in her hands; and as she read it and found there the name of Princess Dowager, she took a pen and dashed out the words, the mark of which indignant ink-stroke may now be seen in the letter from which this account is taken. 444 With the accuracy of the rest she appeared to be satisfied—only when she found again their poor suggestion that she was influenced by vanity, she broke out with a burst of passionate indignation.

"I would rather be a poor beggar's wife," she said, "and be sure of heaven, than queen of all the world, and stand in doubt thereof by reason of my own consent. I stick not so for vain glory, but because I know myself the king's true wife—and while you call me the king's subject, I was his subject while he took me for his wife. But if he take me not for his wife, I came not into this Realm as merchandise, nor to be married to any merchant; nor do I continue in the same but as his lawful wife, and not as a subject to live under his dominion otherwise. I have always demeaned myself well and truly towards the king—and if it can be proved that either in writing to the pope or any other, I have either stirred or procured anything against his Grace, or have been the means to any person to make any motion which might be prejudicial to his Grace or to his Realm, I am content to suffer for it. I have done England little good, and I should be sorry to do it any harm. But if I should agree to your motions and persuasions, I should slander myself, and confess to have been the king's harlot for twenty-four years. The cause, I cannot tell by what subtle means, has been determined here within the king's Realm, before a man of his own making, the Bishop of Canterbury, no person indifferent I think in that behalf; and for the indifference of the place, I think the place had been more indifferent to have been judged in hell; for no truth can be suffered here, whereas the devils themselves I suppose do tremble to see the truth in this cause so sore oppressed." 445

Most noble, spirited, and like a queen. Yet she would never have been brought to this extremity, and she would have shown a truer nobleness, if four years before she could have yielded at the pope's entreaty on the first terms which were proposed to her. Those terms would have required no humiliating confessions; they would have involved no sentence on her marriage nor touched her daughter's legitimacy. She would have broken no law of God, nor seemed to break it. She was required only to forget her own interests; and she would not forget them, though all the world should be wrecked by her refusal. She denied that she was concerned in "motions prejudicial to the king or to the Realm," but she must have placed her own interpretation on the words, and would have considered excommunication and interdict a salutary discipline to the king and parliament. She knew that this sentence was imminent, that in its minor form it had already fallen; and she knew that her nephew and her friends in England were plotting to give effect to the decree. But we may pass over this. It is not for an English writer to dwell upon those faults of Catherine of Arragon, which English remorse has honourably insisted on forgetting. Her injuries, inevitable as they were, and forced upon her in great measure by her own wilfulness, remain among the saddest spots in the pages of our history.

One other brief incident remains to be noticed here, to bring up before the imagination the features of this momentous summer. It is contained in the postscript of a letter of Cranmer to Hawkins the ambassador in

Germany; and the manner in which the story is told is no less suggestive than the story itself.

The immediate present, however awful its import, will ever seem common and familiar to those who live and breathe in the midst of it. In the days of the September massacre at Paris, the theatres were open as usual; men ate, and drank, and laughed, and cried, and went about their common work, unconscious that those days which were passing by them, so much like other days, would remain the *dies nefasti*, accursed in the memory of mankind for ever. Nothing is terrible, nothing is sublime in human things, so long as they are before our eyes. The great man has so much in common with men in general, the routine of daily life, in periods the most remarkable in history, contains so much that is unvarying, that it is only when time has done its work; and all which was unimportant has ceased to be remembered, that such men and such times stand out in their true significance. It might have been thought that to a person like Cranmer, the court at Dunstable, the coronation of the new queen, the past out of which these things had risen, and the future which they threatened to involve, would have seemed at least serious; and that engaged as he had been as a chief actor, in a matter which, if it had done nothing else, had broken the heart of a high-born lady whom once he had honoured as his queen, he would have been either silent about his exploits, or if he had spoken of them, would have spoken not without some show of emotion. We look for a symptom of feeling, but we do not find it. When the coronation festivities were concluded he wrote to his friend an account of what had been done by himself and others in the light gossiping tone of easiest content; as if he were describing the common incidents of a common day. It is disappointing, and not wholly to be approved of. Still less can we approve of the passage with which he concludes his letter.

"Other news we have none notable, but that one Frith, which was in the Tower in prison, 446 was appointed by the King's Grace to be examined before me, my Lord of London, my Lord of Winchester, my Lord of Suffolk, my Lord Chancellor, and my Lord of Wiltshire; whose opinion was so notably erroneous that we could not dispatch him, but were fain to leave him to the determination of his ordinary, which is the Bishop of London. His said opinion is of such nature, that he thought it not necessary to be believed as an article of our faith that there is the very corporeal presence of Christ within the host and sacrament of the altar; and holdeth on this point much after the opinion of Œcolampadius.

"And surely I myself sent for him three or four times to persuade him to leave that imagination. But for all that we could do therein, he would not apply to any counsel. Notwithstanding now he is at a final end with all examinations; for my Lord of London hath given sentence, and delivered him to the secular power when he looketh every day to go unto the fire. And there is also condemned with him one Andrew a tailor for the self-same opinion; and thus fare you well." 447

These victims went as they were sentenced, dismissed to their martyr's crowns at Smithfield, as Queen Anne Boleyn but a few days before had received her golden crown at the altar of Westminster Abbey. Twenty years later another fire was blazing under the walls of Oxford; and the hand which was now writing these light lines was blackening in the flames of it, paying there the penalty of the same "imagination" for which Frith and the poor London tailor were with such cool indifference condemned. It is affecting to know that Frith's writings were the instruments of Cranmer's conversion; and the fathers of the Anglican church have left a monument of their sorrow for the shedding of this innocent blood in the Order of the Communion service, which closes with the very words on which the primate, with his brother bishops, had sate in judgment. 448

CHAPTER VI.
THE PROTESTANTS

Where changes are about to take place of great and enduring moment, a kind of prologue, on a small scale, sometimes anticipates the true opening of the drama; like the first drops which give notice of the coming storm, or as if the shadows of the reality were projected forwards into the future, and imitated in dumb show the movements of the real actors in the story.

Such a rehearsal of the English Reformation was witnessed at the close of the fourteenth century, confused, imperfect, disproportioned, to outward appearance barren of results; yet containing a representative of each one of the mixed forces by which that great change was ultimately effected, and foreshadowing even something of the course which it was to run.

There was a quarrel with the pope upon the extent of the papal privileges; there were disputes between the laity and the clergy,—accompanied, as if involuntarily, by attacks on the sacramental system and the Catholic faith,—while innovation in doctrine was accompanied also with the tendency which characterised the extreme development of the later Protestants—towards political republicanism, the fifth monarchy, and community of goods. Some account of this movement must be given in this place, although it can be but a sketch only. "Lollardry" 449 has a history of its own; but it forms no proper part of the history of the Reformation. It was a separate phenomenon, provoked by the same causes which produced their true fruit at a later period; but it formed no portion of the stem on which those fruits ultimately grew. It was a prelude which was played out, and sank into silence, answering for the time no other end than to make the name of heretic odious in the ears of the English nation. In their recoil from their first failure, the people stamped their hatred of heterodoxy into their language; and in the word *miscreant*, misbeliever, as the synonym of the worst species of reprobate, they left an indelible record of the popular estimate of the followers of John Wycliffe.

The Lollard story opens with the disputes between the crown and the see of Rome on the presentation to English benefices. For the hundred and fifty years which succeeded the Conquest, the right of nominating the archbishops, the bishops, and the mitred abbots, had been claimed and exercised by the crown. On the passing of the great charter, the church had recovered its liberties, and the privilege of free election had been conceded by a special clause to the clergy. The practice which then became established was in accordance with the general spirit of the English constitution. On the vacancy of a see, the cathedral chapter applied to the crown for a congé d'élire. The application was a form; the consent was invariable. A bishop was then elected by a majority of suffrages; his name was submitted to the metropolitan, and by him to the pope. If the pope signified his approval, the election was complete; consecration followed; and the bishop having been furnished with his bulls of investiture, was presented to the king, and from him received "the temporalities" of his see. The mode in which the great abbots were chosen was precisely similar; the superiors of the orders to which the abbeys belonged were the channels of communication with the pope, in the place of the archbishops; but the elections in themselves were free, and were conducted in the same manner. The smaller church benefices, the small monasteries or parish churches, were in the hands of private patrons, lay or ecclesiastical; but in the case of each institution a reference was admitted, or was supposed to be admitted, to the court of Rome.

There was thus in the pope's hand an authority of an indefinite kind, which it was presumed that his sacred office would forbid him to abuse, but which, however, if he so unfortunately pleased, he might abuse at his discretion. He had absolute power over every nomination to an English benefice; he might refuse his consent till such adequate reasons, material or spiritual, as he considered sufficient to induce him to acquiesce, had been submitted to his consideration. In the case of nominations to the religious houses, the superiors of the various orders residing abroad had equal facilities for obstructiveness; and the consequence of so large a confidence in the purity of the higher orders of the Church became visible in an act of parliament which it was found necessary to pass in 1306-7. 450

"Of late," says this act, "it has come to the knowledge of the king, by the grievous complaint of the honourable persons, lords, and other noblemen of his realm, that whereas monasteries, priories, and other religious houses were founded to the honour and glory of God, and the advancement of holy church, by the king and his progenitors, and by the said noblemen and their ancestors; and a very great portion of lands and tenements have been given by them to the said monasteries, priories, and religious houses, and the religious men serving God in them; to the intent that clerks and laymen might be admitted in such houses, and that sick and feeble folk might be maintained, hospitality, almsgiving, and other charitable deeds might be done, and prayers be said for the souls of the founders and their heirs; the abbots, priors, and governors of the said houses, *and certain aliens their superiors*, as the abbots and priors of the Cistertians, the Premonstrants, the orders of Saint Augustine and of Saint Benedict, and many more of other religions and orders have at their own pleasure set divers heavy, unwonted heavy and importable tallages, payments, and impositions upon every of the said monasteries and houses subject unto them, in England, Ireland, Scotland, and Wales, without the privity of the king and his nobility, contrary to the laws and customs of the said realm; and thereby the number of religious persons being oppressed by such tallages, payments, and impositions, the service of God is diminished, alms are not given to the poor, the sick, and the feeble; the healths of the living and the souls of the dead be miserably defrauded; hospitality, alms-giving, and other godly deeds do cease; and so that which in times past was charitably given to godly uses and to the service of God, is now converted to an evil end, by permission whereof there groweth great scandal to the people." To provide against a continuance of these abuses, it was enacted that no "religious" persons should, under any pretence or form, send out of the kingdom any kind of tax, rent, or tallage; and that "priors aliens" should not presume to assess any payment, charge, or other burden whatever upon houses within the realm. 451

The language of this act was studiously guarded. The pope was not alluded to; the specific methods by which the extortion was practised were not explained; the tax upon presentations to benefices, either having not yet distinguished itself beyond other impositions, or the government trusting that a measure of this general kind might answer the desired end. Lucrative encroachments, however, do not yield so easily to treatment; nearly fifty years after it became necessary to re-enact the same statute; and while recapitulating the provisions of it, the parliament found it desirable to point out more specifically the intention with which it was passed.

The popes in the interval had absorbed in their turn from the heads of the religious orders, the privileges which by them had been extorted from the affiliated societies. Each English benefice had become the fountain of a rivulet which flowed into the Roman exchequer, or a property to be distributed as the private patronage of the Roman bishop: and the English parliament for the first time found itself in collision with the Father of Christendom.

"The pope," says the fourth of the twenty-fifth of Edward III., "accroaching to himself the signories of the benefices within the realm of England, doth give and grant the same to aliens which did never dwell in England, and to cardinals which could not dwell here, and to others as well aliens as denizens, whereby manifold inconveniences have ensued." "Not regarding" the statute of Edward I., he had also continued to present to bishoprics, abbeys, priories, and other valuable preferments: money in large quantities was carried out of the realm from the proceeds of these offices, and it was necessary to insist emphatically that the papal nominations should cease. They were made in violation of the law, and were conducted with simony so flagrant that English benefices were sold in the papal courts to any person who would pay for them, whether an Englishman or a stranger. It was therefore decreed that the elections to bishoprics should be free as in time past, that the rights of patrons should be preserved, and penalties of imprisonment, forfeiture, or outlawry, according to the complexion of the offence, should be attached to all impetration of benefices from Rome by purchase or otherwise. 452

If statute law could have touched the evil, these enactments would have been sufficient for the purpose; but the influence of the popes in England was of that subtle kind which was not so readily defeated. The law was still defied, or still evaded; and the struggle continued till the close of the century, the legislature labouring patiently, but ineffectually, to confine with fresh enactments their ingenious adversary. 453

At length symptoms appeared of an intention on the part of the popes to maintain their claims with spiritual censures, and the nation was obliged to resolve upon the course which, in the event of their resorting to that extremity, it would follow. The lay lords 454 and the House of Commons found no difficulty in arriving at a conclusion. They passed a fresh penal statute with prohibitions even more emphatically stringent, and decided that "if any man brought into this realm any sentence, summons, or excommunication, contrary to the effect of the statute, he should incur pain of life and members, with forfeiture of goods; and if any prelate made execution of such sentence, his temporalities should be taken from him, and should abide in the king's hands till redress was made." 455

So bold a measure threatened nothing less than open rupture. The act, however, seems to have been passed in haste, without determined consideration; and on second thoughts, it was held more prudent to attempt a milder course. The strength of the opposition to the papacy lay with the Commons. 456 When the session of parliament was over, a great council was summoned to reconsider what should be done, and an address was drawn up, and forwarded to Rome, with a request that the then reigning pope would devise some manner by which the difficulty could be arranged. 457 Boniface IX. replied with the same want of judgment which was shown afterwards on an analogous occasion by Clement VII. He disbelieved the danger; and daring the government to persevere, he granted a prebendal stall at Wells to an Italian cardinal, to which a presentation had been made already by the king. Opposing suits were instantly instituted between the claimants in the courts of the two countries. A decision was given in England in favour of the nominee of the king, and the bishops agreeing to support the crown were excommunicated. 458 The court of Rome had resolved to try the issue by a struggle of force, and the government had no alternative but to surrender at discretion, or to persevere at all hazards, and resist the usurpation.

The proceedings on this occasion seem to have been unusual, and significant of the importance of the crisis. Parliament either was sitting at the time when the excommunication was issued, or else it was immediately assembled; and the House of Commons drew up, in the form of a petition to the king, a declaration of the circumstances which had occurred. After having stated generally the English law on the presentation to benefices, "Now of late," they added, "divers processes be made by his Holiness the Pope, and censures of excommunication upon certain bishops, because they have made execution of the judgments [given in the king's courts], to the open disherison of the crown; whereby, if remedy be not provided, the crown of England, which hath been so free at all times, that it has been in no earthly subjection, should be submitted to the pope; and the laws and statutes of the realm by him be defeated and avoided at his will, in perpetual destruction of the sovereignty of the king our lord, his crown, his regality, and all his realm." The Commons, therefore, on their part, declared, "That the things so attempted were clearly against the king's crown and his regality, used and approved of in the time of all his progenitors, and therefore they and all the liege commons of the realm would stand with their said lord the king, and his said crown, in the cases aforesaid, to live and die." 459 Whether they made allusion to the act of 1389 does not appear—a measure passed under protest from one of the estates of the realm was possibly held unequal to meet the emergency—at all events they would not rely upon it. For after this peremptory assertion of their own opinion, they desired the king, "and required him in the way of justice," to examine severally the lords spiritual and temporal how they thought, and how they would stand. 460 The examination was made, and the result was satisfactory. The lay lords replied without reservation that they would support the crown. The bishops (they were in a difficulty for which all allowance must be made) gave a cautious, but also a manly answer. They would not affirm, they said, that the pope had a right to excommunicate them in such cases, and they would not say that he had not. It was clear, however, that legal or illegal, such excommunication was against the privileges of the English crown, and therefore that, on the whole, they would and ought to be with the crown, *loialment*, like loyal subjects, as they were bound by their allegiance. 461

In this unusual and emphatic manner, the three estates agreed that the pope should be resisted; and an act passed "that all persons suing at the court of Rome, and obtaining thence any bulls, instruments, sentences of excommunication which touched the king, or were against him, his regality, or his realm, and they which brought the same within the realm, or received the same, or made thereof notification, or any other execution whatever, within the realm or without, they, their notaries, procurators, maintainers and abettors, fautors and counsellors, should be put out of the king's protection, and their lands and tenements, goods and chattels, be forfeited."

The resolute attitude of the country terminated the struggle. Boniface prudently yielded, and for the moment; and indeed for ever under this especial form, the wave of papal encroachment was rolled back. The temper which had been roused in the contest, might perhaps have carried the nation further. The liberties of the crown had been asserted successfully. The analogous liberties of the church might have followed; and other channels, too, might have been cut off, through which the papal exchequer fed itself on English blood. But at this crisis the anti-Roman policy was arrested in its course by another movement, which turned the current of suspicion, and frightened back the nation to conservatism.

While the crown and the parliament had been engaged with the pope, the undulations of the dispute had penetrated down among the body of the people, and an agitation had been commenced of an analogous kind against the spiritual authorities at home. The parliament had lamented that the duties of the religious houses were left unfulfilled, in consequence of the extortions of their superiors abroad. The people, who were equally convinced of the neglect of duty, adopted an interpretation of the phenomenon less favourable to the clergy, and attributed it to the temptations of worldliness, and the self-indulgence generated by enormous wealth.

This form of discontent found its exponent in John Wycliffe, the great forerunner of the Reformation, whose austere figure stands out above the crowd of notables in English history, with an outline not unlike that of another forerunner of a greater change.

The early life of Wycliffe is obscure. Lewis, on the authority of Leland, 462 says that he was born near Richmond, in Yorkshire. Fuller, though with some hesitation, prefers Durham. 463 He emerges into distinct notice in 1360, ten years subsequent to the passing of the first Statute of Provisors, having then acquired a great Oxford reputation as a lecturer in divinity, and having earned for himself powerful friends and powerful enemies. He had made his name distinguished by attacks upon the clergy for their indolence and profligacy: attacks both written and orally delivered—those written, we observe, being written in English, not in Latin. 464 In 1365, Islip, Archbishop of Canterbury, appointed him Warden of Canterbury Hall; the appointment, however, was made with some irregularity, and the following year, Archbishop Islip dying, his successor, Langham, deprived Wycliffe, and the sentence was confirmed by the king. It seemed, nevertheless, that no personal reflection was intended by this decision, for Edward III. nominated the ex-warden one of his chaplains immediately after, and employed him on an important mission to Bruges, where a conference on the benefice question was to be held with a papal commission.

Other church preferment was subsequently given to Wycliffe; but Oxford remained the chief scene of his work. He continued to hold his professorship of divinity; and from this office the character of his history took its complexion. At a time when books were rare and difficult to be procured, lecturers who had truth to communicate fresh drawn from the fountain, held an influence which in these days it is as difficult to imagine as, however, it is impossible to overrate. Students from all Europe flocked to the feet of a celebrated professor, who became the leader of a party by the mere fact of his position.

The burden of Wycliffe's teaching was the exposure of the indolent fictions which passed under the name of religion in the established theory of the church. He was a man of most simple life; austere in appearance, with bare feet and russet mantle. 465 As a soldier of Christ, he saw in his Great Master and his Apostles the patterns whom he was bound to imitate. By the contagion of example he gathered about him other men who thought as he did; and gradually, under his captaincy, these "poor priests," as they were called—vowed to poverty because Christ was poor—vowed to accept no benefice, lest they should misspend the property of the poor, and because, as apostles, they were bound to go where their Master called them, 466 spread out over the country as an army of missionaries, to preach the faith which they found in the Bible—to preach, not of relics and of indulgences, but of repentance and of the grace of God. They carried with them copies of the Bible which Wycliffe had translated, leaving here and there, as they travelled, their costly treasures, as shining seed points of light; and they refused to recognise the authority of the bishops, or their right to silence them.

If this had been all, and perhaps if Edward III. had been succeeded by a prince less miserably incapable than his grandson Richard, Wycliffe might have made good his ground; the movement of the parliament against the pope might have united in a common stream with the spiritual move against the church at home, and the Reformation have been antedated by a century. He was summoned to answer for himself before the Archbishop of

Canterbury in 1377. He appeared in court supported by the presence of John of Gaunt, Duke of Lancaster, the eldest of Edward's surviving sons, and the authorities were unable to strike him behind so powerful a shield.

But the "poor priests" had other doctrines besides those which they discovered in the Bible, relating to subjects with which, as apostles, they would have done better if they had shrunk from meddling. The inefficiency of the clergy was occasioned, as Wycliffe thought, by their wealth and by their luxury. He desired to save them from a temptation too heavy for them to bear, and he insisted that by neglect of duty their wealth had been forfeited, and that it was the business of the laity to take it from its unworthy possessors. The invectives with which the argument was accompanied produced a widely-spread irritation. The reins of the country fell simultaneously into the weak hands of Richard II., and the consequence was a rapid spread of disorder. In the year which followed Richard's accession, consistory judges were assaulted in their courts, sanctuaries were violated, priests were attacked and ill-treated in church, church-yard, and cathedral, and even while engaged in the mass; 467 the contagion of the growing anarchy seems to have touched even Wycliffe himself, and touched him in a point most deeply dangerous.

His theory of property, and his study of the character of Christ, had led him to the near confines of Anabaptism. Expanding his views upon the estates of the church into an axiom, he taught that "charters of perpetual inheritance were impossible;" "that God could not give men civil possessions for ever;" 468 "that property was founded in grace, and derived from God;" and "seeing that forfeiture was the punishment of treason, and all sin was treason against God, the sinner must consequently forfeit his right to what he held of God." These propositions were nakedly true, as we shall most of us allow; but God has his own methods of enforcing extreme principles; and human legislation may only meddle with them at its peril. The theory as an abstraction could be represented as applying equally to the laity as to the clergy, and the new teaching received a practical comment in 1381, in the invasion of London by Wat, the tyler of Dartford, and 100,000 men, who were to level all ranks, put down the church, and establish universal liberty. 469 Two priests accompanied the insurgents, not Wycliffe's followers, but the licentious counterfeits of them, who trod inevitably in their footsteps, and were as inevitably countenanced by their doctrines. The insurrection was attended with the bloodshed, destruction, and ferocity natural to such outbreaks. The Archbishop of Canterbury and many gentlemen were murdered; and a great part of London sacked and burnt. It would be absurd to attribute this disaster to Wycliffe, nor was there any desire to hold him responsible for it; but it is equally certain that the doctrines which he had taught were incompatible, at that particular time, with an effective repression of the spirit which had caused the explosion. It is equally certain that he had brought discredit on his nobler efforts by ambiguous language on a subject of the utmost difficulty, and had taught the wiser and better portion of the people to confound heterodoxy of opinion with sedition, anarchy, and disorder.

So long as Wycliffe lived, his own lofty character was a guarantee for the conduct of his immediate disciples; and although his favour had far declined, a party in the state remained attached to him, with sufficient influence to prevent the adoption of extreme measures against the "poor priests." In the year following the insurrection, an act was passed for their repression in the House of Lords, and was sent down by the king to the Commons. They were spoken of as "evil persons," going from place to place in defiance of the bishops, preaching in the open air to great congregations at markets and fairs, "exciting the people," "engendering discord between the estates of the realm." The ordinaries had no power to silence them, and had therefore desired that commissions should be issued to the sheriffs of the various counties, to arrest all such persons, and confine them, until they would "justify themselves" in the ecclesiastical courts. 470 Wycliffe petitioned against the bill, and it was rejected; not so much perhaps out of tenderness for the reformer, as because the Lower House was excited by the controversy with the pope; and being doubtfully disposed towards the clergy, was reluctant to subject the people to a more stringent spiritual control.

But Wycliffe himself meanwhile had received a clear intimation of his own declining position. His opposition to the church authorities, and his efforts at re-invigorating the faith of the country, had led him into doubtful statements on the nature of the eucharist; he had entangled himself in dubious metaphysics on a subject on which no middle course is really possible; and being summoned to answer for his language before a synod in London, he had thrown himself again for protection on the Duke of Lancaster. The duke (not unnaturally under the circumstances) declined to encourage what he could neither approve nor understand; 471 and Wycliffe, by his great patron's advice, submitted. He read a confession of faith before the bishops, which was held satisfactory; he was forbidden, however, to preach again in Oxford, and retired to his living of Lutterworth, in Leicestershire, where two years later he died.

With him departed all which was best and purest in the movement which he had commenced. The zeal of his followers was not extinguished, but the wisdom was extinguished which had directed it; and perhaps the being treated as the enemies of order had itself a tendency to make them what they were believed to be. They were left unmolested for the next twenty years, the feebleness of the government, the angry complexion which had been assumed by the dispute with Rome, and the political anarchy in the closing decade of the century, combining to give them temporary shelter; but they availed themselves of their opportunity to travel further on the dangerous road on which they had entered; and on the settlement of the country under Henry IV. they fell under the general ban which struck down all parties who had shared in the late disturbances.

They had been spared in 1382, only for more sharp denunciation, and a more cruel fate; and Boniface having healed, on his side, the wounds which had been opened, by well-timed concessions, there was no reason left for leniency. The character of the Lollard teaching was thus described (perhaps in somewhat exaggerated language) in the preamble of the act of 1401. 472

"Divers false and perverse people," so runs the act *De Heretico comburendo*, "of a certain new sect, damnably thinking of the faith of the sacraments of the church, and of the authority of the same, against the law of God and of the church, usurping the office of preaching, do perversely and maliciously, in divers places within the realm, preach and teach divers new doctrines, and wicked erroneous opinions, contrary to the faith and determination of Holy Church. And of such sect and wicked doctrines they make unlawful conventicles, they hold and exercise schools, they make and write books, they do wickedly instruct and inform people, and excite and stir them to sedition and insurrection, and make great strife and division among the people, and other enormities horrible to be heard, daily do perpetrate and commit. The diocesans cannot by their jurisdiction spiritual, without aid of the King's Majesty, sufficiently correct these said false and perverse people, nor refrain their malice, because they do go from diocess to diocess, and will not appear before the said diocesans; but the jurisdiction spiritual, the keys of the church, and the censures of the same, do utterly contemn and despise; and so their wicked preachings and doctrines they do from day to day continue and exercise, to the destruction of all order and rule, right and reason."

Something of these violent accusations is perhaps due to the horror with which false doctrine in matters of faith was looked upon in the Catholic church, the grace by which alone an honest life was made possible being held to be dependent upon orthodoxy. But the Lollards had become political revolutionists as well as religious reformers; the revolt against the spiritual authority had encouraged and countenanced a revolt against the secular; and we cannot be surprised, therefore, that these institutions should have sympathised with each other, and have united to repress a danger which was formidable to both.

The bishops, by this act, received arbitrary power to arrest and imprison on suspicion, without check or restraint of law, at their will and pleasure. Prisoners who refused to abjure their errors, who persisted in heresy, or relapsed into it after abjuration, were sentenced to be burnt at the stake—a dreadful punishment, on the wickedness of which the world has long been happily agreed. Yet we must remember that those who condemned teachers of heresy to the flames, considered that heresy itself involved everlasting perdition; that they were but faintly imitating the severity which orthodoxy still ascribes to Almighty God Himself.

The tide which was thus setting back in favour of the church did not yet, however, flow freely, and without a check. The Commons consented to sacrifice the heretics, but they still cast wistful looks on the lands of the religious houses. On two several occasions, in 1406, and again 1410, spoliation was debated in the Lower House, and representations were made upon the subject to the king. 473 The country, too, continued to be agitated with war and treason; and when Henry V. became king, in 1412, the church was still uneasy, and the Lollards were as dangerous as ever. Whether by prudent conduct they might have secured a repeal of the persecuting act is uncertain; it is more likely, from their conduct, that they had made their existence incompatible with the security of any tolerable government.

A rumour having gone abroad that the king intended to enforce the laws against heresy, notices were found fixed against the doors of the London churches, that if any such measure was attempted, a hundred thousand men would be in arms to oppose it. These papers were traced to Sir John Oldcastle, otherwise called Lord Cobham, a man whose true character is more difficult to distinguish, in the conflict of the evidence which has come down to us about him, than that of almost any noticeable person in history. He was perhaps no worse than a fanatic. He was certainly prepared, if we may trust the words of a royal proclamation (and Henry was personally intimate with Oldcastle, and otherwise was not likely to have exaggerated the charges against him), he was prepared to venture a rebellion, with the prospect of himself becoming the president of some possible Lollard commonwealth. 474 The king, with swift decisiveness, annihilated the incipient treason. Oldcastle was himself arrested. He escaped out of the Tower into Scotland; and while Henry was absent in France he seems to have attempted to organise some kind of Scotch invasion; but he was soon after again taken on the Welsh Border, tried and executed. An act which was passed in 1414 described his proceedings as an "attempt to destroy the king, and all other manner of estates of the realm, as well spiritual as temporal, and also all manner of policy, and finally the laws of the land." The sedition was held to have originated in heresy, and for the better repression of such

mischiefs in time to come, the lord chancellor, the judges, the justices of the peace, the sheriffs, mayors, bailiffs, and every other officer having government of people, were sworn on entering their office to use their best power and diligence to detect and prosecute all persons suspected of so heinous a crime. 475

Thus perished Wycliffe's labour,—not wholly, because his translation of the Bible still remained a rare treasure; as seed of future life, which would spring again under happier circumstances. But the sect which he organised, the special doctrines which he set himself to teach, after a brief blaze of success, sank into darkness; and no trace remained of Lollardry except the black memory of contempt and hatred with which the heretics of the fourteenth century were remembered by the English people, long after the actual Reformation had become the law of the land. 476

So poor a close to a movement of so fair promise was due partly to the agitated temper of the times; partly, perhaps, to a want of judgment in Wycliffe; but chiefly and essentially because it was an untimely birth. Wycliffe saw the evil; he did not see the remedy; and neither in his mind nor in the mind of the world about him, had the problem ripened itself for solution. England would have gained little by the premature overthrow of the church, when the house out of which the evil spirit was cast out could have been but swept and garnished for the occupation of the seven devils of anarchy.

The fire of heresy continued to smoulder, exploding occasionally in insurrection, 477 occasionally blazing up in nobler form, when some poor seeker for the truth, groping for a vision of God in the darkness of the years which followed, found his way into that high presence through the martyr's fire. But substantially, the nation relapsed into obedience—the church was reprieved for a century. Its fall was delayed till the spirit in which it was attacked was winnowed clean of all doubtful elements—until Protestantism had recommenced its enterprise in a desire, not for a fairer adjustment of the world's good things, but in a desire for some deeper, truer, nobler, holier insight into the will of God. It recommenced not under the auspices of a Wycliffe, not with the partial countenance of a government which was crossing swords with the Father of Catholic Christendom, and menacing the severance of England from the unity of the faith, but under a strong dynasty of undoubted Catholic loyalty, with the entire administrative power, secular as well as spiritual, in the hands of the episcopate. It sprung up spontaneously, unguided, unexcited, by the vital necessity of its nature, among the masses of the nation.

Leaping over a century, I pass to the year 1525, at which time, or about which time, a society was enrolled in London calling itself "The Association of Christian Brothers." 478 It was composed of poor men, chiefly tradesmen, artisans, a few, a very few of the clergy; but it was carefully organised, it was provided with moderate funds, which were regularly audited; and its paid agents went up and down the country carrying Testaments and tracts with them, and enrolling in the order all persons who dared to risk their lives in such a cause. The harvest had been long ripening. The records of the bishops' courts 479 are filled from the beginning of the century with accounts of prosecutions for heresy—with prosecutions, that is, of men and women to whom the masses, the pilgrimages, the indulgences, the pardons, the effete paraphernalia of the establishment, had become intolerable; who had risen up in blind resistance, and had declared, with passionate anger, that whatever was the truth, all this was falsehood. The bishops had not been idle; they had plied their busy tasks with stake and prison, and victim after victim had been executed with more than necessary cruelty. But it was all in vain: punishment only multiplied offenders, and "the reek" of the martyrs, as was said when Patrick Hamilton was burnt at St. Andrews, "infected all that it did blow upon." 480

There were no teachers, however, there were no books, no unity of conviction, only a confused refusal to believe in lies. Copies of Wycliffe's Bible remained, which parties here and there, under death penalties if detected, met to read; 481 copies, also, of some of his tracts 482 were extant; but they were unprinted transcripts, most rare and precious, which the watchfulness of the police made it impossible to multiply through the press, and which remained therefore necessarily in the possession of but a few fortunate persons.

The Protestants were thus isolated in single groups or families, without organisation, without knowledge of each other, with nothing to give them coherency as a party; and so they might have long continued, except for an impulse from some external circumstances. They were waiting for direction, and men in such a temper are seldom left to wait in vain.

The state of England did but represent the state of all Northern Europe. Wherever the Teutonic language was spoken, wherever the Teutonic nature was in the people, there was the same weariness of unreality, the same craving for a higher life. England rather lagged behind than was a leader in the race of discontent. In Germany, all classes shared the common feeling; in England it was almost confined to the lowest. But, wherever it existed, it was a free, spontaneous growth in each separate breast, not propagated by agitation, but springing self sown, the expression of the honest anger of honest men at a system which had passed the limits of toleration, and which could be endured no longer. At such times the minds of men are like a train of gunpowder, the isolated grains of which have no relation to

each other, and no effect on each other, while they remain unignited; but let a spark kindle but one of them, and they shoot into instant union in a common explosion. Such a spark was kindled in Germany, at Wittenberg, on the 31st of October, 1517. In the middle of that day Luther's denunciation of Indulgences was fixed against the gate of All Saints church, Wittenberg, and it became, like the brazen serpent in the wilderness, the sign to which the sick spirits throughout the western world looked hopefully and were healed. In all those millions of hearts the words of Luther found an echo, and flew from lip to lip, from ear to ear. The thing which all were longing for was done, and in two years from that day there was scarcely perhaps a village from the Irish Channel to the Danube in which the name of Luther was not familiar as a word of hope and promise. Then rose a common cry for guidance. Books were called for—above all things, the great book of all, the Bible. Luther's inexhaustible fecundity flowed with a steady stream, and the printing presses in Germany and in the Free Towns of the Netherlands, multiplied Testaments and tracts in hundreds of thousands. Printers published at their own expense as Luther wrote. 483 The continent was covered with disfrocked monks who had become the pedlars of these precious wares; 484 and as the contagion spread, noble young spirits from other countries, eager themselves to fight in God's battle, came to Wittenberg to learn from the champion who had struck the first blow at their great enemy how to use their weapons. "Students from all nations came to Wittenberg," says one, "to hear Luther and Melancthon. As they came in sight of the town they returned thanks to God with clasped hands; for from Wittenberg, as heretofore from Jerusalem, proceeded the light of evangelical truth, to spread thence to the utmost parts of the earth." 485 Thither came young Patrick Hamilton from Edinburgh, whose "reek" was of so much potency, a boy-enthusiast of nature as illustrious as his birth; and thither came also from England, which is here our chief concern, William Tyndal, a man whose history is lost in his work, and whose epitaph is the Reformation. Beginning life as a restless Oxford student, he moved thence to Cambridge, thence to Gloucestershire, to be tutor in a knight's family, and there hearing of Luther's doings, and expressing himself with too warm approval to suit his patron's conservatism, 486 he fell into disgrace. From Gloucestershire he removed to London, where Cuthbert Tunstall had lately been made bishop, and from whom he looked for countenance in an intention to translate the New Testament. Tunstall showed little encouragement to this enterprise; but a better friend rose where he was least looked for; and a London alderman, Humfrey Monmouth by name, hearing the young dreamer preach on some occasion at St. Dunstan's, took him to his home for half a year, and kept him there: where "the said Tyndal," as the alderman declared, "lived like a good priest, studying both night and day;

he would eat but sodden meat, by his good will, nor drink but small single beer; nor was he ever seen to wear linen about him all the time of his being there." 487 The half year being passed, Monmouth gave him ten pounds, with which provision he went off to Wittenberg; and the alderman, for assisting him in that business, went to the Tower—escaping, however, we are glad to know, without worse consequences than a short imprisonment. Tyndal saw Luther, 488 and under his immediate direction translated the Gospels and Epistles while at Wittenberg. Thence he returned to Antwerp, and settling there under the privileges of the city, he was joined by Joy, who shared his great work with him. Young Frith from Cambridge came to him also, and Barnes, and Lambert, and many others of whom no written record remains, to concert a common scheme of action.

In Antwerp, under the care of these men, was established the printing press, by which books were supplied, to accomplish for the teaching of England what Luther and Melancthon were accomplishing for Germany. Tyndal's Testament was first printed, then translations of the best German books, reprints of Wycliffe's tracts or original commentaries. Such volumes as the people most required were here multiplied as fast as the press could produce them; and for the dissemination of these precious writings, the brave London Protestants dared, at the hazard of their lives, to form themselves into an organised association.

It is well to pause and look for a moment at this small band of heroes; for heroes they were, if ever men deserved the name. Unlike the first reformers who had followed Wycliffe, they had no earthly object, emphatically none; and equally unlike them, perhaps, because they had no earthly object, they were all, as I have said, poor men—either students, like Tyndal, or artisans and labourers who worked for their own bread, and in tough contact with reality, had learnt better than the great and the educated the difference between truth and lies. Wycliffe had royal dukes and noblemen for his supporters—knights and divines among his disciples—a king and a House of Commons looking upon him, not without favour. The first Protestants of the sixteenth century had for their king the champion of Holy Church, who had broken a lance with Luther; and spiritual rulers over them alike powerful and imbecile, whose highest conception of Christian virtue was the destruction of those who disobeyed their mandates. The masses of the people were indifferent to a cause which promised them no material advantage; and the Commons of Parliament, while contending with the abuses of the spiritual authorities, were laboriously anxious to wash their hands of heterodoxy. "In the crime of heresy, thanked be God," said the bishops in 1529, "there hath no notable person fallen in our time;" no chief priest, chief ruler, or learned Pharisee—not one. "Truth it is that certain apostate friars and monks, lewd priests, bankrupt merchants, vagabonds and lewd idle fellows of corrupt nature, have embraced the abominable and erroneous opinions lately sprung in Germany, and by them have been some seduced in simplicity and ignorance. Against these, if judgment have been exercised according to the laws of the realm, we be without blame. If we have been too remiss or slack, we shall gladly do our duty from henceforth." 489 Such were the first Protestants in the eyes of their superiors. On one side was wealth, rank, dignity, the weight of authority, the majority of numbers, the prestige of centuries; here too were the phantom legions of superstition and cowardice; and here were all the worthier influences so pre-eminently English, which lead wise men to shrink from change, and to cling to things established, so long as one stone of them remains upon another, This was the army of conservatism. Opposed to it were a little band of enthusiasts, armed only with truth and fearlessness; "weak things of the world," about to do battle in God's name; and it was to be seen whether God or the world was the stronger. They were armed, I say, with the truth. It was that alone which could have given them victory in so unequal a struggle. They had returned to the essential fountain of life; they re-asserted the principle which has lain at the root of all religions, whatever their name or outward form, which once burnt with divine lustre in that Catholicism which was now to pass away; the fundamental axiom of all real life, that the service which man owes to God is not the service of words or magic forms, or ceremonies or opinions; but the service of holiness, of purity, of obedience to the everlasting laws of duty.

When we look through the writings of Latimer, the apostle of the English Reformation, when we read the depositions against the martyrs, and the lists of their crimes against the established faith, we find no opposite schemes of doctrine, no "plans of salvation;" no positive system of theology which it was held a duty to believe; these things were of later growth, when it became again necessary to clothe the living spirit in a perishable body. We find only an effort to express again the old exhortation of the Wise Man— "Will you hear the beginning and the end of the whole matter? Fear God and keep his commandments; for that is the whole duty of man."

Had it been possible for mankind to sustain themselves upon this single principle without disguising its simplicity, their history would have been painted in far other colours than those which have so long chequered its surface. This, however, has not been given to us; and perhaps it never will be given. As the soul is clothed in flesh, and only thus is able to perform its functions in this earth, where it is sent to live; as the thought must find a word before it can pass from mind to mind; so every great truth seeks some body, some outward form in which to exhibit its powers. It appears in the world, and men lay hold of it, and represent it to themselves, in histories, in forms of words, in sacramental symbols; and these things which in their proper nature are but illustrations, stiffen into essential fact, and become part of the reality. So arises in era after era an outward and mortal expression of the inward immortal life; and at once the old struggle begins to repeat itself between the flesh and the spirit, the form and the reality. For a while the lower tendencies are held in check; the meaning of the symbolism is remembered and fresh; it is a living language, pregnant and suggestive. Bye and bye, as the mind passes into other phases, the meaning is forgotten; the language becomes a dead language; and the living robe of life becomes a winding-sheet of corruption. The form is represented as everything, the spirit as nothing; obedience is dispensed with; sin and religion arrange a compromise; and outward observances, or technical inward emotions, are converted into jugglers' tricks, by which men are enabled to enjoy their pleasures and escape the penalties of wrong. Then such religion becomes no religion, but a falsehood; and honourable men turn away from it, and fall back in haste upon the naked elemental life.

This, as I understand it, was the position of the early Protestants. They found the service of God buried in a system where obedience was dissipated into superstition; where sin was expiated by the vicarious virtues of other men; where, instead of leading a holy life, men were taught that their souls might be saved through masses said for them, at a money rate, by priests whose licentiousness disgraced the nation which endured it; a system in which, amidst all the trickery of the pardons, pilgrimages, indulgences,— double-faced as these inventions are—wearing one meaning in the apologies of theologians, and quite another to the multitude who live and suffer under their influence—one plain fact at least is visible. The people substantially learnt that all evils which could touch either their spirits or their bodies, might be escaped by means which resolved themselves, scarcely disguised, into the payment of moneys.

The superstition had lingered long; the time had come when it was to pass away. Those in whom some craving lingered for a Christian life turned to the heart of the matter, to the book which told them who Christ was, and what he was; and finding there that holy example for which they longed, they flung aside in one noble burst of enthusiastic passion, the disguise which had concealed it from them. They believed in Christ, not in the bowing rood, or the pretended wood of the cross on which he suffered; and when that saintly figure had once been seen—the object of all love, the pattern of all imitation—thenceforward neither form nor ceremony should stand between them and their God.

Under much confusion of words and thoughts, confusion pardonable in all men, and most of all in them, this seems to me to be transparently visible in the aim of these "Christian Brothers;" a thirst for some fresh and noble enunciation of the everlasting truth, the one essential thing for all men to know and believe. And therefore they were strong; and therefore they at last conquered. Yet if we think of it, no common daring was required in those who would stand out at such a time in defence of such a cause. The bishops might seize them on mere suspicion; and the evidence of the most abandoned villains sufficed for their conviction. 490 By the act of Henry V., every officer, from the lord chancellor to the parish constable, was sworn to seek them out and destroy them; and both bishops and officials had shown no reluctance to execute their duty. Hunted like wild beasts from hiding-place to hiding-place, decimated by the stake, with the certainty that however many years they might be reprieved, their own lives would close at last in the same fiery trial; beset by informers, imprisoned, racked, and scourged; worst of all, haunted by their own infirmities, the flesh shrinking before the dread of a death of agony—thus it was that they struggled on; earning for *themselves* martyrdom—for *us*, the free England in which we live and breathe. Among the great, until Cromwell came to power, they had but one friend, and he but a doubtful one, who long believed the truest kindness was to kill them. Henry VIII. was always attracted towards the persons of the reformers. Their open bearing commanded his respect. Their worst crime in the bishops' eyes—the translating the Bible—was in his eyes not a crime, but a merit; he had himself long desired an authorised English version, and at length compelled the clergy to undertake it; while in the most notorious of the men themselves, in Tyndal and in Frith, he had more than once expressed an anxious interest. 491 But the convictions of his early years were long in yielding. His feeling, though genuine, extended no further than to pity, to a desire to recover estimable heretics out of errors which he would endeavour to pardon. They knew, and all the "brethren" knew, that if they persisted, they must look for the worst from the king and from every earthly power; they knew it, and they made their account with it. An informer deposed to the council, that he had asked one of the society "how the King's Grace did take the matter against the sacrament; which answered, the King's Highness was extreme against their opinions, and would punish them grievously; also that my Lords of Norfolk and Suffolk, my Lord Marquis of Exeter, with divers other great lords, were very extreme against them. Then he (the informer) asked him how he and his fellows would do seeing this, the which answered they had two thousand books out against the Blessed Sacrament, in the commons' hands; and if it were once in the commons' heads, they would have no further care." 492

Tyndal then being at work at Antwerp, and the society for the dispersion of his books thus preparing itself in England, the authorities were not slow in taking the alarm. The isolated discontent which had prevailed hitherto had been left to the ordinary tribunals; the present danger called for measures of more systematic coercion. This duty naturally devolved on Wolsey, and the office of Grand Inquisitor, which he now assumed, could not have fallen into more competent hands.

Wolsey was not cruel. There is no instance, I believe, in which he of his special motion sent a victim to the stake;—it would be well if the same praise could be allowed to Cranmer. There was this difference between the cardinal and other bishops, that while they seemed to desire to punish, Wolsey was contented to silence; while they, in their conduct of trials, made escape as difficult as possible, Wolsey sought rather to make submission easy. He was too wise to suppose that he could cauterise heresy, while the causes of it, in the corruption of the clergy, remained unremoved; and the remedy to which he trusted, was the infusing new vigour into the constitution of the church. 493 Nevertheless, he was determined to repress, as far as outward measures could repress it, the spread of the contagion; and he set himself to accomplish his task with the full energy of his nature, backed by the whole power, spiritual and secular, of the kingdom. The country was covered with his secret police, arresting suspected persons and searching for books. In London the scrutiny was so strict that at one time there was a general flight and panic; suspected butchers, tailors, and carpenters, hiding themselves in the holds of vessels in the river, and escaping across the Channel. 494 Even there they were not safe. Heretics were outlawed by a common consent of the European governments. Special offenders were hunted through France by the English emissaries with the permission and countenance of the court, 495 and there was an attempt to arrest Tyndal at Brussels, from which, for that time, he happily escaped. 496

Simultaneously the English universities fell under examination, in consequence of the appearance of dangerous symptoms among the younger students. Dr. Barnes, returning from the continent, had used violent language in a pulpit at Cambridge; and Latimer, then a neophyte in heresy, had grown suspect, and had alarmed the heads of houses. Complaints against both of them were forwarded to Wolsey, and they were summoned to London to answer for themselves.

Latimer, for some cause, found favour with the cardinal, and was dismissed, with a hope on the part of his judge that his accusers might prove as honest as he appeared to be, and even with a general licence to preach. 497 Barnes was less fortunate; he was far inferior to Latimer; a noisy, unwise man, without reticence or prudence. In addition to his offences in matters of doctrine, he had attacked Wolsey himself with somewhat vulgar personality; and it was thought well to single him out for a public, though not a very terrible admonition. His house had been searched for books, which he was suspected, and justly suspected, of having brought with him from abroad. These, however, through a timely warning of the danger, had been happily secreted, 498 or it might have gone harder with him. As it was, he was committed to the Fleet on the charge of having used heretical language. An abjuration was drawn up by Wolsey, which he signed; and while he remained in prison preparations were made for a ceremony, in which he was to bear a part, in St. Paul's church, by which the Catholic authorities hoped to produce some salutary effect on the disaffected spirits of London.

Vast quantities of Tyndal's publications had been collected by the police. The bishops, also, had subscribed among themselves 499 to buy up the copies of the New Testament before they left Antwerp;—an unpromising method, like an attempt to extinguish fire by pouring oil upon it; they had been successful, however, in obtaining a large immediate harvest, and a pyramid of offending volumes was ready to be consumed in a solemn *auto da fé*.

In the morning of Shrove Sunday, then, 1527, we are to picture to ourselves a procession moving along London streets from the Fleet prison to St. Paul's Cathedral. The warden of the Fleet was there, and the knight marshal, and the tipstaffs, and "all the company they could make," "with bills and glaives;" and in the midst of these armed officials, six men marching in penitential dresses, one carrying a lighted taper five pounds' weight, the others with symbolic fagots, signifying to the lookers-on the fate which their crimes had earned for them, but which this time, in mercy, was remitted. One of these was Barnes; the other five were "Stillyard men," undistinguishable by any other name, but detected members of the brotherhood.

It was eight o'clock when they arrived at St. Paul's. The people had flocked in crowds before them. The public seats and benches were filled. All London had hurried to the spectacle. A platform was erected in the centre of the nave, on the top of which, enthroned in pomp of purple and gold and splendour, sate the great cardinal, supported on each side with eighteen bishops, mitred abbots, and priors—six-and-thirty in all; his chaplains and "spiritual doctors" sitting also where they could find place, "in gowns of damask and satin." Opposite the platform, over the north door of the cathedral, was a great crucifix—a famous image, in those days called the Rood of Northen; and at the foot of it, inside a rail, a fire was burning, with the sinful books, the Tracts and Testaments, ranged round it in baskets, waiting for the execution of sentence.

Such was the scene into the midst of which the six prisoners entered. A second platform stood in a conspicuous place in front of the cardinal's throne, where they could be seen and heard by the crowd; and there upon their knees, with their fagots on their shoulders, they begged pardon of God and the Holy Catholic Church for their high crimes and offences. When the confession was finished Fisher, Bishop of Rochester, preached a sermon: and the sermon over, Barnes turned to the people, declaring that "he was more charitably handled than he deserved, his heresies were so heinous and detestable."

There was no other religious service: mass had perhaps been said previous to the admission into the church of heretics lying under censure; and the knight marshal led the prisoners down from the stage to the fire underneath the crucifix. They were taken within the rails, and three times led round the blazing pile, casting in their fagots as they passed. The contents of the baskets were heaped upon the fagots, and the holocaust was complete. This time, an unbloody sacrifice was deemed sufficient. The church was satisfied with penance, and Fisher pronounced the prisoners absolved, and received back into communion. 500

So ended this strange exhibition, designed to work great results on the consciences of the spectators. It may be supposed, however, that men whom the tragedies of Smithfield failed to terrify, were not likely to be affected deeply by melodrame and blazing paper.

A story follows of far deeper human interest, a story in which the persecution is mirrored with its true lights and shadows, unexaggerated by rhetoric; and which, in its minute simplicity, brings us face to face with that old world, where men like ourselves lived, and worked, and suffered, three centuries ago.

Two years before the time at which we have now arrived, Wolsey, in pursuance of his scheme of converting the endowments of the religious houses to purposes of education, had obtained permission from the pope to suppress a number of the smaller monasteries. He had added largely to the means thus placed at his disposal from his own resources, and had founded the great college at Oxford, which is now called Christchurch. 501 Desiring his magnificent institution to be as perfect as art could make it, he had sought his professors in Rome, in the Italian universities, wherever genius or ability could be found; and he had introduced into the foundation several students from Cambridge, who had been reported to him as being of unusual promise. Frith, of whom we have heard, was one of these. Of the rest, John Clark, Sumner, and Taverner are the most noticeable. At the time at which they were invited to Oxford, they were tainted, or some of them were tainted, in the eyes of the Cambridge authorities, with suspicion of heterodoxy; 502 and it is creditable to Wolsey's liberality, that he set aside these unsubstantiated rumours, not allowing them to weigh against ability, industry, and character. The church authorities thought only of crushing what opposed them, especially of crushing talent, because talent was dangerous. Wolsey's noble anxiety was to court talent, and if possible to win it.

The young Cambridge students, however, ill repaid his confidence (so, at least, it must have appeared to him), and introduced into Oxford the rising epidemic. Clark, as was at last discovered, was in the habit of reading St. Paul's Epistles to young men in his rooms; and a gradually increasing circle of undergraduates, of three or four years' standing, 503 from various colleges, formed themselves into a spiritual freemasonry, some of them passionately insisting on being admitted to the lectures, in spite of warnings from Clark himself, whose wiser foresight knew the risk which they were running, and shrank from allowing weak giddy spirits to thrust themselves into so fearful peril. 504

This little party had been in the habit of meeting for about six months, 505 when at Easter, 1527, Thomas Garret, a fellow of Magdalen, 506 who had gone out of residence, and was curate at All Hallows church, in London, re-appeared in Oxford. Garret was a secret member of the London Society, and had come down at Clark's instigation, to feel his way in the university. So excellent a beginning had already been made, that he had only to improve upon it. He sought out all such young men as were given to Greek, Hebrew, and the polite Latin; 507 and in this visit met with so much encouragement, that the Christmas following he returned again, this time bringing with him treasures of forbidden books, imported by "the Christian Brothers;" New Testaments, tracts and volumes of German divinity, which he sold privately among the initiated.

He lay concealed, with his store, at "the house of one Radley," 508 the position of which cannot now be identified; and there he remained for several weeks, unsuspected by the university authorities, till orders were sent by Wolsey to the Dean of Christchurch, for his arrest. Precise information was furnished at the same time respecting himself, his mission in Oxford, and his place of concealment. 509

The proctors were put upon the scent, and directed to take him; but one of them, Arthur Cole, of Magdalen, by name, not from any sympathy with Garret's objects, as the sequel proved, but probably from old acquaintance, for they were fellows at the same college, gave him information of his danger, and warned him to escape.

His young friends, more alarmed for their companion than for themselves, held a meeting instantly to decide what should be done; and at this meeting was Anthony Dalaber, an undergraduate of Alban Hall, and one of Clark's pupils, who will now tell the story of what followed.

"The Christmas before that time, I, Anthony Dalaber, the scholar of Alban Hall, who had books of Master Garret, had been in my country, at Dorsetshire, at Stalbridge, where I had a brother, parson of this parish, who was very desirous to have a curate out of Oxford, and willed me in any wise to get him one there, if I could. This just occasion offered, it was thought good among the brethren (for so we did not only call one another, but were indeed one to another), that Master Garret, changing his name, should be sent forth with my letters into Dorsetshire, to my brother, to serve him there for a time, until he might secretly convey himself from thence some whither over the sea. According hereunto I wrote my letters in all haste possible unto my brother, for Master Garret to be his curate; but not declaring what he was indeed, for my brother was a rank papist, and afterwards was the most mortal enemy that ever I had, for the Gospel's sake.

"So on Wednesday (Feb. 18), in the morning before Shrovetide, Master Garret departed out of Oxford towards Dorsetshire, with my letter, for his new service."

The most important person being thus, as was supposed, safe from immediate danger, Dalaber was at leisure to think a little about himself; and supposing, naturally, that the matter would not end there, and that some change of residence might be of advantage for his own security, he moved off from Alban Hall (as undergraduates it seems were then at liberty to do) to Gloucester College, 510 under pretence that he desired to study civil law, for which no facilities existed at the hall. This little matter was affected on the Thursday; and all Friday and Saturday morning he "was so much busied in setting his poor stuff in order, his bed, his books, and such things else as he had," that he had no leisure to go forth anywhere those two days, Friday and Saturday.

"Having set up my things handsomely," he continues, "the same day, before noon, I determined to spend that whole afternoon, until evensong time, at Frideswide College, 511 at my book in mine own study; and so shut my chamber door unto me, and my study door also, and took into my head to read Francis Lambert upon the Gospel of St. Luke, which book only I had then within there. All my other books written on the Scriptures, of which I had great numbers, I had left in my chamber at Alban's Hall, where I had made a very secret place to keep them safe in, because it was so dangerous to have any such books. And so, as I was diligently reading in the same book of Lambert upon Luke, suddenly one knocked at my chamber door very hard, which made me astonished, and yet I sat still and would not speak; then he knocked again more hard, and yet I held my peace; and straightway he knocked again yet more fiercely; and then I thought this: peradventure it is somebody that hath need of me; and therefore I thought myself bound to do as I would be done unto; and so, laying my book aside, I came to the door and opened it, and there was Master Garret, as a man amazed, whom I thought to have been with my brother, and one with him."

Garret had set out on his expedition into Dorsetshire, but had been frightened, and had stolen back into Oxford on the Friday, to his old hiding place, where, in the middle of the night, the proctors had taken him. He had been carried to Lincoln, and shut up in a room in the rector's house, where he had been left all day. In the afternoon the rector went to chapel, no one was stirring about the college, and he had taken advantage of the opportunity to slip the bolt of the door and escape. He had a friend at Gloucester College, "a monk who had bought books of him;" and Gloucester lying on the outskirts of the town, he had hurried down there as the readiest place of shelter. The monk was out; and as no time was to be lost, Garret asked the servant on the staircase to show him Dalaber's rooms.

As soon as the door was opened, "he said he was undone, for he was taken." "Thus he spake unadvisedly in the presence of the young man, who at once slipped down the stairs," it was to be feared, on no good errand. "Then I said to him," Dalaber goes on, "alas, Master Garret, by this your uncircumspect coming here and speaking so before the young man, you have disclosed yourself and utterly undone me. I asked him why he was not in Dorsetshire. He said he had gone a day's journey and a half; but he was so fearful, his heart would none other but that he must needs return again unto Oxford. With deep sighs and plenty of tears, he prayed me to help to convey him away; and so he cast off his hood and gown wherein he came to me, and desired me to give him a coat with sleeves, if I had any; and he told me that he would go into Wales, and thence convey himself, if he might, into Germany. Then I put on him a sleeved coat of mine. He would also have had another manner of cap of me, but I had none but priestlike, such as his own was.

"Then kneeled we both down together upon our knees, and lifting up our hearts and hands to God our heavenly Father, desired him, with plenty of tears, so to conduct and prosper him in his journey, that he might well escape the danger of all his enemies, to the glory of His Holy Name, if His good pleasure and will so were. And then we embraced and kissed the one the other, the tears so abundantly flowing out from both our eyes, that we all bewet both our faces, and scarcely for sorrow could we speak one to another. And so he departed from me, apparelled in my coat, being committed unto the tuition of our Almighty and merciful Father.

"When he was gone down the stairs from my chamber, I straightways did shut my chamber door, and went into my study; and taking the New Testament in my hands, kneeled down on my knees, and with many a deep sigh and salt tear, I did, with much deliberation, read over the tenth chapter of St. Matthew's Gospel, 512 praying that God would endue his tender and lately-born little flock in Oxford with heavenly strength by his Holy Spirit; that quietly to their own salvation, with all godly patience, they might bear Christ's heavy cross, which I now saw was presently to be laid on their young and weak backs, unable to bear so huge a burden without the greater help of his Holy Spirit.

"This done, I laid aside my book safe, folded up Master Garret's gown and hood, and so, having put on my short gown, and shut my doors, I went towards Frideswide (Christchurch), to speak with that worthy martyr of God, Master Clark. But of purpose I went by St. Mary's church, to go first unto Corpus Christi College, to speak with Diet and Udal, my faithful brethren and fellows in the Lord. By chance I met by the way a brother of ours, one Master Eden, fellow of Magdalen, who, as soon as he saw me, said, we were all undone, for Master Garret was returned, and was in prison. I said it was not so; he said it was. I heard, quoth he, our Proctor, Master Cole, say and declare the same this day. Then I told him what was done; and so made haste to Frideswide, to find Master Clark, for I thought that he and others would be in great sorrow.

"Evensong was begun; the dean and the canons were there in their grey amices; they were almost at Magnificat before I came thither. I stood in the choir door and heard Master Taverner play, and others of the chapel there sing, with and among whom I myself was wont to sing also; but now my singing and music were turned into sighing and musing. As I there stood, in cometh Dr. Cottisford, 513 the commissary, as fast as ever he could go, bareheaded, as pale as ashes (I knew his grief well enough); and to the dean he goeth into the choir, were he was sitting in his stall, and talked with him, very sorrowfully: what, I know not; but whereof I might and did truly guess. I went aside from the choir door to see and hear more. The commissary and dean came out of the choir, wonderfully troubled as it seemed. About the middle of the church, met them Dr. London, 514 puffing, blustering, and blowing like a hungry and greedy lion seeking his prey. They talked together awhile; but the commissary was much blamed by them, insomuch that he wept for sorrow.

"The doctors departed, and sent abroad their servants and spies everywhere. Master Clark, about the middle of the compline, 515 came forth of the choir. I followed him to his chamber, and declared what had happened that afternoon of Master Garret's escape. Then he sent for one Master Sumner and Master Bets, fellows and canons there. In the meantime he gave me a very godly exhortation, praying God to give us all the wisdom of the serpent and the harmlessness of doves, for we should shortly have much need thereof. When Master Sumner and Master Bets came, he caused me to declare again the whole matter to them two. Then desiring them to tell our other brethren in that college, I went to Corpus Christi College, to comfort our brethren there, where I found in Diet's chamber, looking for me, Fitzjames, Diet, and Udal. They all knew the matter before by Master Eden, whom I had sent unto Fitzjames. So I tarried there and supped with them, where they had provided meat and drink for us before my coming; and when we had ended, Fitzjames would needs have me to lie that night with him in my old lodging at Alban's Hall. But small rest and little sleep took we both there that night."

The next day, which was Sunday, Dalaber rose at five o'clock, and as soon as he could leave the Hall, hastened off to his rooms at Gloucester. The night had been wet and stormy, and his shoes and stockings were covered with mud. The college gates, when he reached them, were still closed, an unusual thing at that hour; and he walked up and down under the walls in the bleak grey morning, till the clock struck seven, "much disquieted, his head full of forecasting cares," but resolved, like a brave man, that come what would, he would accuse no one, and declare nothing but what he saw was already known. The gates were at last opened; he went to his rooms, and for some time his key would not turn in the door, the lock having been meddled with. At length he succeeded in entering, and found everything in confusion, his bed tossed and tumbled, his study door open, and his clothes strewed about the floor. A monk who occupied the opposite rooms, hearing him return, came to him and said that the commissary and the two proctors had been there looking for Garret. Bills and swords had been thrust through the bed-straw, and every corner of the room searched for him. Finding nothing, they had left orders that Dalaber, as soon as he returned, should appear before the prior of the students.

"This so troubled me," Dalaber says, "that I forgot to make clean my hose and shoes, and to shift me into another gown; and all bedirted as I was, I went to the said prior's chamber." The prior asked him where he had slept that night. At Alban's Hall, he answered, with his old bedfellow, Fitzjames. The prior said he did not believe him, and asked if Garret had been at his rooms the day before. He replied that he had. Whither had he gone, then? the prior inquired; and where was he at that time? "I answered," says Dalaber, "that I knew not, unless he was gone to Woodstock; he told me that he would go there, because one of the keepers had promised him a piece of venison to make merry with at Shrovetide. This tale I thought meetest, though it were nothing so." 516

At this moment the university beadle entered with two of the commissary's servants, bringing a message to the prior that he should repair at once to Lincoln, taking Dalaber with him. "I was brought into the chapel," the latter continues, "and there I found Dr. Cottisford, commissary; Dr. Higdon, Dean of Cardinal's College; and Dr. London, Warden of New College; standing together at the altar. They called for chairs and sate down, and then [ordered] me to come to them; they asked me what my name was, how long I had been at the university, what I studied," with various other inquiries: the clerk of the university, meanwhile, bringing pens, ink, and paper, and arranging a table with a few loose boards upon tressels. A mass book, he says, was then placed before him, and he was commanded to lay his hand upon it, and swear that he would answer truly such questions as should be asked him. At first he refused; but afterwards, being persuaded, "partly by fair words, and partly by great threats," he promised to do as they would have him; but in his heart he "meant nothing so to do." "So I laid my hand on the book," he goes on, "and one of them gave me my oath, and commanded me to kiss the book. They made great courtesy between them who should examine me; at last, the rankest Pharisee of them all took upon him to do it.

"Then he asked me again, by my oath, where Master Garret was, and whither I had conveyed him. I said I had not conveyed him, nor yet wist where he was, nor whither he was gone, except he were gone to Woodstock, as I had before said. Surely, they said, I brought him some whither this morning, for they might well perceive by my foul shoes and dirty hosen that I had travelled with him the most part of the night. I answered plainly, that I lay at Alban's Hall with Sir Fitzjames, and that I had good witness thereof. They asked me where I was at evensong. I told them at Frideswide, and that I saw, first, Master Commissary, and then Master Doctor London, come thither to Master Dean. Doctor London and the Dean threatened me that if I would not tell the truth I should surely be sent to the Tower of London, and there be racked, and put into Little-ease. 517

"At last when they could get nothing out of me whereby to hurt or accuse any man, or to know anything of that which they sought, they all three together brought me up a long stairs, into a great chamber, over Master Commissary's chamber, wherein stood a great pair of very high stocks. Then Master Commissary asked me for my purse and girdle, and took away my money and my knives; and then they put my legs into the stocks, and so locked me fast in them, in which I sate, my feet being almost as high as my head; and so they departed, locking fast the door, and leaving me alone.

"When they were all gone, then came into my remembrance the worthy forewarning and godly declaration of that most constant martyr of God, Master John Clark, who, well nigh two years before that, when I did earnestly desire him to grant me to be his scholar, said unto me after this sort: 'Dalaber, you desire you wot not what, and that which you are, I fear, unable to take upon you; for though now my preaching be sweet and pleasant to you, because there is no persecution laid on you for it, yet the time will come, and that, peradventure, shortly, if ye continue to live godly therein, that God will lay on you the cross of persecution, to try you whether you can as pure gold abide the fire. You shall be called and judged a heretic; you shall be abhorred of the world; your own friends and kinsfolk will forsake you, and also hate you; you shall be cast into prison, and none shall dare to help you; you shall be accused before bishops, to your reproach and shame, to the great sorrow of all your friends and kinsfolk. Then will ye wish ye had never known this doctrine; then will ye curse Clark, and wish that ye had never known him because he hath brought you to all these troubles.'

"At which words, I was so grieved that I fell down on my knees at his feet, and with tears and sighs besought him that, for the tender mercy of God, he would not refuse me; saying that I trusted, verily, that he which had begun this in me would not forsake me, but would give me grace to continue therein to the end. When he heard me say so, he came to me, took me in his arms and kissed me, the tears trickling from his eyes; and said unto me: 'The Lord God Almighty grant you so to do; and from henceforth for ever, take me for your father, and I will take you for my son in Christ.'"

In these meditations the long Sunday morning wore away. A little before noon the commissary came again to see if his prisoner was more amenable; finding him, however, still obstinate, he offered him some dinner—a promise which we will hope he fulfilled, for here Dalaber's own narrative abruptly forsakes us, 518 leaving uncompleted, at this point, the most vivid picture which remains to us of a fraction of English life in the reign of Henry VIII. If the curtain fell finally on the little group of students, this narrative alone would furnish us with rare insight into the circumstances under which the Protestants fought their way. The story, however, can be carried something further, and the strangest incident connected with it remains to be told.

Dalaber breaks off on Sunday at noon. The same day, or early the following morning, he was submitted once more to examination: this time, for the discovery of his own offences, and to induce him to give up his confederates. With respect to the latter he proved "marvellous obstinate." "All that was gotten of him was with much difficulty;" nor would he confess to any names as connected with heresy or heretics except that of Clark, which was already known. About himself he was more open. He wrote his "book of heresy," that is, his confession of faith, "with his own hand" —his evening's occupation, perhaps, in the stocks in the rector of Lincoln's house; and the next day he was transferred to prison. 519

This offender being thus disposed of, and strict secrecy being observed to prevent the spread of alarm, a rapid search was set on foot for books in all suspected quarters. The fear of the authorities was that "the infect persons would flee," and "convey" their poison "away with them." 520 The officials, once on the scent of heresy, were skilful in running down the game. No time was lost, and by Monday evening many of "the brethren" had been arrested, their rooms examined, and their forbidden treasures discovered and rifled. Dalaber's store was found "hid with marvellous secresy;" and in one student's desk a duplicate of Garret's list—the titles of the volumes with which the first "Religious Tract Society" set themselves to convert England.

Information of all this was conveyed in haste by Dr. London to the Bishop of Lincoln, as the ordinary of the university; and the warden told his story with much self-congratulation. On one point, however, the news which he had to communicate was less satisfactory. Garret himself was gone—utterly gone. Dalaber was obstinate, and no clue to the track of the fugitive could be discovered. The police were at fault; neither bribes nor threats could elicit anything; and in these desperate circumstances, as he told the bishop, the three heads of houses conceived that they might strain a point of propriety for so good a purpose as to prevent the escape of a heretic. Accordingly, after a full report of the points of their success, Doctor London went on to relate the following remarkable proceeding:

"After Master Garret escaped, *the commissary being in extreme pensiveness, knew no other remedy but this extraordinary, and caused a figure to be made by one expert in astronomy—and his judgment doth continually persist upon this, that he fled in a tawny coat south-eastward, and is in the middle of London, and will shortly to the sea side.* He was curate unto the parson of Honey Lane. 521 It is likely he is privily cloaked there. Wherefore, as soon as I knew the judgment of this astronomer, I thought it expedient and my duty with all speed to ascertain your good lordship of all the premises; that in time your lordship may advertise my lord his Grace, and my lord of London. It will be a gracious deed that he and all his pestiferous works, which he carrieth about, might be taken, to the salvation of his soul, opening of many privy heresies, and extinction of the same." 522

We might much desire to know what the bishop's sensations were in reading this letter—to know whether it occurred to him that in this naïve acknowledgment, the Oxford heresy hunters were themselves confessing to an act of heresy; and that by the law of the church, which they were so eager to administer, they were liable to the same death which they were so zealous to secure for the poor vendors of Testaments. So indeed they really were. Consulting the stars had been ruled from immemorial time to be dealing with the devil; the penalty of it was the same as for witchcraft; yet here was a reverend warden of a college considering it his duty to write eagerly of a discovery obtained by these forbidden means, to his own diocesan, begging him to communicate with the Cardinal of York and the Bishop of London, that three of the highest church authorities in England might become *participes criminis*, by acting on this diabolical information.

Meanwhile, the commissary, not wholly relying on the astrologer, but resolving prudently to make use of the more earthly resources which were at his disposal, had sent information of Garret's escape to the corporations of Dover, Rye, Winchester, Southampton, and Bristol, with descriptions of the person of the fugitive; and this step was taken with so much expedition, that before the end of the week no vessel was allowed to leave either of those harbours without being strictly searched.

The natural method proved more effectual than the supernatural, though again with the assistance of a singular accident. Garret had not gone to London; unfortunately for himself, he had not gone to Wales as he had intended. He left Oxford, as we saw, the evening of Saturday, February 21st. That night he reached a village called Corkthrop, 523 where he lay concealed till Wednesday; and then, not in the astrologer's orange-tawny dress, but in "a courtier's coat and buttoned cap," which he had by some means contrived to procure, he set out again on his forlorn journey, making for the nearest sea-port, Bristol, where the police were looking out to receive him. His choice of Bristol was peculiarly unlucky. The "chapman" of the town was the step-father of Cole, the Oxford proctor: to this person, whose name was Master Wilkyns, the proctor had written a special letter, in addition to the commissary's circular; and the family connection acting as a spur to his natural activity, a coast guard had been set before Garret's arrival, to watch for him down the Avon banks, and along the Channel shore for fifteen miles. All the Friday night "the mayor, with the aldermen, and twenty of the council, had kept privy watch," and searched suspicious houses at Master Wilkyns's instance; the whole population were on the alert, and when the next afternoon, a week after his escape, the poor heretic, footsore and weary, dragged himself into the town, he found that he had walked into the lion's mouth. 524 He quickly learnt this danger to which he was exposed, and hurried off again with the best speed which he could command; but it was too late. The chapman, alert and indefatigable, had heard that a stranger had been seen in the street; the police were set upon his track, and he was taken at Bedminster, a suburb on the opposite bank of the Avon, and hurried before a magistrate, where he at once acknowledged his identity.

With such happy success were the good chapman's efforts rewarded. Yet in this world there is no light without shadow; no pleasure without its alloy. In imagination, Master Wilkyns had thought of himself conducting the prisoner in triumph into the streets of Oxford, the hero of the hour. The sour formality of the law condemned him to ill-merited disappointment. Garret had been taken beyond the liberties of the city; it was necessary, therefore, to commit him to the county gaol, and he was sent to Ilchester. "Master Wilkyns offered himself to be bound to the said justice in three hundred pounds to discharge him of the said Garret, and to see him surely to Master Proctor's of Oxford; yet could he not have him, for the justice said that the order of the law would not so serve." 525 The fortunate captor had therefore to content himself with the consciousness of his exploit, and the favourable report of his conduct which was sent to the bishops; and Garret went first to Ilchester, and thence was taken by special writ, and surrendered to Wolsey.

Thus unkind had fortune shown herself to the chief criminal, guilty of the unpardonable offence of selling Testaments at Oxford, and therefore hunted down as a mad dog, and a common enemy of mankind. He escaped for the present the heaviest consequences, for Wolsey persuaded him to abjure. A few years later we shall again meet him, when he had recovered his better nature, and would not abjure, and died as a brave man should die. In the meantime we return to the university, where the authorities were busy trampling out the remains of the conflagration.

Two days after his letter respecting the astrologer, the Warden of New College wrote again to the Diocesan, with an account of his further proceedings. He was an efficient inquisitor, and the secrets of the poor undergraduates had been unravelled to the last thread. Some of "the brethren" had confessed; all were in prison, and the doctor desired instructions as to what should be done with them. It must be said for Dr. London, that he was anxious that they should be treated leniently. Dalaber described him as a roaring lion, and he was a bad man, and came at last to a bad end. But it is pleasant to find that even he, a mere blustering arrogant official, was not wholly without redeeming points of character; and as little good will be said for him hereafter, the following passage in his second letter may be placed to the credit side of his account. The tone in which he wrote was at least humane, and must pass for more than an expression of natural kindness, when it is remembered that he was addressing a person with whom tenderness for heresy was a crime.

"These youths," he said, "have not been long conversant with Master Garret, nor have greatly perused his mischievous books; and long before Master Garret was taken, divers of them were weary of these works, and delivered them to Dalaber. I am marvellous sorry for the young men. If they be openly called upon, although they appear not greatly infect, yet they shall never avoid slander, because my Lord's Grace did send for Master Garret to be taken. I suppose his Grace will know of your good lordship everything. Nothing shall be hid, I assure your good lordship, an every one of them were my brother; and I do only make this moan for these youths, for surely they be of the most towardly young men in Oxford; and as far as I do yet perceive, not greatly infect, but much to blame for reading any part of these works." 526

Doctor London's intercession, if timid, was generous; he obviously wished to suggest that the matter should be hushed up, and that the offending parties should be dismissed with a reprimand. If the decision had rested with Wolsey, it is likely that this view would have been readily acted upon. But the Bishop of Lincoln was a person in whom the spirit of humanity had been long exorcised by the spirit of an ecclesiastic. He was staggering along the last years of a life against which his own register 527 bears dreadful witness, and he would not burden his conscience with mercy to heretics. He would not mar the completeness of his barbarous career. He singled out three of the prisoners—Garret, Clark, and Ferrars 528—and especially entreated that they should be punished. "They be three perilous men," he wrote to Wolsey, "and have been the occasion of the corruption of youth. They have done much mischief, and for the love of God let them be handled thereafter." 529

Wolsey had Garret in his own keeping, and declined to surrender him. Ferrars had been taken at the Black Friars, in London, 530 and making his submission, was respited and escaped with abjuration. But Clark was at Oxford, in the bishop's power, and the wicked old man was allowed to work his will upon him. A bill of heresy was drawn, which the prisoner was required to sign. He refused, and must have been sent to the stake, had he not escaped by dying prematurely of the treatment which he had received in prison. 531 His last words only are recorded. He was refused the communion, not perhaps as a special act of cruelty, but because the laws of the church would not allow the holy thing to be profaned by the touch of a heretic. When he was told that it would not be suffered, he said "*crede et manducâsti*"—"faith is the communion;" and so passed away; a very noble person, so far as the surviving features of his character will let us judge; one who, if his manhood had fulfilled the promise of his youth, would have taken no common part in the Reformation.

The remaining brethren were then dispersed. Some were sent home to their friends—others, Anthony Dalaber among them, were placed on their trial, and being terrified at their position, recanted, and were sentenced to do penance. Ferrars was brought to Oxford for the occasion, and we discern indistinctly (for the mere fact is all which survives) a great fire at Carfax; a crowd of spectators, and a procession of students marching up High Street with fagots on their shoulders, the solemn beadles leading them with gowns and maces. The ceremony was repeated to which Dr. Barnes had been submitted at St. Paul's. They were taken three times round the fire, throwing in each first their fagot, and then some one of the offending books, in token that they repented and renounced their errors.

Thus was Oxford purged of heresy. The state of innocence which Dr. London pathetically lamented 532 was restored, and the heads of houses had peace till their rest was broken by a ruder storm.

In this single specimen we may see a complete image of Wolsey's persecution, as with varying details it was carried out in every town and village from the Tweed to the Land's End. I dwell on the stories of individual suffering, not to colour the narrative, or to re-awaken feelings of bitterness which may well rest now and sleep for ever; but because, through the years in which it was struggling for recognition, the history of Protestantism is the history of its martyrs. No rival theology, as I have said, had as yet shaped itself into formulas. We have not to trace any slow growing elaboration of opinion. Protestantism, before it became an establishment, was a refusal to live any longer in a lie. It was a falling back upon the undefined untheoretic rules of truth and piety which lay upon the surface of the Bible, and a determination rather to die than to mock with unreality any longer the Almighty Maker of the world. We do not look in the dawning manifestations of such a spirit for subtleties of intellect. Intellect, as it ever does, followed in the wake of the higher virtues of manly honesty and truthfulness. And the evidences which were to effect the world's conversion were so cunningly arranged syllogistic demonstrations, but once more those loftier evidences which lay in the calm endurance by heroic men of the extremities of suffering, and which touched—not the mind with conviction, but the heart with admiring reverence.

In the concluding years of his administration Wolsey was embarrassed with the divorce. Difficulties were gathering round him, from the failure of his hopes abroad and the wreck of his popularity at home; and the activity of the persecution was something relaxed, as the guiding mind of the great minister ceased to have leisure to attend to it. The bishops, however, continued, each in his own diocese, to act with such vigour as they possessed. Their courts were unceasingly occupied with vexatious suits, commenced without reason, and conducted without justice. They summoned arbitrarily as suspected offenders whoever had the misfortune to have provoked their dislike; either compelling them to criminate themselves by questions on the intricacies of theology, 533 or allowing sentence to be passed against them on the evidence of abandoned persons, who would not have been admissible as witnesses before the secular tribunals. 534

It might have been thought that the clear perception which was shown by the House of Commons of the injustice with which the trials for heresy were conducted, the disregard, shameless and flagrant, of the provisions of the statutes under which the bishops were enabled to proceed, might have led them to reconsider the equity of persecution in itself; or, at least, to remove from the office of judges persons who had shown themselves so signally unfit to exercise that office. It would have been indecent, however, if not impossible, to transfer to a civil tribunal the cognisance of opinion; and, on the other hand, there was as yet among the upper classes of the laity no kind of disposition to be lenient towards those who were really unorthodox. The desire so far was only to check the reckless and random accusations of persons whose offence was to have criticised, not the doctrine but the moral conduct, of the church authorities. The Protestants, although from the date of the meeting of the parliament and Wolsey's fall their ultimate triumph was certain, gained nothing in its immediate consequences. They suffered rather from the eagerness of the political reformers to clear themselves from complicity with heterodoxy; and the bishops were even taunted with the spiritual dissensions of the realm as an evidence of their indolence and misconduct. 535 Language of this kind boded ill for the "Christian Brethren;" and the choice of Wolsey's successor for the office of chancellor soon confirmed their apprehensions; Wolsey had chastised them with whips; Sir Thomas More would chastise them with scorpions; and the philosopher of the *Utopia*, the friend of Erasmus, whose life was of blameless beauty, whose genius was cultivated to the highest attainable perfection, was to prove to the world that the spirit of persecution is no peculiar attribute of the pedant, the bigot, of the fanatic, but may co-exist with the fairest graces of the human character. The lives of remarkable men usually illustrate some emphatic truth. Sir Thomas More may be said to have lived to illustrate the necessary tendencies of Romanism in an honest mind convinced of its truth; to show that the test of sincerity in a man who professes to regard orthodoxy as an essential of salvation, is not the readiness to endure persecution, but the courage which will venture to inflict it.

The seals were delivered to the new chancellor in November, 1529. By his oath on entering office he was bound to exert himself to the utmost for the suppression of heretics: 536 he was bound, however, equally to obey the conditions under which the law allowed them to be suppressed. Unfortunately for his reputation as a judge, he permitted the hatred of "that kind of men," which he did not conceal that he felt, 537 to obscure his conscience on this important feature of his duty, and tempt him to imitate the worst iniquities of the bishops. I do not intend in this place to relate the stories of his cruelties in his house at Chelsea, 538 which he himself partially denied, and which at least we may hope were exaggerated. Being obliged to confine myself to specific instances, I choose rather those on which the evidence is not open to question; and which prove against More, not the zealous execution of a cruel law, for which we may not fairly hold him responsible, but a disregard, in the highest degree censurable, of his obligations as a judge.

The acts under which heretics were liable to punishment, were the 15th of the 2nd of Henry IV., and the 1st of the 2nd of Henry V.

By the act of Henry IV., the bishops were bound to bring offenders to trial in open court, within three months of their arrest, if there were no lawful impediment. If conviction followed, they might imprison at their discretion. Except under these conditions, they were not at liberty to imprison.

By the act of Henry V., a heretic, if he was first indicted before a secular judge, was to be delivered within ten days (or if possible, a shorter period) to the bishop, "to be acquit or convict" by a jury in the spiritual court, and to be dealt with accordingly. 539

The secular judge might detain a heretic for ten days before delivering him to the bishop. The bishop might detain him for three months before his trial. Neither the secular judge nor the bishop had power to inflict indefinite imprisonment at will while the trial was delayed; nor if on the trial the bishop failed in securing a conviction, was he at liberty to detain the accused person any longer on the same charge, because the result was not satisfactory to himself. These provisions were not preposterously lenient. Sir Thomas More should have found no difficulty in observing them himself, and in securing the observance of them by the bishops, at least in cases where he was himself responsible for the first committal. It is to be feared that he forgot that he was a judge in his eagerness to be a partisan, and permitted no punctilious legal scruples to interfere with the more important object of ensuring punishment to heretics.

The first case which I shall mention is one in which the Bishop of London was principally guilty; not, however, without More's countenance, and, if Foxe is to be believed, his efficient support.

In December, 1529, the month succeeding his appointment as chancellor, More, at the instance of the Bishop of London, 540 arrested a citizen of London, Thomas Philips by name, on a charge of heresy.

The prisoner was surrendered in due form to his diocesan, and was brought to trial on the 4th of February; a series of articles being alleged against him by Foxford, the bishop's vicar-general. The articles were of the usual kind. The prisoner was accused of having used unorthodox expressions on transubstantiation, on purgatory, pilgrimages, and confession. It does not appear whether any witnesses were produced. The vicar-general brought his accusations on the ground of general rumour, and failed to maintain them. Whether there were witnesses or not, neither the particular offences, nor even the fact of the general rumour, could be proved to the satisfaction of the jury. Philips himself encountered each separate charge with a specific denial, declaring that he neither was, nor ever had been, other than orthodox; and the result of the trial was, that no conviction could be obtained. The prisoner "was found so clear from all manner of infamous slanders and suspicions, that all the people before the said bishop, shouting in judgment as with one voice, openly witnessed his good name and fame, to the great reproof and shame of the said bishop, if he had not been ashamed to be ashamed." 541 The case had broken down; the proceedings were over, and by law the accused person was free. But the law, except when it was on their own side, was of little importance to the church authorities. As they had failed to prove Philips guilty of heresy, they called upon him to confess his guilt by abjuring it; "as if," he says, "there were no difference between a nocent and an innocent, between a guilty and a not guilty." 542

He refused resolutely, and was remanded to prison, in open violation of the law. The bishop, in conjunction with Sir Thomas More, 543 sent for him from time to time, submitting him to private examinations, which again were illegal; and urged the required confession, in order, as Philips says, "to save the bishop's credit."

The further they advanced, the more difficult it was to recede; and the bishop at length, irritated at his failure, concluded the process with an arbitrary sentence of excommunication. From this sentence, whether just or unjust, there was then no appeal, except to the pope. The wretched man, in virtue of it, was no longer under the protection of the law, and was committed to the Tower, where he languished for three years, protesting, but protesting fruitlessly, against the tyranny which had crushed him, and clamouring for justice in the deaf ears of pedants who knew not what justice meant.

If this had occurred at the beginning of the century, the prisoner would have been left to die, as countless multitudes had already died, unheard, uncared for, unthought of; the victim not of deliberate cruelty, but of that frightfullest portent, folly armed with power. Happily the years of his imprisonment had been years of swift revolution. The House of Commons had become a tribunal where oppression would not any longer cry wholly unheard; Philips appealed to it for protection, and recovered his liberty. 544

The weight of guilt in this instance presses essentially on Stokesley; yet a portion of the blame must be borne also by the chancellor, who first placed Philips in Stokesley's hands; who took part in the illegal private examinations, and who could not have been ignorant of the prisoner's ultimate fate. If, however, it be thought unjust to charge a good man's memory with an offence in which his part was only secondary, the following iniquity was wholly and exclusively his own. I relate the story without comment in the address of the injured person to More's successor. 545

"To the Right Hon. the Lord Chancellor of England. (Sir T. Audeley) and other of the King's Council.

"In most humble wise showeth unto your goodness your poor bedeman John Field, how that the next morrow upon twelfth day, 546 in the twenty-first year of our sovereign lord the King's Highness, Sir Thomas More, Knight, then being Lord Chancellor of England, did send certain of his servants, and caused your said bedeman, with certain others, to be brought to his place at Chelsea, and there kept him (after what manner and fashion it were now long to tell), by the space of eighteen days; 547 and then set him at liberty, binding him to appear before him again the eighth day following in the Star Chamber, which was Candlemas eve; at which day your said bedeman appeared, and was then sent to the Fleet, where he continued until Palm Sunday two years after [in violation of both the statutes], kept so close the first quarter that his keeper only might visit him; and always after closed up with those that were handled most straitly; often searched, sometimes even at midnight; besides snares and traps laid to take him in. Betwixt Michaelmas and Allhalloween tide next after his coming to prison there was taken from your bedeman a Greek vocabulary, price five shillings; Saint Cyprian's works, with a book of the same Sir Thomas More's making, named the *Supplication of Souls*. For what cause it was done he committeth to the judgment of God, that seeth the souls of all persons. The said Palm Sunday, which was also our Lady's day, towards night there came two officers of the Fleet, named George Porter and John Butler, and took your bedeman into a ward alone, and there, after long searching, found his purse hanging at his girdle; which they took, and shook out the money to the sum of ten shillings, which was sent him to buy such necessaries as he lacked, and delivered him again his purse, well and truly keeping the money to themselves, as they said for their fees; and forthwith carried him from the Fleet (where he lost such poor bedding as he then had, and could never since get it), and delivered him to the Marshalsea, under our gracious sovereign's commandment and Sir Thomas More's. When the Sunday before the Rogation week following, your bedeman fell sick; and the Whitsun Monday was carried out on four men's backs, and delivered to his friends to be recovered if it so pleased God. At which time the keeper took for your bedeman's fees other ten shillings, when four shillings should have sufficed if he had been delivered in good health.

"Within three weeks it pleased God to set your bedeman on his feet, so that he might walk abroad. Whereof when Sir Thomas More heard (who went out of his chancellorship about the time your bedeman was carried out of prison), although he had neither word nor deed which he could ever truly lay to your bedeman's charge, yet made he such means by the Bishops of Winchester and London, as your bedeman heard say, to the Hon. Lord Thomas Duke of Norfolk, that he gave new commandment to the keeper of the Marshalsea to attach again your said bedeman; which thing was speedily done the Sunday three weeks after his deliverance. And so he continued in prison again until Saint Lawrence tide following; at which time money was given to the keeper, and some things he took which were not given, and then was your bedeman re-delivered through the king's goodness, under sureties bound in a certain sum, that he should appear the first day of the next term following, and then day by day until his dismission. And so hath your bedeman been at liberty now twelve months waiting daily from term to term, and nothing laid to his charge as before.

"Wherefore, the premises tenderly considered, and also your said bedeman's great poverty, he most humbly beseecheth your goodness that he may now be clearly discharged; and if books, money, or other things seem to be taken or kept from him otherwise than justice would, eftsoons he beseecheth you that ye will command it to be restored.

"As for his long imprisonment, with other griefs thereto appertaining, he looketh not to have recompense of man; but committeth his whole cause to God, to whom your bedeman shall daily pray, according as he is bound, that ye may so order and govern the realm that it may be to the honour of God and your heavenly and everlasting reward."

I do not find the result of this petition, but as it appeared that Henry had interested himself in the story, it is likely to have been successful. We can form but an imperfect judgment on the merits of the case, for we have only the sufferer's *ex parte* complaint, and More might probably have been able to make some counter-statement. But the illegal imprisonment cannot be explained away, and cannot be palliated; and when a judge permits himself to commit an act of arbitrary tyranny, we argue from the known to the unknown, and refuse reasonably to give him credit for equity where he was so little careful of law.

Yet a few years of misery in a prison was but an insignificant misfortune when compared with the fate under which so many other poor men were at this time overwhelmed. Under Wolsey's chancellorship the stake had been comparatively idle; he possessed a remarkable power of making recantation easy; and there is, I believe, no instance in which an accused heretic was brought under his immediate cognisance, where he failed to arrange some terms by which submission was made possible. With Wolsey heresy was an error—with More it was a crime. Soon after the seals changed hands the Smithfield fires recommenced; and, the chancellor acting in concert with them, the bishops resolved to obliterate, in these edifying spectacles, the recollection of their general infirmities. The crime of the offenders varied—sometimes it was a denial of the corporal presence, more often it was a reflection too loud to be endured on the character and habits of the clergy; but whatever it was, the alternative lay only between abjuration humiliating as ingenuity could make it, or a dreadful death. The hearts of many failed them in the trial, and of all the confessors those perhaps do not deserve the least compassion whose weakness betrayed them, who sank and died broken-hearted. Of these silent sufferers history knows nothing. A few, unable to endure the misery of having, as they supposed, denied their Saviour, returned to the danger from which they had fled, and washed out their fall in martyrdom. Latimer has told us the story of his friend Bilney—little Bilney, or Saint Bilney, 548 as he calls him, his companion at Cambridge, to whom he owed his own conversion. Bilney, after escaping through Wolsey's hands in 1527, was again cited in 1529 before the Bishop of London. Three times he refused to recant. He was offered a fourth and last chance. The temptation was too strong, and he fell. For two years he was hopelessly miserable; at length his braver nature prevailed. There was no pardon for a relapsed heretic, and if he was again in the bishop's hands he knew well the fate which awaited him.

He told his friends, in language touchingly significant, that "he would go up to Jerusalem;" and began to preach in the fields. The journey which he had undertaken was not to be a long one. He was heard to say In a sermon, that of his personal knowledge certain things which had been offered in pilgrimage had been given to abandoned women. The priests, he affirmed, "take away the offerings, and hang them about their women's necks; and after that they take them off the women, if they please them not, and hang them again upon the images." 549 This was Bilney's heresy, or formed the ground of his arrest; he was orthodox on the mass, and also on the power of the keys; but the secrets of the sacred order were not to be betrayed with impunity. He was seized, and hurried before the Bishop of Norwich; and being found heterodox on the papacy and the mediation of the saints by the Bishop of Norwich he was sent to the stake.

Another instance of recovered courage, and of martyrdom consequent upon it, is that of James Bainham, a barrister of the Middle Temple. This story is noticeable from a very curious circumstance connected with it.

Bainham had challenged suspicion by marrying the widow of Simon Fish, the author of the famous *Beggars' Petition*, who had died in 1528; and, soon after his marriage, was challenged to give an account of his faith. He was charged with denying transubstantiation, with questioning the value of the confessional, and the power of the keys; and the absence of authoritative Protestant dogma had left his mind free to expand to a yet larger belief. He had ventured to assert, that "if a Turk, a Jew, or a Saracen do trust in God and keep his law, he is a good Christian man," 550—a conception of Christianity, a conception of Protestantism, which we but feebly dare to whisper even at the present day. The proceedings against him commenced with a demand that he should give up his books, and also the names of other barristers with whom he was suspected to have held intercourse. He refused; and in consequence his wife was imprisoned, and he himself was racked in the Tower by order of Sir Thomas More. Enfeebled by suffering, he was then brought before Stokesley, and terrified by the cold merciless eyes of his judge, he gave way, not about his friends, but about himself: he abjured, and was dismissed heartbroken. This was on the seventeenth of February. He was only able to endure his wretchedness for a month. At the end of it, he appeared at a secret meeting of the Christian Brothers, in "a warehouse in Bow Lane," where he asked forgiveness of God and all the world for what he had done; and then went out to take again upon his shoulders the heavy burden of the cross.

The following Sunday, at the church of St. Augustine, he rose in his seat with the fatal English Testament in his hand, and "declared openly, before all the people, with weeping tears, that he had denied God," praying them all to forgive him, and beware of his weakness; "for if I should not return to the truth," he said, "this Word of God would damn me, body and soul, at the day of judgment." And then he prayed "everybody rather to die than to do as he did, for he would not feel such a hell again as he did feel for all the world's good." 551

Of course but one event was to be looked for; he knew it, and himself wrote to the bishop, telling him what he had done. No mercy was possible: he looked for none, and he found none.

Yet perhaps he found what the wise authorities thought to be some act of mercy. They could not grant him pardon in this world upon any terms; but they would not kill him till they had made an effort for his soul. He was taken to the Bishop of London's coal cellar at Fulham, the favourite episcopal penance chamber, where he was ironed and put in the stocks; and there was left for many days, in the chill March weather, to bethink himself. This failing to work conviction, he was carried to Sir Thomas More's house at Chelsea, where for two nights he was chained to a post and whipped; thence, again, he was taken back to Fulham for another week of torture; and finally to the Tower, for a further fortnight, again with ineffectual whippings.

The demands of charity were thus satisfied. The pious bishop and the learned chancellor had exhausted their means of conversion; they had discharged their consciences; and the law was allowed to take its course. The prisoner was brought to trial on the 20th of April, as a relapsed heretic. Sentence followed; and on the last of the month the drama closed in the usual manner at Smithfield. Before the fire was lighted Bainham made a farewell address to the people, laying his death expressly to More, whom he called his accuser and his judge. 552

It is unfortunately impossible to learn the feelings with which these dreadful scenes were witnessed by the people. There are stories which show that, in some instances, familiarity had produced the usual effect; that the martyrdom of saints was at times of no more moment to an English crowd than the execution of ordinary felons—that it was a mere spectacle to the idle, the hardened, and the curious. On the other hand, it is certain that the behaviour of the sufferers was the argument which at last converted the nation; and an effect which in the end was so powerful with the multitude, must have been visible long before in the braver and better natures. The increasing number of prosecutions in London shows, also, that the leaven was spreading. There were five executions in Smithfield between 1529 and 1533, besides those in the provinces. The prisons were crowded with offenders who had abjured and were undergoing sentence; and the list of those who were "troubled" in various ways is so extensive, as to leave no doubt of the sympathy which, in London at least, must have been felt by many, very many, of the spectators of the martyrs' deaths. We are left, in this important point, mainly to conjecture; and if we were better furnished with evidence, the language of ordinary narrative would fail to convey any real notion of perplexed and various emotions. We have glimpses, however, into the inner world of men, here and there of strange interest; and we must regret that they are so few.

A poor boy at Cambridge, John Randall, of Christ's College, a relation of Foxe the martyrologist, destroyed himself in these years in religious desperation; he was found in his study hanging by his girdle, before an open Bible, with his dead arm and finger stretched pitifully towards a passage on predestination. 553

A story even more remarkable is connected with Bainham's execution. Among the lay officials present at the stake, was "one Pavier," town clerk of London. This Pavier was a Catholic fanatic, and as the flames were about to be kindled he burst out into violent and abusive language. The fire blazed up, and the dying sufferer, as the red flickering tongues licked the flesh from off his bones, turned to him and said, "May God forgive thee, and shew more mercy than thou, angry reviler, shewest to me." The scene was soon over; the town clerk went home. A week after, one morning when his wife had gone to mass, he sent all his servants out of his house on one pretext or another, a single girl only being left, and he withdrew to a garret at the top of the house, which he used as an oratory. A large crucifix was on the wall, and the girl having some question to ask, went to the room, and found him standing before it "bitterly weeping." He told her to take his sword, which was rusty, and clean it. She went away, and left him; when she returned, a little time after, he was hanging from a beam, dead. He was a singular person. Edward Hall, the historian, knew him, and had heard him say, that "if the king put forth the New Testament in English, he would not live to bear it." 554 And yet he could not bear to see a heretic die. What was it? Had the meaning of that awful figure hanging on the torturing cross suddenly revealed itself? Had some inner voice asked him whether, in the prayer for his persecutors with which Christ had parted out of life, there might be some affinity with words which had lately sounded in his own ears? God, into whose hands he threw himself, self-condemned in his wretchedness, only knows the agony of that hour. Let the secret rest where it lies, and let us be thankful for ourselves that we live in a changed world.

Thus, however, the struggle went forward; a forlorn hope of saints led the way up the breach, and paved with their bodies a broad road into the new era; and the nation the meanwhile was unconsciously waiting till the works of the enemy were won, and they could walk safely in and take possession. While men like Bilney and Bainham were teaching with words and writings, there were stout English hearts labouring also on the practical side of the same conflict, instilling the same lessons, and meeting for themselves the same consequences. Speculative superstition was to be met with speculative denial. Practical idolatry required a rougher method of disenchantment.

Every monastery, every parish church, had in those days its special relics, its special images, its special something, to attract the interest of the people. The reverence for the remains of noble and pious men, the dresses which they had worn, or the bodies in which their spirits had lived, was in itself a natural and pious emotion; but it had been petrified into a dogma; and like every other imaginative feeling which is submitted to that bad process, it had become a falsehood, a mere superstition, a substitute for piety, not a stimulus to it, and a perpetual occasion of fraud. The people brought offerings to the shrines where it was supposed that the relics were of greatest potency. The clergy, to secure the offerings, invented the relics, and invented the stories of the wonders which had been worked by them. The greatest exposure of these things took place at the visitation of the religious houses. In the meantime, Bishop Shaxton's unsavoury inventory of what passed under the name of relics in the diocese of Salisbury, will furnish an adequate notion of these objects of popular veneration. There "be set forth and commended unto the ignorant people," he said, "as I myself of certain which be already come to my hands, have perfect knowledge, stinking boots, mucky combes, ragged rochettes, rotten girdles, pyl'd purses, great bullocks' horns, locks of hair, and filthy rags, gobbetts of wood, under the name of parcels of the holy cross, and such pelfry beyond estimation." 555 Besides matters of this kind, there were images of the Virgin or of the Saints; above all, roods or crucifixes, of especial potency, the virtues of which had begun to grow uncertain, however, to sceptical Protestants; and from doubt to denial, and from denial to passionate hatred, there were but a few brief steps. The most famous of the roods was that of Boxley in Kent, which used to smile and bow, or frown and shake its head, as its worshippers were generous or closehanded. The fortunes and misfortunes of this image I shall by and bye have to relate. There was another, however, at Dovercourt, in Su folk, of scarcely inferior fame. This image was of such power that the door of the church in which it stood was open at all hours to all comers, and no human hand could close it. Dovercourt therefore became a place of great and lucrative pilgrimage, much resorted to by the neighbours on all occasions of difficulty.

Now it happened that within the circuit of a few miles there lived four young men, to whom the virtues of the rood had become greatly questionable. If it could work miracles, it must be capable, so they thought, of protecting its own substance; and they agreed to apply a practical test which would determine the extent of its abilities. Accordingly (about the time of Bainham's first imprisonment), Robert King of Dedham, Robert Debenham of Eastbergholt, Nicholas Marsh of Dedham, and Robert Gardiner of Dedham, "their consciences being burdened to see the honour of Almighty God so blasphemed by such an idol," started off "on a wondrous goodly night" in February, with hard frost and a clear full moon, ten miles across the wolds, to the church.

The door was open as the legend declared; but nothing daunted, they entered bravely, and lifting down the "idol" from its shrine, with its coat and shoes, and the store of tapers which were kept for the services, they carried it on their shoulders for a quarter of a mile from the place where it had stood, "without any resistance of the said idol." There setting it on the ground, they struck a light, fastened the tapers to the body, and with the help of them, sacrilegiously burnt the image down to a heap of ashes; the old dry wood "blazing so brimly," that it lighted them a full mile on their way home. 556

For this night's performance, which, if the devil is the father of lies, was a stroke of honest work against him and his family, the world rewarded these men after the usual fashion. One of them, Robert Gardiner, escaped the search which was made, and disappeared till better times; the remaining three were swinging in chains six months later on the scene of their exploit. Their fate was perhaps inevitable. Men who dare to be the first in great movements are ever self-immolated victims. But I suppose that it was better for them to be bleaching on their gibbets, than crawling at the feet of a wooden rood, and believing it to be God.

These were the first Paladins of the Reformation; the knights who slew the dragons and the enchanters, and made the earth habitable for common flesh and blood. They were rarely, as we have said, men of great ability, still more rarely men of "wealth and station;" but men rather of clear senses and honest hearts. Tyndal was a remarkable person, and so Clark and Frith promised to become; but the two last were cut off before they had found scope to show themselves; and Tyndal remaining abroad, lay outside the battle which was being fought in England, doing noble work, indeed, and ending as the rest ended, with earning a martyr's crown; but taking no part in the actual struggle except with his pen. As yet but two men of the highest order of power were on the side of Protestantism—Latimer and Cromwell. Of them we have already said something; but the time was now fast coming when they were to step forward, pressed by circumstances which could no longer dispense with them, into scenes of far wider activity; and the present seems a fitting occasion to give some closer account of their history. When the breach with the pope was made irreparable, and the papal party at home had assumed an attitude of suspended insurrection, the fortunes of the Protestants entered into a new phase. The persecution ceased; and those who but lately were carrying fagots in the streets, or hiding for their lives, passed at once by a sudden alternation into the sunshine of political favour. The summer was but a brief one, followed soon by returning winter; but Cromwell and Latimer had together caught the moment as it went by; and before it was over, a work had been done in England which, when it was accomplished once, was accomplished for ever. The conservative party recovered their power, and abused it as before; but the chains of the nation were broken, and no craft of kings or priests or statesmen could weld the magic links again.

It is a pity that of two persons to whom England owes so deep a debt, we can piece together such scanty biographies. I must attempt, however, to give some outline of the little which is known.

The father of Latimer was a solid English yeoman, of Thurcaston, in Leicestershire. "He had no lands of his own," but he rented a farm "of four pounds by the year," on which "he tilled so much as kept half a dozen men;" "he had walk for a hundred sheep, and meadow ground for thirty cows." 557 The world prospered with him; he was able to save money for his son's education and his daughters' portions; but he was freehanded and hospitable; he kept open house for his poor neighbours; and he was a good citizen, too, for "he did find the king a harness with himself and his horse," ready to do battle for his country, if occasion called. His family were brought up "in godliness and the fear of the Lord;" and in all points the old Latimer seems to have been a worthy, sound, upright man, of the true English mettle.

There were several children. 558 The Reformer was born about 1490, some five years after the usurper Richard had been killed at Bosworth. Bosworth being no great distance from Thurcaston, Latimer the father is likely to have been present in the battle, on one side or the other—the right side in those times it was no easy matter to choose—but he became a good servant of the new government—and the little Hugh, when a boy of seven years old, helped to buckle 559 on his armour for him, "when he went to Blackheath field." 560 Being a soldier himself, the old gentleman was careful to give his sons, whatever else he gave them, a sound soldier's training. "He was diligent," says Latimer, "to teach me to shoot with the bow: he taught me how to draw, how to lay my body in the bow—not to draw with strength of arm, as other nations do, but with the strength of the body. I had my bows bought me according to my age and strength; as I increased in these, my bows were made bigger and bigger." 561 Under this education, and in the wholesome atmosphere of the farmhouse, the boy prospered well; and by and bye, showing signs of promise, he was sent to school. When he was fourteen, the promises so far having been fulfilled, his father transferred him to Cambridge. 562

He was soon known at the university as a sober, hard-working student. At nineteen, he was elected fellow of Clare Hall; at twenty, he took his degree, and became a student in divinity, when he accepted quietly, like a sensible man, the doctrines which he had been brought up to believe. At the time when Henry VIII. was writing against Luther, Latimer was fleshing his maiden sword in an attack upon Melancthon; 563 and he remained, he said, till he was thirty, "in darkness and the shadow of death." About this time he became acquainted with Bilney, whom he calls "the instrument whereby God called him to knowledge." In Bilney, doubtless, he found a sound instructor; but a careful reader of his sermons will see traces of a teaching for which he was indebted to no human master. His deepest knowledge was that which stole upon him unconsciously through the experience of life and the world. His words are like the clear impression of a seal; the account and the result of observations, taken first hand, on the condition of the English men and women of his time, in all ranks and classes, from the palace to the prison. He shows large acquaintance with books; with the Bible, most of all; with patristic divinity and school divinity; and history, sacred and profane: but if this had been all, he would not have been the Latimer of the Reformation, and the Church of England would not, perhaps, have been here to-day. Like the physician, to whom a year of practical experience in a hospital teaches more than a life of closest study, Latimer learnt the mental disorders of his age in the age itself; and the secret of that art no other man, however good, however wise, could have taught him. He was not an echo, but a voice; and he drew his thoughts fresh from the fountain—from the facts of the era in which God had placed him.

He became early famous as a preacher at Cambridge, from the first, "a seditious fellow," as a noble lord called him in later life, highly troublesome to unjust persons in authority. "None, except the stiff-necked and uncircumcised, ever went away from his preaching, it was said, without being affected with high detestation of sin, and moved to all godliness and virtue." 564 And, in his audacious simplicity, he addressed himself always to his individual hearers, giving his words a personal application, and often addressing men by name. This habit brought him first into difficulty in 1525. He was preaching before the university, when the Bishop of Ely came into the church, being curious to hear him. He paused till the bishop was seated; and when he recommenced, he changed his subject, and drew an ideal picture of a prelate as a prelate ought to be; the features of which, though he did not say so, were strikingly unlike those of his auditor. The bishop complained to Wolsey, who sent for Latimer, and inquired what he had said. Latimer repeated the substance of his sermon; and other conversation then followed, which showed Wolsey very clearly the nature of the person with whom he was speaking. No eye saw more rapidly than the cardinal's the difference between a true man and an impostor; and he replied to the Bishop of Ely's accusations by granting the offender a licence to preach in any church in England. "If the Bishop of Ely cannot abide such doctrine as you have here repeated," he said, "you shall preach it to his beard, let him say what he will." 565

Thus fortified, Latimer pursued his way, careless of the university authorities, and probably defiant of them. He was still orthodox in points of theoretic belief. His mind was practical rather than speculative, and he was slow in arriving at conclusions which had no immediate bearing upon action. No charge could be fastened upon him, definitely criminal; and he was too strong to be crushed by that compendious tyranny which treated as an act of heresy the exposure of imposture or delinquency.

On Wolsey's fall, however, he would have certainly been silenced: if he had fallen into the hands of Sir Thomas More, he would have perhaps been prematurely sacrificed. But, fortunately, he found a fresh protector in the king. Henry heard of him, sent for him, and, with instinctive recognition of his character, appointed him one of the royal chaplains. He now left Cambridge and removed to Windsor, but only to treat his royal patron as freely as he had treated the Cambridge doctors—not with any absence of respect, for he was most respectful, but with that highest respect which dares to speak unwelcome truth where the truth seems to be forgotten. He was made chaplain in 1530—during the new persecution, for which Henry was responsible by a more than tacit acquiescence. Latimer, with no authority but his own conscience, and the strong certainty that he was on God's side, threw himself between the spoilers and their prey, and wrote to the king, protesting against the injustice which was crushing the truest men in his dominions. The letter is too long to insert; the close of it may show how a poor priest could dare to address the imperious Henry VIII.:

"I pray to God that your Grace may take heed of the worldly wisdom which is foolishness before God; that you may do that [which] God commandeth, and not that [which] seemeth good in your own sight, without the word of God; that your Grace may be found acceptable in his sight, and one of the members of his church; and according to the office that he hath called your Grace unto, you may be found a faithful minister of his gifts, and not a defender of his faith: for he will not have it defended by man or man's power, but by his word only, by the which he hath evermore defended it, and that by a way far above man's power or reason.

"Wherefore, gracious king, remember yourself; have pity upon your soul; and think that the day is even at hand when you shall give account for your office, and of the blood that hath been shed by your sword. In which day, that your Grace may stand steadfastly, and not be ashamed, but be clear and ready in your reckoning, and have (as they say), your *quietus est* sealed with the blood of our Saviour Christ, which only serveth at that day, is my daily prayer to Him that suffered death for our sins, which also prayeth to his Father for grace for us continually; to whom be all honour and praise for ever. Amen. The Spirit of God preserve your Grace." 566

These words, which conclude an address of almost unexampled grandeur, are unfortunately of no interest to us, except as illustrating the character of the priest who wrote them, and the king to whom they were written. The hand of the persecutor was not stayed. The rack and the lash and the stake continued to claim their victims. So far it was labour in vain. But the letter remains, to speak for ever for the courage of Latimer; and to speak something, too, for a prince that could respect the nobleness of the poor yeoman's son, who dared in such a cause to write to him as a man to a man. To have written at all in such a strain was as brave a step as was ever deliberately ventured. Like most brave acts, it did not go unrewarded; for Henry remained ever after, however widely divided from him in opinion, his unshaken friend.

In 1531, the king gave him the living of West Kingston, in Wiltshire, where for a time he now retired. Yet it was but a partial rest. He had a special licence as a preacher from Cambridge, which continued to him (with the king's express sanction) 567 the powers which he had received from Wolsey. He might preach in any diocese to which he was invited; and the repose of a country parish could not be long allowed in such stormy times to Latimer. He had bad health, being troubled with headache, pleurisy, colic, stone; his bodily constitution meeting feebly the demands which he was forced to make upon it. 568 But he struggled on, travelling up and down to London, to Kent, to Bristol, wherever opportunity called him; marked for destruction by the bishops, if he was betrayed into an imprudent word, and himself living in constant expectation of death. 569

At length the Bishop of London believed that Latimer was in his power. He had preached at St. Abb's, in the city, "at the request of a company of merchants," 570 in the beginning of the winter of 1531; and soon after his return to his living, he was informed that he was to be cited before Stokesley. His friends in the neighbourhood wrote to him, evidently in great alarm, and more anxious that he might clear himself, than expecting that he would be able to do so; 571 he himself, indeed, had almost made up his mind that the end was coming. 572

The citation was delayed for a few weeks. It was issued at last, on the 10th of January, 1531-2, 573 and was served by Sir Walter Hungerford, of Farley. 574 The offences with which he was charged were certain "excesses and irregularities" not specially defined; and the practice of the bishops in such cases was not to confine the prosecution to the acts committed; but to draw up a series of articles, on which it was presumed that the orthodoxy of the accused person was open to suspicion, and to question him separately upon each. Latimer was first examined by Stokesley; subsequently at various times by the bishops collectively; and finally, when certain formulas had been submitted to him, which he refused to sign, his case was transferred to convocation. The convocation, as we know, were then in difficulty with their premunire; they had consoled themselves in their sorrow with burning the body of Tracy; and they would gladly have taken further comfort by burning Latimer. 575 He was submitted to the closest cross-questionings, in the hope that he would commit himself. They felt that he was the most dangerous person to them in the kingdom, and they laboured with unusual patience to ensure his conviction. 576 With a common person they would have rapidly succeeded. But Latimer was in no haste to be a martyr; he would be martyred patiently when the time was come for martyrdom; but he felt that no one ought "to consent to die," as long as he could honestly live; 577 and he baffled the episcopal inquisitors with their own weapons. He has left a most curious account of one of his interviews with them.

"I was once in examination," he says, 578 "before five or six bishops, where I had much turmoiling. Every week, thrice, I came to examination, and many snares and traps were laid to get something. Now, God knoweth, I was ignorant of the law; but that God gave me answer and wisdom what I should speak. It was God indeed, for else I had never escaped them. At the last, I was brought forth to be examined into a chamber hanged with arras, where I was before wont to be examined, but now, at this time, the chamber was somewhat altered: for whereas before there was wont ever to be a fire in the chimney, 579 now the fire was taken away, and an arras hanging hanged over the chimney; and the table stood near the chimney's end, so that I stood between the table and the chimney's end. There was among these bishops that examined me one with whom I had been very familiar, and took him for my great friend, an aged man, and he sate next the table end. Then, among all other questions, he put forth one, a very subtle and crafty one, and such one indeed as I could not think so great danger in. And when I would make answer, 'I pray you, Master Latimer,' said he, 'speak out; I am very thick of hearing, and here be many that sit far off.' I marvelled at this, that I was bidden to speak out, and began to misdeem, and gave an ear to the chimney; and, sir, there I heard a pen walking in the chimney, behind the cloth. They had appointed one there to write all mine answers; for they made sure work that I should not start from them: there was no starting from them: God was my good Lord, and gave me answer; I could never else have escaped it. The question was this: 'Master Latimer, do you not think, on your conscience, that you have been suspected of heresy?' — a subtle question — a very subtle question. There was no holding of peace would serve. To hold my peace had been to grant myself faulty. To answer was every way full of danger. But God, which hath always given rile answer, helped me, or else I could never have escaped it. *Ostendite mihi numisma census.* Shew me, said he, a penny of the tribute money. They laid snares to destroy him, but he overturneth them in their own traps." 580

The bishops, however, were not men who were nice in their adherence to the laws; and it would have gone ill with Latimer, notwithstanding his dialectic ability. He was excommunicated and imprisoned, and would soon have fallen into worse extremities; but at the last moment he appealed to the king, and the king, who knew his value, would not allow him to be sacrificed. He had refused to subscribe the articles proposed to him. 581 Henry intimated to the convocation that it was not his pleasure that the matter should be pressed further; they were to content themselves with a general submission, which should be made to the archbishop, without exacting more special acknowledgments. This was the reward to Latimer for his noble letter. He was absolved, and returned to his parish, though snatched as a brand out of the fire.

Soon after, the tide turned, and the Reformation entered into a new phase.

Such is a brief sketch of the life of Hugh Latimer, to the time when it blended with the broad stream of English history. With respect to the other very great man whom the exigencies of the state called to power simultaneously with him, our information is far less satisfactory. Though our knowledge of Latimer's early story comes to us in fragments only, yet there are certain marks in it by which the outline can be determined with certainty. A cloud rests over the youth and early manhood of Thomas Cromwell, through which, only at intervals, we catch glimpses of authentic facts; and these few fragments of reality seem rather to belong to a romance than to the actual life of a man.

Cromwell, the *malleus monachorum*, was of good English family, belonging to the Cromwells of Lincolnshire. One of these, probably a younger brother, moved up to London and conducted an ironfoundry, or other business of that description, at Putney. He married a lady of respectable connections, of whom we know only that she was sister of the wife of a gentleman in Derbyshire, but whose name does not appear. 582 The old Cromwell dying early, the widow was re-married to a cloth-merchant; and the child of the first husband, who made himself so great a name in English story, met with the reputed fortune of a stepson, and became a vagabond in the wide world. The chart of his course wholly fails us. One day in later life he shook by the hand an old bell-ringer at Sion House before a crowd of courtiers, and told them that "this man's father had given him many a dinner in his necessities." And a strange random account is given by Foxe of his having joined a party in an expedition to Rome to obtain a renewal from the pope of certain immunities and indulgences for the town of Boston; a story which derives some kind of credibility from its connection with Lincolnshire, but is full of incoherence and unlikelihood. Following still the popular legend, we find him in the autumn of 1515 a ragged stripling at the door of Frescobaldi's banking-house in Florence, begging for help. Frescobaldi had an establishment in London, 583 with a large connection there; and seeing an English face, and seemingly an honest one, he asked the boy who and what he was. "I am, sir," quoth he, "of England, and my name is Thomas Cromwell; my father is a poor man, and by occupation a cloth-shearer; I am strayed from my country, and am now come into Italy with the camp of Frenchmen that were overthrown at Garigliano, where I was page to a footman, carrying after him his pike and burganet." Something in the boy's manner was said to have attracted the banker's interest; he took him into his house, and after keeping him there as long as he desired to stay, he gave him a horse and sixteen ducats to help him home to England. 584 Foxe is the first English authority for the story; and Foxe took it from Bandello, the novelist; but it is confirmed by, or harmonises with, a sketch of Cromwell's early life in a letter of Chappuys, the imperial ambassador, to Chancellor Granvelle. "Master Cromwell," wrote Chappuys in 1535, "is the son of a poor blacksmith, who lived in a small village four miles from London, and is buried in a common grave in the parish churchyard. In his youth, for some offence, he was imprisoned, and had to leave the country. He went to Flanders, and thence to Rome and other places in Italy." 585

Returning to England, he married the daughter of a woollen-dealer, and became a partner in the business, where he amassed or inherited a considerable fortune. 586 Circumstances afterwards brought him, while still young, in contact with Wolsey, who discovered his merit, took him into service, and in 1525, employed him in the most important work of visiting and breaking up the small monasteries, which the pope had granted for the foundation of the new colleges. He was engaged with this business for two years, and was so efficient that he obtained an unpleasant notoriety, and complaints of his conduct found their way to the king. Nothing came of these complaints, however, and Cromwell remained with the cardinal till his fall. 587

It was then that the truly noble nature which was in him showed itself. He accompanied his master through his dreary confinement at Esher, 588 doing all that man could do to soften the outward wretchedness of it; and at the meeting of parliament, in which he obtained a seat, he rendered him a still more gallant service. The Lords had passed a bill of impeachment against Wolsey, violent, vindictive, and malevolent. It was to be submitted to the Commons, and Cromwell prepared to attempt an opposition. Cavendish has left a most characteristic description of his leaving Esher at this trying time. A cheerless November evening was closing in with rain and storm. Wolsey was broken down with sorrow and sickness; and had been unusually tried by parting with his retinue, whom he had sent home, as unwilling to keep them attached any longer to his fallen fortunes. When they were all gone, "My lord," says Cavendish, "returned to his chamber, lamenting the departure of his servants, making his moan unto Master Cromwell, who comforted him the best he could, and desired my lord to give him leave to go to London, where he would either make or mar before he came again, which was always his common saying. Then after long communication with my lord in secret, he departed, and took his horse and rode to London; at whose departing I was by, whom he bade farewell, and said, ye shall hear shortly of me, and if I speed well I will not fail to be here again within these two days." 589 He did speed well. "After two days he came again with a much pleasanter countenance, and meeting with me before he came to my lord, said unto me, that he had adventured to put in his foot where he trusted shortly to be better regarded or all were done." He had stopped the progress of the impeachment in the Lower House, and was answering the articles one by one. In the evening he rode down to Esher for instructions. In the morning he was again at his place in Parliament; and he conducted the defence so skilfully, that finally he threw out the bill, saved Wolsey, and himself "grew into such estimation in every man's opinion, for his honest behaviour in his master's cause, that he was esteemed the most faithfullest servant, [and] was of all men greatly commended." 590

Henry admired his chivalry, and perhaps his talent. The loss of Wolsey had left him without any very able man, unless we may consider Sir Thomas More such, upon his council, and he could not calculate on More for support in his anti-Roman policy; he was glad, therefore, to avail himself of the service of a man who had given so rare a proof of fidelity, and who had been trained by the ablest statesman of the age. 591

To Wolsey Cromwell could render no more service except as a friend, and his warm friend he remained to the last. He became the king's secretary, representing the government in the House of Commons, and was at once on the high road to power. I cannot call him ambitious; an ambitious man would scarcely have pursued so refined a policy, or have calculated on the admiration which he gained by adhering to a fallen minister. He did not seek greatness—greatness rather sought him as the man in England most fit to bear it. His business was to prepare the measures which were to be submitted to Parliament by the government. His influence, therefore, grew necessarily with the rapidity with which events were ripening; and when the conclusive step was taken, and the king was married, the virtual conduct of the Reformation passed into his hands. His Protestant tendencies were unknown as yet, perhaps, even to his own conscience; nor to the last could he arrive at any certain speculative convictions. He was drawn towards the Protestants as he rose into power by the integrity of his nature, which compelled him to trust only those who were honest like himself.

APPENDIX TO CHAPTER VI

WILL OF THOMAS CROMWELL—1529.

In the name of God, Amen. The 12th day of July, in the year of our Lord God MCCCCCXXIX., and in the 21st year of the reign of our Sovereign Lord, King Henry VIII., I, Thomas Cromwell, of London, Gentleman, being whole in body and in good and perfect memory, lauded be the Holy Trinity, make, ordain, and declare this my present testament, containing my last will, in manner as following:—First I bequeath my soul to the great God of heaven, my Maker, Creator, and Redeemer, beseeching the most glorious Virgin and blessed Lady Saint Mary the Virgin and Mother, with all the holy company of heaven, to be mediators and intercessors for me to the Holy Trinity, so that I may be able, when it shall please Almighty God to call me out of this miserable world and transitory life, to inherit the kingdom of heaven amongst the number of good Christian people; and whensoever I shall depart this present life I bequeath my body to be buried where it shall please God to ordain me to die, and to be ordered after the discretion of mine executors undernamed. And for my goods which our Lord hath lent me in this world, I will shall be ordered and disposed in manner and form as hereafter shall ensue. First I give and bequeath unto my son Gregory Cromwell six hundred threescore six pounds, thirteen shillings, and fourpence, of lawful money of England, with the which six hundred threescore six pounds, thirteen shillings, and fourpence, I will mine executors undernamed immediately or as soon as they conveniently may after my decease, shall purchase lands, tenements, and hereditaments to the clear yearly value of £33 6s. 8d. by the year above all charges and reprises to the use of my said son Gregory, for term of his life; and after the decease of the said Gregory to the heirs male of his body lawfully to be begotten, and for lack of heirs male of the body of the said Gregory, lawfully begotten, to the heirs general of his body lawfully begotten. And for lack of such heirs to the right heirs of me the said Thomas Cromwell, in fee. I will also that immediately and as soon as the said lands, tenements, and hereditaments shall be so purchased after my death as is aforesaid by mine executors, that the yearly profits thereof shall be wholly spent and employed in and about the education and finding honestly of my said son Gregory, in virtue, good learning, and manners, until such time as he shall come to the full age of 24 years. During which time I heartily desire and require my said executors to be good unto my said you Gregory, and to see he do lose no time, but to see him virtuously ordered and brought up according to my trust.

Item. I give and bequeath to my said son Gregory, (when he shall come to his full age of 24 years), two hundred pounds of lawful English money to order them as our Lord shall give him grace and discretion, which £200 I will shall be put in surety to the intent the same may come to his hands at his said age of 24 years. Item. I give and bequeath to my said son Gregory of such household stuff as God hath lent me, three of my best featherbeds with their bolsters; and, the best pair of blankets of fustian, my best coverlet of tapestry, and my quilt of yellow Turkey satin; one pair of my best sheets, four pillows of down, with four pair of the best pillowberes, four of my best table-cloths, four of my best towels, two dozen of my finest napkins, and two dozen of my other napkins, two garnish of my best vessel, three of my best brass pots, three of my best brass pans, two of my best kettles, two of my best spits, my best joined bed of Flanders work, with the best − − and tester, and other the appurtenances thereto belonging; my best press, carven of Flanders work, and my best cupboard, carven of Flanders work, with also six joined stools of Flanders work, and six of my best cushions. Item. I give and bequeath to my said son Gregory a basin with an ewer parcel-gilt, my best salt gilt, my best cup gilt, three of my best goblets; three other of my goblets parcel-gilt, twelve of my best silver spoons, three of my best drinking ale-pots gilt; all the which parcels of plate and household stuff I will shall be safely kept to the use of my said you Gregory till he shall come to his said full age of 24. And all the which plate, household stuff, napery, and all other the premises, I will mine executors do put in safe keeping until my said son come to the said years or age of 24. And if he die before the age of 24, then I will all the said plate, vessel, and household stuff shall be sold by mine executors. And the money thereof coming to be given and equally divided amongst my poor kinsfolk, that is to say, amongst the children as well of mine own sisters Elizabeth and Katherine, as of my late wife's sister Joan, wife to John Williamson; 592 and if it happen that all the children of my said sisters and sister-in-law do die before the partition be made, and none of them be living, then I will that all the said plate, vessel, and household stuff shall be sold and given to other my poor kinsfolk then being in life, and other poor and indigent people, in deeds of charity for my soul, my father and mother their souls, and all Christian souls.

[593 Item. I give and bequeath to my daughter Anne an hundred marks of lawful money of England when she shall come to her lawful age or happen to be married, and £40 toward her finding until the time that she shall be of lawful age or be married, which £40 I will shall be delivered to my friend John Cook, one of the six Clerks of the King's Chancery, to the intent he may order the same and cause the same to be employed in the best wise he can devise about the virtuous education and bringing up of my said daughter till she shall come to her lawful age or marriage. Then I will that the said 100 marks, and so much of the said £40 as then shall be unspent and unemployed at the day of the death of my said daughter Anne, I will it shall remain to Gregory my son, if he then be in life; and if he be dead, the same hundred marks, and also so much of the said £40 as then shall be unspent, to be departed amongst my sisters' children, in manner and form aforesaid. And if it happen my said sisters' children then to be all dead, then I will the said 100 marks and so much of the said £40 as shall be unspent, shall be divided amongst my kinsfolk, such as then, shall be in life.] Item. I give and bequeath unto my sister Elizabeth Wellyfed £40, three goblets without a cover, a mazer, and a nut. Item. I give and bequeath to my nephew Richard Willyams [594 servant with my Lord Marquess Dorset, £66 13s. 4d.], £40 sterling, my [594 fourth] best gown, doublet, and jacket. Item. I give and bequeath to my nephew, Christopher Wellyfed £40, [594 £20] my fifth gown, doublet, and jacket. Item. I give and bequeath to my nephew William Wellyfed the younger £20, [594 £40]. Item. I give and bequeath to my niece Alice Wellyfed, to her marriage, £20. And if it happen her to die before marriage, then I will that the said £20 shall remain to her brother Christopher. And if it happen him to die, the same £20 to remain to Wm. Wellyfed the younger, his brother. And if it happen them all to die before their lawful age or marriage, then I will that all their parts shall remain to Gregory my son. And if it happen him to die before them, then I will all the said parts shall remain [594 to Anne and Grace, my daughters] to Richard Willyams and Walter Willyams, my nephews. And if it happen them to die, then I will that all the said parts shall be distributed in deeds of charity for my soul, my father's and mother's souls, and all Christian souls. Item. I give and bequeath to my mother-in-law Mercy Prior, £40 of lawful English money, and her chamber, with certain household stuff; that is to say, a featherbed, a bolster, two pillows with their beres, six pair of sheets, a pair of blankets, a garnish of vessel, two pots, two pans, two spits, with such other of my household stuff as shall be thought meet for her by the discretion of mine executors, and such as she will reasonably desire, not being bequeathed to other uses in this my present testament and last will. Item. I give and bequeath to my said mother-in-law a little salt of silver, a mazer, six silver spoons, and a drinking-pot of silver. And also I charge mine executors to be good unto her during her life. Item. I give and bequeath to my brother-in-law William Wellyfed, £20, my third gown, jacket, and doublet. Item. I give and bequeath to John Willyams my brother-in-law, 100 marks, a gown, a doublet, a jacket, a featherbed, a bolster, six pair of sheets, two table-cloths, two dozen napkins, two towels, two brass pots, two brass pans, a silver pot, a nut parcel-gilt; and to Joan, his wife, £40. Item. I give and bequeath to Joan Willyams, their daughter, to her marriage, £20, and to every other of their children, £12 13s. 4d. Item. I bequeath to Walter Willyams, my nephew, £20. item. I give and bequeath to Ralph Sadler, my servant, 200 marks of lawful English money, my second gown, jacket, and doublet, and all my books. Item. I give and bequeath to Hugh Whalley, my servant, £6 13s. 4d. Item. I give and bequeath to Stephen Vaughan, sometime my servant, 100 marks, a gown, jacket, and doublet. Item. I give and bequeath to Page, my servant, otherwise called John De Fount, £6 13s. 4d. [594 Item. I give and bequeath to Elizabeth Gregory, sometime my servant, £20, six pair of sheets, a featherbed, a pair of blankets, a coverlet, two table-cloths, one dozen napkins, two brass pots, two pans, two spits.] And also to Thomas Averey, my servant, £6 13s.4d. [Item. I give and bequeath to John Cooke, one of the six Master Clerks of the Chancery, £10, my second gown, doublet, and jacket. Item. I give and bequeath to Roger More, servant of the King's bakehouse, £6 13s. 4d., three yards of satin; and to Maudelyn, his wife, £3 6s. 8d.] Item. I give and bequeath to John Horwood, £6 13s. 4d. [Item. I give and bequeath to my little daughter Grace 100 marks of lawful English money when she shall come to her lawful age or marriage; and also £40 towards her exhibition and finding until such time she shall be of lawful age or be married, which £40 I will shall be delivered to my brother-in-law, John Willyams, to the intent he may order and cause the same to be employed in and about the virtuous education and bringing up of my said daughter, till she shall come to her lawful age of marriage. And if it happen my said daughter to die before she come to her lawful age or marriage, then I will that the said 100 marks, and so much of the said £40 as shall then be unspent and unemployed about the finding of my said daughter at the day of the death of my said daughter shall remain and be delivered to Gregory my son, if he then shall happen to be in life; and if he be dead, then the said 100 marks, and the said residue of the said £40, to be evenly departed among my grown kinsfolk—that is to say, my sisters' children aforesaid] Item. That the rest of mine apparel before not given or bequeathed in this my testament and last will shall be given and equally departed amongst my servants after the order and discretion of mine executors. Item. I will also that mine executors shall take the yearly profits above the charges of my farm of Carberry, and all other things contained in my said lease of Carberry, in the county of Middlesex, and with the profits thereof shall yearly pay unto my brother-in-law William (Wellyfed) and Elizabeth his wife, mine only sister, twenty pounds; give and distribute for my soul quarterly 40 shillings during their lives and the longer of them; and after the decease of the said William and Elizabeth, the profits of the said farm over and above the yearly rent to be kept to the use of my son Gregory till he be come to the age of 24 years. And at the years of 24 the said lease and farm of Carberry, I do give and bequeath to my son Gregory, to have the same to him, his executors and assigns. And if it fortune the said Gregory my son to die before, my said brother-in-law and sister being dead, he shall come to the age of 24 years, then I will my said cousin Richard Willyams shall have the farm with the appurtenances to him and to his executors and assigns; and if it happen my said brother-in-law, my sister, my son Gregory, and my said cousin Richard, to die before the accomplishment of this my will touching the said farm, then I will mine executors shall sell the said farm, and the money thereof coming to employ in deeds of charity, to pray for my soul and all Christian souls. Item. I will mine executors shall conduct and hire a priest, being an honest person of continent and good living, to sing for my soul by the space of seven years next after my death, and to give him for the same £6 13s. 4d. for his stipend. Item. I give and bequeath towards the making of highways in this realm, where it shall be thought most necessary, £20 to be disposed by the discretion of mine executors. Item. I give and bequeath to every the five orders of Friars within the City of London, to pray for my soul, 20 shillings. Item. I give and bequeath to 60 poor maidens in marriage, £40, that is to say, 13s. 4d. to every of the said poor maidens, to be given and distributed by the discretion of mine executors. Item. I will that there shall be dealt and given after my decease amongst poor people householders, to pray for my soul, £20, such as by mine executors shall be thought most needful. Item. I give and bequeath to the poor parishioners of the parish where God shall ordain me to have my dwellingplace at the time of my death, £10, to be truly distributed amongst them by the discretion of mine executors. Item. I give and bequeath to my parish church for my tithes forgotten, 20 shillings. Item. To the poor prisoners of Newgate, Ludgate, King's Bench, and Marshalsea, to be equally distributed amongst them, £10. Willing, charging, and desiring mine executors underwritten, that they shall see this my will performed in every point according to my true meaning and intent as they will answer to God, and discharge their consciences. The residue of all my goods, chattels, and debts not bequeathed, my funeral and burial performed, which I will shall be done without any earthly pomp, and my debts paid, I will shall be sold, and the money thereof coming, to be distributed in works of charity and pity, after the good discretion of mine executors undernamed. Whom I make and ordain, Stephen Vaughan, Ralph Sadler, my servants, and John Willyams my brother-in-law. Praying and desiring the same mine executors to be good unto my son Gregory, and to all other my poor friends and kinsfolk and servants aforenamed in this my testament. And of this my present testament and last will I make Roger More mine overseer; unto whom and also to every of the other mine executors I give and bequeath £6 13s. 4d. for their pains to be taken in the execution of this my last will and testament, over and above such legacies as herebefore I have bequeathed them in this same testament and will. In witness whereof, to this my present testament and last will I have set to my hand in every leaf contained in this book, the day and year before limited.

THOMAS CROMWELL.

Item. I give and bequeath to William Brabazon, my servant, £20 8s., a gun, a doublet, a jacket, and my second gelding.

It. to John Avery, Yeoman of the Bedchamber with the King's Highness, £6 13s. 4d., and a doublet of satin.

It. to Thurston, my cook. £6 13s. 4d.

It. to William Body, my servant, £6 13s. 4d.

It. to Peter Mewtas, my servant, £6 13s. 4d.

It. to Ric. Sleysh, my servant, £6 13s. 4d.

It. to George Wilkinson, my servant, £6 13s. 4d.

It. to my friend, Thomas Alvard. £10, and my best gelding.

It. to my friend, Thomas Rush, £10.

It. to my servant, John Hynde, my horsekeeper, £3 6s. 8d.

Item. I will that mine executors shall safely keep the patent of the manor of Romney to the use of my son Gregory, and the money growing thereof, till he shall come to his lawful age, to be yearly received to the use of my said son, and the whole revenue thereof coming to be truly paid unto him at such time as he shall come to the age of 24 years.

CHAPTER VII.
THE LAST EFFORTS OF DIPLOMACY

I have now to resume the thread of the political history where it was dropped at the sentence of divorce pronounced by Cranmer, and the coronation of the new queen. The effect was about to be ascertained of these bold measures upon Europe; and of what their effect would be, only so much could be foretold with certainty, that the time for trifling was past, and the pope and Francis of France would be compelled to declare their true intentions. If these intentions were honest, the subordination of England to the papacy might be still preserved in a modified form. The papal jurisdiction was at end, but the spiritual supremacy of the Bishop of Rome, with a diminished but considerable revenue attached to it, remained unaffected; and it was for the pope to determine whether, by fulfilling at last his original engagements, he would preserve these remnants of his power and privileges, or boldly take up the gage, excommunicate his disobedient subjects, and attempt by force to bring them back to their allegiance.

The news of what had been done did not take him wholly by surprise. It was known at Brussels at the end of April that the king had married. The queen regent 595 spoke of it to the ambassador sternly and significantly, not concealing her expectation of the mortal resentment which would be felt by her brothers; 596 and the information was forwarded with the least possible delay to the cardinals of the imperial faction at Rome. The true purposes which underlay the contradiction of Clement's language are undiscoverable. Perhaps in the past winter he had been acting out a deep intrigue—perhaps he was drifting between rival currents, and yielded in any or all directions as the alternate pressure varied; yet whatever had been the meaning of his language, whether it was a scheme to deceive Henry, or was the expression only of weakness and good-nature desiring to avoid a quarrel to the latest moment, the decisive step which had been taken in the marriage, even though it was nominally undivulged, obliged him to choose his course and openly adhere to it. After the experience of the past, there could be no doubt what that course would be.

On the 12th of May a citation was issued against the King of England, summoning him to appear by person or proxy at a stated day. It had been understood that no step of such a kind was to be taken before the meeting of the pope and Francis; Bennet, therefore, Henry's faithful secretary, hastily inquired the meaning of this measure. The pope told him that it could not be avoided, and the language which he used revealed to the English agent the inevitable future. The king, he said, had defied the inhibitory brief which had been lately issued, and had incurred excommunication; the imperialists insisted that he should be proceeded against for contempt, and that the excommunication should at once be pronounced. However great might be his own personal reluctance, it was not possible for him to remain passive; and if he declined to resort at once to the more extreme exercise of his power, the hesitation was merely until the emperor was prepared to enforce the censures of the church with the strong hand. It stood not "with his honour to execute such censures," he said, "and the same not to be regarded." 597 But there was no wish to spare Henry; and if Francis could be detached from his ally, and if the condition of the rest of Christendom became such as to favour the enterprise, England might evidently look for the worst which the pope, with the Catholic powers, could execute. If the papal court was roused into so menacing a mood by the mere intimation of the secret marriage, it was easy to foresee what would ensue when the news arrived of the proceedings at Dunstable. Bennet entreated that the process should be delayed till the interview; but the pope answered coldly that he had done his best and could do no more; the imperialists were urgent, and he saw no reason to refuse their petition. 598 This was Clement's usual language, but there was something peculiar in his manner. He had been often violent, but he had never shown resolution, and the English agents were perplexed. The mystery was soon explained. He had secured himself on the side of France; and Francis, who at Calais had told Henry that his negotiations with the see of Rome were solely for the interests of England, that for Henry's sake he was marrying his son into a family beneath him in rank, that Henry's divorce was to form the especial subject of his conference with the pope, had consented to allow these dangerous questions to sink into a secondary place, and had relinquished his intention, if he had ever seriously entertained it, of becoming an active party in the English quarrel.

The long-talked-of interview was still delayed. First it was to have taken place in the winter, then in the spring; June was the date last fixed for it, and now Bennet had to inform the king that it would not take place before September; and that, from the terms of a communication which had just passed between the parties who were to meet, the subjects discussed at the conference would not be those which he had been led to expect. Francis, in answer to a question from the pope, had specified three things which he proposed particularly to "intreat." The first concerned the defence of

Christendom against the Turks, the second concerned the general council, and the third concerned "the extinction of the Lutheran sect." 599 These were the points which the Most Christian king was anxious to discuss with the pope. For the latter good object especially, "he would devise and treat for the provision of an army." In the King of England's cause, he trusted "some means might be found whereby it might be compounded;" 600 but if persuasion failed, there was no fear lest he should have recourse to any other method.

It was this which had given back to the pope his courage. It was this which Bennet had now to report to Henry. The French alliance, it was too likely, would prove a broken reed, and pierce the hand that leant upon it.

Henry knew the danger; but danger was not a very terrible thing either to him or to his people. If he had conquered his own reluctance to risk a schism in the church, he was not likely to yield to the fear of isolation; and if there was something to alarm in the aspect of affairs, there was also much to encourage. His parliament was united and resolute. His queen was pregnant. The Nun of Kent had assigned him but a month to live after his marriage; six months had passed, and he was alive and well; the supernatural powers had not declared against him; and while safe with respect to enmity from above, the earthly powers he could afford to defy. When he finally divorced Queen Catherine, he must have foreseen his present position at least as a possibility, and if not prepared for so swift an apostasy in Francis, and if not yet wholly believing it, we may satisfy ourselves he had never absolutely trusted a prince of metal so questionable.

The Duke of Norfolk was waiting at the French court, with a magnificent embassy, to represent the English king at the interview. The arrival of the pope had been expected in May. It was now delayed till September; and if Clement came after all, it would be for objects in which England had but small concern. It was better for England that there should be no meeting at all, than a meeting to devise schemes for the massacre of Lutherans. Henry therefore wrote to the Duke, telling him generally what he had heard from Rome; he mentioned the three topics which he understood were to form the matter of discussion; but he skilfully affected to regard them as having originated with the imperialists, and not with the French king. In a long paper of instructions, in which earnestness and irony were strangely blended, he directed the ambassador to treat his good brother as if he were still exclusively devoted to the interests of England; and to urge upon him, on the ground of this fresh delay, that the interview should not take place at all. 601

"Our pleasure is," he wrote, "that ye shall say—that we be not a little moved in our heart to see our good brother and us, being such princes of Christendom, to be so handled with the pope, so much to our dishonour, and to the pope's and the emperor's advancement; seeming to be at the pope's commandment to come or tarry as he or his cardinals shall appoint; and to depend upon his pleasure when to meet—that is to say, when he list or never. If our good brother and we were either suitors to make request, the obtaining whereof we did much set by, or had any particular matter of advantage to entreat with him, these proceedings might be the better tolerated; but our good brother having no particular matter of his own, and being ... that [no] more glory nor surety could happen to the emperour than to obtain the effect of the three articles moved by the pope and his cardinals, we think it not convenient to attend the pleasure of the pope, to go or to abyde. We could have been content to have received and taken at the pope's hand, jointly with our good brother, pleasure and friendship in our great cause; [but] on the other part, we cannot esteem the pope's part so high, as to have our good brother an attendant suitor therefore ... desiring him, therefore, in anywise to disappoint for his part the said interview; and if he have already granted thereto—upon some new good occasion, which he now undoubtedly hath—to depart from the same.

"For we, ye may say, having the justness of our cause for us, with such an entire and whole consent of our nobility and commons of our realm and subjects, and being all matters passed, and in such terms as they now be, do not find such lack and want of that the pope might do, with us or against us, as we would for the obtaining thereof be contented to have a French king our so perfect a friend, to be not only a mediator but a suitor therein, and a suitor attendant to have audience upon liking and after the advice of such cardinals as repute it among pastymes to play and dally with kings and princes; whose honour, ye may say, is above all things, and more dear to us in the person of our good brother, than is any piece of our cause at the pope's hands. And therefore, if there be none other thing but our cause, and the other causes whereof we be advertised, our advice, counsel, special desire also and request is, [that our good brother shall] break off the interview, unless the pope will make suit to him; and [unless] our said good brother hath such causes of his own as may particularly tend to his own benefit, honour, and profit—wherein he shall do great and singular pleasure unto us; *giving to understand to the pope, that me know ourselves and him both, and look to be esteemed accordingly.*"

Should it appear that on receipt of this communication, Francis was still resolved to persevere, and that he had other objects in view to which Henry had not been made privy, the ambassadors were then to remind him of the remaining obligations into which he had entered; and to ascertain to what degree his assistance might be calculated upon, should the pope pronounce Henry deposed, and the emperor attempt to enforce the sentence.

After forwarding these instructions, the king's next step was to anticipate the pope by an appeal which would neutralise his judgment should he venture upon it; and which offered a fresh opportunity of restoring the peace of Christendom, if there was true anxiety to preserve that peace. The hinge of the great question, in the form which at last it assumed, was the validity or invalidity of the dispensation by which Henry had married his brother's widow. Being a matter which touched the limit of the pope's power, the pope was himself unable to determine it in his own favour; and the only authority by which the law could be ruled, was a general council. In the preceding winter, the pope had volunteered to submit the question to this tribunal; but Henry believing that it was on the point of immediate solution in another way, had then declined, on the ground that it would cause a needless delay. He was already married, and he had hoped that sentence might be given in his favour in time to anticipate the publication of the ceremony. But he was perfectly satisfied that justice was on his side; and was equally confident of obtaining the verdict of Europe, if it could be fairly pronounced. Now, therefore, under the altered circumstances, he accepted the offered alternative. He anticipated with tolerable certainty the effect which would be produced at Rome, when the news should arrive there of the Dunstable divorce; and on the 29th of June, he appealed formally, in the presence of the Archbishop of York, from the pope's impending sentence, to the next general council. 602

Of this curious document the substance was as follows:—It commenced with a declaration that the king had no intention of acting otherwise than became a good Catholic prince; or of injuring the church or attacking the privileges conceded by God to the Holy See. If his words could be lawfully shown to have such a tendency he would revoke, emend, and correct them in a Catholic spirit.

The general features of the case were then recapitulated. His marriage with his brother's wife had been pronounced illegal by the principal universities of Europe, by the clergy of the two provinces of the Church of England, by the most learned theologians and canonists, and finally, by the public judgment of the church. 603 He therefore had felt himself free; and, "by the inspiration of the Host High, had lawfully married another woman." Furthermore, "for the common weal and tranquillity of the realm of England, and for the wholesome rule and government of the same, he had caused to be enacted certain statutes and ordinances, by authority of parliaments lawfully called for that purpose." "Now, however," he continued, "we fearing that his Holyness the Pope ... having in our said cause treated us far otherwise than either respect for our dignity and desert, or the duty of his own office required at his hands, and having done us many injuries which we now of design do suppress, but which hereafter we shall be ready, should circumstances so require, to divulge ... may now proceed to acts of further injustice, and heaping wrong on wrong, may pronounce the censures and other penalties of the spiritual sword against ourselves, our realm, and subjects, seeking thereby to deprive us of the use of the sacraments, and to cut us off, in the sight of the world, from the unity of the church, to the no slight hurt and injury of our realm and subjects:

"Fearing these things, and desiring to preserve from detriment not only ourselves, our own dignity and estimation, but also our subjects, committed to us by Almighty God; to keep them in the unity of the Christian faith, and in the wonted participation in the sacraments; that, when in truth they be not cut off from the integrity of the church, nor can nor will be so cut off in any manner, they may not appear to be so cut off in the estimation of men; [desiring further] to check and hold back our people whom God has given to us, lest, in the event of such injury, they refuse utterly to obey any longer the Roman Pontiff, as a hard and cruel pastor: [for these causes] and believing, from reasons probable, conjectures likely, and words used to our injury by his Holiness the Pope, which in divers manners have been brought to our ears, that some weighty act may be committed by him or others to the prejudice of ourselves and of our realm;—We, therefore, in behalf of all and every of our subjects, and of all persons adhering to us in this our cause, do make our appeal to the next general council, which shall be lawfully held, in place convenient, with the consent of the Christian princes, and of such others as it may concern—not in contempt of the Holy See, but for defence of the truth of the Gospel, and for the other causes afore rehearsed. And we do trust in God that it shall not be interpreted as a thing ill done on our part, if preferring the salvation of our soul and the relief of our conscience to any mundane respects or favours, we have in this cause regarded more the Divine law than the laws of man, and have thought it rather meet to obey God than to obey man." 604

By the appeal and the causes which were assigned for it, Henry pre-occupied the ground of the conflict; he entrenched himself in the "debateable land" of legal uncertainty; and until his position had been pronounced untenable by the general voice of Christendom, any sentence which the pope could issue would have but a doubtful validity. It was, perhaps, but a slight advantage; and the niceties of technical fencing might soon resolve themselves into a question of mere strength; yet, in the opening of great conflicts, it is well, even when a resort to force is inevitable, to throw on the opposing party the responsibility of violence; and Henry had been led, either by a refinement of policy, or by the plain straightforwardness of his intentions, into a situation where he could expect without alarm the unrolling of the future.

The character of that future was likely soon to be decided. The appeal was published on the 29th of June; and as the pope must have heard, by the middle of the month at latest, of the trial and judgment at Dunstable, a few days would bring an account of the manner in which he had received the intelligence. Prior to the arrival of the couriers, Bennet, with the assistance of Cardinal Tournon, had somewhat soothed down his exasperation. Francis, also, having heard that immediate process was threatened, had written earnestly to deprecate such a measure; 605 and though he took the interference "very displeasantly," 606 the pope could not afford to lose, by premature impatience; the fruit of all his labour and diplomacy, and had yielded so far as to promise that nothing of moment should be done. To this state of mind he had been brought one day in the second week of June. The morning after, Bennet found him "sore altered." The news of "my Lord of Canterbury's proceedings" had arrived the preceding night; and "his Holiness said that [such] doings were too sore for him to stand still at and do nothing." 607 It was "against his duty towards God and the world to tolerate them." The imperialist cardinals, impatient before, clamoured that the evil had been caused by the dilatory timidity with which the case had been handled from the first. 608 The consistory sate day after day with closed doors; 609 and even such members of it as had before inclined to the English side, joined in the common indignation. "Some extreme process" was instantly looked for, and the English agents, in their daily interviews with the pope, were forced to listen to language which it was hard to bear with equanimity. Bennet's well-bred courtesy carried him successfully through the difficulty; his companion Bonner was not so fortunate. Bonner's tongue was insolent, and under bad control. He replied to menace by impertinence; and on one occasion was so exasperating, that Clement threatened to burn him alive, or boil him in a caldron of lead. 610 When fairly roused, the old man was dangerous; and the future Bishop of London wrote to England in extremity of alarm. His letter has not been found, but the character of it may be perceived from the reassuring reply of the king. The agents, Henry said, were not to allow themselves to be frightened; they were to go on calmly, with their accustomed diligence and dexterity, disputing the ground from point to point, and trust to him. Their cause was good, and, with God's help, he would be able to defend them from the malice of their adversaries. 611

Fortunately for Bonner, the pope's passion was of brief duration, and the experiment whether Henry's arm could reach to the dungeons of the Vatican remained untried. The more moderate of the cardinals, also, something assuaged the storm; and angry as they all were, the majority still saw the necessity of prudence. In the heat of the irritation, final sentence was to have been pronounced upon the entire cause, backed by interdict, excommunication, and the full volume of the papal thunders. At the close of a month's deliberation they resolved to reserve judgement on the original question, and to confine themselves for the present to revenging the insult to the pope by "my Lord of Canterbury." Both the king and the archbishop had disobeyed a formal inhibition. On the 12th of July, the pope issued a brief, declaring Cranmer's judgment to have been illegal, the English process to have been null and void, and the king, by his disobedience, to have incurred, *ipso facto*, the threatened penalties of excommunication. Of his clemency he suspended these censures till the close of the following September, in order that time might be allowed to restore the respective parties to their old positions: if within that period the parties were not so restored, the censures would fall. 612 This brief was sent into Flanders, and fixed in the usual place against the door of a church in Dunkirk.

Henry was prepared for a measure which was no more than natural. He had been prepared for it as a possibility when he married. Both he and Francis must have been prepared for it on their meeting at Calais, when the French king advised him to marry, and promised to support him through the consequences. His own measures had been arranged beforehand, and he had secured himself in technical entrenchments by his appeal. After the issue of the brief, however, he could allow no English embassy to compliment Clement by its presence on his visit to France. He "knew the pope," as he said. Long experience had shown him that nothing was to be gained by yielding in minor points; and the only chance which now remained of preserving the established order of Christendom, was to terrify the Vatican court into submission by the firmness of his attitude. For the present complications, the court of Rome, not he, was responsible. The pope, with a culpable complacency for the emperor, had shrunk from discharging a duty which his office imposed upon him; and the result had been, that the duty was discharged by another. Henry could not blame himself for the consequences of Clement's delinquency. He rather felt himself wronged in having been driven to so extreme a measure against his will. He resolved, therefore, to recall the embassy, and once more, though with no great hope that he would be successful, to invite Francis to fulfil his promise, and to unite with himself in expressing his resentment at the pope's conduct.

His despatch to the Duke of Norfolk on this occasion was the natural sequel of what he had written a few weeks previously. That letter had failed wholly of its effect. The interview was resolved upon for quite other reasons than those which were acknowledged, and therefore was not to be given up. A promise, however, had been extracted, that it should be given up, if in the course of the summer the pope "innovated anything" against the King of England; and Henry now required, formally, that this engagement should be observed. "A notorious and notable innovation" had been made, and Francis must either deny his words, or adhere to them. It would be evident to all the world, if the interview took place under the present circumstances, that the alliance with England was no longer of the importance with him which it had been; that his place in the struggle, when the struggle came, would be found on the papal side.

The language of Henry throughout this paper was very fine and noble. He reminded Francis that substantially the cause at issue was the cause of all princes; the pope claiming a right to summon them to plead in the courts of Rome, and refusing to admit their exemption as sovereign rulers. He had been required not only to undo his marriage, and cancel the sentence of divorce, but, as a condition of reconciliation with the Holy See, to undo also, the Act of Appeals, and to restore the papal jurisdiction. He desired it to be understood, with emphasis, that these points were all equally sacred, and the repeal of the act was as little to be thought of as the annulling the marriage. "The pope," he said, "did inforce us to excogitate some new thing, whereby we might be healed and relieved of that continual disease, to care for our cause at Rome, where such defence was taken from us, as by the laws of God, nature, and man, is due unto us. Hereupon depended the wealth of our realm; hereupon consisted the surety of our succession, which by no other means could be well assured." "And therefore," he went on, "you [the Duke] shall say to our good brother, that the pope persisting in the ways he hath entered, ye must needs despair in any meeting between the French king and the pope, to produce any such effect as to cause us to meet in concord with the pope; but we shall be even as far asunder as is between yea and nay. For to the pope's enterprise to revoke or put back anything that is done here, either in marriage, statute, sentence, or proclamation 613—of which four members is knit and conjoined the surety of our matter, nor any can be removed from the other, lest thereby the whole edifice should be destroyed—we will and shall, by all ways and means say nay, and declare our nay in such sort as the world shall hear, and the pope feel it. Wherein ye may say our firm trust, perfect hope, and assured confidence is, that our good brother will agree with us; as well for that it should be partly dishonourable for him to see decay the thing that was of his own foundation and planting: as also that it should be too much dishonourable for us—having travelled so far in this matter, and brought it to this point, that all the storms of the year passed, it is now come to harvest, trusting to see shortly the fruit of our marriage, to the wealth, joy, and comfort of all our realm, and our own singular consolation—that anything should now be done by us to impair the same, and to put our issue either in peril of bastardy, or otherwise disturb that [which] is by the whole agreement of our realm established for their and our commodity, wealth, and benefit. And in this determination ye know us to be so fixed, and the contrary hereof to be so infeasible, either at our hands, or by the consent of the realm, that ye must needs despair of any order to be taken by the French king with the pope. For if any were by him taken wherein any of these four pieces should be touched—that is to say, the marriage of the queen our wife, the revocation of the Bishop of Canterbury's sentence, the statute of our realm, or our late proclamation, which be as it were one—and as walls, covering, the foundation make a house, so they knit together, establish, and make one matter—ye be well assured, and be so ascertained from us, that in no wise we will relent, but will, as we have before written, withstand the same. Whereof ye may say that ye have thought good to advertise him, to the intent he make no farther promise to the pope therein than may be performed."

The ambassadors were the more emphatically to insist on the king's resolution, lest Francis, in his desire for conciliation, might hold out hopes to the pope which could not be realised. They were to say, however, that the King of England still trusted that the interview would not take place. The see of Rome was asserting a jurisdiction which, if conceded, would encourage an unlimited usurpation. If princes might be cited to the papal courts in a cause of matrimony, they might be cited equally in other causes at the pope's pleasure; and the free kingdoms of Europe would be converted into dependent provinces of the see of Rome. It concerned alike the interest and the honour of all sovereigns to resist encroachments which pointed to such an issue; and, therefore, Henry said he hoped that his good brother would use the pope as he had deserved, "doing him to understand his folly, and [that] unless he had first made amends, he could not find in his heart to have further amity with him."

If notwithstanding, the instructions concluded, "all these persuasions cannot have place to let the said meeting, and the French king shall say it is expedient for him to have in his hands the duchess, 614 under pretence of marriage for his son, which he cannot obtain but by this means, ye shall say that ye remember ye heard him say once he would never conclude that marriage but to do us good, which is now infaisible; and now in the voice of the world shall do us both more hurt in the diminution of the reputation of our amity than it should do otherwise profit. Nevertheless, [if] ye cannot let his precise determination, [ye] can but lament and bewail your own chance to depart home in this sort; and that yet of the two inconvenients, it is to you more tolerable to return to us nothing done, than to be present at the interview and to be compelled to look patiently upon your master's enemy."

After having entered thus their protest against the French king's conduct, the embassy was to return to England, leaving a parting intimation of the single condition under which Henry would consent to treat. If the pope would declare that "the matrimony with the Lady Catherine was and is nought, he should do somewhat not to be refused;" except with this preliminary, no offer whatever could be entertained. 615

This communication, as Henry anticipated, was not more effectual than the former in respect of its immediate object. At the meeting of Calais the interests of Francis had united him with England, and in pursuing the objects of Henry he was then pursuing his own. The pope and the emperor had dissolved the coalition by concessions on the least dangerous side. The interests of Francis lay now in the other direction, and there are few instances in history in which governments have adhered to obligations against their advantage from a spirit of honour, when the purposes with which they contracted those obligations have been otherwise obtained. The English embassy returned as they were ordered; the French court pursued their way to Marseilles; not quarrelling with England; intending to abide by the alliance, and to give all proofs of amity which did not involve inconvenient sacrifices; but producing on the world at large by their conduct the precise effect which Henry had foretold. The world at large, looking to acts rather than to words, regarded the interview as a contrivance to reconcile Francis and the emperor through the intervention of the pope, as a preliminary for a packed council, and for a holy war against the Lutherans 616—a combination of ominous augury to Christendom, from the consequences of which, if Germany was to be the first sufferer, England would be inevitably the second.

Meanwhile, as the French alliance threatened to fail, the English government found themselves driven at last to look for a connection among those powers from whom they had hitherto most anxiously disconnected themselves. At such a time. Protestant Germany, not Catholic France, was England's natural friend. The Reformation was essentially a Teutonic movement; the Germans, the English, the Scotch, the Swedes, the Hollanders, all were struggling on their various roads towards an end essentially the same. The same dangers threatened them, the same inspiration moved them; and in the eyes of the orthodox Catholics they were united in a black communion of heresy. Unhappily, though this identity was obvious to their enemies, it was far from obvious to themselves. The odium theologicum is ever hotter between sections of the same party which are divided by trifling differences, than between the open representatives of antagonist principles; and Anglicans and Lutherans, instead of joining hands across the Channel, endeavoured only to secure each a recognition of themselves at the expense of the other. The English plumed themselves on their orthodoxy. They were "not as those publicans," heretics, despisers of the keys, disobedient to authority; they desired only the independence of their national church, and they proved their zeal for the established faith with all the warmth of persecution. To the Germans national freedom was of wholly minor moment, in comparison with the freedom of the soul; the orthodoxy of England was as distasteful to the disciples of Luther as the orthodoxy of Rome—and the interests of Europe were sacrificed on both sides to this foolish and fatal disunion. Circumstances indeed would not permit the division to remain in its first intensity, and their common danger compelled the two nations into a partial understanding. Yet the reconciliation, imperfect to the last, was at the outset all but impossible. Their relations were already embittered by many reciprocal acts of hostility. Henry VIII. had won his spurs as a theologian by an attack on Luther. Luther had replied by a hailstorm of invectives. The Lutheran books had been proscribed, the Lutherans themselves had' been burnt by Henry's bishops. The Protestant divines in Germany had attempted to conciliate the emperor by supporting the cause of Catherine; and Luther himself had spoken loudly in condemnation of the king. The elements of disunion were so many and so powerful, that there was little hope of contending against them successfully. Nevertheless, as Henry saw, the coalition of Francis and the emperor, if the pope succeeded in cementing it, was a most serious danger, to which an opposite alliance would alone be an adequate counterpoise; and the experiment might at least be tried whether such an alliance was possible. At the beginning of August, therefore, Stephen Vaughan was sent on a tentative mission to the Elector of Saxe, John Frederick, at Weimar. 617 He was the bearer of letters containing a proposal for a resident English ambassador; and if the elector gave his consent, he was to proceed with similar offers to the courts of the Landgrave of Hesse and the Duke of Lunenberg. 618 Vaughan arrived in due time at the elector's court, was admitted to audience and delivered his letters. The prince read them, and in the evening of the same day returned for answer a polite but wholly absolute refusal. Being but a prince elector, he said, he might not aspire to so high an honour as to be favoured with the presence of an English ambassador. It was not the custom in Germany, and he feared that if he consented he should displease the emperor. 619 The meaning of such a reply delivered in a few hours was not to be mistaken, however disguised in courteous language. The English emissary saw that he was an unwelcome visitor, and that he must depart with the utmost celerity. "The elector," he wrote, 620 "thirsted to have me gone from him, which I right well perceived by evident tokens which declared unto me the same." He had no anxiety to expose to hazard the toleration which the Protestant dukedoms as yet enjoyed from the emperor, by committing himself to a connection with a prince with whose present policy he had no sympathy, and whose conversion to the cause of the Reformation he had as yet no reason to believe sincere. 621

The reception which Vaughan met with at Weimar satisfied him that he need go no further; neither the Landgrave nor the Duke of Lunenberg would be likely to venture on a course which the elector so obviously feared. He, therefore, gave up his mission, and returned to England.

The first overtures in this direction issued in complete failure, nor was the result wholly to be regretted. It taught Henry (or it was a first commencement of the lesson) that so long as he pursued a merely English policy he might not expect that other nations would embroil themselves in his defence. He must allow the Reformation a wider scope, he must permit it to comprehend within its possible consequences the breaking of the chains by which his subjects' minds were bound—not merely a change of jailors. Then perhaps the German princes might return some other answer.

The disappointment, however, fell lightly; for before the account of the failure had reached England, an event had happened, which, poor as the king might be in foreign alliances, had added most material strength to his position in England. The full moment of that event he had no means of knowing. In its immediate bearing it was matter for most abundant satisfaction. On the seventh of September, between three and four in the afternoon, at the palace of Greenwich, was born a princess, named three days later in her baptism, after the king's mother, Elizabeth. 622 A son had been hoped for. The child was a daughter only; yet at least Providence had not pronounced against the marriage by a sentence of barrenness; at least there was now an heir whose legitimacy the nation had agreed to accept. Te Deums were sung in all the churches; again the river decked itself in splendour; again all London steeples were musical with bells. A font of gold was presented for the christening. Francis, in compensation for his backslidings, had consented to be godfather; and the infant, who was soon to find her country so rude a stepmother, was received with all the outward signs of exulting welcome. To Catherine's friends the offspring of the rival marriage was not welcome, but was an object rather of bitter hatred; and the black cloud of a sister's jealousy gathered over the cradle whose innocent occupant had robbed her of her title and her expectations. To the king, to the parliament, to the healthy heart of England, she was an object of eager hope and an occasion for thankful gratitude; but the seeds were sown with her birth of those misfortunes which were soon to overshadow her, and to form the school of the great nature which in its maturity would re-mould the world.

Leaving Elizabeth for the present, we return to the continent, and to the long-promised interview, which was now at last approaching. Henry made no further attempt to remonstrate with Francis; and Francis assured him, and with all sincerity, that he would use his best efforts to move the pope to make the necessary concessions. The English embassy meanwhile was withdrawn. The excommunication had been received as an act of hostility, of which Henry would not even condescend to complain; and it was to be understood distinctly that in any exertions which might be made by the French king, the latter was acting without commission on his own responsibility. The intercession was to be the spontaneous act of a mutual friend, who, for the interests of Christendom, desired to heal a dangerous wound; but neither directly nor indirectly was it to be interpreted as an expression of a desire for a reconciliation on the English side.

It was determined further, on the recal of the Duke of Norfolk, that the opportunity of the meeting should be taken to give a notice to the pope of the king's appeal to the council; and for this purpose, Bennet and Bonner were directed to follow the papal court from Rome. Bennet never accomplished this journey, dying on the route, worn out with much service. 623 His death delayed Bonner, and the conferences had opened for many days before his arrival. Clement had reached Marseilles by ship from Genoa, about the 20th of October. As if pointedly to irritate Henry, he had placed himself under the conduct of the Duke of Albany. 624 He was followed two days later by his fair niece, Catherine de Medici; and the preparations for the marriage were commenced with the utmost swiftness and secrecy. The conditions of the contract were not allowed to transpire, but they were concluded in three days; and on this 25th of October the pope bestowed his precious present on the Duke of Orleans, he himself performing the nuptial ceremony, and accompanying it with his paternal benediction on the young pair, and on the happy country which was to possess them for its king and queen. France being thus securely riveted to Rome, other matters could be talked of more easily. Francis made all decent overtures to the pope in behalf of Henry; if the pope was to be believed indeed, he was vehemently urgent. 625 Clement in turn made suggestions for terms of alliance between Francis and Charles, "to the advantage of the Most Christian king;" 626 and thus parried the remonstrances. The only point positively clear to the observers, was the perfect understanding which existed between the King of France and his spiritual father. 627 Unusual activity was remarked in the dockyards;

Italian soldiers of fortune were about the court in unusual numbers, and apparently in favour. 628 An invasion of Lombardy was talked of among the palace retinue; and the emperor was said to distrust the intentions of the conference. Possibly experience had taught all parties to doubt each other's faith. Possibly they were all in some degree waiting upon events; and had not yet resolved upon their conduct.

In the midst of this scene arrived Doctor Bonner, in the beginning of November, with Henry's appeal. He was a strange figure to appear in such a society. There was little probity, perhaps, either in the court of France, or in their Italian visitors: but of refinement, of culture, of those graces which enable men to dispense with the more austere excellences of character—which transform licentiousness into elegant frailty, and treachery and falsehood into pardonable finesse—of these there was very much: and when a rough, coarse, vulgar Englishman was plunged among these delicate ladies and gentlemen, he formed an element which contrasted strongly with the general environment. Yet Banner, perhaps, was not without qualifications which fitted him for his mission. He was not, indeed, virtuous; but he had a certain downright honesty about him, joined with an entire insensibility to those finer perceptions which would have interfered with plain speaking, where plain speaking was desirable; he had a broad, not ungenial humour, which showed him things and persons in their genuine light, and enabled him to picture them for us with a distinctness for which we owe him lasting thanks.

He appeared at Marseilles on the 7th of November, and had much difficulty in procuring an interview. At length, weary of waiting, and regardless of the hot lead with which he had been lately threatened, he forced his way into the room where "the pope was standing, with the Cardinals De Lorraine and Medici, ready apparelled with his stole to go to the consistory."

"Incontinently upon my coming thither," he wrote to Henry, 629 "the pope, whose sight is incredulous quick, eyed me, and that divers times; making a good pause in one place; at which time I desired the datary to advertise his Holiness that I would speak with him; and albeit the datary made no little difficulty therein, yet perceiving that upon refusal I would have gone forthwith to the pope, he advertised the pope of my said desire. His Holiness dismissing as then the said cardinals, and letting his vesture fall, went to a window in the said chamber, calling me unto him. At which time I showed unto his Holiness how that your Highness had given me express and strait commandment to intimate unto him how that your Grace had solemnly provoked and appealed unto the general council; submitting yourself to the tuition and defence thereof; which provocation and appeal I had under authentic writings then with me, to show for that purpose. And herewithal I drew out the said writing, showing his said Holiness that I brought the same in proof of the premises, and that his Holiness might see and perceive all the same. The pope having this for a breakfast, only pulled down his head to his shoulders, after the Italian fashion, and said that because he was as then fully ready to go into the consistory, he would not tarry to hear or see the said writings, but willed me to come at afternoon."

The afternoon came, and Bonner returned, and was admitted. There was some conversation upon indifferent matters; the pope making good-natured inquiries about Bennet, and speaking warmly and kindly of him.

"Presently," Bonner continues, "falling out of that, he said that he marvelled your Highness would use his Holiness after such sort as it appears ye did. I said that your Highness no less did marvel that his Holiness having found so much benevolence and kindness at your hands in all times past, would for acquittal show such unkindness as of late he did. And here we entered in communication upon two points: one was that his Holiness, having committed in times past, and in most ample form, the cause into the realm, promising not to revoke the said commission, and over that, to confirm the process and sentence of the commissaries, should not at the point of sentence have advoked the cause, retaining it at Rome—forasmuch as Rome was a place whither your Highness could not, ne yet ought, personally to come unto, and also was not bound to send thither your proctor. The second point was, that your Highness's cause being, in the opinion of the best learned men in Christendom, approved good and just, and so [in] many ways known unto his Holiness, the same should not so long have retained it in his hands without judgment.

"His Holiness answering the same, as touching the first point, said that if the queen (meaning the late wife of Prince Arthur, calling her always in his conversation the queen) had not given an oath refusing the judges as suspect, he would not have advoked the matter at all, but been content that it should have been determined and ended in your realm. But seeing she gave that oath, appealing also to his court, he might and ought to hear her, his promise made to your Highness, which was qualified, notwithstanding. As touching the second point, his Holiness said that your Highness only was the default thereof, because ye would not send a proxy to the cause. These matters, however, he said, had been many times fully talked upon at Rome; and therefore [he] willed me to omit further communication thereupon, and to proceed to the doing of such things that I was specially sent for.

"Whereupon making protestation of your Highness's mind and intent towards the see apostolic—not intending anything to do in contempt of the same—I exhibited unto his Holiness the commission which your Highness had sent unto me; and his Holiness delivering it to the datary, commanded him to read it; and hearing in the same the words (referring to the injuries which he had done to your Highness), he began to look up after a new sort, and said, 'O questo et multo vero! (this is much true!)' meaning that it was not true indeed. And verily, sure not only in this, but also in many parts of the said commission, he showed himself grievously offended; insomuch that, when those words, 'To the next general council which shall be lawfully held in place convenient,' were read, he fell in a marvellous great choler and rage, not only declaring the same by his gesture and manner, but also by words: speaking with great vehemence, and saying, 'Why did not the king, when I wrote to my nuncio this year past, to speak unto him for this general council, give no answer unto my said nuncio, but referred him for answer to the French king? at what time he might perceive by my doing, that I was very well disposed, and much spake for it.' 'The thing so standing, now to speak of a general council! Oh, good Lord! but well! his commission and all his other writings cannot be but welcome unto me;' which words methought he spake willing to hide his choler, and make me believe that he was nothing angry with their doings, when in vary deed I perceived, by many arguments, that it was otherwise. And one among others was taken here for infallible with them that knoweth the pope's conditions, that he was continually folding up and unwinding of his handkerchief, which he never doth but when he is tickled to the very heart with great choler."

At length the appeal was read through; and at the close of it Francis entered, and talked to the pope for some time, but in so low a voice that Bonner could not hear what was passing. When he had gone, his Holiness said that he would deliberate upon the appeal with the consistory, and after hearing their judgments would return his answer.

Three days passed, and then the English agent was informed that he might again present himself. The pope had recovered his calmness. When he had time to collect himself, Clement could speak well and with dignity; and if we could forget that his conduct was substantially unjust, and that in his conscience he knew it to be unjust, he would almost persuade us to believe him honest. "He said," wrote Bonner, "that his mind towards your Highness always had been to minister justice, and to do pleasure to you; albeit it hath not been so taken: and he never unjustly grieved your Grace that he knoweth, nor intendeth hereafter to do. As concerning the appeal, he said that, forasmuch as there was a constitution of Pope Pius, his predecessor, that did condemn and reprove all such appeals, he did therefore reject your Grace's appeal as frivolous, forbidden, and unlawful." As touching the council, he said generally, that he would do his best that it should meet; but it was to be understood that the calling a general council belonged to him, and not to the King of England.

The audience ended, and Bonner left the pope convinced that he intended, on his return to Rome, to execute the censures and continue the process without delay. That the sentence which he would pronounce would be against the king appeared equally certain.

It appeared certain, yet after all no certain conclusion is possible. Francis I., though not choosing to quarrel with the see of Rome to do a pleasure to Henry, was anxious to please his ally to the extent of his convenience; at any rate, he would not have gratuitously deceived him; and still less would he have been party to an act of deliberate treachery. When Bonner was gone he had a last interview with the pope, in which he urged upon him the necessity of complying with Henry's demands; and the pope on this occasion said that he was satisfied that the King of England was right; that his cause was good; and that he had only to acknowledge the papal jurisdiction by some formal act, to find sentence immediately pronounced in his favour. Except for his precipitation, and his refusal to depute a proxy to plead for him, his wishes would have been complied with long before. In the existing posture of affairs, and after the measures which had been passed in England with respect to the see of Rome, he himself, the pope said, could not make advances without some kind of submission; but a single act of acknowledgment was all which he required. 630

Extraordinary as it must seem, the pope certainly bound himself by this engagement: and who can tell with what intention? To believe him sincere and to believe him false seems equally impossible. If he was persuaded that Henry's cause *was* good, why did he in the following year pronounce finally for Catherine? why had he imperilled so needlessly the interests of the papacy in England? why had his conduct from the beginning pointed steadily to the conclusion at which he at last arrived? and why throughout Europe were the ultramontane party, to a man, on Catherine's side? On the other hand, what object at such a time can be conceived for falsehood? Can we suppose that he designed to dupe Henry into submission by a promise which he had predetermined to break? It is hard to suppose even Clement capable of so elaborate an act of perfidy; and it is, perhaps, idle to waste conjectures on the motives of a weak, much-agitated man. He was, probably, but giving a fresh example of his disposition to say at each moment whatever would be most agreeable to his hearers. This was his unhappy habit, by which he earned for himself a character for dishonesty, I labour to think, but half deserved.

If, however, Clement meant to deceive, he succeeded, undoubtedly, in deceiving the French king. Francis, in communicating to Henry the language which the pope had used, entreated him to reconsider his resolution. The objection to pleading at Rome might be overcome; for the pope would meet him in a middle course. Judges could be appointed, who should sit at Cambray, and pass a sentence in condemnation of the original marriage; with a definite promise that their sentence should not again be called in question. To this arrangement there could be no reasonable objection; and Francis implored that a proposal so liberal should not be rejected. Sufficient danger already threatened Christendom, from heretics within and from the Turks without; and although the English parliament were agreed to maintain the second marriage, it was unwise to provoke the displeasure of foreign princes. To allow time for the preliminary arrangements, the execution of the censures had been further postponed; and if Henry would make up the quarrel, the French monarch was commissioned to offer a league, offensive and defensive, between England, France, and the Papacy. He himself only desired to be faithful to his engagements to his good brother; and as a proof of his good faith, he said that he had been offered the Duchy of Milan, if he would look on while the emperor and the pope attacked England. 631

This language bears all the character of sincerity; and when we remember that it followed immediately upon a close and intimate communication of three weeks with Clement, it is not easy to believe that he could have mistaken the extent of the pope's promises. We may suppose Clement for the moment to have been honest, or wavering between honesty and falsehood; we may suppose further that Francis trusted him because it was undesirable to be suspicious, in the belief that he was discharging the duty of a friend to Henry, and of a friend to the church, in offering to mediate upon these terms.

But Henry was far advanced beyond the point at which fair words could move him. He had trusted many times, and had been many times deceived. It was not easy to entangle him again. It mattered little whether Clement was weak or false; the result was the same—he could not be trusted. To an open English understanding there was something monstrous in the position of a person professing to be a judge, who admitted that a cause which lay before him was so clear that he could bind himself to a sentence upon it, and could yet refuse to pronounce that sentence, except upon conditions. It was scarcely for the interests of justice to leave the distribution of it in hands so questionable.

Instead, therefore, of coming forward, as Francis hoped, instead of consenting to entangle himself again in the meshes of diplomatic intrigue, the king returned a peremptory refusal.

The Duke of Norfolk, and such of the council as dreaded the completion of the schism, assured d'Inteville, the French ambassador, that for themselves they considered Francis was doing the best for England which could be done, and that they deprecated violent measures as much as possible; but in all this party there was a secret leaning to Queen Catherine, a dislike of Queen Anne and the whole Boleyn race, and a private hope and belief that the pope would after all be firm. Their tongues were therefore tied. They durst not speak except alone in whispers to each other; and the French ambassador, who did dare, only drew from Henry a more determined expression of his resolution.

As to his measures in England, the king said, the pope had begun the quarrel by issuing censures and by refusing to admit his reasons for declining to plead at Rome. He was required to send a proctor, and was told that the cause should be decided in favour of whichever party was so represented there. For the sake of all other princes as well as himself, he would send no proctor, nor would he seem to acquiesce in the pretences of the papal see. The King of France told him that the pope admitted the justice of his cause. Let the pope do justice, then. The laws passed in parliament were for the benefit of the commonwealth, and he would never revoke them. He demanded no reparation, and could make no reparation. He asked only for his right, and if he could not obtain it, he had God and truth on his side, and that was enough. In vain d'Inteville answered feebly, that his master had done all that was in his power; the king replied that the French council wished to entangle him with the pope; but for his own part he would never more acknowledge the pope in his pretended capacity. He might be bishop of Rome, or pope also, if he preferred the name; but the see of Rome should have no more jurisdiction in England, and he thought he would be none the worse Christian on that account, but rather the better. Jesus Christ he would acknowledge, and him only, as the true Lord of Christian men, and Christ's word only should be preached in England. The Spaniards might invade him as they threatened. He did not fear them. They might come, but they might not find it so easy to return. 632

The King had taken his position and was prepared for the consequences. He had foreseen for more than a year the possibility of an attempted invasion; and since his marriage, he had been aware that the chances of success in the adventure had been discussed on the Continent by the papal and imperial party. The pope had spoken of his censures being enforced, and Francis had revealed to Henry the nature of the dangerous overtures which had been made to himself. The Lutheran princes had hurriedly declined to connect themselves in any kind of alliance with England; and on the 25th of September, Stephen Vaughan had reported that troops were being raised in Germany, which rumour destined for Catherine's service. 633 Ireland, too, as we shall hear in the next chapter, was on the verge of an insurrection, which had been fomented by papal agents.

Nevertheless, there was no real danger from an invasion, unless it was accompanied with an insurrection at home, or with a simultaneous attack from Scotland; and while of the first there appeared upon the surface no probability, with Scotland a truce for a year had been concluded on the 1st of October. 634 The king, therefore, had felt himself reasonably secure. Parliament had seemed unanimous; the clergy were submissive; the nation acquiescent or openly approving; 635 and as late as the beginning of November, 1533, no suspicion seems to have been entertained of the spread of serious disaffection. A great internal revolution had been accomplished; a conflict of centuries between the civil and spiritual powers had been terminated without a life lost or a blow struck. Partial murmurs there had been, but murmurs were inevitable, and, so far as the government yet knew, were harmless. The Scotch war had threatened to be dangerous, but it had been extinguished. Impatient monks had denounced the king from the pulpits, and disloyal language had been reported from other quarters, which had roused vigilance, but had not created alarm. The Nun of Kent had forced herself into the royal presence with menacing prophecies; but she had appeared to be a harmless dreamer, who could only be made of importance by punishment. The surface of the nation was in profound repose. Cromwell, like Walsingham after him, may perhaps have known of the fire which was smouldering below, and have watched it silently till the moment came at which to trample it out; but no symptom of uneasiness appears either in the conduct of the government or in the official correspondence. The organisation of the friars, the secret communication of the Nun with Catherine and the Princess Mary, with the papal nuncio, or with noble lords and reverend bishops, was either unknown, or the character of those communications was not suspected. That a serious political conspiracy should have shaped itself round the ravings of a seeming lunatic, to all appearance had not occurred as a possibility to a single member of the council, except to those whose silence was ensured by their complicity.

So far as we are able to trace the story (for the links of the chain which led to the discovery of the design's which were entertained, are something imperfect), the suspicions of the government were first roused in the following manner:

Queen Catherine, as we have already seen, had been called upon, at the coronation of Anne Boleyn, to renounce her title, and she had refused. Mary had been similarly deprived of her rank as princess; but either her disgrace was held to be involved in that of her mother, or some other cause, perhaps the absence of immediate necessity, had postponed the demand for her own personal submission. As, however, on the publication of the second marriage, it had been urged on Catherine that there could not be two queens in England, so on the birth of the Princess Elizabeth, an analogous argument required the disinheritance of Mary. It was a hard thing; but her mother's conduct obliged the king to be peremptory. She might have been legitimatised by act of parliament, if Catherine would have submitted. The consequences of Catherine's refusal might be cruel, but they were unavoidable.

Mary was not with her mother. It had been held desirable to remove her from an influence which would encourage her in a useless opposition; and she was residing at Beaulieu, afterwards New Hall, in Essex, under the care of Lord Hussey and the Countess of Salisbury. Lord Hussey was a dangerous guardian; he was subsequently executed for his complicity in the Pilgrimage of Grace, the avowed object of which was the restoration of Mary to her place as heir-apparent. We may believe, therefore, that while under his surveillance she experienced no severe restraint, nor received that advice with respect to her conduct which prudence would have dictated. Lord Hussey, however, for the present enjoyed the confidence of the king, and was directed to inform his charge, that for the future she was to consider herself not as princess, but as the king's natural daughter, the Lady Mary Tudor. The message was a painful one; painful, we will hope, more on her mother's account than on her own; but her answer implied that, as yet, Henry VIII. was no object of especial terror to his children.

"Her Grace replied," wrote Lord Hussey to the council in communicating the result of his undertaking, 636 that "she could not a little marvel that I being alone, and not associate with some other the king's most honourable council, nor yet sufficiently authorised neither by commission not by any other writing from the King's Highness, would attempt to declare such a high enterprise and matter of no little weight and importance unto her Grace, in diminishing her said estate and name; her Grace not doubting that she is the king's true and legitimate daughter and heir procreate in good and lawful matrimony; [and] further adding, that unless she were advertised from his Highness by his writing that his Grace was so minded to diminish her estate, name, and dignity, which she trusteth his Highness will never do, she would not believe it."

Inasmuch as Mary was but sixteen at this time, the resolution which she displayed in sending such a message was considerable. The early English held almost Roman notions on the nature of parental authority, and the tone of a child to a father was usually that of the most submissive reverence. Nor was she contented with replying indirectly through her guardian. She wrote herself to the king, saying that she neither could nor would in her conscience think the contrary, but that she was his lawful daughter born in true matrimony, and that she thought that he in his own conscience did judge the same. 637

Such an attitude in so young a girl was singular, yet not necessarily censurable. Henry was not her only parent, and if we suppose her to have been actuated by affection for her mother, her conduct may appear not pardonable only, but spirited and creditable. In insisting upon her legitimacy, nevertheless, she was not only asserting the good name and fame of Catherine of Arragon, but unhappily her own claim to the succession to the throne. It was natural that under the circumstances she should have felt her right to assert that claim; for the injury which she had suffered was patent not only to herself, but to Europe. Catherine might have been required to give way that the king might have a son, and that the succession might be established in a prince; but so long as the child of the second marriage was a daughter only, it seemed substantially monstrous to set aside the elder for the younger. Yet the measure was a harsh necessity; a link in the chain which could not be broken. The harassed nation insisted above all things that no doubt should hang over the future, and it was impossible in the existing complications to recognise the daughter of Catherine without excluding Elizabeth, and excluding the prince who was expected to follow her. By asserting her title, Mary was making herself the nucleus of sedition, which on her father's death would lead to a convulsion in the realm. She might not mean it, but the result would not be affected by a want of purpose in herself; and it was possible that her resolution might create immediate and far more painful complications. The king's excommunication was imminent, and if the censures were enforced by the emperor, she would be thrust into the unpermitted position of her father's rival.

The political consequences of her conduct, notwithstanding, although evident to statesmen, might well be concealed from a headstrong, passionate girl. There was no suspicion that she herself was encouraging any of these dangerous thoughts, and Henry looked upon her answer to Lord Hussey and her letter to himself as expressions of petulant folly. Lord Oxford, the Earl of Essex, and the Earl of Sussex were directed to repair to Beaulieu, and explain to her the situation in which she had placed herself.

"Considering," wrote the king to them, "how highly such contempt and rebellion done by our daughter and her servants doth touch not only us, and the surety of our honour and person, but also the tranquillity of our realm; and not minding to suffer the pernicious example hereof to spread far abroad, but to put remedy to the same in due time, we have given you commandment to declare to her the great folly, temerity, and indiscretion that she hath used herein, with the peril she hath incurred by reason of her so doing. By these her ungodly doings hitherto she hath most worthily deserved our high indignation and displeasure, and thereto no less pain and punition than by the order of the laws of our realm doth appertain in case of high treason, unless our mercy and clemency should be shewed in that behalf. [If, however, after] understanding our mind and pleasure, [she will] conform herself humbly and obediently to the observation of the same, according to the office and duty of a natural daughter, and of a true and faithful subject, she may give us cause hereafter to incline our fatherly pity to her reconciliation, her benefit and advancement." 638

The reply of Mary to this message is not discoverable; but it is certain that she persisted in her resolution, and clung either to her mother's "cause" or to her own rank and privilege, in sturdy defiance of her father. To punish her insubordination or to tolerate it was equally difficult; and the government might have been in serious embarrassment had not a series of discoveries, following rapidly one upon the other, explained the mystery of these proceedings, and opened a view with alarming clearness into the under-currents of the feeling of the country.

Information from time to time had reached Henry from Rome, relating to the correspondence between Catherine and the pope. Perhaps, too, he knew how assiduously she had importuned the emperor to force Clement to a decision. 639 No effort, however, had been hitherto made to interfere with her hospitalities, or to oblige her visitors to submit to scrutiny before they could be admitted to her presence. She was the mistress of her own court and of her own actions; and confidential agents, both from Rome, Brussels, and Spain, had undoubtedly passed and repassed with reciprocal instructions and directions.

The crisis which was clearly approaching had obliged Henry, in the course of this autumn, to be more watchful; and about the end of October, or the beginning of November, 640 two friars were reported as having been at Bugden, whose movements attracted suspicion from their anxiety to escape observation. Secret agents of the government, who had been "set" for the purpose, followed the friars to London, and notwithstanding "many wiles and cautells by them invented to escape," the suspected persons were arrested and brought before Cromwell. Cromwell, "upon examination" could gather nothing from them of any moment or great importance; but, "entering on further communication," he said, "he found one of them a very seditious person, and so committed them to ward." The king was absent from London, but had left directions that, in the event of any important occurrence of the kind, Archbishop Cranmer should be sent for; but Cranmer not being immediately at hand, Cromwell wrote to Henry for instructions;

inasmuch as, he said, "it is undoubted that they (the monks) have intended, and would confess, some great matter, if they might be examined as they ought to be—that is to say, by pains."

The curtain here falls over the two prisoners; we do not know whether they were tortured, whether they confessed, or what they confessed; but we may naturally connect this letter, directly or indirectly, with the events which immediately followed. In the middle of November we find a commission sitting at Lambeth, composed of Cromwell, Cranmer, and Latimer, ravelling out the threads of a story, from which, when the whole was disentangled, it appeared that by Queen Catherine, the Princess Mary, and a large and formidable party in the country, the king, on the faith of a pretended revelation, was supposed to have forfeited the crown; that his death, either by visitation of God or by visitation of man, was daily expected; and that whether his death took place or not, a revolution was immediately looked for, which would place the princess on the throne.

The Nun of Kent, as we remember, had declared that if Henry persisted in his resolution of marrying Anne, she was commissioned by God to tell him that he should lose his power and authority. She had not specified the manner in which the sentence would be carried into effect against him. The form of her threats had been also varied occasionally; she said that he should die, but whether by the hands of his subjects, or by a providential judgment, she left to conjecture; 641 and the period within which his punishment was to fall upon him was stated variously at one month or at six. 642 She had attempted no secresy with these prophecies; she had confined herself in appearance to words; and the publicity which she courted having prevented suspicion of secret conspiracy, Henry quietly accepted the issue, and left the truth of the prophecy to be confuted by the event. He married. The one month passed; the six months passed; eight—nine months. His child was born and was baptised, and no divine thunder had interposed; only a mere harmless verbal thunder, from a poor old man at Rome. The illusion, as he imagined, had been lived down, and had expired of its own vanity.

But the Nun and her friar advisers were counting on other methods of securing the fulfilment of the prophecy than supernatural assistance. It is remarkable that hypocrites and impostors as they knew themselves to be, they were not without a half belief that some supernatural intervention was imminent; but the career on which they had entered was too fascinating to allow them to forsake it when their expectation failed them. They were swept into the stream which was swelling to resist the Reformation, and allowed themselves to be hurried forward either to victory or to destruction.

The first revelation being apparently confuted by facts, a second was produced as an interpretation of it; which, however, was not published like the other, but whispered in secret to persons whose dispositions were known. 643

"When the King's Grace," says the report of the commissioners, "had continued in good health, honour, and prosperity more than a month, Dr. Bocking shewed the said Nun, that as King Saul, abjected from his kingdom by God, yet continued king in the sight of the world, so her said revelations might be taken. And therefore the said Nun, upon this information, forged another revelation, that her words should be understood to mean that the King's Grace should not be king in the reputation or acceptation of God, not one month or one hour after that he married the Queen's Grace that now is. The first revelation had moved a great number of the king's subjects, both high and low, to grudge against the said marriage before it was concluded and perfected; and also induced such as were stiffly bent against that marriage, daily to look for the destruction of the King's Grace within a month after he married the Queen's Grace that now is. And when they were deluded in that expectation, the second revelation was devised not only as an interpretation of the former, but to the intent to induce the king's subjects to believe that God took the King's Grace for no king of this realm, and that they should likewise take him for no righteous king, and themselves not bounden to be his subjects; which might have put the King and the Queen's Grace in jeopardy of their crown and of their issue, and the people of this realm in great danger of destruction." 644

It was no light matter to pronounce the king to be in the position of Saul after his rejection; and read by the light of the impending excommunication, the Nun's words could mean nothing but treason. The speaker herself was in correspondence with the pope; she had attested her divine commission by miracles, and had been recognised as a saint by an Archbishop of Canterbury; the regular orders of the clergy throughout the realm were known to regard her as inspired; and when the commission recollected that the king was threatened further with dying "a villain's death;" and that these and similar prophecies were carefully written out, and were in private circulation through the country, the matter assumed a dangerous complexion: it became at once essential to ascertain how far, and among what classes of the state, these things had penetrated. The Friars Mendicant were discovered to be in league with her, and these itinerants were ready-made missionaries of sedition. They had privilege of vagrancy without check or limit; and owing to their universal distribution and the freemasonry among themselves, the secret disposition of every family in England was intimately known to them. No movement, therefore, could be securely over-looked in which these orders had a share; the country might be undermined in secret; and the government might only learn their danger at the moment of explosion.

No sooner, therefore, were the commissioners in possession of the general facts, than the principal parties—that is to say, the Nun herself and five of the monks of Christ Church at Canterbury—with whom her intercourse was most constant, were sent to the Tower to be "examined"—the monks it is likely by "torture," if they could not otherwise be brought to confession. The Nun was certainly not tortured. On her first arrest, she was obstinate in maintaining her prophetic character; and she was detected in sending messages to her friends, "to animate them to adhere to her and to her prophecies." 645 But her courage ebbed away under the hard reality of her position. She soon made a full confession, in which her accomplices joined her; and the half-completed web of conspiracy was ravelled out. They did not attempt to conceal that they had intended, if possible, to create an insurrection. The five monks—Father Bocking, Father Rich, Father Rysby, Father Dering, and Father Goold—had assisted the Nun in inventing her "Revelations;" and as apostles, they had travelled about the country to communicate them in whatever quarters they were likely to be welcome. When we remember that Archbishop Warham had been a dupe of this woman, and that even Wolsey's experience and ability had not prevented him from believing in her power, we are not surprised to find high names among those who were implicated. Vast numbers of abbots and priors, and of regular and secular clergy, had listened eagerly; country gentlemen also, and London merchants. The Bishop of Rochester had "wept for joy" at the first utterances of the inspired prophetess; and Sir Thomas More, "who at first did little regard the said revelations, afterwards did greatly rejoice to hear of them." 646 We learn, also, that the Nun had continued to *communicate with "the Lady Princess Dowager" and "the Lady Mary, her daughter."* 647

These were names which might have furnished cause for regret, but little for surprise or alarm. The commissioners must have found occasion for other feelings, however, when among the persons implicated were found the Countess of Salisbury and the Marchioness of Exeter, with their chaplains, households, and servants; Sir Thomas Arundel, Sir George Carew, and "many of the nobles of England." 648 A combination headed by the Countess of Salisbury, if she were supported even by a small section of the nobility, would under any circumstances have been dangerous; and if such a combination was formed in support of an invasion, and was backed by the blessings of the pope and the fanaticism of the clergy, the result might be serious indeed. So careful a silence is observed in the official papers on this feature of the Nun's conspiracy, that it is uncertain how far the countess had committed herself; but she had listened certainly to avowals of treasonable intentions without revealing them, which of itself was no slight evidence of disloyalty; and that the government were really alarmed may be gathered from the simultaneous arrest of Sir William and Sir George Neville, the brothers of Lord Latimer. The connection and significance of these names I shall explain presently; in the meantime I return to the preparations which had been made by the Nun.

As the final judgment drew near—which, unless the king submitted, would be accompanied, with excommunication, and a declaration that the English nation was absolved from allegiance,—"the said false Nun," says the report, "surmised herself to have made a petition to God to know, when fearful war should come, whether any man should take my Lady Mary's part or no; and she feigned herself to have answer by revelation that no man should fear but that she should have succour and help enough; and that no man should put her from her right that she was born unto. And petitioning next to know when it was the pleasure of God that her revelations should be put forth to the world, she had answer that knowledge should be given to her ghostly father when it should be time." 649

With this information Father Goold had hastened down to Bugden, encouraging Catherine to persevere in her resistance; 650 and while the imperialists at Rome were pressing the pope for sentence (we cannot doubt at Catherine's instance), the Nun had placed herself in readiness to seize the opportunity when it offered, and to blow the trumpet of insurrection in the panic which might be surely looked for when that sentence should be published.

For this purpose she had organised, with considerable skill, a corps of fanatical friars, who, when the signal was given, were simultaneously to throw themselves into the midst of the people, and call upon them to rise in the name of God. "To the intent," says the report, "to set forth this matter, certain spiritual and religious persons were appointed, as they had been chosen of God, to preach the false revelations of the said Nun, when the time should require, if warning were given them; and some of these preachers have confessed openly, and subscribed their names to their confessions, that if the Nun had so sent them word, they would have preached to the king's subjects that the pleasure of God was that they should take him no longer for their king; and some of these preachers were such as gave themselves to great fasting, watching, long prayers, wearing of shirts of hair and great chains of iron about their middle, whereby the people had them in high estimation of their great holiness,—and this strait life they took on them by the counsel and exhortation of the said Nun." 651

Here, then, was the explanation of the attitude of Catherine and Mary. Smarting under injustice, and most naturally blending their private quarrel with the cause of the church, they had listened to these disordered visions as to a message from heaven, and they had lent themselves to the first of those religious conspiracies which held England in chronic agitation for three quarters of a century. The innocent Saint at Bugden was the forerunner of the prisoner at Fotheringay; and the Observant friars, with their chain girdles and shirts of hair, were the antitypes of Parsons and Campion. How critical the situation of England really was, appears from the following letter of the French ambassador. The project for the marriage of the Princess Mary with the Dauphin had been revived by the Catholic party; and a private arrangement, of which this marriage was to form the connecting link, was contemplated between the Ultramontanes in France, the pope, and the emperor.

D'Inteville to Cardinal Tournon. 652

"MY LORD,—You will be so good as to tell the Most Christian king that the emperor's ambassador has communicated with the old queen. The emperor sends a message to her and to her daughter, that he will not return to Spain till he has seen them restored to their rights.

"The people are so much attached to the said ladies that they will rise in rebellion, and join any prince who will undertake their quarrel. You probably know from other quarters the intensity of this feeling. It is shared by all classes, high and low, and penetrates even into the royal household.

"The nation is in marvellous discontent. Every one but the relations of the present queen, is indignant on the ladies' account. Some fear the overthrow of religion; others fear war and injury to trade. Up to this time, the cloth, hides, wool, lead, and other merchandise of England have found markets in Flanders, Spain, and Italy; now it is thought navigation will be so dangerous that English merchants must equip their ships for war if they trade to foreign countries; and besides the risk of losing all to the enemy, the expense of the armament will swallow the profits of the voyage. In like manner, the emperor's subjects and the pope's subjects will not be able to trade with England. The coasts will be blockaded by the ships of the emperor and his allies; and at this moment men's fears are aggravated by the unseasonable weather throughout the summer, and the failure of the crops. There is not corn enough for half the ordinary consumption.

"The common people, foreseeing these inconveniences, are so violent against the queen, that they say a thousand shameful things of her, and of all who have supported her in her intrigues. On them is cast the odium of all the calamities anticipated from the war.

"When the war comes, no one doubts that the people will rebel as much from fear of the dangers which I have mentioned, as from the love which is felt for the two ladies, and especially for the Princess. She is so entirely beloved that, notwithstanding the law made at the last Parliament, and the menace of death contained in it, they persist in regarding her as Princess. No Parliament, they say, can make her anything but the king's daughter, born in marriage; and so the king and every one else regarded her before that Parliament.

"Lately, when she was removed from Greenwich, a vast crowd of women, wives of citizens and others, walked before her at their husbands' desire, weeping and crying that notwithstanding all she was Princess. Some of them were sent to the Tower, but they would not retract.

"Things are now so critical, and the fear of war is so general, that many of the greatest merchants in London have placed themselves in communication with the emperor's ambassador, telling him, that if the emperor will declare war, the English nation will join him for the love they bear the Lady Mary.

"You, my Lord, will remember that when you were here, it was said you were come to tell the king that he was excommunicated, and to demand the hand of the Princess for the Dauphin. The people were so delighted that they have never ceased to pray for you. We too, when we arrived in London, were told that the people were praying for us. They thought our embassy was to the Princess. They imagined her marriage with the Dauphin had been determined on by the two kings, and the satisfaction was intense and universal.

"They believe that, except by this marriage, they cannot possibly escape war; whereas, can it be brought about, they will have peace with the emperor and all other Christian princes. They are now so disturbed and so desperate that, although at one time they would have preferred a husband for her from among themselves, that they might not have a foreign king, there now is nothing which they desire more. Unless the Dauphin will take her, they say she will continue disinherited; or, if she come to her rights, it can only be by battle, to the great incommodity of the country. The Princess herself says publicly that the Dauphin is her husband, and that she has no hope but in him. I have been told this by persons who have heard it from her own lips.

"The emperor's ambassador inquired, after you came, whether we had seen her. He said he knew she was most anxious to speak with us; she thought we had permission to visit her, and she looked for good news. He told us, among other things, that she had been more strictly guarded of late, by the orders of the queen that now is, who, knowing her feeling for the

Dauphin, feared there might be some practice with her, or some attempt to carry her off.

"The Princess's ladies say that she calls herself the Dauphin's wife. A time will come, she says, when God will see that she has suffered pain and tribulation sufficient; the Dauphin will then demand her of the king her father, and the king her father will not be able to refuse.

"The lady who was my informant heard, also, from the Princess, that her governess, and the other attendants whom the queen had set to watch her, had assured her that the Dauphin was married to the daughter of the emperor; but she, the Princess, had answered it was not true—the Dauphin could not have two wives, and they well knew that she was his wife: they told her that story, she said, to make her despair, and agree to give up her rights; but she would never part with her hopes.

"You may have heard of the storm that broke out between her and her governess when we went to visit her little sister. She was carried off by force to her room, that she might not speak with us; and they could neither pacify her nor keep her still, till the gentleman who escorted us told her he had the king's commands that she was not to show herself while we were in the house. You remember the message the same gentleman brought to you from her, and the charge which was given by the queen.

"Could the king be brought to consent to the marriage, it could be a fair union of two realms, and to annex Britain to the crown of France would be a great honour to our Sovereign; the English party desire nothing better; the pope will be glad of it; the pope fears that, if war break out again, France will draw closer to England on the terms which the King of England desires; and he may thus lose the French tribute as he has lost the English. He therefore will urge the emperor to agree, and the emperor will assist gladly for the love which he bears to his cousin.

"If the emperor be willing, the King of England can then be informed; and he can be made to feel that, if he will avoid war, he must not refuse his consent. The king, in fact, has no wish to disown the Princess, and he knows well that the marriage with the Dauphin was once agreed on.

"Should he be unwilling, and should his wife's persuasions stil have influence with him, he will hesitate before he will defy, for her sake, the King of France and the emperor united. His regard for the queen is less than it was, and diminishes every day. He has a new fancy, 653 as you are aware."

The actual conspiracy, in the form which it had so far assumed, was rather an appeal to fanaticism than a plot which could have laid hold of the deeper mind of the country; but as an indication of the unrest which was stealing over the minds of men, it assumed an importance which it would not have received from its intrinsic character.

The guilt of the principal offenders admitted of no doubt. As soon as the commissioners were satisfied that there was nothing further to be discovered, the Nun, with the monks, was brought to trial before the Star Chamber; and conviction followed as a matter of course. 654

The unhappy girl finding herself at this conclusion, after seven years of vanity, in which she had played with popes, and queens, and princesses, and archbishops, now, when the dream was thus rudely broken, in the revulsion of feeling could see nothing in herself but a convicted impostor. We need not refuse to pity her. The misfortunes of her sickness had exposed her to temptations far beyond the strength of an ordinary woman: and the guilt which she passionately claimed for herself rested far more truly with the knavery of the Christ Church monks and the incredible folly of Archbishop Warham. 655 But the times were too stern to admit of nice distinctions. No immediate sentence was pronounced, but it was thought desirable for the satisfaction of the people that a confession should be made in public by the Nun and her companions. The Sunday following their trial they were placed on a raised platform at Paul's Cross by the side of the pulpit, and when the sermon was over they one by one delivered their "bills" to the preacher, which by him were read to the crowd. 656

After an acknowledgment of their imposture the prisoners were remanded to the Tower, and their ultimate fate reserved for the consideration of parliament, which was to meet in the middle of January.

The chief offenders being thus disposed of, the council resolved next that peremptory measures should be taken with respect to the Princess Mary. 657 Her establishment was broken up, and she was sent to reside as the Lady Mary in the household of the Princess Elizabeth—a hard but not unwholesome discipline. 658 As soon as this was done, being satisfied that the leading shoot of the conspiracy was broken, and that no immediate danger was now to be feared, they proceeded leisurely to follow the clue of the Nun's confession, and to extend their inquiries. The Countess of Salisbury was mentioned as one of the persons with whom the woman had been in correspondence. This lady was the daughter of the Duke of Clarence, brother of Edward IV. Her mother was a Neville, a child of Richard the Kingmaker, the famous Earl of Warwick, and her only brother had been murdered to secure the shaking throne of Henry VII. Margaret Plantagenet, in recompense for the lost honours of the house, was made Countess of Salisbury in her own right. The title descended from her grandfather, who was Earl of Salisbury and Warwick; but the prouder title had been dropped as suggestive of dangerous associations. The Earldom of Warwick remained in abeyance, and the castle and the estates attached to it were forfeited to the Crown. The countess was married after her brother's death to a Sir Richard Pole, a supporter and relation 659 of the king; and when left a widow she received from Henry VIII. the respectful honour which was due to the most nobly born of his subjects, the only remaining Plantagenet of unblemished descent. In his kindness to her children the king had attempted to obliterate the recollection of her brother's wrongs, and she had been herself selected to preside over the household of the Princess Mary. During the first twenty years of Henry's reign the countess seems to have acknowledged his attentions with loyal regard, and if she had not forgotten her birth and her childhood, she never connected herself with the attempts which during that time were made to revive the feuds of the houses. Richard de la Pole, nephew of Edward IV., 660 and called while he lived "the White Rose," had more than once endeavoured to excite an insurrection in the eastern counties; but Lady Salisbury was never suspected of holding intercourse with him; she remained aloof from political disputes, and in lofty retirement she was contented to forget her greatness for the sake of the Princess Mary, to whom she and her family were deeply attached. Her relations with the king had thus continued undisturbed until his second marriage. As the representative of the House of York she was the object of the hopes and affections of the remnants of their party, but she had betrayed no disposition to abuse her influence, or to disturb the quiet of the nation for personal ambition of her own.

If it be lawful to interpret symptoms in themselves trifling by the light of later events, it would seem as if her attitude now underwent a material change. Her son Reginald had already quarrelled with the king upon the divorce. He was in suspicious connection with the pope, and having been required to return home upon his allegiance, had refused obedience. His mother, and his mother's attached friend, the Marchioness of Exeter, we now find among those to whom the Nun of Kent communicated her prophecies and her plans. It does not seem that the countess thought at any time of reviving her own pretensions; it does seem that she was ready to build a throne for the Princess Mary out of the ruined supporters of her father's family. The power which she could wield might at any moment become formidable. She had two sons in England, Lord Montague and Sir Geoffrey Pole. Her cousin, the Marquis of Exeter, a grandson himself of Edward IV., 661 was, with the exception of the Duke of Norfolk, the most powerful nobleman in the realm; and he, to judge by events, was beginning to look coldly on the king. 662 We find her surrounded also by the representatives of her mother's family—Lord Abergavenny, who had been under suspicion when the Duke of Buckingham was executed, Sir Edward Neville, afterwards executed, Lord Latimer, Sir George and Sir William Neville, all of them were her near connections, all collateral heirs of the King-maker, inheriting the pride of their birth, and resentfully conscious of their fallen fortunes. The support of a party so composed would have added formidable strength to the preaching friars of the Nun of Kent; and as I cannot doubt that the Nun was endeavouring to press her intrigues in a quarter where disaffection if created would be most dangerous, so the lady who ruled this party with a patriarchal authority had listened to her suggestions; and the repeated interviews with her which were sought by the Marchioness of Exeter were rendered more than suspicious by the secresy with which these interviews were conducted. 663

These circumstances explain the arrest, to which I alluded above, of Sir William and Sir George Neville, brothers of Lord Latimer. They were not among "the many noblemen" to whom the commissioners referred; for their confessions remain, and contain no allusion to the Nun; but they were examined at this particular time on general suspicion; and the arrest, under such circumstances, of two near relatives of Lady Salisbury, indicates clearly an alarm in the council, lest she might be contemplating some serious movements. At any rate, either on her account or on their own, the Nevilles fell under suspicion, and while they had no crimes to reveal, their depositions, especially that of Sir William Neville, furnish singular evidence of the temper of the times.

The confession of the latter begins with an account of the loss of certain silver spoons, for the recovery of which Sir William sent to a wizard who resided in Cirencester. The wizard took the opportunity of telling Sir William's fortune: his wife was to die, and he himself was to marry an heiress, and be made a baron; with other prospective splendours. The wizard concluded, however, with recommending him to pay a visit to another dealer in the dark art more learned than himself, whose name was Jones, at Oxford.

"So after that," said Sir William [Midsummer, 1532], "I went to Oxford, intending that my brother George and I should kill a buck with Sir Simon Harcourt, which he had promised me; and there at Oxford, in the said Jones's chamber, I did see certain stillatories, alembics, and other instruments of glass, and also a sceptre and other things, which he said did appertain to the conjuration of the four kings; and also an image of white metal; and in a box, a serpent's skin, as he said, and divers books and things, whereof one was a book which he said was my Lord Cardinal's, having pictures in it like angels. He told me he could make rings of gold, to obtain favour of great men; and said that my Lord Cardinal had such; and promised my said brother and me, either of us, one of them; and also he showed me a round thing like a ball of crystal.

"He said that if the King's Grace went over to France [the Calais visit of October, 1532], his Grace should marry my Lady Marchioness of Pembroke before that his Highness returned again; and that it would be dangerous to his Grace, and to the most part of the noblemen that should go with him; saying also that he had written to one of the king's council to advise his Highness not to go over, for if he did, it should not be for his Grace's profit."

The wizard next pretended that he had seen a vision of a certain room in a tower, in which a spirit had appeared with a coat of arms in his hand, and had "delivered the same to Sir William Neville." The arms being described as those of the Warwick family, Sir William, his brother, and Jones rode down from Oxford to Warwick, where they went over the castle. The wizard professed to recognise in a turret chamber the room in which he had seen the spirit, and he prophesied that Sir William should recover the earldom, the long-coveted prize of all the Neville family.

On their return to Oxford, Jones, continues Sir William, said further, "That there should be a field in the north about a se'n-night before Christmas, in which my Lord my brother [Lord Latimer] should be slain; the realm should be long without a king; and much robbery would be within the realm, specially of abbeys and religious houses, and of rich men, as merchants, graziers, and others; so that, if I would, he at that time would advise me to find the means to enter into the said castle for mine own safeguard, and divers persons would resort unto me. *None of Cadwallader's blood,* he told me, *should reign more than twenty-four years;* and also that Prince Edward [son of Henry VI. and Margaret of Anjou, killed at Tewkesbury], had issue a son which was conveyed over sea; and there had issue a son which was yet alive, either in Saxony or Almayne; and that either he or the King of Scots should reign next after the King's Grace that now is. To all which I answered," Sir William concluded, "that there is nothing which the will of God is that a man shall obtain, but that he of his goodness will put in his mind the way whereby he shall come by it; and that surely I had no mind to follow any such fashion; and that, also, the late Duke of Buckingham and others had cast themselves away by too much trust in prophecies, and other jeoparding of themselves, and therefore I would in no wise follow any such way. He answered, if I would not, it would be long ere I obtained it. Then I said I believed that well, and if it never came, I trusted to God to live well enough." 664

Sir George Neville confirmed generally his brother's story, protesting that they had never intended treason, and that "at no time had he been of counsel" when any treason was thought of. 665

The wizard himself was next sent for. The prophecies about the king he denied wholly. He admitted that he had seen an angel in a dream giving Sir William Neville the shield of the earldom in Warwick Castle, and that he had accompanied the two brothers to Warwick, to examine the tower. Beyond that, he said that he knew nothing either of them or of their intentions. He declared himself a good subject, and he would "jeopard his life" to make the philosopher's stone for the king in twelve months if the king pleased to command him. He desired "no longer space than twelve months upon silver and twelve and a half upon gold;" to be kept in prison till he had done it; and it would be "better to the King's Grace than a thousand men." 666

The result of these examinations does not appear, except it be that the Nevilles were dismissed without punishment; and the story itself may be thought too trifling to have deserved a grave notice. I see in it, however, an illustration very noticeworthy of the temper which was working in the country. The suspicion of treason in the Neville family may not have been confirmed, although we see them casting longing looks on the lost inheritance of Warwick; but their confessions betray the visions of impending change, anarchy, and confusion, which were haunting the popular imagination. A craving after prophecies, a restless eagerness to search into the future by abnormal means, had infected all ranks from the highest to the lowest; and such symptoms, when they appear, are a sure evidence of approaching disorder, for they are an evidence of a present madness which has brought down wisdom to a common level with folly. At such times, the idlest fancy is more potent with the mind than the soundest arguments of reason. The understanding abdicates its functions; and men are given over, as if by magic, to the enchantments of insanity.

Phenomena of this eccentric kind always accompany periods of intellectual change. Most men live and think by habit; and when habit fails them, they are like unskilful sailors who have lost the landmarks of their course, and have no compass and no celestial charts by which to steer. In the years which preceded the French Revolution, Cagliostro was the companion of princes—at the dissolution of paganism the practicers of curious arts, the watches and the necromancers, were the sole objects of reverence in the Roman world;—and so, before the Reformation, archbishops and cardinals saw an inspired prophetess in a Kentish servant girl; Oxford heads of colleges sought out heretics with the help of astrology; Anne Boleyn blessed a basin of rings, her royal fingers pouring such virtue into the metal that no disorder could resist it; 667 Wolsey had a magic crystal; and Cromwell, while in Wolsey's household, "did haunt to the company of a wizard." 668 These things were the counterpart of a religion which taught that slips of paper, duly paid for, could secure indemnity for sin. It was well for England that the chief captain at least was proof against the epidemic—no random scandal seems ever to have whispered that such delusions had touched the mind of the king. 669

While the government were prosecuting these inquiries at home, the law at the Vatican had run its course; November passed, and as no submission had arrived, the sentence of the 12th of July came into force, and the king, the queen, and the Archbishop of Canterbury were declared to have incurred the threatened censures.

The privy council met on the 2nd of December, and it was determined in consequence that copies of the "Act of Appeals," and of the king's "provocation" to a general council, should be fixed without delay on every church door in England. Protests were at the same time to be drawn up and sent into Flanders, and to the other courts in Europe, "to the intent the falsehood and injustice of the Bishop of Rome might appear to all the world." The defences of the country were to be looked to; and "spies" to be sent into Scotland to see "what they intended there," "and whether they would confeder themselves with any outward princes." Finally, it was proposed that the attempt to form an alliance with the Lutheran powers should be renewed on a larger scale; that certain discreet and grave persons should be appointed to conclude "some league or amity with the princes of Germany"—"that is to say, the King of Poland, the King of Hungary, 670 the Duke of Saxony, the Duke of Bavaria, the Duke of Brandenburg, the Landgrave of Hesse, and other potentates." 671 Vaughan's mission had been merely tentative, and had failed. Yet the offer of a league, offensive and defensive, the immediate and avowed object of which was a general council at which the Protestants should be represented, might easily succeed where vague offers of amity had come to nothing. The formation of a Protestant alliance, however, would have been equivalent to a declaration of war against Catholic Europe; and it was a step which could not be taken, consistently with the Treaty of Calais,—without first communicating with Francis.

Henry, therefore, by the advice of the council, wrote a despatch to Sir John Wallop, the ambassador at Paris, which was to be laid before the French court. He explained the circumstances in which he was placed, with the suggestion which the council had made to him. He gave a list of the princes with whom he had been desired by his ministers to connect himself— and the object was nothing less than a coalition of Northern Europe. He recapitulated the injuries which he had received from the pope, who at length was studying "to subvert the rest and peace of the realm;" "yea, and so much as in him was, utterly to destroy the same." The nobles and council, he said, for their own sake as well as for the sake of the kingdom, had entreated him to put an end, once for all, to the pope's usurpation; and to invite the Protestant princes, for the universal weal of Christendom, to unite in a common alliance. In his present situation he was inclined to act upon this advice. "As concerning his own realm, he had already taken such order with his nobles and subjects, as he would shortly be able to give to the pope such a buffet as he never had heretofore;" but as a German alliance was a matter of great weight and importance, "although," he concluded, "we consider it to be right expedient to set forth the same with all diligence, yet we intend nothing to do therein without making our good brother first privy thereunto. And for this cause and consideration only, you may say that we have at this time addressed these letters unto you, commanding you to declare our said purpose unto our good brother, and to require of him on our behalf his good address and best advice. Of his answer we require you to advertise us with all diligence, for according thereunto we intend to attemper our proceedings. We have lately had advertisements how that our said good brother should, by the labour of divers affectionate Papists, be minded to set forth something with his clergy in advancement of the pope and his desires. This we cannot believe that he will do." 672

The meaning of this letter lies upon the surface. If the European powers were determined to leave him no alternative, the king was prepared to ally himself with the Lutherans. But however he might profess to desire that alliance, it was evident that he would prefer, if possible, a less extreme resource. The pope had ceased to be an object of concern to him; but he could not contemplate, without extreme unwillingness, a separation from the orderly governments who professed the Catholic faith. The pope had injured him; Francis had deceived him; they had tempted his patience because they knew his disposition. The limit of endurance had been reached at length; yet, on the verge of the concluding rupture, he turned once more, as if to offer a last opportunity of peace.

The reply of Francis was an immediate mission of the Bishop of Bayonne (now Bishop of Paris), first into England, and from England to Rome, where he was to endeavour, to the best of his ability, to seam together the already gaping rent in the church with fair words—a hopeless task—the results of which, however, were unexpectedly considerable, as will be presently seen.

Meanwhile, on the side of Flanders, the atmosphere was dubious and menacing. The refugee friars, who were reported to be well supplied with money from England, were labouring to exasperate the people, Father Peto especially distinguishing himself upon this service. 673 The English ambassador, Sir John Hacket, still remained at Brussels, and the two governments were formally at peace; but when Hacket required the queen-regent to forbid the publication of the brief of July in the Netherlands, he was met with a positive refusal. "M. Ambassador," she said, "the Emperor, the King of Hungary, the Queen of France, the King of Portugal, and I, understand what are the rights of our aunt—our duty is to her—and such letters of the pope as come hither in her favour we shall obey. Your master has no right to complain either of the emperor or of myself, if we support our aunt in a just cause." 674 At the same time, formal complaints were made by Charles of the personal treatment of Queen Catherine, and the clouds appeared to be gathering for a storm. Yet here, too, there was an evident shrinking from extremities. A Welsh gentleman had been at Brussels to offer his services against Henry, and had met with apparent coldness. Sir John Hacket wrote, on the 15th of December, that he was assured by well-informed persons, that so long as Charles lived, he would never be the first to begin a war with England, "which would rebound to the destruction of the Low Countries." 675 A week later, when the queen-regent was suffering from an alarming illness, he said it was reported that, should she die, Catherine or Mary, if either of them was allowed to leave England, would be held "meet to have governance of the Low Countries." 676 This was a generous step, if the emperor seriously contemplated it. The failure of the Nun of Kent had perhaps taught him that there was no present prospect of a successful insurrection. In his conduct towards England, he was seemingly governing himself by the prospect which might open for a successful attack upon it. If occasion offered to strike the government in connection with an efficient Catholic party in the nation itself, he would not fail to avail himself of it. 677 Otherwise, he would perhaps content himself with an attitude of inactive menace; unless menaced himself by a Protestant confederation.

Amidst these uneasy symptoms at home and abroad, parliament re-assembled on the 15th of January. It was a changed England since these men first came together on the fall of Wolsey. Session after session had been spent in clipping the roots of the old tree which had overshadowed them for centuries. On their present meeting they were to finish their work, and lay it prostrate for ever. Negotiations were still pending with the See of Rome, and this momentous session had closed before the final catastrophe. The measures which were passed in the course of it are not, therefore, to be looked upon as adopted hastily, in a spirit of retaliation, but as the consistent accomplishment of a course which had been deliberately adopted, to reverse the positions of the civil and spiritual authority within the realm, and to withdraw the realm itself from all dependence on a foreign power.

The Annates and Firstfruits' Bill had not yet received the royal assent; but the pope had refused to grant the bulls for bishops recently appointed, and he was no longer to receive payment for services which he refused to render. Peter's pence were still paid, and might continue to be paid, if the pope would recollect himself; but, like the Sibyl of Cuma, Henry destroyed some fresh privilege with each delay of justice, demanding the same price for the preservation of what remained. The secondary streams of tribute now only remained to the Roman See; and communion with the English church, which it was for Clement to accept or refuse.

The circumstances under which the session opened were, however, grave and saddening. Simultaneously with the concluding legislation on the church, the succession to the throne was to be determined in terms which might, perhaps, be accepted as a declaration of war by the emperor; and the affair of the Nun of Kent had rendered necessary an inquiry into the conduct of honoured members of the two Houses, who were lying under the shadow of high treason. The conditions were for the first time to be plainly seen under which the Reformation was to fight its way. The road which lay before it was beset not merely with external obstacles, which a strong will and a strong hand could crush, but with the phantoms of dying faiths, which haunted the hearts of all living men; the superstitions, the prejudices, the hopes, the fears, the passions, which swayed stormily and fitfully through the minds of every actor in the great drama.

The uniformity of action in the parliament of 1529, during the seven years which it continued, is due to the one man who saw his way distinctly, Thomas Cromwell. The nation was substantially united in the divorce question, could the divorce be secured without a rupture with the European powers. It was united also on the necessity of limiting the jurisdiction of the clergy, and cutting short the powers of the consistory courts. But in questions of "opinion" there was the most sensitive jealousy; and from the combined instincts of prejudice and conservatism, the majority of the country in a count of heads would undoubtedly have been against a separation from Rome.

The clergy professed to approve the acts of the government, but it was for the most part with the unwilling acquiescence of men who were without courage to refuse. The king was divided against himself. Nine days in ten he was the clear-headed, energetic, powerful statesman; on the tenth he was looking wistfully to the superstition which he had left, and the clear sunshine was darkened with theological clouds, which broke in lightning and persecution. Thus there was danger at any moment of a reaction, unless opportunity was taken at the flood, unless the work was executed too completely to admit of reconsideration, and the nation committed to a course from which it was impossible to recede. The action of the conservatives was paralysed for the time by the want of a fixed purpose. The various parts of the movement were so skilfully linked together, that partial opposition to it was impossible; and so long as the people had to choose between the pope and the king, their loyalty would not allow them to hesitate. But very few men actively adhered to Cromwell. Cromwell had struck the line on which the forces of nature were truly moving—the resultant, not of the victory of either of the extreme parties, but of the joint action of their opposing forces. To him belonged the rare privilege of genius, to see what other men could not see; and therefore he was condemned to rule a generation which hated him, to do the will of God, and to perish in his success. He had no party. By the nobles he was regarded with the same mixed contempt and fear which had been felt for Wolsey. The Protestants, perhaps, knew what he was, but he could only purchase their toleration by himself checking their extravagance. Latimer was the only person of real power on whose friendship he could calculate, and Latimer was too plain spoken on dangerous questions to be useful as a political supporter.

The session commenced on the 15th of January.

The first step was to receive the final submission of convocation. The undignified resistance was at last over, and the clergy had promised to abstain for the future from unlicensed legislation. To secure their adherence to their engagements, an act 678 was passed to make the breach of that engagement penal; and a commission of thirty-two persons, half of whom were to be laymen, was designed for the revision of the Canon law. 679

The next most important movement was to assimilate the trials for heresy with the trials for other criminal offences. I have already explained at length the manner in which the bishops abused their judicial powers. These powers were not absolutely taken away, but ecclesiastics were no longer permitted to arrest *ex officio* and examine at their pleasure. Where a charge of heresy was to be brought against a man, presentments were to be made by lawful witnesses before justices of the peace; and then, and not otherwise, he might fall under the authority of the "ordinary." Secret examinations were declared illegal. The offender was to be tried in open court, and, previous to his trial, had a right to be admitted to bail, unless the bishop could show cause to the contrary to the satisfaction of two magistrates. 680

This was but a slight instalment of lenity; but it was an indication of the turning tide. Limited as it was, the act operated as an effective check upon persecution till the passing of the Six Articles Bill.

Turning next to the relations between England and Rome, the parliament reviewed the Annates Act, 681 which had been left unratified in the hope that the pope might have consented to a compromise, and that "by some gentle ways the said exaction might have been redressed and reformed." The expectation had been disappointed. The pope had not condescended to reply to the communication which had been made to him, and the act had in consequence received the royal assent. An alteration had thus become necessary in the manner of presentation to vacant bishoprics. The anomalies of the existing practice have been already described. By the Great Charter the chapters had acquired the right of free election. A *congé d'élire* was granted by the king on the occurrence of a vacancy, with no attempt at a nomination. The chapters were supposed to make their choice freely, and the name of the bishop-elect was forwarded to the pope, who returned the Pallium and the Bulls, receiving the Annates in exchange. The pope's part in the matter was now terminated. No Annates would be sent any longer to Rome, and no Bulls would be returned from Rome. The appointments lay between the chapters and the crown; and it might have seemed, at first sight, as if it would have been sufficient to omit the reference to the papacy, and as if the remaining forms might continue as they were. The chapters, however, had virtually long ceased to elect freely; the crown had absorbed the entire functions of presentation, sometimes appointing foreigners, 682 sometimes allowing the great ecclesiastical ministers to nominate themselves; 683 while the rights of the chapters, though existing in theory, were not officially recognised either by the pope or by the crown. The king affected to accept the names of the prelates-elect, when returned to him from Rome, as nominations by the pope; and the pope, in communicating with the chapters, presented them with their bishops as from himself. 684 The papal share in the matter was a shadow, but it was acknowledged under the forms of courtesy; the share of the chapters was wholly and absolutely ignored. The crisis of a revolution was not the moment at which their legal privileges could be safely restored to them. The problem of re-arrangement was a difficult one, and it was met in a manner peculiarly English. The practice of granting the *congé d'élire* to the chapters on the occurrence of a vacancy, which had fallen into desuetude, was again adopted, and the church resumed the forms of liberty: but the licence to elect a bishop was to be accompanied with the name of the person whom the chapter was required to elect; and if within twelve days the person so named had not been chosen, the nomination of the crown was to become absolute, and the chapter would incur a Premunire. 685

This act, which I conceive to have been more arbitrary in form than in intention, was followed by a closing attack upon the remaining "exactions" of the Bishop of Rome. The Annates were gone. There were yet to go, "Pensions, Censes, Peter's Pence, Procurations, Fruits, Suits for Provision, Delegacies and Rescripts in causes of Contention and Appeals, Jurisdictions legatine—also Dispensations, Licenses, Faculties, Grants, Relaxations, Writs called Perinde valere, Rehabilitations, Abolitions," with other unnamed (the parliament being wearied of naming them) "infinite sorts of Rules, Briefs, and instruments of sundry natures, names, and kinds." All these were perennially open sluices, which had drained England of its wealth for centuries, returning only in showers of paper, and the Commons were determined that streams so unremunerative should flow no longer. They conceived that they had been all along imposed upon, and that the "Bishop of Rome was to be blamed for having allured and beguiled the English nation, persuading them that he had power to dispense with human laws, uses, and customs, contrary to right and conscience." If the king so pleased, therefore, they would not be so beguiled any more. These and all similar exactions should cease; and all powers claimed by the Bishop of Rome within the realm should cease, and should be transferred to the crown. At the same time they would not press upon the pope too hardly; they would repeat the same conditions which they had offered with the Annates. He had received these revenues as the supreme judge in the highest court in Europe, and he might retain his revenues or receive compensation for them, if he dared to be just. It was for himself to resolve, and three months were allowed for a final decision.

In conclusion, the Commons thought it well to assert that they were separating, not from the church of Christ, but only from the papacy. A judge who allowed himself to be overawed against his conscience by a secular power, could not any longer be recognised; but no thing or things contained in the act should be afterwards "interpreted or expounded, that his Grace (the king), his nobles and subjects, intended by the same to decline or vary from the congregation of Christ's church in anything concerning the articles of the Catholic faith of Christendom, or in any other things declared by the Holy Scripture and the Word of God necessary for salvation; but only to make an ordinance, by policies necessary and convenient, to repress vice, and for the good conservation of the realm in peace, unity, and tranquillity, from ravin and spoil—ensuing much the old antient customs of the realm in that behalf." 686

The most arduous business was thus finished—the most painful remained. The Nun of Kent and her accomplices were to be proceeded against by act of parliament; and the bill of their attainder was presented for the first time in the House of Lords, on the 18th of February. The offence of the principal conspirators was plainly high treason; their own confessions removed uncertainty; the guilt was clear—the sentence was inevitable. But the fault of those who had been listeners only was less easy of measurement, and might vary from comparative innocence to a definite breach of allegiance.

The government were unwilling to press with severity on the noble lords and ladies whose names had been unexpectedly brought to light; and there were two men of high rank only, whose complicity it was thought necessary to notice. The Bishop of Rochester's connection with the Nun had been culpably encouraging; and the responsibility of Sir Thomas More was held also to be very great in having countenanced, however lightly, such perilous schemers.

In the bill, therefore, as it was first read, More and Fisher found themselves declared guilty of misprision of treason. But the object of this measure was rather to warn than to punish, nor was there any real intention of continuing their prosecution. Cromwell, under instructions from the king, had communicated privately with both of them. He had sent a message to Fisher through his brother, telling him that he had only to ask for forgiveness to receive it; 687 and he had begged More through his son-in-law, Mr. Roper, to furnish him with an explicit account of what had passed at any time between himself and the Nun, 688 with an intimation that, if honestly made, it would be accepted in his favour.

These advances were met by More in the spirit in which they were offered. He heartily thanked Cromwell, "reckoning himself right deeply beholden to him;" 689 and replied with a long, minute, and evidently veracious story, detailing an interview which he had held with the woman in the chapel of Sion Monastery. He sent at the same time a copy of a letter which he had written to her, and described various conversations with the friars who were concerned in the forgery. He did not deny that he had believed the Nun to have been inspired, or that he had heard of the language which she was in the habit of using respecting the king. He protested, however, that he had himself never entertained a treasonable thought. He told Cromwell that "he had done a very meritorious deed in bringing forth to light such detestable hypocrisy, whereby every other wretch might take warning, and be feared to set forth their devilish dissembled falsehoods under the manner and colour of the wonderful work of God." 690 More's offence had not been great. His acknowledgments were open and unreserved; and Cromwell laid his letter before the king, adding his own intercession that the matter might be passed over. Henry consented, expressing only his grief and concern that Sir Thomas More should have acted so unwisely. 691 He required, nevertheless, as Cromwell suggested, that a formal letter should be written, with a confession of fault, and a request for forgiveness. More obeyed; he wrote, gracefully reminding the king of a promise when he resigned the chancellorship, that in any suit which he might afterwards have to his

Grace, either touching his honour or his profit, he should find his Highness his good and gracious lord. 692 Henry acknowledged his claim; his name was struck out of the bill, and the prosecution against him was dropped.

Fisher's conduct was very different; his fault had been far greater than More's, and promises more explicit had been held out to him of forgiveness. He replied to these promises by an elaborate and ridiculous defence—not writing to the king, as Cromwell desired him, but vindicating himself as having committed no fault; although he had listened eagerly to language which was only pardonable on the assumption that it was inspired, and had encouraged a nest of fanatics by his childish credulity. The Nun "had showed him not," he said, "that any prince or temporal lord should put the king in danger of his crown." He knew nothing of the intended insurrection. He believed the woman to have been a saint; he supposed that she had herself told the king all which she had told to him; and therefore he said that he had nothing for which to reproach himself. 693 He was unable to see that the exposure of the imposture had imparted a fresh character to his conduct, which he was bound to regret. Knowingly or unknowingly, he had lent his countenance to a conspiracy; and so long as he refused to acknowledge his indiscretion, the government necessarily would interpret his actions in the manner least to his advantage.

If he desired that his conduct should be forgotten, it was indispensable that he should change his attitude, and so Cromwell warned him. "Ye desire," the latter wrote, "for the passion of Christ, that ye be no more quickened in this matter; for if ye be put to that strait ye will not lose your soul, but ye will speak as your conscience leadeth you; with many more words of great courage. My Lord, if ye had taken my counsel sent unto you by your brother, and followed the same, submitting yourself by your letter to the King's Grace for your offences in this behalf, I would have trusted that ye should never be quickened in the matter more. But now where ye take upon you to defy the whole matter as ye were in no default, I cannot so far promise you. Wherefore, my Lord, I would eftsoons advise you that, laying apart all such excuses as ye have alleged in your letters, which in my opinion be of small effect, ye beseech the King's Grace to be your gracious lord and to remit unto you your negligence, oversight, and offence committed against his Highness in this behalf; and I dare undertake that his Highness shall benignly accept you into his gracious favour, all matter of displeasure past afore this time forgotten and forgiven." 694

Fisher must have been a hopelessly impracticable person. Instead of following More's example, and accepting well-meant advice, he persisted in the same tone, and drew up an address to the House of Lords, in which he repeated the defence which he had made to Cromwell. He expressed no sorrow that he had been engaged in a criminal intrigue, no pleasure that the intrigue had been discovered; and he doggedly adhered to his assertions of his own innocence. 695

There was nothing to be done except to proceed with his attainder. The bill passed three readings, and the various prisoners were summoned to the Star Chamber to be heard in arrest of judgment. The Bishop of Rochester's attendance was dispensed with on the ground of illness, and because he had made his defence in writing. 696 Nothing of consequence was urged by either of the accused. The bill was most explicit in its details, going carefully through the history of the imposture, and dwelling on the separate acts of each offender. They were able to disprove no one of its clauses, and on the 12th of March it was read a last time. On the 21st it received the royal assent, and there remained only to execute the sentence. The Nun herself, Richard Masters, and the five friars being found guilty of high treason, were to die; the Bishop of Rochester, Father Abel, Queen Catherine's confessor, and four more, were sentenced for misprision of treason to forfeiture of goods and imprisonment. All other persons implicated whose names did not appear, were declared pardoned at the intercession of Queen Anne. 697

The chief offenders suffered at Tyburn on the 21st of April, meeting death calmly, as it appears; receiving a fate most necessary and most deserved, 698 yet claiming from us that partial respect which is due to all persons who will risk their lives in an unselfish cause. For the Nun herself, we may feel even a less qualified regret. Before her death she was permitted to speak a few words to the people, which at the distance of three centuries will not be read without emotion.

"Hither am I come to die," she said, "and I have not been the only cause of mine own death, which most justly I have deserved; but also I am the cause of the death of all these persons which at this time here suffer. And yet I am not so much to be blamed, considering that it was well known unto these learned men that I was a poor wench without learning; and therefore they might have easily perceived that the things which were done by me could not proceed in no such sort; but their capacities and learning could right well judge that they were altogether feigned. But because the things which I feigned were profitable unto them, therefore they much praised me, and bare me in hand that it was the Holy Ghost and not I that did them. And I being puffed up with their praises, fell into a pride and foolish fantasye with myself, and thought I might feign what I would, which thing hath brought me to this case, and for the which I now cry God and the King's Highness most heartily mercy, and desire all you good people to pray to God to have mercy on me, and on all them that here suffer with me." 699

And now the closing seal was to be affixed to the agitation of the great question of the preceding years. I have said that throughout these years the uncertainty of the succession had been the continual anxiety of the nation. The birth of a prince or princess could alone provide an absolute security; and to beget a prince appeared to be the single feat which Henry was unable to accomplish. The marriage so dearly bought had been followed as yet only by a girl; and if the king were to die, leaving two daughters circumstanced as Mary and Elizabeth were circumstanced, a dispute would open which the sword only could decide. To escape the certainty of civil war, therefore, it was necessary to lay down the line of inheritance by a peremptory order; to cut off resolutely all rival claims; and in legislating upon a matter so vital, and hitherto so uncertain and indeterminate, to enforce the decision with the most stringent and exacting penalties. From the Heptarchy downwards English history furnished no fixed rule of inheritance, but only a series of precedents of uncertainty; and while at no previous time had the circumstances of the succession been of a nature so legitimately embarrassing, the relations of England with the pope and with foreign powers doubly enhanced the danger. But I will not use my own language on so important a subject. The preamble of the Act of Succession is the best interpreter of the provisions of that act.

"In their most humble wise show unto your Majesty your most humble and obedient subjects, the Lords Spiritual and Temporal and the Commons, in this present parliament assembled; that since it is the natural inclination of every man gladly and willingly to provide for the safety of both his title and succession, although it touch only his private cause; we therefore, most rightful and dreadful Sovereign Lord, reckon ourselves much more bounden to beseech and intreat your Highness (although we doubt not of your princely heart and wisdom, mixed with a natural affection to the same) to foresee and provide for the most perfect surety of both you and of your most lawful successors and heirs, upon which dependeth all our joy and wealth; in whom also is united and knit the only mere true inheritance and title of this realm without any contradiction. We, your said most humble and obedient servants, call to our remembrance the great divisions which in times past hath been in this realm by reason of several titles pretended to the imperial crown of the same; which some time and for the most part ensued by occasion of ambiguity, and [by] doubts then not so perfectly declared but that men might upon froward intents expound them to every man's sinister appetite and affection after their senses; whereof hath ensued great destruction and effusion of man's blood, as well of a great number of the nobles as of other the subjects and specialty inheritors in the same. The greatest occasion thereof hath been because no perfect and substantial provision by law hath been made within this realm itself when doubts and questions have been moved; by reason whereof the Bishops of Rome and See Apostolic have presumed in times past to invest who should please them to inherit in other men's kingdoms and dominions, which thing we your most humble subjects, both spiritual and temporal, do much abhor and detest. And sometimes other foreign princes and potentates of sundry degrees, minding rather dissension and discord to continue in the realm than charity, equity, or unity, have many times supported wrong titles, whereby they might the more easily and facilly aspire to the superiority of the same.

"The continuance and sufferance of these things, deeply considered and pondered, is too dangerous and perilous to be suffered any longer; and too much contrary to unity, peace, and tranquillity, being greatly reproachable and dishonourable to the whole realm. And in consideration thereof, your said subjects, calling further to their remembrance, that the good unity, peace, and wealth of the realm, specially and principally, above all worldly things, consisteth in the surety and certainty of the procreation and posterity of your Highness, in whose most Royal person at this time is no manner of doubt, do therefore most humbly beseech your Highness that it may be enacted, with the consent of the Lords Spiritual and Temporal and the Commons in this present parliament assembled—

"1. That the marriage between your Highness and the Lady Catherine, widow of the late Prince Arthur, be declared to have been from the beginning, null, the issue of it illegitimate, and the separation pronounced by the Archbishop of Canterbury good and valid.

"2. That the marriage between your Highness and your most dear and entirely beloved wife, Queen Anne, be established and held good, and taken for undoubtful, true, sincere, and perfect, ever hereafter." 701

The act then assumed a general character, laying down a table of prohibited degrees, within which marriage might not under any pretence be in future contracted; and demanding that any marriage which might already exist within those degrees should be at once dissolved. After this provision, it again returned to the king, and fixed the order in which his children by Queen Anne were to succeed. The details of the regulations were minute and elaborate, and the rule to be observed was the same as that which exists at present. First, the sons were to succeed with their heirs. If sons failed, then the daughters, with their heirs; and, in conclusion, it was resolved that any person who should maliciously do anything by writing, printing, or other external act or deed to the peril of the king, or to the prejudice of his marriage with Queen Anne, or to the derogation of the issue of that marriage, should be held guilty of high treason; and whoever should speak against that marriage, should be held guilty of misprision of treason—severe enactments, such as could not be justified at ordinary times, and such as, if the times had been ordinary, would not have been thought necessary—but the exigencies of the country could not tolerate an uncertainty of title in the heir to the crown; and the title could only be secured by prohibiting absolutely the discussion of dangerous questions.

The mere enactment of a statute, whatever penalties were attached to the violation of it, was still, however, an insufficient safeguard. The recent investigation had revealed a spirit of disloyalty, where such a spirit had not been expected. The deeper the inquiry had penetrated, the more clearly appeared tokens, if not of conspiracy, yet of excitement, of doubt, of agitation, of alienated feeling, if not of alienated act. All the symptoms were abroad which provide disaffection with its opportunity; and in the natural confusion which attended the revolt from the papacy, the obligations of duty, both political and religious, had become indefinite and contradictory, pointing in all directions, like the magnetic needle in a thunderstorm.

It was thought well, therefore, to vest a power in the crown, of trying the tempers of suspected persons, and examining them upon oath, as to their willingness to maintain the decision of parliament. This measure was a natural corollary of the statute, and depended for its justification on the extent of the danger to which the state was exposed. If a difference of opinion on the legitimacy of the king's children, or of the pope's power in England, was not dangerous, it was unjust to interfere with the natural liberty of speech or thought. If it was dangerous, and if the state had cause for supposing that opinions of the kind might spread in secret so long as no opportunity was offered for detecting their progress, to require the oath was a measure of reasonable self-defence, not permissible only, but in a high degree necessary and right.

Under the impression, then, that the circumstances of the country demanded extraordinary precautions, a commission was appointed, consisting of the Archbishop of Canterbury, the Lord Chancellor, the Duke of Norfolk, and the Duke of Suffolk; and these four, or any three of them, were empowered to administer, at the pleasure of the king, "to all and singular liege subjects of the realm," the following oath:—

"Ye shall swear to bear your faith, truth, and obedience only to the King's Majesty, and to the heirs of his body, according to the limitation and rehearsal within the statute of succession; and not to any other within this realm, or foreign authority, prince, or potentate: and in case any oath be made or hath been made by you to any other person or persons, that then you do repute the same as vain and annihilate: and that to your cunning, wit, and utmost of your power, without guile, fraud, or other undue means, ye shall observe, keep, maintain, and defend this act above specified, and all the whole contents and effects thereof; and all other acts and statutes made since the beginning of this present parliament, in confirmation or for due execution of the same, or of anything therein contained. And thus ye shall do against all manner of persons, of what estate, dignity, degree, or condition soever they be; and in no wise do or attempt, or to your power suffer to be done or attempted, directly or indirectly, any thing or things, privily or apertly, to the let, hindrance, damage, or derogation thereof, by any manner of means, or for any pretence or cause, so help you God and all saints." 702

With this last resolution the House rose, having sat seventy-five days, and despatched their business swiftly. A week later, the news arrived from Rome that there too all was at length over; that the cause was decided, and decided against the king. The history of the closing catastrophe is as obscure as it is strange, and the account of the manner in which it was brought about is unfortunately incomplete in many important particulars. The outline only can be apprehended, and that very imperfectly.

On the receipt in Paris of the letter in which Henry threatened to organise a Protestant confederacy, Du Bellay, in genuine anxiety for the welfare of Christendom, had volunteered his services for a final effort. Not a moment was to be lost, for the courts of Rome were already busy with the great cause; but the king's evident reluctance to break with the Catholic powers, gave room for hope that something might still be done; and going in person to England, the bishop had induced Henry, at the last extremity, either to entrust him with representative powers, or else to allow him after all to make some kind of concession. I am unable to learn the extent to which Henry yielded, but that an offer was made of some kind is evident from the form of the story. 703 The winter was very cold, but the bishop made his way to Rome with the haste of good will, and arrived in time to stay judgment, which was on the point of being pronounced. It seemed, for the moment, as if he would succeed. He was permitted to make engagements on the part of Henry; and that time might be allowed for communication with England, the pope agreed to delay sentence till the 23rd of March. This bishop's terms were approved by the king, and a courier was sent off with letters of confirmation; Sir Edward Karne and Dr. Revett following leisurely, with a more ample commission. The stone which had been laboriously rolled to the summit of the hill was trembling on the brink, and in a moment might rebound into the plain.

But this was not to be the end. Some accidental cause delayed the courier; the 23rd of March came, and he had not arrived. Du Bellay implored a further respite. The King of England, he said, had waited six years; it was not a great thing for the papal council to wait six days. The cardinals were divided; but the Spanish party were the strongest, and when the votes were taken carried the day. The die was cast, and the pope, in spite of himself, his promises, and his conscience, drove at length upon the rocks to which he had been so long drifting. 704 In deference to the opinion of the majority of the cardinals, he pronounced the original marriage to have been valid, the dispensation by which it was permitted to have been legal; and, as a natural consequence, Henry, King of England, should he fail in obedience to this judgment, was declared to be excommunicate from the fellowship of the church, and to have forfeited the allegiance of his subjects.

Lest the censures should be discredited by a blank discharge, engagements were entered into, that within four months of the promulgation of the sentence, the emperor would invade England, and Henry should be deposed. 705 The imperialists illuminated Rome; cannon were fired; bonfires blazed; and great bodies of men paraded the streets with shouts of "the Empire and Spain." 706 Already, in their eager expectation, England was a second Netherlands, a captured province under the regency of Catherine or Mary.

Two days later, the courier arrived. The pope, at the entreaties of the Bishop of Paris, re-assembled the consistory, to consider whether the steps which had been taken should be undone. They sat debating all night, and the result was nothing. No dependence could be placed on the cardinals, Du Bellay said, for they spoke one way, and voted another. 707

Thus all was over. In a scene of general helplessness the long drama closed, and, what we call accident, for want of some better word, cut the knot at last over which human incapacity had so vainly laboured. The Bishop of Paris retired from Rome in despair. On his way back, he met the English commissioners at Bologna, and told them that their errand was hopeless, and that they need not proceed. "When we asked him," wrote Sir Edward Karne to the king, "the cause of such hasty process, he made answer that the imperialists at Rome had strengthened themselves in such a manner, that they coacted the said Bishop of Rome to give sentence contrary to his own mind, and the expectation of himself and of the French king. He showed us also that the Lady Princess Dowager sent lately, in the month of March past, letters to the Bishop of Rome, and also to her proctors, whereby the Bishop of Rome was much moved for her part. The imperials, before the sentence was given, promised, in the emperor's behalf, that he would be the executor of the sentence." 708

This is all which we are able to say of the immediate catastrophe which decided the fate of England, and through England, of the world. The deep impenetrable falsehood of the Roman ecclesiastics prevents us from discovering with what intentions the game of the last few weeks or months had been played; it is sufficient for Englishmen to remember that, whatever may have been the explanation of his conduct, the pope, in the concluding passage of his connection with this country, furnished the most signal justification which was ever given for the revolt from an abused authority. The supreme judge in Christendom had for six years trifled with justice, out of fear of an earthly prince; he concluded these years with uniting the extreme of folly with the extreme of improbity, and pronounced a sentence, willingly or unwillingly, which he had acknowledged to be unjust.

Charity may possibly acquit Clement of conscious duplicity. He was one of those men who waited upon fortune, and waited always without success; who gave his word as the interest of the moment suggested, trusting that it might be convenient to observe it; and who was too long accustomed to break his promises to look with any particular alarm on that contingency. It is possible, also,—for of this Clement was capable—that he knew from the beginning the conclusion to which he would at last be driven; that he had engaged himself with Charles to decide in Catherine's favour as distinctly as he had engaged himself with Francis to decide against her; and that all his tortuous scheming was intended either to weary out the patience of the King of England, or to entangle him in acknowledgments from which he would not be able to extricate himself.

He was mistaken, certainly, in the temper of the English nation; he believed what the friars told him; and trusting to the promises of disaffection, insurrection, invasion—those *ignes fatui* which for sixty years floated so delusively before the Italian imagination, he imagined, perhaps, that he might trifle with Henry with impunity. This only is impossible, that, if he had seriously intended to fulfil the promises which he had made to the French king, the accidental delay of a courier could have made so large a difference in his determination. It is not possible that, if he had assured himself, as he pretended, that justice was on the side against which he had declared, he would not have availed himself of any pretext to retreat from a position which ought to have been intolerable to him.

The question, however, had ended, "as all things in this world do have their end." The news of the sentence arrived in England at the beginning of April, with an intimation of the engagements which had been entered upon by the imperial ambassador for an invasion. Du Bellay returned to Paris at the same time, to report the failure of his undertaking; and Francis, disappointed, angry, and alarmed, sent the Duke of Guise to London with promises of support if an attempt to invade was really made, and with a warning at the same time to Henry to prepare for danger. Troops were gathering in Flanders; detachments were on their way out of Italy, Germany, and Bohemia, to be followed by three thousand Spaniards, and perhaps many more; and the object avowed for these preparations was wholly incommensurate with their magnitude. 709 For his own sake Francis could not permit a successful invasion of England, unless, indeed, he himself was to take part in it; and therefore, with entire sincerity, he offered his services. The cordial understanding for which Henry had hoped was at an end; but the political confederacy remained, which the interests of the two countries combined for the present to preserve unbroken.

Guise proposed another interview at Calais between the sovereigns. The king for the moment was afraid to leave England, 710 lest the opportunity should be made use of for an insurrection; but prudence taught him, though disappointed in Francis, to make the best of a connection too convenient to be sacrificed. The German league was left in abeyance till the immediate danger was passed, and till the effect of the shock in England itself had been first experienced. He gladly accepted, in lieu of it, an offer that the French fleet should guard the Channel through the summer; and meanwhile, he collected himself resolutely, to abide the issue, whatever the issue was to be.

The Tudor spirit was at length awake in the English sovereign. He had exhausted the resources of patience; he had stooped even to indignity to avoid the conclusion which had come at last. There was nothing left but to meet defiance by defiance, and accept the position to which the pope had driven him. In quiet times occasionally wayward and capricious, Henry, like Elizabeth after him, reserved his noblest nature for the moment of danger, and was ever greatest when peril was most immediate. Woe to those who crossed him now, for the time was grown stern, and to trifle further was to be lost. The suspended act of parliament was made law on the day (it would seem) of the arrival of the sentence. Convocation, which was still sitting, hurried through a declaration that the pope had no more power in England than any other bishop. 711 Five years before, if a heretic had ventured so desperate an opinion, the clergy would have shut their ears and run upon him: now they only contended with each other in precipitate obsequiousness. The houses of the Observants at Canterbury and Greenwich, which had been implicated with the Nun of Kent, were suppressed, and the brethren were scattered among monasteries where they could be under surveillance. The Nun and her friends were sent to execution. 712 The ordnance stores were examined, the repairs of the navy were hastened, and the garrisons were strengthened along the coast. Everywhere the realm armed itself for the struggle, looking well to the joints of its harness and to the temper of its weapons.

The commission appointed under the Statute of Succession opened its sittings to receive the oaths of allegiance. Now, more than ever, was it necessary to try men's dispositions, when the pope had challenged their obedience. In words all went well: the peers swore; bishops, abbots, priors, heads of colleges swore 713 with scarcely an exception,—the nation seemed to unite in an unanimous declaration of freedom. In one quarter only, and that a very painful one, was there refusal. It was found solely among the persons who had been implicated in the late conspiracy. Neither Sir Thomas More nor the Bishop of Rochester could expect that their recent conduct would exempt them from an obligation which the people generally accepted with good will. They had connected themselves, perhaps unintentionally, with a body of confessed traitors. An opportunity was offered them of giving evidence of their loyalty, and escaping from the shadow of distrust. More had been treated leniently; Fisher had been treated far more than leniently. It was both fair and natural that they should be called upon to give proof that their lesson had not been learnt in vain; and, in fact, no other persons, if they had been passed over, could have been called upon to swear, for no other persons had laid themselves open to so just suspicion.

Their conduct so exactly tallied, that they must have agreed beforehand on the course which they would adopt; and in following the details, we need concern ourselves only with the nobler figure.

The commissioners sate at the archbishop's palace at Lambeth; and at the end of April, Sir Thomas More received a summons to appear before them. 714 He was at his house at Chelsea, where for the last two years he had lived in deep retirement, making ready for evil times. Those times at length were come. On the morning on which he was to present himself, he confessed and received the sacrament in Chelsea church; and "whereas," says his great-grandson, "at other times, before he parted from his wife and children, they used to bring him to his boat, and he there kissing them bade them farewell, at this time he suffered none of them to follow him forth of his gate, but pulled the wicket after him, and with a heavy heart he took boat with his son Roper." 715 He was leaving his home for the last time, and he knew it. He sat silent for some minutes, and then, with a sudden start, said, "I thank our Lord, the field is won." Lambeth Palace was crowded with people who had come on the same errand with himself. More was called in early, and found Cromwell present with the four commissioners, and also the Abbot of Westminster. The oath was read to him. It implied that he should keep the statute of succession in all its parts, and he desired to see the statute itself. He read it through, and at once replied that others might do as they pleased; he would blame no one for taking the oath; but for himself it was impossible. He would swear willingly to the part of it which secured the succession to the children of Queen Anne. 716 That was a matter on which parliament was competent to decide, and he had no right to make objections. If he might be allowed to take an oath to this portion of the statute in language of his own, he would do it; but as the words stood, he would "peril his soul" by using them. The Lord Chancellor desired him to re-consider his answer. He retired to the garden, and in his absence others were called in; among them the Bishop of Rochester, who refused in the same terms. More was then recalled. He was asked if he persisted in his resolution; and when he replied that he did, he was requested to state his reasons. He said that he was afraid of increasing the king's displeasure, but if he could be assured that he might explain himself safely he was ready to do so. If his objection could then be answered to his satisfaction, he would swear; in the meantime, he repeated, very explicitly, that he judged no one—he spoke only for himself.

An opening seemed to be offered in these expressions which was caught at by Cranmer's kind-hearted casuistry. If Sir Thomas More could not condemn others for taking the oath, the archbishop said, Sir Thomas More could not be sure that it was sin to take it; while his duty to his king and to the parliament was open and unquestioned.

More hesitated for an instant, but he speedily recovered his firmness. He had considered what he ought to do, he said; his conscience was clear about it, and he could say no more than he had said already. They continued to argue with him, but without effect; he had made up his mind; the victory, as he said, had been won.

Cromwell was deeply affected. In his passionate regret, he exclaimed, that he had rather his only son had lost his head than that More should have refused the oath. No one knew better than Cromwell that intercession would be of no further use; that he could not himself advise the king to give way. The parliament, after grave consideration, had passed a law which they held necessary to secure the peace of the country; and two persons of high rank refused obedience to it, whose example would tell in every English household. Either, therefore, the act was not worth the parchment on which it was written, or the penalties of it must be enforced: no middle way, no compromise, no acquiescent reservations, could in such a case be admitted. The law must have its way.

The recusants were committed for four days to the keeping of the Abbot of Westminster; and the council met to determine on the course to be pursued. Their offence, by the act, was misprision of treason. On the other hand, they had both offered to acknowledge the Princess Elizabeth as the lawful heir to the throne; and the question was raised whether this offer should be accepted. It was equivalent to a demand that the form should be altered, not for them only, but for every man. If persons of their rank and notoriety were permitted to swear with a qualification, the same privilege must be conceded to all. But there was so much anxiety to avoid extremities, and so warm a regard was personally felt for Sir Thomas More, that this objection was not allowed to be fatal. It was thought that possibly an exception might be made, yet kept a secret from the world; and the fact that they had sworn under any form might go far to silence objectors and reconcile the better class of the disaffected. 717 This view was particularly urged by Cranmer, always gentle, hoping, and illogical. 718 But, in fact, secresy was impossible. If More's discretion could have been relied upon, Fisher's babbling tongue would have trumpeted his victory to all the winds. Nor would the government consent to pass censure on its own conduct by evading the question whether the act was or was not just. If it was not just, it ought not to be: maintained at all; if it was just, there must be no respect of persons.

The clauses to which the bishop and the ex-chancellor declined to bind themselves were those which declared illegal the marriage of the king with Catherine, and the marriage legal between the king and Queen Anne. To refuse these was to declare Mary legitimate, to declare Elizabeth illegitimate, and would do more to strengthen Mary's claims than could be undone by a thousand oaths. However large might be More's estimate of the power of parliament, he could have given no clear answer—and far less could Fisher have given a clear answer—if they had been required to say the part which they would take, should the emperor invade the kingdom under the pope's sanction. The emperor would come to execute a sentence which in their consciences they believed to be just; how could they retain their allegiance to Henry, when their convictions must be with the invading army?

What ought to have been done let those say who disapprove of what was actually done. The high character of the prisoners, while it increased the desire, increased the difficulty of sparing them; and to have given way would have been a confession of a doubtful cause, which at such a time would not have been dangerous, but would have been fatal. Anne Boleyn is said to have urged the king to remain peremptory; 719 but the following letter of Cromwell's explains the ultimate resolution of the council in a very reasonable manner. It was written to Cranmer in reply to his arguments for concession.

"My Lord, after mine humble commendation, it may please your Grace to be advertised that I have received your letter, and showed the same to the King's Highness; who, perceiving that your mind and opinion is, that it were good that the Bishop of Rochester and Master More should be sworn to the act of the king's succession, and not to the preamble of the same, thinketh that if their oaths should be taken, it were an occasion to all men to refuse the whole, or at least the like. For, in case they be sworn to the succession, and not to the preamble, it is to be thought that it might be taken not only as a confirmation of the Bishop of Rome's authority, but also as a reprobation of the king's second marriage. Wherefore, to the intent that no such things should be brought into the heads of the people, by the example of the said Bishop of Rochester and Master More, the King's Highness in no wise willeth but that they shall be sworn as well to the preamble as to the act. Wherefore his Grace specially trusteth that ye will in no wise attempt to move him to the contrary; for as his Grace supposeth, that manner of swearing, if it shall be suffered, may be an utter destruction to his whole cause, and also to the effect of the law made for the same." 720

Thus, therefore, with much regret the council decided—and, in fact, why should they have decided otherwise? They were satisfied that they were right in requiring the oath; and their duty to the English nation obliged them to persevere. They must go their way; and those who thought them wrong must go theirs; and the great God would judge between them. It was a hard thing to suffer for an opinion; but there are times when opinions are as dangerous as acts; and liberty of conscience was a plea which could be urged with a bad grace for men who, while in power, had fed the stake with heretics. They were summoned for a last time, to return the same answer as they had returned before; and nothing remained but to pronounce against them the penalties of the statute, imprisonment at the king's pleasure, and forfeiture. The latter part of the sentence was not enforced. More's family were left in the enjoyment of his property. Fisher's bishoprick was not taken from him. They were sent to the Tower, where for the present we leave them.

Meanwhile, in accordance with the resolution taken in council on the and of December, 721 but which seems to have been suspended till the issue of the trial at Rome was decided, the bishops, who had been examined severally on the nature of the papal authority, and whose answers had been embodied in the last act of parliament, were now required to instruct the clergy throughout their dioceses—and the clergy in turn to instruct the people—in the nature of the changes which had taken place. A bishop was to preach each Sunday at Paul's Cross, on the pope's usurpation. Every secular priest was directed to preach on the same subject week after week, in his parish church. Abbots and priors were to teach their convents; noblemen and gentlemen their families and servants; mayors and aldermen the boroughs. In town and country, in all houses, at all dinner-tables, the conduct of the pope and the causes of the separation from Rome were to be the one subject of conversation; that the whole nation might be informed accurately and faithfully of the grounds on which the government had acted. No wiser method could have been adopted. The imperial agents would be busy under the surface; and the mendicant friars, and all the missionaries of insurrection. The machinery of order was set in force to counteract the machinery of sedition.

Further, every bishop, in addition to the oath of allegiance, had sworn obedience to the king as Supreme Head of the Church; 722 and this was the title under which he was to be spoken of in all churches of the realm. A royal order had been issued, "that all manner of prayers, rubrics, canons of Mass books, and all other books in the churches wherein the Bishop of Rome was named, or his presumptuous and proud pomp and authority preferred, should utterly be abolished, eradicated, and rased out, and his name and memory should be never more, except to his contumely and reproach, remembered; but perpetually be suppressed and obscured." 723

Nor were these mere idle sounds, like the bellow of unshotted cannon; but words with a sharp, prompt meaning, which the king intended to be obeyed. He had addressed his orders to the clergy, because the clergy were the officials who had possession of the pulpits from which the people were to be taught; but he knew their nature too well to trust them. They were too well schooled in the tricks of reservation; and, for the nonce, it was necessary to reverse the posture of the priest and of his flock, and to set the honest laymen to overlook their pastors.

With the instructions to the bishops circulars went round to the sheriffs of the counties, containing a full account of these instructions, and an appeal to their loyalty to see that the royal orders were obeyed. "We," the king wrote to them, "seeing, esteeming, and reputing you to be of such singular and vehement zeal and affection towards the glory of Almighty God, and of so faithful, loving, and obedient heart towards us, as you will accomplish, with all power, diligence, and labour, whatsoever shall be to the preferment and setting forth of God's word, have thought good, not only to signify unto you by these our letters, the particulars of the charge given by us to the bishops, but also to require and straitly charge you, upon pain of your allegiance, and as ye shall avoid our high indignation and displeasure, [that] at your uttermost peril, laying aside all vain affections, respects, and other carnal considerations, and setting only before your eyes the mirrour of the truth, the glory of God, the dignity of your Sovereign Lord and King, and the great concord and unity, and inestimable profit and utility, that shall by the due execution of the premises ensue to yourselves and to all other faithful and loving subjects, ye make or cause to be made diligent search and wait, whether the said bishops do truly and sincerely, without all manner of cloke, colour, or dissimulation, execute and accomplish our will and commandment, as is aforesaid. And in case ye shall hear that the said bishops, or any other ecclesiastical person, do omit and leave undone any part or parcel of the premises, or else in the execution and setting forth of the same, do coldly and feignedly use any manner of sinister addition, wrong interpretation, or painted colour, then we straitly charge and command you that you do make, undelayedly, and with all speed and diligence, declaration and advertisement to us and to our council of the said default.

"And forasmuch as we upon the singular trust which we have in you, and for the special love which we suppose you bear towards us, and the weal and tranquillity of this our realm, have specially elected and chosen you among so many for this purpose, and have reputed you such men as unto whose wisdom and fidelity we might commit a matter of such great weight and importance: if ye should, contrary to our expectation and trust which we have in you, and against your duty and allegiance towards us, neglect, or omit to do with all your diligence, whatsoever shall be in your power for the due performance of our pleasure to you declared, or halt or stumble at any part or specialty of the same; Be ye assured that we, like a prince of justice, will so extremely punish you for the same, that all the world beside shall take by you example, and beware contrary to their allegiance to disobey the lawful commandment of their Sovereign Lord and Prince.

"Given under our signet, at our Palace of Westminster, the 9th day of June, 1534." 724

So Henry spoke at last. There was no place any more for nice distinctions and care of tender consciences. The general, when the shot is flying, cannot qualify his orders with dainty periods. Swift command and swift obedience can alone be tolerated; and martial law for those who hesitate.

This chapter has brought many things to a close. Before ending it we will leap over three months, to the termination of the career of the pope who has been so far our companion. Not any more was the distracted Clement to twist his handkerchief, or weep, or flatter, or wildly wave his arms in angry impotence; he was to lie down in his long rest, and vex the world no more. He had lived to set England free—an exploit which, in the face of so persevering an anxiety to escape a separation, required a rare genius and a combination of singular qualities. He had finished his work, and now he was allowed to depart.

In him, infinite insincerity was accompanied with a grace of manner which regained confidence as rapidly as it was forfeited. Desiring sincerely, so far as he could be sincere in anything, to please every one by turns, and reckless of truth to a degree in which he was without a rival in the world, he sought only to escape his difficulties by inactivity, and he trusted to provide himself with a refuge against all contingencies by waiting upon time. Even when at length he was compelled to act, and to act in a distinct direction, his plausibility long enabled him to explain away his conduct; and, honest in the excess of his dishonesty, he wore his falsehood with so easy a grace that it assumed the character of truth. He was false, deceitful, treacherous; yet he had the virtue of not pretending to be virtuous. He was a real man, though but an indifferent one; and we can refuse to no one, however grave his faults, a certain ambiguous sympathy, when in his perplexities he shows us features so truly human in their weakness as those of Clement VII.

Notes.

1 Printed in FOXE, vol. iv. p. 659, Townsend's edition.

2 24 Hen. VIII. cap. 4.

3 Bishop Latimer, in a sermon at Paul's Cross, suggested another purpose which this act might answer. One of his audience, writing to the Mayor of Plymouth, after describing the exceedingly disrespectful language in which he spoke of the high church dignitaries, continues, "The king," quoth he, "made a marvellous good act of parliament that certain men should sow every of them two acres of hemp; but it were all too little were it so much more to hang the thieves that be in England." — *Suppression of the Monasteries*, Camden Society's publications, p. 38.

4 32 Hen. VIII. cap. 18.

5 25 Hen. VIII. cap. 18.

6 *Antiquities of Hengrave*, by Sir T. GAGE.

7 See especially 2 Hen. VII. capp. 16 and 19.

8 24 Hen. VIII. cap. 9.

9 See especially the 4th of the 5th of Elizabeth.

10 10 Ed. III. cap. 3.

11 Statutes of the Realm, vol. i. (edit. 1817), pp. 227-8.

12 "The artificers and husbandmen make most account of such meat as they may soonest come by and have it quickliest ready. Their food consisteth principally in beef, and such meat as the butcher selleth, that is to say, mutton, veal, lamb, pork, whereof the one findeth great store in the markets adjoining; besides souse, brawn, bacon, fruit, pies of fruit, fowls of sundry sorts, as the other wanteth it not at home by his own provision, which is at the best hand and commonly least charge. In feasting, this latter sort—I mean the husbandmen—do exceed after their manner, especially at bridals and such odd meetings, where it is incredible to tell what meat is consumed and spent." — HARRISON'S *Description of England*.

The Spanish nobles who came into England with Philip were astonished at the diet which they found among the poor.

"These English," said one of them, "have their houses made of sticks and dirt, but they fare commonly so well as the king." —Ibid. p. 313.

13 *State Papers*, Hen. VIII. vol. ii. p. 10.

14 HALL, p. 646.

15 25 Ed. III. cap. I.

16 *Statutes of the Realm*, vol. i. p. 199.

17 3 Ed. IV. cap. 2.

18 10 Hen. VI. cap. 2.

19 STOW'S *Chronicle*.

20 *Statutes of Philip and Mary*.

21 From 1565 to 1575 there was a rapid and violent rise in the prices of all kinds of grain. Wheat stood at four and five times its earlier rates; and in 1576, when Harrison wrote, was entirely beyond the reach of the labouring classes. "The poor in some shires," he says, "are enforced to content themselves with rye or barley, yea, and in time of dearth many with bread made either of peas, beans, or oats, or of all together and some acorns among, of which scourge the poorest do soonest taste, sith they are least able to provide themselves of better. I will not say that this extremity is oft so well seen in time of plenty as of dearth, but if I should I could easily bring my trial. For, albeit that there be much more ground eared now almost in every place than hath been of late years, yet such a price of corn continues in each town and market, that the artificer and poor labouring man is not able to reach to it, but is driven to content himself with beans, peas, oats, tares, and lentils." —HARRISON. The condition of the labourer was at this period deteriorating rapidly. The causes will be described in the progress of this history.

22 *Chronicle*

23 33 Hen. VIII. cap. II. The change in the prices of such articles commenced in the beginning of the reign of Edward VI., and continued till the close of the century. A discussion upon the subject, written in 1581 by Mr. Edward Stafford, and containing the clearest detailed account of the alteration, is printed in the *Harleian Miscellany*, vol. ix. p.139, etc.

24 Leland, *Itin.*, vol. vi. p.17. In large households beef used to be salted in great quantities for winter consumption. The art of fatting cattle in the stall was imperfectly understood, and the loss of substance in the destruction of fibre by salt was less than in the falling off of flesh on the failure of fresh grass. The Northumberland Household Book describes the storing of salted

provision for the earl's establishment at Michaelmas; and men now living can remember the array of salting tubs in old-fashioned country houses. So long as pigs, poultry, and other articles of food, however, remained cheap and abundant, the salt diet could not, as Hume imagines, have been carried to an extent injurious to health; and fresh meat, beef as well as mutton, was undoubtedly sold in all markets the whole year round in the reign of Henry VIII., and sold at a uniform price, which it could not have been if there had been so much difficulty in procuring it. Latimer (*Letters*, p.412), writing to Cromwell on Christmas Eve, 1538, speaks of his winter stock of "beeves" and muttons as a thing of course.

25 STAFFORD'S *Discourse on the State of the Realm*. It is to be understood, however, that these rates applied only to articles of ordinary consumption. Capons fatted for the dinners of the London companies were sometimes provided at a shilling apiece. Fresh fish was also extravagantly dear, and when two days a week were observed strictly as fasting days, it becomes a curious question to know how the supply was kept up. The inland counties were dependent entirely on ponds and rivers. London was provided either from the Thames or from the coast of Sussex. An officer of the Fishmongers' Company resided at each of the Cinque Ports whose business it was to buy the fish wholesale from the boats and to forward it on horseback. Three hundred horses were kept for this service at Rye alone. And when an adventurous fisherman, taking advantage of a fair wind, sailed up the Thames with his catch and sold it first hand at London Bridge, the innovation was considered dangerous, and the Mayor of Rye petitioned against it.

Salmon, sturgeon, porpoise, roach, dace, flounders, eels, etc., were caught in considerable quantities in the Thames, below London Bridge, and further up, pike and trout. The fishermen had great nets that stretched all across Limehouse-reach four fathoms deep.

Fresh fish, however, remained the luxury of the rich, and the poor were left to the salt cod, ling, and herring brought in annually by the Iceland fleet.

Fresh herrings sold for five or six a penny in the time of Henry VIII., and were never cheaper. Fresh salmon five and six shillings apiece. Roach, dace, and flounders from two to four shillings a hundred. Pike and barbel varied with their length. The barbel a foot long sold for five-pence, and twopence was added for each additional inch: a pike a foot long sold for sixteen pence, and increased a penny an inch. — *Guildhall MSS. Journals* 12, 13, 14, 15.

26 "When the brewer buyeth a quarter of malt for two shillings, then he shall sell a gallon of the best ale for two farthings; when he buyeth a quarter malt for four shillings, the gallon shall be four farthings, and so forth... and

that he sell a quart of ale upon his table for a farthing." — Assize of Brewers: from a MS. in Balliol College, Oxford.

By an order of the Lord Mayor and Council of the City of London, in September, 1529, the price of a kilderkin of single beer was fixed at a shilling, the kilderkin of double beer at two shillings; but this included the cask; and the London brewers replied with a remonstrance, saying that the casks were often destroyed or made away with, and that an allowance had to be made for bad debts. "Your beseechers," they said, "have many city debtors, for many of them which have taken much beer into their houses suddenly goeth to the sanctuary, some keep their houses—some purchase the king's protection, and some, when they die, be reckoned poor, and of no value, and many of your said beseechers be for the most part against such debtors remediless and suffer great losses."

They offered to supply then: customers with sixteen gallon casks of single beer for eleven pence, and the same quantity of double beer for a shilling, the cask included. And this offer was accepted.

The corporation, however, returned two years after to their original order. *Guildhall Records*, MS. Journal 13.

27 28 Hen. VIII. cap. 14.

The prices assessed, being a maximum, applied to the best wines of each class. In 1531, the mayor and corporation "did straitly charge and command that all such persons as sold wines by retail within the city and liberties of the same, should from henceforth sell two gallons of the best red wine for eightpence, and not above; the gallon of the best white wine for eightpence, and not above; the pottle, quart, and pint after the same rate, upon pain of imprisonment."

The quality of the wine sold was looked into from time to time, and when found tainted, or unwholesome, "according to the antient customs of the city," the heads of the vessels were broken up, and the wines in them put forth open into the kennels, in example of all other offenders. *Guildhall MS.* Journals 12 and 13.

28 *Sermons*, p.101.

29 See HARRISON. At the beginning of the century farms let for four pounds a year, which in 1576 had been raised to forty, fifty, or a hundred. The price of produce kept pace with the rent. The large farmers prospered; the poor forfeited their tenures.

30 The wages were fixed at a maximum, showing that labour was scarce, and that its natural tendency was towards a higher rate of remuneration.

Persons not possessed of other means of subsistence were punishable if they refused to work at the statutable rate of payment; and a clause in the act of Hen. VIII. directed that where the practice had been to give lower wages, lower wages should be taken. This provision was owing to a difference in the value of money in different parts of England. The price of bread at Stratford, for instance, was permanently twenty-five per cent. below the price in London. (Assize of Bread in England: *Balliol MS.*) The statute, therefore, may be taken as a guide sufficiently conclusive as to the practical scale. It is of course uncertain how far work was constant. The ascending tendency of wages is an evidence, so far as it goes, in the labourer's favour; and the proportion between the wages of the household farm servant and those of the day labourer, which furnishes a further guide, was much the same as at present. By the same statute of Henry VIII. the common servant of husbandry, who was boarded and lodged at his master's house, received 16s. 8d. a year in money, with 4s. for his clothes; while the wages of the out-door labourer, supposing his work constant, would have been £5 a year. Among ourselves, on an average of different counties, the labourer's wages are £25 to £30 a year, supposing his work constant. The farm servant, unless in the neighbourhood of large towns, receives about £6, or from that to £8.

Where meat and drink was allowed it was calculated at 2d. a day, or 1s. 2d. a week. In the household of the Earl of Northumberland the allowance was 2½d. Here, again, we observe an approach to modern proportions. The estimated cost of the board and lodging of a man servant in an English gentleman's family is now about £25 a year.

31 Mowers, for instance, were paid 8d. a day.—*Privy Purse Expenses of Henry VIII.*

32 In 1581 the agricultural labourer, as he now exists, was only beginning to appear. "There be such in the realm," says Stafford, "as live only by the labour of their hands and the profit which they can make upon the commons."—STAFFORD'S *Discourse*. This novel class had been called into being by the general raising of rents, and the wholesale evictions of the smaller tenantry which followed the Reformation. The progress of the causes which led to the change can be traced from the beginning of the century. Harrison says he knew old men who, comparing things present with things past, spoke of two things grown to be very grievous—to wit, "the enhancing of rents, and the daily oppression of copyholders, whose lords seek to bring their poor tenants almost into plain servitude and misery, daily devising new means, and seeking up all the old, how to cut them shorter and shorter; doubling, trebling, and now and then seven times increasing their fines; driving them also for every trifle to lose and forfeit their tenures, by whom the greatest part of the realm doth stand and is maintained, to the end they

may fleece them yet more: which is a lamentable hearing." — *Description of England*.

33 HALL, p. 581. Nor was the act in fact observed even in London itself, or towards workmen employed by the Government. In 1538, the Corporation of London, "for certain reasonable and necessary considerations," assessed the wages of common labourers at 7*d.* and 8*d.* the day, classing them with carpenters and masons. — *Guildhall MSS. Journal* 14, fol. 10. Labourers employed on Government works in the reign of Hen. VIII. never received less than 6*d.* a day, and frequently more. — *Chronicle of Calais*, p. 197, etc. Sixpence a day is the usual sum entered as the wages of a day's labour in the innumerable lists of accounts in the Record Office. And 6*d.* a day again was the lowest pay of the common soldier, not only on exceptional service in the field, but when regularly employed in garrison duty. Those who doubt whether this was really the practice, may easily satisfy themselves by referring to the accounts of the expenses of Berwick, or of Dover, Deal, or Walmer Castles, to be found in the Record Office in great numbers. The daily wages of the soldier are among the very best criteria for determining the average value of the unskilled labourer's work. No government gives higher wages than it is compelled to give by the market rate.

34 The wages of the day labourer in London, under this act of Elizabeth, were fixed at 9*d.* the day, and this, after the restoration of the depreciated currency. — *Guildhall MSS. Journal* 18, fol. 157, etc.

35 4 Hen. VII. cap. 16. By the same parliament these provisions were extended to the rest of England. 4 Hen. VII. cap. 19.

36 HALL, p. 863.

37 27 Hen. VIII. cap. 22.

38 There is a cause of difficulty "peculiar to England, the increase of pasture, by which sheep may be now said to devour men and unpeople not only villages but towns. For wherever it is found that the sheep yield a softer and richer wool than ordinary, there the nobility and gentry, and even those holy men the abbots, not contented with the old rents which their farms yielded, nor thinking it enough that they, living at their ease, do no good to the public, resolve to do it hurt instead of good. They stop the course of agriculture.... One shepherd can look after a flock which will stock an extent of ground that would require many hands if it were ploughed and reaped. And this likewise in many places raises the price of corn. The price of wool is also risen ... since, though sheep cannot be called a monopoly, because they are not engrossed by one person; yet they are in so few hands, and these are so rich, that as they are not prest to sell them sooner than they

have a mind to it, so they never do it till they have raised the price as high as possible." —Sir THOMAS MORE'S *Utopia*, Burnet's Translation.

39 I find scattered among the *State Papers* many loose memoranda, apparently of privy councillors, written on the backs of letters, or on such loose scraps as might be at hand. The following fragment on the present subject is curious. I do not recognise the hand:—

"Mem. That an act may be made that merchants shall employ their goods continually in the traffic of merchandise, and not in the purchasing of lands; and that craftsmen, also, shall continually use their crafts in cities and towns, and not leave the same and take farms in the country; and that no merchant shall hereafter purchase above £40 lands by the year." —*Cotton MS.* Titus, b. i. 160.

40 When the enclosing system was carried on with greatest activity and provoked insurrection. In expressing a sympathy with the social policy of the Tudor government, I have exposed myself to a charge of opposing the received and ascertained conclusions of political economy. I disclaim entirely an intention so foolish; but I believe that the science of political economy came into being with the state of things to which alone it is applicable. It ought to be evident that principles which answer admirably when a manufacturing system capable of indefinite expansion multiplies employment at home—when the soil of England is but a fraction of its empire, and the sea is a highway to emigration—would have produced far different effects, in a condition of things which habit had petrified into form, when manufactures could not provide work for one additional hand, when the first colony was yet unthought of, and where those who were thrown out of the occupation to which they had been bred could find no other. The tenants evicted, the labourers thrown out of employ, when the tillage lands were converted into pastures, had scarcely an alternative offered them except to beg, to rob, or to starve.

41 *Lansdowne MS.* No. I. fol. 26.

42 GIUSTINIANI'S *Letters from the Court of Henry VIII.*

43 Ibid.

44 22 Hen. VIII. cap. 18.

45 Under Hen. VI. the household expenses were £23,000 a year—Cf. *Proceedings and Ordinances of the Privy Council*, vol. vi. p. 35. The particulars of the expenses of the household of Hen. VIII. are in an MS. in the Rolls House. They cover the entire outlay except the personal expenditure of the king, and the sum total amounts to £14,365 10s. 7d. This would leave above £5000 a year for the privy purse, not, perhaps, sufficient to cover Henry's

gambling extravagances in his early life. Curious particulars of his excesses in this matter will be found in a publication wrongly called *The Privy Purse Expenses of Henry the Eighth*. It is a diary of general payments, as much for purposes of state as for the king himself. The high play was confined for the most part to Christmas or other times of festivity, when the statutes against unlawful games were dispensed with for all classes.

46 18 Hen. VI. cap. 11.

47 4 Hen. VII. cap. 12.

48 During the quarter sessions time they were allowed 4s. a day.—Ric. II. xii. 10.

49 The rudeness of the furniture in English country houses has been dwelt upon with much emphasis by Hume and others. An authentic inventory of the goods and chattels in a parsonage in Kent proves that there has been much exaggeration in this matter. It is from an MS. in the Rolls House.

The Inventory of the Goods and Catales of Richd. Master, Clerk, Parson of Aldington, being in his Parsonage on the 20th Day of April, in the 25th Year of the Reign of our Sovereign Lord King Henry VIII.

Plate
Silver spoons, twelve.

In the Hall
Two tables and two forms.
Item, a painted cloth hanging at the upper part of the hall.
Item, a green banker hung on the bench in the hall.
Item, a laver of laten.

In the Parlour
A hanging of old red and green saye.
Item, a banker of woven carpet of divers colours.
Item, two cushions.
Item, one table, two forms, one cupboard, one chair.
Item, two painted pictures and a picture of the names of kings of England
pinned on the said hanging.

In the Chamber on the North Side of the said Parlour
A painted hanging.

Item, a bedstedyll with a feather bed, one bolster, two pillows, one blanket,
one roulett of rough tapestry, a testner of green and red saye.
Item, two forms.
Item, one jack to set a basin on.

In the Chamber over the Parlour
Two bedsteads.
Item, another testner of painted cloth.
Item, a painted cloth.
Item, two forms.

At the Stairs' Hed beside the Parson's Bedchamber
One table, two trestylls, four beehives.

In the Parson's Lodging-chamber
A bedstedyll and a feather bed, two blankets, one payr of sheets, one
coverlet of tapestry lined with canvas, one bolster, one pillow with
a pillocote.
Item, one gown of violet cloth lined with red saye.
Item, a gown of black cloth, furred with lamb.
Item, two hoods of violet cloth, whereof one is lined with green sarsenet.
Item, one jerkyn of tawny camlet.
Item, a jerkyn of cloth furred with white.
Item, a jacket of cloth furred.
Item, a sheet to put in cloth.
Item, one press.
Item, a leather mail.
Item, one table, two forms, four chairs, two trestylls.
Item, a tester of painted cloth.
Item, a pair of hangings of green saye, with two pictures thereupon.
Item, one cupboard, two chests.
Item, a little flock bed, with a bolster and a coverlet.
Item, one cushion, one mantell, one towel, and, by estimation, a pound
of wax candles.
Item, Greek books covered with boards, 42.

Item, small books covered with boards, 33.
Item, books covered with leather and parchment, 38.

In the said Chest in the said Chamber
Three pieces of red saye and green.
Item, one tyke for a bolster, two tykes for pillows.
Item, a typpett of cloth.
Item, diaper napkins, 4, diaper towels, 2.
Item, four pairs of sheets, and one shete, two tablecloths.

In the other Chest in the same Chamber
One typpett of sarsenett.
Item, two cotes belonging to the crosse of Underbill, whereupon hang
thirty-three pieces of money, rings, and other things, and three
crystal stones closed in silver.

In the Study
Two old boxes, a wicker hamper full of papers.

In the Chamber behind the Chimney
One seam and a half of old malt.
Item, a trap for rats.
Item, a board of three yards length.

In the Chamber next adjoining westwards
One bedstedyll, one flock bed, one bolster.
One form, two shelf boards, one little table, two trestylls, two awgyes, one
nett, called a stalker, a well rope, five quarters of hemp.

In the Buttery
Three basino of pewter, five candlesticks, one ewer of lateen, one chafing
dish, two platters, one dish, one salter, three podingers [? porringer],
a saltseller of pewter, seven kilderkyns, three keelers, one form, five
shelves, one byn, one table, one glasse bottell.

In the Priest's Chamber
One bedstedyll, one feather bed, two forms, one press.

In the Woman's Keeping

Two tablecloths, two pairs of sheets.

In the Servant's Chamber
One painted hanging, a bedstedyll, one feather bed, a press, and a shelf.

In the Kitchen
Eight bacon flitches, a little brewing lead, three brass pots, three kettles,
one posnett, one frying-pan, a dripping-pan, a great pan, two trivetts,
a chopping knife, a skimmer, one fire rake, a pothanger, one pothooke,
one andiron, three spits, one gridiron, one firepan, a coal rake of iron,
two bolts [? butts], three wooden platters, six boldishes, three forms,
two stools, seven platters, two pewter dishes, four saucers, a covering
of a saltseller, a podynger, seven tubbs, a caldron, two syffs, a capon
cope, a mustard quern, a ladder, two pails, one beehive.

In the Mill-house
Seven butts, two cheeses, an old sheet, an old brass pan, three podyngers,
a pewter dish.

In the Boulting-house
One brass pan, one quern, a boulting hutch, a boulting tub, three little
tubbys, two keelers, a tolvett, two boulters, one tonnell.

In the Larder
One sieve, one bacon trough, a cheese press, one little tub, eight shelves,
one graper for a well.

Wood
Of tall wood ten load, of ash wood a load and a half.

Poultry
Nine hens, eight capons, one cock, sixteen young chickens, three old
geese, seventeen goslings, four ducks.

Cattle
Five young hoggs, two red kyne, one red heifer two years old, one bay
gelding lame of spavins, one old grey mare having a mare colt.

In the Entries
Two tubbs, one trough, one ring to bear water and towel, a chest to keep

cornes.

In the same House
Five seams of lime.

In the Woman's Chamber
One bedstedyll of hempen yarn, by estimation 20 lbs.

Without the House
Of tyles, — —, of bricks, — —, seven planks, three rafters, one ladder.

In the Gate-house
One form, a leather sack, three bushels of wheat.

In the Still beside the Gate
Two old road saddles, one bridle, a horse-cloth.

In the Barn next the Gate
Of wheat unthrashed, by estimation, thirty quarters, of barley unthrashed,
by estimation, five quarters.

In the Cartlage
One weene with two whyles, one dung-cart without whyles, two shod-whyles,
two yokes, one sledge.

In the Barn next the Church
Of oats unthrashed, by estimation, one quarter.

In the Garden-house
Of oats, by estimation, three seams four bushels.

In the Court
Two racks, one ladder.

50 Two hundred poor were fed daily at the house of Tomas Cromwell. This fact is perfectly authenticated. Stowe the historian, who did not like Cromwell, lived in an adjoining house, and reports it as an eye witness.—See STOWE'S *Survey of London*.

51 HARRISON'S *Description of Britain*.

52 The Earl and Countess of Northumberland breakfasted together alone at seven. The meal consisted of a quart of ale, a quart of wine, and a chine of beef: a loaf of bread is not mentioned, but we hope it may be presumed. On fast days the beef was exchanged for a dish of sprats or herrings, fresh or salt.—*Northumberland Household Book*, quoted by Hume.

53 Some notice of the style of living sometimes witnessed in England in the old times may be gathered from the details of a feast given at the installation of George Neville, brother of Warwick the King Maker, when made Archbishop of York.

The number of persons present including servants was about 3500.

The provisions were as follow—

Wheat, 300 quarters.
Ale, 300 tuns.
Wine, 104 tuns.
Ipocras, 1 pipe.
Oxen, 80.
Wild bulls, 6.
Muttons, 1004.
Veal, 300.
Porkers, 300.
Geese, 3000.
Capons, 2300.
Pigs, 2000.
Peacocks, 100.
Cranes, 200.
Kids, 200.
Chickens, 2000.
Pigeons, 4000.
Conies, 4000.
Bitterns, 204.
Mallards and teals, 4000.
Heronshaws, 4000.
Fesants, 200.

Partridges, 500.

Woodcocks, 400.

Plovers, 400.

Curlews, 100.

Quails, 100.

Egrets, 1000

Rees, 200.

Harts, bucks, and roes, 400 and odd.

Pasties of venison, cold, 4000.

Pasties of venison, hot, 1506.

Dishes of jelly, pasted, 1000.

Plain dishes of jelly, 4000.

Cold tarts, baken, 4000.

Cold custards, 4000.

Custards, hot, 2000.

Pikes, 300.

Breams, 300.

Seals, 8.

Porpoises, 4.

54 LATIMER'S *Sermons*, p. 64.

55 *Statutes of the Realm*, 1 Ed. VI. cap. 12.

56 HOOKER'S *Life of Sir Peter Carew*.

57 In a subsequent letter he is described as learning French, etymology, casting of accounts, playing at weapons, and other such exercises.—ELLIS, third series, vol. i. p. 342-3.

58 It has been objected that inasmuch as the Statute Book gives evidence of extensive practices of adulteration, the guild system was useless, nay, it has been even said that it was the cause of the evil. Cessante causâ cessat effectus; when the companies lost their authority, the adulteration ought to have ceased, which in the face of recent exposures will be scarcely maintained. It would be as reasonable to say that the police are useless because we have still burglars and pickpockets among us.

59 Throughout the old legislation, morality went along with politics and economics, and formed the life and spirit of them. The fruiterers in the streets were prohibited from selling plums and apples, because the apprentices played dice with them for their wares, or because the temptation induced children and servants to steal money to buy. When Parliament came to be held regularly in London, an order of Council fixed the rates

which the hotel-keeper might charge for dinners. Messes were served for four at twopence per head; the bill of fare providing bread, fish, salt and fresh, two courses of meat, ale, with fire and candles. And the care of the Government did not cease with their meals, and in an anxiety that neither the burgesses nor their servants should be led into sin, stringent orders were issued against street-walkers coming near their quarters.—*Guildhall MSS. Journals* 12 and 15.

The sanitary regulations for the city are peculiarly interesting. The scavengers, constables and officers of the wards were ordered, "on pain of death," to see all streets and yards kept clear of dung and rubbish and all other filthy and corrupt things. Carts went round every Monday, Wednesday, and Saturday, to carry off the litter from the houses, and on each of those days twelve buckets of water were drawn for "every person," and used in cleaning their rooms and passages.

Particular pains were taken to keep the Thames clean, and at the mouth of every sewer or watercourse there was a strong iron grating two feet deep.—*Guildhall MSS. Journal* 15.

60 And not in England alone, but throughout Europe.

61 27 Hen. VIII. cap. 25.

62 Ibid.

63 Ibid.

64 22 Hen. VIII. cap. 4; 28 Hen. VIII. cap. 5.

65 *Statut. Winton.* 13 Edw. I. cap. 6.

66 12 Rich. II. cap. 6: 11 Hen. IV. cap. 4.

67 ELLIS'S *Original Letters*, first series, vol. i. p. 226.

68 It has been stated again and again that the policy of Henry the Eighth was to make the crown despotic by destroying the remnants of the feudal power of the nobility. How is such a theory to be reconciled with statutes the only object of which was the arming and training of the country population, whose natural leaders were the peers, knights, and gentlemen? We have heard too much of this random declamation.

69 33 Hen. VIII. cap. 9.

70 From my experience of modern archery I found difficulty in believing that these figures were accurately given. Few living men could send the lightest arrow 220 yards, even with the greatest elevation, and for effective use it must be delivered nearly point blank. A passage in HOLINSHED'S *Description of Britain*, however, prevents me from doubting that the words

of the statute are correct. In his own time, he says that the strength of the English archers had so notoriously declined that the French soldiers were in the habit of disrespectfully turning their backs, at long range, "bidding them shoot," whereas, says Holinshed, "had the archers been what they were wont to be, these fellows would have had their breeches nailed unto their buttocks." In an order for bowstaves, in the reign of Henry the Eighth, I find this direction: "Each bowstave ought to be *three fingers thick* and squared, and *seven feet long*: to be got up well polished and without knots." —Butler to Bullinger: *Zurich Letters*.

71 Page 735, quarto edition.

72 The Personages, Dresses, and Properties of a Mystery Play, acted at Greenwich, by command of Henry VIII. *Rolls House MS.*

73 Hall says "collar of the *garter* of St. Michael," which, however, I venture to correct.

74 Rich. II. 12, cap. 7, 8, 9; Rich. II. 15, cap. 6.

75 *Lansdowne MSS.* 1, fol. 26.

76 Injunctions to the Monasteries: BURNET'S *Collect.*

77 Letter of Thomas Dorset to the Mayor of Plymouth: *Suppression of the Monasteries*.

78 "Divers of your noble predecessors, kings of this realm, have given lands to monasteries, to give a certain sum of money yearly to the poor people, whereof for the anciety of the time they never give one penny. Wherefore, if your Grace will build to your poor bedemen a sure hospital that shall never fail, take from them these things.... Tie the holy idle thieves to the cart to be whipped, naked, till they fall to labour, that they, by their importunate begging take not away the alms that the good charitable people would give unto us sore, impotent, miserable people, your bedemen." — FISH'S *Supplication*: FOXE, vol. iv. p. 664.

79 27 Hen. VIII. cap. 25.

80 Roads, harbours, embankments, fortifications at Dover and at Berwick, etc. —STRYPE's *Memorials*, vol. 1. p. 326 and 419.

81 It is to be remembered that the criminal law was checked on one side by the sanctuary system, on the other by the practice of benefit of clergy. Habit was too strong for legislation, and these privileges continued to protect criminals long after they were abolished by statute. There is abundant evidence that the execution of justice was as lax in practice as it was severe in theory.

82 27 Ed. III. stat. 1; 38 Ed. III. stat. 2; 16 Rich. cap. 5.

83 25 Ed. III. stat. 4; stat. 5, cap. 22; 13 Rich. II. stat. 2, cap. 2; 2 Hen. IV. cap. 3; 9 Hen. IV. cap. 8.

84 See p. 42.

85 *Lansdowne MS.* 1, fol. 26; STOW'S *Chron.* ed. 1630, p. 338.

86 2 Hen. IV. cap. 3; 9 Hen. IV. cap. 8.

87 2 Hen. IV. cap. 15.

88 Hen. VII. cap. 4. Among the miscellaneous publications of the Record Commission, there is a complaint presented during this reign, by the gentlemen and the farmers of Carnarvonshire, accusing the clergy of systematic seduction of their wives and daughters.

89 Hen. IV. cap. 15.

90 MORTON'S *Register*, MS. Lambeth. See vol. ii. cap. 10, of the second edition of this work for the results of Morton's investigation.

91 MORTON'S *Register*; and see WILKINS'S *Concilia*, vol. iii. pp. 618-621.

92 Quibus Dominus intimavit qualis infamia super illos in dictâ civitate crescit quod complures eorundem tabernas pandoxatorias, sive caupones indies exerceant ibidem expectando fere per totum diem. Quare Dominus consuluit et monuit eosdem quod in posterum talia dimittant, et quod dimittant suos longos crines et induantur togis non per totum apertis.

93 The expression is remarkable. They were not to dwell on the offences of their brethren coram laicis qui semper clericis sunt infesti.—WILKINS, vol. iii. p. 618.

94 Johannes permissione divinâ Cantuar. episcop. totius Angliæ primas cum in præsenti convocatione pie et salubriter consideratum fuit quod nonnulli sacerdotes et alii clerici ejusdem nostræ provinciæ in sacris ordinibus constituti honestatem clericalem in tantum abjecerint ac in comâ tonsurâque et superindumentis suis quæ in anteriori sui parte totaliter aperta existere dignoscuntur, sic sunt dissoluti et adeo insolescant quod inter eos et alios laicos et sæculares viros nulla vel modica comæ vel habituum sive vestimentorum distinctio esse videatur quo fiet in brevi ut a multis verisimiliter formidatur quod sicut populus ita et sacerdos erit, et nisi celeriori remedio tantæ lasciviæ ecclesiasticarum personarum quanto ocyus obviemus et clericorum mores hujusmodi maturius compescamus,

Ecclesia Anglicana quæ superioribus diebus vitâ famâ et compositis moribus floruisse dignoscitur nostris temporibus quod Deus avertat, præcipitanter ruet;

Desiring, therefore, to find some remedy for these disorders, lest the blood of those committed to him should be required at his hands, the archbishop decrees and ordains, —

Ne aliquis sacerdos vel clericus in sacris ordinibus constitutus togam gerat nisi clausam a parte anteriori et non totaliter apertam neque utatur ense nec sicâ nec zonâ aut marcipio deaurato vel auri ornatum habente. Incedent etiam omnes et singuli presbyteri et clerici ejusdem nostræ provinciæ coronas et tonsuras gerentes aures patentes ostendendo juxta canonicas sanctiones.—WILKINS, vol. iii. p. 619.

95 See WARHAM'S *Register*, MS. Lambeth.

96 21 Hen. VIII. cap. 13.

97 ROY'S *Satire against the Clergy*, written about 1528, is so plain-spoken, and goes so directly to the point of the matter, that it is difficult to find a presentable extract. The following lines on the bishops are among the most moderate in the poem: —

> "What are the bishops divines—
> Yea, they can best skill of wines
> Better than of divinity;
> Lawyers are they of experience,
> And in cases against conscience
> They are parfet by practice.
> To forge excommunications,
> For tythes and decimations
> Is their continual exercise.
> As for preaching they take no care,
> They would rather see a course at a hare;
> Rather than to make a sermon
> To follow the chase of wild deer,
> Passing the time with jolly cheer.
> Among them all is common
> To play at the cards and dice;
> Some of them are nothing nice
> Both at hazard and momchance;
> They drink in golden bowls
> The blood of poor simple souls
> Perishing for lack of sustenance.

Their hungry cures they never teach,
Nor will suffer none other to preach," etc.

98 LATIMER'S *Sermons*, pp. 70, 71.

99 A peculiarly hateful form of clerical impost, the priests claiming the last dress worn in life by persons brought to them for burial.

100 Fitz James to Wolsey, FOXE, vol. iv. p. 196.

101 *Supplication of the Beggars*; FOXE, vol. iv. p. 661. The glimpses into the condition of the monasteries which had been obtained in the imperfect visitation of Morton, bear out the pamphleteer too completely. See chapter x. of this work, second edition.

102 FOXE, vol. iv. p. 658.

103 13 Ric. II. stat. ii. c. 2; 2 Hen. IV. c. 3; 9 Hen. IV. c. 8. Lingard is mistaken in saying that the Crown had power to dispense with these statutes. A dispensing power was indeed granted by the 12th of the 7th of Ric. II. But by the 2nd of the 13th of the same reign, the king is expressly and by name placed under the same prohibitions as all other persons.

104 HALL, p. 784.

105 25 Hen. VIII. c. 22.

106 28 Hen. VIII. c. 24. Speech of Sir Ralph Sadler in parliament, *Sadler Papers*, vol. iii. p. 323.

107 Nor was the theory distinctly admitted, or the claim of the house of York would have been unquestionable.

108 25 Hen. VIII. c. 22, Draft of the Dispensation to be granted to Henry VIII. *Rolls House MS.* It has been asserted by a writer in the *Tablet* that there is no instance in the whole of English history where the ambiguity of the marriage law led to a dispute of title. This was not the opinion of those who remembered the wars of the fifteenth century. "Recens in quorundam vestrorum animis adhuc est illius cruenti temporis memoria," said Henry VIII. in a speech in council, "quod a Ricardo tertio cum avi nostri materni Edwardi quarti statum in controversiam vocâsset ejusque heredes regno atque vitâ privâsset illatum est."-WILKINS'S *Concilia*, vol. iii. p. 714. Richard claimed the crown on the ground that a precontract rendered his brother's marriage invalid, and Henry VII. tacitly allowed the same doubt to continue. The language of the 22nd of the 25th of Hen. VIII. is so clear as to require no additional elucidation; but another distinct evidence of the belief of the time upon the subject is in one of the papers laid before Pope Clement.

"Constat, in ipso regno quam plurima gravissima bella sæpe exorta, confingentes ex justis et legitimis nuptiis quorundam Angliæ regum procreatos illegitimos fore propter aliquod consangunitatis vel affinitatis confictum impedimentum et propterea inhabiles esse ad regni successionem."—*Rolls House MS.*; WILKINS'S *Concilia*, vol. iii. p. 707.

109 28 Hen. VIII. c. 24.

110 *Appendix 2 to the Third Report of the Deputy-Keeper of the Public Records.*

111 *Sadler Papers*, vol. iii. p. 323.

112 28 Hen. VIII. c. 24.

113 *Four Years at the Court of Henry the Eighth*, vol. ii. pp. 315-16.

114 Sir Charles Brandon, created Duke of Suffolk, and married to Mary Tudor, widow of Louis XII.

115 28 Hen. VIII. c. 24.

116 The treaty was in progress from Dec. 24, 1526, to March 2, 1527 [LORD HERBERT], and during this time the difficulty was raised. The earliest intimation which I find of an intended divorce was in June, 1527, at which time Wolsey was privately consulting the bishops.—*State Papers* vol. i. p. 189.

117 It was for some time delayed; and the papal agent was instructed to inform Ferdinand that a marriage which was at variance a jure et laudabilibus moribus could not be permitted nisi maturo consilio et necessitatis causâ.— Minute of a brief of Julius the Second, dated March 13, 1504, *Rolls House MS.*

118 LORD HERBERT, p. 114.

119 LORD HERBERT, p. 117, Kennett's edition. The act itself is printed in BURNET'S *Collectanea*, vol. iv. (Nares' edition) pp. 5, 6. It is dated June 27, 1505. Dr. Lingard endeavours to explain away the renunciation as a form. The language of Moryson, however, leaves no doubt either of its causes or its meaning. "Non multo post sponsalia contrahuntur," he says, "Henrico plus minus tredecim annos jam nato. Sed rerum non recte inceptarum successus infelicior homines non prorsus oscitantes plerumque docet quid recte gestum quid perperam, quid factum superi volunt quid infectum. Nimirum Henricus Septimus nullâ ægritudinis prospecta causâ repente in deteriorem valetudinem prolapsus est, nec unquam potuit affectum corpus pristinum statum recuperare. Uxor in aliud ex alio malum regina omnium laudatissimia non multo post morbo periit. Quid mirum si Rex tot irati numinis indiciis admonitus cœperit cogitare rem male illis succedere qui vellent hoc nomine cum Dei legibus litem instituere ut diutius cum homine

amicitiam gerere possent. Quid deinceps egit? Quid aliud quam quod decuit Christianissimum regem? Filium ad se accersiri jubet, accersitur. Adest, adsunt et multi nobilissimi homines. Rex filium regno natum hortatur ut secum una cum doctissimis ac optimis viris cogitavit nefarium esse putare leges Dei leges Dei non esse cum papa volet. Non ita longâ oratione usus filium patri obsequentissimum a sententiâ nullo negotio abduxit. Sponsalia contracta infirmantur, pontificiæque auctoritatis beneficio palam renunciatum est. Adest publicus tabellio—fit instrumentum. Rerum gestarum testes rogati sigilla apponunt. Postremo filius patri fidem se illam uxorem nunquam ducturum." —*Apomaxis* RICARDI MORYSINI. Printed by Berthelet, 1537.

120 See LINGARD, sixth edition, vol. iv. p. 164.

121 HALL, p. 507.

122 He married Catherine, June 3, 1509. Early in the spring of 1510 she miscarried.—*Four Years at the Court of Henry VIII.* vol. i. p. 83.

Jan. 1, 1511. A prince was born, who died Feb. 22.—HALL.

Nov. 1513. Another prince was born, who died immediately.— LINGARD, vol. iv, p. 290.

Dec. 1514. Badoer, the Venetian ambassador, wrote that the queen had been delivered of a still-born male child, to the great grief of the whole nation.

May 3, 1515. The queen was supposed to be pregnant. If the supposition was right, she must have miscarried.—*Four Years at the Court of Henry VIII.* vol. i. p. 81.

Feb. 18, 1516. The Princess Mary was born.

July 3, 1518. "The Queen declared herself quick with child." (Pace to Wolsey: *State Papers*, vol. i. p. 2,) and again miscarried.

These misfortunes we are able to trace accidentally through casual letters, and it is probable that these were not all. Henry's own words upon the subject are very striking:—

"All such issue male as I have received of the queen died incontinent after they were born, so that I doubt the punishment of God in that behalf. Thus being troubled in waves of a scrupulous conscience, and partly in despair of any issue male by her, it drove me at last to consider the estate of this realm, and the danger it stood in for lack of issue male to succeed me in this imperial dignity."—CAVENDISH.

123 "If a man shall take his brother's wife it is an unclean thing. He hath uncovered his brother's nakedness. They shall be childless." —*Leviticus* xx.

21. It ought to be remembered, that if the present law of England be right, the party in favour of the divorce was right.

124 *Letters of the Bishop of Bayonne*, LEGRAND, vol. iii.

125 Legates to the Pope, printed in BURNET'S *Collectanea*, p. 40.

126 *State Papers*, vol. vii. p. 117.

127 *Letters of the Bishop of Bayonne*, LEGRAND, vol. iii.; HALL, 669.

128 They were shut up in the Castle of St. Angelo.

129 *State Papers*, vol. vii. pp. 18, 19.

130 The fullest account of Wolsey's intentions on church reform will be found in a letter addressed to him by Fox, the old blind Bishop of Winchester, in 1528. The letter is printed in STRYPE'S *Memorials Eccles.* vol. i. Appendix 10.

131 *Letters of the Bishop of Bayonne*, LEGRAND, vol. iii. It is not uncommon to find splendid imaginations of this kind haunting statesmen of the 16th century; and the recapture of Constantinople always formed a feature in the picture. *A Plan for the Reformation of Ireland*, drawn up in 1515, contains the following curious passage: "The prophecy is, that the King of England shall put this land of Ireland into such order that the wars of the land, whereof groweth the vices of the same, shall cease for ever; and after that God shall give such grace and fortune to the same king that he shall with the army of England and of Ireland subdue the realm of France to his obeysance for ever, and shall rescue the Greeks, and recover the great city of Constantinople, and shall vanquish the Turks and win the Holy Cross and the Holy Land, and shall die Emperor of Rome, and eternal blisse shall be his end." — *State Papers*, vol. ii. pp. 30, 31.

132 Knight to Henry: *State Papers*, vol. vii. pp. 2, 3.

133 Wolsey to Cassalis: Ibid. p. 26.

134 The dispensing power of the popes was not formally limited. According to the Roman lawyers, a faculty lay with them of granting extraordinary dispensations in cases where dispensations would not be usually admissible—which faculty was to be used, however, dummodo causa cogat urgentissima ne regnum aliquod funditus pereat; the pope's business being to decide on the question of urgency. — Sir Gregory Cassalis to Henry VIII., Dec. 26, 1532. *Rolls House MS.*

135 Knight and Cassalis to Wolsey: BURNET'S *Collect.* p. 12.

136 STRYPE'S *Memorials*, vol. i., Appendix p. 66.

137 Sir F. Bryan and Peter Vannes to Henry; *State Papers*, vol. vii. p. 144.

138 STRYPE'S *Memorials*, Appendix, vol. i. p. 100.

139 Ibid. Appendix, vol. i. pp. 105-6; BURNET'S *Collectanea*, p. 13.

140 Wolsey to the Pope, BURNET'S *Collectanea*, p. 16: Vereor quod tamen nequeo tacere, ne Regia Majestas, humano divinoque jure quod habet ex omni Christianitate suis his actionibus adjunctum freta, postquam viderit sedis Apostolicæ gratiam et Christi in terris Vicarii clementiam desperatam Cæsaris intuitu, in cujus manu neutiquam est tam sanctos conatus reprimere, ea tunc moliatur, ea suæ causæ perquirat remedia, quæ non solum huic Regno sed etiam aliis Christianis principibus occasionem subministrarent sedis Apostolicæ auctoritatem et jurisdictionem imminuendi et vilipendendi.

141 BURNET'S *Collectanea*, p. 20. Wolsey to John Cassalis: "If his Holyness, which God forbid, shall shew himself unwilling to listen to the king's demands, to me assuredly it will be but grief to live longer, for the innumerable evils which I foresee will then follow. One only sure remedy remains to prevent the worst calamities. If that be neglected, there is nothing before us but universal and inevitable ruin."

142 Gardiner and Fox to Wolsey; STRYPE'S *Memorials*, vol. i. Appendix, p. 92.

143 His Holiness being yet in captivity, as he esteemed himself to be, so long as the Almayns and Spaniards continue in Italy, he thought if he should grant this commission that he should have the emperour his perpetual enemy without any hope of reconciliation. Notwithstanding he was content rather to put himself in evident ruin, and utter undoing, than the king or your Grace shall suspect any point of ingratitude in him; heartily desiring with sighs and tears that the king and your Grace which have been always fast and good to him, will not now suddenly precipitate him for ever: which should be done if immediately on receiving the commission your Grace should begin process. He intendeth to save all upright thus. If M. de Lautrec would set forwards, which he saith daily that he will do, but yet he doth not, at his coming the Pope's Holiness may have good colour to say, "He was required of the commission by the ambassador of England, and denying the same, he was, eftsoons, required by M. de Lautrec to grant the said commission, inasmuch as it was but a letter of justice." And by this colour he would cover the matter so that it might appear unto the emperour that the pope did it not as he that would gladly do displeasure unto the emperour, but as an indifferent judge, that could not nor might deny justice, specially being required by such personages; and immediately he would

despatch a commission bearing date after the time that M. de Lautrec had been with him or was nigh unto him. The pope most instantly beseecheth your Grace to be a mean that the King's Highness may accept this in a good part, and that he will take patience for this little time, which, as it is supposed, will be but short. —Knight to Wolsey and the King, Jan. 1, 1527-8: BURNET *Collections*, 12, 13.

144 Such at least was the ultimate conclusion of a curious discussion. When the French herald declared war, the English herald accompanied him into the emperor's presence, and when his companion had concluded, followed up his words with an intimation that unless the French demands were complied with, England would unite to enforce them. The Emperor replied to Francis with defiance. To the English herald he expressed a hope that peace on that side would still be maintained. For the moment the two countries were uncertain whether they were at war or not. The Spanish ambassador in London did not know, and the court could not tell him. The English ambassador in Spain did not leave his post, but he was placed under surveillance. An embargo on Spanish and English property was laid respectively in the ports of the two kingdoms; and the merchants and residents were placed under arrest. Alarmed by the outcry in London, the king hastily concluded a truce with the Regent of the Netherlands, the language of which implied a state of war; but when peace was concluded between France and Spain, England appeared only as a contracting party, not as a principal, and in 1542 it was decided that the antecedent treaties between England and the empire continued in force. —See LORD HERBERT; HOLINSHED; *State Papers*, vols. vii. viii. and ix.; with the treaties in RYMER, vol. vi. part 2.

145 Gardiner to the King: BURNET'S *Collectanea*, p. 426.

146 Duke of Suffolk to Henry the Eighth: *State Papers*, vol. vii, p. 183.

147 Duke of Suffolk to Henry VIII.: *State Papers*, vol. vii. p. 183.

148 HALL, p. 744.

149 When the clothiers of Essex, Kent, Wiltshire, Suffolk, and other shires which are clothmaking, brought cloths to London to be sold, as they were wont, few merchants or none bought any cloth at all. When the clothiers lacked sale, then they put from them their spinners, carders, tuckers, and such others that lived by clothworking, which caused the people greatly to murmur, and specially in Suffolk, for if the Duke of Norfolk had not wisely appeased them, no doubt but they had fallen to some rioting. When the king's council was advertised of the inconvenience, the cardinal sent for a great number of the merchants of London, and to them said, "Sirs, the king is informed that you use not yourselves like merchants, but like graziers

and artificers; for where the clothiers do daily bring cloths to the market for your ease, to their great cost, and then be ready to sell them, you of your wilfulness will not buy them, as you have been accustomed to do. What manner of men be you?" said the cardinal. "I tell you that the king straitly commandeth you to buy their cloths as beforetime you have been accustomed to do, upon pain of his high displeasure." —HALL, p. 746.

150 LEGRAND, vol. iii. p. 157. By manners and customs he was referring clearly to his intended reformation of the church. See the letter of Fox, Bishop of Winchester (STRYPE'S *Memorials*, vol. ii. p. 25), in which Wolsey's intentions are dwelt upon at length.

151 Ibid. pp. 136, 7.

152 *State Papers*, vol. vii. pp. 96, 7.

153 Wolsey to Cassalis: Ibid. p. 100.

154 State Papers, vol. vii. pp. 106, 7

155 Ibid. p. 113.

156 Ibid. vii. p. 113.

157 Take the veil.

158 Instruction to the Ambassadours at Rome: *State Papers*, vol. vii. p. 136.

159 *Letters of the Bishop of Bayanne*, LEGRAND, vol. iii.

160 LEGRAND, vol. iii. 231.

161 Instrucion para Gonzalo Fernandez que se envoie a Ireland al Conde de Desmond, 1529. —MS. Archives at Brussels. —*The Pilgrim*, note 1, p. 169.

162 Henrici regis octavi de repudiandâ dominâ Catherinâ oratio Idibus Novembris habita 1528.

Veneranda et chara nobis præsulum procerum atque consiliariorum cohors quos communis reipublicæ atque regni nostri administrandi cura conjunxit. Haud vos latet divinâ nos Providentiâ viginti jam ferme annis hanc nostram patriam tantâ felicitate rexisse ut in illâ ab hostilibus incursionibus tuta semper interea fuerit et nos in his bellis quæ suscepimus victores semper evasimus; et quanquam in eo gloriâri jure possumus majorem tranquillitatem opes et honores prioribus huc usque ductis socculis, nunquam subditis a majoribus parentibusque nostris Angliâ regibus quam a nobis provenisse, tamen quando cum hâc gloriâ in mentem una venit ac concurrit mortis cogitatio, veremur ne nobis sine prole legitimâ decedentibus majorem ex morte nostrâ patiamini calamitatem quam ex vitâ fructum ac emolumentum percepistis. Recens enim in quorundam vestrorum animis adhuc est illius cruenti temporis memoria quod a Ricardo tertio cum avi nostri materni Edwardi Quarti statum in controversiam vocasset ejusque heredes regno atque vitâ privâsset illatum est. Tum ex historiis notæ sunt illæ diræ strages quæ a clarissimis Angliæ gentibus Eboracensi atque Lancastrensi, dum inter se de regno et imperio multis ævis contenderent, populo evenerunt. Ac illæ ex justis nuptiis inter Henricum Septimum et dominam Elizabetham clarissimos nostros parentes contractis in nobis inde legitimâ natâ sobole sopitæ tandem desierunt. Si vero quod absit, regalis ex nostris nuptiis stirps quæ jure deinceps regnare possit non nascatur, hoc regnum civilibus atque intestinis se versabit tumultibus aut in exterorum dominationem atque potestatem veniet. Nam quanquam formâ atque venustate singulari, quæ magno nobis solatio fuit filiam Dominam Mariam ex nobilissimâ fœminâ Dominâ Catherinâ procreavimus, tamen a piis atque eruditis theologis nuper accepimus quia eam quæ Arturi fratris nostri conjux ante fuerat uxorem duximus nostras nuptias jure divino esse vetitas, partumque inde editum non posse censeri legitimum. Id quod eo vehementius nos angit et excruciat, quod cum superiori anno legatos ad conciliandas inter Aureliensem ducem et filiam nostram Mariam nuptias ad Franciscum Gallorum regem misissemus a quodam ejus consiliario responsum est, "antequam de hujusmodi nuptiis agatum inquirendum esse prius an Maria fuerit filia nostra legitima; constat enim 'inquit,' quod exdominâ Catherinâ fratris sui viduâ cujusmodi nuptiæ jure divino interdictæ sunt suscepta est." Quæ oratio quanto metu ac horrore animum nostrum turbaverit quia res ipsa æternæ tam animi quam corporis salutis periculum in se continet, et quam perplexis cogitationibus conscientiam occupat, vos quibus et capitis aut fortunæ ac multo magis animarum jactura immineret, remedium nisi adhibere velitis, ignorare non posse arbitror. Hæc una res—quod Deo teste et in Regis oraculo affirmamus— nos impulit ut per legatos doctissimorum per totum orbem Christianum theologorum sententias exquireremus et Romani Pontificis legatum verum atque æquum judicium de tantâ causâ laturum ut tranquillâ deinceps et intergà conscientiâ in conjugio licito vivere possimus accerseremus. In quo si ex sacris litteris hoc quo viginti jam fere annis gavisi sumus matrimonium jure divino permissum esse manifeste liquidoque constabit, non modo ob conscientiæ tranquillitatem, verum etiam ob amabiles mores virtutesque quibus regina prædita et ornata est, nihil optatius nihilque jucundius accidere nobis potest. Nam præterquam quod regali atque nobili genere prognata est, tantâ præterea comitate et obsequio conjugali tum cæteris animi morumque ornamentis quæ nobilitatem illustrant omnes fœminas his viginti annis sic mihi anteire visa est ut si a conjugio liber essem ac solutus, si jure divino liceret, hanc solam præ cæteris fœminis stabili mihi jure ac fœdere matrimoniali conjungerem. Si vero in hoc judicio matrimonium nostrum jure divino prohibitum, ideoque ab initio nullum irritumque fuisse pronuncietur, infelix hic meus casus multis lacrimis lugendus ac deplorandus erit. Non modo quod a tam illustris et amabilis mulieris consuetudine et consortio divertendum sit, sed multo magis quod specie ad similitudinem veri conjugii decepti in amplexibus plusquam fornicariis tam multos annos trivimus nullâ legitimâ prognatâ nobis sobole quæ nobis mortuis hujus inclyti regni hereditatem capessat.

Hæ nostræ curæ istæque solicitudines sunt quæ mentem atque conscientiam nostram dies noctesque torquent et excurciant, quibus auferendis et profligandis remedium ex hâc legatione et judicio opportunum quærimus. Ideoque vos quorum virtuti atque fidei multum attribuimus rogamus ut certum atque genuinum nostrum de hâc re sensum quem ex nostro sermone percepistis populo declaretis: eumque excitetis ut nobiscum una oraret ut ad conscientiæ nostræ pacem atque tranquillitatem in hoc judicio veritas multis jam annis tenebris involuta tandem patefiat.— WILKINS'S *Concilia*, vol. iii. p. 714.

163 HALL, *Letters of the Bishop of Bayonne*, LEGRAND, vol. iii.

164 LEGRAND, vol. iii.

165 Ibid. vol. iii. pp. 232, 3.

166 *State Papers*, vol. vii. p. 120; Ibid. p. 186.

167 BURNET'S *Collectanea*, p. 41.

168 *State Papers*, vol. vii. p. 193.

169 The Emperor could as little trust Clement as the English, and to the last moment could not tell how he would act.

"Il me semble," wrote Inigo di Mendoza to Charles on the 17th of June, 1529,—"il me semble que Sa Sainteté differe autant qu'il peut ce qu' auparavant il avoit promis, et je crains qu'il n'ait ordonné aux legatz ce qui jusques à present avoit resté en suspens qu'ils procedent par la première commission. Ce qui faisant votre Majesté peut tenir la Reine autant que condamné."—*MS. Archives at Brussels.*

The sort of influence to which the See of Rome was amenable appears in another letter to the Emperor, written from Rome itself on the 4th of October. The Pope and cardinals, it is to be remembered, were claiming to be considered the supreme court of appeal in Christendom.

"Si je ne m'abuse tous ou la pluspart du Saint College sont plus affectionnez à vostre dite Majesté que à autre Prince Chrestien: de vous escrire, Sire, particulièrement toutes leurs responses seroit chose trop longue. Tant y a que elles sont telles que votre Majesté a raison doùbt grandement se contenter d'icelles.

"... Seulement diray derechief à vostre Majesté, et me souvient l'avoir dict plusieurs fois, qu'il est en vostre Majesté gaigner et entretenir perpetuellement ce college en vostre devotion en distribuant seulement entre les principaulx d'eulx en pensions et benefices la somme de vingt mille ducas, l'ung mille, l'autre deulx ou trois mille. Et est cecy chose, Sire, que plus vous touche que à autre Prince Chrestien pour les affaires que vostre Majesté a journellement à despescher en ceste court." —M. de Præt to Charles V. August 5th, 1529. MS. Ibid.

170 LEGRAND, vol. iii. p. 377.

171 Ibid. vol. iii. p. 374.

172 Ibid. vol. iii. p. 355.

173 Ibid.

174 Memorandum relating to the Society of Christian Brethren. *Rolls House MS.*

175 DALABER'S *Narrative*, printed in FOXE, vol. iv. Seeley's Ed.

176 All authorities agree in the early account of Henry, and his letters provide abundant proof that it is not exaggerated. The following description of him in the despatches of the Venetian ambassador shows the effect which he produced on strangers in 1515:—

"Assuredly, most serene prince, from what we have seen of him, and in conformity, moreover, with the report made to us by others, this most serene king is not only very expert in arms and of great valour and most excellent in his personal endowments, but is likewise so gifted and adorned with mental accomplishments of every sort, that we believe him to have few equals in the world. He speaks English, French, Latin, understands Italian well; plays almost on every instrument; sings and composes fairly; is prudent, and sage, and free from every vice." —*Four Years at the Court of Henry VIII.* vol. i. p. 76.

Four years later, the same writer adds,—

"The king speaks good French, Latin, and Spanish; is very religious; hears three masses a day when he hunts, and sometimes five on other days; he hears the office every day in the queen's chamber—that is to say, vespers and complins." —Ibid. vol. ii. p. 312. William Thomas, who must have seen him, says,

"Of personage he was one of the goodliest men that lived in his time; being high of stature, in manner more than a man, and proportionable in all his members unto that height; of countenance he was most amiable; courteous and benign in gesture unto all persons and specially unto strangers; seldom or never offended with anything; and of so constant a nature in himself that I believe few can say that ever he changed his cheer for any novelty how contrary or sudden so ever it were. Prudent he was in council and forecasting; most liberal in rewarding his faithful servants, and even unto his enemies, as it behoveth a prince to be. He was learned in all sciences, and had the gift of many tongues. He was a perfect theologian, a good philosopher, and a strong man at arms, a jeweller, a perfect builder as well of fortresses as of pleasant palaces, and from one to another there was no necessary kind of knowledge, from a king's degree to a carter's, but he had an honest sight in it." — *The Pilgrim* p. 78.

177 Exposition of the Commandments, set forth by Royal authority, 1536. This treatise was drawn up by the bishops, and submitted to, and revised by, the king.

178 SAGUDINO'S *Summary. Four Years at the Court of Henry VIII.* vol. ii. P. 75.

179 "The truth is, when I married my wife, I had but fifty pounds to live on for me and my wife so long as my father lived, and yet she brought me forth every year a child." — Earl of Wiltshire to Cromwell: ELLIS, third series, vol. iii. pp. 22, 3.

180 BURNET, vol. i. p. 69.

181 Thomas Allen to the Earl of Shrewsbury: LODGE'S *Illustrations*, vol. i. p. 20.

182 Earl of Northumberland to Cromwell: printed by LORD HERBERT and by BURNET.

183 28 Hen. VIII. cap. 7.

184 Since these words were written, I have discovered among the Archives of Simancas what may perhaps be some clue to the mystery, in an epitome of a letter written to Charles V. from London in May, 1536: —-

"His Majesty has letters from England of the 11th of May, with certain news that the paramour of the King of England, who called herself queen, has been thrown into the Tower of London for adultery. The partner of her guilt was an organist of the Privy Chamber, who is in the Tower as well. An officer of the King's wardrobe has been arrested also for the same offence with her, and one of her brothers for having been privy to her offences without revealing them. They say, too, that if the adultery had not been discovered, the King was determined to put her away, having been informed by competent witnesses that she was married and had consummated her marriage nine years before, with the Earl of Northumberland."

185 ELLIS, third series, vol. ii. p. 131.

186 Wyatt's Memorials, printed in Singer's CAVENDISH, p. 420.

187 ELLIS, third series, vol. ii. p. 132.

188 ELLIS, first series, vol. i. p. 135. "My Lord, in my most humblest wise that my poor heart can think, I do thank your Grace for your kind letter, and for your rich and goodly present; the which I shall never be able to deserve without your great help; of the which I have hitherto had so great plenty, that all the days of my life I am most bound of all creatures, next to the King's Grace, to love and serve your Grace. Of the which I beseech you never to doubt that ever I shall vary from this thought as long as any breath is in my body."

189 CAVENDISH *Life of Wolsey*, p. 316. Singer's edition.

190 CAVENDISH, pp. 364, 5.

191 *Letters of the Bishop of Bayonne*, LEGRAND, vol. iii. pp. 368, 378, etc.

192 See HALE'S *Criminal Causes from the Records of the Consistory Court of London.*

193 Petition of the Commons, infra, p. 191, etc.

194 Reply of the Ordinaries to the petition of the Commons, infra, p. 202, etc.

195 Petition of the Commons. 23 Hen. VIII. c. 9.

196 HALE'S *Criminal Causes*, p.4.

197 An Act that no person committing murder, felony, or treason should be admitted to his clergy under the degree of sub-deacon.

198 In May, 1528, the evil had become so intolerable, that Wolsey drew the pope's attention to it. Priests, he said, both secular and regular, were in the habit of committing atrocious crimes, for which, if not in orders, they would have been promptly executed; and the laity were scandalised to see such persons not only not degraded, but escaping with complete impunity. Clement something altered the law of degradation in consequence of this representation, but quite inadequately.—RYMER, vol. vi. part 2, p. 96.

199 Thomas Cowper et ejus uxor Margarita pronubæ horribiles, et instigant mulieres ad fornicandum cum quibuscunque laicis, religiosis, fratribus minoribus, et nisi fornicant in domo suâ ipsi diffamabunt nisi voluerint dare eis ad voluntatem eorum; et vir est pronuba uxori, et vult relinquere eam apud fratres minores pro peccatis habendis.—HALE, *Criminal Causes*, p. 9.

Joanna Cutting communis pronuba at præsertim inter presbyteros fratres monachos et canonicos et etiam inter Thomam Peise et quandam Agnetam, etc.—HALE, *Criminal Causes*, p. 28.

See also Ibid. pp. 15, 22, 23, 39, etc.

In the first instance the parties accused "made their purgation" and were dismissed. The exquisite corruption of the courts, instead of inviting evidence and sifting accusations, allowed accused persons to support their own pleas of not guilty by producing four witnesses, not to disprove the charges, but to swear that they believed the charges untrue. This was called "purgation."

Clergy, it seems, were sometimes allowed to purge themselves simply on their own word.—HALE, p. 22; and see the Preamble of the 1st of the 23rd of Henry VIII.

200 Complaints of iniquities arising from confession were laid before Parliament as early as 1394.

"Auricularis confessio quæ dicitur tam necessaria ad salvationem hominis, cum fictâ potestate absolutionis exaltat superbiam sacerdotum, et dat illis opportunitatem secretarum sermocinationum quas nos nolumus dicere, quia domini et dominæ attestantur quod pro timore confessorum suorum non audent dicere veritatem; et in tempore confessionis est opportunum tempus procationis id est of wowing et aliarum secretarum conventionum ad peccata mortalia. Ipsi dicunt quod sunt commissarii Dei ad judicandum de omni peccato perdonandum et mundandum quemcunque eis placuerint. Dicunt quod habent claves cœli et inferni et possunt excommunicare et benedicere ligare et solvere in voluntatem eorum; in tantum quod pro bussello vel 12 denariis volunt vendere benedictionem cœli per chartam et clausulam de warrantiâ sigillitâ sigillo communi. Ista conclusio sic est in usu quod non eget probatione aliquâ."—Extract from a Petition presented to Parliament: WILKINS, vol. iii. p. 221.

This remarkable paper ends with the following lines:—

"Plangunt Anglorum gentes crimen Sodomorum
Paulus fert horum sunt idola causa malorum
Surgunt ingrati Giezitæ Simone nati

Nomine prælati hoc defensare parati
Qui reges estis populis quicunque præstis
Qualiter his gestis gladios prohibere potestis."

See also HALE, p. 42, where an abominable instance is mentioned, and a still worse in the *Suppression of the Monasteries*.

201 HALE, p. 12.

202 Ibid. pp. 75, 83; *Suppression of the Monasteries, p. 47.*

203 Ibid. p. 80.

204 Ibid. p. 83.

205 I have been taunted with my inability to produce more evidence. For the present I will mention two additional instances only, and perhaps I shall not be invited to swell the list further.

1. In the State Paper Office is a report to Cromwell by Adam Bekenshaw, one of his diocesan visitors, in which I find this passage:—

"There be knights and divers gentlemen in the diocese of Chester who do keep concubines and do yearly compound with the officials for a small sum without monition to leave their naughty living."

2. In another report I find also the following:—

"The names of such persons as be permitted to live in adultery and fornication for money:—

"The Vicar of Ledbury.
The Vicar of Brasmyll.
The Vicar of Stow.
The Vicar of Cloune.
The Parson of Wentnor.
The Parson of Rusbury.
The Parson of Plowden.
The Dean of Pountsbury.
The Parson of Stratton.
Sir Matthew of Montgomery.
Sir — — of Lauvange.
Sir John Brayle.
Sir Morris of Clone.
Sir Adam of Clone.
Sir Pierce of Norbury.
Sir Gryffon ap Egmond.
Sir John Orkeley.

Sir John of Mynton.

Sir John Reynolds.

Sir Morris of Knighton, priest.

Hugh Davis.

Cadwallader ap Gern.

Edward ap Meyrick.

With many others of the diocese of Hereford."

The originals of both these documents are in the State Paper Office. There are copies in the Bodleian Library.—*MS. Tanner*, 105.

206 Skelton gives us a specimen of the popular criticisms:—

"Thus I, Colin Clout,
As I go about,
And wondering as I walk,
I hear the people talk:
Men say for silver and gold
Mitres are bought and sold:
A straw for Goddys curse,
What are they the worse?

"What care the clergy though Gill sweat,
Or Jack of the Noke?
The poor people they yoke
With sumners and citacions,
And excommunications.
About churches and markets
The bishop on his carpets
At home soft doth sit.
This is a fearful fit,
To hear the people jangle.
How wearily they wrangle!
But Doctor Bullatus

"Parum litteratus,
Dominus Doctoratus
At the broad gate-house.
Doctor Daupatus
And Bachelor Bacheleratus,
Drunken as a mouse
At the ale-house,

Taketh his pillion and his cap
At the good ale-tap,
For lack of good wine.
As wise as Robin Swine,
Under a notary's sign,
Was made a divine;
As wise as Waltham's calf,
Must preach in Goddys half;
In the pulpit solemnly;
More meet in a pillory;
For by St. Hilary
He can nothing smatter
Of logic nor school matter.

"Such temporal war and bate
As now is made of late
Against holy church estate,
Or to mountain good quarrels;
The laymen call them barrels
Full of gluttony and of hypocrisy,
That counterfeits and paints
As they were very saints.

"By sweet St. Marke,
This is a wondrous warke,
That the people talk this.
Somewhat there is amiss.
The devil cannot stop their mouths,
But they will talk of such uncouths
All that ever they ken
Against spiritual men."

I am unable to quote more than a few lines from ROY'S *Satire*. At the close of a long paragraph of details an advocate of the clergy ventures to say that the bad among them are a minority. His friend answers:—

"Make the company great or small,
Among a thousand find thou shall
Scant one chaste of body or mind."

207 Answer of the Bishops to the Commons' Petition: *Rolls House MS.*

208 Joanna Leman notatur officio quod non venit ad ecclesiam parochialem; et dicit se nolle accipere panem benedictum a manibus rectoris; et vocavit eum "horsyn preste." —HALE, p. 99.

209 HALE, p. 63.

210 Ibid. p. 98.

211 Ibid. p. 38.

212 Ibid. p. 67.

213 Ibid. p. 100.

214 CAVENDISH, *Life of Wolsey*, p. 251.

215 HALL, p. 764.

216 Ibid. p. 764.

217 *State Papers*, vol. vii. p. 361.

218 6 Hen. VIII. cap. 16.

219 The session lasted six weeks only, and several of the subjects of the petition were disposed of in the course of it, as we shall see.

220 The MS. from which I have transcribed this copy is itself imperfect, as will be seen in the "reply of the Bishops," which supplies several omitted articles. See p. 137, et seq. It is in the Rolls House.

221 The penny, as I have shown, equalled, in terms of a poor man's necessities, a shilling. See chap. i.

222 See instance's in HALE: p, 62, *Omnium Sanctorum in muro.* —M. Gulielmus Edward curatus notatur officio quod recusat ministrare sacramenta ecelesiastica ægrotantibus nisi prius habitis pecuniis pro suo labore: p. 64, *St. Mary Magdalen.* —Curatus notatur officio prbpter quod recusavit solemnizare matrrimonium quousque habet pro hujusmodi solemnizatione, *3s. 8d.*; and see pp. 52, 75.

223 I give many instances of this practice in my sixth chapter. It was a direct breach of the statute of Henry IV., which insists on all examinations for heresy being conducted in open court. "The diocesan and his commissaries," says that act, "shall openly and judicially proceed against persons arrested." —2 Hen. IV. c. 15.

224 Again breaking the statute of Hen. IV., which limited the period of imprisonment previous to public trial to three months. —2 Hen. IV. c. 15.

225 To be disposed of at Smithfield. Abjuration was allowed once. For a second offence there was no forgiveness.

226 Petition of the Commons. *Rolls House MS.*

227 See STRYPE, *Eccles. Memorials*, vol. i. p. 191-2, — who is very eloquent in his outcries upon his subject.

228 *Answer of the Bishops*, p. 204, etc.

229 Explanations are not easy; but the following passage may suggest the meaning of the House of Commons: — "The holy Father Prior of Maiden Bradley hath but six children, and but one daughter married yet of the goods of the monastery; trusting shortly to marry the rest." — Dr. Leyton to Cromwell: *Suppression of the Monasteries*, p. 58.

230 Reply of the Bishops, infra.

231 CAVENDISH, *Life of Wolsey*, p. 390. MORE'S *Life of More*, p. 109.

232 Populus diu oblatrans. Fox to Wolsey. STRYPE, *Eccl. Mem.* vol. i. Appendix, p. 27.

233 RYMER, vol. vi. part 2, p. 119.

234 The answer of the Ordinaries to the supplication of the worshipful the Commons of the Lower House of Parliament offered to our Sovereign Lord the King's most noble Grace. — *Rolls House MS.*

235 The terms of the several articles of complaint are repeated verbally from the petition. I condense them to spare recapitulation.

236 2 Hen. IV. cap. 15; 2 Hen. V. cap. 7.

237 An Act that no person shall be cited out of the diocese in which he dwells, except in certain cases. It received the Royal assent two years later. See 23 Hen. VIII. cap. 9.

238 21 Hen. VIII. cap. 5. An Act concerning fines and sums of money to be taken by the ministers of bishops and other ordinaries of holy church for the probate of testaments.

239 HALE, *Precedents*, p. 86.

240 Ibid.

241 21 Hen. VIII. cap. 6. An Act concerning the taking of mortuaries, or demanding, receiving, or claiming the same.

In Scotland the usual mortuary was, a cow and the uppermost cloth or counterpane on the bed in which the death took place. A bishop reprimanding a suspected clergyman for his leaning toward the Reformation, said to him:—

"My joy, Dean Thomas, I am informed that ye preach the epistle and gospel every Sunday to your parishioners, and that ye take not the cow nor the upmost cloth from your parishioners; which thing is very prejudicial to the churchmen. And therefore, Dean Thomas, I would ye took your cow and upmost cloth, or else it is too much to preach every Sunday, for in so doing ye may make the people think we should preach likewise."—CALDERWOOD, vol. i. p. 126.

The bishop had to burn Dean Thomas at last, being unable to work conviction into him in these matters.

242 21 Hen. VIII. cap. 13. An Act that no spiritual person shall take farms; or buy and sell for lucre and profit; or keep tan-houses or breweries. And for pluralities of benefices and for residence.

243 HALL, p. 767.

244 Ibid. 766

245 Ibid. 767.

246 Ibid. 766.

247 Ibid. 768.

248 So reluctant was he, that at one time he had resolved, rather than compromise the unity of Christendom, to give way. When the disposition of the court of Rome was no longer doubtful, "his difficultatibus permotus, cum in hoc statu res essent, dixerunt qui ejus verba exceperunt, post profundam secum de universo negotio deliberationem et mentis agitationem, tandem in hæc verba prorupisse, se primum tentâsse illud divortium persuasum ecclesiam Romanam hoc idem probaturum—quod si ita ilia abhorreret ab illâ sententiâ ut nullo modo permittendum censeret se nolle cum eâ contendere neque amplius in illo negotio progredi."

Pole, on whose authority we receive these words, says that they were heard with almost unanimous satisfaction at the council board. The moment of hesitation was, it is almost certain, at the crisis which preceded or attended Wolsey's fall. It endured but for three days, and was dispelled by the influence of Cromwell, who tempted both the king and parliament into their fatal revolt.—POLI *Apologia ad Carolum Quintum*.

249 LEGRAND, vol. iii. p. 446. The censures were threatened in the first brief, but the menace was withdrawn under the impression that it was not needed.

250 Ibid. The second brief is dated March 7, and declares that the king, if he proceeds, shall incur ipso facto the greater excommunication; that the kingdom will fall under an interdict.

251 Cranmer was born in 1489, and was thus forty years old when he first emerged into eminence.

252 *State Papers*, vol. vii. p. 226.

253 Je croy qu'il ne feist en sa vie ceremonie qui luy touchast si prés du cœur, ne dont je pense qu'il luy doive advenir moins du bien. Car aucunes fois qu'il pensoit qu'on ne le regardast, il faisoit de si grands soupirs que pour pesante que fust sa chappe, il la faisoit bransler à bon escient.—*Lettre de M. de Gramont, Evêque de Tarbès*. LEGRAND, vol. iii. p. 386.

254 ELLIS, *Third Series*, vol. ii. p. 98. "In the letters showed us by M. de Buclans from the emperor, of the which mention was made in ciphers, it was written in terms that the French king would offer unto your Grace the papalite of France vel Patriarchate, for the French men would no more obey the Church of Rome."—Lee to Wolsey.

255 A ce qu'il m'en a declaré des fois plus de trois en secret, il seroit content que le dit mariage fust ja faict, ou par dispense du Legat d'Angleterre ou autrement; mais que ce ne fust par son autorité, in aussi diminuant sa puissance, quant aux dispenses, et limitation de droict divin.—*Dechiffrement de Lettres de M. de Tarbès.*—LEGRAND, vol. iii. p. 408.

256 LEGRAND, vol. iii. p. 408.

257 *State Papers*, vol. vii. p. 230.

258 The Bishop of Tarbès to the King of France. LEGRAND, vol. iii. p. 401.

259 *State Papers*, vol. vii. p. 234.

260 Ibid. p. 235.

261 We demand a service of you which it is your duty to concede; and your first thought is lest you should offend the emperor. We do not blame *him*. That in such a matter he should be influenced by natural affection is intelligible and laudable. But for that very reason we decline to submit to so partial a judgment.—Henry VIII. to the Pope: BURNET'S *Collectanea*, p. 431.

262 LEGRAND, vol. iii. p. 394.

263 *State Papers*, vol. vii. p. 317.

264 For Croke's Mission, see BURNET, vol. i. p. 144 e.

265 *State Papers*, vol. vii. p. 241.

266 Friar Pallavicino to the Bishop of Bath. *Rolls House MS.*

267 Croke and Omnibow to the King. *Rolls House MS.*

268 Generalis magister nostri ordinis mandavit omnibus suæ religionis professoribus, ut nullus audeat de auctoritate Pontificis quicquam loqui. Denique Orator Cæsareus in talia verba prorupit, quibus facile cognovi ut me a Pontifice vocari studeat et tunc timendum esset saluti meæ. Father Omnibow to Henry VIII. *Rolls House MS.*

269 BURNET'S *Collect.* p. 50. Burnet labours to prove that on Henry's side there was no bribery, and that the emperor was the only offender; an examination of many MS. letters from Croke and other agents in Italy leads me to believe that, although the emperor only had recourse to intimidation, because he alone was able to practise it, the bribery was equally shared between both parties.

270 LEGRAND, vol. iii. p. 458. The Grand Master to the King of France:— De l'autre part, adventure il n'est moins a craindre, que le Roy d'Angleterre, irrité de trop longues dissimulations, trouvast moyen de parvenir a ses intentions du consentement de l'Empereur, et que par l'advenement d'un tiers *se fissent ami, Herode et Pilate.*

271 Ibid. vol. iii. p. 467, etc.

272 Letter from the King of France to the President of the Parliament of Paris. *Rolls House MS.*

273 Letter from Reginald Pole to Henry VIII. *Rolls House MS.*

274 Pole to Henry VIII. *Rolls House MS.*

275 BURNET, *Collectanea*, p. 429.

276 *State Papers*, vol. i. p. 377.

277 BURNET'S *Collectanea*, p. 436; *State Papers*, vol. i. p. 378.

278 It is not good to stir a hornet's nest.

279 BURNET'S *Collectanea*, p. 431.

280 Ibid. p. 48.

281 Preface to LATIMER'S *Sermons*. Parker Society's edition, p. 3.

282 "King Harry loved a man," was an English proverb to the close of the century. See SIR ROBERT NAUNTON'S *Fragmenta Regalia*, London, 1641, p. 14.

283 Sir George Throgmorton, who distinguished himself by his opposition to the Reformation in the House of Commons.

284 BURNET'S *Collect*, p. 429.

285 *A Glasse of Truth.*

286 Ibid. p. 144.

287 35 Ed. I.; 25 Ed. III. stat. 4; stat. 5, cap. 22; 27 Ed. III. stat. 1; 13 Ric. II. stat. 2, cap. 2; 16 Ric. II. cap. 5; 9 Hen. IV. cap. 8.

288 CAVENDISH, p. 276.

Gardiner has left some noticeable remarks on this subject.

"Whether," he says, "a king may command against a common law or an act of parliament, there is never a judge or other man in the realm ought to know more by experience of that the laws have said than I.

"First, my Lord Cardinal, that obtained his legacy by our late Sovereign Lord's requirements at Rome, yet, because it was against the laws of the realm, the judges concluded the offence of Premunire, which matter I bare away, and took it for a law of the realm, because the lawyers said so, but my reason digested it not. The lawyers, for confirmation of their doings, brought in the case of Lord Tiptoft. An earl he was, and learned in the civil laws, who being chancellor, because in execution of the king's commandment he offended the laws of the realm, suffered on Tower Hill. They brought in examples of many judges that had fines set on their heads in like cases for transgression of laws by the king's commandment, and this I learned in that case.

"Since that time being of the council, when many proclamations were devised against the carriers out of corn, when it came to punish the offender, the judges would answer it might not be by the law, because the Act of Parliament gave liberty, wheat being under a price. Whereupon at last followed the Act of Proclamations, in the passing whereof were many large words spoken."

After mentioning other cases, he goes on:—

"I reasoned once in the parliament house, where there was free speech without danger, and the Lord Audely, to satisfy me, because I was in some secret estimation, as he knew, 'Thou art a good fellow, Bishop,' quoth he; 'look at the Act of Supremacy, and there the king's doings be restrained to spiritual jurisdiction; and in another act no spiritual law shall have place contrary to a common law, or an act of parliament. And this were not,' quoth he, 'you bishops would enter in with the king, and by means of his supremacy order the laws as ye listed. But we will provide,' quoth he, 'that the premunire shall never go off your heads.' This I bare away then, and held my peace." — Gardiner to the Protector Somerset: *MS. Harleian*, 417.

289 13 Ric. II. stat. 2, cap. 2. Et si le Roi envoie par lettre on en autre maniere a la Courte du Rome al excitacion dascune person, parount que la contrarie de cest estatut soit fait touchant ascune dignité de Sainte Eglise, si celuy qui fait tiel excitacion soit Prelate de Sainte Eglise, paie au Roy le value de ses temporalitees dun an. The petition of parliament which occasioned the statute is even more emphatic: Perveuz tout foitz que par nulle traite ou composition a faire entre le Seint Pere le Pape et notre Seigneur le Roy que riens soit fait a contraire en prejudice de cest Estatute a faire. Et si ascune Seigneur Espirituel ou Temporel ou ascune persone quiconque de qu'elle condition q'il soit, enforme, ensence ou excite le Roi ou ses heirs, l'anientiser, adnuller ou repeller cest Estatut a faire, et de ceo soit atteint par due proces du loy que le Seigneur Espirituel eit la peyne sus dite, etc. — *Rolls of Parliament*, Ric. II. 13.

290 Even further, as chancellor the particular duty had been assigned to him of watching over the observance of the act.

Et le chancellor que pur le temps serra a quelle heure que pleint a luy ou a conseill le Roy soit fait d'ascunes des articles sus ditz par ascune persone que pleindre soy voudra granta briefs sur le cas ou commissions a faire au covenables persones, d'oier et terminer les ditz articles sur peyne de perdre son office et jamais estre mys en office le Roy et perdre mille livres a lever a l'oeps le Roy si de ce soit atteint par du proces. — *Rolls of Parliament*, Ric. II. 13.

291 BURNET, vol. iii. p. 77. See a summary of the acts of this Convocation in a sermon of Latimer's preached before the two Houses in 1536. LATIMER'S *Sermons*, p. 45.

292 The king, considering what good might come of reading of the New Testament and following the same; and what evil might come of the reading of the same if it were evil translated, and not followed; came into the Star Chamber the five-and-twentieth day of May; and then communed with his council and the prelates concerning the cause. And after long debating, it was alleged that the translations of Tyndal and Joy were not truly translated, and also that in them were prologues and prefaces that sounded unto heresy, and railed against the bishops uncharitably. Wherefore all such books were prohibited, and commandment given by the king to the bishops, that they, calling to them the best learned men of the universities, should cause a new translation to be made, so that the people should not be ignorant of the law of God. — HALL, p. 771. And see WARHAM'S *Register* for the years 1529-1531. MS. Lambeth.

293 22 Hen. VIII. cap. 15.

294 BURNET, vol. iii. p. 78.

295 *State Papers*, vol. vii. 457.

296 Memoranda relating to the Clergy: *Rolls House MS.*

297 BURNET, vol. iii. p. 80.

298 The King's Highness, having always tender eyes with mercy and pity and compassion towards his spiritual subjects, minding of his high goodness and great benignity so always to impart the same unto them, as justice being duly administered, all rigour be excluded; and the great benevolent minds of his said subjects [having been] largely and many times approved towards his Highness, and specially in their Convocation and Synod now presently being in the Chapter House of Westminster, his Highness, of his said benignity and high liberality, in consideration that the said Convocation has given and granted unto him a subsidy of one hundred thousand pounds, is content to grant his general pardon to the clergy and the province of Canterbury, for all offences against the statute and premunire.—22 Hen. VIII. cap. 15.

299 BURNET, vol. 1. p. 185.

300 An instance is reported in the Chronicle of the Grey Friars ten years previously. The punishment was the same as that which was statutably enacted in the case of Rouse.

301 HALL, p. 781.

302 Most shocking when the *wrong persons* were made the victims; and because clerical officials were altogether incapable of detecting the *right persons*, the memory of the practice has become abhorrent to all just men. I suppose, however, that, if the *right persons* could have been detected, even the stake itself would not have been too tremendous a penalty for the destroying of human souls.

303 22 Hen. VIII. cap. 10.

304 See a very curious pamphlet on this subject, by SIR FRANCIS PALGRAVE. It is called *The Confessions of Richard Bishop, Robert Seymour, and Sir Edward Neville, before the Privy Council, touching Prophecie, Necromancy, and Treasure-trove.*

305 Miscellaneous Depositions on the State Of the Country: *Rolls House MS.*

306 See the Preamble of the Bill against conjurations, witchcraft, sorceries, and enchantments.—33 Hen. VIII. cap. 8.

Also "the Bill touching Prophecies upon Arms and Badges."—33 Hen. VIII. cap. 14.

A similar edict expelled the gipsies from Germany. At the Diet of Spires, June 10, 1544.

Statutum est ne vagabundum hominum genus quos vulgo Saracenos vocant per Germaniam oberrare sinatur *usu enim compertum est eos exploratores et proditores esse.*—*State Papers,* vol. ix. p. 705.

307 ELLIS, first series, vol. ii. p. 101.

308 Bulla pro Johanne Scot, qui sine cibo et potu per centum et sex dies vixerat.-RYMER, vol. vi. part 2, p. 176.

309 BUCHANAN, *History of Scotland,* vol. ii. p. 156.

310 *Letter of Archbishop Cranmer.*—ELLIS, second series, vol. ii. p. 314.

311 *Statutes of the Realm.* 25 Hen. VIII. cap. 12.

312 Extracts from a Narrative containing an Account of Elizabeth Barton: *Rolls House MS.*

313 *Statutes of the Realm.*

314 *Rolls House MS.*

315 Ibid.

316 *Suppression of the Monasteries,* p. 19.

317 Ibid.

318 Proceedings connected with Elizabeth Barton: *Rolls House MS.*

319 25 Hen. VIII. cap. 12.

320 Ibid.

321 Ibid.

322 *Cranmer's Letter.* ELLIS, third series, vol. iii. p. 315.

323 More to Cromwell: BURNET'S *Collectanea,* p. 350.

324 25 Hen. VIII. cap. 12.

325 Confessions of Elizabeth Barton: *Rolls House MS.* Sir Thomas More gave her a double ducat to pray for him and his. BURNET'S *Collectanea,* p. 352. Moryson, in his *Apomaxis,* declares that she had a regular understanding with the confessors at the Priory. When penitents came to confess, they were detained while a priest conveyed what they had acknowledged to the Nun; and when afterwards they were admitted to her presence, she amazed them with repeating their own confessions.

326 The said Elizabeth subtilly and craftily conceiving the opinion and mind of the said Edward Bocking, willing to please him, revealed and showed unto the said Edward that God was highly displeased with our said sovereign lord the king for this matter; and in case he desisted not from his proceeding in the said divorce and separation, but pursued the same and married again, that then within one month after such marriage, he should no longer be king of this realm; and in the reputation of Almighty God he should not be a king one day nor one hour, and that he should die a villain's death. Saying further, that there was a root with three branches, and till they were plucked up it should never be merry in England: interpreting the root to be the late lord cardinal, and the first branch to be the king our sovereign lord, the second the Duke of Norfolk, and the third the Duke of Suffolk.—25 Hen. VIII. cap. 12.

327 Revelations of Elizabeth Barton: *Rolls House MS.* In the epitome of the book of her Revelations it is stated that there was a story in it "of an angel that appeared, and bade the Nun go unto the king, that infidel prince of England, and say that I command him to amend his life, and that he leave three things which he loveth and pondereth upon, *i.e.*, that he take none of the pope's right nor patrimony from him; the second that he destroy all these new folks of opinion and the works of their new learning; the third, that if he married and took Anne to wife, the vengeance of God should plague him; and as she sayth she shewed this unto the king."—Paper on the Nun of Kent: *MS. Cotton, Cleopatra*, E 4.

328 ELLIS, third series, vol. ii. p. 137. Warham had promised to marry Henry to Anne Boleyn. The Nun frightened him into a refusal by a pretended message from an angel.—*MS. ibid.*

329 The Nun hath practised with two of the pope's ambassadors within this realm, and hath sent to the pope that if he did not do his duty in reformation of kings, God would destroy him at a certain day which he had appointed. By reason whereof it is supposed that the pope hath showed himself so double and so deceivable to the King's Grace in his great cause of marriage as he hath done, contrary to all truth, justice, and equity. As likewise the late cardinal of England, and the Archbishop of Canterbury, being very well-minded to further and set at an end the marriage which the King's Grace now enjoyeth, according to their spiritual duty, were prevented by the false revelations of the said Nun. And that the said Bishop of Canterbury was so minded may be proved by divers which knew then his towardness.—Narrative of the Proceedings of Elizabeth Barton: *Rolls House MS.*

330 Note of the Revelations of Elizabeth Barton: *Rolls House MS.*

331 HALL, p. 780.

332 RYMER, vol. vi. p. 160. We are left to collateral evidence to fix the place of this petition, the official transcriber having contented himself with the substance, and omitted the date. The original, as appears from the pope's reply (LORD HERBERT, p. 145), bore the date of July 13; and unless a mistake was made in transcribing the papal brief, this was July, 1530. I have ventured to assume a mistake, and to place the petition in the following year, because the judgment of the universities, to which it refers, was not completed till the winter of 1530; they were not read in parliament till March 30, 1531; and it seems unlikely that a petition of so great moment would have been presented on an incomplete case, or before the additional support of the House of Commons had been secured. I am far from satisfied, however, that I am right in making the change. The petition must have been drawn up (though it need not have been presented) in 1530; since it bears the signature of Wolsey, who died in the November of that year.

333 Mademoiselle de Boleyn est venue; et l'a le Roy logée en fort beau logis; et qu'il a faict bien accoustrer tout auprés du sien. Et luy est la cour faicte ordinairement tous les jours plus grosse que de long temps elle ne fut faicte a la Royne. Je crois bien qu'on veult accoutumer par les petie ce peuple à l'endurer, afin que quand ivendra à donner les grands coups, il ne les trouve si estrange. Toutefois il demeure tous jours endurcy, et croy bien qu'il feroit plus qu'il ne faict si plus il avoit de puissance; mais grand ordre se donne par tout.—Bishop of Bayonne to the Grand Master: LEGRAND, vol. iii. p. 231.

334 HALL, p. 781.

335 It seems to have been his favourite place of retirement. The gardens and fishponds were peculiarly elaborate and beautiful.—Sir John Russell to Cromwell: MS. State Paper Office.

336 Also it is a proverb of old date—"The pride of France, the treason of England, and the war of Ireland, shall never have end." State Papers, vol. ii. p. 11

337 There was a secret ambassador with the Scots king from the emperour, who had long communicated with the king alone in his privy chamber. And after the ambassador's departure the king, coming out into his outer chamber, said to his chancellor and the Earl Bothwell, "My lords, how much are we bounden unto the emperour that in the matter concerning our style, which so long he hath set about for our honour, that shall be by him discussed on Easter day, and that we may lawfully write ourself Prince of England and Duke of York." To which the chancellor said, "I pray God

the pope confirm the same." The Scots king answered, "Let the emperour alone."—Earl of Northumberland to Henry VIII.: *State Papers*, vol. iv. p. 599.

338 HALL, p. 783.

339 "The bishop was brought in desperation of his life."—*Rolls House MS.*, second series, 532. This paper confirms Hall's account in every point.

340 HALL, p. 796.

341 BURNET, vol. iii. p. 115.

342 Warham was however fined £300 for it.—HALL, 796. A letter of Richard Tracy, son of the dead man, is in the *MS. State Paper Office*, first series, vol. iv. He says the King's Majesty had committed the investigation of the matter to Cromwell.

343 LATIMER'S *Sermons*, p. 46.

344 Cap. iii.

345 23 Hen. VIII. cap. 1.

346 23 Hen. VIII. cap. 9.

347 Be it further enacted that no archbishop or bishop, official, commissary, or any other minister, having spiritual jurisdiction, shall ask, demand, or receive of any of the king's subjects any sum or sums of money for the seal of any citizen, but only threepence sterling.—23 Hen. VIII. cap. 9.

348 23 Hen. VIII. cap. 10.—By a separate clause all covenants to defraud the purposes of this act were declared void, and the act itself was to be interpreted "as beneficially as might be, to the destruction and utter avoiding of such uses, intents, and purposes."

349 Annates or firstfruits were first suffered to be taken within the realm for the only defence of Christian people against infidels, and now they be claimed and demanded as mere duty only for lucre, against all right and conscience.—23 Hen. VIII. cap. 20.

350 23 Hen. VIII. cap. 20.

351 It hath happened many times by occasion of death unto archbishops or bishops newly promoted within two or three years after their consecration, that their friends by whom they have been holpen to make payment have been utterly undone and impoverished.—23 Henry VIII. cap. 20.

352 *M. de la Pomeroy to Cardinal Tournon.*

"London, March 23, 1531-2.

"My Lord,—I sent two letters to your lordship on the 20th of this month. Since that day Parliament has been prorogued, and will not meet again till after Easter.

"It has been determined that the Pope's Holiness shall receive no more annates, and the collectors' office is to be abolished. Everything is turning against the Holy See, but the King has shown no little skill; the Lords and Commons have left the final decision of the question at his personal pleasure, and the Pope is to understand that, if he will do nothing for the King, the King has the means of making him suffer. The clergy in convocation have consented to nothing, nor will they, till they know the pleasure of their master the Holy Father; but the other estates being agreed, the refusal of the clergy is treated as of no consequence.

"Many other rights and privileges of the Church are abolished also, too numerous to mention."—MS. Bibliot. Impér. Paris.

353 STRYPE, *Eccles. Mem.*, vol. i. part 2, p. 158.

354 Ibid.

355 Sir George Throgmorton, Sir William Essex, Sir John Giffard, Sir Marmaduke Constable, with many others, spoke and voted in opposition to the government. They had a sort of club at the Queen's Head by Temple Bar, where they held discussions in secret, "and when we did commence," said Throgmorton, "we did bid the servants of the house go out, and likewise our own servants, because we thought it not convenient that they should hear us speak of such matters."—Throgmorton to the King: *MS. State Paper Office.*

356 23 Hen. VIII. cap. 20.

357 Printed in STRYPE, *Eccles. Mem.*, vol. i. p. 201. Strype, knowing nothing of the first answer, and perceiving in the second an allusion to one preceding, has supposed that this answer followed the third and last, and was in fact a retractation of it. All obscurity is removed when the three replies are arranged in their legitimate order.

358 STRYPE, *Eccles. Mem.*, vol. i. p. 199, etc.

359 23 Hen. VIII. cap. 20.

360 STOW, p. 562.

361 "In connection with the Annates Act, the question of appeals to Rome had been discussed in the present session. Sir George Throgmorton had spoken on the papal side, and in his subsequent confession he mentioned a remarkable interview which he had had with More.

"After I had reasoned to the Bill of Appeals," he said, "Sir Thomas More, then being chancellor, sent for me to come and speak with him in the parliament chamber. And when I came to him he was in a little chamber within the parliament chamber, where, as I remember, stood an altar, or a thing like unto an altar, whereupon he did lean and, as I do think, the same time the Bishop of Bath was talking with him. And then he said this to me, I am very glad to hear the good report that goeth of you, and that ye be so good a Catholic man as ye be. And if ye do continue in the same way that ye begin, and be not afraid to say your conscience, ye shall deserve great reward of God, and thanks of the King's Grace at length, and much worship to yourself."—Throgmorton to the King: *MS. State Paper Office.*

362 In part of it he speaks in his own person. Vide supra, cap. 3.

363 BURNET'S *Collectanea*, p. 435.

364 Note of the Revelations of Elizabeth Barton: *Rolls House MS.*

365 It has been thought that the Tudor princes and their ministers carried out the spy system to an iniquitous extent,—that it was the great instrument of their Machiavellian policy, introduced by Cromwell, and afterwards developed by Cecil and Walsingham. That both Cromwell and Walsingham availed themselves of secret information, is unquestionable,—as I think it is also unquestionable that they would have betrayed the interests of their country if they had neglected to do so. Nothing, in fact, except their skill in fighting treason with its own weapons, saved England from a repetition of the wars of the Roses, envenomed with the additional fury of religious fanaticism. But the agents of Cromwell, at least, were all volunteers;—their services were rather checked than encouraged; and when I am told, by high authority, that in those times an accusation was equivalent to a sentence of death, I am compelled to lay so sweeping a charge of injustice by the side of a document which forces me to demur to it. "In the reign of the Tudors," says a very eminent writer, "the committal, arraignment, conviction, and execution of any state prisoner, accused or *suspected, or under suspicion of being suspected* of high treason, were only the regular terms in the series of judicial proceedings." This is scarcely to be reconciled with the 10th of the 37th of Hen. VIII., which shows no desire to welcome accusations, or exaggerated readiness to listen to them.

"Whereas," says that Act, "divers malicious and evil disposed persons of their perverse, cruel, and malicious intents, minding the utter undoing of some persons to whom they have and do bear malice, hatred, and evil will, have of late most devilishly practised and devised divers writings, wherein hath been comprised that the same persons to whom they bear malice should speak traitorous words against the King's Majesty, his crown and dignity, or commit divers heinous and detestable treasons against the King's Highness, where, in very deed, the persons so accused never spake nor committed any such offence; by reason whereof divers of the king's true, faithful, and loving subjects have been put in fear and dread of their lives and of the loss and forfeiture of their lands and chattels—for reformation hereof, be it enacted, that if any person or persons, of what estate, degree, or condition he or they shall be, shall at any time hereafter devise, make, or write, or cause to be made any manner of writing comprising that any person has spoken, committed, or done any offence or offences which now by the laws of this realm be made treason, or that hereafter shall be made treason, and do not subscribe, or cause to be subscribed, his true name to the said writing, and within twelve days next after ensuing do not personally come before the king or his council, and affirm the contents of the said writings to be true, and do as much as in him shall be for the approvement of the same, that then all and every person or persons offending as aforesaid, shall be deemed and adjudged a felon or felons; and being lawfully convicted of such offence, after the laws of the realm, shall suffer pains of death and loss and forfeiture of lands, goods, and chattels, without benefit of clergy or privilege of sanctuary to be admitted or allowed in that behalf."

366 Accusation brought by Robert Wodehouse, Prior of Whitby, against the Abbot, for slanderous words against Anne Boleyn: *Rolls House MS.*

367 Deposition of Robert Legate concerning the Language of the Monks of Furness: *Rolls House MS.*

368 ELLIS, third series, vol. ii. p. 254.

369 Father Forest hath laboured divers manner of ways to expulse Father Laurence out of the convent, and his chief cause is, because he knoweth that Father Laurence will preach the king's matter whensoever it shall please his Grace to command him.—Ibid. p. 250.

370 Ibid. p. 251.

371 Lyst to Cromwell. Ibid. p. 255. STRYPE, *Eccles. Memor.*, vol. i. Appendix, No. 47.

372 STOW'S *Annals*, p. 562. This expression passed into a proverb, although the words were first spoken by a poor friar; they were the last which the good Sir Humfrey Gilbert was heard to utter before his ship went down.

373 Vaughan to Cromwell: *State Papers*, vol. vii. p. 489-90. "I learn that this book was first drawn by the Bishop of Rochester, and so being drawn, was by the said bishop afterwards delivered in England to two Spaniards, being secular and laymen. They receiving his first draught, either by themselves

or some other Spaniards, altered and perfinished the same into the form that it now is; Peto and one Friar Elstowe of Canterbury, being the only men that have and do take upon themselves to be conveyers of the same books into England, and conveyers of all other things into and out of England. If privy search be made, and shortly, peradventure in the house of the same bishop shall be found his first copy. Master More hath sent oftentimes and lately books unto Peto, in Antwerp—as his book of the confutation of Tyndal, and of Frith's opinion of the sacrament, with divers other books. I can no further learn of More's practices, but if you consider this well, you may perchance espy his craft. Peto laboureth busylier than a bee in the setting forth of this book. He never ceaseth running to and from the court here. The king never had in his realm traitors like his friars—[Vaughan wrote "clergy." The word in the original is dashed through, and "friars" is substituted, whether by Cromwell or by himself in an afterthought, I do not know]—and so I have always said, and yet do. Let his Grace look well about him, for they seek to devour him. They have blinded his Grace."

374 ELLIS, third series, vol. ii. p. 262, etc.

375 The wishes of the French Court had been expressed emphatically to Clement in the preceding January. Original copies of the two following letters are in the Bibliothèque Impérial at Paris:—

The Cardinal of Lorraine to Cardinal — — at Rome.

"Paris, Jan. 8, 1531-2.

"RIGHT REVEREND FATHER AND LORD IN CHRIST.—After our most humble commendations—The King of England complains loudly that his cause is not remanded into his own country; he says that it cannot be equitably dealt with at Rome, where he cannot be present. He himself, the Queen, and the other witnesses, are not to be dragged into Italy to give their evidence; and the suits of the Sovereigns of England and France have always hitherto been determined in their respective countries.

"Nevertheless, by no entreaty can we prevail on the Pope to nominate impartial judges who will decide the question in England.

"The King's personal indignation is not the only evil which has to be feared. When these proceedings are known among the people, there will, perhaps, be a revolt, and the Apostolic See may receive an injury which will not afterwards be easily remedied.

"I have explained these things more at length to his Holiness, as my duty requires. Your affection towards him, my lord, I am assured is no less than mine. I beseech you, therefore, use your best endeavours with his Holiness, that the King of England may no longer have occasion to exclaim against him. In so doing you will gratify the Most Christian King, and you will follow the course most honourable to yourself and most favourable to the quiet of Christendom.

"From Abbeville."

Francis the First to Pope Clement the Seventh.

"Paris, Jan. 10, 1531-2.

"MOST HOLY FATHER,—You are not ignorant what our good brother and ally the King of England demands at your hands. He requires that the cognisance of his marriage be remanded to his own realm, and that he be no further pressed to pursue the process at Rome. The place is inconvenient from its distance, and there are other good and reasonable objections which he assures us that he has urged upon your Holiness's consideration.

"Most Holy Father, we have written several times to you, especially of late from St. Cloud, and afterwards from Chantilly, in our good brother's behalf; and we have further entreated you, through our ambassador residing at your Court, to put an end to this business as nearly according to the wishes of our said good brother as is compatible with the honour of Almighty God. We have made this request of you as well for the affection and close alliance which exist between ourselves and our brother, as for the filial love and duty with which we both in common regard your Holiness.

"Seeing, nevertheless, Most Holy Father, that the affair in question is still far from settlement, and knowing our good brother to be displeased and dissatisfied, we fear that some great scandal and inconvenience may arise at last which may cause the diminution of your Holiness's authority. There is no longer that ready obedience to the Holy See in England which was offered to your predecessors; and yet your Holiness persists in citing my good brother the King of England to plead his cause before you in Rome. Surely it is not without cause that he calls such treatment of him unreasonable. We have ourselves examined into the law in this matter, and we are assured that your Holiness's claim is unjust and contrary to the privilege of kings. For a sovereign to leave his realm and plead as a suitor in Rome, is a thing wholly impossible,377 and therefore, Holy Father, we have thought good to address you once more in this matter. Bear with us, we entreat you. Consider our words, and recall to your memory what by letter and through our ministers we have urged upon you. Look promptly to our brother's matter, and so act that your Holiness may be seen to value and esteem our friendship. What you do for him, or what you do against him, we shall take it as done to ourselves.

"Holy Father, we will pray the Son of God to pardon and long preserve your Holiness to rule and govern our Holy Mother the Church.—FRANCIS."

376 *State Papers*, vol. vii. p. 428. LEGRAND, vol. iii.

377 Chose beaucoup plus impossible que possible.

378 LORD HERBERT, p. 160. RYMER, vol. vi. part ii. p. 171.

379 Francis seems to have desired that the intention of the interview should be kept secret. Henry found this impossible. "Monseigneur," wrote the Bishop of Paris to the Grand Master, "quant à tenir la chose secrette comme vous le demandez, il est mal aisé; combien que ce Roy fust bien de cest advis, sinon qu'il le treuve impossible; car a cause de ces provisions et choses, qu'il fault faire en ce Royaulme, incontinent sera sceu a Londres, et de la par tout le monde. Pourquoy ne faictes vostre compte qu'on le puisse tenir secret.

"Monseigneur, je sçay veritablement et de bon lieu que le plus grant plaisir que le Roy pourroit faire au Roy son frere et a Madame Anne, c'est que le dit seigneur m'escripre que je requiere le Roy son dit frere qu'il veuille mener la dicte Dame Anne avec luy a Callais pour la veoir et pour la festoyer, afin qu'ils ne demeurrent ensembles sans compagnie de dames, pour ce que les bonnes cheres en sont tous jours meilleures: mais il fauldroit que en pareil le Roy menast la Royne de Navarre à Boulogne, pour festoyer le Roy d'Angleterre.

"Quant à la Royne pour rien ce Roy ne vouldroit qu'elle vint: Il häit cest habillement à l'Espagnolle, tant qu'il luy semble veoir un diable. Il desireroit qu'il pleust au Roy mener à Boulogne, messeigneurs ses enfans pour les veoir.

"Surtout je vous prie que vous ostez de la court deux sortes de gens, ceulx qui sont imperiaulx, s'aucuns en y a, et ceux qui ont la reputation d'estre mocqueurs et gaudisseurs, car c'est bien la chose en ce monde autant häie de ceste nation."—Bishop of Paris to the Grand Master: LEGRAND, vol. iii. pp. 555, 556.

380 Sir Gregory Cassalis to Henry VIII.: BURNET'S *Collectanea*, p. 433. Valde existimabam necessarium cum hoc Principe (*i.e.*, Francis) agere ut duobus Cardinalibus daret in mandatis ut ante omnes Cardinalis de Monte meminissent, eique pensionem annuam saltem trium millium aureorum ex quadraginta millibus quæ mihi dixerat velle in Cardinales distribuere, assignaret. Et Rex quidem hæc etiam scribi ad duos Cardinales jussit secretario Vitandri. Quicum ego postmodo super iis pensionibus sermonem habui, cognovique sic in animo Regem habere ut duo Cardinales cum Romæ fuerint, videant, qui potissimum digni hâc Regiâ sint liberalitate;

in eosque quum quid in Regno Galliæ ecclesiasticum vacare contigerit ex meritis uniuscujusque pensiones conferantur. Tunc autem nihil in promptu haberi quod Cardinali de Monte dari possit—verum Regio nomine illi de futuro esse promittendum quod mihi certe summopere displicuit; et secretario Vitandri non reticui ostendens pollicitationes hujusmodi centies jam Cardinali de Monte factas fuisse; et modo si iterum fiant nihil effecturas nisi ut illius viri quasi ulcera pertractent; id quod Vitandris verum esse fatebatur pollicitusque est se, quum Rex a venatu rediisset velle ei suadere ut Cardinalem de Monte aliquâ presenti pensione prosequatur; quâ quidem tibi nihil conducibilius aut opportunius fieri possit.

381 *State Papers*, vol. iv. p. 612.

382 Ibid, p. 616.

383 The *State Papers* contain a piteous picture of this business, the hereditary feuds of centuries bursting out on the first symptoms of ill-will between the two governments, with fire and devastation.—*State Papers*, vol. iv. p. 620-644.

384 If the said Earl of Angus do make unto us oath of allegiance, and recognises us as Supreme Lord of Scotland, and as his prince and sovereign, we then, the said earl doing the premises, by these presents bind ourself to pay yearly to the said earl the sum of one thousand pounds sterling.— Henry VIII. to the Earl of Angus: *State Papers*, vol. iv. p. 613.

385 A letter of Queen Catherine to the Emperor, written on the occasion of this visit, will be read with interest:—

"HIGH AND MIGHTY LORD,—Although your Majesty is occupied with your own affairs and with your preparations against the Turk, I cannot, nevertheless, refrain from troubling you with mine, which perhaps in substance and in the sight of God are of equal importance. Your Majesty knows well, that God hears those who do him service, and no greater service can be done than to procure an end in this business. It does not concern only ourselves—it concerns equally all who fear God. None can measure the woes which will fall on Christendom, if his Holiness will not act in it and act promptly. The signs are all around us in new printed books full of lies and dishonesty—in the resolution to proceed with the cause here in England— in the interview of these two princes, where the king, my lord, is covering himself with infamy through the companion which he takes with him. The country is full of terror and scandal; and evil may be looked for if nothing be done, and inasmuch as our only hope is in God's mercy, and in the favour of your Majesty, for the discharge of my conscience, I must let you know the strait in which I am placed.

"I implore your Highness for the service of God, that you urge his Holiness to be prompt in bringing the cause to a conclusion. The longer the delay the harder the remedy will be.

"The particulars of what is passing here are so shocking, so outrageous against Almighty God, they touch so nearly the honour of my Lord and husband, that for the love I bear him, and for the good that I desire for him, I would not have your Highness know of them from me. Your ambassador will inform you of all."—Queen Catherine to Charles V. September 18.—MS. Simancas.

The Emperor, who was at Mantua, was disturbed at the meeting at Boulogne, on political grounds as well as personal. On the 24th of October he wrote to his sister, at Brussels.

Charles the Fifth to the Regent Mary.

Mantua, October 16, 1532.

I found your packets on arriving here, with the ambassadors' letters from France and England. The ambassadors will themselves have informed you of the intended conference of the Kings. The results will make themselves felt ere long. We must be on our guard, and I highly approve of your precautions for the protection of the frontiers.

As to the report that the King of England means to take the opportunity of the meeting to marry Anne Boleyn, I can hardly believe that he will be so blind as to do so, or that the King of France will lend himself to the other's sensuality. At all events, however, I have written to my ministers at Rome, and I have instructed them to lay a complaint before the Pope, that, while the process is yet pending, in contempt of the authority of the Church, the King of England is scandalously bringing over the said Anne with him, as if she were his wife.

His Holiness and the Apostolic See will be the more inclined to do us justice, and to provide as the case shall require.

Should the King indeed venture the marriage—as I cannot think he will—I have desired his Holiness not only not to sanction such conduct openly, but not to pass it by in silence. I have demanded that severe and fitting sentence be passed at once on an act so wicked and so derogatory to the Apostolic See.—*The Pilgrim*, p. 89.

386 There can be little doubt of this. He was the child of the only intrigue of Henry VIII. of which any credible evidence exists. His mother was Elizabeth, daughter of Sir John Blunt, an accomplished and most interesting person; and the offspring of the connection, one boy only, was brought up

with the care and the state of a prince. Henry FitzRoy, as he was called, was born in 1519, and when six years old was created Earl of Nottingham and Duke of Richmond and Somerset, the title of the king's father.

In 1527, before the commencement of the disturbance on the divorce, Henry endeavoured to negotiate a marriage for him with a princess of the imperial blood; and in the first overtures gave an intimation which could not be mistaken, of his intention, if possible, to place him in the line of the succession. After speaking of the desire which was felt by the King of England for some connection in marriage of the Houses of England and Spain, the ambassadors charged with the negotiation were to say to Charles, that—

"His Highness can be content to bestow the Duke of Richmond and Somerset (who is near of his blood, and of excellent qualities, and is already furnished to keep the state of a great prince, *and yet may be easily by the king's means exalted to higher things*) to some noble princess of his near blood." — ELLIS, third series, vol. ii. p. 121.

He was a gallant, high-spirited boy. A letter is extant from him to Wolsey, written when he was nine years old, begging the cardinal to intercede with the king, "for an harness to exercise myself in arms according to my erudition in the Commentaries of Cæsar." —Ibid. p. 119.

He was brought up with Lord Surrey, who has left a beautiful account of their boyhood at Windsor—their tournaments, their hunts, their young loves, and passionate friendship. Richmond married Surrey's sister, but died the year after, when only seventeen; and Surrey revisiting Windsor, recalls his image among the scenes which they had enjoyed together, in the most interesting of all his poems. He speaks of

> The secret grove, which oft we made resound
> Of pleasant plaint and of our ladies' praise;
> Recording oft what grace each one had found,
> What hope of speed, what dread of long delays.
> The wild forest; the clothed holts with green;
> With reins availed, and swift y-breathed horse,
> With cry of hounds, and merry blasts between,
> Where we did chase the fearful hart of force.
> The void walls eke that harboured us each night,
> Wherewith, alas! reviveth in my breast
> The sweet accord, such sleeps as yet delight
> The pleasant dream, the quiet bed of rest;
> The secret thought imparted with such trust.

The wanton talk, the divers change of play,
The friendship sworn, each promise kept so just,
Wherewith we past the winter nights away.

387 Compare LORD HERBERT with A Paper of Instructions to Lord Rochfort on his Mission to Paris: *State Papers*, vol. vii. p. 427, etc.; and A Remonstrance of Francis I. to Henry VIII.: LEGRAND, vol. iii. p. 571, etc. It would be curious to know whether Francis ever actually wrote to the pope a letter of which Henry sent him a draft. If he did, there are expressions contained in it which amount to a threat of separation. In case the pope was obstinate Francis was to say, "Lors force seroit de pourvoir audict affaire, par autres voyes et façons, qui peut etre, ne vous seroint gueres agreable." — *State Papers*, vol. vii. p. 436.

388 A nostre derniere entrevue sur la fraternelle et familiere communication que nous eusmes ensemble de noz affaires venant aux nostres, Luy declarasmes comme a tord et injustment nous estions affligez, dilayez, et fort ingratemeut manniez et troublez, en nostre dicte grande et pesante matiere de marriage par la particuliere affection de l'empereur et du pape. Lesquelz sembloient par leurs longues retardations de nostre dicte matiere ne sercher autre chose, sinon par longue attente et laps de temps, nous frustrer malicieusement du propoz, qui plus nous induict a poursuivir et mettre avant la dicte matiere; c'est davoir masculine succession et posterite en laquelle nous etablirons (Dieu voulant) le quiet repoz et tranquillite de notre royaulme et dominion. Son fraternel, plain, et entier advis (et a bref dire le meilleur qui pourroit estre) fut tel; il nous conseilla de ne dilayer ne protractor le temps plus longuement, mais en toute celerite proceder effectuellement a laccomplisment et consummation de nostre marriage. — Henry VIII. to Rochfort: *State Papers*, vol. vii. p. 428-9.

389 The extent of Francis's engagements, as Henry represents them, was this:— He had promised qu'en icelle nostre dicte cause jamais ne nous abandonneroit quelque chose que sen ensuyst; ainsi de tout son pouvoir l'establiroit, supporteroit, aideroit et maintiendroit notre bon droict, et le droict de la posterite et succession qui sen pourroit ensuyr; et a tous ceulz qui y vouldroyent mettre trouble, empeschement, encombrance, ou y procurer deshonneur, vitupere, ou infraction, il seroit enemy et adversaire de tout son pouvoir, de quelconque estat qu'il soit, fust pape ou empereur, — avecque plusieurs autres consolatives paroles. This he wished Francis to commit to paper. Car autant de fois, que les verrions, he says, qui seroit tous les jours, nous ne pourrions, si non les liscent, imaginer et reduire a notre souvenance la bonne grace facunde et geste, dont il les nous prononçait, et estimer estre comme face a face, parlans avecque luy. — *State Papers*, vol. vii. p. 437. Evidently language of so wide a kind might admit of many interpretations.

390 LEGRAND, vol. iii. p. 571, etc.

391 Note of the Revelations of Eliz. Barton: *Rolls House MS. Suppression of the Monasteries*, p. 17.

The intention was really perhaps what the nun said. An agent of the government at Brussels, who was watching the conference, reported on the 12th of November: — "The King of England did really cross with the intention of marrying; but, happily for the emperor, the ceremony is postponed. Of other secrets, my informant has learned thus much. They have resolved to demand as the portion of the Queen of France, Artois, Tournay, and part of Burgundy. They have also sent two cardinals to Rome to require the Pope to relinquish the tenths, which they have begun to levy for themselves. If his Holiness refuse, the King of England will simply appropriate them throughout his dominions. Captain — — heard this from the king's proctor at Rome, who has been with him at Calais, and from an Italian named Jeronymo, whom the Lady Anne has roughly handled for managing her business badly. She trusted that she would have been married in September.

"The proctor told her the Pope delayed sentence for fear of the Emperor. The two kings, when they heard this, despatched the cardinals to quicken his movements; and the demand for the tenths is thought to have been invented to frighten him.

"They are afraid that the Emperor may force his Holiness into giving sentence before the cardinals arrive. Jeronymo has been therefore sent forward by post to give him notice of their approach, and to require him to make no decision till they have spoken with him." — *The Pilgrim*, p. 89.

392 25 Hen. VIII. cap. 12.

393 Revelations of Eliz. Barton: *Rolls House MS.*

394 *State Papers*, vol. vii. pp. 435, 468.

395 Letter from — —, containing an account of an interview with his Holiness: *Rolls House MS.*

396 This proposal was originally the king's (see chapter 2), but it had been dropped because one of the conditions of it had been Catherine's "entrance into religion." The pope, however, had not lost sight of the alternative, as one of which, in case of extremity, he might avail himself; and, in 1530, in a short interval of relaxation, he had definitely offered the king a dispensation to have two wives, at the instigation, curiously, of the imperialists. The following letter was written on that occasion to the king by Sir Gregory Cassalis: —

Serenissime et potentissime domine rex, domine mi supreme humillimâ commendatione premissâ, salutem et felicitatem. Superioribus diebus Pontifex secreto, veluti rem quam magni faceret, mihi proposuit conditionem hujusmodi; concedi posse vestræ majestati, ut duas uxores habeat; cui dixi nolle me provinciam suscipere eâ de re scribendi, ob eam causam quod ignorarem an inde vestræ conscientiæ satisfieri posset quam vestra majestas imprimis exonerare cupit. Cur autem sic responderem, illud in causâ fuit, quod ex certo loco, unde quæ Cæsariani moliantur aucupari soleo exploratum certumque habebam Cæsarianos illud ipsum quærere et procurare. Quem vero ad finem id quærant pro certo exprimere non ausim. Id certe totum vestræ prudentiæ considerandum relinquo. Et quamvis dixerim Pontifici, nihil me de eo scripturum, nolui tamen majestati vestræ hoc reticere; quæ sciat omni me industriâ laborâsse in iis quæ nobis mandat exequendis et cum Anconitano qui me familiariter uti solet, omnia sum conatus. De omnibus autem me ad communes literas rejicio. Optime valeat vestra majestas.—Romæ die xviii. Septembris, 1530.

Clarissimi vestrai Majestatis, Humillimus servus,

GREGORIUS CASSALIS,

—LORD HERBERT, p. 140.

397 *State Papers*, vol. vii. p. 394, etc.

398 The obtaining the opinion in writing of the late Cardinal of Ancona, and submitting it to the emperor. This minister, the most aged as well as the most influential member of the conclave, had latterly been supposed to be inclined to advise a conciliatory policy towards England; and his judgment was of so much weight that it was thought likely that the emperor would have been unable to resist the publication of it, if it was given against him. At the critical moment of the Bologna interview this cardinal unfortunately died: he had left his sentiments, however, in the hands of his nephew, the Cardinal of Ravenna, who, knowing the value of his legacy, was disposed to make a market of it. It was a knavish piece of business. The English ambassadors offered 3000 ducats; Charles bid them out of the field with a promise of church benefices to the extent of 6000 ducats; he did not know precisely the terms of the judgment, or even on which side it inclined, but in either case the purchase was of equal importance to him, either to produce it or to suppress it. The French and English ambassadors then combined, and bid again with church benefices in the two countries, of equal value with those offered by Charles, with a promise of the next English bishopric which fell vacant, and the original 3000 ducats as an initiatory fee. There was a difficulty in the transaction, for the cardinal would not part with the paper till he had received the ducats, and the ambassadors would not pay the

ducats till they had possession of the paper. The Italian, however, proved an overmatch for his antagonists. He got his money, and the judgment was not produced after all.—*State Papers*, vol. vii. pp. 397-8, 464. BURNET, vol. iii. p. 108.

399 Bennet to Henry VIII.: *State Papers*, vol. vii. p. 402.

400 Sir Gregory Cassalis to the King: *Rolls House M.S.*, endorsed by Henry, Litteræ in Pontificis dicta declaratoriæ quæ maxime causam nostram probant.

401 There was a tradition (it cannot be called more), that no Englishman could be compelled against his will to plead at a foreign tribunal. "Ne Angli extra Angliam litigare cogantur."

402 Henry VIII. to the Ambassadors with the Pope: *Rolls House M.S.*

403 Ibid.

404 So at least the English government was at last convinced, as appears in the circular to the clergy, printed in BURNET'S *Collectanea*, p. 447, etc. I try to believe, however, that the pope's conduct was rather weak than treacherous.

405 So at least Cranmer says; but he was not present, nor was he at the time informed that it was to take place.—ELLIS, first series, vol. ii. p. 32. The belief, however, generally was, that the marriage took place in November; and though Cranmer's evidence is very strong, his language is too vague to be decisive.

406 Individual interests have to yield necessarily and justly to the interests of a nation, provided the conduct or the sacrifice which the nation requires is not sinful. That there would have been any sin on Queen Catherine's part if she had consented to a separation from the king, was never pretended; and although it is a difficult and delicate matter to decide how far unwilling persons may be compelled to do what they ought to have done without compulsion, yet the will of a single man or woman cannot be allowed to constitute itself an irremovable obstacle to a great national good.

407 It is printed by LORD HERBERT, and in LEGRAND, vol. iii.

408 LEGRAND, vol. iii. p. 558, etc.

409 Ye may show unto his Holiness that ye have heard from a friend of yours in Flanders lately, that there hath been set up certain writings from the See Apostolic, in derogation both of justice and of the affection lately showed by his Holiness unto us; which thing ye may say ye can hardly believe to be true, but that ye reckon them rather to be counterfeited. For if it should be true, it is a thing too far out of the way, specially considering

that you and other our ambassadors be there, and have heard nothing of the matter. We send a copy of these writings unto you, which copy we will in no wise that ye shall show to any person which might think that ye had any knowledge from us nor any of our council, marvelling greatly if the same hath proceeded indeed from the pope; [and] willing you expressly not to show that ye had it of us.—*State Papers*, vol. vii. p. 421.

410 *State Papers*, vol. vii. p. 454.

411 Sir John Wallop to Henry: *State Papers*, vol. vii. p. 422.

412 Francis represented himself to Henry as having refused with a species of bravado. "He told me," says Sir John Wallop, "that he had announced previously that he would consent to no such interview, unless your Highness were also comprised in the same; and if it were so condescended that your Highness and he should be then together, yet you two should go after such a sort and with such power that you would not care whether the pope and emperor would have peace or else *coups de baston*."—Wallop to Henry, from Paris, Feb. 22. But this was scarcely a complete account of the transaction; it was an account only of so much of it as the French king was pleased to communicate. The emperor was urgent for a council. The pope, feeling the difficulty either of excluding or admitting the Protestant representatives, was afraid of consenting to it, and equally afraid of refusing. The meeting proposed to Francis was for the discussion of this difficulty; and Francis, in return, proposed that the great Powers, Henry included, should hold an interview, and arrange beforehand the conclusions at which the council should arrive. This naïve suggestion was waived by Charles, apparently on grounds of religion. LORD HERBERT, Kennet's Edit. p. 167.

413 The emperor's answer touching this interview is come, and is, in effect, that if the pope shall judge the said interview to be for the wealth and quietness of Christendom, he will not be seen to dissuade his Holiness from the same; but he desired him to remember what he showed to his Holiness when he was with the same, at what time his Holiness offered himself for the commonwealth to go to any place to speak with the French king.—Bennet to Henry VIII.; *State Papers*, vol. vii. p. 464.

414 The estrapade was an infernal machine introduced by Francis into Paris for the better correction of heresy. The offender was slung by a chain over a fire, and by means of a crane was dipped up and down into the flame, the torture being thus prolonged for an indefinite time. Francis was occasionally present in person at these exhibitions, the executioner waiting his arrival before commencing the spectacle.

415 24 Hen. VIII. cap. 13.

416 24 Hen. VIII. cap. 12

417 *State Papers*, vol. vii. p. 441.

418 D'Inteville to Francis the First: MS. Bibliothèque Impérial, Paris—*Pilgrim*, p. 92.

419 24 Hen. VIII. cap. 12.

420 He had been selected as Warham's successor; and had been consecrated on the 30th of March, 1533. On the occasion of the ceremony when the usual oath to the Pope was presented to him, he took it with a declaration that his first duty and first obedience was to the crown and laws of his own country. It is idle trifling, to build up, as too many writers have attempted to do, a charge of insincerity upon an action which was forced upon him by the existing relation between England and Rome. The Act of Appeals was the law of the land. The separation from communion with the papacy was a contingency which there was still a hope might be avoided. Such a protest as Cranmer made was therefore the easiest solution of the difficulty. See it in STRYPE'S *Cranmer*, Appendix, p. 683.

421 BURNET, Vol. iii. pp. 122-3

422 Bennet to Henry VIII.: *State Papers*, vol. vii. p. 402. Sir Gregory Cassalis to the same: *Rolls House MS.*

423 BURNET, vol. iii. p. 123.

424 Ibid. vol. i. p. 210.

425 See *State Papers*, vol. i. pp. 415, 420, etc.

426 BURNET'S *Collectanea*, p. 22. It is very singular that in the original Bull of Julius, the expression is "forsan consummavissetis;" while in the brief, which, if it was genuine, was written the same day, and which, if forged, was forged by Catherine's friends, there is no forsan. The fact is stated absolutely.

427 LORD HERBERT, p. 163. BURNET. vol. iii. p. 123.

428 *State Papers*, vol. i. pp. 390. 391.

429 Ye therefore duly recognising that it becometh you not, being our subject, to enterprise any part of your said office in so weighty and great a cause pertaining to us being your prince and sovereign, without our licence obtained so to do; and therefore in your most humble wise ye supplicate us to grant unto you our licence to proceed.—*State Papers*, vol. i. p. 392.

430 *State Papers*, vol. i. p. 392.

431 Cromwell to the King on his Committal to the Tower: BURNET, *Collectanea*, p. 500.

432 So at least she called him a few days later.—*State Papers*, vol. i. p. 420. We have no details of her words when she was summoned; but only a general account of them.—*State Papers*, vol. i. p. 394-5.

433 The words of the sentence may be interesting:—"In the name of God, Amen. We, Thomas, by Divine permission Archbishop of Canterbury, Primate of all England, and Legate of the Apostolic See, in a certain cause of inquiry of and concerning the validity of the marriage contracted and consummated between the most potent and most illustrious Prince, our Sovereign Lord, Henry VIII., by the grace of God King of England and France, Defender of the Faith, and Lord of Ireland, and the most serene Princess, Catherine, daughter of his Most Catholic Majesty, Ferdinand, King of Spain, of glorious memory, we proceeding according to law and justice in the said cause which has been brought judicially before us in virtue of our office, and which for some time has lain under examination, as it still is, being not yet finally determined and decided; having first seen all the articles and pleas which have been exhibited and set forth of her part, together with the answers made thereto on the part of the most illustrious and powerful Prince, Henry VIII.; having likewise seen and diligently inspected the informations and depositions of many noblemen and other witnesses of unsuspected veracity exhibited in the said cause; having also seen and in like manner carefully considered not only the censures and decrees of the most famous universities of almost the whole Christian world, but likewise the opinions and determinations both of the most eminent divines and civilians, as also the resolutions and conclusions of the clergy of both Provinces of England in Convocation assembled, and many other wholesome instructions and doctrines which have been given in and laid before us concerning the said marriage; having further seen and in like manner inspected all the treaties and leagues of peace and amity on this account entered upon and concluded between Henry VII., of immortal fame, late King of England, and the said Ferdinand, of glorious memory, late King of Spain; having besides seen and most carefully weighed all and every of the acts, debates, letters, processes, instruments, writs, arguments, and all other things which have passed and been transacted in the said cause at any time; in all which thus seen and inspected, our most exact care in examining, and our most mature deliberation in weighing them hath by us been used, and all other things have been observed by us, which of right in this matter were to be observed; furthermore, the said most illustrious Prince, Henry VIII., in the forementioned cause, by his proper Proctor having appeared before us, but the said most serene Lady Catherine in contempt absenting herself (whose

absence we pray that the divine presence may compensate) [cujus absentia Divinâ repleatur præsentiâ. Lord Herbert translates it, "whose absence may the Divine presence attend," missing, I think, the point of the Archbishop's parenthesis] by and with the advice of the most learned in the law, and of persons of most eminent skill in divinity whom we have consulted in the premises, we have found it our duty to proceed to give our final decree and sentence in the said cause, which, accordingly, we do in this manner.

"Because by acts, warrants, deductions, propositions, exhibitions, allegations, proofs and confessions, articles drawn up, answers of witnesses, depositions, informations, instruments, arguments, letters, writs, censures, determinations of professors, opinions, councils, assertions, affirmations, treaties, and leagues of peace, processes, and other matters in the said cause, as is above mentioned, before us laid, had, done, exhibited, and respectively produced, as also from the same and sundry other reasons, causes, and considerations, manifold arguments, and various kinds of proof of the greatest evidence, strength, and validity, of which in the said cause we have fully and clearly informed ourselves, we find, and with undeniable evidence and plainness see that the marriage contracted and consummated, as is aforesaid, between the said most illustrious Prince, Henry VIII., and the most serene Lady Catherine, was and is null and invalid, and that it was contracted and consummated contrary to the law of God: therefore, we, Thomas, Archbishop, Primate, and Legate aforesaid, having first called upon the name of Christ for direction herein, and having God altogether before our eyes, do pronounce sentence, and declare for the invalidity of the said marriage, decreeing that the said pretended marriage always was and still is null and invalid; that it was contracted and consummated contrary to the will and law of God, that it is of no force or obligation, but that it always wanted, and still wants, the strength and sanction of law; and therefore we sentence that it is not lawful for the said most illustrious Prince, Henry VIII., and the said most serene Lady Catherine, to remain in the said pretended marriage; and we do separate and divorce them one from the other, inasmuch as they contracted and consummated the said pretended marriage de facto, and not de jure; and that they so separated and divorced are absolutely free from all marriage bond with regard to the foresaid pretended marriage, we pronounce, and declare by this our definitive sentence and final decree, which we now give, and by the tenour of these present writings do publish. May 23rd, 1533." —BURNET'S *Collectanea*, p. 68, and LORD HERBERT.

434 HALL.

435 Ibid.

436 Ibid. p. 801. Hall was most likely an eye-witness, and may be thoroughly trusted in these descriptions. Whenever we are able to test him, which sometimes happens, by independent contemporary accounts, he proves faithful in the most minute particulars.

437 FOXE, vol. v. p. III.

438 Northumberland to Henry VIII.: *State Papers*, vol. iv. pp. 598-9.

439 Hawkins to Henry VIII.: *Ibid.* vol. vii. p. 488.

440 BURNET. vol. iii. p. 115.

441 *State Papers*, vol. i. p. 398.

442 Papers relating to the Nun of Kent: *Rolls House MS.*

443 ELLIS, first series, vol. ii. p. 43.

444 *Cotton M.S.* Otho X, p. 199. *State Papers*, vol. i. p. 397.

445 *State Papers*, vol. i. p. 403.

446 Cromwell had endeavoured to save Frith, or at least had been interested for him. Sir Edmund Walsingham, writing to him about the prisoners in the Tower, says:—"Two of them wear irons, and Frith weareth none. Although he lacketh irons, he lacketh not wit nor pleasant tongue. His learning passeth my judgment. Sir, as ye said, it were great pity to lose him if he may be reconciled."—Walsingham to Cromwell: *M.S. State Paper Office*, second series, vol. xlvi.

447 ELLIS, first series, vol. ii. p. 40.

448 "The natural body and blood of our Saviour Christ are in Heaven, and not here, it being against the truth of Christ's natural body to be at one time in more places than one." The argument and the words in which it is expressed were Frith's.—See FOXE, vol. v. p. 6.

449 The origin of the word Lollards has been always a disputed question. I conceive it to be from Lolium. They were the "tares" in the corn of Catholicism.

450 35 Ed. I.; Statutes of Carlisle, cap. 1-4.

451 Ibid.

452 25 Ed. III. stat. 4. A clause in the preamble of this act bears a significantly Erastian complexion: *come seinte Eglise estoit founde en estat de prelacie deins le royaulme Dengleterre par le dit Roi et ses progenitours, et countes, barons, et nobles de ce Royaulme et lours ancestres, pour eux et le poeple enfourmer de la lei Dieu.* If the Church of England was held to have been, founded not

by the successors of the Apostles, but by the king and the nobles, the claim of Henry VIII. to the supremacy was precisely in the spirit of the constitution.

453 38 Ed. III. stat. 2; 3 Ric. II. cap. 3; 12 Ric. II. cap. 15; 13 Ric. II. stat. 2. The first of these acts contains a paragraph which shifts the blame from the popes themselves to the officials of the Roman courts. The statute is said to have been enacted en eide et confort du pape qui moult sovent a estee trublez par tieles et semblables clamours et impetracions, et qui y meist voluntiers covenable remedie, si sa seyntetee estoit sur ces choses enfournee. I had regarded this passage as a fiction of courtesy like that of the Long Parliament who levied troops in the name of Charles I. The suspicious omission of the clause, however, in the translation of the statutes which was made in the later years of Henry VIII. justifies an interpretation more favourable to the intentions of the popes.

454 The abbots and bishops decently protested. Their protest was read in parliament, and entered on the Rolls. *Rot. Parl.* iii. [264] quoted by Lingard, who has given a full account of these transactions.

455 13 Ric. II. stat. 2.

456 See 16 Ric. II. cap. 5.

457 This it will be remembered was the course which was afterwards followed by the parliament under Henry VIII. before abolishing the payment of first-fruits.

458 Lingard says, that "there were rumours that if the prelates executed the decree of the king's courts, they would be excommunicated." —Vol. iii. p. 172. The language of the act of parliament, 16 Ric. II. cap. 5, is explicit that the sentence was pronounced.

459 16 Ric. II. cap. 5.

460 Ibid.

461 Ibid.

462 LEWIS, *Life of Wycliffe.*

463 If such *scientia media* might be allowed to man, which is beneath certainty and above conjecture, such should I call our persuasion that he was born in Durham.—FULLER'S *Worthies*, vol. i. p. 479.

464 *The Last Age of the Church* was written in 1356. See LEWIS, p. 3.

465 LELAND.

466 LEWIS, p. 287.

467 1 Ric. II. cap. 13.

468 WALSINGHAM, 206-7, apud LINGARD. It is to be observed, however, that Wycliffe himself limited his arguments strictly to the property of the clergy. See MILMAN'S *History of Latin Christianity*, vol. v. p. 508.

469 WALSINGHAM, p. 275, apud LINGARD.

470 5 Ric. II. cap. 5.

471 WILKINS, *Concilia*, iii. 160-167.

472 *De Heretico comburendo*. 2 Hen. IV. cap. 15.

473 STOW, 330, 338.

474 *Rot. Parl.* iv. 24, 108, apud LINGARD; RYMER, ix. 89, 119, 129, 170, 193; MILMAN, Vol. v. p. 520-535.

475 2 Hen. V. stat. 1, cap. 7.

476 There is no better test of the popular opinion of a man than the character assigned to him on the stage; and till the close of the sixteenth century Sir John Oldcastle remained the profligate buffoon of English comedy. Whether in life he bore the character so assigned to him, I am unable to say. The popularity of Henry V., and the splendour of his French wars, served no doubt to colour all who had opposed him with a blacker shade than they deserved: but it is almost certain that Shakspeare, though not intending Falstaff as a portrait of Oldcastle, thought of him as he was designing the character; and it is altogether certain that by the London public Falstaff was supposed to represent Oldcastle. We can hardly suppose that such an expression as "my old lad of the castle," should be accidental; and in the epilogue to the Second Part of *Henry the Fourth*, when promising to reintroduce Falstaff once more, Shakspeare says, "where for anything I know he shall die of the sweat, for Oldcastle died a martyr, and this is not the man." He had, therefore, certainly been supposed to *be the man*, and Falstaff represented the English conception of the character of the Lollard hero. I should add, however, that Dean Milman, who has examined the records which remain to throw light on the character of this remarkable person with elaborate care and ability, concludes emphatically in his favour.

477 Two curious letters of Henry VI. upon the Lollards, written in 1431, are printed in the *Archæologia*, vol. xxiii. p. 339, etc. "As God knoweth," he says of them, "never would they be subject to his laws nor to man's, but would be loose and free to rob, reve, and dispoil, slay and destroy all men of thrift and worship, as they proposed to have done in our father's days; and of lads and lurdains would make lords."

478 Proceedings of an organised Society in London called the Christian Brethren, supported by voluntary contributions, for the dispersion of tracts against the doctrines of the Church: *Rolls House MS.*

479 HALE'S *Precedents*. The London and Lincoln Registers, in FOXE, vol. iv.; and the MS. Registers of Archbishops Morton and Warham, at Lambeth.

480 KNOX'S *History of the Reformation in Scotland*.

481 Also we object to you that divers times, and specially in Robert Durdant's house, of Iver Court, near unto Staines, you erroneously and damnably read in a great book of heresy, all [one] night, certain chapters of the Evangelists, in English, containing in them divers erroneous and damnable opinions and conclusions of heresy, in the presence of divers suspected persons.—Articles objected against Richard Butler—London Register: FOXE, vol. iv. p. 178.

482 FOXE, vol. iv. p. 176.

483 MICHELET, *Life of Luther*, p. 71.

484 Ibid.

485 Ibid. p. 41.

486 WOOD'S *Athenæ Oxonienses*.

487 FOXE, vol. iv. p. 618.

488 The suspicious eyes of the Bishops discovered Tyndal's visit, and the result which was to be expected from it.

On Dec. 2nd, 1525, Edward Lee, afterwards Archbishop of York, then king's almoner, and on a mission into Spain, wrote from Bordeaux to warn Henry. The letter is instructive: •

"Please your Highness to understand that I am certainly informed as I passed in this country, that an Englishman, your subject, at the solicitation and instance of Luther, with whom he is, hath translated the New Testament into English; and within few days intendeth to return with the same imprinted into England. I need not to advertise your Grace what infection and danger may ensue hereby if it be not withstanded. This is the next way to fulfil your realm with Lutherians. For all Luther's perverse opinions be grounded upon bare words of Scripture, not well taken, ne understanded, which your Grace hath opened in sundry places of your royal book. All our forefathers, governors of the Church of England, hath with all diligence forbid and eschewed publication of English Bibles, as appeareth in constitutions provincial of the Church of England. Nowe, sure, as God hath endued your Grace with Christian courage to sett forth the standard against these Philistines and to vanquish them, so I doubt not but that he will assist your Grace to prosecute and perform the same—that is, to undertread them that they shall not now lift up their heads; which they endeavour by means of English Bibles. They know what hurt such books hath done in your realm in times past."—Edward Lee to Henry VIII.: ELLIS, third series, vol. ii. p. 71.

489 Answer of the Bishops: *Rolls House MS.* See cap. 3.

490 Answer of the Bishops, vol. i. cap. 3.

491 See, particularly, *State Papers*, vol. vii. p. 302.

492 Proceedings of the Christian Brethren: *Rolls House MS.*

493 See the letter of Bishop Fox to Wolsey: STRYPE'S *Memorials*, vol. i. Appendix.

494 Particulars of Persons who had dispersed Anabaptist and Lutheran Tracts: *Rolls House MS.*

495 Dr. Taylor to Wolsey: *Rolls House MS.* Clark to Wolsey: *State Papers*, vol. vii. pp. 80, 81.

496 ELLIS, third series, vol. ii. p. 189.

497 Memoirs of Latimer prefixed to *Sermons*, pp. 3, 4; and see STRYPE'S *Memorials*, vol. i.

498 FOXE, vol. v. p. 416.

499 Tunstall, Bishop of London, has had the credit hitherto of this ingenious folly, the effect of which, as Sir Thomas More warned him, could only be to supply Tyndal with money.—HALL, 762, 763. The following letter from the Bishop of Norwich to Warham shows that Tunstall was only acting in canonical obedience to the resolution of his metropolitan:—

"In right humble manner I commend me unto your good Lordship, doing the same to understand that I lately received your letters, dated at your manor of Lambeth, the 26th day of the month of May, by the which I do perceive that your Grace hath lately gotten into your hands all the books of the New Testament, translated into English, and printed beyond the sea; as well those with the glosses joined unto them as those without the glosses.

"Surely, in myn opinion, you have done therein a gracious and a blessed deed; and God, I doubt not, shall highly reward you therefore. And when, in your said letters, ye write that, insomuch as this matter and the danger thereof, if remedy had not been provided, should not only have touched you, but all the bishops within your province; and that it is no reason that the holle charge and cost thereof should rest only in you; but that they and every of them, for their part, should advance and contribute certain sums of money towards the same: I for my part will be contented to advance in this behalf, and to make payment thereof unto your servant, Master William Potkyn.

"Pleaseth it you to understand, I am well contented to give and advance in this behalf ten marks, and shall cause the same to be delivered shortly; the which sum I think sufficient for my part, if every bishop within your province make like contribution, after the rate and substance of their benefices. Nevertheless, if your Grace think this sum not sufficient for my part in this matter, your further pleasure known, I shall be as glad to conform myself thereunto in this, or any other matter concerning the church, as any your subject within your province; as knows Almighty God, who long preserve you. At Hoxne in Suffolk, the 14th day of June, 1527. Your humble obedience and bedeman,

"R. NORWICEN."

500 FOXE, vol. iv.

501 The papal bull, and the king's licence to proceed upon it, are printed in *Rymer*, vol. vi. part ii. pp. 8 and 17. The latter is explicit on Wolsey's personal liberality in establishing this foundation. Ultro et ex propriâ liberalitate et munificentiâ, nec sine gravissimo suo sumptu et impensis, collegium fundare conatur.

502 Would God my Lord his Grace had never been motioned to call any Cambridge man to his most towardly college. It were a gracious deed if they were tried and purged and restored unto their mother from whence they came, if they be worthy to come thither again. We were clear without blot or suspicion till they came, and some of them, as Master Dean hath known a long time, hath had a shrewd name.—Dr. London to Archbishop Warham: *Rolls House MS.*

503 Dr. London to Warham: *Rolls House MS.*

504 DALABER'S *Narrative.*

505 Clark seems to have taken pupils in the long vacation. Dalaber at least read with him all one summer in the country.—Dr. London to Warham: *Rolls House MS.*

506 The Vicar of Bristol to the Master of Lincoln College, Oxford: *Rolls House MS.*

507 Dr. London to Warham: *Rolls House MS.*

508 Radley himself was one of the singers at Christchurch: London to Warham. *MS.*

509 Dr. London to Warham: *Rolls House MS.*

510 On the site of the present Worcester College. It lay beyond the walls of the town, and was then some distance from it across the fields.

511 Christchurch, where Dalaber occasionally sung in the quire. Vide infra.

512 Some part of which let us read with him. "I send you forth as sheep in the midst of wolves; be ye therefore wise as serpents and harmless as doves. But beware of men, for they will deliver you up to the councils, and they will scourge you in their synagogues; and ye shall be brought before governors and kings for my sake, for a testimony against them and the gentiles. But when they deliver you up, take no thought how or what ye shall speak, for it shall be given you in that same hour what ye shall speak; for it is not ye that speak, but the Spirit of your Father which speaketh in you. And the brother shall deliver up the brother to death; and the father the child; and the children shall rise up against their parents, and cause them to be put to death. And ye shall be hated of all men for my name's sake: but he that endureth to the end shall be saved. Whosoever shall confess me before men, him will I confess also before my Father which is in heaven. Whosoever shall deny me before men, him will I also deny before my Father which is in heaven. Think not that I am come to send peace on earth; I came not to send peace, but a sword. For I am come to set a man at variance against his father, and the daughter against her mother, and the daughter-in-law against her mother-in-law. And a man's foes shall be they of his own household. He that loveth father or mother more than me is not worthy of me. He that loveth son or daughter more than me is not worthy of me. He that taketh not his cross and followeth after me is not worthy of me. He that findeth his life shall lose it, and he that loseth his life for my sake shall find it."

513 Rector of Lincoln.

514 Warden of New College.

515 The last prayer.

516 Dr. Maitland, who has an indifferent opinion of the early Protestants, especially on the point of veracity, brings forward this assertion of Dalaber as an illustration of what he considers their recklessness. It seems obvious, however, that a falsehood of this kind is something different in kind from what we commonly mean by unveracity, and has no affinity with it. I do not see my way to a conclusion; but I am satisfied that Dr. Maitland's strictures are unjust. If Garret was taken, he was in danger of a cruel death, and his escape could only be made possible by throwing the bloodhounds off the

scent. A refusal to answer would not have been sufficient; and the general laws by which our conduct is ordinarily to be directed, cannot be made so universal in their application as to meet all contingencies. It is a law that we may not strike or kill other men, but occasions rise in which we may innocently do both. I may kill a man in defence of my own life or my friend's life, or even of my friend's property; and surely the circumstances which dispense with obedience to one law may dispense equally with obedience to another. If I may kill a man to prevent him from robbing my friend, why may I not deceive a man to save my friend from being barbarously murdered? It is possible that the highest morality would forbid me to do either. I am unable to see why, if the first be permissible, the second should be a crime. Rahab of Jericho did the same thing which Dalaber did, and on that very ground was placed in the catalogue of saints.

517 A cell in the Tower, the nature of which we need not inquire into.

518 FOXE, vol. v. p. 421.

519 Dr. London to the Bishop of Lincoln: *Rolls House MS.*

520 Ibid.

521 Dr. Forman, rector of All Hallows, who had himself been in trouble for heterodoxy.

522 Dr. London to the Bishop of Lincoln, Feb. 20, 1528: *Rolls House MS.*

523 Now Cokethorpe Park, three miles from Stanton Harcourt, and about twelve from Oxford. The village has disappeared.

524 Vicar of All Saints, Bristol, to the Rector of Lincoln: *Rolls House MS.*

525 The Vicar of All Saints to the Rector of Lincoln: *Rolls House MS.*

526 Dr. London to the Bishop of Lincoln: *Rolls House MS.*

527 Long extracts from it are printed in FOXE, vol. iv.

528 Another of the brethren, afterwards Bishop of St. David's, and one of the Marian victims.

529 Bishop of Lincoln to Wolsey, March 5, 1527-8: *Rolls House MS.*: and see ELLIS, third series, vol. ii. p. 77.

530 ELLIS, third series, vol. ii. p. 77.

531 With some others he "was cast into a prison where the saltfish lay, through the stink whereof the most part of them were infected; and the said Clark, being a tender young man, died in the same prison."—FOXE, vol. iv. p. 615.

532 London to Warham: *Rolls House MS.*

533 Petition of the Commons, vol. i. cap. 3.

534 Ibid. And, as we saw in the bishops' reply, they considered their practice in these respects wholly defensible.—See *Reply of the Bishops*, cap. 3.

535 Petition of the Commons, cap. 3.

536 Hen. V. stat. 1.

537 He had been "troublesome to heretics," he said, and he had "done it with a little ambition;" for "he so hated this kind of men, that he would fie the sorest enemy that they could have, if they would not repent."—MORE'S *Life of More*, p. 211.

538 See FOXE:, vol. iv. pp. 689, 698, 705.

539 2 Hen. V. stat. 1.

540 John Stokesley.

541 Petition of Thomas Philips to the House of Commons: *Rolls House MS.*

542 Ibid.

543 FOXE, vol. v. pp. 29, 30.

544 The circumstances are curious. Philips begged that he might have the benefit of the king's writ of corpus cum causâ, and be brought to the bar of the House of Commons, where the Bishop of London should be subpœnaed to meet him. [Petition of Thomas Philips: *Rolls House MS.*] The Commons did not venture on so strong a measure; but a digest of the petition was sent to the Upper House, that the bishop might have an opportunity of reply. The Lords refused to receive or consider the case: they replied that it was too "frivolous an affair" for so grave an assembly, and that they could not discuss it. [*Lords' Journals*, vol. i. p. 66.] A deputation of the Commons then waited privately upon the bishop, and being of course anxious to ascertain whether Philips had given a true version of what had passed, they begged him to give some written explanation of his conduct, which might be read in the Commons' House. [*Lords' Journals*, vol. i. p. 71.] The request was reasonable, and we cannot doubt that, if explanation had been possible, the bishop would not have failed to offer it; but he preferred to shield himself behind the judgment of the Lords. The Lords, he said, had decided that the matter was too frivolous for their own consideration; and without their permission, he might not set a precedent of responsibility to the Commons by answering their questions.

This conduct met with the unanimous approval of the Peers. [*Lords' Journals*, vol. i. p. 71. Omnes proceres tam spirituales quam temporales unâ, voce dicebant, quod non consentaneum fuit aliquem procerum prædictorum alicui in eo loco responsurum.] The demand for explanation was treated as a breach of privilege, and the bishop was allowed to remain silent. But the time was passed for conduct of this kind to be allowed to triumph. If the bishop could not or would not justify himself, his victim might at least be released from unjust imprisonment. The case was referred to the king: and by the king and the House of Commons Philips was set at liberty.

545 Petition of John Field: *Rolls House MS.*

546 Jan. 1529-30.

547 Illegal. See 2 Hen. V. stat. 1.

548 Seventh Sermon before King Edward. First Sermon before the Duchess of Suffolk.

549 FOXE, vol. iv. p. 649.

550 Articles against James Bainham: FOXE, vol. iv. p. 703.

551 FOXE, vol. iv. p. 702.

552 Ibid. vol. iv. p. 705.

553 Ibid. vol. iv. p. 694.

554 HALL, p. 806; and see FOXE, vol iv. p. 705.

555 Instructions given by the Bishop of Salisbury: BURNET'S *Collectanea*, p. 493.

556 From a Letter of Robert Gardiner: FOXE, vol. iv. p. 706.

557 LATIMER'S *Sermons*, p. 101.

558 Latimer speaks of sons and daughters.—Ibid. p. 101.

559 Ibid.

560 Where the Cornish rebels came to an end in 1497.—BACON'S *History of Henry the Seventh.*

561 LATIMER'S *Sermons*, p. 197.

562 On which occasion, old relations perhaps shook their heads, and made objection to the expense. Some such feeling is indicated in the following glimpse behind the veil of Latimer's private history:—

"I was once called to one of my kinsfolk," he says ("it was at that time when I had taken my degree at Cambridge); I was called, I say, to one of my kinsfolk which was very sick, and died immediately after my coming. Now, there was an old cousin of mine, which, after the man was dead, gave me a wax candle in my hand, and commanded me to make certain crosses over him that was dead; for she thought the devil should run away by and bye. Now, I took the candle, but I could not cross him as she would have me to do; for I had never seen it before. She, perceiving I could not do it, with great anger took the candle out of my hand, saying, 'It is pity that thy father spendeth so much money upon thee;' and so she took the candle, and crossed and blessed him; so that he was sure enough."—LATIMER'S *Sermons*, p. 499.

563 "I was as obstinate a papist as any was in England, insomuch that, when I should be made Bachelor of Divinity, my whole oration went against Philip Melancthon and his opinions."—LATIMER'S *Sermons*, p. 334.

564 *Jewel of Joy*, p. 224, et seq.: Parker Society's edition. LATIMER'S *Sermons*, p. 3.

565 LATIMER'S *Remains*, pp. 27-31.

566 Ibid. pp. 308-9.

567 LATIMER to Sir Edward Baynton: *Letters*, p. 329.

568 *Letters*, p. 323.

569 He thought of going abroad. "I have trust that God will help me," he wrote to a friend; "if I had not, I think the ocean sea should have divided my Lord of London and me by this day."—*Remains*, p. 334.

570 Latimer to Sir Edward Baynton.

571 See Latimer's two letters to Sir Edward Baynton: *Remains*, pp. 322-351.

572 "As ye say, the matter is weighty, and ought substantially to be looked upon, even as weighty as my life is worth; but how to look substantially upon it otherwise know not I, than to pray my Lord God, day and night, that, as he hath emboldened me to preach his truth, so he will strengthen me to suffer for it.

"I pray you pardon me that I write no more distinctly, for my head is [so] out of frame, that it would be too painful for me to write it again. If I be not prevented shortly, I intend to make merry with my parishioners, this Christmas, for all the sorrow, *lest perchance I never return to them again*; and I have heard say that a doe is as good in winter as a buck in summer."—Latimer to Sir Edward Baynton, p. 334.

573 LATIMER'S *Remains*, p. 334.

574 Ibid. p. 350.

575 "I pray you, in God's name, what did you, so great fathers, so many, so long season, so oft assembled together? What went you about?

What would ye have brought to pass? Two things taken away—the one that ye (which I heard) burned a dead man,—the other, that ye (which I felt) went about to burn one being alive. Take away these two noble acts, and there is nothing else left that ye went about that I know," etc., etc.—Sermon preached before the Convocation: LATIMER'S *Sermons*, p. 46.

576 "My affair had some bounds assigned to it by him who sent for me up, but is now protracted by intricate and wily examinations, as if it would never find a period; while sometimes one person, sometimes another, ask me questions, without limit and without end."—Latimer to the Archbishop of Canterbury: *Remains*, p. 352.

577 *Remains*, p. 222.

578 *Sermons*, p. 294.

579 The process lasted through January, February, and March.

580 *Sermons*, p. 294.

581 He subscribed all except two—one apparently on the power of the pope, the other I am unable to conjecture. Compare the Articles themselves—printed in LATIMER'S *Remains*, p. 466—with the Sermon before the Convocation.—*Sermons*, p. 46; and BURNET, vol. iii. p. 116.

582 Nicholas Glossop to Cromwell: ELLIS, third series, vol. ii. p. 237.

583 Where he was known among the English of the day as Master Frisky-all.

584 See FOXE. vol. v. p. 392.

585 Eustace Chappuys to Chancellor Granvelle: *MS. Archiv. Brussels: Pilgrim*, p. 106.

586 See Cromwell's will in an appendix to this chapter. This document, lately found in the Rolls House, furnishes a clue at last to the connections of the Cromwell family.

587 Are we to believe Foxe's story that Cromwell was with the Duke of Bourbon at the storming of Rome in May, 1527? See FOXE, vol. v. p. 365. He was with Wolsey in January, 1527. See ELLIS, third series, vol. ii. p. 117. And he was again with him early in 1528. Is it likely that he was in Italy on such an occasion in the interval? Foxe speaks of it as one of the random exploits of Cromwell's youth, which is obviously untrue; and the natural impression which we gather is, that he was confusing the expedition of the Duke of Bourbon with some earlier campaign. On the other hand Foxe's authority was Cranmer, who was likely to know the truth; and it is not impossible that, in the critical state of Italian politics, the English government might have

desired to have some confidential agent in the Duke of Bourbon's camp. Cromwell, with his knowledge of Italy and Italian, and his adventurous ability, was a likely man to have been sent on such an employment; and the story gains additional probability from another legend about him, that he once saved the life of Sir John Russell, in some secret affair at Bologna. See FOXE, vol. v. p. 367. Now, although Sir John Russell had been in Italy several times before (he was at the Battle of Pavia, and had been employed in various diplomatic missions), and Cromwell might thus have rendered him the service in question on an earlier occasion, yet he certainly was in the Papal States, on a most secret and dangerous mission, in the months preceding the capture of Rome. *State Papers*, vol. vi. p. 560, etc. The probabilities may pass for what they are worth till further discovery.

588 A damp, unfurnished house belonging to Wolsey, where he was ordered to remain till the government had determined upon their course towards him. See CAVENDISH.

589 CAVENDISH, pp. 269-70.

590 Ibid. p. 276.

591 Chappuys says, that a quarrel with Sir John Wallop first introduced Cromwell to Henry. Cromwell, "not knowing how else to defend himself, contrived with presents and entreaties to obtain an audience of the king, whom he promised to make the richest sovereign that ever reigned in England." —Chappuys to Granvelle: *The Pilgrim*, p. 107.

592 Or Willyams. The words are used indifferently.

593 The clause enclosed between brackets is struck through.

594 Struck through.

595 Mary, widow of Louis of Hungary, sister of the emperor, and Regent of the Netherlands.

596 She was much affected when the first intimation of the marriage reached her. "I am informed of a secret friend of mine," wrote Sir John Hacket, "that when the queen here had read the letters which she received of late out of England, the tears came to her eyes with very sad countenance. But indeed this day when I spake to her she showed me not such countenance, but told me that she was not well pleased.

"At her setting forward to ride at hunting, her Grace asked me if I had heard of late any tidings out of England. I told her Grace, as it is true, that I had none. She gave me a look as that she should marvel thereof, and said to me, 'Jay des nouvelles qui ne me semblent point trop bonnes,' and told me touching the King's Highness's marriage. To the which I answered her

Grace and said, 'Madame, je ne me doute point syl est faict, et quand le veult prendre et entendre de bonne part et au sain chemyn, sans porter faveur parentelle que ung le trouvera tout lente et bien raysonnable par layde de Dieu et de bonne conscience.' Her Grace said to me again, 'Monsieur l'ambassadeur, c'est Dieu qui le scait que je vouldroye que le tout allysse bien, mais ne scaye comment l'empereur et le roy mon frere entendront l'affaire car il touche a eulx tant que a moy.' I answered and said, 'Madame, il me semble estre assuree que l'empereur et le roy vostre frere qui sont deux Prinssys tres prudens et sayges, quant ilz auront considere indifferentement tout l'affaire qu ilz ne le deveroyent prendre que de bonne part.' And hereunto her Grace made me answer, saying, 'Da quant de le prendre de bonne part ce la, ne sayge M. l'ambassadeur.'" —Hacket to the Duke of Norfolk: *State Papers*, vol. vii. p. 452.

597 *State Papers*, vol. vii. p. 457.

598 Sir Gregory Cassalis to the Duke of Norfolk. Ad pontificem accessi et mei sermonis illa summa fuit, vellet id præstare ut serenissimum regem nostrum certiorem facere possemus, in suâ causâ nihil innovatum iri. Hic ille, sicut solet, respondit, nescire se quo pacto possit Cæsarianis obsistere,— *State Papers*, vol. vii. p. 461.

599 Bennet to Henry: *State Papers*, vol. vii. p. 462.

600 Ibid.

601 Letter undated, but written about the middle of June: *State Papers*, vol. vii. p. 474

602 Of the Archbishop of York, not of Canterbury: which provokes a question. Conjectures are of little value in history, but inasmuch as there must have been some grave reason for the substitution, a suggestion of a possible reason may not be wholly out of place. The appeal in itself was strictly legal; and it was of the highest importance to avoid any illegality of form. Cranmer, by transgressing the inhibition which Clement had issued in the winter, might be construed by the papal party to have virtually incurred the censures threatened, and an escape might thus have been furnished from the difficulty in which the appeal placed them.

603 Publico ecclesiæ judicio.

604 RYMER, vol. vi. part 2, p. 188.

605 The French king did write unto Cardinal Tournon (not, however, of his own will, but under pressure from the Duke of Norfolk), very instantly, that he should desire the pope, in the said French king's name, that his Holyness would not innovate anything against your Highness any wise

till the congress: adding, withal, that if his Holyness, notwithstanding his said desire, would proceed, he could not less do, considering the great and indissoluble amity betwixt your Highnesses, notorious to all the world, but take and recognise such proceeding for a fresh injury.—Bennet to Henry VIII.: *State Papers*, vol. vii. p. 468.

606 Ibid. p. 469.

607 Ibid. p. 469.

608 Ibid. p. 470.

609 Ibid. p. 467, note, and p. 470.

610 BURNET, vol. i. p. 221.

611 We only desire and pray you to endeavour yourselves in the execution of that your charge—easting utterly away and banishing from you such fear and timorousness, or rather despair, as by your said letters we perceive ye have conceived—reducing to your memories in the lieu and stead thereof, as a thing continually lying before your eyes and incessantly sounded in your ears, the justice of our cause, which cannot at length be shadowed, but shall shine and shew itself to the confusion of our adversaries. And we having, as is said, truth for us, with the help and assistance of God, author of the same, shall at all times be able to maintain you.—Henry VIII. to Bonner: *State Papers*, vol. vii. p. 485.

612 Bonner to Cromwell: Ibid. vol. vii. p. 481.

613 The proclamation ordering that Catherine should be called not queen, but Princess Dowager.

614 Catherine de Medici.

615 Henry VIII. to the Duke of Norfolk: *State Papers*, vol. vii. p. 493.

616 Sir John Rackct, writing fiom Ghent on the 6th of September, describes as the general impression that the Pope's "trust was to assure his alliance on both sides." "He trusts to bring about that his Majesty the French king and he shall become and remain in good, fast, and sure alliance together; and so ensuring that they three (the Pope, Francis, and Charles V.) shall be able to reform and set good order in the rest of Christendom. But whether his Unhappiness's—I mean his Holiness's—intention, is set for the welfare and utility of Christendom, or for his own insincerity and singular purpose, I remit that to God and to them that know more of the world than I do."—Hacket to Cromwell: *State Papers*, vol. vii. p. 506.

617 John the Magnanimous, son of John the Steadfast, and nephew of the Elector Frederick, Luther's first protector.

618 *State Papers*, vol. vii. pp. 499-501.

619 Princeps Elector ducit se imparem ut Regiæ Celsitudinis vel aliorum regum oratores eâ lege in aulâ suâ degerent; vereturque ne ob id apud Cæsaream majestatem unicum ejus Dominum et alios male audiret, possetque sinistre tale institutum interpretari.—Reply of the Elector: *State Papers*, vol. vii. p. 503.

620 Vaughan to Cromwell: *State Papers*, vol vii. p. 509.

621 I consider the man, with other two—that is to say, the Landgrave von Hesse and the Duke of Lunenberg—to be the chief and principal defenders and maintainers of the Lutheran sect: who considering the same with no small difficulty to be defended, as well against the emperor and the bishops of Germany, his nigh and shrewd neighbours, as against the most opinion of all Christian men, feareth to raise any other new matter whereby they should take a larger and peradventure a better occasion to revenge the same. The King's Highness seeketh to have intelligence with them, as they conjecture to have them confederate with him; yea, and that against the emperor, if he would anything pretend against the king.—Here is the thing which I think feareth the duke.—Vaughan to Cromwell: *State Papers*, vol. vii. pp. 509-10.

622 HALL, p. 805.

623 *State Papers*, vol. vii. p. 512.

624 The Duke of Albany, during the minority of James V., had headed the party in Scotland most opposed to the English. He expelled the queen-mother, Margaret, sister of Henry; he seized the persons of the two young princes, whom he shut up in Stirling, where the younger brother died under suspicion of foul play (*Despatches of* GIUSTINIANI, vol. i. p. 157); and subsequently, in his genius for intrigue, he gained over the queen dowager herself in a manner which touched her honour.—Lord Thomas Dacre to Queen Margaret: ELLIS, second series, vol. i. p. 279.

625 Ex his tamen, qui hæc a Pontifice, audierunt, intelligo regem vehementissime instare, ut vestræ majestatis expectatione satisfiat Pontifex.—Peter Vannes to Henry VIII.: *State Papers*, vol. vii. p. 518.

626 *State Papers*, vol. vii. p. 520.

627 Hoc dico quod video inter regem et pontificem conjunctissime et amicissime hic agi.—Vannes to Cromwell: Ibid.

628 Vannes to Cromwell: Ibid. pp. 522-3.

629 BURNET, *Collectanea*, p. 436.

630 Letter of the King of France: LEGRAND, vol. iii. Reply of Henry: FOXE, vol. v. p. 110.

631 Commission of the Bishop of Paris: LEGRAND, vol. iii; BURNET, vol. iii. p. 128; FOXE, vol. v. p. 106-111. The commission of the Bishop of Bayonne is not explicit on the extent to which the pope had bound himself with respect to the sentence. Yet either in some other despatch, or verbally through the Bishop, Francis certainly informed Henry that the Pope had promised that sentence should be given in his favour. We shall find Henry assuming this in his reply; and the Archbishop of York declared to Catherine that the pope "said at Marseilles, that if his Grace would send a proxy thither he would give sentence for his Highness against her, because that he knew his cause to be good and just." — *State Papers*, vol. i. p. 421.

632 MS. Bibl. Impér. Paris. — *The Pilgrim*, pp. 97, 98. Cf. FOXE, vol. v. p. 110.

633 I hear of a number of Gelders which be lately reared; and the opinion of the people here is that they shall go into England. All men there speak evil of England, and threaten it in their foolish manner. — Vaughan to Cromwell: *State Papers*, vol. vii. p. 511.

634 RYMER, vol. vi. part 2, p. 189.

635 Parties were so divided in England that lookers-on who reported any one sentiment as general there, reported in fact by their own wishes and sympathies. D'Inteville, the French ambassador, a strong Catholic, declares the feeling to have been against the revolt. Chastillon, on the other hand, writing at the same time from the same place (for he had returned from France, and was present with d'Inteville at the last interview), says, "The King has made up his mind to a complete separation from Rome; and the lords and the majority of the people go along with him." — Chastillon to the Bishop of Paris: *The Pilgrim*, p. 99.

636 STRYPE, *Eccles. Memor.*, vol. i. p. 224.

637 Instructions to the Earls of Oxford, Essex, and Sussex, to remonstrate with the Lady Mary: *Rolls House MS.*

638 Ibid.

639 On the 15th of November, Queen Catherine wrote to the Emperor, and after congratulating him on his successes against the Turks, she continued,

"And as our Lord in his mercy has worked so great a good for Christendom by your Highness's hands, so has he enlightened also his Holiness; and I and all this realm have now a sure hope that, with the grace of God, his Holiness will slay this second Turk, this affair between the King my Lord and me. Second Turk, I call it, from the misfortunes which, through his Holiness's long delay, have grown out of it, and are now so vast and of so ill example that I know not whether this or the Turk be the worst. Sorry am I to have been compelled to importune your Majesty so often in this matter, for sure I am you do not need my pressing. But I see delay to be so calamitous, my own life is so unquiet and so painful, and the opportunity to make an end now so convenient, that it seems as if God of his goodness had brought his Holiness and your Majesty together to bring about so great a good. I am forced to be importunate, and I implore your Highness for the passion of our Lord Jesus Christ, that in return for the signal benefits which God each day is heaping on you, you will accomplish for me this great blessing, and bring his Holiness to a decision. Let him remember what he promised you at Bologna. The truth here is known, and he will thus destroy the hopes of those who persuade the King my Lord that he will never pass judgment."—Queen Catherine to Charles V.: *MS. Simancas*, November 15, 1533.

640 Letter to the King, giving an account of certain Friars Observants who had been about the Princess Dowager: *Rolls House MS.*

641 We remember the northern prophecy, "In England shall be slain the decorate Rose in his mother's belly," which the monks of Furness interpreted as meaning that "the King's Grace should die by the hands of priests."—Vol. i. cap. 4.

642 Statutes of the Realm, 25 Henry VIII. cap. 12. State Papers relating to Elizabeth Barton: *Rolls House MS.* Prior of Christ Church, Canterbury, to Cromwell: *Suppression of the Monasteries*, p. 20.

643 Thus Cromwell writes to Fisher: "My Lord, [the outward evidences that she was speaking truth] moved you not to give credence to her, but only the very matter whereupon she made her false prophecies, to which matter ye were so affected—as ye be noted to be on all matters which ye once enter into—that nothing could come amiss that made for that purpose."— *Suppression of the Monasteries*, p. 30.

644 Papers relating to the Nun of Kent: *Rolls House MS.*

645 Ibid.

646 Ibid.

647 25 Hen. VIII. cap. 12.

648 Papers relating to the Nun of Kent: *Rolls House MS.* 25 Hen. VIII. cap. 12. The "many" nobles are not more particularly designated in the

official papers. It was not desirable to mention names when the offence was to be passed over.

649 Report of the Commissioners—Papers relating to the Nun of Kent: *Rolls House MS.*

650 Goold, says the Act of the Nun's attainder, travelled to Bugden, "to animate the said Lady Princess to make commotion in the realm against our sovereign lord; surmitting that the said Nun should hear by revelation of God that the said Lady Catherine should prosper and do well, and that her issue, the Lady Mary, should prosper and reign in the realm."—25 Henry VIII. cap. 13.

651 Report of the Proceedings of the Nun of Kent: *Rolls House MS.*

652 MS. Bibliot. Impér., Paris. The letter is undated. It was apparently written in the autumn of 1533.

653 Il a des nouvelles amours. In a paper at Simancas, containing Nuevas de Inglaterra, written about this time, is a similar account of the dislike of Anne and her family, as well as of the king's altered feelings towards her. Dicano anchora che la Anna è mal voluta degli Si. di Inghilterra si per la sua superbia, si anche per l'insolentia e mali portamenti che fanno nel regno li fratelli e parenti di Anna; e che per questo il Re non la porta la affezione que soleva per che il Re festeggia una altra Donna della quale se mostra esser inamorato, e molti Si. di Inghilterra lo ajutano nel seguir el predito amor per deviar questo Re dalla pratica di Anna.

654 HALL.

655 "I, dame Elizabeth Barton," she said, "do confess that I, most miserable and wretched person, have been the original of all this mischief, and by my falsehood I have deceived all these persons (the monks who were her accomplices), and many more; whereby I have most grievously offended Almighty God, and my most noble sovereign the King's Grace. Wherefore I humbly, and with heart most sorrowful, desire you to pray to Almighty God for my miserable sins, and make supplication for me to my sovereign for his gracious mercy and pardon."—Confession of Elizabeth Barton: *Rolls House MS.*

656 Papers relating to Elizabeth Barton: Ibid.

657 *State Papers*, vol. i. p. 415.

658 A curious trait in Mary's character may be mentioned in connection with this transfer. She had a voracious appetite; and in Elizabeth's household expenses an extra charge was made necessary of £26 a year for the meat breakfasts and meat suppers "served into the Lady Mary's chamber."—

Statement of the expenses of the Household of the Princess Elizabeth: *Rolls House MS.*

659 He is called *frater consobrinus.* See FULLER'S *Worthies,* vol. iii. p. 128.

660 He was killed at the battle of Pavia.

661 Courtenay, Earl of Devonshire, married Catherine, daughter of Edward.

662 Believe me, my lord, there are some here, and those of the greatest in the land, who will be indignant if the Pope confirm the sentence against the late Queen.—D'Inteville to Montmorency: *The Pilgrim,* p. 97.

663 She once rode to Canterbury, disguised as a servant, with only a young girl for a companion.—Depositions of Sir Geoffrey Pole: *Rolls House MS.*

664 Confession of Sir William Neville: *Rolls House MS.*

665 Confession of Sir George Neville: Ibid.

666 Confession of the Oxford Wizard: Ibid.

667 Queen Anne Boleyn to Gardiner: BURNET'S *Collectanea,* p. 355. Office for the Consecration of Cramp Rings: Ibid.

668 So at least the Oxford Wizard said that Sir William Neville had told him.—Confession of the Wizard: *Rolls House MS.* But the authority is not good.

669 Henry alone never listened seriously to the Nun of Kent.

670 John of Transylvania, the rival of Ferdinand. His designation by the title of king in an English state paper was a menace that, if driven to extremities, Henry would support him against the empire.

671 Acts of Council: *State Papers,* vol. i. pp. 414-15.

672 Henry VIII. to Sir John Wallop: *State Papers,* vol. vii. p. 524.

673 Stephen Vaughan to Cromwell: *State Papers,* vol. vii. p. 517. Vaughan describes Peto with Shakespearian raciness. "Peto is an ipocrite knave, as the most part of his brethren be; a wolf; a tiger clad in a sheep's skin. It is a perilous knave—a raiser of sedition—an evil reporter of the King's Highness—a prophecyer of mischief—a fellow I would wish to be in the king's hands, and to be shamefully punished. Would God I could get him by any policy—I will work what I can. Be sure he shall do nothing, nor pretend to do nothing, in these parts, that I will not find means to cause the King's Highness to know. I have laid a bait for him. He is not able to wear the clokys and cucullys that be sent him out of England, they be so many."

674 Hacket to Henry VIII.: *State Papers*, vol. vii. p. 528.

675 Ibid. p. 530.

676 Hacket to Cromwell: *State Papers*, vol. vii. p. 531.

677 So at least Henry supposed, if we may judge by the resolutions of the Council "for the fortification of all the frontiers of the realm, as well upon the coasts of the sea as the frontiers foreanenst Scotland." The fortresses and havens were to be "fortefyed and munited;" and money to be sent to York to be in readiness "if any business should happen." — Ibid. vol. i. p. 411.

678 25 Hen. VIII. cap. 19.

679 A design which unfortunately was not put in effect. In the hurry of the time it was allowed to drop.

680 25 Henry VIII. cap. 14.

681 23 Henry VIII. cap. 20.

682 At this very time Campeggio was Bishop of Salisbury, and Ghinucci, who had been acting for Henry at Rome, was Bishop of Worcester. The Act by which they were deprived speaks of these two appointments as *nominations* by the king. — 25 Henry VIII. cap. 27.

683 Wolsey held three bishoprics and one archbishopric, besides the abbey of St. Albans.

684 Thus when Wolsey was presented, in 1514, to the See of Lincoln, Leo X. writes to his beloved son Thomas Wolsey how that in his great care for the interests of the Church, "Nos hodie Ecclesiæ Lincolniensi, te in episcopum et pastorem præficere intendimus." He then informs the Chapter of Lincoln of the appointment; and the king, in granting the temporalities, continues the fiction without seeming to recognise it: — "Cum dominus summus Pontifex nuper vacante Ecclesiâ cathedrali personam fidelis clerici nostri Thomæ Wolsey, in ipsius Ecclesiæ episcopum præfecerit, nos," etc. — See the Acts in RYMER, vol. vi. part 1, pp. 55-7.

685 25 Henry VIII. cap. 20. The pre-existing, unrealities with respect to the election of bishops explain the unreality of the new arrangement, and divest it of the character of wanton tyranny with which it appeared *primâ facie* to press upon the Chapters. The history of this statute is curious, and perhaps explains the intentions with which it was originally passed. It was repealed by the 2nd of the 1st of Edward VI. on the ground that the liberty of election was merely nominal, and that the Chapters ought to be relieved of responsibility when they had no power of choice. Direct nomination by the crown was substituted for the *congé d'élire*, and remained the practice till the reaction under Mary, when the indefinite system was resumed which had

existed before the Reformation. On the accession of Elizabeth, the statute of 25 Henry VIII. was again enacted. The more complicated process of Henry was preferred to the more simple one of Edward, and we are naturally led to ask the reason of so singular a preference. I cannot but think that it was this. The Council of Regency under Edward VI. treated the Church as an institution of the State, while Henry and Elizabeth endeavoured (under difficulties) to regard it under its more Catholic aspect of an organic body. So long as the Reformation was in progress, it was necessary to prevent the intrusion upon the bench of bishops of Romanising tendencies, and the deans and chapters were therefore protected by a strong hand from their own possible mistakes. But the form of liberty was conceded to them, not, I hope, to place deliberately a body of clergymen in a degrading position, but in the belief that at no distant time the Church might be allowed without danger to resume some degree of self-government.

686 25 Henry VIII. cap. 21.

687 I sent you no heavy words, but words of great comfort; willing your brother to shew you how benign and merciful the prince was; and that I thought it expedient for you to write unto his Highness, and to recognise your offence and to desire his pardon, which his Grace would not deny you how in your age and sickness.—Cromwell to Fisher: *Suppression of the Monasteries*, p. 27.

688 Sir Thomas More to Cromwell: BURNET'S *Collectanea*, p. 350.

689 Ibid.

690 Ibid.

691 More to Cromwell: STRYPE'S *Memorials*, vol. i. Appendix, p. 195.

692 More to the King: ELLIS, first series, vol. ii. p. 47.

693 Cromwell to Fisher: *Suppression of the Monasteries*, p. 27, et seq.

694 *Suppression of the Monasteries*, p. 27, et seq.

695 John Fisher to the Lords in Parliament: ELLIS, third series, vol. ii. p. 289.

696 *Lords' Journals*, p. 72.

697 25 Hen. VIII. cap. 12.

698 In a tract written by a Dr. Moryson in defence of the government, three years later, I find evidence that a distinction was made among the prisoners, and that Dr. Bocking was executed with peculiar cruelty. "Solus in crucem actus est Bockingus," are Moryson's words, though I feel uncertain of the nature of the punishment which he meant to designate.

"Crucifixion" was unknown to the English law; and an event so peculiar as the "crucifixion" of a monk would hardly have escaped the notice of the contemporary chroniclers. In a careful diary kept by a London merchant during these years, which is in MS. in the Library of Balliol College, Oxford, the whole party are said to have been hanged.—See, however, *Morysini Apomaxis*, printed by Berthelet, 1537.

699 HALL, p. 814.] The inferior confederates were committed to their prisons with the exception only of Fisher, who, though sentenced, found mercy thrust upon him, till by fresh provocation the miserable old man forced himself upon his fate. 700

700 LORD HERBERT says he was pardoned; I do not find, however, on what authority: but he was certainly not imprisoned, nor was the sentence of forfeiture enforced against him.

701 This is the substance of the provisions, which are, of course, much abridged.

702 *Lords' Journals*, vol. i. p. 82. An act was also passed in this session "against the usurped power of the Bishop of Rome." We trace it in its progress through the House of Lords. (*Lords' Journals*, Parliament of 1533-4.) It received the royal assent (ibid.), and is subsequently alluded to in the both of the 28th of Henry VIII., as well as in a Royal Proclamation dated June, 1534; and yet it is not on the Roll, nor do I anywhere find traces of it. It is not to be confounded with the act against payment of Peter's Pence, for in the *Lords' Journals* the two acts are separately mentioned. It received the royal assent on the 30th of March, while that against Peter's Pence was suspended till the 7th of April. It contained, also, an indirect assertion that the king was Head of the English Church, according to the title which had been given him by Convocation. (King's Proclamation: FOXE, vol. v. p. 69.) For some cause or other, the act at the last moment must have been withdrawn.

703 See BURNET, vol. i. pp. 220-1: vol. iii p. 135; and LORD HERBERT. Du Bellay's brother, the author of the memoirs, says that the king, at the bishop's entreaty, promised that if the pope would delay sentence, and send "judges to hear the matter, he would himself forbear to do what he proposed to do"—that is, separate wholly from the See of Rome. If this is

true, the sending "judges" must allude to the "sending them to Cambray," which had been proposed at Marseilles.

704 See the letter of the Bishop of Bayonne, dated March 23, in LEGRAND. A paraphrase is given by BURNET, vol. iii. p. 132.

705 Promisistis predecessori meo quod si sententiam contra regem Angliæ tulisset, Cæsar illum infra quatuor menses erat invasurus, et regno expulsurus.—*State Papers*, vol. vii. p. 579.

706 Letter of Du Bellay in LEGRAND.

707 Ibid.

708 Sir Edward Karne and Dr. Revett to Henry VIII.: *State Papers*, vol. vii. pp. 553-4.

709 State Papers, vol. vii. p. 560, et seq.

710 His Highness, considering the time and the malice of the emperour, cannot conveniently pass out of the realm—since he leaveth behind him another daughter and a mother, with their friends, maligning his enterprises in this behalf—who bearing no small grudge against his most entirely beloved Queen Anne, and his young daughter the princess, might perchance in his absence take occasion to excogitate and practise with their said friends matters of no small peril to his royal person, realm, and subjects.—*State Papers*, vol. vii. p. 559.

711 LORD HERBERT.

712 I mentioned their execution in connection with their sentence; but it did not take place till the 20th of April, a month after their attainder: and delay of this kind was very unusual in cases of high treason. I have little doubt that their final sentence was in fact pronounced by the pope.

713 The oaths of a great many are in RYMER, vol. vi. part 2, p. 195, et seq.

714 His great-grandson's history of him (*Life of Sir Thomas More,*, by CRESACRE MORE, written about 1620, published 1627, with a dedication to Henrietta Maria) is incorrect in so many instances that I follow it with hesitation; but the account of the present matter is derived from Mr. Roper, More's son-in-law, who accompanied him to Lambeth, and it is incidentally confirmed in various details by More himself.

715 MORE'S *Life of More*, p. 232.

716 More held extreme republican opinions on the tenure of kings, holding that they might be deposed by act of parliament.

717 MORE'S *Life of More*, p. 237.

718 BURNET, vol. i. p. 255.

719 MORE'S *Life of More*, p. 237.

720 Cromwell to the Archbishop of Canterbury: *Rolls House MS.*

721 *State Papers*, vol. i. p. 411, et seq.

722 Royal Proclamation, June, 1534.

723 Ibid.

724 FOXE, vol. v. p. 70.